POINTS UNKNOWN

POINTS UNKNOWN

A Century of Great Exploration

Edited by David Roberts

W. W. Norton & Company New York London

Library of Congress Cataloging-in-Publication Data
Points unknown : a century of great exploration / edited by David Roberts.
p. cm.
"An Outside book."
ISBN 0-393-05000-9
1. Voyages and travels.   2. Explorers.   3. Adventure and adventurers.
I. Roberts, David, 1943–   II. Title.
G525 .P56 2000
910'.92—dc21
00-032915
W. W. Norton & Company, Inc., 500 Fifth Avenue, New York, N.Y. 10110
wwww.wwnorton.com
W. W. Norton & Company Ltd., 10 Coptic Street, London WC1A 1PU
2 3 4 5 6 7 8 9 0

Turn to page 608 for the balance of the credits.

Contents

5

PART II　Idylls

Introduction

Every generation of adventurers laments the fact that it was born too late. At the beginning of the twentieth century, as they set their sights on the great empty spaces of the Earth—the Poles, the high mountains, the deserts, the open seas—the best Victorian explorers wondered aloud whether their quests were perverse; for their predecessors had regarded those empty spaces as barren wastelands, not worth the trouble to investigate. Yet by 1900, there was no longer a Great West, unknown to all but Indians, for a latter-day Lewis and Clark to discover; no chain of South Sea Islands awaiting their Captain Cook; no unguessed source of the Nile for Burton and Speke to battle over.

So, at the beginning of the twenty-first century, the young adventurer, trying to find a new route to put up ten feet away from a classic line on El Capitan or conjuring up a slickrock itinerary that no one has mountain biked before, rues the fact that long before he was born, luckier explorers knocked off the Poles, Everest and Annapurna, the Empty Quarter and the

Northwest Passage. There seems little left for him to accomplish but to fill in the lacunae between the bold lines written by his elders and betters.

It is the premise of this anthology, however, that in the year 2000 adventure is alive and well. It would be amiss, of course, to ignore the revolutions in our relationship to planet Earth that our century has wrought—upheavals that, like those of no previous century, have truly changed the nature of exploration and adventure.

Consider the plights of two brave men who met their deaths at the heart of their quests, one in 1912, the other in 1996. Returning from the South Pole with his four companions, demoralized to discover Amundsen's tent mocking him at 90°S., Captain Robert Falcon Scott ran out of food, strength, and good weather only eleven miles short of a depot that would have saved his team's lives. For eight months through the Antarctic winter, Scott's teammates at McMurdo base worried and speculated. Only when a relief party found his last camp the next summer did those teammates learn what had happened to the polar party. It would take another three months for news of the tragedy to make its way home to England.

In May 1996, high on the South Col route on Everest, veteran guide Rob Hall found himself in trouble after refusing to abandon his exhausted client, Doug Hansen. Where Scott's denouement had played itself out in the utter privacy of an icy grave, Hall's ordeal was broadcast to the world. Over two-way radio, his colleagues in lower camps cajoled him to get up and start moving down. When it was too late for that, Hall's pregnant wife in New Zealand was patched through to him: their poignant farewell was eavesdropped on by climbers all over the mountain, as the archivists of Everest's deadliest season took notes.

The difference is not one of degree, but a truly qualitative one. Yet Scott and Hall shared an exigency that explorers have always demanded to keep adventure real. No matter how many ears could listen in on Hall's dying moments, in the midst of the storm that trapped him, the strongest climbers in the world were powerless to go to his aid. Rob Hall was on his own.

To be sure, the inventions that have transformed our access to the last blank places on Earth during this tumultuous century—from the airplane to the radio, from the submersible to the sat phone, from the four-wheel-drive vehicle to the GPS—run the risk at times of emasculating adventure. The hiker in the woods who, soaked in a downpour, pulls out his cell phone and calls for a rescue; the Caribbean sailor who, becalmed, starts up his auxiliary engine and chugs into port—these and their brethren are merely playing at a toothless facsimile of adventure, like kids camping out in the backyard who crawl back to bed after getting spooked in the dark.

One measure of the threat of modern technology to corrupt adventure comes in the proliferation of adventure travel companies during the last two decades. By processing a Bolivian trek or an Alaskan river run into a tidy two-week holiday package, with the guides buying and cooking the food, bargaining with the locals, and making all the decisions, these outfits perform the clever trick of giving the client the illusion that he's had a real adventure, while the true experience is more akin to a cruise on the QE2. Tourism dates, historians reassure us, at least to the Middle Ages and maybe to ancient Rome; but never before has a whole industry so deliberately blurred the boundary between tourism and exploration as to convince a wine taster biking through France or a rafter bouncing down the Colorado that he's danced on the edge of risk and ordeal.

The onslaught of technology has dictated to true adventurers a new stratagem, which might be called "arbitrary self-limitation." As recently as 1953, the summit of Mount Everest was still so redoubtable that the British expedition attacking it could use every means at its disposal—bottled oxygen, miles of fixed ropes, metal ladders across crevasses, an army of porters and Sherpas, tons of food and gear—and yet gain no guarantee of success. In 1996, on the other hand, to keep the game a good one, the lone Swede Goran Kropp bicycled from his native country to Everest and climbed it solo without oxygen, refusing so much as a spoonful of another team's dinner, to ensure his self-sufficiency.

Arbitrarily limiting themselves, adventurers now decide to climb without pitons, bolts, or fixed ropes; to ski to the Pole without dogs; to swim a strait without a support boat. Having entered into the new wilderness that their own ground rules have posited, these men and women discover a freedom as heady as Columbus or Magellan knew. Thus Peter Boardman and Joe Tasker, resolving to climb the savage west wall of Changabang in 1976 without support or the chance of rescue, or Eric Hansen, walking into the rain forest of Borneo in 1982, surrendering his fate to the whims of his Penan hosts—such travelers plunge into the heart of an indelible adventure, with the outcome uncertain, the epiphanies unpredictable, and life or death genuinely in the balance. In the twenty-first century, an incalculable richness of comparable journeys awaits.

Certain places on Earth, moreover, remain truly unknown at the end of the second millennium. Cavers today are only beginning to enter the golden age of their sport, for the deepest and most intricate underground labyrinths have yet to be plumbed. The depths of the ocean floor are still all but unknown, though whether humans or only unmanned submersibles will reveal them remains to be seen. Surely no exploratory venture ever undertaken provides more thrilling discoveries at the cost of more fiendish dangers than the nascent pastime of cave diving.

Some aspects of adventure, alas, will never be the same. In our impatient century, we have relentlessly whittled down the spans of time we are willing to expend on any quest. In the 1900s, polar explorers accepted the notion that to find anything really new, they must devote two, three, or even four years in the ice to their enterprise. Today, few expeditions anywhere last longer than three months. No intensity of experience can replace the impact of enduring for years in a truly hostile place. It is no accident that some of the masterpieces of early-twentieth-century adventure writing, such as Apsley Cherry-Garrard's *The Worst Journey in the World*, have a lordly amplitude in the telling that mirrors those years of endurance.

Not all adventure need be extreme, of course, to be memorable. Toward the end of the twentieth century, a flowering of ironic narratives that celebrate the less-than-heroic exploits of would-be adventurers claims a rightful place beside the classics. Books such as Eric Newby's *A Short Walk in the Hindu Kush* or Redmond O'Hanlon's *Into the Heart of Borneo* capture the humor of ordinary folks blundering their way into extraordinary pickles. Before the twentieth century, there were isolated examples of this comic genre, such as Jerome K. Jerome's *Three Men in a Boat,* but its proliferation in the last decades of the twentieth century no doubt says something about the Age of Self-Consciousness all our tinkering has spawned.

Meanwhile, the adventurers of the next generation can lay aside their angst and doubt and, with a little imagination, invent the journeys that will provoke the adventure classics of the twenty-first century. At one of his lectures on some recent voyage, the great British climber and sailor H. W. Tilman was asked by an earnest youth, "But, sir, how does one get on an expedition such as yours?" Tilman bellowed, "Put on your boots and go!"

A FEW WORDS about the scope of this book. In choosing the forty-one excerpts for the anthology, neither I nor my editor nor a panel of consultants from *Outside* magazine claims that these are the forty-one finest pieces of adventure writing our century has produced. Any such claim would be foolish in the first place. Taste varies wildly, "classics" go in and out of favor, and no reader can be conversant with all the literature in a single field—say, long-distance single-handed sailing—let alone with adventure as a whole.

For several reasons, we have chosen to include only works written originally in English, even though that means omitting such otherwise obvious candidates as Maurice Herzog's *Annapurna* or Heinrich Harrer's *Seven Years in Tibet.* If no single reader can be *au courant* in adventure writing in English, to claim a grasp of the landmarks in Russian or Chinese would be ludicrous. (Just last year, I was made aware of one of the true masterpieces of Arctic literature, a book written in Russian and translated into French, published in 1917, called *Au Pays de la Mort Blanche,* by one Valerian Ivanovitch Albanov. I had never before heard of the book, or even of the disastrous journey it chronicled. The copy I found in Widener Library at Harvard had not been checked out in sixty-eight years.)

Furthermore, just as Robert Frost once said, "Poetry is what evaporates in translation," so it is hard to judge the quality of writing in an adventure classic after it has been translated (more or less felicitously) into English. Is Thor Heyerdahl a good writer in Norwegian, or is his popularity in large part due to a series of skillful translators?

There is a temptation, in assembling an anthology such as this one, to choose great adventures rather than great adventure writing. One must resist the urge. Many stylish exploits have produced only mediocre accounts. The first ascent of Everest by Edmund Hillary and Tenzing Norgay in 1953 exemplified expeditionary mountaineering at its blithest, yet Sir John Hunt's *The Ascent of Everest* is a plodding book. (Wilfrid Noyce's memoir of that expedition, *South Col*, came close to making the list.)

That great explorer and curmudgeon Vilhjalmur Stefansson was fond of arguing that adventure was always a mistake—adventure was what happened when you screwed up. Accordingly, he was proudest of the journeys he prosecuted in the Arctic that ran (and read) like clockwork. It must be confessed that an inordinate number of the excerpts in this book spring from dire predicaments their authors would just as soon have avoided—such as Art Davidson's grim bivouac in winter at Denali Pass or, for that matter, Scott's perishing on his return from the South Pole. This state of affairs cannot be helped: just as it takes interpersonal conflict to animate a novel, so danger and failure often give the spark to a journey that turns it into a memorable adventure.

Lest the anthology be all hairbreadth escapes, however, we have kept our eyes out for whimsical, lighthearted, even satiric adventures. Redmond O'Hanlon's stumbling through Borneo could have made for a tedious narrative rather than a hilarious one. Tom Patey's attempt on the north face of the Eiger could have read like a journal note rather than a Quixotic epic. The difference is in the writing.

We considered restricting our choices to first-person accounts by the adventurers themselves. Yet in certain cases—David Howarth's *We Die Alone*, Piers Paul Read's *Alive*, Sebastian Junger's *The Perfect Storm*—it takes an outside observer to capture the essence of a dramatic adventure. These excerpts, in fact, with their assumption of a disinterested, omniscient narrator surveying such highly controversial events as the survivors of an Andean plane crash cannibalizing their dead comrades, make for a beguiling change of pace from the necessarily subjective first-person accounts.

Many of the great adventures of our century have been the work of what we sometimes call "Third World peoples." Alas, their own tellings of these vivid events seldom find the printed page, getting passed down orally instead, generation after generation, by elders retelling the stories to the young. To try to do a modicum of justice to such exploits, we have included two passages that, though recorded by Anglos, spring straight from the peoples' own narratives. They are of the Apache warrior Massai's twenty-five-year survival as a hunted outcast in white America, in Eve Ball's *Indeh*, and of the profound discovery of the outside world thrust on the highlanders of New Guinea by a handful of Australian gold miners, in Bob Connolly and Robin Anderson's *First Contact*.

The most vexing problem we faced in compiling this anthology was the dearth of narratives by women that met our criteria. There is no shortage of fine writing by ambitious women travelers in our century, wonderful books by Dervla Murphy, Rebecca West, and Mary Morris, among others. In the end, we rejected such choices for the same reason we excluded the comparable accounts by Graham Greene and Evelyn Waugh and Patrick Leigh Fermor: they remain exemplars of the genre of travel writing, not of adventure writing per se.

Oddly, had we compiled an anthology of nineteenth-century adventure writing, we would have faced no such dearth, for that era produced an abundance of splendid narratives from the likes of Mary Kingsley, Isabella Bird, and Fanny Bullock Workman. What was it about the Victorian age that allowed so many women to adventure so boldly and to write about it so well? Having made our selections for this anthology, we (including our women consultants) can only plead that at least we have avoided the temptation to toss in marginal narratives simply because they were written by women.

Readers may notice a disproportionate number of accounts in this book from the worlds of mountaineering and polar exploration. I confess that those realms are the ones of my greatest expertise. Were I an aficionado of jungle travel, no doubt I would have come up with some narratives that have otherwise escaped my sleuthing (as well as that of our panel of thoughtful experts). In defense of this possible imbalance, however, I would argue that mountaineering and polar exploration have each produced a strikingly rich literature. Caving and undersea exploration may be among the most vital forms of adventure taking place at the end of the twentieth century, but so far those enterprises have not given birth to a great deal of first-rate writing in English.

Rather than organize the excerpts by discipline or chronology, we have grouped them under three rubrics: Obsessions, Idylls, and Ordeals. Just how arbitrary these rubrics might be can be seen by pondering how easily an idyll can turn into an ordeal (as when Robert Marshall gets stranded on a sandbar in his beloved Brooks Range, with the river rising about him) or an ordeal can devolve into an obsession (as with Wilfred Thesiger's addiction to the Empty Quarter that nearly kills him). These rubrics, we hope, free us up both to pair like journeys undertaken by diametrically different adventurers (Bertram Thomas and Wilfred Thesiger, Joshua Slocum and Francis Chichester), and to avoid the plodding pace of six climbing narratives in a row or three all-but-fatal scrapes back to back. With these categories, we hope also to invite the reader to dip into the book wherever he or she pleases, rather than feel any obligation to read it from start to finish. If a collection such as this one succeeds, it is not so much because it represents a definitive gathering as because it delights the reader with the richness of little-known stories, thereby surprising us with the freshness—which adventure at its best opens up to us—of new ways of seeing the world.

Finally, I would like to acknowledge and thank my judicious and indefatigable editor at W. W. Norton, John Barstow; Anne Majusiak, who tirelessly hunted down permissions to reprint these excerpts; Ann R. Tappert, our diligent copy editor; and our panel of experts—most of them editors and writers at *Outside* magazine—who gave so generously of their advice and expertise: John Atwood, John Brant, Nancy Shute, Dan Coyle, Tad Friend, Michel Guérin, Vaughn Hadenfeldt, Karen Karbo, Jon Krakauer, Bucky McMahon, David Noland, Meg Lukens Noonan, David Quammen, Marshall Sella, Peter Shelton, and Randy White.

PART I

Obsessions

ROBERT FALCON SCOTT

(1868–1912)

From *Scott's Last Expedition*

The tragic story of Captain Robert Falcon Scott and his four teammates reaching the South Pole in early 1912, only to discover that they had been beaten in the race to reach that goal by Roald Amundsen's Norwegian team, and then struggling valiantly to retrace their outward track back to base camp at McMurdo Sound, is one of the canonic sagas in exploration. Scott's diary, which he kept faithfully to the end, is the most vivid and detailed account of slow deterioration and inevitable death in polar annals. For decades, its last page has lain open, under glass, in the British Museum, not far from the case displaying the only known signature of William Shakespeare.

Recently Roland Huntford, in his well-researched book Scott and Amundsen, *has seized on several critical "mistakes"—taking five men with only four pairs of skis, man-hauling sledges rather than using dogs—to paint a very one-sided portrait of Scott as an incompetent bungler. Whatever the merits of Huntford's revisionism, there is no denying*

the heroism of Edgar Evans, Titus Oates, Bill Wilson, Birdie Bowers,
and Scott himself on that hopeless return journey. Nor is there any deny-
ing the understated nobility of Scott's account. The last of the five men
to die, he managed, after five days' silence in the last camp, to rouse
himself for one last entry, giving the world two of the most memorable
closing lines in exploratory history.

I t is wonderful to think that two long marches would land us at the Pole. We left our depôt to-day with nine days' provisions, so that it ought to be a certain thing now, and the only appalling possibility the sight of the Norwegian flag forestalling ours. Little Bowers continues his indefatigable efforts to get good sights, and it is wonderful how he works them up in his sleeping-bag in our congested tent. (Minimum for night −27.5°.)[1] Only 27 miles from the Pole. We *ought* to do it now.

Tuesday, January 16. —Camp 68. Height 9760. T. −23.5°. The worst has happened, or nearly the worst. We marched well in the morning and covered 7½ miles. Noon sight showed us in Lat. 89° 42' S., and we started off in high spirits in the afternoon, feeling that to-morrow would see us at our destination. About the second hour of the March Bowers' sharp eyes detected what he thought was a cairn; he was uneasy about it, but argued that it must be a sastrugus.[2] Half an hour later he detected a black speck ahead. Soon we knew that this could not be a natural snow feature. We marched on, found that it was a black flag tied to a sledge bearer; near by the remains of a camp; sledge tracks and ski tracks going and coming and the clear trace of dogs' paws—many dogs. This told us the whole story. The Norwegians have forestalled us and are first at the Pole. It is a terrible disappointment, and I am very sorry for my loyal companions. Many thoughts come and much discussion have we had. To-morrow we must march on to the Pole

---

[1]Fahrenheit.

[2]A small fin of wind-sculpted snow.

and then hasten home with all the speed we can compass. All the day dreams must go; it will be a wearisome return. We are descending in altitude—certainly also the Norwegians found an easy way up.

Wednesday, January 17.—Camp 69. T. −22° at start. Night −21°. The Pole. Yes, but under very different circumstances from those expected. We have had a horrible day—add to our disappointment a head wind 4 to 5, with a temperature −22°, and companions labouring on with cold feet and hands.

We started at 7.30, none of us having slept much after the shock of our discovery. We followed the Norwegian sledge tracks for some way; as far as we make out there are only two men. In about three miles we passed two small cairns. Then the weather overcast, and the tracks being increasingly drifted up and obviously going too far to the west, we decided to make straight for the Pole according to our calculations. At 12.30 Evans had such cold hands we camped for lunch—an excellent "week-end one." We had marched 7.4 miles. Lat. sight gave 89° 53' 37". We started out and did 6½ miles due south. To-night little Bowers is laying himself out to get sights in terrible difficult circumstances; the wind is blowing hard, T. −21°, and there is that curious damp, cold feeling in the air which chills one to the bone in no time. We have been descending again, I think, but there looks to be a rise ahead; otherwise there is very little that is different from the awful monotony of past days. Great God! this is an awful place and terrible enough for us to have laboured to it without the reward of priority. Well, it is something to have got here, and the wind may be our friend to-morrow. We have had a fat Polar hoosh in spite of our chagrin, and feel comfortable inside—added a small stick of chocolate and the queer taste of a cigarette brought by Wilson. Now for the run home and a desperate struggle. I wonder if we can do it.

Thursday morning, January 18.—Decided after summing up all observations that we were 3.5 miles away from the Pole—one mile beyond it and 3 to the right. More or less in this direction Bowers saw a cairn or tent.

We have just arrived at this tent, 2 miles from our camp, therefore about

1½ miles from the Pole. In the tent we find a record of five Norwegians hav-ing been here, as follows:

> Roald Amundsen
> Olav Olavson Bjaaland
> Hilmer Hanssen
> Sverre H. Hassel
> Oscar Wisting.
>   *16 Dec. 1911.*

The tent is fine—a small compact affair supported by a single bamboo. A note from Amundsen, which I keep, asks me to forward a letter to King Haakon![3]

The following articles have been left in the tent: 3 half bags of reindeer containing a miscellaneous assortment of mits and sleeping socks, very var-ious in description, a sextant, a Norwegian artificial horizon and a hyp-someter without boiling-point thermometers, a sextant and hypsometer of English make.[4]

Left a note to say I had visited the tent with companions. Bowers pho-tographing and Wilson sketching. Since lunch we have marched 6.2 miles S.S.E. by compass (i.e. northwards). Sights at lunch gave us ½ to ¾ of a mile from the Pole, so we call it the Pole Camp. (Temp. Lunch −21°.) We built a cairn, put up our poor slighted Union Jack, and photographed our-selves—mighty cold work all of it—less than ½ a mile south we saw stuck up an old underrunner of a sledge. This we commandeered as a yard for a floorcloth sail. I imagine it was intended to mark the exact spot of the Pole as near as the Norwegians could fix it. (Height 9500.) A note attached talked of the tent as being 2 miles from the Pole. Wilson keeps the note. There is no doubt that our predecessors have made thoroughly sure of their mark and fully carried out their programme. I think the Pole is about 9500

[3]King of Norway 1905–57.

[4]A hypsometer is a type of altimeter.

feet in height; this is remarkable, considering that in Lat. 88° we were about 10,500.

We carried the Union Jack about ¾ of a mile north with us and left it on a piece of stick as near as we could fix it. I fancy the Norwegians arrived at the Pole on the 15th Dec. and left on the 17th, ahead of a date quoted by me in London as ideal, viz. Dec. 22. It looks as though the Norwegian party expected colder weather on the summit than they got; it could scarcely be otherwise from Shackleton's account.[5] Well, we have turned our back now on the goal of our ambition and must face our 800 miles of solid dragging— and good-bye to most of the daydreams!

• • •

Saturday, February 17.—A very terrible day. Evans looked a little better after a good sleep, and declared, as he always did, that he was quite well. He started in his place on the traces, but half an hour later worked his ski shoes adrift, and had to leave the sledge. The surface was awful, the soft recently fallen snow clogging the ski and runners at every step, the sledge groaning, the sky overcast, and the land hazy. We stopped after about one hour, and Evans came up again, but very slowly. Half an hour later he dropped out again on the same plea. He asked Bowers to lend him a piece of string. I cautioned him to come on as quickly as he could, and he answered cheer- fully as I thought. We had to push on, and the remainder of us were forced to pull very hard, sweating heavily. Abreast the Monument Rock we stopped, and seeing Evans a long way astern, I camped for lunch. There was no alarm at first, and we prepared tea and our own meal, consuming the latter. After lunch, and Evans still not appearing, we looked out, to see him still afar off. By this time we were alarmed, and all four started back on ski. I was first to reach the poor man and shocked at his appearance; he was on his knees with clothing disarranged, hands uncovered and frostbitten, and a wild look in his eyes. Asked what was the matter, he replied with a slow speech that he didn't know, but thought he must have fainted. We got him

[5]Scott's chief British rival, Sir Ernest Shackleton had led an expedition that reached a point only ninety-seven miles from the Pole in 1909.

on his feet, but after two or three steps he sank down again. He showed every sign of complete collapse. Wilson, Bowers, and I went back for the sledge, whilst Oates remained with him. When we returned he was practically unconscious, and when we got him into the tent quite comatose. He died quietly at 12.30 A.M. On discussing the symptoms we think he began to get weaker just before we reached the Pole, and that his downward path was accelerated first by the shock of his frostbitten fingers, and later by falls during rough travelling on the glacier, further by his loss of all confidence in himself. Wilson thinks it certain he must have injured his brain by a fall. It is a terrible thing to lose a companion in this way, but calm reflection shows that there could not have been a better ending to the terrible anxieties of the past week. Discussion of the situation at lunch yesterday shows us what a desperate pass we were in with a sick man on our hands at such a distance from home.

At 1 A.M. we packed up and came down over the pressure ridges, finding our depôt easily.

Sunday, February 18.—R.32.[6] Temp. −5.5°. At Shambles Camp. We gave ourselves 5 hours' sleep at the lower glacier depôt after the horrible night, and came on at about 3 to-day to this camp, coming fairly easily over the divide. Here with plenty of horsemeat we have had a fine supper,[7] to be followed by others such, and so continue a more plentiful era if we can keep good marches up. New life seems to come with greater food almost immediately, but I am anxious about the Barrier surfaces.

Monday, February 19.—Lunch T. −16°. It was late (past noon) before we got away to-day, as I gave nearly 8 hours sleep, and much camp work was done shifting sledges[†] and fitting up new one with mast, &c., packing

[†] Sledges were left at the chief depôts to replace damaged ones. [Footnotes preceded by symbols are editor Leonard Huxley's.]

---

[6] "R" stands for return camp; return camps were numbered sequentially.

[7] Scott's party had brought ponies to Antarctica, hoping to use them to haul loads, but after the animals proved useless, they were slaughtered for meat.

horsemeat and personal effects. The surface was every bit as bad as I expected, the sun shining brightly on it and its covering of soft loose sandy snow. We have come out about 2' on the old tracks. Perhaps lucky to have a fine day for this and our camp work, but we shall want wind or change of sliding conditions to do anything on such a surface as we have got. I fear there will not be much change for the next 3 or 4 days.

R. 33. Temp. −17°. We have struggled out 4.6 miles in a short day over a really terrible surface — it has been like pulling over desert sand, not the least glide in the world. If this goes on we shall have a bad time, but I sincerely trust it is only the result of this windless area close to the coast and that, as we are making steadily outwards, we shall shortly escape it. It is perhaps premature to be anxious about covering distance. In all other respects things are improving. We have our sleeping-bags spread on the sledge and they are drying, but, above all, we have our full measure of food again. To-night we had a sort of stew fry of pemmican and horseflesh, and voted it the best hoosh we had ever had on a sledge journey. The absence of poor Evans is a help to the commissariat, but if he had been here in a fit state we might have got along faster. I wonder what is in store for us, with some little alarm at the lateness of the season.

Monday, February 20. — R.34. Lunch Temp. −13°; Supper Temp. −15°. Same terrible surface; four hours' hard plodding in morning brought us to our Desolation Camp, where we had the four-day blizzard. We looked for more pony meat, but found none. After lunch we took to ski with some improvement of comfort. Total mileage for day 7 — the ski tracks pretty plain and easily followed this afternoon. We have left another cairn behind. Terribly slow progress, but we hope for better things as we clear the land. There is a tendency to cloud over in the S.E. to-night, which may turn to our advantage. At present our sledge and ski leave deeply ploughed tracks which can be seen winding for miles behind. It is distressing, but as usual trials are forgotten when we camp, and good food is our lot. Pray God we get better travelling as we are not fit as we were, and the season is advancing apace.

Tuesday, February 21.—R.35. Lunch Temp. −9½°; Supper Temp. −11°. Gloomy and overcast when we started; a good deal warmer. The marching almost as bad as yesterday. Heavy toiling all day, inspiring gloomiest thoughts at times. Rays of comfort when we picked up tracks and cairns. At lunch we seemed to have missed the way, but an hour or two after we passed the last pony walls,[8] and since, we struck a tent ring, ending the march actually on our old pony-tracks. There is a critical spot here with a long stretch between cairns. If we can tide that over we get on the regular cairn route, and with luck should stick to it; but everything depends on the weather. We never won a march of 8½ miles with greater difficulty, but we can't go on like this. We are drawing away from the land and perhaps may get better things in a day or two. I devoutly hope so.

Wednesday, February 22.—R.36. Supper Temp. −2°. There is little doubt we are in for a rotten critical time going home, and the lateness of the season may make it really serious. Shortly after starting to-day the wind grew very fresh from the S.E. with strong surface drift. We lost the faint track immediately, though covering ground fairly rapidly. Lunch came without sight of the cairn we had hoped to pass. In the afternoon, Bowers being sure we were too far to the west, steered out. Result, we have passed another pony camp without seeing it. Looking at the map to-night there is no doubt we are too far to the east. With clear weather we ought to be able to correct the mistake, but will the weather get clear? It's a gloomy position, more especially as one sees the same difficulty returning even when we have corrected the error. The wind is dying down to-night and the sky clearing in the south, which is hopeful. Meanwhile it is satisfactory to note that such untoward events fail to damp the spirit of the party. To-night we had a pony hoosh so excellent and filling that one feels really strong and vigorous again.

Thursday, February 23.—R.37. Lunch Temp. −9.8°; Supper Temp. −12°. Started in sunshine, wind almost dropped. Luckily Bowers took a round of

---

[8]Ice-block walls to keep the ponies out of the wind.

angles and with help of the chart we fogged out that we must be inside rather than outside tracks. The data were so meagre that it seemed a great responsibility to march out and we were none of us happy about it. But just as we decided to lunch, Bowers' wonderful sharp eyes detected an old double lunch cairn, the theodolite telescope confirmed it, and our spirits rose accordingly. This afternoon we marched on and picked up another cairn; then on and camped only 2½ miles from the depôt. We cannot see it, but, given fine weather, we cannot miss it. We are, therefore, extraordinarily relieved. Covered 8.2 miles in 7 hours, showing we can do 10 to 12 on this surface. Things are again looking up, as we are on the regular line of cairns, with no gaps right home, I hope.

Friday, February 24. — Lunch. Beautiful day — too beautiful — an hour after starting loose ice crystals spoiling surface. Saw depôt and reached it middle forenoon. Found store in order except shortage oil[9] — shall have to be *very* saving with fuel — otherwise have ten full days' provision from to-night and shall have less than 70 miles to go. Note from Meares who passed through December 15, saying surface bad; from Atkinson, after fine marching (2¼ days from pony depôt), reporting Keohane better after sickness. Short note from Evans,[10] not very cheerful, saying surface bad, temperature high. Think he must have been a little anxious.[†] It is an immense relief to have picked up this depôt and, for the time, anxieties are thrust aside. There is no doubt we have been rising steadily since leaving the Shambles Camp. The coastal Barrier descends except where glaciers press out. Undulation still but flattening out. Surface soft on top, curiously hard below. Great difference now between night and day temperatures. Quite warm as I write in tent. We are on tracks with half-march cairn ahead; have covered 4½ miles. Poor Wilson has a fearful attack snow-blindness consequent on yesterday's efforts. Wish we had more fuel.

[†]It will be remembered that he was already stricken with scurvy.

---

[9]Cooking fuel (paraffin).

[10]Edward Evans, member of a support team that had laid depots of supplies in advance of the polar party; not to be confused with Edgar Evans of the polar party.

Night camp R.38. Temp. −17°. A little despondent again. We had a really terrible surface this afternoon and only covered 4 miles. We are on the track just beyond a lunch cairn. It really will be a bad business if we are to have this pulling all through. I don't know what to think, but the rapid closing of the season is ominous. It is great luck having the horsemeat to add to our ration. To-night we have had a real fine "hoosh." It is a race between the season and hard conditions and our fitness and good food.

Saturday, February 25.—Lunch Temp. −12°. Managed just 6 miles this morning. Started somewhat despondent; not relieved when pulling seemed to show no improvement. Bit by bit surface grew better, less sastrugi, more glide, slight following wind for a time. Then we began to travel a little faster. But the pulling is still *very* hard; undulations disappearing but inequalities remain.

Twenty-six Camp walls about 2 miles ahead, all tracks in sight—Evans' track very conspicuous.[11] This is something in favour, but the pulling is tiring us, though we are getting into better ski drawing again. Bowers hasn't quite the trick and is a little hurt at my criticisms, but I never doubted his heart. Very much easier—write diary at lunch—excellent meal—now one pannikin very strong tea—four biscuits and butter.

Hope for better things this afternoon, but no improvement apparent. Oh! for a little wind—E. Evans evidently had plenty.

R.39. Temp. −20°. Better march in afternoon. Day yields 11.4 miles— the first double figure of steady dragging for a long time, but it meant and will mean hard work if we can't get a wind to help us. Evans evidently had a strong wind here, S.E. I should think. The temperature goes very low at night now when the sky is clear as at present. As a matter of fact this is wonderfully fair weather—the only drawback the spoiling of the surface and absence of wind. We see all tracks very plain, but the pony-walls have evidently been badly drifted up. Some kind people had substituted a cairn at last camp 27. The old cairns do not seem to have suffered much.

[11]Edward Evans's team's track returning from the depot-laying mission.

Sunday, February 26. — Lunch Temp. −17°. Sky overcast at start, but able see tracks and cairn distinct at long distance. Did a little better, 6½ miles to date. Bowers and Wilson now in front. Find great relief pulling behind with no necessity to keep attention on track. Very cold nights now and cold feet starting march, as day footgear doesn't dry at all. We are doing well on our food, but we ought to have yet more. I hope the next depôt, now only 50 miles, will find us with enough surplus to open out. The fuel shortage still an anxiety.

R.40. Temp. −21°. Nine hours' solid marching has given us 11½ miles. Only 43 miles from the next depôt. Wonderfully fine weather but cold, very cold. Nothing dries and we get our feet cold too often. We want more food yet and especially more fat. Fuel is woefully short. We can scarcely hope to get a better surface at this season, but I wish we could have some help from the wind, though it might shake us badly if the temp. didn't rise.

Monday, February 27. — Desperately cold last night: −33° when we got up, with −37° minimum. Some suffering from cold feet, but all got good rest. We *must* open out on food soon. But we have done 7 miles this morning and hope for some 5 this afternoon. Overcast sky and good surface till now, when sun shows again. It is good to be marching the cairns up, but there is still much to be anxious about. We talk of little but food, except after meals. Land disappearing in satisfactory manner. Pray God we have no further set-backs. We are naturally always discussing possibility of meeting dogs, where and when, &c. It is a critical position. We may find ourselves in safety at next depôt, but there is a horrid element of doubt.

Camp R.41. Temp. −32°. Still fine clear weather but very cold — absolutely calm to-night. We have got off an excellent march for these days (12.2) and are much earlier than usual in our bags. 31 miles to depôt, 3 days' fuel at a pinch, and 6 days' food. Things begin to look a little better; we can open out a little on food from to-morrow night, I think.

Very curious surface — soft recent sastrugi which sink underfoot, and between, a sort of flaky crust with large crystals beneath.

Tuesday, February 28.—Lunch. Thermometer went below –40° last night; it was desperately cold for us, but we had a fair night. I decided to slightly increase food; the effect is undoubtedly good. Started marching in –32° with a slight north-westerly breeze—blighting. Many cold feet this morning; long time over foot gear, but we are earlier. Shall camp earlier and get the chance of a good night, if not the reality. Things must be critical till we reach the depôt, and the more I think of matters, the more I anticipate their remaining so after that event. Only 24½ miles from the depôt. The sun shines brightly, but there is little warmth in it. There is no doubt the middle of the Barrier is a pretty awful locality.

Camp 42. Splendid pony hoosh sent us to bed and sleep happily after a horrid day, wind continuing; did 11½ miles. Temp. not quite so low, but expect we are in for cold night (Temp. –27°).

Wednesday, February 29.—Lunch. Cold night. Minimum Temp. –37.5°; –30° with north-west wind, force 4, when we got up. Frightfully cold starting; luckily Bowers and Oates in their last new finnesko;[12] keeping my old ones for present. Expected awful march and for first hour got it. Then things improved and we camped after 5½ hours marching close to lunch camp—22½. Next camp is our depôt and it is exactly 13 miles. It ought not to take more than 1½ days; we pray for another fine one. The oil will just about spin out in that event, and we arrive 3 clear days' food in hand. The increase of ration has had an enormously beneficial result. Mountains now looking small. Wind still very light from west—cannot understand this wind.

Thursday, March 1.—Lunch. Very cold last night—minimum –41.5°. Cold start to march, too, as usual now. Got away at 8 and have marched within sight of depôt; flag something under 3 miles away. We did 11½ yesterday and marched 6 this morning. Heavy dragging yesterday and *very* heavy this morning. Apart from sledging considerations the weather is wonderful.

[12]Fur boots.

Cloudless days and nights and the wind trifling. Worse luck, the light airs come from the north and keep us horribly cold. For this lunch hour the exception has come. There is a bright and comparatively warm sun. All our gear is out drying.

Friday, March 2.—Lunch. Misfortunes rarely come singly. We marched to the (Middle Barrier) depôt fairly easily yesterday afternoon, and since that have suffered three distinct blows which have placed us in a bad position. First we found a shortage of oil; with most rigid economy it can scarce carry us to the next depôt on this surface (71 miles away). Second, Titus Oates disclosed his feet, the toes showing very bad indeed, evidently bitten by the late temperatures. The third blow came in the night, when the wind, which we had hailed with some joy, brought dark overcast weather. It fell below −40° in the night, and this morning it took 1½ hours to get our foot gear on, but we got away before eight. We lost cairn and tracks together and made as steady as we could N. by W., but have seen nothing. Worse was to come— the surface is simply awful. In spite of strong wind and full sail we have only done 5½ miles. We are in a *very* queer street since there is no doubt we cannot do the extra marches and feel the cold horribly.

Saturday, March 3.—Lunch. We picked up the track again yesterday, finding ourselves to the eastward. Did close on 10 miles and things looked a trifle better; but this morning the outlook is blacker than ever. Started well and with good breeze; for an hour made good headway; then the surface grew awful beyond words. The wind drew forward; every circumstance was against us. After 4¼ hours things so bad that we camped, having covered 4½ miles. (R.46.) One cannot consider this a fault of our own—certainly we were pulling hard this morning—it was more than three parts surface which held us back—the wind at strongest, powerless to move the sledge. When the light is good it is easy to see the reason. The surface, lately a very good hard one, is coated with a thin layer of woolly crystals, formed by radiation no doubt. These are too firmly fixed to be removed by the wind and cause impossible friction on the runners. God help us, we can't keep up this pulling, that is certain. Amongst ourselves we are unendingly cheerful, but what each man feels in his heart I can only guess. Pulling on foot gear in the morning is getting slower and slower, therefore every day more dangerous.

Sunday, March 4. — Lunch. Things looking *very* black indeed. As usual we forgot our trouble last night, got into our bags, slept splendidly on good hoosh, woke and had another, and started marching. Sun shining brightly, tracks clear, but surface covered with sandy frostrime. All the morning we had to pull with all our strength, and in 4½ hours we covered 3½ miles. Last night it was overcast and thick, surface bad; this morning sun shining and surface as bad as ever. One has little to hope for except perhaps strong dry wind — an unlikely contingency at this time of year. Under the immediate surface crystals is a hard sastrugi surface, which must have been excellent for pulling a week or two ago. We are about 42 miles from the next depôt and have a week's food, but only about 3 to 4 days' fuel — we are as economical of the latter as one can possibly be, and we cannot afford to save food and pull as we are pulling. We are in a very tight place indeed, but none of us despondent *yet*, or at least we preserve every semblance of good cheer, but one's heart sinks as the sledge stops dead at some sastrugi behind which the surface sand lies thickly heaped. For the moment the temperature is on the −20° — an improvement which makes us much more comfortable, but a colder snap is bound to come again soon. I fear that Oates at least will weather such an event very poorly. Providence to our aid! We can expect little from man now except the possibility of extra food at the next depôt. It will be real bad if we get there and find the same shortage of oil. Shall we get there? Such a short distance it would have appeared to us on the summit! I don't know what I should do if Wilson and Bowers weren't so determinedly cheerful over things.

Monday, March 5. — Lunch. Regret to say going from bad to worse. We got a slant of wind yesterday afternoon, and going on 5 hours we converted our wretched morning run of 3½ miles into something over 9. We went to bed on a cup of cocoa and pemmican solid with the chill off. (R.47.) The result is telling on all, but mainly on Oates, whose feet are in a wretched condition. One swelled up tremendously last night and he is very lame this morning. We started march on tea and pemmican as last night—we pretend to prefer the pemmican this way. Marched for 5 hours this morning over a slightly better surface covered with high moundy sastrugi. Sledge capsized twice; we pulled on foot, covering about 5½ miles. We are two pony marches and 4 miles about from our depôt. Our fuel dreadfully low and the poor Soldier nearly done.[13] It is pathetic enough because we can do nothing for him; more hot food might do a little, but only a little, I fear. We none of us expected these terribly low temperatures, and of the rest of us Wilson is feeling them most; mainly, I fear, from his self-sacrificing devotion in doctoring Oates' feet. We cannot help each other, each has enough to do to take care of himself. We get cold on the march when the trudging is heavy, and the wind pierces our warm garments. The others, all of them, are unendingly cheerful when in the tent. We mean to see the game through with a proper spirit, but it's tough work to be pulling harder than we ever pulled in our lives for long hours, and to feel that the progress is so slow. One can only say "God help us!" and plod on our weary way, cold and very miserable, though outwardly cheerful. We talk of all sorts of subjects in the tent, not much of food now, since we decided to take the risk of running a full ration. We simply couldn't go hungry at this time.

Tuesday, March 6. —Lunch. We did a little better with help of wind yesterday afternoon, finishing 9½ miles for the day, and 27 miles from depôt. (R.48.) But this morning things have been awful. It was warm in the night and for the first time during the journey I overslept myself by more than an hour; then we were slow with foot gear; then, pulling with all our might (for our lives) we could scarcely advance at rate of a mile an hour; then it grew thick and three times we had to get out of harness to search for tracks. The result is something less than 3½ miles for the forenoon. The sun is shin-

---

[13] "The Soldier" is Titus Oates.

ing now and the wind gone. Poor Oates is unable to pull, sits on the sledge when we are track-searching—he is wonderfully plucky, as his feet must be giving him great pain. He makes no complaint, but his spirits only come up in spurts now, and he grows more silent in the tent. We are making a spirit lamp to try and replace the primus when our oil is exhausted. It will be a very poor substitute and we've not got much spirit. If we could have kept up our 9-mile days we might have got within reasonable distance of the depôt before running out, but nothing but a strong wind and good surface can help us now, and though we had quite a good breeze this morning, the sledge came as heavy as lead. If we were all fit I should have hopes of getting through, but the poor Soldier has become a terrible hindrance, though he does his utmost and suffers much I fear.

Wednesday, March 7.—A little worse I fear. One of Oates' feet *very* bad this morning; he is wonderfully brave. We still talk of what we will do together at home.

We only made 6½ miles yesterday. (R.49.) This morning in 4½ hours we did just over 4 miles. We are 16 from our depôt. If we only find the correct proportion of food there and this surface continues, we may get to the next depôt [Mt. Hooper, 72 miles farther] but not to One Ton Camp. We hope against hope that the dogs have been to Mt. Hooper; then we might pull through. If there is a shortage of oil again we can have little hope. One feels that for poor Oates the crisis is near, but none of us are improving, though we are wonderfully fit considering the really excessive work we are doing. We are only kept going by good food. No wind this morning till a chill northerly air came ahead. Sun bright and cairns showing up well. I should like to keep the track to the end.

Thursday, March 8.—Lunch. Worse and worse in morning; poor Oates' left foot can never last out, and time over foot gear something awful. Have to wait in night foot gear for nearly an hour before I start changing, and then am generally first to be ready. Wilson's feet giving trouble now, but this mainly because he gives so much help to others. We did 4½ miles this morning and are now 8½ miles from the depôt—a ridiculously small distance to feel in difficulties, yet on this surface we know we cannot equal half our old marches, and that for that effort we expend nearly double the energy. The great question is, What shall we find at the depôt? If the dogs have visited it we may get along a good distance, but if there is another short allowance of fuel, God help us indeed. We are in a very bad way, I fear, in any case.

Saturday, March 10.—Things steadily downhill. Oates' foot worse. He has rare pluck and must know that he can never get through. He asked Wilson if he had a chance this morning, and of course Bill had to say he didn't know. In point of fact he has none. Apart from him, if he went under now, I doubt whether we could get through. With great care we might have a dog's chance, but no more. The weather conditions are awful, and our gear gets steadily more icy and difficult to manage. At the same time of course poor Titus is the greatest handicap. He keeps us waiting in the morning until we have partly lost the warming effect of our good breakfast, when the only wise policy is to be up and away at once; again at lunch. Poor chap! it is too pathetic to watch him; one cannot but try to cheer him up.

Yesterday we marched up the depôt, Mt. Hooper. Cold comfort. Shortage on our allowance all round. I don't know that anyone is to blame. The dogs which would have been our salvation have evidently failed.[†] Meares had a bad trip home I suppose.

[†] For the last six days the dogs had been waiting at One Ton Camp under Cherry-Garrard and Demetri. The supporting party had come out as arranged on the chance of hurrying the Pole travellers back over the last stages of their journey in time to catch the ship. Scott had dated his probable return to Hut Point anywhere between mid-March and early April. Calculating from the speed of the other return parties, Dr. Atkinson looked for him to reach One Ton Camp between March 3 and 10. Here Cherry-Garrard met four days of blizzard; then there remained little more than enough dog food to bring the teams home. He could either push south one more march and back, at imminent risk of missing Scott on the way, or stay two days at the Camp where Scott was bound to come, if he came at all."

This morning it was calm when we breakfasted, but the wind came from W.N.W. as we broke camp. It rapidly grew in strength. After travelling for half an hour I saw that none of us could go on facing such conditions. We were forced to camp and are spending the rest of the day in a comfortless blizzard camp, wind quite foul. (R.52.)

Sunday, March 11.—Titus Oates is very near the end, one feels. What we or he will do, God only knows. We discussed the matter after breakfast; he is a brave fine fellow and understands the situation, but he practically asked for advice. Nothing could be said but to urge him to march as long as he could. One satisfactory result to the discussion; I practically ordered Wilson to hand over the means of ending our troubles to us, so that anyone of us may know how to do so. Wilson had no choice between doing so and our ransacking the medicine case. We have 30 opium tabloids apiece and he is left with a tube of morphine. So far the tragical side of our story. (R.53.)

The sky completely overcast when we started this morning. We could see nothing, lost the tracks, and doubtless have been swaying a good deal since—3.1 miles for the forenoon—terribly heavy dragging—expected it. Know that 6 miles is about the limit of our endurance now, if we get no help from wind or surfaces. We have 7 days' food and should be about 55 miles from One Ton Camp to-night, $6 \times 7 = 42$, leaving us 13 miles short of our distance, even if things get no worse. Meanwhile the season rapidly advances.

Monday, March 12.—We did 6.9 miles yesterday, under our necessary average. Things are left much the same, Oates not pulling much, and now with hands as well as feet pretty well useless. We did 4 miles this morning in 4 hours 20 min.—we may hope for 3 this afternoon, $7 \times 6 = 42$. We shall be 47 miles from the depôt. I doubt if we can possibly do it. The surface remains awful, the cold intense, and our physical condition running down. God help us! Not a breath of favourable wind for more than a week, and apparently liable to head winds at any moment.

Wednesday, March 14. — No doubt about the going downhill, but everything going wrong for us. Yesterday we woke to a strong northerly wind with temp. −37°. Couldn't face it, so remained in camp (R.54) till 2, then did 5¼ miles. Wanted to march later, but party feeling the cold badly as the breeze (N.) never took off entirely, and as the sun sank the temp. fell. Long time getting supper in dark. (R.55.)

This morning started with southerly breeze, set sail and passed another cairn at good speed; half-way, however, the wind shifted to W. by S. or W.S.W., blew through our wind clothes and into our mits. Poor Wilson horribly cold, could not get off ski for some time. Bowers and I practically made camp, and when we got into the tent at last we were all deadly cold. Then temp. now midday down −43° and the wind strong. We *must* go on, but now the making of every camp must be more difficult and dangerous. It must be near the end, but a pretty merciful end. Poor Oates got it again in the foot. I shudder to think what it will be like to-morrow. It is only with greatest pains rest of us keep off frostbites. No idea there could be temperatures like this at this time of year with such winds. Truly awful outside the tent. Must fight it out to the last biscuit, but can't reduce rations.

Friday, March 16 or Saturday 17. — Lost track of dates, but think the last correct. Tragedy all along the line. At lunch, the day before yesterday, poor Titus Oates said he couldn't go on; he proposed we should leave him in his sleeping-bag. That we could not do, and induced him to come on, on the afternoon march. In spite of its awful nature for him he struggled on and we made a few miles. At night he was worse and we knew the end had come.

Should this be found I want these facts recorded. Oates' last thoughts were of his Mother, but immediately before he took pride in thinking that his regiment would be pleased with the bold way in which he met his death. We can testify to his bravery. He has borne intense suffering for weeks without complaint, and to the very last was able and willing to discuss outside subjects. He did not — would not — give up hope to the very end. He was a brave soul. This was the end. He slept through the night before last, hoping not to wake; but he woke in the morning—yesterday. It was blowing a blizzard. He said, "I am just going outside and may be some time." He went out into the blizzard and we have not seen him since.

I take this opportunity of saying that we have stuck to our sick companions to the last. In case of Edgar Evans, when absolutely out of food and he lay insensible, the safety of the remainder seemed to demand his abandonment, but Providence mercifully removed him at this critical moment. He died a natural death, and we did not leave him till two hours after his death. We knew that poor Oates was walking to his death, but though we tried to dissuade him, we knew it was the act of a brave man and an English gentleman. We all hope to meet the end with a similar spirit, and assuredly the end is not far.

I can only write at lunch and then only occasionally. The cold is intense, −40° at midday. My companions are unendingly cheerful, but we are all on the verge of serious frostbites, and though we constantly talk of fetching through I don't think anyone of us believes it in his heart.

We are cold on the march now, and at all times except meals. Yesterday we had to lay up for a blizzard and to-day we move dreadfully slowly. We are at No. 14 pony camp, only two pony marches from One Ton Depôt. We leave here our theodolite, a camera, and Oates' sleeping-bags. Diaries, &c., and geological specimens carried at Wilson's special request, will be found with us or on our sledge.

Sunday, March 18.—To-day, lunch, we are 21 miles from the depôt. Ill fortune presses, but better may come. We have had more wind and drift from ahead yesterday; had to stop marching; wind N.W., force 4, temp. −35°. No human being could face it, and we are worn out *nearly.*

My right foot has gone, nearly all the toes—two days ago I was proud possessor of best feet. These are the steps of my downfall. Like an ass I mixed a small spoonful of curry powder with my melted pemmican—it gave me violent indigestion. I lay awake and in pain all night; woke and felt done on the march; foot went and I didn't know it. A very small measure of neglect and have a foot which is not pleasant to contemplate. Bowers takes first place in condition, but there is not much to choose after all. The others are still confident of getting through—or pretend to be—I don't know! We have the last *half* fill of oil in our primus and a very small quantity of spirit—this alone between us and thirst. The wind is fair for the moment, and that is perhaps a fact to help. The mileage would have seemed ridiculously small on our outward journey.

Monday, March 19.—Lunch. We camped with difficulty last night, and were dreadfully cold till after our supper of cold pemmican and biscuit and a half a pannikin of cocoa cooked over the spirit. Then, contrary to expectation, we got warm and all slept well. To-day we started in the usual dragging manner. Sledge dreadfully heavy. We are 15½ miles from the depôt and ought to get there in three days. What progress! We have two days' food but barely a day's fuel. All our feet are getting bad—Wilson's best, my right foot worst, left all right. There is no chance to nurse one's feet till we can get hot food into us. Amputation is the least I can hope for now, but will the trouble spread? That is the serious question. The weather doesn't give us a chance—the wind from N. to N.W. and –40° temp. to-day.

Wednesday, March 21.—Got within 11 miles of depôt Monday night;[†] had to lay up all yesterday in severe blizzard. To-day forlorn hope, Wilson and Bowers going to depôt for fuel.

Thursday, March 22 and 23.—Blizzard bad as ever—Wilson and Bowers unable to start—to-morrow last chance—no fuel and only one or two of food left—must be near the end. Have decided it shall be natural—we shall march for the depôt with or without our effects and die in our tracks.

Thursday, March 29.—Since the 21st we have had a continuous gale from W.S.W. and S.W. We had fuel to make two cups of tea apiece and bare food

†The 60th camp from the Pole.

for two days on the 20th. Every day we have been ready to start for our depôt 11 *miles* away, but outside the door of the tent it remains a scene of whirling drift. I do not think we can hope for any better things now. We shall stick it out to the end, but we are getting weaker, of course, and the end cannot be far.

It seems a pity, but I do not think I can write more.

R. Scott.

For God's sake look after our people.

APSLEY CHERRY-GARRARD

(1886–1959)

From *The Worst Journey in the World*

Remarkable though Scott's diary may be (see previous selection), it is not even the best book to emerge from the 1910–13 British Antarctic Expedition. The chronicle of Apsley Cherry-Garrard, which he waited ten years to write, is one of the indisputable masterpieces of exploration history. Many experts consider it the finest polar narrative ever published. Magisterial, comprehensive, yet vividly written, at 652 pages in the Penguin edition, the book has (as Schumann wrote on rediscovering Schubert's last symphony) "a heavenly length."

The centerpiece of the chronicle is not Scott's ill-fated polar push but a sledge journey undertaken in midwinter 1911 by Cherry-Garrard, Bill Wilson, and Birdie Bowers (the latter two to die eight months later on the return from the Pole with Robert Falcon Scott) from base camp in McMurdo Sound to Cape Crozier, in order to gather penguin eggs, which those odd-looking birds hatch only during the coldest and darkest months of the year. The effort expended by the three men to get the *eggs bears witness to the faith in scientific inquiry that turn-of-the-century explorers cherished (including Scott, who died with thirty pounds of rocks—geological samples—still on his sledge). Fortunately, Cherry-Garrard did not live to learn that the scientific theory on which the quest was based—that penguin embryos, as the most "primitive" known, cast light on the early stages of evolution—was rubbish.*

The "worst journey" refers, strictly speaking, not to the whole expedition but to the midwinter jaunt. In this excerpt, Cherry-Garrard details the ordeal that began when a Force 11 gale tore away the three men's tent.

That night we took much of our gear into the tent and lighted the blubber stove. I always mistrusted that stove, and every moment I expected it to flare up and burn the tent. But the heat it gave, as it burned furiously, with the double lining of the tent to contain it, was considerable.

It did not matter, except for a routine which we never managed to keep, whether we started to thaw our way into our frozen sleeping-bags at 4 in the morning or 4 in the afternoon. I think we must have turned in during the afternoon of that Friday, leaving the cooker, our finnesko,[1] a deal of our foot-gear, Bowers's bag of personal gear, and many other things in the tent. I expect we left the blubber stove there too, for it was quite useless at present to try and warm the igloo. The tent floor-cloth was under our sleeping-bags in the igloo.

"Things must improve," said Bill. After all there was much for which to be thankful. I don't think anybody could have made a better igloo with the hard snow blocks and rocks which were all we had: we would get it air-tight by degrees. The blubber stove was working, and we had fuel for it: we had also found a way down to the penguins and had three complete, though frozen eggs: the two which had been in my mitts smashed when I fell about

[1] Fur boots.

because I could not wear spectacles. Also the twilight given by the sun below the horizon at noon was getting longer.

But already we had been out twice as long in winter as the longest previous journeys in spring. The men who made those journeys had daylight where we had darkness, they had never had such low temperatures, generally nothing approaching them, and they had seldom worked in such difficult country. The nearest approach to healthy sleep we had had for nearly a month was when during blizzards the temperature allowed the warmth of our bodies to thaw some of the ice in our clothing and sleeping-bags into water. The wear and tear on our minds was very great. We were certainly weaker. We had a little more than a tin of oil to get back on, and we knew the conditions we had to face on that journey across the Barrier: even with fresh men and fresh gear it had been almost unendurable.

And so we spent half an hour or more getting into our bags. Cirrus cloud was moving across the face of the stars from the north, it looked rather hazy and thick to the south, but it is always difficult to judge weather in the dark. There was little wind and the temperature was in the minus twenties. We felt no particular uneasiness. Our tent was well dug in, and was also held down by rocks and the heavy tank off the sledge which were placed on the skirting as additional security. We felt that no power on earth could move the thick walls of our igloo, nor drag the canvas roof from the middle of the embankment into which it was packed and lashed.

"Things must improve," said Bill.

I do not know what time it was when I woke up. It was calm, with that absolute silence which can be so soothing or so terrible as circumstances dictate. Then there came a sob of wind, and all was still again. Ten minutes and it was blowing as though the world was having a fit of hysterics. The earth was torn in pieces: the indescribable fury and roar of it all cannot be imagined.

"Bill, Bill, the tent has gone," was the next I remember—from Bowers shouting at us again and again through the door. It is always these early morning shocks which hit one hardest: our slow minds suggested that this might mean a peculiarly lingering form of death. Journey after journey

Birdie and I fought our way across the few yards which had separated the tent from the igloo door. I have never understood why so much of our gear which was in the tent remained, even in the lee of the igloo. The place where the tent had been was littered with gear, and when we came to reckon up afterwards we had everything except the bottom piece of the cooker, and the top of the outer cooker. We never saw these again. The most wonderful thing of all was that our finnesko were lying where they were left, which happened to be on the ground in the part of the tent which was under the lee of the igloo. Also Birdie's bag of personal gear was there, and a tin of sweets.

Birdie brought two tins of sweets away with him. One we had to celebrate our arrival at the Knoll: this was the second, of which we knew nothing, and which was for Bill's birthday, the next day. We started eating them on Saturday, however, and the tin came in useful to Bill afterwards.

To get that gear in we fought against solid walls of black snow which flowed past us and tried to hurl us down the slope. Once started nothing could have stopped us. I saw Birdie knocked over once, but he clawed his way back just in time. Having passed everything we could find in to Bill, we got back into the igloo, and started to collect things together, including our very dishevelled minds.

There was no doubt that we were in the devil of a mess, and it was not altogether our fault. We had had to put our igloo more or less where we could get rocks with which to build it. Very naturally we had given both our tent and igloo all the shelter we could from the full force of the wind, and now it seemed we were in danger not because they were in the wind, but because they were not sufficiently in it. The main force of the hurricane, deflected by the ridge behind, fled over our heads and appeared to form by suction a vacuum below. Our tent had either been sucked upwards into this, or had been blown away because some of it was in the wind while some of it was not. The roof of our igloo was being wrenched upwards and then dropped back with great crashes: the drift was spouting in, not it seemed because it was blown in from outside, but because it was sucked in from within: the lee, not the weather, wall was the worst. Already everything was six or eight inches under snow.

Very soon we began to be alarmed about the igloo. For some time the heavy snow blocks we had heaved up on to the canvas roof kept it weighted down. But it seemed that they were being gradually moved off by the hurricane. The tension became well-nigh unendurable: the waiting in all that welter of noise was maddening. Minute after minute, hour after hour—those snow blocks were off now anyway, and the roof was smashed up and down—no canvas ever made could stand it indefinitely.

We got a meal that Saturday morning, our last for a very long time as it happened. Oil being of such importance to us we tried to use the blubber stove, but after several preliminary spasms it came to pieces in our hands, some solder having melted; and a very good thing too, I thought, for it was more dangerous than useful. We finished cooking our meal on the primus. Two bits of the cooker having been blown away we had to balance it on the primus as best we could. We then settled that in view of the shortage of oil we would not have another meal for as long as possible. As a matter of fact God settled that for us.

We did all we could to stop up the places where the drift was coming in, plugging the holes with our socks, mitts and other clothing. But it was no real good. Our igloo was a vacuum which was filling itself up as soon as possible: and when snow was not coming in a fine black moraine dust took its place, covering us and everything. For twenty-four hours we waited for the roof to go: things were so bad now that we dare not unlash the door.

Many hours ago Bill had told us that if the roof went he considered that our best chance would be to roll over in our sleeping-bags until we were lying on the openings, and get frozen and drifted in.

Gradually the situation got more desperate. The distance between the taut-sucked canvas and the sledge on which it should have been resting became greater, and this must have been due to the stretching of the canvas itself and the loss of the snow blocks on the top: it was not drawing out of the walls. The crashes as it dropped and banged out again were louder.

There was more snow coming through the walls, though all our loose mitts, socks and smaller clothing were stuffed into the worst places: our pyjama jackets were stuffed between the roof and the rocks over the door. The rocks were lifting and shaking here till we thought they would fall.

We talked by shouting, and long before this one of us proposed to try and get the Alpine rope lashed down over the roof from outside. But Bowers said it was an absolute impossibility in that wind. "You could never ask men at sea to try such a thing," he said. He was up and out of his bag continually, stopping up holes, pressing against bits of roof to try and prevent the flapping and so forth. He was magnificent.

And then it went.

Birdie was over by the door, where the canvas which was bent over the lintel board was working worse than anywhere else. Bill was practically out of his bag pressing against some part with a long stick of some kind. I don't know what I was doing but I was half out of and half in my bag.

The top of the door opened in little slits and that green Willesden canvas flapped into hundreds of little fragments in fewer seconds than it takes to read this. The uproar of it all was indescribable. Even above the savage thunder of that great wind on the mountain came the lash of the canvas as it was whipped to little tiny strips. The highest rocks which we had built into our walls fell upon us, and a sheet of drift came in.

Birdie dived for his sleeping-bag and eventually got in, together with a terrible lot of drift. Bill also—but he was better off: I was already half into mine and all right, so I turned to help Bill. "Get into your own," he shouted, and when I continued to try and help him, he leaned over until his mouth was against my ear. "*Please*, Cherry," he said, and his voice was terribly anxious. I know he felt responsible: feared it was he who had brought us to this ghastly end.

The next I knew was Bowers's head across Bill's body. "We're all right," he yelled, and we answered in the affirmative. Despite the fact that we knew we only said so because we knew we were all wrong, this statement was helpful. Then we turned our bags over as far as possible, so that the bottom of the bag was uppermost and the flaps were more or less beneath us. And we lay and thought, and sometimes we sang.

I suppose, wrote Wilson, we were all revolving plans to get back without a tent: and the one thing we had left was the floor-cloth upon which we were actually lying. Of course we could not speak at present, but later after the blizzard had stopped we discussed the possibility of digging a hole in the snow each night and covering it over with the floor-cloth. I do not think we had any idea that we could really get back in those temperatures in our present state of ice by such means, but no one ever hinted at such a thing. Birdie and Bill sang quite a lot of songs and hymns, snatches of which reached me every now and then, and I chimed in, somewhat feebly I suspect. Of course we were getting pretty badly drifted up. "I was resolved to keep warm," wrote Bowers, "and beneath my debris covering I paddled my feet and sang all the songs and hymns I knew to pass the time. I could occasionally thump Bill, and as he still moved I knew he was alive all right—what a birthday for him!" Birdie was more drifted up than we, but at times we all had to hummock ourselves up to heave the snow off our bags. By opening the flaps of our bags we could get small pinches of soft drift which we pressed together and put into our mouths to melt. When our hands warmed up again we got some more; so we did not get very thirsty. A few ribbons of canvas still remained in the wall over our heads, and these produced volleys of cracks like pistol shots hour after hour. The canvas never drew out from the walls, not an inch. The wind made just the same noise as an express train running fast through a tunnel if you have both the windows down.

I can well believe that neither of my companions gave up hope for an instant. They must have been frightened, but they were never disturbed. As for me I never had any hope at all; and when the roof went I felt that this was the end. What else could I think? We had spent days in reaching this place through the darkness in cold such as had never been experienced by human beings. We had been out for four weeks under conditions in which no man had existed previously for more than a few days, if that. During this time we had seldom slept except from sheer physical exhaustion, as men sleep on the rack; and every minute of it we had been fighting for the bed-rock necessaries of bare existence, and always in the dark. We had kept ourselves going by enormous care of our feet and hands and bodies, by burning oil, and by having plenty of hot fatty food. Now we had no tent, one tin of oil left out of six, and only part of our cooker. When we were lucky and not too cold we could almost wring water from our clothes, and directly we got out of our sleeping-bags we were frozen into solid sheets of armoured ice. In cold temperatures with all the advantages of a tent over our heads we were already taking more than an hour of fierce struggling and cramp to get into our sleeping-bags—so frozen were they and so long did it take us to thaw our way in. No! Without the tent we were dead men.

And there seemed not one chance in a million that we should ever see our tent again. We were 900 feet up on the mountain side, and the wind blew about as hard as a wind can blow straight out to sea. First there was a steep slope, so hard that a pick made little impression upon it, so slippery that if you started down in finnesko you never could stop: this ended in a great ice-cliff some hundreds of feet high, and then came miles of pressure ridges, crevassed and tumbled, in which you might as well look for a daisy as a tent: and after that the open sea. The chances, however, were that the tent had just been taken up into the air and dropped somewhere in this sea well on the way to New Zealand. Obviously the tent was gone.

Face to face with real death one does not think of the things that torment the bad people in the tracts, and fill the good people with bliss. I might have speculated on my chances of going to Heaven; but candidly I did not care. I could not have wept if I had tried. I had no wish to review the evils of my past. But the past did seem to have been a bit wasted. The road to Hell may be paved with good intentions: the road to Heaven is paved with lost opportunities.

I wanted those years over again. What fun I would have with them: what glorious fun! It was a pity. Well has the Persian said that when we come to die we, remembering that God is merciful, will gnaw our elbows with remorse for thinking of the things we have not done for fear of the Day of Judgement.

And I wanted peaches and syrup—badly. We had them at the hut, sweeter and more luscious than you can imagine. And we have been without sugar for a month. Yes—especially the syrup.

Thus impiously I set out to die, making up my mind that I was not going to try and keep warm, that it might not take too long, and thinking I would try and get some morphia from the medical case if it got very bad. Not a bit heroic, and entirely true! Yes! comfortable, warm reader. Men do not fear death, they fear the pain of dying.

And then quite naturally and no doubt disappointingly to those who would like to read of my last agonies (for who would not give pleasure by his death?) I fell asleep. I expect the temperature was pretty high during this great blizzard, and anything near zero was very high to us. That and the snow which drifted over us made a pleasant wet kind of snipe marsh inside our sleeping-bags, and I am sure we all dozed a good bit. There was so much to worry about that there was not the least use in worrying: and we were so *very* tired. We were hungry, for the last meal we had had was in the morning of the day before, but hunger was not very pressing.

And so we lay, wet and quite fairly warm, hour after hour while the wind roared round us, blowing storm force continually and rising in the gusts to something indescribable. Storm force is force 11, and force 12 is the biggest wind which can be logged: Bowers logged it force 11, but he was always so afraid of overestimating that he was inclined to underrate. I think it was blowing a full hurricane. Sometimes awake, sometimes dozing, we had not a very uncomfortable time so far as I can remember. I knew that parties which had come to Cape Crozier in the spring had experienced blizzards which lasted eight or ten days. But this did not worry us as much as I think it did Bill: I was numb. I vaguely called to mind that Peary had survived a blizzard in the open: but wasn't that in the summer?

It was in the early morning of Saturday (22 July) that we discovered the loss of the tent. Some time during that morning we had had our last meal. The roof went about noon on Sunday and we had had no meal in the interval because our supply of oil was so low; nor could we move out of our bags except as a last necessity. By Sunday night we had been without a meal for some thirty-six hours.

The rocks which fell upon us when the roof went did no damage, and

though we could not get out of our bags to move them, we could fit ourselves into them without difficulty. More serious was the drift which began
to pile up all round and over us. It helped to keep us warm of course, but
at the same time in these comparatively high temperatures it saturated our
bags even worse than they were before. If we did not find the tent (and its
recovery would be a miracle) these bags and the floor-cloth of the tent on
which we were lying were all we had in that fight back across the Barrier
which could, I suppose, have only had one end.

Meanwhile we had to wait. It was nearly 70 miles home and it had taken
us the best part of three weeks to come. In our less miserable moments we
tried to think out ways of getting back, but I do not remember very much
about that time. Sunday morning faded into Sunday afternoon,—into Sunday night,—into Monday morning. Till then the blizzard had raged with
monstrous fury; the winds of the world were there, and they had all gone
mad. We had bad winds at Cape Evans this year, and we had far worse the
next winter when the open water was at our doors. But I have never heard
or felt or seen a wind like this. I wondered why it did not carry away the
earth.

In the early hours of Monday there was an occasional hint of a lull. Ordinarily in a big winter blizzard, when you have lived for several days and
nights with that turmoil in your ears, the lulls are more trying than the noise:
"the feel of not to feel it." I do not remember noticing that now. Seven or
eight more hours passed, and though it was still blowing we could make
ourselves heard to one another without great difficulty. It was two days and
two nights since we had had a meal.

We decided to get out of our bags and make a search for the tent. We
did so, bitterly cold and utterly miserable, though I do not think any of us
showed it. In the darkness we could see very little, and no trace whatever
of the tent. We returned against the wind, nursing our faces and hands, and
settled that we must try and cook a meal somehow. We managed about the
weirdest meal eaten north or south. We got the floor-cloth wedged under
our bags, then got into our bags and drew the floor-cloth over our heads.
Between us we got the primus alight somehow, and by hand we balanced

the cooker on top of it, minus the two members which had been blown away. The flame flickered in the draughts. Very slowly the snow in the cooker melted, we threw in a plentiful supply of pemmican, and the smell of it was better than anything on earth. In time we got both tea and pemmican, which was full of hairs from our bags, penguin feathers, dirt and debris, but delicious. The blubber left in the cooker got burnt and gave the tea a burnt taste. None of us ever forgot that meal: I enjoyed it as much as such a meal could be enjoyed, and that burnt taste will always bring back the memory.

It was still dark and we lay down in our bags again, but soon a little glow of light began to come up, and we turned out to have a further search for the tent. Birdie went off before Bill and me. Clumsily I dragged my eider-down out of my bag on my feet, all sopping wet: it was impossible to get it back and I let it freeze: it was soon just like a rock. The sky to the south was as black and sinister as it could possibly be. It looked as though the blizzard would be on us again in a moment.

I followed Bill down the slope. We could find nothing. But, as we searched, we heard a shout somewhere below and to the right. We got on a slope, slipped, and went sliding down quite unable to stop ourselves, and came upon Birdie with the tent, the outer lining still on the bamboos. Our lives had been taken away and given back to us.

We were so thankful we said nothing.

The tent must have been gripped up into the air, shutting as it rose. The bamboos, with the inner lining lashed to them, had entangled the outer cover, and the whole went up together like a shut umbrella. This was our salvation. If it had opened in the air nothing could have prevented its de-struction. As it was, with all the accumulated ice upon it, it must have weighed the best part of 100 lbs. It had been dropped about half a mile away, at the bottom of a steep slope: and it fell in a hollow, still shut up. The main force of the wind had passed over it, and there it was, with the bamboos and fastenings wrenched and strained, and the ends of two of the poles bro-ken, but the silk untorn.

If that tent went again we were going with it. We made our way back up the slope with it, carrying it solemnly and reverently, precious as though it

were something not quite of the earth. And we dug it in as tent was never
dug in before; not by the igloo, but in the old place farther down where we
had first arrived. And while Bill was doing this Birdie and I went back to
the igloo and dug and scratched and shook away the drift inside until we
had found nearly all our gear. It is wonderful how little we lost when the
roof went. Most of our gear was hung on the sledge, which was part of the
roof, or was packed into the holes of the hut to try and make it drift-proof,
and the things must have been blown inwards into the bottom of the hut
by the wind from the south and the back draught from the north. Then they
were all drifted up. Of course a certain number of mitts and socks were
blown away and lost, but the only important things were Bill's fur mitts,
which were stuffed into a hole in the rocks of the hut. We loaded up the
sledge and pushed it down the slope. I don't know how Birdie was feeling,
but I felt so weak that it was the greatest labour. The blizzard looked right
on top of us.

We had another meal, and we wanted it: and as the good hoosh ran down
into our feet and hands, and up into our cheeks and ears and brains, we
discussed what we would do next. Birdie was all for another go at the Em-
peror penguins. Dear Birdie, he never would admit that he was beaten—I
don't know that he ever really was! "I think he (Wilson) thought he had
landed us in a bad corner and was determined to go straight home, though
I was for one other tap at the Rookery. However, I had placed myself under
his orders for this trip voluntarily, and so we started the next day for home."[†]
There could really be no common-sense doubt: we had to go back, and we
were already very doubtful whether we should ever manage to get into our
sleeping-bags in very low temperature, so ghastly had they become.

I don't know when it was, but I remember walking down that slope—I
don't know why, perhaps to try and find the bottom of the cooker—and
thinking that there was nothing on earth that a man under such circumstances would not give for a good warm sleep. He would give everything
he possessed: he would give—how many—years of his life. One or two at
any rate—perhaps five? Yes—I would give five. I remember the sastrugi, the

---

†Bowers. [Footnotes preceded by symbols are the author's.]

view of the Knoll, the dim hazy black smudge of the sea far away below: the tiny bits of green canvas that twittered in the wind on the surface of the snow: the cold misery of it all, and the weakness which was biting into my heart.

For days Birdie had been urging me to use his eider-down lining—his beautiful dry bag of the finest down—which he had never slipped into his own fur bag. I had refused: I felt that I should be a beast to take it.

We packed the tank ready for a start back in the morning and turned in, utterly worn out. It was only $-12°$[2] that night, but my left big-toe was frost-bitten in my bag which I was trying to use without an eider-down lining, and my bag was always too big for me. It must have taken several hours to get it back, by beating one foot against the other. When we got up, as soon as we could, as we did every night, for our bags were nearly impossible, it was blowing fairly hard and looked like blizzing. We had a lot to do, two or three hours' work, packing sledges and making a depot of what we did not want, in a corner of the igloo. We left the second sledge, and a note tied to the handle of the pickaxe.

We started down the slope in a wind which was rising all the time and $-15°$. My job was to balance the sledge behind: I was so utterly done I don't believe I could have pulled effectively. Birdie was much the strongest of us. The strain and want of sleep was getting me in the neck, and Bill looked very bad. At the bottom we turned our faces to the Barrier, our backs to the penguins, but after doing about a mile it looked so threatening in the south that we camped in a big wind, our hands going one after the other. We had nothing but the hardest wind-swept sastrugi, and it was a long business: there was only the smallest amount of drift, and we were afraid the icy snow blocks would chafe the tent. Birdie lashed the full biscuit tin to the door to prevent its flapping, and also got what he called the tent downhaul round the cap and then tied it about himself outside his bag: if the tent went he was going too.

I was feeling as if I should crack, and accepted Birdie's eider-down. It was wonderfully self-sacrificing of him: more than I can write. I felt a brute to take it, but I was getting useless unless I got some sleep which my big

[2]Fahrenheit.

bag would not allow. Bill and Birdie kept on telling me to do less: that I was doing more than my share of the work: but I think that I was getting more and more weak. Birdie kept wonderfully strong: he slept most of the night: the difficulty for him was to get into his bag without going to sleep. He kept the meteorological log untiringly, but some of these nights he had to give it up for the time because he could not keep awake. He used to fall asleep with his pannikin in his hand and let it fall: and sometimes he had the primus.

Bill's bag was getting hopeless: it was really too small for an eider-down and was splitting all over the place: great long holes. He never consciously slept for nights: he did sleep a bit, for we heard him. Except for this night, and the next when Birdie's eider-down was still fairly dry, I never consciously slept; except that I used to wake for five or six nights running with the same nightmare—that we were drifted up, and that Bill and Birdie were passing the gear into my bag, cutting it open to do so, or some other variation,—I did not know that I had been asleep at all.[†]

"We had hardly reached the pit," wrote Bowers,

when a furious wind came on again and we had to camp. All that night the tent flapped like the noise of musketry, owing to two poles having been broken at the ends and the fit spoilt. I thought it would end matters by going altogether and lashed it down as much as I could, attaching the apex to a line round my own bag. The wind abated after 1½ days and we set out, doing five or six miles before we found ourselves among crevasses.[††]

We had plugged ahead all that day (26 July) in a terrible light, blundering in among pressure and up on to the slopes of Terror.[3] The temperature dropped from −21° to −45°.

†My own diary.
††Bowers.

---

[3]A conspicuous 10,750-foot mountain named by the team.

Several times [we] stepped into rotten-lidded crevasses in smooth wind-swept ice. We continued, however, feeling our way along by keeping always off hard ice-slopes and on the crustier deeper snow which characterizes the hollows of the pressure ridges, which I believed we had once more fouled in the dark. We had no light, and no landmarks to guide us, except vague and indistinct silhouetted slopes ahead, which were always altering and whose distance and character it was impossible to judge. We never knew whether we were approaching a steep slope at close quarters or a long slope of Terror, miles away, and eventually we travelled on by the ear, and by the feel of the snow under our feet, for both the sound and the touch told one much of the chances of crevasses or of safe going. We continued thus in the dark in the hope that we were at any rate in the right direction.[†]

And then we camped after getting into a bunch of crevasses, completely lost. Bill said, "At any rate I think we are well clear of the pressure." But there were pressure pops all night, as though someone was whacking an empty tub.

It was Birdie's picture hat which made the trouble next day. "What do you think of *that* for a hat, sir?" I heard him say to Scott[4] a few days before we started, holding it out much as Lucille displays her latest Paris model. Scott looked at it quietly for a time: "I'll tell you when you come back, Birdie," he said. It was a complicated affair with all kinds of nose-guards and buttons and lanyards: he thought he was going to set it to suit the wind much as he would set the sails of a ship. We spent a long time with our housewifes before this and other trips, for everybody has their own ideas as to how to alter their clothing for the best. When finished some looked neat, like Bill: others baggy, like Scott or Seaman Evans:[5] others rough and ready, like Oates and Bowers: a few perhaps more rough than ready, and I will not men-

[†]Wilson in *Scott's Last Expedition*.

---

[4]Robert Falcon Scott, leader of the expedition.

[5]Edgar Evans, later to die with Scott on the return from the Pole.

tion names. Anyway Birdie's hat became improper immediately it was well
iced up.

When we got a little light in the morning we found we were a little
north of the two patches of moraine on Terror. Though we did not know
it, we were on the point where the pressure runs up against Terror, and
we could dimly see that we were right up against something. We started
to try and clear it, but soon had an enormous ridge, blotting out the
moraine and half Terror, rising like a great hill on our right. Bill said the
only thing was to go right on and hope it would lower; all the time, however, there was a bad feeling that we might be putting any number of
ridges between us and the mountain. After a while we tried to cross this
one, but had to turn back for crevasses, both Bill and I putting a leg down.
We went on for about twenty minutes and found a lower place, and
turned to rise up it diagonally, and reached the top. Just over the top Birdie
went right down a crevasse, which was about wide enough to take him.
He was out of sight and out of reach from the surface, hanging in his harness. Bill went for his harness, I went for the bow of the sledge: Bill told
me to get the Alpine rope and Birdie directed from below what we could
do. We could not possibly haul him up as he was, for the sides of the
crevasse were soft and he could not help himself.[†]

"My helmet was so frozen up," wrote Bowers,

that my head was encased in a solid block of ice, and I could not look
down without inclining my whole body. As a result Bill stumbled one foot
into a crevasse and I landed in it with both mine [even as I shouted a warn-
ing],[††] the bridge gave way and down I went. Fortunately our sledge harness is made with a view to resisting this sort of thing, and there I hung
with the bottomless pit below and the ice-crusted sides alongside, so narrow that to step over it would have been quite easy had I been able to see

†My own diary.
††Wilson.

it. Bill said, "What do you want?" I asked for an Alpine rope with a bowline for my foot: and taking up first the bowline and then my harness they got me out.[†]

Meanwhile on the surface I lay over the crevasse and gave Birdie the bowline: he put it on his foot: then he raised his foot, giving me some slack: I held the rope while he raised himself on his foot, thus giving Bill some slack on the harness: Bill then held the harness, allowing Birdie to raise his foot and give me some slack again. We got him up inch by inch, our fingers getting bitten, for the temperature was −46°. Afterwards we often used this way of getting people out of crevasses, and it was a wonderful piece of presence of mind that it was invented, so far as I know, on the spur of the moment by a frozen man hanging in one himself.

In front of us we could see another ridge, and we did not know how many lay beyond that. Things looked pretty bad. Bill took a long lead on the Alpine rope and we got down our present difficulty all right. This method of the leader being on a long trace in front we all agreed to be very useful. From this moment our luck changed and everything went for us to the end. When we went out on the sea-ice the whole experience was over in a few days, Hut Point[6] was always in sight, and there was daylight. I always had the feeling that the whole series of events had been brought about by an extraordinary run of accidents, and that after a certain stage it was quite beyond our power to guide the course of them. When on the way to Cape Crozier the moon suddenly came out of the cloud to show us a great crevasse which would have taken us all with our sledge without any difficulty, I felt that we were not to go under this trip after such a deliverance. When we had lost our tent, and there was a very great balance of probability that we should never find it again, and we were lying out the blizzard in our bags, I saw that we were face to face

†Bowers.

---

[6]A landmark near the party's base camp.

with a long fight against cold which we could not have survived. I cannot write how helpless I believed we were to help ourselves, and how we were brought out of a very terrible series of experiences. When we started back I had a feeling that things were going to change for the better, and this day I had a distinct idea that we were to have one more bad experience and that after that we could hope for better things.

By running along the hollow we cleared the pressure ridges, and continued all day up and down, but met no crevasses. Indeed, we met no more crevasses and no more pressure. I think it was upon this day that a wonderful glow stretched over the Barrier edge from Cape Crozier: at the base it was the most vivid crimson it is possible to imagine, shading upwards through every shade of red to light green, and so into a deep blue sky. It is the most vivid red I have ever seen in the sky.[†]

It was −49° in the night and we were away early in −47°. By midday we were rising Terror Point, opening Erebus rapidly,[7] and got the first really light day, though the sun would not appear over the horizon for another month. I cannot describe what a relief the light was to us. We crossed the point outside our former track, and saw inside us the ridges where we had been blizzed for three days on our outward journey.

The minimum was −66° the next night and we were now back in the windless bight of Barrier with its soft snow, low temperatures, fogs and mists, and lingering settlements of the inside crusts. Saturday and Sunday, the 29th and 30th, we plugged on across this waste, iced up as usual but always with Castle Rock[8] getting bigger. Sometimes it looked like fog or wind, but it always cleared away. We were getting weak, how weak we can only realize now, but we got in good marches, though slow—days when we did 4½, 7¼, 6¾, 6½, 7½ miles. On our outward journey we had been relaying and getting forward about 1½ miles a day at this point. The surface which we had dreaded so much was not so sandy or soft as when we had

†My own diary.

[7]At 13,350 feet, Erebus is the highest mountain near McMurdo Sound.
[8]Another landmark near base camp.

come out, and the settlements were more marked. These are caused by a crust falling under your feet. Generally the area involved is some twenty yards or so round you, and the surface falls through an air space for two or three inches with a soft "crush" which may at first make you think there are crevasses about. In the region where we now travelled they were much more pronounced than elsewhere, and one day, when Bill was inside the tent lighting the primus, I put my foot into a hole that I had dug. This started a big settlement: sledge, tent and all of us dropped about a foot, and the noise of it ran away for miles and miles: we listened to it until we began to get too cold. It must have lasted a full three minutes.

In the pauses of our marching we halted in our harness, the ropes of which lay slack in the powdery snow. We stood panting with our backs against the mountainous mass of frozen gear which was our load. There was no wind, at any rate no more than light airs: our breath crackled as it froze. There was no unnecessary conversation: I don't know why our tongues never got frozen, but all my teeth, the nerves of which had been killed, split to pieces. We had been going perhaps three hours since lunch.

"How are your feet, Cherry?" from Bill.

"Very cold."

"That's all right; so are mine." We didn't worry to ask Birdie: he never had a frost-bitten foot from start to finish.

Half an hour later, as we marched, Bill would ask the same question. I tell him that all feeling has gone: Bill still has some feeling in one of his but the other is lost. He settled we had better camp: another ghastly night ahead.

We started to get out of our harnesses, while Bill, before doing anything else, would take the fur mitts from his hands, carefully shape any soft parts as they froze (generally, however, our mitts did not thaw on our hands), and lay them on the snow in front of him—two dark dots. His proper fur mitts were lost when the igloo roof went: these were the delicate dog-skin linings we had in addition, beautiful things to look at and to feel when new, excellent when dry to turn the screws of a theodolite, but too dainty for straps and lanyards. Just now I don't know what he could have done without them.

Working with our woollen half-mitts and mitts on our hands all the time, and our fur mitts over them when possible, we gradually got the buckles undone, and spread the green canvas floor-cloth on the snow. This was also fitted to be used as a sail, but we never could have rigged a sail on this journey. The shovel and the bamboos, with a lining, itself lined with ice, lashed to them, were packed on the top of the load and were now put on the snow until wanted. Our next job was to lift our three sleeping-bags one by one on to the floor-cloth: they covered it, bulging over the sides—those obstinate coffins which were all our life to us. . . . One of us is off by now to nurse his fingers back. The cooker was unlashed from the top of the instrument box; some parts of it were put on the bags with the primus, methylated spirit can, matches and so forth; others left to be filled with snow later. Taking a pole in each hand we three spread the bamboos over the whole. "All right? Down!" from Bill; and we lowered them gently on to the soft snow, that they might not sink too far. The ice on the inner lining of the tent was formed mostly from the steam of the cooker. This we had been unable to beat or chip off in the past, and we were now, truth to tell, past worrying about it. The little ventilator in the top, made to let out this steam, had been tied up in order to keep in all possible heat. Then over the outer cover, and for one of us the third worst job of the day was to begin. The worst job was to get into our bags: the second or equal worst was to lie in them for six hours (we had brought it down to six): this third worst was to get the primus lighted and a meal on the way.

As cook of the day you took the broken metal framework, all that remained of our candlestick, and got yourself with difficulty into the funnel which formed the door. The enclosed space of the tent seemed much colder than the outside air: you tried three or four match-boxes and no match would strike: almost desperate, you asked for a new box to be given you from the sledge and got a light from this because it had not yet been in the warmth, so called, of the tent. The candle hung by a wire from the cap of the tent. It would be tedious to tell of the times we had getting the primus alight, and the lanyards of the weekly food bag unlashed. Probably by now the other two men have dug in the tent; squared up outside; filled and passed in the cooker; set the thermometer under the sledge and so forth. There were always one or two odd jobs which wanted doing as well: but you may be sure they came in as soon as possible when they heard the primus hissing, and saw the glow of light inside. Birdie made a bottom for the cooker out of an empty biscuit tin to take the place of the part which was blown away. On the whole this was a success, but we had to hold it steady—on Bill's sleeping-bag, for the flat frozen bags spread all over the floor space. Cooking was a longer business now. Someone whacked out the biscuit, and the cook put the ration of pemmican into the inner cooker which was by now half full of water. As opportunity offered we got out of our day, and into our night foot-gear—fleecy camel-hair stockings and fur boots. In the dim light we examined our feet for frost-bite.

I do not think it took us less than an hour to get a hot meal to our lips: pemmican followed by hot water in which we soaked our biscuits. For lunch we had tea and biscuits: for breakfast, pemmican, biscuits and tea. We could not have managed more food bags—three were bad enough, and the lashings of everything were like wire. The lashing of the tent door, however, was the worst, and it *had* to be tied tightly, especially if it was blowing. In the early days we took great pains to brush rime from the tent before packing it up, but we were long past that now.

The hoosh got down into our feet: we nursed back frost-bites: and we were all the warmer for having got our dry foot-gear on before supper. Then we started to get into our bags.

Birdie's bag fitted him beautifully, though perhaps it would have been a little small with an eider-down inside. He must have had a greater heat supply than other men; for he never had serious trouble with his feet, while ours were constantly frost-bitten: he slept, I should be afraid to say how much, longer than we did, even in these last days: it was a pleasure, lying awake practically all night, to hear his snores. He turned his bag inside out from fur to skin, and skin to fur, many times during the journey, and thus got rid of a lot of moisture which came out as snow or actual knobs of ice. When we did turn our bags the only way was to do so directly we turned out, and even then you had to be quick before the bag froze. Getting out of the tent at night it was quite a race to get back to your bag before it hardened. Of course this was in the lowest temperatures.

We could not burn our bags and we tried putting the lighted primus into them to thaw them out, but this was not very successful. Before this time, when it was very cold, we lighted the primus in the morning while we were still in our bags: and in the evening we kept it going until we were just getting or had got the mouths of our bags levered open. But returning we had no oil for such luxuries, until the last day or two.

I do not believe that any man, however sick he is, has a much worse time than we had in those bags, shaking with cold until our backs would almost break. One of the added troubles which came to us on our return was the sodden condition of our hands in our bags at night. We had to wear our mitts and half-mitts, and they were as wet as they could be: when we got up in the morning we had washerwomen's hands—white, crinkled, sodden. That was an unhealthy way to start the day's work. We really wanted some bags of saennegrass for hands as well as feet; one of the blessings of that kind of bag being that you can shake the moisture from it: but we only had enough for our wretched feet.

The horrors of that return journey are blurred to my memory and I know they were blurred to my body at the time. I think this applies to all of us, for we were much weakened and callous. The day we got down to the penguins I had not cared whether I fell into a crevasse or not. We had been through a great deal since then. I know that we slept on the march; for I woke up when I bumped against Birdie, and Birdie woke when he bumped against me. I think Bill steering out in front managed to keep awake. I know we fell asleep if we waited in the comparatively warm tent when the primus was alight—with our pannikins or the primus in our hands. I know that our sleeping-bags were so full of ice that we did not worry if we spilt water or hoosh over them as they lay on the floor-cloth, when we cooked on them with our maimed cooker. They were so bad that we never rolled them up in the usual way when we got out of them in the morning: we opened their mouths as much as possible before they froze, and hoisted them more or less flat on to the sledge. All three of us helped to raise each bag, which looked rather like a squashed coffin and was probably a good deal harder. I know that if it was only −40° when we camped for the night we considered quite seriously that we were going to have a warm one, and that when we got up in the morning if the temperature was in the minus sixties we did not inquire what it was. The day's march was bliss compared to the night's rest, and both were awful. We were about as bad as men can be and do good travelling: but I never heard a word of complaint, nor, I believe, an oath, and I saw self-sacrifice standing every test.

Always we were getting nearer home: and we were doing good marches. We were going to pull through; it was only a matter of sticking this for a few more days; six, five, four . . . three perhaps now, if we were not blizzed. Our main hut was behind that ridge where the mist was always forming and blowing away, and there was Castle Rock: we might even see Observation Hill tomorrow, and the *Discovery* Hut[9] furnished and trim was behind it, and they would have sent some dry sleeping-bags from Cape Evans to greet us there. We reckoned our troubles over at the Barrier edge, and assuredly it was not far away. "You've got it in the neck, stick it, you've got it in the neck"—it was always running in my head.

And we *did* stick it. How good the memories of those days are. With jokes about Birdie's picture hat: with songs we remembered off the gramophone: with ready words of sympathy for frost-bitten feet: with generous smiles for poor jests: with suggestions of happy beds to come. We did not forget the Please and Thank You, which means much in such circumstances, and all the little links with decent civilization which we could still keep going. I'll swear there was still a grace about us when we staggered in. And we kept our tempers—even with God.

We *might* reach Hut Point tonight: we were burning more oil now, that one-gallon tin had lasted us well: and burning more candle too; at one time we feared they would give out. A hell of a morning we had: −57° in our present state. But it was calm, and the Barrier edge could not be much far-

---

[9]A base-camp hut, built originally by Scott in 1902, named after that previous expedition's ship, the *Discovery*. It was not used in 1910–13.

ther now. The surface was getting harder: there were a few wind-blown furrows, the crust was coming up to us. The sledge was dragging easier: we always suspected the Barrier sloped downwards hereabouts. Now the hard snow was on the surface, peeping out like great inverted basins on which we slipped, and our feet became warmer for not sinking into soft snow. Suddenly we saw a gleam of light in a line of darkness running across our course. It was the Barrier edge: we were all right now.

We ran the sledge off a snow-drift on to the sea-ice, with the same cold stream of air flowing down it which wrecked my hands five weeks ago: pushed out of this, camped and had a meal: the temperature had already risen to −43°. We could almost feel it getting warmer as we went round Cape Armitage on the last three miles. We managed to haul our sledge up the ice foot, and dug the drift away from the door. The old hut struck us as fairly warm.

Bill was convinced that we ought not to go into the warm hut at Cape Evans when we arrived there—tomorrow night! We ought to get back to warmth gradually, live in a tent outside, or in the annexe for a day or two. But I'm sure we never meant to do it. Just now Hut Point did not prejudice us in favour of such abstinence. It was just as we had left it: there was nothing sent down for us there—no sleeping-bags, nor sugar: but there was plenty of oil. Inside the hut we pitched a dry tent left there since Depot Journey days, set two primuses going in it; sat dozing on our bags; and drank cocoa without sugar so thick that next morning we were gorged with it. We were very happy, falling asleep between each mouthful, and after several hours discussed schemes of not getting into our bags at all. But someone would have to keep the primus going to prevent frost-bite, and we could not trust ourselves to keep awake. Bill and I tried to sing a part-song. Finally we sopped our way into our bags. We only stuck *them* three hours, and thankfully turned out at 3 A.M., and were ready to pack up when we heard the wind come away. It was no good, so we sat in our tent and dozed again. The wind dropped at 9.30: we were off at 11. We walked out into what seemed to us a blaze of light. It was not until the following year that I understood that a great part of such twilight as there is in the latter part of the winter was cut off from us by the mountains under which we travelled. Now, with nothing between us and the northern horizon below which lay the sun, we saw as we had not seen for months, and the iridescent clouds that day were beautiful.

We just pulled for all we were worth and did nearly two miles an hour: for two miles a baddish salt surface, then big undulating hard sastrugi and good going. We slept as we walked. We had done eight miles by 4 P.M. and were past Glacier Tongue. We lunched there.

As we began to gather our gear together to pack up for the last time, Bill said quietly, "I want to thank you two for what you have done. I couldn't have found two better companions—and what is more I never shall."

I am proud of that.

Antarctic exploration is seldom as bad as you imagine, seldom as bad as it sounds. But this journey had beggared our language: no words could express its horror.

We trudged on for several more hours and it grew very dark. There was a discussion as to where Cape Evans lay. We rounded it at last: it must have been ten or eleven o'clock, and it was possible that someone might see us as we pulled towards the hut. "Spread out well," said Bill, "and they will be able to see that there are three men." But we pulled along the cape, over the tide-crack, up the bank to the very door of the hut without a sound. No noise from the stable, nor the bark of a dog from the snow drifts above us. We halted and stood there trying to get ourselves and one another out of our frozen harnesses—the usual long job. The door opened—"Good God! here is the Crozier Party," said a voice, and disappeared.

Thus ended the worst journey in the world.

• • •

ERNEST SHACKLETON

(1874–1922)

From *South: The Story of Shackleton's Last Expedition
1914–1917*

*After Roald Amundsen and Robert Falcon Scott both reached the South
Pole in the summer of 1911–12, concluding a decade and a half of
efforts to attain the most remote spot on Earth, exploratory interest in
Antarctica waned. But Sir Ernest Shackleton, who in 1909 had pushed
farther south than anyone before him, returned to the icy continent in
1914 with a "last great journey" as a goal that was breathtaking in its
audacity: to traverse Antarctica from sea to sea. (That exploratory deed
would not be performed until the late 1950s, when Sir Vivian Fuchs
and Sir Edmund Hillary used motorized tractors to make the crossing.)*

*By most reckonings, Shackleton's 1914–17 expedition might have
gone down as one of the all-time polar fiascos, for the* Endurance *never
even reached the Antarctic shore, getting frozen into sea ice and drifting with the currents for months before breaking up and sinking. Instead, Shackleton turned his disaster into an escape so brilliant that
almost nine decades later it still inspires readers. Dragging and sailing*

their three lifeboats, the party struggled to uninhabited Elephant Island. There, twenty-two men wintered over as five volunteers led by Shackleton set out in a single boat, the James Caird, *to sail some eight hundred miles to South Georgia Island, where a forlorn whaling station formed the nearest outpost of civilization. Frank Worsley's solving the route of that passage, with only a chronometer and a few sextant readings, is still regarded as one of the finest feats of open-boat navigation ever performed.*

Shackleton not only reached South Georgia Island but organized a rescue mission that eventually saved the twenty-two men on Elephant Island. In the whole perilous expedition, not a single life was lost.

In recent years, a kind of Shackleton mania has put secondhand accounts by Caroline Alexander and Alfred Lansing on the best-seller list. The truest narrative of the expedition, however, remains Shackleton's own book South, *no matter how understated its telling of that heroic adventure. In this excerpt, Shackleton recounts the bold traverse of heavily glaciated, mountainous South Georgia Island that formed the climax of the escape from Antarctic ice. Leaving the three weakest men from the boat party on shore, Shackleton set off across the island with Worsley and second officer Tom Crean.*

The sun rose in the sky with every appearance of a fine day, and we grew warmer as we toiled through the soft snow. Ahead of us lay the ridges and spurs of a range of mountains, the transverse range that we had noticed from the bay. We were travelling over a gently rising plateau, and at the end of an hour we found ourselves growing uncomfortably hot. Years before, on an earlier expedition, I had declared that I would never again growl at the heat of the sun, and my resolution had been strengthened during the boat journey. I called it to mind as the sun beat fiercely on the blinding white snow-slope. After passing an area of crevasses we paused for our first meal. We dug a hole in the snow about three feet deep with the adze and put the Primus into it. There was no wind at the moment, but a gust might come suddenly. A hot hoosh was soon eaten and we plodded on towards a sharp ridge between two of the peaks already mentioned. By 11 A.M. we were almost at the crest. The slope had become precipitous and it was necessary to cut steps as we advanced. The adze proved an excellent instrument for this purpose, a blow sufficing to provide a foothold. Anxiously but hopefully I cut the last few steps and stood upon the razor-back, while the other men held the rope and waited for my news. The outlook was disappointing. I looked down a sheer precipice to a chaos of crumpled ice 1500 ft. below. There was no way down for us. The country to the east was a great snow upland, sloping upwards for a distance of seven or eight miles to a height of over 4000 ft. To the north it fell away steeply in glaciers into the bays, and to the south it was broken by huge outfalls from the inland ice-sheet. Our path lay between the glaciers and the outfalls, but first we had to descend from the ridge on which we stood.

Cutting steps with the adze, we moved in a lateral direction round the base of a dolomite,[1] which blocked our view to the north. The same precipice confronted us. Away to the north-east there appeared to be a snow-slope that might give a path to the lower country, and so we retraced our steps down the long slope that had taken us three hours to climb. We were at the bottom in an hour. We were now feeling the strain of the unaccustomed marching. We had done little walking since January and our muscles were out of tune. Skirting the base of the mountain above us, we came to a gigantic bergschrund,[2] a mile and a half long and 1000 ft. deep. This tremendous gully, cut in the snow and ice by the fierce winds blowing round the mountain, was semicircular in form, and it ended in a gentle incline. We passed through it, under the towering precipice of ice, and at the far end we had another meal and a short rest. This was at 12.30 P.M. Half a pot of steaming Bovril ration[3] warmed us up, and when we marched again ice-inclines at angles of 45 degrees did not look quite as formidable as before.

---

[1] A limestone outcrop.

[2] A crevasse that separates the mountain proper from the glacier beneath it.

[3] A hot drink.

Once more we started for the crest. After another weary climb we reached the top. The snow lay thinly on blue ice at the ridge, and we had to cut steps over the last fifty yards. The same precipice lay below, and my eyes searched vainly for a way down. The hot sun had loosened the snow, which was now in a treacherous condition, and we had to pick our way carefully. Looking back, we could see that a fog was rolling up behind us and meeting in the valleys a fog that was coming up from the east. The creeping grey clouds were a plain warning that we must get down to lower levels before becoming enveloped.

The ridge was studded with peaks, which prevented us getting a clear view either to the right or to the left. The situation in this respect seemed no better at other points within our reach, and I had to decide that our course lay back the way we had come. The afternoon was wearing on and the fog was rolling up ominously from the west. It was of the utmost importance for us to get down into the next valley before dark. We were now up 4500 ft. and the night temperature at that elevation would be very low. We had no tent and no sleeping-bags, and our clothes had endured much rough usage and had weathered many storms during the last ten months. In the distance, down the valley below us, we could see tussock-grass close to the shore, and if we could get down it might be possible to dig out a hole in one of the lower snow-banks, line it with dry grass, and make ourselves fairly comfortable for the night. Back we went, and after a detour we reached the top of another ridge in the fading light. After a glance over the top I turned to the anxious faces of the two men behind me and said, "Come on, boys." Within a minute they stood beside me on the ice-ridge. The surface fell away at a sharp incline in front of us, but it merged into a snow-slope. We could not see the bottom clearly owing to mist and bad light, and the possibility of the slope ending in a sheer fall occurred to us; but the fog that was creeping up behind allowed no time for hesitation. We descended slowly at first, cutting steps in the hard snow; then the surface became softer, indicating that the gradient was less severe. There could be no turning back now, so we unroped and slid in the fashion of youthful days. When we stopped on a snow-bank at the foot of the slope we found that we had descended at least 900 ft. in two or three minutes. We looked back and saw the grey fingers of the fog appearing on the ridge, as though reaching after the intruders into untrodden wilds. But we had escaped.

The country to the east was an ascending snow upland dividing the glaciers of the north coast from the outfalls of the south. We had seen from the top that our course lay between two huge masses of crevasses, and we thought that the road ahead lay clear. This belief and the increasing cold made us abandon the idea of camping. We had another meal at 6 P.M. A little breeze made cooking difficult in spite of the shelter provided for the cooker by a hole. Crean was the cook, and Worsley and I lay on the snow to windward of the lamp so as to break the wind with our bodies. The meal over, we started up the long, gentle ascent. Night was upon us, and for an hour we plodded along in almost complete darkness, watching warily for signs of crevasses. Then about 8 P.M. a glow which we had seen behind the jagged peaks resolved itself into the full moon, which rose ahead of us and made a silver pathway for our feet. Along that pathway in the wake of the moon we advanced in safety, with the shadows cast by the edges of crevasses showing black on either side of us. Onwards and upwards through soft snow we marched, resting now and then on hard patches which had revealed themselves by glittering ahead of us in the white light. By midnight we were again at an elevation of about 4000 ft. Still we were following the light, for as the moon swung round towards the north-east our path curved in that direction. The friendly moon seemed to pilot our weary feet. We could have had no better guide. If in bright daylight we had made that march we would have followed the course that was traced for us that night.

Midnight found us approaching the edge of a great snow-field, pierced by isolated nunataks which cast long shadows like black rivers across the white expanse. A gentle slope to the north-east lured our all-too-willing feet in that direction. We thought that at the base of the slope lay Stromness Bay.[4] After we had descended about 300 ft. a thin wind began to attack us. We had now been on the march for over twenty hours, only halting for our oc-

---

[4]On which the whaling station was located.

casional meals. Wisps of cloud drove over the high peaks to the southward, warning us that wind and snow were likely to come. After 1 A.M. we cut a pit in the snow, piled up loose snow around it, and started the Primus again. The hot food gave us another renewal of energy. Worsley and Crean sang their old songs when the Primus was going merrily. Laughter was in our hearts, though not on our parched and cracked lips.

We were up and away again within half an hour, still downward to the coast. We felt almost sure now that we were above Stromness Bay. A dark object down at the foot of the slope looked like Mutton Island, which lies off Husvik.[5] I suppose our desires were giving wings to our fancies, for we pointed out joyfully various landmarks revealed by the now vagrant light of the moon, whose friendly face was cloud-swept. Our high hopes were soon shattered. Crevasses warned us that we were on another glacier, and soon we looked down almost to the seaward edge of the great riven ice-mass. I knew there was no glacier in Stromness and realized that this must be For-tuna Glacier. The disappointment was severe. Back we turned and tramped up the glacier again, not directly tracing our steps but working at a tangent to the south-east. We were very tired.

At 5 A.M. we were at the foot of the rocky spurs of the range. We were tired, and the wind that blew down from the heights was chilling us. We decided to get down under the lee of a rock for a rest. We put our sticks and the adze on the snow, sat down on them as close to one another as possi-ble, and put our arms round each other. The wind was bringing a little drift with it and the white dust lay on our clothes. I thought that we might be able to keep warm and have half an hour's rest this way. Within a minute my two companions were fast asleep. I realized that it would be disastrous if we all slumbered together, for sleep under such conditions merges into death. After five minutes I shook them into consciousness again, told them that they had slept for half an hour, and gave the word for a fresh start. We were so stiff that for the first two or three hundred yards we marched with our knees bent. A jagged line of peaks with a gap like a broken tooth con-

[5]The whaling station.

fronted us. This was the ridge that runs in a southerly direction from For-tuna Bay, and our course eastward to Stromness lay across it. A very steep slope led up to the ridge and an icy wind burst through the gap.

We went through the gap at 6 A.M. with anxious hearts as well as weary bodies. If the farther slope had proved impassable our situation would have been almost desperate; but the worst was turning to the best for us. The twisted, wave-like rock-formations of Husvik Harbour appeared right ahead in the opening of dawn. Without a word we shook hands with one another. To our minds the journey was over, though as a matter of fact twelve miles of difficult country had still to be traversed. A gentle snow-slope descended at our feet towards a valley that separated our ridge from the hills immedi-ately behind Husvik, and as we stood gazing Worsley said solemnly, "Boss, it looks too good to be true!" Down we went, to be checked presently by the sight of water 2500 ft. below. We could see the little wave-ripples on the black beach, penguins strutting to and fro, and dark objects that looked like seals lolling lazily on the sand. This was an eastern arm of Fortuna Bay, sep-arated by the ridge from the arm we had seen below us during the night. The slope we were traversing appeared to end in a precipice above this beach. But our revived spirits were not to be damped by difficulties on the last stage of the journey, and we camped cheerfully for breakfast. Whilst Worsley and Crean were digging a hole for the lamp and starting the cooker I climbed a ridge above us, cutting steps with the adze, in order to secure an extended view of the country below. At 6.30 A.M. I thought I heard the sound of a steam-whistle. I dared not be certain, but I knew that the men at the whaling-station would be called from their beds about that time. De-scending to the camp I told the others, and in intense excitement we watched the chronometer for seven o'clock, when the whalers would be summoned to work. Right to the minute the steam-whistle came to us, borne clearly on the wind across the intervening miles of rock and snow. Never had any one of us heard sweeter music. It was the first sound created by out-side human agency that had come to our ears since we left Stromness Bay in December 1914. That whistle told us that men were living near, that ships were ready, and that within a few hours we should be on our way back to Elephant Island to the rescue of the men waiting there under the watch and ward of Wild.[6] It was a moment hard to describe. Pain and ache, boat journeys, marches, hunger and fatigue seemed to belong to the limbo of forgotten things, and there remained only the perfect contentment that comes of work accomplished.

My examination of the country from a higher point had not provided definite information, and after descending I put the situation before Worsley and Crean. Our obvious course lay down a snow-slope in the direction of Husvik. "Boys," I said, "this snow-slope seems to end in a precipice, but perhaps there is no precipice. If we don't go down we shall have to make a detour of at least five miles before we reach level going. What shall it be?" They both replied at once, "Try the slope." So we started away again downwards. We abandoned the Primus lamp, now empty, at the breakfast camp and carried with us one ration and a biscuit each. The deepest snow we had yet encountered clogged our feet, but we plodded downward, and after descending about 500 ft., reducing our altitude to 2000 ft. above sea-level, we thought we saw the way clear ahead. A steep gradient of blue ice was the next obstacle. Worsley and Crean got a firm footing in a hole excavated with the adze and then lowered me as I cut steps until the full 50 ft. of our alpine rope was out. Then I made a hole big enough for the three of us, and the other two men came down the steps. My end of the rope was anchored to the adze and I had settled myself in the hole braced for a strain in case they slipped. When we all stood in the second hole I went down again to make more steps, and in this laborious fashion we spent two hours descending about 500 ft. Halfway down we had to strike away diagonally to the left, for we noticed that the fragments of ice loosened by the adze were taking a leap into space at the bottom of the slope. Eventually we got off the steep ice, very gratefully, at a point where some rocks protruded, and we could see then that there was a perilous precipice directly below the point where we had started to cut steps. A slide down a slippery slope, with the adze and our cooker going ahead, completed this

---

[6] Frank Wild, second-in-command on the expedition.

descent, and incidentally did considerable damage to our much-tried trousers.

When we picked ourselves up at the bottom we were not more than 1500 ft. above the sea. The slope was comparatively easy. Water was running beneath the snow, making "pockets" between the rocks that protruded above the white surface. The shells of snow over these pockets were traps for our feet; but we scrambled down, and presently came to patches of tussock. A few minutes later we reached the sandy beach. The tracks of some animals were to be seen, and we were puzzled until I remembered that reindeer, brought from Norway, had been placed on the island and now ranged along the lower land of the eastern coast. We did not pause to investigate. Our minds were set upon reaching the haunts of man, and at our best speed we went along the beach to another rising ridge of tussock. Here we saw the first evidence of the proximity of man, whose work, as is so often the case, was one of destruction. A recently killed seal was lying there, and presently we saw several other bodies bearing the marks of bullet-wounds. I learned later that men from the whaling-station at Stromness sometimes go round to Fortuna Bay by boat to shoot seals.

Noon found us well up the slope on the other side of the bay working east-south-east, and half an hour later we were on a flat plateau, with one more ridge to cross before we descended into Husvik. I was leading the way over this plateau when I suddenly found myself up to my knees in water and quickly sinking deeper through the snow-crust. I flung myself down and called to the others to do the same, so as to distribute our weight on the treacherous surface. We were on top of a small lake, snow-covered. After lying still for a few moments we got to our feet and walked delicately, like Agag,[7] for 200 yds., until a rise in the surface showed us that we were clear of the lake.

At 1.30 P.M. we climbed round a final ridge and saw a little steamer, a whaling-boat, entering the bay 2500 ft. below. A few moments later, as he hurried forward, the masts of a sailing-ship lying at a wharf came in sight.

[7]Reference to 1 Sam. 15.32: "And Agag came unto him delicately."

Minute figures moving to and fro about the boats caught our gaze, and then we saw the sheds and factory of Stromness whaling-station. We paused and shook hands, a form of mutual congratulation that had seemed necessary on four other occasions in the course of the expedition. The first time was when we landed on Elephant Island, the second when we reached South Georgia, and the third when we reached the ridge and saw the snow-slope stretching below on the first day of the overland journey, then when we saw Husvik rocks.

Cautiously we started down the slope that led to warmth and comfort. The last lap of the journey proved extraordinarily difficult. Vainly we searched for a safe, or a reasonably safe, way down the steep ice-clad mountain-side. The sole possible pathway seemed to be a channel cut by water running from the upland. Down through icy water we followed the course of this stream. We were wet to the waist, shivering, cold, and tired. Presently our ears detected an unwelcome sound that might have been musical under other conditions. It was the splashing of a waterfall, and we were at the wrong end. When we reached the top of this fall we peered over cautiously and discovered that there was a drop of 25 or 30 ft., with impassable ice-cliffs on both sides. To go up again was scarcely thinkable in our utterly wearied condition. The way down was through the waterfall itself. We made fast one end of our rope to a boulder with some difficulty, due to the fact that the rocks had been worn smooth by the running water. Then Worsley and I lowered Crean, who was the heaviest man. He disappeared altogether in the falling water and came out gasping at the bottom. I went next, sliding down the rope, and Worsley, who was the lightest and most nimble member of the party, came last. At the bottom of the fall we were able to stand again on dry land. The rope could not be recovered. We had flung down the adze from the top of the fall and also the logbook and the cooker wrapped in one of our blouses. That was all, except our wet clothes, that we brought out of the Antarctic, which we had entered a year and a half before with well-found ship, full equipment, and high hopes. That was all of tangible things; but in memories we were rich. We had pierced the veneer of outside things. We had "suffered, starved, and triumphed, grovelled down yet grasped at glory, grown bigger in the bigness of the whole." We had seen God in his splendours, heard the text that Nature renders. We had reached the naked soul of man.

Shivering with cold, yet with hearts light and happy, we set off towards the whaling-station, now not more than a mile and a half distant. The difficulties of the journey lay behind us. We tried to straighten ourselves up a bit, for the thought that there might be women at the station made us painfully conscious of our uncivilized appearance. Our beards were long and our hair was matted. We were unwashed and the garments that we had worn for nearly a year without a change were tattered and stained. Three more unpleasant-looking ruffians could hardly have been imagined. Worsley produced several safety-pins from some corner of his garments and effected some temporary repairs that really emphasized his general disrepair. Down we hurried, and when quite close to the station we met two small boys ten or twelve years of age. I asked these lads where the manager's house was situated. They did not answer. They gave us one look—a comprehensive look that did not need to be repeated. Then they ran from us as fast as their legs would carry them. We reached the outskirts of the station and passed through the "digesting-house," which was dark inside. Emerging at the other end, we met an old man, who started as if he had seen the Devil himself and gave us no time to ask any question. He hurried away. This greeting was not friendly. Then we came to the wharf, where the man in charge stuck to his station. I asked him if Mr. Sorlle (the manager) was in the house.

"Yes," he said as he stared at us.

"We would like to see him," said I.

"Who are you?" he asked.

"We have lost our ship and come over the island," I replied.

"You have come over the island?" he said in a tone of entire disbelief.

The man went towards the manager's house and we followed him. I learned afterwards that he said to Mr. Sorlle: "There are three funny-looking men outside, who say they have come over the island and they know you. I have left them outside." A very necessary precaution from his point of view.

Mr. Sorlle came out to the door and said, "Well?"

"Don't you know me?" I said.

"I know your voice," he replied doubtfully. "You're the mate of the *Daisy.*"

"My name is Shackleton," I said.

Immediately he put out his hand and said, "Come in. Come in."

"Tell me, when was the war over?" I asked.

"The war is not over," he answered. "Millions are being killed. Europe is mad. The world is mad."

• • •

BERTRAM THOMAS

(1892–1950)

From *Arabia Felix: Across the "Empty Quarter" of Arabia*

The Rub' al Khali, or Empty Quarter, in southern Arabia—probably the world's most inhospitable desert—will forever be associated with the great English traveler Sir Wilfred Thesiger. But Thesiger was not the first Westerner to cross the Empty Quarter. That honor fell to Bertram Thomas in 1931, after a number of other European veterans had been defeated.

In Arabian Sands, Thesiger pays tribute to Thomas for having seized "the final and greatest prize of Arabian exploration." In the next breath, however, he downplays the achievement: "His object was to cross the Empty Quarter, and naturally he crossed it by the easiest way, where the dunes were small and the wells, known to his Rashid guides, were frequent."

In any event, Thomas's traverse by "the easiest way" came only at the cost of an exhausting and perilous journey. It is characteristic of Thomas's modest account that he subsumes the ordeal beneath his in-

satiable curiosity—about meteorites, prehistoric artifacts, place names, Bedouin tracking techniques, and camels' homing instinct. T. E. Lawrence hailed Thomas's deed as "the finest thing in Arabian exploration," the man himself as "a master of every desert art."

An early start was made on the 19th January, our course still northwest. The absence of grazing in our way and our camels' thirst from their recent saline pastures made for fast marching. Leaving Umm Quraiyin on our right hand—a reported water-hole that marked the northward limit of Munajjar—we came to the sand region of Sanam, white and rolling in a gentle swell. This region—the word itself means camel's hump—is conspicuous for the comparative sweetness of its water-holes and their abnormal depth, an average being eleven fathoms, and some there are of fifteen and seventeen fathoms in the west.

The shallower wells of the southern sands are sometimes filled in after watering to obstruct a possible pursuer. But here the water-holes are roofed to protect them, for great labour, skill and courage have gone in their making. Indeed the deep water-holes of Tuwal exact a toll of life, for the soft sides are prone to slip and entomb the miners, and all that avails for revetment is the coiled branches of some wretched bush of the sands. As we passed Safif, a Murri turned to me. "Four of my brothers" (i.e. Murra tribesmen) "lie in the bottom there. Two of them had descended to clean it out and were overwhelmed by slipping sand, and their companions, following to rescue them, were engulfed too. Safif is a tomb; we have abandoned it."

The fasting month of Ramadhan was upon us. No crescent moon had been seen on the morning of 20th January, so hopes were set upon the evening. We halted in good time, all eyes towards the western sky in the wake of the setting sun. The first appearance of the Ramadhan moon excites intense eagerness on the part of the Faithful, and in Oman its entry and exit are accompanied by the booming of more than a monarch's salute. This evening disappointment was in store for us. The saffron sky turned to slaty grey and then to darkness, but there was no moon; to-morrow my companions would not be glorifying God in the Fast.

Farajja, our next water-hole, lay a nine and a half hours' march distant, and we were obliged to make it because our water-skins were empty. We were thus still in the saddle when just after sunset rifle shots rang out from ahead, and a faint wisp of the crescent moon showed in the pale sky. With cries of "Glory to God," my companions couched their camels and prostrated themselves in prayer, one or two of them first sticking their rifles barrel downwards into the sands. Our course had veered due west in the track of our advance party and thus continued until after dark, when the flare of a distant camp-fire was the beacon for our night's halting-place. My companions being on a journey had a right to break or postpone fasting till they regained their homes, but none elected to do so. They all fasted on the march, as my Bait Kathiris[1] had done at Mugshin a year before. Hitherto they had availed themselves of the prayer concession of the march, running the five occasions into three, but now in Ramadhan they observed the entire number. Scarcely in keeping with this increased religious zeal was the change in the food _régime_. Dinner had formerly followed the joint evening prayer; now it followed the sunset Credo of the _mu'ed-hdhin_[2] and was sandwiched between it and the prayer that normally would follow.

Scouts for pastures may postpone the Ramadhan fast, but the rule for the raider is different. He may enjoy the concession only on the return from the raid; during the approach and the attack he must fast.

The sand tribes have also a peculiar marital observance. In Ramadhan sexual relations are only permissible if ablution can follow, that is, when near or carrying water.

At other times of the year the religious injunction regarding this greater ablution is disregarded. When they are away from water, sand is used before prayer, but nothing after the sexual act. It thus comes about that while

[1]Desert Bedouins of the Bait Kathir tribe.
[2]Muslim call to prayer.

there is no rule against marriage in Ramadhan such marriages in the sands are rare, if not unheard of.

The months of the desert are lunar months, but known by names not always according with the usual Muslim calendar. The word Muharram, for instance, is never used by them, and they reckon the year, so far as they date it at all, from the Fast month or the Pilgrimage month.

Here in lat. 21° 30' the sands of Sanam must be shallowing because for the first time the hard flat floor emerged in circular patches from the sands.

One of my Badawin[3] found and brought me some potsherds and bits of broken old dull glass from the surface of one such place. I looked but could see no trace of an artificial mound, but only apparently natural undulations, and I was incredulous that the region could have had any considerable settlement, preferring the theory that *dibbis*—syrup of dates—had been brought out here in pots from Hasa, for some bygone Ramadhan perhaps, before the kerosene tin became the common receptacle of Arabia. The possibility of archæological remains in Sanam should not, on the other hand, be ruled out. The Murra indeed have a tradition of the foundations of a fort once to be seen but now covered over by sand. Umm al Hadid, a water-hole, is also said to have a tradition of remains—two large blocks of so-called iron-stone—whence its name. These, however, may have been meteorites.

I had collected a fragment of black meteorite in the Buwah region of Suwahib. It was found lying on the sands as we passed, the Badu[4] who picked it up calling it an "iron stone" presumably on account of its great weight. Its nature proved difficult to establish at first on account of its irregular shape and sharp angles, for the meteorite is commonly a rounded stone, sometimes pitted with holes. My Buwah specimen is thought to be part of a much larger meteorite which burst into pieces on its passage through the atmosphere.

At Farajja our camels were taken off to water in the forenoon, and this provided me with an opportunity of collecting data for my map—the names

[3]I.e., Bedouins.
[4]Bedouin.

and direction and distance of sands and water-holes that must be recorded as we went along and worked out by a process of arithmetical triangulation. But Badawin are apt to fret under too close and long cross-questioning and the most profitable information is obtained when the Arab can be encouraged to discourse. The occasion was one for a story too—the tale of Bu Zaid and his two brothers Yusif and Baraiga and their encounter with a *jinn*.

• • •

BEFORE THE STORY was ended our camels, coming back from water, appeared across the sands. Hamad and I walked out to meet them. As we went we crossed many recent camel tracks which showed Farajja to be a popular water-hole. The grouped tracks of four camels walking in line arrested my companion's attention, and he turned to me and asked me in play which camel I saw in the sands to be best. I pointed—pardonably, I persuaded myself—to the wrong one. "There," he said, "do you see that cuffing up of the toes? It is a good sign: but not that skidding," pointing to mine, "between the footmarks." "That," he said of the third, "is an animal that has recently been in the steppe. Do you see the rugged impressions of her feet? Camels that have long been in the sands leave smooth impressions, and that" (pointing to the fourth) "is her baby. Your camel is big with young— see the deep impressions of her small hind feet." And thus and thus. It was not the least important part of Hamad's lore—a lore shared by nearly every dweller of the sands in varying degree—to read the condition of the strange camel, as yet unseen, from her marks, and hence to know whether to flee or to pursue.

Tracking in Arabia is an exact science, beside which the finger-print methods of the West are limited in scope, for the sands are a perfect medium.

In the more sophisticated parts of the peninsula—Oman, for example, a Court of Justice acts upon a foot-tracker's evidence, though there the *qaffar*, as he is called, has gifts not possessed, as in the sands, by the world at large. A case occurred during my service in Muscat. A Chinaman who had come to buy pearls and sea-slugs was murdered one night while he slept on the roof of his house in the Muscat bazaar. The murderer had apparently been surprised in the act, for he had jumped from the roof (it was a single-storey building) in his flight. The imprint of his foot remained in the lane beneath. On discovery next morning a pot was placed over it, sentries were posted at either end of the lane to prevent people passing that way, and a famous foot-tracker sent for, from up country. Meanwhile the days passed and the town grew nervous, for the murder had been a particularly brutal one—the neck had been cut with a sharp dagger from ear to ear—and the murderer was still at large.

The foot-tracker arrived and visited the footprint two or three times, on each occasion spending some minutes down on his hands and knees over it, as though to memorise it.

The next day the Council ordered that every male in the town must pass for inspection by the *qaffar*; quarter by quarter sent their tale of men. Some days had thus passed, till at last the *qaffar* gave the sign.

It was a young man in his twenties, an African slave, indeed a Court slave, and therefore not a safe person to charge in error. He was immediately arrested and sent to the Prison Fort, where charged with the crime he flatly denied all knowledge of it, and affirmed his innocence.

The clothes he was supposed to have been wearing were sent to the Public Analyst in Bombay and no blood stains were found, but other circumstantial evidence supported the foot-tracker. The slave was a notorious character; he was the sole occupant of the next house, so that he could have kept a careful watch on the movements of his intended victim; he could also have jumped easily from his upstairs veranda on to the roof where the murder took place, but he could not have jumped back.

The Indian Apothecary looked at the foot-impression too. There in the middle was an edge of splintered stone, and his opinion was that the man who had dropped from the roof on to the stone must have a slight cut in the sole of his right foot.

The prisoner was brought before me and I asked him to show me the bottom of his foot. He lifted the left one promptly. Examination of the right foot showed the cut mark there, and my head callipers confirmed that the position of it corresponded exactly with the position of the splintered stone in the foot impression. The slave suffered the prescribed penalty in public at the hands of a firing squad. The foot-tracker had not read the marks in vain.

And now six months later, in the centre of Rub' al Khali I was enjoying serener moments studying the tracks of the smaller animals. To a Badu, their simple story is immediately intelligible. For a European they have another appeal, the charm of graceful line or subtle invention; the sweep of droop-ing *gasis* in the wind makes a tiny picture of the prayer-ring the Badu sweeps with his cane towards the setting sun; the straight stride of birds' claws spaced one immediately before the other, a contrast with the earthy me-anderings of some small quadruped; the neat little rosette pattern of a rat leads to a thicket, where you will find its tiny hole, a heap of newly turned red sand at the entrance; the crooked but beautiful intricacies of a lizard like a miniature arabesque lead to a sprig of herbage where it has played maypole and rolled over in joyous repletion; that futuristic riot marks the fallen twigs bowled over and over by the whims of the wind.

The morrow was intensely cold. Our course at first due east obliquely across the strong north wind, then turned into the face of it, and I was glad of my greatcoat. A large hawk, the first I had seen in the sands, circled about our heads to sail swiftly down wind as we passed an encampment of Murra with some fifty black camels. The great camel herds of the Murra are said to be mostly black, whence the tents of the sands are generally of that colour, in sharp contrast with the colour of the wild animals of the sands, particularly the mammals, which is that of their environment.

We made a wide detour to avoid these Murra. They were ostensibly a friendly section, but it was declared unwise that I be seen or heard of, lest news of me get ahead with mischievous results.

Shaikh Salih as he rode at my side shivered, but would not bemoan the cold, lest he affront the Almighty, the All Knowing, who had sent it. I told Salih of the cold of an English winter.

"Do you hear that?"—he turned to Mubarak. "In the Wazir's country the water that is cut off from the sea (a pond) becomes solid with the cold so that the Arabs and horses and donkeys can walk upon it."

"There is no god but God," returned Mubarak, and I detected in his expression a fear lest I be the advance guard of a party of invaders, anxious to forsake such misery for their own delectable sands.

Long hungry hours in the saddle and the cold north wind made life at this stage uncomfortable, the night temperature falling to 40° F., and having no tent or other overhead covering, I found it necessary to sleep in all my clothes plus three blankets.

On 22nd January in the red rolling sand-hills of Ubaila we met the first of a series of sandstorms. We were sitting round the camp fire after the evening meal. Two nights before there had been a heavy dew, our first since leaving the Qara Mountains. To-night a cold wind from the north was blowing, but nothing presaged a coming storm. Suddenly the flames swept this way and that as though the wind blew from everywhere in turn. We all covered our faces with our hands to save our eyes from the smoke. My companions leapt up and rushed off in the darkness to bring in their grazing camels, for the sandstorm is one of their worst enemies. The storm grew fiercer; the Badawin, with their poor mantles wrapped round them, huddled together for warmth.

I slept fitfully. The hissing of the sand-laden wind, the rattling of my camp cordage and the cold of my feet made sleep impossible. When my face was exposed the gritty blast struck it with the sharpness of a knife. The temperature fell to 37° F. dry, 35° F. wet. I dozed off just before dawn and woke soon after to find my saddle and baggage embedded in driven sand. The wind had dropped and round the camp-fires clustered huddled and shivering Badawin. Soon they were rousing their camels that had been rounded up overnight for safety, and the wretched beasts shuffled, shivering, away to feed and to feel the warmth of the rising sun.

To me the night had disastrous results. The sand had got into some of my instruments. My small cinema camera was out of action, and my two aneroids no longer tallied, so that I was obliged thereafter to record two different readings, not knowing which, if either, was right till the end of the journey.

"I bring you good tidings of the *shamal*! I bring you good tidings of the shamal!" shouted a young Badu next morning in ironical reference to the bitter north wind, the temperature standing within 5° F. of freezing-point.

> "But for the north wind
> There would be no increase,"

retorted Shaikh Salih, quoting a desert rhyme upon the wind's stimulus to the bull-camel.

The rolling reds of Ubaila had given place again to the more typical white open spaces of Sanam as we approached the water-hole of Jahaishi. A chill depressing day with the plain a white smoke-screen that swept towards us and past us filming our camels' feet, the wind had stung my poor companions, who, muffled up in their scanty garments sat shivering as we rode along.

"Couch her, Sahib! Couch Agaba," they cried, "it is the hour of the midday prayer." Here beside the abandoned water-hole of Duwairis were firewood and a little grazing, and I realised we were halting for the day. Sand filled my eyes, and my note-books; sand was everywhere; note-taking with numbed fingers was impossible, and all that could be done was to sit idly in the swirl of sand and cold discomfort, and wish for a lull.

The Badawin collected brushwood from the thickets and piled it in a strong hedge twenty yards long. It was *gadha*, a considerable bush which we here met for the first time. Behind this shelter the camels were couched huddled together, only a few hardy brutes electing to stand and graze. Later in the day when the sun made itself felt and the wind dropped a little, they hobbled off to some near pastures, but when the wind again rose they were promptly brought back, their masters fearing to lose them, if left out, for the wind immediately effaced all tracks.

The homing instinct of the camel—if the absence of an established home does not make the term a paradox—is amazing. Her fixed idea apparently is to regain the fat pastures and main herds she had just left. During the preoccupations of marching, she may forget, but when a halt is called and she is turned out to graze unfettered, she will wander back alone the way she has come. Her master means nothing to her. She has no affection for him and never learns to know more of him than the sound of his voice. Yet she is utterly dependent upon him for her watering, being powerless to fend for herself even at the shallowest water-hole. She is excessively stupid except for an uncanny sense of direction, but is none the less "*Ata Y' Allah*"—the Gift of God—in his eyes.

"If you leave Agaba to herself," said Shaikh Salih, "she will go off across the sands directly under that star back to Dakaka and her companions, though she has never come this way before."

"But how will she fare for water?"

"She will wander back without water and arrive safely in the winter time, but in summer she will perish of thirst before a quarter of the way."

Our march during the past two days had afforded an instance of this. A strange camel, a cow big with calf, had joined our party, or rather led the way, for she bounced along ahead of us, making straight for Qatar where her camel brand showed her to belong. She was presumably anxious for dates or sardines, the local delicacies she missed in the sands; lucky for her that the season was winter!

"Do not let your camel eat of this *gadha*," shouted a Murri next day as we passed through a verdant plain of it; "it is *jinn* haunted."

"But only these *gadha* pastures of Al Hirra and Banaiyan," explained Hamad to me, "elsewhere it is good enough fodder. Here five camels died in one night, and on another occasion two became ill and their milk dried up."

I had also found this idea, that *jinns* could affect the wholesomeness of vegetation, at Mugshin, where it caused a magnificent grove of acacias to be largely neglected. My Badawin's invariable habit of picking the juiciest herbage for hand-feeding their camels was there suspended, nor would they shoot the hares of this grove for the pot. The Kathiris had another strange belief, that a camel hand-fed at Mugshin instead of grazing for itself would suffer misfortune.

The famous water-hole of Banaiyan lay but a day's march ahead. An hour and a half after leaving our overnight's *hadh* pastures,[5] we breasted the red

---

[5] A type of flora found in the sands.

sand-hills of Khiyut al Buraidan that marked the northern border of Sanam. The wind had dropped and the pure smooth surface of the rosy sand-hills—here called Hamarur—was in refreshing contrast to the white smoking plains of the recent marches. Patches of vivid green *haram*[6] lined the gravelly troughs in the sand-hills and our hungry camels occasionally snatched at a tuft as we passed, though without encouragement, for *haram* is a saline feed which does no good to the animal not used to it. "Now the Manasir," said a Badu with a sweep of his arm to the eastwards, "have little else and their camels are reared on it and grow humps like this"—here he caught the elbow of one arm held out before him, the forearm bent upwards on the palm of the other hand—a favourite gesture to indicate a large hump and therefore a thriving animal.

Rare ridges of red sand in the plain, long and low, and patches of *gadha* growing out of elephant-mask accretions of sand about their roots, formed an area called Qadha Za'aza and brought us to more rolling red hills. In the midst of these we halted over the water-hole of Banaiyan. The caravan had dragged out, as all tired caravans do. Ramadhan was telling on the men, the saline pastures on the camels, and the long marches and cold north wind on both. Hamad and I were the first arrivals.

"Drink, Sahib," he said, "the water of Banaiyan is good."

Hamad, even had it not been the fast month, would himself have forborne. It was their code after a thirsty day's march that when we arrived at a water-hole no drop of water should pass the lips of the advance party until those in the rear had come up, nor would any man eat a crust with me on the march unless his companions were there to share it. If this precarious condition of life produces savagery between enemies, it breeds none the less a fine humanity among friends.

Banaiyan was a real well, stone-lined and therefore unlike the mere pits in the sand that are the water-holes of the south. As my party straggled in there was a visible change in their mood. Cheerfulness prevailed with the merry shouts and noise of spilling water that they love to make, while their

---

[6]Another sands flora.

great thirsty brutes with long necks stretched down to the scooped-out water trough gurgled their fill.

The want of pastures forbade a halt in these barren, rolling hills, and the first animals to be watered were already on the march before the last had come up. I delayed to accompany the rear party. Soon we had to halt for the sunset prayer, and after that we found growing difficulty in following the tracks of our advance guard; the failing light soon made it impossible. So with Polaris before our left shoulder—as the Badu has it, with his hand over his corresponding collar-bone so that you shall not err—we made our way through the night. An hour had passed when there was a shout from a man behind me. Turning, I saw the glimmer of a camp fire away to the eastwards. We turned and made camp at seven o'clock. I was thoroughly exhausted after ten and a half hours in the saddle, but comfort came from the realisation that the great central wastes of Rub' al Khali lay behind me, the sea was but eighty miles to the northward, success was in sight.

WILFRED THESIGER

(b. 1910)

From *Arabian Sands*

Wilfred Thesiger made his first crossing of the Empty Quarter, in 1946–47, by a much longer and far more difficult route than Bertram Thomas had followed in 1931 (see preceding selection). The climactic episode in his journey, chronicled in this passage, came with the crossing of the great range of little-known dunes called the Uruq al Shaiba. By this point, Thesiger's party had been reduced to four Bedouins (or Bedu, as he calls them) and himself, after the desertion of five other companions. What was more, the travelers were now running seriously short of both food and water. They were too far into the desert to retrace their steps: their only options were to break through to the well at Khaba, or die.

Undaunted by the narrow escape he so understatedly narrates in Arabian Sands, Thesiger went on to make a second crossing of the Empty Quarter the following year, by an entirely different route. Adapting himself completely to the Bedouin life, resigning himself to its Muslim idea of fate, Thesiger became the finest Western explorer of the desert who ever lived.

We stopped at sunset for the evening meal, and fed to our camels the tribulus[1] we had brought with us. All the skins were sweating and we were worried about our water. There had been a regular and ominous drip from them throughout the day, a drop falling on to the sand every few yards as we rode along, like blood dripping from a wound that could not be staunched. There was nothing to do but to press on, and yet to push the camels too hard would be to founder them. They were already showing signs of thirst. Al Auf had decided to go on again after we had fed, and while Musallim and bin Kabina baked bread I asked him about his former journeys through these Sands. "I have crossed them twice," he said. "The last time I came this way was two years ago. I was coming from Abu Dhabi." I asked, "Who was with you?" and he answered, "I was alone." Thinking that I must have misunderstood him, I repeated, "Who were your companions?" "God was my companion." To have ridden alone through this appalling desolation was an incredible achievement. We were travelling through it now, but we carried our own world with us: a small world of five people, which yet provided each of us with companionship, with talk and laughter and the knowledge that others were there to share the hardship and the danger. I knew that if I travelled here alone the weight of this vast solitude would crush me utterly.

I also knew that al Auf had used no figure of speech when he said that God was his companion. To these Bedu,[2] God is a reality, and the conviction of his presence gives them the courage to endure. For them to doubt his existence would be as inconceivable as for them to blaspheme. Most of them pray regularly, and many keep the fast of Ramadhan, which lasts for a whole month, during which time a man may not eat or drink from dawn

[1]A desert plant.
[2]Bedouins.

till sunset. When this fast falls in summer—and the Arab months being lunar it is eleven days earlier each year—they make use of the exemption which allows travellers to observe the fast when they have finished their journey, and keep it in the winter. Several of the Arabs whom we had left at Mughshin were fasting to compensate for not having done so earlier in the year. I have heard townsmen and villagers in the Hadhramaut and the Hajaz[3] disparage the Bedu, as being without religion. When I have protested, they have said, "Even if they pray, their prayers are not acceptable to God, since they do not first perform the proper ablutions."

These Bedu are not fanatical. Once I was travelling with a large party of Rashid,[4] one of whom said to me, "Why don't you become a Muslim and then you would really be one of us?" I answered, "God protect me from the Devil!" They laughed. This invocation is one which Arabs invariably use in rejecting something shameful or indecent. I would not have dared to make it if other Arabs had asked me this question, but the man who had spoken would certainly have used it if I had suggested that he should become a Christian.

AFTER THE MEAL we rode for two hours along a salt-flat. The dunes on either side, colourless in the moonlight, seemed higher by night than by day. The lighted slopes looked very smooth, the shadows in their folds inky black. Soon I was shivering uncontrollably from the cold. The others roared out their songs into a silence, broken otherwise only by the crunch of salt beneath the camels' feet. The words were the words of the south, but the rhythm and intonation were the same as in the songs which I had heard other Bedu singing in the Syrian desert. At first sight the Bedu of southern

---

[3]Or Hajar, a mountainous region in Oman. Hadhramaut: a region near the coast in eastern Yemen.

[4]Nomadic goat-herding Arabs who migrated to Arabia from Eritrea and southern Sudan in the nineteenth century; described by Thesiger as "the most authentic of the Bedu, the least affected by the outside world."

Arabia had appeared to be very different from those of the north, but I now realized that this difference was largely superficial and due to the clothes which they wore. My companions would not have felt out of place in an encampment of the Rualla,[5] whereas a townsman from Aden or Muscat would be conspicuous in Damascus.

Eventually we halted and I dismounted numbly. I would have given much for a hot drink but I knew that I must wait eighteen hours for that. We lit a small fire and warmed ourselves before we slept, though I slept little. I was tired; for days I had ridden long hours on a rough camel, my body racked by its uneven gait. I suppose I was weak from hunger, for the food which we ate was a starvation ration, even by Bedu standards. But my thirst troubled me most; it was not bad enough really to distress me but I was always conscious of it. Even when I was asleep I dreamt of racing streams of ice-cold water, but it was difficult to get to sleep. Now I lay there trying to estimate the distance we had covered and the distance that still lay ahead. When I had asked al Auf how far it was to the well, he had answered, "It is not the distance but the great dunes of the Uruq al Shaiba that may destroy us." I worried about the water which I had watched dripping away on to the sand, and about the state of our camels. They were there, close beside me in the dark. I sat up and looked at them. Mabkhaut stirred and called out, "What is it, Umbarak?" I mumbled an answer and lay down again. Then I worried whether we had tied the mouth of the skin properly when we had last drawn water and wondered what would happen if one of us was sick or had an accident. It was easy to banish these thoughts in daylight, less easy in the lonely darkness. Then I thought of al Auf travelling here alone and felt ashamed.

The others were awake at the first light, anxious to push on while it was still cold. The camels sniffed at the withered tribulus but were too thirsty to eat it. In a few minutes we were ready. We plodded along in silence. My eyes watered with the cold; the jagged salt-crusts cut and stung my feet. The world was grey and dreary. Then gradually the peaks ahead of us stood out

[5] A northern Bedouin tribe, from Syria.

against a paling sky; almost imperceptibly they began to glow, borrowing the colours of the sunrise which touched their crests.

A high unbroken dune-chain stretched across our front. It was not of uniform height, but, like a mountain range, consisted of peaks and connecting passes. Several of the summits appeared to be seven hundred feet above the salt-flat on which we stood. The southern face confronting us was very steep, which meant that this was the lee side to the prevailing winds. I wished we had to climb it from the opposite direction, for it is easy to take a camel down these precipices of sand but always difficult to find a way up them.

Al Auf told us to wait while he went to reconnoitre. I watched him walking away across the glistening salt-flat, his rifle on his shoulder and his head thrown back as he scanned the slopes above. He looked superbly confident, but as I viewed this wall of sand I despaired that we would ever get the camels up it. Mabkhaut evidently thought the same, for he said to Musallim, "We will have to find a way round. No camel will ever climb that." Musallim answered, "It is al Auf's doing. He brought us here. We should have gone much farther to the west, nearer to Dakaka." He had caught a cold and was snuffling, and his rather high-pitched voice was hoarse and edged with grievance. I knew that he was jealous of al Auf and always ready to disparage him, so unwisely I gibed, "We should have got a long way if you had been our guide!" He swung round and answered angrily, "You don't like the Bait Kathir.[6] I know that you only like the Rashid. I defied my tribe to bring you here and you never recognize what I have done for you."

For the past few days he had taken every opportunity of reminding me that I could not have come on from Ramlat al Ghafa without him. It was done in the hope of currying favour and of increasing his reward, but it only irritated me. Now I was tempted to seek relief in angry words, to welcome the silly, bitter squabble which would result. I kept silent with an effort and

---

[6]Another Bedouin tribe, kinsmen of the Rashid. Thesiger is accompanied by both Rashid and Bait Kathir Bedouins on his first crossing of the Empty Quarter. Musallim is of the Bait Kathir, whereas al Auf is of the Rashid. Despite their kinship, there is rivalry between the two tribes.

moved apart on the excuse of taking a photograph. I knew how easily, under conditions such as these, I could take a violent dislike to one member of the party and use him as my private scapegoat. I thought, "I must not let myself dislike him. After all, I do owe him a great deal; but I wish to God he would not go on reminding me of it."

I went over to a bank and sat down to wait for al Auf's return. The ground was still cold, although the sun was now well up, throwing a hard, clear light on the barrier of sand ahead of us. It seemed fantastic that this great rampart which shut out half the sky could be made of wind-blown sand. Now I could see al Auf, about half a mile away, moving along the salt-flat at the bottom of the dune. While I watched him he started to climb a ridge, like a mountaineer struggling upward through soft snow towards a pass over a high mountain. I even saw the tracks which he left behind him. He was the only moving thing in all that empty, silent landscape.

What were we going to do if we could not get the camels over it? I knew that we could not go any farther to the east, for al Auf had told me that the quicksands of Umm al Samim were in that direction. To the west the easier sands of Dakaka, where Thomas had crossed, were more than two hundred miles away. We had no margin, and could not afford to lengthen our journey. Our water was already dangerously short, and even more urgent than our own needs were those of the camels, which would collapse unless they were watered soon. We *must* get them over this monstrous dune, if necessary by unloading them and carrying the loads to the top. But what was on the other side? How many more of these dunes were there ahead of us? If we turned back now we might reach Mughshin, but I knew that once we crossed this dune the camels would be too tired and thirsty to get back even to Ghanim. Then I thought of Sultan and the others who had deserted us, and of their triumph if we gave up and returned defeated. Looking again at the dune ahead I noticed that al Auf was coming back. A shadow fell across the sand beside me. I glanced up and bin Kabina stood there. He smiled, said "Salam Alaikum,"[7] and sat down. Urgently I turned to him and

[7]"Peace be with you," a Muslim salutation.

asked, "Will we ever get the camels over that?" He pushed the hair back from his forehead, looked thoughtfully at the slopes above us, and answered, "It is very steep but al Auf will find a way. He is a Rashid; he is not like these Bait Kathir." Unconcernedly he then took the bolt out of his rifle and began to clean it with the hem of his shirt, while he asked me if all the English used the same kind of rifle.

When al Auf approached we went over to the others. Mabkhaut's camel had lain down; the rest of them stood where we had left them, which was a bad sign. Ordinarily they would have roamed off at once to look for food. Al Auf smiled at me as he came up but said nothing, and no one questioned him. Noticing that my camel's load was unbalanced he heaved up the saddle-bag from one side, and then picking up with his toes the camel-stick which he had dropped, he went over to his own camel, caught hold of its head-rope, said "Come on," and led us forward.

It was now that he really showed his skill. He picked his way unerringly, choosing the inclines up which the camels could climb. Here on the lee side of this range a succession of great faces flowed down in unruffled sheets of sand, from the top to the very bottom of the dune. They were unscalable, for the sand was poised always on the verge of avalanching, but they were flanked by ridges where the sand was firmer and the inclines easier. It was possible to force a circuitous way up these slopes, but not all were practicable for camels, and from below it was difficult to judge their steepness. Very slowly, a foot at a time, we coaxed the unwilling beasts upward. Each time we stopped I looked up at the crests where the rising wind was blowing streamers of sand into the void, and wondered how we should ever reach the top. Suddenly we were there. Before slumping down on the sand I looked anxiously ahead of us. To my relief I saw that we were on the edge of rolling downs, where the going would be easy among shallow valleys and low, rounded hills. "We have made it. We are on top of Uruq al Shaiba," I thought triumphantly. The fear of this great obstacle had lain like a shadow on my mind ever since al Auf had first warned me of it, the night we spoke together in the sands of Ghanim. Now the shadow had lifted and I was confident of success.

We rested for a while on the sand, not troubling to talk, until al Auf rose to his feet and said "Come on." Some small dunes built up by cross-winds ran in curves parallel with the main face across the back of these downs. Their steep faces were to the north and the camels slithered down them without difficulty. These downs were brick-red, splashed with deeper shades of colour; the underlying sand, exposed where it had been churned up by our feet, showing red of a paler shade. But the most curious feature was a number of deep craters resembling giant hoof-prints. These were unlike normal crescent-dunes, since they did not rise above their surroundings, but formed hollows in the floor of hard undulating sand. The salt-flats far below us looked very white.

We mounted our camels. My companions had muffled their faces in their head-cloths and rode in silence, swaying to the camels' stride. The shadows on the sand were very blue, of the same tone as the sky; two ravens flew northward, croaking as they passed. I struggled to keep awake. The only sound was made by the slap of the camels' feet, like wavelets lapping on a beach.

To rest the camels we stopped for four hours in the late afternoon on a long gentle slope which stretched down to another salt-flat. There was no vegetation on it and no salt-bushes bordered the plain below us. Al Auf announced that we would go on again at sunset. While we were feeding I said to him cheerfully, "Anyway, the worst should be over now that we are across the Uruq al Shaiba." He looked at me for a moment and then answered, "If we go well tonight we should reach them tomorrow." I said, "Reach what?" and he replied, "The Uruq al Shaiba," adding, "Did you think what we crossed today was the Uruq al Shaiba? That was only a dune. You will see them tomorrow." For a moment, I thought he was joking, and then I realized that he was serious, that the worst of the journey which I had thought was behind us was still ahead.

It was midnight when at last al Auf said, "Let's stop here. We will get some sleep and give the camels a rest. The Uruq al Shaiba are not far away now." In my dreams that night they towered above us higher than the Himalayas.

Al Auf woke us again while it was still dark. As usual bin Kabina made coffee, and the sharp-tasting drops which he poured out stimulated but did not warm. The morning star had risen above the dunes. Formless things regained their shape in the first dim light of dawn. The grunting camels heaved themselves erect. We lingered for a moment more beside the fire; then al Auf said "Come," and we moved forward. Beneath my feet the gritty sand was cold as frozen snow.

We were faced by a range as high as, perhaps even higher than, the range we had crossed the day before, but here the peaks were steeper and more pronounced, rising in many cases to great pinnacles, down which the flowing ridges swept like draperies. These sands, paler coloured than those we had crossed, were very soft, cascading round our feet as the camels struggled up the slopes. Remembering how little warning of imminent collapse the dying camels had given me twelve years before in the Danakil country,[8] I wondered how much more these camels would stand, for they were trembling violently whenever they halted. When one refused to go on we heaved on her head-rope, pushed her from behind, and lifted the loads on either side as we manhandled the roaring animal upward. Sometimes one of them lay down and refused to rise, and then we had to unload her, and carry the water-skins and the saddle-bags ourselves. Not that the loads were heavy. We had only a few gallons of water left and some handfuls of flour.

We led the trembling, hesitating animals upward along great sweeping ridges where the knife-edged crests crumbled beneath our feet. Although it was killing work, my companions were always gentle and infinitely patient. The sun was scorching hot and I felt empty, sick, and dizzy. As I struggled up the slope, knee-deep in shifting sand, my heart thumped wildly and my thirst grew worse. I found it difficult to swallow; even my ears felt blocked, and yet I knew that it would be many intolerable hours before I could drink. I would stop to rest, dropping down on the scorching sand, and

---

[8]A desert region in northeastern Ethiopia that Thesiger had been one of the first Westerners to penetrate in the early 1930s. He had been warned that the Danakil would certainly castrate and most likely murder him.

immediately it seemed I would hear the others shouting, "Umbarak, Umbarak"; their voices sounded strained and hoarse.

It took us three hours to cross this range.

On the summit were no gently undulating downs such as we had met the day before. Instead, three smaller dune-chains rode upon its back, and beyond them the sand fell away to a salt-flat in another great empty trough between the mountains. The range on the far side seemed even higher than the one on which we stood, and behind it were others. I looked round, seeking instinctively for some escape. There was no limit to my vision. Somewhere in the ultimate distance the sands merged into the sky, but in that infinity of space I could see no living thing, not even a withered plant to give me hope. "There is nowhere to go," I thought. "We cannot go back and our camels will never get up another of these awful dunes. We really are finished." The silence flowed over me, drowning the voices of my companions and the fidgeting of their camels.

We went down into the valley, and somehow—and I shall never know how the camels did it—we got up the other side. There, utterly exhausted, we collapsed. Al Auf gave us each a little water, enough to wet our mouths. He said, "We need this if we are to go on." The midday sun had drained the colour from the sands. Scattered banks of cumulus cloud threw shadows across the dunes and salt-flats, and added an illusion that we were high among Alpine peaks, with frozen lakes of blue and green in the valley, far below. Half asleep, I turned over, but the sand burnt through my shirt and woke me from my dreams.

Two hours later al Auf roused us. As he helped me load my camel, he said, "Cheer up, Umbarak. This time we really are across the Uruq al Shaiba," and when I pointed to the ranges ahead of us, he answered, "I can find a way through those; we need not cross them." We went on till sunset, but we were going with the grain of the country, following the valleys and no longer trying to climb the dunes. We should not have been able to cross another. There was a little fresh *qassis*[9] on the slope where we halted. I

[9]A desert plant.

hoped that this lucky find would give us an excuse to stop here for the night, but, after we had fed, al Auf went to fetch the camels, saying, "We must go on again while it is cool if we are ever to reach Dhafara."

We stopped long after midnight and started again at dawn, still exhausted from the strain and long hours of yesterday, but al Auf encouraged us by saying that the worst was over. The dunes were certainly lower than they had been, more uniform in height and more rounded, with fewer peaks. Four hours after we had started we came to rolling uplands of gold and silver sand, but still there was nothing for the camels to eat.

A hare jumped out from under a bush, and al Auf knocked it over with his stick. The others shouted "God has given us meat." For days we had talked of food; every conversation seemed to lead back to it. Since we had left Ghanim I had been always conscious of the dull ache of hunger, yet in the evening my throat was dry even after my drink, so that I found it difficult to swallow the dry bread Musallim set before us. All day we thought and talked about that hare, and by three o'clock in the afternoon could no longer resist stopping to cook it. Mabkhaut suggested, "Let's roast it in its skin in the embers of a fire. That will save our water—we haven't got much left." Bin Kabina led the chorus of protest. "No, by God! Don't even suggest such a thing"; and turning to me he said, "We don't want Mabkhaut's charred meat. Soup. We want soup and extra bread. We will feed well today even if we go hungry and thirsty later. By God, I am hungry!" We agreed to make soup. We were across the Uruq al Shaiba and intended to celebrate our achievement with this gift from God. Unless our camels foundered we were safe; even if our water ran out we should live to reach a well.

Musallim made nearly double our usual quantity of bread while bin Kabina cooked the hare. He looked across at me and said, "The smell of this meat makes me faint." When it was ready he divided it into five portions. They were very small, for an Arabian hare is no larger than an English rabbit, and this one was not even fully grown. Al Auf named the lots and Mabkhaut drew them. Each of us took the small pile of meat which had fallen to him. Then bin Kabina said, "God! I have forgotten to divide the liver," and the others said, "Give it to Umbarak." I protested, saying that they should divide it, but they swore by God that they would not eat it and that I was to have it. Eventually I took it, knowing that I ought not, but too greedy for this extra scrap of meat to care.

OUR WATER WAS nearly finished and there was only enough flour for about another week. The starving camels were so thirsty that they had refused to eat some half-dried herbage which we had passed. We must water them in the next day or two or they would collapse. Al Auf said that it would take us three more days to reach Khaba well in Dhafara, but that there was a very brackish well not far away. He thought that the camels might drink its water.

That night after we had ridden for a little over an hour it grew suddenly dark. Thinking that a cloud must be covering the full moon, I looked over my shoulder and saw that there was an eclipse and that half the moon was already obscured. Bin Kabina noticed it at the same moment and broke into a chant which the others took up.

> God endures for ever.
> The life of man is short.
> The Pleiades are overhead.
> The moon's among the stars.

Otherwise they paid no attention to the eclipse (which was total), but looked around for a place to camp.

We started very early the next morning and rode without a stop for seven hours across easy rolling downs. The colour of these sands was vivid, varied, and unexpected: in places the colour of ground coffee, elsewhere brick-red, or purple, or a curious golden-green. There were small white gypsum-flats, fringed with *shanan*, a grey-green salt-bush, lying in hollows in the downs. We rested for two hours on sands the colour of dried blood and then led our camels on again.

Suddenly we were challenged by an Arab lying behind a bush on the crest of a dune. Our rifles were on our camels, for we had not expected to meet anyone here. Musallim was hidden behind mine. I watched him draw his rifle clear. But al Auf said, "It is the voice of a Rashid," and walked forward. He spoke to the concealed Arab, who rose and came to meet him. They embraced and stood talking until we joined them. We greeted the man, and al Auf said, "This is Hamad bin Hanna, a sheikh of the Rashid." He was a heavily-built bearded man of middle age. His eyes were set close together and he had a long nose with a blunt end. He fetched his camel from behind the dune while we unloaded.

We made coffee for him and listened to his news. He told us that he had been looking for a stray camel when he crossed our tracks and had taken us for a raiding party from the south. Ibn Saud's tax-collectors were in Dhafara and the Rabadh, collecting tribute from the tribes;[10] and there were Rashid, Awamir, Murra, and some Manahil to the north of us.

We had to avoid all contact with Arabs other than the Rashid, and if possible even with them, so that news of my presence would not get about among the tribes, for I had no desire to be arrested by Ibn Saud's tax-collectors and taken off to explain my presence here to Ibn Jalawi, the formidable Governor of the Hasa.[11] Karab[12] from the Hadhramaut had raided these sands the year before, so there was also a serious risk of our being mistaken for raiders, since the tracks of our camels would show that we had come from the southern steppes. This risk would be increased if it appeared that we were avoiding the Arabs, for honest travellers never pass an encampment without seeking news and food. It was going to be very difficult to escape detection. First we must water our camels and draw water for ourselves. Then we must lie up as close as possible to Liwa and send a party to the villages to buy us enough food for at least another month. Hamad told me that Liwa belonged to the Al bu Falah of Abu Dhabi. He said that

[10]Ibn Saud was then king of Saudi Arabia.

[11]Al Hasa, a region in eastern Saudi Arabia, along the Persian Gulf.

[12]A Bedouin tribe from farther west than the Rashid or the Bait Kathir.

they were still fighting Said bin Maktum of Dibai, and that, as there was a lot of raiding going on, the Arabs would be very much on the alert.

We started again in the late afternoon and travelled till sunset. Hamad came with us and said he would stay with us until we had got food from Liwa. Knowing where the Arabs were encamped he could help us to avoid them. Next day, after seven hours' travelling, we reached Khaur Sabakha on the edge of the Dhafara sands. We cleaned out the well and found brackish water at seven feet, so bitter that even the camels only drank a little before refusing it. They sniffed thirstily at the water with which al Auf tried to coax them from a leather bucket, but only dipped their lips into it. We covered their noses but still they would not drink. Yet al Auf said that Arabs themselves drank this water mixed with milk, and when I expressed my disbelief he added that if an Arab was really thirsty he would even kill a camel and drink the liquid in its stomach, or ram a stick down its throat and drink the vomit. We went on again till nearly sunset.

The next day when we halted in the afternoon al Auf told us we had reached Dhafara and that Khaba well was close. He said that he would fetch water in the morning. We finished what little was left in one of our skins. Next day we remained where we were. Hamad said that he would go for news and return the following day. Al Auf, who went with him, came back in the afternoon with two skins full of water which, although slightly brackish, was delicious after the filthy evil-smelling dregs we had drunk the night before.

It was 12 December, fourteen days since we had left Khaur bin Atarit in Ghanim.

In the evening, now that we needed no longer measure out each cup of water, bin Kabina made extra coffee, while Musallim increased our rations of flour by a mugful. This was wild extravagance, but we felt that the occasion called for celebration. Even so, the loaves he handed us were woefully inadequate to stay our hunger, now that our thirst was gone.

The moon was high above us when I lay down to sleep. The others still talked round the fire, but I closed my mind to the meaning of their words, content to hear only the murmur of their voices, to watch their outlines sharp against the sky, happily conscious that they were there and beyond them the camels to which we owed our lives.

For years the Empty Quarter had represented to me the final, unattainable challenge which the desert offered. Suddenly it had come within my reach. I remembered my excitement when Lean[13] had casually offered me the chance to go there, the immediate determination to cross it, and then the doubts and fears, the frustrations, and the moments of despair. Now I had crossed it. To others my journey would have little importance. It would produce nothing except a rather inaccurate map which no one was ever likely to use. It was a personal experience, and the reward had been a drink of clean, nearly tasteless water. I was content with that.

Looking back on the journey I realized that there had been no high moment of achievement such as a mountaineer must feel when he stands upon his chosen summit. Over the past days new strains and anxieties had built up as others eased, for, after all, this crossing of the Empty Quarter was set in the framework of a longer journey, and already my mind was busy with the new problems which our return journey presented.

[13]O. B. Lean, Desert Locust Specialist of the British Food and Agriculture Organization. It was Lean who gave Thesiger his official charge to explore the Empty Quarter and report on locust movements.

GEOFFREY MOORHOUSE

(b. 1931)

From *The Fearful Void*

*Geoffrey Moorhouse set out in 1972 to perform a journey every bit the
equal of Bertram Thomas's and Wilfred Thesiger's — he hoped to become
the first man to traverse the Sahara from west to east, a full three thousand miles as the crow flies (and much longer as the camel wanders)
from the Atlantic to the Nile. He planned, moreover, to go alone, with
at most a pair of Tuareg guides. The motive for this outlandish challenge, Moorhouse insisted, was "not to establish a record" but to dissolve an existential pool of fear that he felt had dominated his life for
forty years.*

*Unlike Thesiger, Moorhouse was no expert in desert travel but sim-
ply a journalist with a penchant for adventure. To prepare for his trek,
he learned Arabic and taught himself navigation. He also consulted
Thesiger, only to be put off by the veteran's "spectacular pessimism."
Informed of Moorhouse's intention to go alone, Thesiger was aghast.
"You don't seem to realize," he lectured the neophyte, "that camels rep-*

resent wealth to the Tuareg, and if they see a lone Englishman cross-
ing their territory with a string of beasts, they'll bump you off without
compunction."

Moorhouse ignored the warning and set off on his perilous voyage.
A succession of guides led him from oasis to oasis, and at intervals other
travelers joined his trek (for the Sahara is more populated than the
Empty Quarter of Arabia). Although in the end the great desert defeated
him, he covered some two thousand miles, from central Mauritania to
southern Algeria. The journey not only provided its share of close brushes
with death: it furnished the narrative of a book that wonderfully min-
gles self-irony with high adventure.

In this passage, the exhausted author completes his aborted journey
with his last guide, Ibrahim, in March 1973, arriving at the historic
oasis town of Tamanrasset, in southern Algeria.

A t a little after three o'clock we prepared to start under a moon that
was something from fantasy. Never in my life had I seen it looming as large as when it topped the horizon. It seemed to fill a quarter of the heavens, a full circle which itself was encircled by a colossal and
golden penumbra. It was a moon from a children's picture book, with the
colour of a Gloucester cheese. There was a sleepy farewell salute from the
bundle of blankets nearby as we set off. It was unlikely that we should see
the three[1] again, with a four-hour start, in conditions ideal for a night
march. There was not a breath of wind, though it was excessively cold. Even
with my howli[2] muffled thickly between chin and eyes under a bare head,
my face was numb for hours, as well as hands and feet. Had I been snow-
balling in an English winter, I could scarcely have been colder. In this condition we attacked the dunes and it was heavy work, headhauling the beasts

---

[1] A man, youth, and young boy leading a string of camels whom Moorhouse had encountered the previous day.

[2] Headcloth.

one at a time up the steeper slopes, the brown bull and the broken-toothed white frequently falling to their knees. Dawn found us on the gravel reg[3] again, and all day we plodded across its flat and featureless surface, blistered now as fiercely by the sun as we had been frozen by night under the moon.

Slumped that evening against the unloaded baggage, I was beyond responding to the sunset. On days without number I had been revived by the magical half hour of the sun's decline: most beautiful of all were those evenings when the horizon glowed with green, yellow and blood-red rays, in which the very thin crescent of a new moon rose a trifle above the ground before slipping back again in pursuit of the sun, without the strength yet to climb into the sky. On this evening the colours stained some wisps of high, stratospheric cloud that a remote wind was unravelling towards the west. But I was too weary to delight in it.

I awoke at 3:30, shivering in spite of a great blaze of grass that Ibrahim had started beside us; its light leapt and flickered upon the four camels, which we had couched on the spot before going to sleep. There was a stiffness in my body that came not from the cold nor yet from long exertions, but seemed to issue now from the deepest fibres of my being in a translated protest of the soul at the very thought of movement. I felt as though I were inhabiting a spent and useless contraption of tissue and bone which no longer had any relevance to me and what I really was. Was this, I wondered, why the mystics came to the desert: to be so alienated from their own flesh, at a distance that was beyond repugnance, that they might dwell, without alternative, upon and within the boundaries of the spirit?

We marched until after seven o'clock across the barren reg in close order, with Ibrahim on the leading headrope and myself bringing up the rear. My old white from Tombouctou was the first camel in line, the two beasts from Tessalit in the middle, Sid' Ahmed's brown bull behind them. When camels are healthy and led in a train like this, their heads tend to strain forward and low to reduce the pull of the ropes on their nose rings. They look a bit like a line of angry geese as they pad along. When they are

[3]Flat gravel plain.

exhausted, their heads are held high on curving necks, trying to resist the awful dragging of their bodies even when their nostrils are almost being pulled out, the pain of the one seeming much greater than that of the other. Our camels were now marching like this. I was belabouring them from behind with my riding stick in an effort to keep them going, offering them a third pain that might be worse than the other two, to reduce the strain on the ropes and persuade them to go forward.

There was nothing but pain in this desert for human beings and animals alike. Life was pain. Only in death was there relief.

We stopped for half an hour to make tea and eat dates. Then we marched on as before. The brown bull, which had carried nothing two days, now began to move at an angle to the other three, his head still tethered to the saddle ahead, his rump swinging out to the right. He went forward in little rushes each time I clouted his haunch. Suddenly I heard a sound like that of a breathless runner, panting hard. It came not from his head but from under his tail, where his anus had started to throb violently, working in and out like a piston out of control. At the same time I was aware of an appalling smell, which I had come across once or twice before. Somewhere inside, this poor creature was already as putrefied as the overblown corpses I had passed outside Tombouctou. Then he went down with a thump, the head-rope breaking with a twang. Ibrahim stopped the train at my shout and came back to help me get the bull to his feet again. We refastened the broken rope and continued, but almost at once the beast went down again. We raised him once more, and something very curious happened. Before we could attach the severed ends of rope, the brown bull cantered forward, past the two camels from Tessalit, to the beast which had shared the long journey from Tombouctou with him. He rubbed his shoulder against that of the white. Then he turned at a right angle, facing it, and sat down again.

Ibrahim shrugged. "He's finished," he said.

I had been unmoved when one of my camels foundered before. This time I felt sadness hanging like a weight on my throat. The brown bull had been such a gallant animal, with much more spirit than any other beast I had used. Most camels roared with indignation when being loaded, but he had been a snarler and a snapper, too, twisting his head right round to menace the rider about to mount. On the move, most beasts bore their riders along at a steady lope, but there had always been something frisky about his trot. He had travelled an intolerable distance to serve my purpose. Now I was abandoning him in the middle of the most barren wilderness we had crossed together, just as the day's heat was beginning to burn, where there was not a vestige of shade from either rock, dune or vegetation as far as the eye could see. Ibrahim said that he would be dead by nightfall. As we moved off, two men and three camels now, the brown bull turned his head slowly to watch our going. Then he turned away again, his back to the sun, his head pointing to the west.

We marched on, and by that day's end I wondered how much farther I could continue myself. Waves of nausea flowed through my stomach and there was a heavy ache around my kidneys. My left leg had started to drag, so that I was consciously trying to bring it forward with each step. At our midday camp I had felt as though the sun were burning a hole through my skull, thickly wrapped in a headcloth though it was. When we moved away I hung the map case on one of the saddles. I had never done this before, but now it seemed far too much to carry. By the time the sun was setting, we had been walking for more than twelve hours—almost fifteen if we counted the stops. Ibrahim wanted to continue for another two, but I couldn't take any more and said so peevishly.

His own strength was draining, too. His face was now strained, and his lips, I noticed, had changed colour to grey. Yet not once had he faltered in anything; never had he responded to cross words of mine with anything but his usual calm and careful attention to whatever he was doing. He was almost as different from my previous companions as I was myself. Not only did he eat his food with a spoon, but he took his share in a brass dish of his own, which he also used as a drinking vessel; I never saw him sup water straight from the neck of a guerba,[4] as others were accustomed to. Where others had lain close beside me at night, for mutual warmth, Ibrahim had

[4]Goatskin water bag.

always rolled into his blanket at some distance. He was the one man who had consistently refused to take anything from the tassoufra[5] containing our shared supplies, even when I asked him to, always waiting for me to apportion the food. He was the only person I had heard say "Thank you" for anything. I could not tell to what extent these habits were Tuareg ways in general, to what degree they belonged singularly to Ibraham Ag Sowanaki, who had a wife and three children, four camels of his own and a small garden in which he grew vegetables for the military garrison at Tessalit.

We started the next day's march in the night again and, when dawn came, there were three or four great mountains ahead, all but hull down on the horizon. I was reminded how once, in the Navy, my ship had approached Gibraltar from the Atlantic and how I had watched the great rock slowly rise from the depths of the sea, first a misty pinnacle, then a solid bastion, finally a towering cliff. The sensation this day was much the same, though the approach of the mountains was much slower. It was late in the afternoon before we were hard against them. Two of them barred our way, set close together, perhaps fifteen hundred feet high. As we made for the gap between them, we passed great outcrops which had been eroded marvellously into sensuous and bulbous shapes that might easily have been original studies for Henry Moore. The two mountain shoulders, we could now see, consisted of colossal black boulders piled on top of each other, some so finely balanced that they looked as if a fingertip would send them crashing down. We could also see that the gap, which at a distance had promised enough width to drive anything through, was in fact very narrow indeed, barely a passage at all. It was no more than a hundred yards long, but was itself a rubble of black boulders which offered a decent scramble for an unhindered man.

The camels made it plain that they were unwilling to try it. I hauled hard on the headrope of the Tombouctou white, while Ibrahim thrashed it from behind with his stick. Weary as the beast was, it kicked viciously with its rear quarters, narrowly missing Ibrahim's head. It was otherwise immovable. I

[5]Leather bag, for food carried behind camel saddle.

told Ibrahim to do nothing while I tried another tack. Still pulling firmly on the rope, I began to murmur to the camel as though it were a child. Slowly it started to come forward, roaring and grunting with fear. Then it had to rush down a rock to avoid slipping, almost knocking me off my stance as it came. But, committed, it came forward in more rushes and careful pauses while it felt nervously for a foothold with a foreleg. Within half an hour I had it through the gap. The broken-toothed beast from Tessalit was persuaded to follow the same way. Only the strongest of the camels refused to budge in response either to beating or gentling. Ibrahim said he would lead it back round the mountain and meet me somewhere on the other side.

A couple of hours later, with the sun almost gone, I saw him emerge far behind me, from the shelter of the hillside. He was not alone. There were more camels with him and a figure riding the leader. It was the youth we had first met at In Azaoua, with most of the beasts in the caravan. There was no sign of the man or the small boy. They, he said, were following him somewhere behind, with one camel and the goats. We pressed on in twilight, into rising stony ground. We had been moving for an hour in darkness before we found a clump of trees and stopped. It was then that Ibrahim told me we had no water left. Nor had the youth; his supplies were on the camel accompanying the father and the child. But they never appeared.

Ibrahim and I set off at dawn. The youth said he would wait for the others to catch up. Presumably they had camped when night fell, not wishing to lose our tracks in the darkness. Our camels were twitching and shaking as we loaded them up, the broken-toothed beast swaying perceptibly on his feet. God knows how he had got this far, for neither of us had expected it. By the middle of the morning we were beginning to stagger as badly as the beasts and there was no tension on any of the headropes, for neither of us had the strength to pull them from the front. We were just managing to walk, and that was all. Ibrahim complained of pains in his head, and mine was throbbing dully, as it had for several days. I was no longer walking straight, but progressed in long ellipses like a drunken man who is determined not to show it. When Ibrahim said we must ride, I did not even nod. I waited for the beasts to couch, hauled myself slowly up, and hung onto the saddle as my camel got to his feet. We rode for perhaps an hour, the relief tremendous, towards a full-blooded range of mountains which was beyond our immediate goal. It was the edge of the Hoggar, and Silet was somewhere on this side of it.

We walked again, casually, incapable of anything more as the creeping paralysis of dehydration spread through our limbs. A hot wind flared murderously at us from the west. I had known its scorching threat for many months now, and the sound that betrayed it for the monster that it was: it was a dull sound, a muted booming, as though half a dozen old-fashioned bombers were flying high above, or a convoy of heavy lorries were rumbling several miles away. It would be a killer, this wind, during March in the desert. It was the first day of March now, and the wind had me within its range.

Almost unconscious even of my mind, I was aware of trees somewhere ahead, somewhere beyond Ibrahim and the camels, who seemed to be a great distance ahead. Then there was a tent. Ibrahim was squatting by it, drinking from his brass bowl. Then a small boy was running towards me, trying not to spill what was in the bowl. The water in it was the colour of diluted blood.[†]

This was the most beautiful thing in the world, more beautiful by far than the stained glass of Chartres, than a fugue by Bach, than the moment after ecstasy with the woman you loved, or the moment when your son scrambled to squeeze the breath out of you and say, "I think you're smashing, Dad." There was nothing in the world as beautiful as this bowlful of water.

It was a little before two, and for the next three hours we lay inert beneath bushes, drinking much water and eating dates. We had been there some time when a liquid blur in the heat haze was transformed into substantial shape and eventually became a group of camels proceeding along our tracks. The youth was still mounted on the leading beast, but of the fa-

---

†Water from a new guerba is sometimes tinted by a residue of oil or other substance used in dressing the leather. [Footnotes preceded by symbols are the author's.]

ther, the child and the goats there was still no sign. We couched the beasts while the young fellow drank his fill outside the tent. After speaking with him for a while, Ibrahim told me the others were coming, and I relaxed into semicoma again.

As the heat wore out of the day, we thanked the people of the tent for their kindness and moved on, the youth and his camels with us. Within the hour we were in the oasis, a sprawling rudimentary settlement of tents with only a small collection of buildings in the middle. There the camels slaked their thirst and we refilled our guerbas, at a watercourse that did service as the well of Silet. I had seen nothing like this before. It had evidently been channelled from some spring which issued from the earth among a clump of palms. In England it would have been called a ditch, a sluggish thing half-choked with weed, containing the odd tin can, but the water itself was clean and sweet enough. Kneeling by it that evening, as the camels sucked at the surface and shook their jowls endlessly around me, it seemed the greatest bounty I had known for a long time. When the beasts were done, we ambled on a little way to make our camp on the far side of the settlement.

Only then did I really begin to worry about the missing pair. Neither Ibrahim nor the youth had showed signs of alarm, and I had easily accepted their assurance that the others were following us. Too easily, perhaps. I was still unsure where the limits of endurance lay for people born and bred in the desert, though I was clear enough now about my own. Reason told me that the man and the child had water, as well as goats that could give them milk and meat. Our tracks were vivid enough to follow and there had been no wind strong enough to wipe them out. Yet the fact was that they had not now been seen for a day and a half. They could quite easily have had some accident, the father falling from his camel and breaking his leg or worse. That tiny boy, younger than my son Michael, might still be out there alone in that awful emptiness which had come close enough to imperilling me again. Guilt suddenly engulfed me in a wave. I should have insisted on staying put this morning until the others appeared, or I should have insisted that we turn back to look for them. It was absolutely no excuse that I was too weary to think straight, that I relied on the judgement of Ibrahim and the youth. I had an instinct—I had believed I had an instinct—and it had failed most miserably.

I turned to my companion in the darkness. If the two didn't show up in the morning, I said, we must do something to organise a search party from the oasis. That, said Ibrahim, wouldn't be necessary: the youth could attend to them; we must go on. Something thudded sickeningly close to my heart. This man, whom I had come to admire and to love as if he were my brother, had betrayed himself with a few words; just as I had betrayed myself with wilful indecision. I said nothing and tried to sleep, with Ibrahim on one side of me and the youth on the other. When I awoke, it was long past dawn and the youth was missing. He had gone, said Ibrahim, to look for the others.

I told him to wait until I returned. Then I walked back to the oasis. I remembered seeing a Land-Rover parked outside the buildings in the centre. I now hurried to this place, past men who eyed me curiously as they paused in their bricklaying of a new wall. In the main structure I found two people in western dress, dapper officials down from Algiers to advise the local people on planting crops in the oasis. They examined my papers and watched me keenly as I explained what had happened and what I feared. Would it be possible, I asked, for some men to take the Land-Rover across the ground we had covered, beyond those two mountains in the distance? I told them as best I could where the youth had parted company with the missing pair after the noon camp two days before. A foreman, one of the locals, was summoned and went off to fetch the vehicle. I paused, wondering whether I should go with him.

One of the agriculturists said, "Thank you. We'll find them." As I shifted, still half undecided whether to leave, he added, "They're very tough, these people, even the little boys. Tougher than you. . . ." He grinned, disarmingly. "Tougher than me, too."

It was midmorning when Ibrahim and I set off again, slogging towards the range of mountains whose scale and height were almost exactly that of the English Lake District. By midafternoon we were amongst them, creeping up a long hill of slaggy rock whose summit was littered with a great number of cairns and grave slabs. How very symbolic, I thought, of what this journey had become. Behind me lay the corpses of two camels that had died on my behalf. At any moment now, they might be joined by another, or even two; there were spots of blood on the rocks again, and the broken-toothed bull was rearing his head back continuously in that desperate, straining effort that heralded the end. Somewhere out there, in the place from whence we came, that small boy might even now be dying in a heap of dust, the Land-Rover too late to help him, or even failing to find his body at all. I was haunted by the chance of tragedy and my own part in its making.

I was suddenly, furiously, abysmally certain that I could go no further than Tamanrasset. I had, at last, discovered beauty in the desert. It was around me now, the familiar beauty of mountains. But all I could feel was agony, suffering, pain, mindlessness, endlessness, futility. Under the dreadful, drilling heat of this appalling sun I had become an automaton that marched. I was scarcely recognisable as a human being, with the responses that alone distinguished us from the animals. I wondered whether I had forfeited a little of my soul to the desert—maybe the greater part of it.

We stopped among the cairns. Ibrahim, as he had never failed to do from the first day of our passage together, was testing ropes, examining feet, sweeping away ticks from the underbellies of beasts which no longer had the strength to do it themselves, so that the insects hung vilely in thick clusters, surfeited with blood. Ibrahim himself needed rest as badly as any camel. His lips were now cracked open, with blood dried around the edges, and the tip of his nose had turned grey. His face was as taut as any of the ropes he was fixing. As we began to move slowly downhill, towards the long gash of the Oued Abalessa, he told me to hit the broken-toothed white, at the back of the line, in order to keep him going. I did so, and there was the awful crack of hard wood upon bone that was no longer covered in anything but hide.

We camped that night in a grove of trees before one of the most breathtaking views I could remember in many years of roaming the world. Far ahead was the full flourish of the Hoggar, an enormous mountain range of jagged peaks that radiated the light of the setting sun, glowing white against the deep blue sky. It was like looking at a bundle of Matterhorns, each vying with the next for prominence, stature and elegance. They were formidable in their presence and they were operatic in their grandeur. Deep inside that bastion of rock was the place where Charles de Foucauld[6] had made his hermitage. Something stirred within me, a genuflection to his memory, to be sure, but also a desire to touch and clasp those rocks and know them well. I would not reach the Nile now. The Hoggar would be my prize.

We walked down to Abalessa next morning. I had known no oasis more fruitful than this. There were small fields on the outskirts, head high in crops that were thick and ripening and vividly green. The place was superbly irrigated, with a stream that wound around and between the houses. There we watered the camels again and topped up the guerbas. We left almost as soon as we had finished and moved into a line of thorn trees to make our midday camp. When we had unloaded the baggage, two of the camels began to snatch at the abundant leaves. The broken-toothed bull, which we did not bother to hobble, meandered very slowly to the shade of the thickest branches and settled down without a sound. We never got him up again. We did not even try very hard this time. He could go no further, and we knew it. Ibrahim thought that, sitting in the shade, the bull might last a couple of days longer before he keeled over and died. No more. Someone might come across him, just as I had come across a camel awaiting death by the well of Chig so very long ago. But they would leave him be, too, as I had done the other.

We rearranged the baggage, discarding some things that were heavy and no longer of importance to us. In a couple of days we should reach Tamanrasset. Already I could feel myself becoming limp in the knowledge of danger past. We were safe now, whatever happened. There was another well between this place and journey's end, if we needed it.

---

[6]A French explorer who in 1905 had built a hermitage in Tamanrasset. He compiled a Tuareg grammar and dictionary but was assassinated in 1916.

"Supposing," I asked Ibrahim as we prepared to leave, "supposing these two camels drop dead tonight. What shall we do?"

He looked at me as levelly as he had always done. "You carry some food," he replied, "and I carry some water. We walk to Tamanrasset." He would have said the same thing in the same tone, I knew, if we had lost all our camels a hundred miles ago.

We walked to Tamanrasset. We left the broken-toothed bull beneath the thorn tree and began the long trudge up a wadi,[7] over the wretched coarse-grained sand that flayed the soles of the feet. Our two remaining beasts now moved better than before, without the almost dead weight of invalids pulling at them from behind. We entered rocky hills again, following a track that rose and fell around headlands and into gulleys, the main range of the Hoggar hidden for long hours as we worked our way through its foothills, then appearing once more as we crested some summit and passed over to its other side. It would have been exhilarating had mind and body not been so desperately fixed upon movement, any kind of movement, even the awful dragging movement of limbs that no longer functioned as they ought. Relief now consisted not in rest but in the knowledge that each step forward took us almost within sight of our goal. In that and in our water, which we could drink as freely as we wished.

Yet I, at least, was still conditioned by the long months of scarcity, in which each mouthful was a rare and blessed gift that might disastrously be withdrawn at any time. In the afternoon of our second day from Abalessa, we stopped to check the loads. Being by then too weary to stretch for my water bottle, which hung high upon my saddle, I asked Ibrahim to draw me some water in his bowl, which dangled lower down among the guerbas. I drank half of it and then, in a reflex, I handed him the rest. He did not, as it happened, wish to drink, having taken some a little time before. But, mistaking my gesture for one of excess, he tossed the rest onto the ground with an arrogant, princely turn of his wrist—the motion of a man who has everything he wants, casting out a surplus. I let out a cry of shock,

[7]Dry riverbed or valley.

and for a split second I could have hit him. I looked down at the dark puddle on the ground. No man on earth, it seemed to me, had any right to waste something so precious.

On Monday, March 5, we moved away from a camp we had made for the night behind some rocks by the side of the highway that ran through Tamanrasset on its way south across the Sahara from Algeria to Niger. It was much more used than the westerly route up which Ould Mohammed[8] and I had laboured three weeks before; several trucks had gone up and down it during the night, and in the space of an hour this morning we had to step aside half a dozen times to allow great petrol tankers and other heavy vehicles to thunder past and smother us with dust. Presently we cut away from the road and headed for the long slab of mountain which stood well behind Tamanrasset. We came to the perimeter of the airport, the most sophisticated thing I had seen since Dakar, complete with a control tower and a tarmacadamed runway. We ignored the warning notices and plodded straight across. A line of electricity pylons began at the other side, and we followed them over several ridges of sand. We marched past the municipal garbage dump, and I had not seen anything so loathsome for years; it defiled this place much more than the wasteland of refuse outside Nouakchott,[9] for everything here was beautiful, whereas there all had been barren. The town itself was all but concealed, even at this distance, in a small forest of trees, every one of them heavy with leaves.

We walked through the trees and suddenly, as if some magician had waved his wand, I found myself leading two camels and a companion in torn and dusty desert clothes down a surfaced street. It was lined with trees, whitewashed halfway up their trunks. Inside the lines of trees were pavements. There were tables set out at intervals along these pavements and people were sitting at them, drinking coffee. They stared at me open-mouthed, as though I were a strange animal they had never seen before. I walked on,

---

[8]One of Moorhouse's Tuareg guides earlier during the journey. "Ould" means "son of."
[9]The seacoast town in Mauritania where Moorhouse had begun his journey.

not daring to speak to any of them, not at all sure where I was going or what I was seeking. Towards the end of the street, I noticed a long low building with a courtyard and a crude sign which called it an hotel. In a reflex from a world apart from the one I had just crossed, I stopped and couched the camels. It was not the ending I had wished.

BOB CONNOLLY (b. 1945) AND ROBIN ANDERSON (b. 1950)

From *First Contact: New Guinea's Highlanders Encounter the Outside World*

⊕

Remarkably, by the end of the 1920s, the highlands of New Guinea still lay completely unknown to the outside world—and the outside world to the natives who lived there. Planes could by then have flown over the jagged valleys and misty plateaus and discovered the evidence of many flourishing tribes, but the wisdom of the day declared the highlands uninhabited.

It took a pair of Australian gold miners, Michael Leahy and Michael Dwyer, to blunder by accident upon these isolated people. In the summer of 1930, having gotten lost on a reconnaissance of new goldfields, the pair and their bearers (from the acculturated seacoast, along the Waria River) ended up traversing the island, following the Purari River. Astonished and intrigued by their contact with the highlanders, Leahy and Dwyer and a handful of cronies returned year after year, photographing and even filming the natives in the act of trying to comprehend this alien invasion.

Fifty years later, two Australian filmmakers, Bob Connolly and Robin Anderson, visited the highlands to seek out the elders who still remembered the world-changing incursion. Having rediscovered Leahy's lost film footage, Connolly and Anderson were able to film natives watching themselves on film shot a half century before. Their stunning documentary, First Contact, *was nominated for an Academy Award.*

In this excerpt from Connolly and Anderson's equally compelling companion book, the filmmakers synthesize hours of oral history to present a narrative of that invasion from the point of view of the highlanders, who, before Leahy and Dwyer arrived, thought they were the only people in the world. One senses the inevitable tragedy looming as the natives begin to deduce that the strange white men are not after all gods or ancestors brought back from the dead. Within months, the gold miners would shoot and kill the bolder highlanders as they pushed inside the rope boundary the Australians had erected around their camp to keep their own fragile autonomy intact.

There is no great difficulty today in finding highlanders who participated in these events of fifty years ago. It is simply a matter of following Michael Leahy's well documented line of march and talking to people along the way. In most cases the villages bear the same or similar names to those listed by Leahy in his diary. Some of them, like Kirupano Eza'e's village, are close to present-day administrative centres, and others lie along paved or dirt roads. Some are more remote, but in all of them, the response to our arrival is much the same. Young children converge from everywhere, and our interpreter sends them into the houses or vegetable gardens to find the old people who remember the *Taim wait man ikamap pastaim long hilans*—the first coming of the Australians. Invariably in each location there are men and women willing to tell their personal history of first contact with the representatives of the outside world. They may not know Leahy or his companions by name, but their descriptions of events invariably coincide, and virtually all use the word *spirit* to describe the strangers and their sudden arrival. The explanation for this is not hard to find. All highlanders shared their existence with the unseen world of the dead. "We had experienced the presence of dead people before," says Gopie Ataiamelaho of Gama Village near Goroka, "but we'd never actually seen them in their physical form. We knew of their presence, by hearing them whistle, or hearing their voices singing. That's how we knew the dead were present. Other times we would feel the dead around us when someone was sick, and one of the ritual experts was performing ceremonies over him. Sometimes then we would feel the presence of the dead."

And the dead could not be ignored. The spirits could be benevolent and protective, or malevolent and destructive. Human well-being depended upon their continued goodwill. Generally speaking, at death a person's soul took its place in the spirit world, and it was to this community of ancestral spirits that the people applied to improve the welfare of their lives. There were other spirits as well—gods, giants, ogres, legendary figures, mythological personifications of the sun, the moon, lightning.

The highlanders' universe, then, was made up of themselves, their allies, their enemies and the spirits. And then came the Australians. Obviously not their allies. Enemies perhaps? That assumption was quickly dispelled. The only other explanation was that the strangers were spirits—either their reincarnated relatives and ancestors, or some other spirit disguised in human form.

Fifty years later the highland people recall these events with a certain wry amusement. But their belief in a spirit world gave them a ready-made framework into which the coming of the Australians and their carriers fitted easily, enabling them to come to terms quickly with an event for which they were otherwise totally unprepared—to make explicable the inexplicable.

On his second journey through the Goroka and Asaro valleys, in November 1930, Michael Leahy passed close by the village of Kirupano Eza'e on November 6 and continued on past the present-day town of Goroka as he travelled west. It was at this time that Sole Sole of Gorohonota Village in the Goroka Valley heard news of the strangers. "We believed that when people died they went in that direction," he said, pointing to the east. "So we immediately thought they were ghosts or dead people." When the strangers were interpreted to be the returning dead, they were greeted with tearful elation—fear of the spirits, joy at the return of loved ones or revered ancestors. It was only a short step for the highlanders to imagine that they recognized particular individuals—prominent men, fathers, brothers, sons.

"So we sent messages out in all directions," says Sole Sole, "telling everybody around. And everybody came, and we all gathered to look at them. This was the time when we gave them a pig and also one of our men stole a knife from them. We all gathered around to look, we were pointing at them and we were saying, 'Aah, that one—that must be . . .' and we named one of our people who had died before. 'That must be him.' And we'd point to another one and say that that must be this other dead person we knew had died before . . . and we were naming them.' "

Gopie, from Gama Village near Goroka, heard the calls that strangers were coming and rushed down to where they had camped. He was confused about the identity of the white men but had no doubt who the black carriers were. They were dead clansmen. One was his late cousin Ulaline. The evidence was overwhelming. "My cousin had been killed in a tribal fight. When he came towards me I saw half his finger missing, and I recognised him as my dead cousin. The reason his finger was cut off was that [when alive] he'd had too many children with his wife. His people had punished him by cutting off his little finger. When he came towards me I said to him, 'Cousin!' And he lifted his eyebrows. So I knew it was definitely him. He was the same colour, the very same man. His facial expression, the way he talked, laughed—exactly the same. And it wasn't only me who thought this, everyone did. Today I tell this story to the pastors at the Seventh Day Adventist Church—but they just laugh at me."

At first Michael Leahy did not fully comprehend the underlying nature of his reception by the highlanders. He believed his initial passage was made easier (and safer) by the mere novelty of his arrival. In fact, even his most ordinary everyday activities were being analysed for a deeper meaning. Kize Kize Obaneso of Asariufa Village near Goroka remembers that "after they had built their tents one of them took an axe and went across to an old, dead, dry tree that had been planted long ago by a man who had since died. We thought this old man, whose name was Vojavona, had come back from the dead to cut down his own tree for firewood. We were very pleased that he knew his own tree."

Leahy's companion Michael Dwyer had false teeth, which he utilised on several occasions to disperse the crowd of onlookers. "We were all gathered there watching these strange people," says Sole Sole from Gorohonota, "when one of the white men pulled out his teeth. When we saw this everyone just ran in all directions." This was further incontrovertible evidence. Teeth might fall from a dead man's skull, but surely not from the living.

One man said that when the strangers gestured to their bodies, they interpreted this as the dead person telling of the wounds that had killed him. Any gesture of familiarity was seized upon, but also the reverse. Another man remembers that when the white men looked at them and then looked away, it was assumed to be deliberate: the dead were attempting to move about without being recognised by their living relatives. The dead, after all, did not always have the best interests of the living at heart.

Nor, for that matter, did the nonhuman entities of the spirit world, some of whom were known to be wild and distinctly ill disposed towards mortals. While Leahy's coastal carriers were almost invariably taken as the returning dead, sometimes the white man's appearance and behaviour coincided more closely with one or another of these mythological figures.

Gopie's first interpretation, before other evidence convinced him that the white men were ancestral dead, was that they were sky beings. "I asked myself: who are these people? They must be somebody from the heavens. Have they come to kill us or what? We wondered if this could be the end of us, and it gave us a feeling of sorrow. We said: 'We must not touch them!' We were terribly frightened." Others in the Asaro took the white men to be Hasu Hasu—the mythical being who expressed its power in lightning.

What counted in these situations was the peoples' attitude towards the spirit figure, or rather its attitude towards them. Among the Mikaru people on the southern fringes of the highlands, the arrival of white men heralded a catastrophe—nothing less than the end of their world. The white men of course were Leahy and Dwyer on their anxious trek down the Purari River, but word had reached the Mikaru before their arrival that strangers were coming with large and fierce dogs. Men owning large dogs had status among the Mikaru, and in their feverish excitement they speculated whether what they were facing was the return of the fearsome giant known as Souw, the principal figure in their creation story. Souw was known to be angry with the Mikaru. In the distant past when he lived among them a party of their ancestors had caught him copulating with his daughter, a grave crime. Souw was ashamed and enraged at being caught, and the people still retained the belief that one day he would come back to earth and punish them for shaming him. When Leahy and Dwyer, both tall men, arrived, the Mikaru were full of fear. Their white skin (Souw had white skin) their big dogs, and their clothing (Souw ensured his immortality by changing his skin like a snake) stamped them as reincarnations of Souw. The Mikaru fled in terror, although a few very brave men came back and met the white men.

At this point in their journey, Leahy and Dwyer were worried men them-selves—hopelessly lost but committed to going on—and they moved quickly through Mikaru territory. But not before the people saw Leahy's men wield-ing their steel axes, felling saplings for tent poles. Further terror for the Mikaru. They believed that the sky itself was supported by certain trees grow-ing along the horizon. The strangers were heading quickly and purposefully in that direction. Did Souw intend wreaking his vengeance upon them by cutting down the trees and allowing the sky to fall upon them?

At about the time Leahy was passing through Mikaru territory, he was making diary references to the timidity of the people, unaware of what was really going on. In first contact situations the intruders often made judge-ments of the people they were meeting in terms of whether they were friendly, timid or hostile, while being unaware of the deeper reasons behind these responses.

When Michael Leahy passed through the Mikaru country in July 1930 survival was uppermost in his mind, not the search for gold. In October and November 1930, back in the Goroka and Asaro valleys, Leahy was much more in control of the situation. The usual practice was to pull up and camp in the early afternoon, before the regular afternoon rain showers made things uncomfortable. The camp was usually sited close to a village and stream. The choice of a campsite involved pantomimed negotiations with the gathered crowd, and once the area was chosen, poles were cut and a rope line stretched around them to mark the boundary. Leahy had trained several ferocious dogs to attack the highlanders if they came into the camp enclosure. The dogs could distinguish them by their scanty clothing—the carriers all wore the skirtlike *lap lap*.

Each of Leahy's Waria men had their assigned jobs in the camp: bartering for food, erecting tents, digging latrine pits, cooking, guard duty. All this was done quickly, and under the intense scrutiny of hundreds, sometimes thousands of onlookers. As the afternoon wore on word would spread through the countryside and newcomers would join the crowds pressing up against the rope boundary.

If there was no prospecting work to be done Leahy might use these afternoons to photograph the scene outside the rope line, often developing the film himself in a nearby stream. In the late afternoon he would take to his tent and write his diary entry for the day. November 1, 1930, reads: "About three hundred men and marys [*meri* is the pidgin word for women] all outside our roped area, gazing at us like prize cattle at a country show." The terse entries in Leahy's diaries suggest he was already becoming aware that he was participating in a singular historical event and that he had an unparalleled opportunity to record it. He later sent away to America for correspondence courses in writing and photography and there was to be a growing sophistication over the years in the quality of his visual and written output.

Meals were eaten before sundown. As there was no necessity to carry any more than emergency food supplies, Leahy travelled comfortably. The white men ate at camp tables, seated on folding chairs, and slept on comfortable stretchers. At dusk guards were posted, and it was now time to disperse the dense crowds of onlookers, if necessary, by loosing the savage dogs trained to attack anyone not wearing a *lap lap*.

Today many highland people clearly recall the detail of the camps—the tents, the rope line, the dogs, the impossibility of closer inspection. Kize Kize Obaneso says his people stood outside the rope line looking in at their dead relatives. "Our older people wanted to go and hug and hold them—so they built a fence around with rope to keep us out." Apart from the rope, Kize Kize remembers that the strange smell of the white people had a powerful deterrent effect, as well. It was like nothing they had ever smelled before and it frightened them. The feeling was mutual. "Nigs pong woefully," wrote Leahy in his diary at one point.

Gavey Akamo remembers the white men camping a few hundred yards away from his village in the middle of the Asaro Valley. "They smelt so differently, these strange people. We thought it would kill us, so we covered our noses with the leaves from a special bush that grows near cucumbers. It had a particularly nice smell, and it covered up theirs."

When on the march the strangers would pass quickly through the crowds of highlanders and disappear as mysteriously as they came. The people would be left, as was Kirupano's clan, to "sit down and develop stories." But when they camped for the night, here was an opportunity to examine the strangers more closely and explore initial assumptions. A striking example of this investigative process was told by Gavey Akamo and his wife Sirizo Gavey.

Sirizo recounted a story well known to her people in the precontact times of a beautiful young widow who had decided it was time to look for a new husband. After much travelling the widow reached the top of a distant mountain, and there she saw a young man lying on the grass. He invited her on a journey, and for days the pair travelled through a beautiful region of flowers. Eventually they arrived at the man's village, and the girl joined his other wives. That night they lay down together, but after a time the girl woke up, looked to her husband and saw only his white skeleton lying there. In the morning there was nothing at all. The woman was shocked, and realised that she was in a place where everybody was dead. To join her dead husband she had no choice but to kill herself. Meanwhile her brothers, concerned that she had not returned, followed her trail and came upon her dead body. They carried it back to their village, and buried it in the traditional way.

So it was thought that the dead could take human form by day, and become skeletons by night. Sirizo's husband Gavey says his people thought that when the strangers lay down to sleep at night, the flesh would go from their bones and they would turn back into skeletons. And they set about proving it.

Gavey was a small boy at the time of contact, but he vividly remembers the older people speculating about the skeletons and trying to work out some way of getting in close enough to the camp to see. He says two redoubtable warriors came forward and declared their willingness to take on the mission. "They were very daring," says Gavey, "famous for their night raiding and feared by all our enemies. Death meant nothing to them. For them night was like daytime and they were the ones to dare find out about these white men. Their names were Gapumbarihe and Nigamangule.

"There were guard dogs in the camp during the night, but these two men were very careful. They crept very quietly, so as not to break any twigs. If the dogs approached they would lie quietly until they went away, and then gradually creep closer. They spent the whole night trying to peep inside the tent, as close as they dared go. They watched and watched, and they expected to see bones in there, but they could see none. They saw no changes taking place. The strangers stayed the same. So they said we should stop this belief that they were dead people."

Gavey suggests his people came quite quickly to the conclusion the strangers were not dead people. Often this process took a lot longer, sometimes years. After fifty years it is difficult to be precise. But the notion of white men turning into skeletons at night was recalled by old people from the Asaro right through to Kerowagi in the Chimbu, contacted by Leahy the following year. Most had little opportunity to put the matter to the test. Korul Korul from Oknel Village in the Chimbu recalls that "at night we used to wonder whether their flesh stayed on their bones or departed. But we couldn't get in to see because they had this big rope around their tents, men on guard. We thought they were dead people but we just lived in doubt about this."

The highlanders were anxious to detect any areas of similarity between themselves and the strangers. Did they eat? Drink? Sleep? Defecate? "Because they wore *lap laps* and trousers," says Kirupano Eza'e of Seigu, "the people said, 'We think they have no wastes in them. How could they when they were wrapped up so neatly and completely?' We wondered how the excreta could be passed. We wondered much about that."

On the march, Leahy and Dwyer found it necessary to choose a secluded spot and post a guard when they wanted to relieve themselves. Ideally they waited until the camp was set up in the afternoon. A screened latrine pit was dug within the roped-off area. But the highlanders' curiosity could not be left unsatisfied for long. "One of the people hid," recalls Kirupano, "and watched them going to excrete. He came back and said, 'Those men from heaven went to excrete over there.' Once they had left many men went to take a look. When they saw that it smelt bad, they said, 'Their skin might be different, but their shit smells bad like ours.' "

In the Enga district, far to the west, Naia Imulan from Tori Village, contacted by Leahy in 1934, says his people entertained one theory that the strangers were skypeople. If they were, it was reasoned that their excreta should look like that of birds, and when the people subsequently dug it up they were surprised to discover otherwise. The interest in excreta went beyond merely establishing the similarity of human functions, as throughout the highlands, bodily wastes were an important element in sorcery. A man became very vulnerable, for example, if his enemies got hold of his faeces, semen or saliva.

The strangers' bodies were covered in a strange material. They must have something important to hide. "We had only our traditional dress to cover our private parts," says Gasowe of Makiroka Village in the Asaro. "So when we saw these new strangers, with clothes and belts all over them, we thought they must have a huge penis they were trying to cover up. We thought it must be so long it was wrapped round and round their waists. It was because they were wearing these strange clothes and belts. The thought of that really used to scare us. The women used to be on the lookout and they would run away."

Reinforcing these assumptions were more mythological stories dealing with the exploits of men with giant penises. In the past, say the Kafe people for example, Hefioza lived alone on a mountain near the village of Henganofi (now a small settlement around a high school on the road between Kainantu and Goroka), prevented from travelling far by the enormous length of his penis. When he did travel he carried it coiled in a basket slung over his shoulder. One morning, Hefioza looked down from his mountain and saw a woman working her garden in the valley below. His penis slowly uncoiled and slid down the mountain, all the way to the woman. When she felt it between her legs she grabbed a stone axe and chopped it into pieces. The first piece turned into taro, and the others into yams, bananas, tapioca and sugarcane, which later became the peoples' staple foods. The woman, however, did not stop at this point, but kept chopping away until poor Hefioza's penis was down to a normal length. But by this time he was dead. So the woman poured a magic potion down his throat, brought him to life, married him, copulated, and brought forth many children who became ancestors of the Kafe people.

Many Eastern Highlands people remember speculating about the size of the strangers' penises. Enlightenment came to some when the white men were observed washing in the river. "When they had their bath," says Gasowe, "we used to peep at them and that's when we found out we were wrong. In fact they were just the same as all us men." But the sight of the strangers washing themselves provoked considerable consternation. "When we saw them using the soap in the river," says Gasowe, "and we saw all the foam that was on their bodies, we thought it was the pus coming from a dead person's skin, like the milky part from the rotten flesh. Our minds were in a turmoil when we saw such things!"

Leahy spent a great deal of his time testing the river and creeks for gold. In the time honoured fashion of prospectors, he would scoop up gravel and water in his pan and repeatedly swirl it round, gradually isolating specks of gold in the bottom, peering intently, of course, at the result. Good prospects would bring excited comments from Leahy and Dwyer and more speculation from their ever-present highland audience. "When the white men first came to the highlands," says Kirupano Eza'e, "they filled their dishes with sand and washed that in the water. They washed and washed, poured it out again, washed, poured off, washed, poured off. They did that on and on. And we watched, and thought like this: in the past, our ancestors, our forefathers and foremothers, when they died their bodies were burnt, and we used to pick up the bones and ashes and throw them in the river. And so we thought those ancestors of ours had come back to collect and wash their ashes and bones.

"Some men thought like that, and others thought, 'Did they want to wash the bones to make them come back to life?' We weren't clear on things then. But we know now. They got money from our ground. Now we think straight—that's how they made money, but before we didn't think like that. We had many wild thoughts."

For the highlanders almost everything the Europeans brought with them was new and mystifying—not only the items themselves, but the very substances with which they were made; the woven canvas of the tent, the cloth of their shirts, trousers and *lap laps,* their leather shoes and steel axes. (Leahy occasionally came across well-worn steel axes, traded up from the coast, but these were very rare.) To people who had never seen these things before, there was great difficulty in even describing them. One man could only liken Leahy's tents to clouds from the sky, because no natural material known to them could approach the canvas in whiteness. The functions and mechanisms of the white man's goods were equally mystifying—their guns, matches, torches, mirrors, watches, binoculars, cameras, writing paper, pens, rucksacks. Kirupano says his people thought the strangers carried their women in the bags strapped to their shoulders, as there appeared to be no women walking in the line. Obviously the women were let out at night, inside the tents. As for the night lanterns, says Kirupano, it seemed these men from heaven had brought the moon with them, or a piece of it.

But of all the wondrous objects possessed by the white man none could compare to their store of shells. Ranging in size and value from the tiny giri giri to the majestic gold-lipped mother-of-pearl shells, these, together with pigs, were the major wealth objects of the highlands. They were used for personal adornment, for ceremonial exchange, as a measure of personal prestige. A man could marry with contributions of pigs and shells to the woman's family. He would surrender them as compensation payments in disputes, or to allies for assistance given in battle. As the Australian penetration of the highlands increased, the area would be flooded by shells used as barter payments, but at the time of first contact they were quite rare, especially those most highly valued by the people—cowries, giant bailers, and gold-lipped pearlshells (*kina* shells in pidgin).

When Leahy first entered the highlands in June 1930 he took with him as trade goods axes and jews harps, large and small knives, glass beads, three bolts of cheap cloth and, on the advice of his friend Helmuth Baum, a bag of dog's teeth. This was the sort of trade that had passed muster in other parts of New Guinea over the years and Leahy thought he had everything he would need. But when he saw the shell decoration worn by the highlanders he realised he had omitted the most sought after item of all. The dogs' teeth were a definite failure. When Leahy offered them as trade for food, the people rounded up all their dogs and presented them for eating.

When Leahy returned to the highlands in late 1930 he was much better prepared, having scoured Salamaua for shells, particularly the cowries and tiny giri giri popular in the Goroka, Bena Bena and Asaro valleys. Each region had its preferred varieties, and Leahy gradually learnt by trial and error which ones were valuable.

Sometimes the initial fear of newly contacted people made them difficult to approach, but a display of shells usually achieved the desired result. "I would pick out someone," says Ewunga Goiba, the man responsible for buying food, "and as he backed away I would tie the shell onto a stick and try to make him take it. When I approached him he would move back further and further, and I'd move backwards! Then the fellow would come forward again, and I would move forward with encouraging gestures for him to take the shell. 'Oh Papa, you come. Get this good thing.'

"Eventually he would swell up with the desire to have the shell, and he would come and feel it with his hands. Then he would hold it, and then come and hold my hands. Then he would bring us food and I would buy it."

The shells used mostly by Leahy in the Eastern highlands were small giri giri, bought on the coast for six pence a pound, with three hundred to the pound. A few handfuls would buy the prospectors all the daily food they needed. Everyone recalls their amazement when they saw what the white men had with them: "We were all exclaiming and crying out in excitement! We couldn't believe it!" says one man. "They were so precious to us," says another, "and we said, 'Ahhh! Look at these!' " "We held them in our hands so carefully," adds a third, "and then we would wrap them up in leaves and put them in a house. And then we would have to go and have a look at them so we'd unwrap them again and look at them. We couldn't believe how wonderful they were."

Highlanders believed their ancestral spirits exerted control over human well-being—healthy children, good crops, big pigs and shell wealth. The Australians entered the highlands carrying what amounted to a treasure trove of the most highly prized items of wealth. The peoples' realisation that the strangers were enormously wealthy was a profoundly significant one influencing not only their immediate reaction to explorers like the Leahys, but the whole process of European colonization.

Shells were not the only effective trade items. European salt was highly prized everywhere, the highlanders considering it an improvement over their locally produced variety, made by burning vegetable matter and straining the ashes. But then there was steel—axes, tomahawks, long bush knives, smaller knives, even the tiny blades used in wood planes. When first shown them, some highlanders could not immediately comprehend their value, preferring their own familiar stone axes. In June 1930, on his way down the Purari, Leahy wrote testily in his diary: "They all use stone axes and are too stupid to sell a pig for a tomahawk, asking instead for tambu shell for their personal adornment." (He had no shells then.) But the people usually needed only a demonstration before they realised the value of what was being offered.

Isakoa Hepu of Magitu Village in the Bena Bena Valley was a small boy when he first saw the Australians, but he gives a comprehensive account of his people's reaction to the white man's cornucopia of exotic novelties and familiar treasures: "When the white man came here the people were really afraid of him. He put some salt in his hands and put it on their tongues. They tasted it and said, 'This is good,' and jumped about making noises like this, 'Sssss! Sssss!' Then they came forward and held on to the white man's legs, saying, 'This is a good thing.' Our way of making fire was by pulling hard on a strip of bamboo. The white man got a matchbox and stroked it. He gave them the matchbox and they too stroked it, and the fire flared out. They held the box to their hearts and they were filled with joy. Then the white man got the tambu shells and the tomahawks and gave them to the men around, to even old men. He got a piece of wood and he cut it and the men saw that and were crazy about it. One took the tomahawk and held it gently near his heart, and then went off. We thought he had gone for good, but he came back with a huge pig."

In the initial encounters any scrap or bauble from the Europeans was likely to be highly prized, invested as it was with great spiritual significance. The item's potential as a spiritual source of wealth and strength was often more important to the highlanders than the actual item itself.

LEAHY AND DWYER moved quickly, anxious to prospect as much of the country as possible. Most initial encounters were simply fleeting glimpses as the white men and their carrier line strode across the countryside. Rarely would the prospectors camp in one place for more than a night, and as Michael Leahy liked to be on the move as soon as there was light enough to see the path, the nearby people would normally still be sleeping when they left, with only the beaten ground of their campsite as evidence of their passing.

Not quite. Ulka Wena of Kundiawa in the Chimbu gives an account of what usually happened when the white men left. In March 1933 on his expedition to the Wahgi Valley, Leahy camped within a few hundred yards of Ulka Wena's home. "The next morning," says Ulka, "the white man packed up and went, and we came back to where he had slept. And we searched. Our old men believed that these were lightning beings from the sky, with special powers, and so they advised us to collect everything they had left behind. We swept the place and collected everything, tea leaves, matches, tin cans. And we went to the place where he had made his toilet and collected the excreta as well.

"Then we put these special things in a *bilum* [string bag]. We knotted the bilum and hung it on a post where everyone could see it. Then we brought pigs and killed them, placing the dead pigs against the white man's things, along with our weapons. The blood was draining from the pig. We cooked it, and cut it up, and everybody had some. Our old men said: 'We'll use these white man's things in the fights.' Now that we had these special powers we decided to go to war against the Kamenaku and the Naredu. We took the spears and gave them to the best warriors and told them to kill our enemies. When we were successful we knew the white man's power was working with us. We held on to this belief for a long time, until more white men came, when we realised these things were nothing special, just ordinary rubbish, so we threw them away."

The heavens may have opened and brought forth skymen or the living dead, but almost immediately the ever pragmatic highlanders were looking for ways in which these momentous events could be turned to their own advantage in everyday life. Mirami Gena, also of the Chimbu, tells how pieces of toilet paper were collected and burnt with pig's blood on the fire. Men then held their bows and arrows and their hands above the rising smoke to gain strength in preparation for going to war. Gena says one man took a razor blade he had found and scraped it along the bamboo strings of the bows, hoping to impart its magic strength into their weapons.

"The useless end of the matchstick," says Kirupano, "which the strangers had thrown away, was taken by the people, who said, 'These men from heaven threw this thing away so we must take it and eat it later, and we will

become like them. And when we go to fight our enemies we will win because this thing is going to help us.' That was the useless end of the used
matchstick. But the people took it with care."

THE SPIRITS HAD appeared among them, and then just as mysteriously had gone again, leaving the highlanders to ponder the meaning of
it all.

JOE KANE
(b. 1953)

From *Running the Amazon*

In joining the Amazon Source to Sea Expedition in 1985, which hoped to make the first complete descent of the mightiest river in the Americas, Joe Kane had the great advantage that he was friends with none of the team members beforehand. Kane was invited for that most postmodern of reasons—the team leader's hope that publicity might help pay for the expedition.

Thus the author was able to portray the tedious, much-interrupted descent simultaneously as an epic journey and as an ongoing fiasco rife with deep personality clashes. The twin camps among the team members polarized around Piotr Chmielinski, the Polish white-water ace who was the driving force behind the descent, and the fussy, fretful leader, Afrikaner Dr. François Odendaal, a control freak who was often terrified of the Amazon. Zbigniew ("Zbyszek") Bzdak, Tim Biggs, and Jerome Truran were the other expert rafters and kayakers. Pierre Van Heerden and Jack Jourgensen were along to make a film. Kane himself,

far from an expert paddler, was tempted often to throw in the towel but
found himself oddly committed to a voyage that mingled transcendent
moments with sheer terror.

In this excerpt, Kane narrates the most dangerous and exciting seg-
ment of the journey—running the Acobamba Gorge on the Apurimac
River, as the Amazon is known just below its headwaters in Peru.

Below us lay three bad rapids, a short stretch of calm water, and then, where the gorge suddenly narrowed, a single, twenty-foot-wide chute through which the whole frustrated Apurimac poured in un-heeding rage. The river was whipped so white over the next half mile that it looked like a snowfield. The thrashing cascades raised a dense mist, ren-dering the dark canyon cold and clammy. Their roar made my head ache.

"You swim in that,' " Bzdak shouted in my ear, "you don't get out!"

But the gorge walls were nearly vertical. We could not portage, we could not climb out, we could not pitch camp. Even had we found a relatively flat area, as the gorge cooled through the night boulders would pop out of the ramparts. The rock shower would be deadly.

We had no choice but to attempt to "line" the raft, a tedious, nerve-racking procedure in which we sent the raft downriver unmanned at the end of Chmielinski's one-hundred-fifty-foot climbing rope a length at a time.

While I stood on a boulder on the left bank and held the Riken in place by a short, thin line tied to its stern, the two Poles affixed the heavy climb-ing rope to the bow and worked downstream with it as far as they could. At Chmielinski's signal I dropped my line and kicked the raft into the first rapid. Within seconds the boat was hurtling through the rapid at what must have been twenty knots, leaping wildly. I shuddered when I imagined rid-ing it.

In the middle of the second rapid, the raft flipped. As it passed the Poles, half the bow line snagged underwater, tautened, and though rated with an "impact force" of more than a ton snapped as if it were mere sewing thread.

Unleashed, the raft sped down the river.

Truran, who had run the first rapid in his kayak, was waiting on a boulder near the calm water above the terrible chute. When he saw the raft break free, he dove into the river, swam for the raft as it drifted toward the chute, and managed briefly to deflect it from its course. He scrambled aboard, and as the raft accelerated toward the chute he caught a rescue line thrown like a football by Chmielinski. The Pole arrested the raft as it teetered on the chute's lip, and slowly hauled Truran back from the edge of disaster. (Chmielinski later described Truran's effort as one of the bravest he had seen on a river.)

Draining as all that was, we still had to get the boat through the chute, somehow hold it to the wall and board it, and then run the ugly water below. The lower rapid could not be scouted. We could only hope that it held no surprises—no waterfalls, no deadly holes.

Jourgensen and Van Heerden slowly worked their way down to the chute, creeping along the boulders that sat at the foot of the gorge's left wall. When they arrived, Chmielinski told them to rest. Then he and Truran anchored the raft with the stern line while Bzdak took the bow line, now shorter by some forty feet, and climbed hand over hand up the two-story boulder that formed the chute's left gate. From the boulder Bzdak then climbed to a foot-wide ledge that ran along the left wall.

At Chmielinski's command I followed Bzdak. I ascended the boulder easily enough, but negotiating the wet, slick wall was something else. It was so sheer that I couldn't find a solid grip, and I quickly developed what rock climbers call "sewing-machine legs," an uncontrollable, fear-induced, pistonlike shaking. I felt cut off and alone. One misstep and I was in the river, which now churned angrily fifteen feet straight below.

Bzdak stopped on the ledge three feet in front of me and looked back. He shouted to me, but I couldn't hear him above the river's tumult. He inched his way back and put his head next to mine.

"DON'T LOOK DOWN!"

We wormed along the ledge until we could lower ourselves onto a one-foot-square rock at the base of the wall and a few feet in front of the gate boulder. We squeezed onto that small rock, each of us with one foot on it and one in the air, and braced ourselves as best we could, trying all the while to ignore the exploding river next to us.

Bzdak twirled the climbing rope up off the top of the gate boulder and tugged on it, signaling Chmielinski to send the raft. I wrapped my arms around Bzdak's waist and leaned back like a counterweight. The raft vaulted the chute. Hand over hand, Bzdak reeled in slack line as fast as he could. I tensed, anticipating the jolt we were about to receive. The raft approached us, shot past, and BOOM! the line straightened and stretched, the raft hurtled down the rapid, I tried to calibrate my backward lean—

"HOLD ME, JOSE!"[1]

I couldn't. We were going in.

Yet somehow Bzdak was hauling the raft toward us, fighting it home inch by inch. Then the line was in my hands and he was in the raft, tearing a paddle loose from beneath the center net. The raft smashed up against the left wall. The river pounded through the chute, curled into the raft, knocked Bzdak flat, and buried him.

Trying to hold the raft was like pulling against a tractor. I couldn't do it. But the raft bailed itself quickly, and Bzdak rose from the floor and paddled toward the rock. When he was five feet away he leapt for it. How he managed to land on that tiny space I do not know, but we made our stand there, anchoring the bucking raft from what seemed like the head of a pin.

We watched Van Heerden help a ghost-white Jourgensen over the boulder and along the wall, then down the wall into the raft. The two men took up positions in the front of the raft. Then Chmielinski climbed over the gate boulder with . . .

. . . I read Bzdak's lips: "Shit!" . . .

. . . Odendaal's kayak.

Its owner appeared behind Chmielinski and stared at us. Chmielinski took aim and shoved the kayak down the boulder's face, dead on into the center of the lurching raft. Then he signaled me into the raft, but the rope

---

[1]Joe's nickname among the team.

had sawed my hands to bloody pulp and I couldn't uncurl them. Bzdak shook the rope loose. I dove the five feet from the wall to the raft and crawled to the left rear. Chmielinski worked his way down the wall and took Bzdak's spot. Bzdak jumped into the raft. With Jourgensen squeezed between them, he and Van Heerden got their paddles ready on front. I reached beneath the center net and yanked out a paddle for me and one for Chmielinski.

"What are we doing?" I yelled to Chmielinski.

He yelled back, "François goes alone, he dies!"

Biggs and Truran had managed to traverse the river above the chute and sneak down the far side of the rapid, but it was too risky for Odendaal. Were he to make a single mistake during the traverse he would plunge through the chute and into what we could now see was a deadly hole a few feet below it. Instead, Chmielinski intended to mount Odendaal and his kayak on the raft and run the rapid.

Chmielinski had tried that strategy with an overwhelmed kayaker once before, in the Colca canyon. Like Odendaal's, that kayak had been almost as long as the raft, and with it strapped over the center net the wildly top-heavy raft had flipped moments after it entered the rapid. Everyone had taken a bad swim, Bzdak the worst of his life. If that happened here, we would drown in the hole. But Chmielinski reasoned that it was better that six men risk their lives than that one be condemned to a near-certain death.

I looked up at Odendaal, standing atop the boulder. His eyes were frozen. He looked paralyzed. I knew the feeling.

Chmielinski screamed at Odendaal. He inched his way to the raft and into it and mounted himself spread-eagled on top of his kayak, facing to the rear.

"Squeeze on that kayak like it is your life!" Chmielinski yelled.

Chmielinski could not hold Odendaal's added weight. He leapt and landed in the raft as it bucked away from the wall. Seconds later, even before I could thrust Chmielinski's paddle at him, we were sucked into the heart of the current. With Chmielinski screaming at the top of his lungs—"LEFTLEFTLEFT!"—we managed to turn hard and get the nose of the boat heading downstream. We skirted the ugly hole, but it shoved the raft sideways. We found ourselves bearing down on a "stopper" rock no one had seen, a rock that would upend us if we hit it.

Chmielinski screamed "RIGHTRIGHTRIGHT!" and we were sideways, then "INININ!," a steering command intended for me, and I hung far to my left and chopped down into the water and pulled my paddle straight in toward me so the rear end of the boat swung left and the front end right. Then a wall of water engulfed me and all I saw was white.

Somehow we shot around the stopper rock's left side but we were still sideways in the rapid "GOGOGOGO!" paddling hard forward fighting in vain for control and the river slammed us up against another rock, this one sloping toward us, Chmielinski's side of the raft shot up on the rock, mine lowered to the river coming behind us, the water punched at the low end, drove it into the rock and stood the raft up on its side, teetering, "UP-UPUPUPUP!" and I fought to climb the high side, to push it back down with my weight, but Odendaal and his kayak had me blocked and I saw Bzdak trapped the same way on the front end, the water pouring in knocked me off my feet, the boat started to flip "GOGOGOGO!" and all I could do was try to paddle free of the rock digging blindly with my paddle "GOGOGOGO!" and BOOM! we were free and bouncing off the left gorge wall and then heading straight for the gentle tail at the end of the rapid and the calm flat water beyond.

JUST ABOVE THE rapid's last one hundred yards we found an eddy and put Odendaal out of the boat to walk along a sandy bank that ran almost, but not quite, to the end of the rapid. We ran the rest of it, two small chutes *boom-boom*, and met Truran in the softly purling water below. He pointed overhead, to the narrow crack of sky between the gorge walls. Storm clouds were snagged on a dark peak. We had to find a campsite quickly, before the boulder-loosening rain hit.

But Odendaal had run out of walking room and stood stiff as a statue thirty yards upstream of us, at the rapid's tail. Biggs sat in his kayak in an eddy near Odendaal, shouting at him to jump in the rapid and swim. Odendaal refused. The exchange continued for ten, fifteen minutes. Then, as the sky darkened, we all began to yell at the Afrikaner. He looked up. He slipped. He was in the river. He bounced through the rapid unharmed and Biggs fished him out at the bottom. After we put his kayak on the water Biggs escorted him downstream.

We got lucky—the gorge widened and we found a generous expanse of sandy beach. But after we unloaded our gear Odendaal lambasted Biggs over the scene at the last rapid, saying that as the expedition leader it was his right to have stood there two hours if he so chose. Disgusted, Biggs walked away and joined the rest of us around the fire. When Chmielinski had dinner ready Odendaal sat down but did not speak, choosing instead to play Biggs's harmonica softly to himself.

Chmielinski guessed that we had covered barely a mile that day. This was disappointing, but for the time being we relaxed. The storm clouds evaporated and we sat by the fire on that fine beach and watched a star show in the thin opening overhead, the river that short hours before had been a deafening monster now bubbling along tranquilly beside us.

DURING THE MORNING run on our second day in the abyss the gorge walls closed in on us once again, narrowing to perhaps thirty feet. At first this was a shock, but the river ran smooth and fast, and we calmed down. Truran, Biggs, and Odendaal paddled their kayaks ahead of the raft and disappeared around a bend.

Fifteen minutes later a gnawing worry gripped the five of us on the raft. Four hundred feet ahead of us the river appeared simply to stop. The gorge turned left, and the wall that crossed in front of us seemed to swallow the river. We expected to see a white line between the river and the wall, a line of riffles, the tops of rapids. The absence of such riffles suggested a waterfall.

We drifted, tense and uncertain. In the front of the raft Bzdak and Van Heerden shipped their paddles. I used mine as a rudder, keeping the bow pointed downstream while Chmielinski stood up and studied the river before us. After a few minutes he said, "Okay, I see a white line." Then we saw it, too, but it looked strange, too hard and unwavering to be riffles.

Jourgensen, sitting between Chmielinski and me, asked, "What if that line is part of the rock formations on the wall?"

We drifted in silence. After about a minute, Chmielinski said, "Shit!" I had never heard him use the word. "It *is* a rock formation! To the bank, fast!"

We paddled urgently for the left wall, and when we gained it Bzdak and I dug in the slippery rock for fingerholds. While we held the raft Chmielinski stood up and tried to determine what lay below the natural dam we assumed we were now approaching.

"This is the thing you are always afraid of," he said. "You cannot go back, you cannot portage, you cannot climb out, the water is dropping away in front of you. Even if that is a waterfall, the only thing we can do is go."

We set off uneasily, no one speaking, all eyes on the water line. Where were the kayakers? Now the river ended fifty, now forty feet in front of us. We went to the wall again, found a crack, inserted fingers. Chmielinski climbed the crack, but when he was fifteen feet above us he fell, returning to the river in a dark blur that ended with a splash and his red-helmeted head bobbing toward the falls.

Bzdak and I paddled furiously. Van Heerden unclipped a rescue line and threw it downstream. We hauled the raft captain aboard just as we began to shoot over the falls . . .

. . . but it was not a waterfall at all, just a long, gentle rapid. Steep—hence no riffle tops—but straight, no boulders, all lazy, harmless waves. And luck.

THEN OUR LUCK ran out. We reentered pinball country. We lined the raft through a cluster of gargantuan boulders, hour after hour of whipsawing rope, bloody hands, and bruised shins, and at the end of the day had to negotiate an ugly rapid that took an hour to scout and half a minute to run.

Something happened to me in that half minute. The rapid was a tricky one. It had three chutes and a dozen turns, the last around a broad hole. We handled the first two chutes well, but the third had a ten-foot drop—a small waterfall. At the top of that last chute Chmielinski yelled "OUT!," a signal to me to set the raft's nose straight, and I managed two correcting strokes before we hit the chute's left wall.

Then the raft burst through the chute, a wave broke over the top of the raft, I saw nothing but water, and I heard Chmielinski screaming "OUT-OUTOUT!" I dug with my paddle and managed three more strokes before we hit the edge of the big hole and the force of the currents spinning around the hole jerked the raft and threw me into the center net.

Or had I *jumped* into the net?

I could not honestly tell. The rapid had been a difficult one, that much was clear, and when we completed it Biggs and Truran shouted congratulations to us. Chmielinski was jubilant, beaming, charged with adrenaline. "Perfect," he said as he shook my hand.

I wasn't so sure. I suspected I was beginning to crack.

IN GENERAL, HOWEVER, that run buoyed our hopes—perhaps we would break free of the abyss the next day. There was a good feeling in camp that night, except for my self-doubts and a blowup between Biggs and Odendaal over Odendaal's failure to follow Biggs's instructions in a difficult rapid.

"Tim's in a terrible spot," Truran said to me as we sipped tea before dinner. "He's like a veterinarian injecting his own dog. If Frans drowns,[2] the responsibility is on Tim. People will say to him, you were the river captain, why didn't you take Frans off the water? But Tim really cares for Frans. He wants him to have a good outing, so he's reluctant to send him off. Maybe the lesson in all this is that if you can't do the job yourself, you don't put a friend in charge. You look for someone impartial."

[2]I.e., François (Odendaal).

That night Odendaal came to my tent. He was smoking his pipe and seemed pensive and subdued.

"Is my behavior on the river causing you rafters worry?" he asked. Speaking for myself, I said, I was concerned mainly with running each rapid, with getting through the abyss alive. He was an afterthought, except when we had to carry him on the raft.

"That's good," he said. "I was afraid . . . well, Tim's being too emotional. I am paddling at my best, but Biggsy is overworried. In a good way, of course. I know he acts as he does because he cares for me."

I said Biggs certainly did appear to care for him. Then he wished me good night.

Thinking about it later, I found his assertion that he was "paddling at my best" surprising. As far as I could tell he was portaging any rapid he could. However, I did not think less of him for this. If anything I admired his prudence, and at times was envious that he could portage his kayak around many rapids that, with our much bigger raft, we had no choice but to run.

I worked on my notes, but this did not distract me from questioning my own behavior on the river, especially on that last rapid. I had always assumed (without ever really testing that assumption) that the one thing I had control over was my nerve, my ability to act under pressure. Now I wondered if I had misled myself.

WE HAD ADVANCED one mile our first day in the abyss, two miles the second day. Our third day started off with no more promise. A hard rain had fallen through the night, and by morning the river had risen six inches. Biggs estimated that it had come up 20 percent overnight, from four thousand cubic feet a second to five thousand. We were awake at dawn and on the water by 8 A.M. By 11 A.M., lining the raft through three unrunnable rapids, we had progressed a grand total of about four hundred yards.

And then we encountered a chute almost identical to the one at the entrance to the abyss. The Apurimac compressed to about twenty feet wide, and the walls rose not just vertically but in fact narrowed—the powerful river had cut its gorge faster than gravity could bring the upper ramparts tumbling down. The kayakers found what they called a "sneak" along the right wall, a small chute next to the main chute that was an easy run for them but too small for the raft. Meanwhile, we couldn't scout the rapid and we couldn't line the raft through it.

Once again Bzdak and I climbed the gate boulder, inched along a thin ledge on the left wall, and retrieved the raft after Chmielinski shoved it through the chute. Once again Van Heerden and Jourgensen worked their way down the wall and into the raft. Once again we bore down on a monstrous hole. In fact, it was the biggest hole I'd seen, a gargantuan churning turbine easily thirty feet across, its eye sunk a good five feet below its outer lip. With Chmielinski screaming furiously we managed to skirt the hole, but as we did I had the distinct impression of it as a demon lurking over my right shoulder.

We shot past the hole, bounced off both walls and spun clockwise in a circle. With the portly Jourgensen riding on my corner of the raft we sat low in the water and the river pelted us constantly over the stern. Now, as we spun, he lost his balance and with an assist from the water beating me on the back sent me flying out of the raft. On my way out Chmielinski reached across and jerked me back in.

Just as I got back into position I saw that we were bearing down on Biggs, who was in his kayak, in a tiny eddy right in the middle of the rapid, poised to rescue one of us in the event of a spill. Bzdak screamed a warning, but in the narrow gorge Biggs had nowhere to go—we had come on him too fast. We ran him down, trapped him beneath the raft, and hauled him fifteen yards before his boat popped out, riderless, from beneath ours. Then Chmielinski managed to reach under the raft, grab Biggs by the life jacket, and yank him free, alive but distraught.

We broke for lunch exhausted and demoralized. After five hours of work we had advanced perhaps eight hundred yards. Food went down hard, because each man felt within his gut a stone of fear and fatigue. To our right, in the east, the sight of snow-capped 21,000-foot Auzangate hovering over the gorge brought little joy, for it reminded us that we were still some six thousand difficult feet above sea level.

After lunch Chmielinski, Truran, and I scouted downriver and discovered our worst rapids yet. Four thundering drops, each at least two hundred yards long, with so much white water that at first they appeared to be one continuous froth.

Truran broke the rapid down into distinct runs: "Ballroom, Milk Shake, Liquidizer, Dead Man." He turned to me. "Whatever you do, *keep paddling*. Keep control of the raft. And *do not swim*."

Bzdak joined us on the rock and appraised the river. "What do you think?" I asked.

He shook his head slowly. "Don't swim. My god, don't swim."

He and I climbed back to the raft and sat on it, waiting for Chmielinski. From utter emotional exhaustion I fell asleep, and awoke to Chmielinski splashing water in my face. He ordered Van Heerden to accompany Biggs, Truran, and Odendaal, who had found a portage route too tight for the raft but adequate for their kayaks. The cover was that Van Heerden could film the rapid. The reality was that by now Chmielinski did not trust Van Heerden. The Afrikaner would not respond to Chmielinski's commands, and his habit of smoking on the raft, and of tossing the empty cigarette packages in the river, had already led to harsh words between the two.

After the kayakers and Van Heerden left, Chmielinski said to Bzdak, Jourgensen, and me, "Okay, guys, looks good. All we do is keep straight in the top chute." He paused. "If you swim, try to go to the right." I had never heard him suggest the possibility of swimming a rapid.

We paddled upstream, turned into the current, maneuvered above the chute, and slowed slightly as we dipped into it. Then the river picked us up and heaved us forward. We were airborne. The only time I had felt a similar sensation was as a teenager, when I had ridden a motorcycle off a small cliff.

The raft hit the water, jackknifed, spun one hundred eighty degrees. We went backward into the Ballroom. Chmielinski and I cracked heads and then I was on my way out of the raft. I grabbed netting as I went over the side.

"Jack!" someone screamed, and for a split second I saw Jourgensen in the heart of the rapid. He was under, up, under again, helpless, his life jacket his only hope, for he could barely swim. His face looked bloodless and frozen, his eyes blank. But he wasn't struggling. It was as if he had resigned himself to the inevitable.

The raft pitched, heaved, scooped me up. Chmielinski lay sprawled across the net, and at first I thought the force of our collision had knocked him out. The raft bolted up, then down. Bzdak, standing in the bucking bow like a defiant warrior, reached into the river and with one hand plucked Jourgensen back from eternity. He dropped the big man on the floor of the raft as if he were no heavier than a trout.

Two seconds later we plunged into Milk Shake.

"FORWARDFORWARDFORWARD!" Chmielinski yelled as he scrambled back into paddling position. We paddled hard to try to regain control of the raft, but it was too late. The front right rose and we began to flip. Jourgensen struggled up from the floor, climbed Bzdak's back, and nearly knocked him out of the boat. Bzdak wrestled him off and threw himself at the high side with Chmielinski. The raft leveled for a moment, then started to spin left to right.

"SWITCH!" Chmielinski yelled. That was a new one. He and I turned on the tubes and became front men, Bzdak the lone driver.

We handled the third rapid, Liquidizer, but lurched out of control as we tumbled over a short waterfall into Dead Man. We bounced off the left wall, hit a rock, spun a three-sixty, hit the right wall—and somehow ricocheted right across the hole. I got one terrifying glance at its ugly swirling eye, and then we shot into the calm water below it.

We paddled to some boulders along the right bank, climbed out of the raft and sat in silence. You could almost hear the nerves jangling. Then Bzdak said, slowly, "Those were the biggest holes I have ever run."

Chmielinski agreed but didn't elaborate, which was unusual for him.

Jourgensen said nothing, but with shaky hands tried to light his pipe. After a while Bzdak said, "We call that Wet Pipe Rapid, Jackie."

And then the laughter started, nervous titters at first, then low howls, then wild insane roaring.

HAVING ONCE AGAIN advanced but a mile over the course of an entire day on the river, we finally began to understand how long a distance forty miles could be. On flat land you could walk that far in two days. We might well need two weeks to travel it on water. We resigned ourselves to a long haul.

That night Chmielinski instructed me to cut our already-lean rations by half. We would fill out the cookpot with our one surplus ingredient, water. Nobody was happy with this, but none opposed it.

As bats wheeled above us we ate a thin gruel—three packages space-age chili, one package powdered soup, water, water, water, eight bowls—then huddled on a granite slab along the river, watching the stars in the slit overhead, following them down to the top of the gorge wall, which in turn was lit up with fireflies. It seemed as if the stars fell right to the river.

"I don't think I've ever seen a more brilliant canyon," Tim Biggs said. Grunts along the rock affirmed that all shared his thought. We were scared and tired, but those emotions concentrated our attention, told us that we were in a sacred place, a place untouched by humans and perhaps, until then, unseen.

"Rivers have their own language," Truran said. "Their own culture. We're not in Peru. We're in a place that speaks in eddies and currents, drops and chutes and pools. So we only made a mile today. Can you think of a finer mile?"

I walked back to my tent and worked on my notes. An hour later, when I crawled into my sleeping bag, I heard the heavy breathing of Jack Jourgensen, who had pitched his tent near mine. I could not forget the look on his face that afternoon when he'd fallen into the rapid, the blankness of it, the resignation.

Jourgensen was nearly fifty-two, and at a crossroads. He'd been reading Leo Buscaglia's *Personhood* and wondering, as he put it, "What does it mean to get in touch with the world and yourself?" He wanted to be more than a man who got rich selling highway paint. His presence on the Apurímac said he was a filmmaker, an explorer, an adventurer—"Viking" was the word he liked to use in the diary he kept for his seven children, the youngest of whom, Leif, was only five months old.

I think all of us were inspired by the fact that Jourgensen would attempt a journey that scared the wits out of men two decades younger and in much better condition, but I know that I, for one, felt guilty about his being there. The cold truth was that he did not belong on the river. He was overweight, with a degenerating disc, arthritic hips, and a history of gout, and the swimming and climbing taxed him much more than it did the rest of us. Back home, he had a huge family depending on him. Yet in Cuzco, when Durrant[3] had said that as the expedition doctor she considered it imprudent to allow him on the raft—"What will you do if he breaks a leg, or has a heart attack? You could kill him trying to get him out of the canyon"—no one had responded. No one had wanted to lose the golden goose.

I SLEPT FITFULLY that night, my body bruised from the bad rapids. At first light I got up and checked the food bags for mildew. Bzdak was up, too, on breakfast duty. He made a pot of instant coffee and poured me a cup, although anticipation of the impending confrontation with the Apurímac already had my stomach in knots. We ladled the rest of the coffee into cups and distributed them to the tents.

"Zbyszek," I said when we had finished, "if we have another rapid like those ones yesterday, will you run it?"

"If there is no choice. Otherwise, no. What if someone breaks his leg? No way out. We put him to the raft and keep pushing. Not so good."

---

[3]Dr. Kate Durrant, the only woman on the expedition, absent during the running of the Acobamba Gorge.

That morning the river's gradient increased, and supported by the rain that had fallen over the last three days, the water rose another six inches and grew more volatile. We encountered rapid after rapid that was off the scale of difficulty—Class Sixes. For five straight hours the kayakers portaged and we worked the raft downriver on the end of Chmielinski's mountain-climbing rope.

This time, however, Chmielinski added a new twist to the lining procedure. He directed Bzdak to ride the raft and paddle it as we tethered him from shore. Chmielinski provided the bulk of the brains and muscle, but it was Bzdak who took the brunt of the risk. These were rapids a man could not swim and survive. The velocity of the water, let alone the rocks and boulders into which it would drive one, would crush a skull as easily as an eggshell. Yet all Chmielinski had to say was, "Zbyszek, go there," and point to a boulder in the middle of the river, or to an eddy far downstream, and Bzdak was in the raft and flying, with no more response than a hand signal to ask, "At which eddy should I stop?"

During six years in some of the wildest, most unforgiving places in the Western Hemisphere, these two disparate men had learned to depend on each other utterly. Despite the terrible risks they were running, despite our dire straits, it was wonderful to watch them work the precious raft down the beastly river. The only sign of the tremendous emotional pressure they were under was an occasional frenzied exchange in Polish.

By the afternoon of our fourth day in the abyss (and our sixth since leaving Cunyac bridge), Bzdak was exhausted. His eyes were red and puffy and his paddle responded too slowly to the raging water. I felt I should spell him on the raft, but Chmielinski would not hear of it. "This is a special thing between me and Zbyszek," he said. "We have many years together. It is correct for me to ask him to go, but not to ask you."

Chmielinski's reply came as a relief. I was more than grateful to scramble along the boulders behind him, hauling in slack line, paying out line as the raft took off, anchoring him so the speeding raft did not drag him into the river. I preferred the feel of rock under my feet, for by now fear of the river dominated my thoughts. My nerves were so raw from the white water that each afternoon, when the word came down that we were stopping to make camp, a wave of gratitude, of recognition that I had survived one more day, washed over me with a feeling that was palpable—it felt as if my body, one big knot of fear the day through, had suddenly come untied. The simple act of sipping my evening cup of coffee gave me immense pleasure.

Part of my fear was due to the fact that I could not get comfortable on the raft, which was packed in such a way that the fifth, nonpaddling man, either Jourgensen or Van Heerden, was crammed into my left rear quadrant. When Jourgensen rode next to me, weighing down our corner of the boat, I always felt that I was about to be pitched into the river. Van Heerden rode in back when he wanted to film, and jumped around constantly. Once, as we bounced through a rapid, he hit me with his camera, knocking me out of the boat and stamping my right temple with a purple wound. The tiny Riken, the agent of my salvation, of my deliverance through the terrible river, now seemed dangerously overburdened.

In all, it appeared that we might never escape the abyss, that it would never end. There was simply no flat water. It was rapid after rapid, mile after mile, driven by what Conrad described as nature's "sinister violence of intention—that indefinable something, . . . in unheralded cruelty that means to tear out of [a man] all he has seen, known, loved, enjoyed or hated . . . which means to sweep the whole precious world utterly away from his sight by the simple and appalling act of taking his life."

"What do you think, Tim?" I asked Biggs later that day.

"I don't know, mate," he said. "But I'd be lying if I didn't say the river had me a bit scared."

RAINY SEASON HAD begun in the high Andes. Influenced by tributaries miles above us, the river changed color daily. At times she appeared a coffee-and-cream brown, at others emerald green, still others a glacial gray. In the early evening she might run smooth and unthreatening past the camp, yet by morning, having come up a foot during the night, be thundering and powerful. In some places she was studded with three- and four-story boulders, in others her banks were packed with crushed gravel. Given these changes in mood, in appearance, it was impossible not to think of the river as having a will and intent of her own. In the end, however, it was sound, a voice, that most gave her life—she *roared* as she charged through her canyon. She seemed not only willful but demonic, bent on the simple act of drowning us. You could shout at her, curse her, plead with her, all to the same effect: nothing. She barreled on indifferent, unrelenting.

And so, inevitably, we turned our frustrations inward. On the river a shouted instruction might end as a yell and a grumbled epithet. In easier times, choice tent sites had been shared or left for another; now, as soon as we found a camp each man scrambled for the best land. Food was eyed greedily and served in strict portions.

In the abyss the competition between Chmielinski and Odendaal festered into open hostility. The Afrikaner's insecurity over his titular role as expedition leader manifested itself as a kind of delight when the Chmielinski-led raft encountered trouble. This attitude, though hardly admirable, was understandable. Several times a day Truran, Biggs, and the raft team would run rapids that Odendaal couldn't, and his solitary portages seemed to set him apart, to isolate him.

Chmielinski, for his part, had no respect for Odendaal as a riverman, and did not go out of his way to hide his disdain. "He is afraid of the water," he would mutter on the raft as he watched Odendaal portage yet another rapid he considered easily runnable. He did not regard Odendaal as his equal, let alone his superior, in any way.

At the end of our fourth day in the abyss, when it appeared that both Odendaal and the raft team would have to make a long portage, Odendaal's face cracked in satisfaction. "I'll be in camp two hours ahead of you!" he said, and laughed. Then he clambered up a boulder, hauled his kayak after him, and set off.

This goading was more than Chmielinski could stand, for the raft carried all of Odendaal's food and most of his gear. After the Pole scouted the route, we portaged the food and equipment bags downstream in three back-breaking trips, heaving them up and over boulders and nursing them along jagged crags. Odendaal did not see us and did not know that we had managed to put the lightened raft on the river instead of portaging it.

Kayaking downriver ahead of us, Biggs had found a tiny cave with a soft, sandy floor. We reached this camp well ahead of Odendaal. He looked shocked when he arrived, and without a word left to set up his tent.

The next morning I awoke to the sound of Odendaal's voice at Biggs's tent, which was pitched near mine. Odendaal wanted Biggs, the river captain, to command Chmielinski to deflate the raft and portage it over the next few kilometers. This, he argued, would be faster than lining. Biggs was noncommittal.

On the face of it, Odendaal's was a strange bit of logic. We lined the raft much faster than we could portage it, and as we had demonstrated the day before, we portaged our equipment and lined the lightened raft faster than Odendaal portaged his kayak.

However, if it came down to portaging the raft without the option of lining—if we deflated the raft—Odendaal would certainly move faster than we. And for Chmielinski, there was a world of symbolic difference between carrying a deflated raft overland and working an inflated one down the river. Deflating the raft would be humiliating, an admission of defeat.

Biggs fetched Chmielinski, who had a mumbled exchange with Odendaal that quickly escalated into a shouting match. Chmielinski told Odendaal that he knew nothing about white water. Odendaal threatened to throw Chmielinski off the expedition at Cachora.[4]

I left then, and went to the cave. Truran was making coffee.

"If anyone goes at Cachora it should be François," he said. He was silent for a moment as he filled my cup, then said, "It's a constant game of one-upmanship with those two. They've got to get over that, or we'll put ourselves in even more danger than we already are."

Chmielinski did not deflate the raft, but that morning, as we attempted to line it through a rapid, it lunged around a boulder and pulled up short, teetering on its nose. Using one of our rescue lines, Bzdak, Truran, and I

[4]The next village and resupply point.

lowered Chmielinski thirty feet down the boulder's face. He freed the raft by slashing the snagged climbing rope, but the rope then ricocheted into aquatic oblivion. Suddenly, all we had left in the way of rope was our five short, thin rescue lines, which were dangerously frayed from overuse. Soon, unable to line the raft, we would be forced to portage. It would be slow, difficult, nasty work.

By lunch we had not advanced five hundred yards. Chmielinski sat by himself and spoke to no one.

That afternoon the rapids got worse. We would fight through a few hundred yards of bad water, lining some rapids, running others, but always hoping that beyond the next bend we'd find a calm, clear stretch. Then we'd peek around the bend and think, "This is getting *ridiculous*." The rapids only got bigger, meaner, and longer.

Late in the afternoon we faced yet another monstrous rapid around which we could not portage the Riken. Chmielinski picked a rafting route, and then, in an attempt at conciliation, consulted with Biggs and Odendaal, who concurred. "You'll do well," Odendaal said to us as he set off to portage his kayak along a thin ledge on the canyon's left wall. Biggs agreed: "You've run much worse." He and Truran shouldered their boats and went with Odendaal, and Chmielinski instructed Jourgensen to follow them. (He feared that Jourgensen's next swim would be his last.) Bzdak, Van Heerden, and I waited for Truran to reach the bottom of the rapid and position himself to rescue us. Then we took up our paddles.

No one had read the current moving left to right just beneath the top of the rapid. I'm not exactly sure what happened when we hit it. One moment I was in the boat, the next all was darkness and silence. I grabbed for what I thought was the raft and got river. The water grew cold, colder, frigid. I tried to swim, but I couldn't tell if I was going up or down, and in any case my flimsy strokes were useless against the powerful current. Something squeezed the wind out of me like a giant fist. Again I tried to swim, searching for light, and again I was dragged down and flipped over and over and over.

I had taken some bad swims before, but this one was different. In a moment of surprising peace and clarity I understood that I was drowning. I grew angry. Then I quit. I knew that it was my time to die.

Suddenly, as if rejecting such sorry sport, the river released her grip.

I saw light. Kick. Pull. Pull toward the light. A lungful of water. Pull. AIR!

Then the river sucked me back down again. Blackness, tumbling, head crashing off rocks.

AIR!

LIGHT!

I surfaced to find the gorge wall hurtling past me. I hit a rock, snagged for a second, and managed to thrust my head out of the water long enough to spot Truran in his kayak at the foot of the rapid, holding in an eddy.

"Swim!" he yelled.

A blast in the back and I was in again. Everything went black. I sucked water up my nose and into my lungs. I bounced off something hard and surfaced next to Truran.

"Grab my waist!" he shouted. I wriggled onto the stern of his kayak and clamped my arms around him. He deposited me near a sandy bank on the river's left side and told me to wait there.

I knelt in the sand and vomited. When Truran returned, I waded into the river, stopped, and turned back to shore.

"Get in the water!" he yelled. "*Now!*"

Then we were in the rapid, and I was hugging him with whatever strength I had left, and the river was beating over me, as if angry she had not claimed me. Long minutes later I stood at the foot of the gorge's right-hand wall.

Van Heerden was smoking a cigarette rapidly and shaking. Chmielinski looked at me as if at a ghost. When the raft had flipped the alert Poles had grabbed onto it again immediately and been yanked from the hole. Van Heerden had been tossed clear and driven toward a flat-faced boulder. The river went directly under the boulder. If Van Heerden had gone with it he would have been shoved under the boulder and killed, but as he was about to hit it Truran, scouting in his kayak, had yelled to him. Van Heerden had turned and reached for the raft, which was trailing him. The raft had slammed into the wall and pinned him. Van Heerden had been sucked under, but Chmielinski had managed to grab a hand, and Bzdak his head. When the raft bounced off the wall they wrestled him free. They assumed I had gone under ahead of him.

Chmielinski said, "Guys, in the boat." Either we got right back in or maybe we would never have the nerve to get in it again.

It was dark when we made camp, on tiny patches of sand hidden among boulders. We managed to eat about half our thin dinner before Truran accidentally upended the cookpot. No one spoke, except Chmielinski, to announce that we had advanced all of one mile that day.

Cold, hungry, and scared, I doubted whether I, or any of us, would survive the abyss. And though I knew it was self-pity, I resented the fact that everyone in that sad little camp but me had at least one partner with him, someone who would have to face family and friends and say, *This is how he died.*

The skies opened up and rain fell hard. We bolted for our tents. I hurried into mine, lit a candle, and stared at it until it had burned almost all the way down. When I blew it out the darkness terrified me—it reminded me of the darkness inside the river. I searched frantically for matches and burned two more candles one after another. I lit a fourth, my last. When it burned out I lay awake in the dark, eyes open, and felt my body tumbling, tumbling, tumbling.

NOEL ODELL

(1890–1987)

"Mallory and Irvine's Attempt"

From *The Fight for Everest*

On June 8, 1924, George Leigh Mallory and Andrew Irvine set out from Camp VI at 26,800 feet on the north side of Mount Everest, determined to climb to the highest point on Earth. They never returned—leaving not only their teammates but the whole world to puzzle over their fate.

That day, Noel Odell climbed alone from Camp V to Camp VI in support of his teammates. As he paused on a rocky rib at 26,000 feet, he caught sight of his friends, outlined against the skyline far above, moving quickly upward. Then the clouds closed in. Odell's fugitive glimpse remains perhaps the most haunting sighting in exploration history. And for seventy-five years, until Mallory's body was discovered on May 1, 1999, that sighting was the chief clue to the mystery of Mallory and Irvine's demise.

By all rights, Odell should have been on the summit push instead of Irvine, a twenty-two-year-old Oxford undergraduate with very limited mountaineering experience. Except for Mallory, Odell was the best

*climber on the team, and after a slow start, he had rounded into superb
shape on the mountain. But Mallory had formed a special bond with
Irvine, whose near genius at tinkering with the faulty oxygen apparatus made him invaluable high on Everest.*

*Odell's deeds in support of his friends, as he lingered for eleven days
above the North Col, climbing twice to Camp VI in a vain search for
an explanation of the tragedy, are virtually without parallel in Himalayan history. And his climactic chapter in the official expedition
book,* The Fight for Everest, *remains a canonic text in mountaineering literature.*

T hat evening as I looked out from the little rock ledge on which my
tent was situated,[1] the weather seemed most promising, and I knew
with what hopeful feelings and exultant cheer Mallory and Irvine
would take their last look around before closing themselves in their tiny tent
at VI that night. My outlook, situated though I was 2,000 feet lower down
the mountain-side than they, was nevertheless commanding and impressive in the extreme, and the fact that I was quite alone certainly enhanced
the impressiveness of the scene. To the westward was a savagely wild jumble of peaks towering above the upper Rongbuk Glacier and its many af-
fluents, culminating in the mighty Cho-uyo (26,750 feet) and Gyachung
Kang (25,910 feet), bathed in pinks and yellows of the most exquisite tints.
Right opposite were the gaunt cliffs of Everest's North Peak, their banded
structure pregnant with the more special and esoteric interest of their past
primeval history, and in this respect not detracting by its impression from
the vision of such as can behold with more than single eye. This massive
pyramid of rock, the one near thing on God's earth, seemed only to lend
greater distance to the wide horizon which it intercepted, and its dark bulk
the more exaggerate the brilliant opalescence of the far northern horizon
of Central Tibet, above which the sharp-cut crests of distant peaks thrust

[1]At Camp V, at 24,800 feet.

their purple fangs, one in particular rising supreme among them. To the eastward, floating in thin air, 100 miles away, the snowy top of Kanchen-junga appeared,[2] and nearer, the beautifully varied outline of the Gyankar Range, that guards the tortuous passages of the Arun in its headlong plunge towards the lowlands of Nepal. It has been my good fortune to climb many peaks alone and witness sunset from not a few, but this was the crowning experience of them all, an ineffable transcendent experience that can never fade from memory.

A meal of "Force"[3] and a little jam varied with macaroni and tomatoes completed my supper, and then by dint of two sleeping-bags and the adoption of a position to avoid the larger stones of the floor I stretched myself diagonally across the tiny tent in an endeavour to obtain what sleep I might pending a visit from the notorious Sukpas, or even the watchdogs of Chomolungma![4] For all I know none put in an appearance, and even the wind did not attain its usual boisterous degree, or threaten to start the some-what precarious built-up platform on which the tent was perched from a glissade down the mountain-side. I kept reasonably warm and consequently had a fair amount of sleep. I was up at 6, but the great efforts necessitated and energy absorbed at these altitudes, by the various little obligations of breakfast and putting on one's boots, etc., prevented my starting off before eight o'clock. Carrying a rucksack with provisions in case of shortage at Camp VI, I made my solitary way up the steep slope of snow and rock behind Camp V and so reached the crest of the main North Ridge. The earlier morning had been clear and not unduly cold, but now rolling banks of mist commenced to form and sweep from the westward across the great face of the mountain. But it was fortunate that the wind did not increase. There were indications though that this mist might be chiefly confined to the lower

[2]Third-highest mountain in the world.

[3]Forcemeat, a finely chopped and seasoned meat or fish.

[4]"Goddess Mother of the Mountain Snows," the Tibetan name for Everest. "Sukpa" is another native word for the Yeti (the "Abominable Snowman"). The king of the Sukpas is believed to live on the top of Everest.

half of the mountain, as on looking up one could see a certain luminosity that might mean comparatively clear conditions about its upper half. This appearance so impressed me that I had no qualms for Mallory and Irvine's progress upward from Camp VI, and I hoped by this time that they would be well on their way up the final pyramid of the summit. The wind being light, they should have made good progress and unhampered by their intended route along the crest of the north-east shoulder.

My plan was to make a rather circuitous route outwards over the northern face in order to examine the geological structure of the mountain. The lower part of it is formed of a variety of gneisses, and on these rest a mass of rocks, mainly highly altered limestones, which compose the greater part of its upper half, and here and there are to be seen in small amount light granitoid rocks which break across, or are interbedded with, all the other series. . . . The whole series dips outwards from the mountain at about 30°, and since the general slope of this face, above 25,000 feet, is about 40° to 45°, the effect is to make a series of overlapping slabs nearly parallel with the slope, and presenting a number of little faces often up to 50 feet in height, which can be climbed, usually by an easy though sometimes steepish route, while most can be entirely circumvented. The rocks are not on the whole rotten in texture since they have been considerably hardened by the igneous intrusions of granitoid rocks. But the slabs are often sprinkled to a varying degree with débris from above, and when to this is added freshly fallen snow, the labour and toil of climbing at these altitudes may perhaps be imagined. It is not so much the technical difficulty as the awkwardness of a slope of uncertain footing not quite steep enough for the use of one's hands.

At about 26,000 feet I climbed a little crag which could possibly have been circumvented, but which I decided to tackle direct, more perhaps as a test of my condition than for any other reason. There was scarcely 100 feet of it, and as I reached the top there was a sudden clearing of the atmosphere above me and I saw the whole summit ridge and final peak of Everest unveiled. I noticed far away on a snow slope leading up to what seemed to me to be the last step but one from the base of the final pyramid, a tiny object moving and approaching the rock step. A second object followed, and then the first climbed to the top of the step. As I stood intently watching this dramatic appearance, the scene became enveloped in cloud once more, and I could not actually be certain that I saw the second figure join the first. It was of course none other than Mallory and Irvine, and I was surprised above all to see them so late as this, namely 12.50, at a point which, if the "second rock step," they should have reached according to Mallory's schedule by 8 A.M. at latest, and if the "first rock step" proportionately earlier.[5] The "second rock step" is seen prominently in photographs of the North Face from the Base Camp, where it appears a short distance from the base of the final pyramid down the snowy first part of the crest of the North-east Arête. The lower "first rock step" is about an equivalent distance again to the left. Owing to the small portion of the summit ridge uncovered I could not be precisely certain at which of these two "steps" they were, as in profile and from below they are very similar, but at the time I took it for the upper "second step." However, I am a little doubtful now whether the latter would not be hidden by the projecting nearer ground from my position below on the face. I could see that they were moving expeditiously as if endeavouring to make up for lost time. True, they were moving one at a time over what was apparently but moderately difficult ground, but one cannot definitely conclude from this that they were roped together—a not unimportant consideration in any estimate of what may have eventually befallen them. I had seen that there was a considerable quantity of new snow covering some of the upper rocks near the summit ridge, and this may well have caused delay in the ascent. Burdened as they undoubtedly would be with the oxygen apparatus, these snow-covered débris-sprinkled slabs may have given much trouble. The oxygen apparatus itself may have needed repair or readjustment either before or after they left Camp VI, and so have delayed them. Though rather unlikely, it is just conceivable that the zone of mist and clouds I had experienced below may have extended up to their

---

[5]Mallory had sent down a note in which he indicated that he thought he and Irvine ought to be visible along the summit ridge by 8 A.M.

level and so have somewhat impeded their progress. Any or all of these factors may have hindered them and prevented their getting higher in the time.

I continued my way up to Camp VI, and on arrival there about two o'clock snow commenced to fall and the wind increased. I placed my load of fresh provisions, etc., inside the tiny tent and decided to take shelter for a while. Within were a rather mixed assortment of spare clothes, scraps of food, their two sleeping-bags, oxygen cylinders, and parts of apparatus; outside were more parts of the latter and of the duralumin carriers. It might be supposed that these were undoubted signs of reconstructional work and probable difficulties with the oxygen outfit. But, knowing Irvine's propensities, I had at the time not the slightest qualms on that score. Nothing would have amused him more—as it ever had, though with such good results— than to have spent the previous evening on a job of work of some kind or other in connection with the oxygen apparatus, or to have invented some problem to be solved even if it never really had turned up! He loved to dwell amongst, nay, revelled in, pieces of apparatus and a litter of tools, and was never happier than when up against some mechanical difficulty! And here to 27,000 feet he had been faithful to himself and carried his usual traits, though his workshop for the purpose would be decidedly limited, and could not have run to much more than a spanner and possibly a pair of pliers! But it was wonderful what he could do with these. I found they had left no note, which left me ignorant as to the time they had actually started out, or what might have intervened to cause delay. The snow continued, and after a while I began to wonder whether the weather and conditions higher up would have necessitated the party commencing their return. Camp VI was in rather a concealed position on a ledge and backed by a small crag, and in the prevailing conditions it seemed likely they would experience considerable difficulty in finding it. So I went out along the mountain-side in the direction of the summit and having scrambled up about 200 feet, and whistled and jodelled meanwhile in case they should happen to be within hearing, I then took shelter for a while behind a rock from the driving sleet. One could not see more than a few yards ahead so thick was the atmosphere, and in an endeavour to forget the cold I examined the rocks around me in case some new point of geological significance could be found. But in the flurry of snow and the biting wind even my accustomed ardour for this pursuit began to wane, and within an hour I decided to turn back, realizing that even if Mallory and Irvine were returning they could hardly yet be within call, and less so under the existing conditions. As I reached Camp VI the squall, which had lasted not more than two hours, blew over, and before long the whole north face became bathed in sunshine, and the freshly fallen snow speedily evaporated, there being no intermediate melting phase as takes place at lower altitudes. The upper crags became visible, but I could see no signs of the party. I waited for a time, and then I remembered that Mallory had particularly requested me in his last note to return to the North Col as he specially wished to reach there, and presumably if possible evacuate it and reach Camp III that same night, in case the monsoon should suddenly break. But besides this the single small tent at Camp VI was only just large enough for two, and if I remained and they returned, one of us would have had to sleep outside in the open—a hazardous expedient in such an exposed position. I placed Mallory's retrieved compass that I had brought up from Camp V in a conspicuous place in the corner of the tent by the door, and after partaking of a little food and leaving ample provisions against their return, I closed up the tent. Leaving Camp VI therefore about 4.30, I made my way down by the extreme crest of the North Ridge, halting now and again to glance up and scan the upper rocks for some signs of the party, who should by now, it seemed to me, be well on their downward tracks. But I looked in vain: I could, at that great distance and against such a broken background, little hope to pick them out, except by some good chance they should be crossing one of the infrequent patches of snow, as had happened that morning, or be silhouetted on the crest of the North-east Arête, if they should be making their way back by that of their ascent, as seemed most likely. . . .

Next morning [back at the North Col] we scrutinized through field-glasses the tiny tents of those camps far up above us, thinking they must be at one or other, and would not as yet have started down. But no movement at all could be seen, and at noon I decided to go up in search. Before leav-

ing, Hazard[6] and I drew up a code of signals so that we could communi-
cate to some extent in case of necessity: this was by a fixed arrangement of
sleeping-bags placed against the snow for day signals, and as far as I was concerned Hazard was to look out for them at stated times at either of the upper
camps. Answering signals from him were also arranged. For use after dark
we arranged a code of simple flash signals, which included, of course, in
case of need, the International Alpine Distress Signal. We had by this time
three porters at the North Col Camp, and two of these I managed after some
difficulty to persuade to come with me. We started off at 12.15, and on our
way up the North Ridge we encountered that bitter cross-wind from the west
that almost always prevails, and which had really been the means of ren-
dering abortive Mallory and Bruce's earlier attempt.[7] I found my two Sherpas repeatedly faltering, and it was with difficulty that one in particular could
be persuaded to proceed. We reached Camp V, however, where the night
was to be spent, in the fairly good time of three and a quarter hours. I hardly
expected, I must admit, to find that Mallory and Irvine had returned here,
for if they had, some movement must have been seen from below. And now
one's sole hopes rested on Camp VI, though in the absence of any signal
from here earlier in the day, the prospects could not but be black. And time
would not allow, even if I could have induced my men to continue in the
conditions, of our proceeding on to Camp VI that evening. We made ourselves as comfortable at V as the boisterous wind would permit, but gusts
sweeping over the North Ridge would now and again threaten to uproot
our small tents bodily from the slender security of the ledges on which they
rested, and carry them and us down the mountain-side. Fleeting glimpses
of stormy sunset could at intervals be seen through the flying scud, and as
the night closed in on us the wind and the cold increased. The porters in
their tent below mine were disinclined for much food, and were soon curled
up in their sleeping-bags, and I went down and added a stone or two to the

[6]Team member John de Vere Hazard, waiting at the North Col.

[7]Another team member, Geoffrey Bruce, and Mallory had made the first attempt on the
summit on June 1.

guys for the security of their tent. I did likewise to mine and then repaired inside, and fitted up for use next day the oxygen apparatus that had lain idle here since I brought it from the ridge two days previously: having with me another mouthpiece, it was now ready for use. I managed to cook a little macaroni and tomatoes on the Meta stove,[8] and that with tea and "Force" comprised my meal. The cold was intense that night and aggravated by the high wind, and one remained chilled and unable to sleep—even inside two sleeping-bags and with all one's clothes on.

By morning the wind was as strong and bitter as ever, and on looking in at the porters' tent I found them both heavy and disinclined to stir. I tried to rouse them, but both seemed to be suffering from extreme lassitude or nausea. After partaking of a little food myself I indicated that we must make a start, but they only made signs of being sick and wishing to descend. The cold and stormy night and lack of sleep had hardly been conducive to their well-being, and to proceed under these conditions was more than they could face. I told them, therefore, to return without delay to Camp IV, and seeing them well on their way downwards I then set off for Camp VI. This time with an artificial oxygen supply available I hoped to make good time on my upward climb. But the boisterous and bitter wind, blowing as ever from the west athwart the ridge, was trying in the extreme, and I could only make slow progress. Now and then I had to take shelter behind rocks, or crouch low in some recess to restore warmth. Within an hour or so of Camp VI, I came to the conclusion that I was deriving but little benefit from the oxygen, which I had been taking only in moderate quantities from the single cylinder that I carried. I gave myself larger quantities and longer in-spirations of it, but the effect seemed almost negligible: perhaps it just allayed a trifle the tire in one's legs. I wondered at the claims of others re-garding its advantages, and could only conclude that I was fortunate in having acclimatized myself more thoroughly to the air of these altitudes and to its small percentage of available oxygen. I switched the oxygen off and experienced none of those feelings of collapse and panting that one had

[8]A brand of stove used at high altitude; it burned a cake of solid fuel.

been led to believe ought to result. I decided to proceed with the apparatus on my back, but without the objectionable rubber mouthpiece between my lips, and depend on direct breathing from the atmosphere. I seemed to get on quite as well, though I must admit the hard breathing at these altitudes would surprise even a long-distance runner.

On reaching the tent at Camp VI, I found everything as I had left it: the tent had obviously not been touched since I was there two days previously: one pole had, however, given way in the wind, though the anchorages had prevented a complete collapse. I dumped the oxygen apparatus and immediately went off along the probable route Mallory and Irvine had taken, to make what search I could in the limited time available. This upper part of Everest must be indeed the remotest and least hospitable spot on earth, but at no time more emphatically and impressively so than when a darkened atmosphere hides its features and a gale races over its cruel face. And how and when more cruel could it ever seem than when balking one's every step to find one's friends? After struggling on for nearly a couple of hours looking in vain for some indication or clue, I realized that the chances of finding the missing ones were indeed small on such a vast expanse of crags and broken slabs, and that for any more expensive search towards the final pyramid a further party would have to be organized. At the same time I considered, and still do consider, that wherever misfortune befell them some traces of them would be discovered on or near the ridge of the North-east Arête: I saw them on that ridge on the morning of their ascent, and presumably they would descend by it. But in the time available under the prevailing conditions, I found it impossible to extend my search. Only too reluctantly I made my way back to Camp VI, and took shelter for a while from the wind, which showed signs of relenting its force. Seizing the opportunity of this lull, with a great effort I dragged the two sleeping-bags from the tent and up the precipitous rocks behind to a steep snow-patch plastered on a bluff of rocks above. It was the only one in the vicinity to utilize for the purpose of signalling down to Hazard at the North Col Camp the results of my search. It needed all my efforts to cut steps out over the steep snow slope and then fix the sleeping-bags in position, so boisterous was the wind. Placed in the form of a **T**, my signal with the sleeping-bags conveyed the news that no trace of the missing party could be found. Fortunately the signal was seen 4,000 feet below at the North Col, though Hazard's answering signal, owing to the bad light, I could not make out. I returned to the tent, and took from within Mallory's compass that I had brought up at his request two days previously. That and the oxygen set of Irvine's design alone seemed worth while to retrieve. Then, closing up the tent and leaving its other contents as my friends had left them, I glanced up at the mighty summit above me, which ever and anon deigned to reveal its cloud-wreathed features. It seemed to look down with cold indifference on me, mere puny man, and howl derision in wind-gusts at my petition to yield up its secret—this mystery of my friends. What right had we to venture thus far into the holy presence of the Supreme Goddess, or, much more, sling at her our blasphemous challenges to "sting her very nose-tip"? If it were indeed the sacred ground of Chomolungma—Goddess Mother of the Mountain Snows, had we violated it—was I now violating it? Had we approached her with due reverence and singleness of heart and purpose? And yet as I gazed again another mood appeared to creep over her haunting features. There seemed to be something alluring in that towering presence. I was almost fascinated. I realized that no mere mountaineer alone could but be fascinated, that he who approaches close must ever be led on, and oblivious of all obstacles seek to reach that most sacred and highest place of all. It seemed that my friends must have been thus enchanted also: for why else should they tarry? In an effort to suppress my feelings, I turned my gaze downwards to the North Col far below, and I remembered that other of my companions would be anxiously awaiting my return, eager to hear what tidings I carried. How then could I justify my wish, in face of such anxiety, to remain here the night, and prolong my search next day? And what hope, if I did, of finding them yet alive?

Alone and in meditation I slowly commenced my long descent. . . .

Hence I incline to the view first expressed that they met their death by being benighted. I know that Mallory had stated he would take no risks in any attempt on the final peak; but in action the desire to overcome, the craving for the victory that had become for him, as Norton has put it, an obsession, may have been too strong for him. The knowledge of his own proved powers of endurance, and those of his companion, may have urged him to make a bold bid for the summit. Irvine I know was willing, nay, determined, to expend his last ounce of energy, to "go all out," as he put it, in an utmost effort to reach the top: for had not his whole training in another hardy pursuit been to inculcate the faculty of supreme final effort?[9] And who of us that has wrestled with some Alpine giant in the teeth of a gale, or in a race with the darkness, could hold back when such a victory, such a triumph of human endeavour, was within our grasp?

The question remains, "Has Mount Everest been climbed?" It must be left unanswered, for there is no direct evidence. But bearing in mind all the circumstances that I have set out above, and considering their position when last seen, I think myself there is a strong probability that Mallory and Irvine succeeded.

[9]Irvine rowed crew at Oxford University.

COLIN FLETCHER

(b. 1922)

From *The Man Who Walked Through Time*

Sometimes a great adventure is born of an idea so inspired—and in retrospect, so obvious—that one wonders why it took so long to think of it. By the mid-1960s, the Grand Canyon was already swarmed over by some two million tourists a year (five million today). The Colorado River had first been run almost a century before, in 1869, on John Wesley Powell's epic rafting journey. Yet before Colin Fletcher set out on his marathon walk, no one had ever attempted to hike the canyon from end to end, between river and rim.

Fletcher found one man, Harvey Butchart, who had hiked the canyon in pieces, on three- to four-day trips strung out over many years. Instead of regarding Butchart as a rival, Fletcher sought him out as a mentor. The man was glad to share his knowledge. The key to Fletcher's pilgrimage was a series of caches laid beforehand, an airdrop, and the author's decision to undertake the trip alone.

With his novel approach to the Grand Canyon, Fletcher discovered

an immense solitude that no tourist could savor. All those days of
monotonous hiking, beset by worries about food and water and route,
served to open Fletcher's senses. The clarity of his narrative—watching
a lizard as he never had before turns into an epiphany about feeling
"knife-edge alive"—allows the reader to see an apparently familiar, even
hackneyed place with fresh eyes. The surprises of Fletcher's tale are one
of its chief virtues—such as the beguiling fact that the Grand Canyon
is so convoluted and huge that for days at a time, Fletcher never caught
a glimpse of the Colorado.

As I stood watching the plane contract to a speck and finally dissolve in the blue distance, I think I already knew that my journey had moved on. It was no picnic yet, let alone a pilgrimage. But I had taken the critical steps. I had crossed the amphitheaters. And by taking my airdrop at the alternate site I had proved beyond all reasonable doubt that I could meet the Canyon's physical challenge.

It was not until evening, though, just after sunset, that I really grasped what the airdrop had meant. I was stretched out on top of my sleeping bag and doing nothing but gaze up into the pale sky when, far overhead, a jet airliner glinted briefly in the rays of the already hidden sun. But the plane was flying so high that its whisper did not really damage the silence. And its remote presence did not even touch the solitude.

And all at once I realized that the airdrop had not touched my solitude either. Had not penetrated my cocoon of peace and simplicity. For there had been no feeling of personal contact. Even on the Cessna's final run I had, curiously, seen no figures in the plane's cabin. And I realized now that I had not really connected the plane and its roar with actual happenings in the outside world. I had seen it as a mere convenience. As an impersonal instrument fulfilling my personal needs. And now, looking up at the remote speck that was the airliner, I saw, in the sudden and overwhelming way you do when the obvious at last forces itself on your awareness, that the important thing was my cocoon of peace and solitude. The fact that a cocoon existed. I had, I saw, finally escaped from the paradox of simple living. The trivia were still there, and would be until the end of my journey. But I had overcome them. Had broken free at last from the din and deadline of the outside world.

I promptly held a celebration: I prefaced dinner with the week's menu-spicing delicacy, a can of smoked sliced lobster, and afterward I tempered the pemmican and dehydrated potatoes with claret. At the meal's end, for a semidelightful five minutes, I was half-canyons over.

Yet the turning point that I had sensed did not immediately materialize. I even managed to spend the next three days pressed tighter than ever to the sweaty world of effort.

All through those three days I reconnoitered, hard, in Fossil Canyon. No one, it seemed, had ever found a way down this narrow cleavage in the rock, almost two thousand feet deep. But I knew that if I succeeded I would be able to travel beside the Colorado and avoid the appallingly long and apparently waterless extension of the Esplanade that still separated me from the cache I had hidden just below the Rim near Bass Camp. (As far as I knew this terrace was quite without any natural water source; but halfway along, just below the Rim at Apache Point, I had put out my only other cache, and it included four gallons of water.)

The idea of pioneering a route down Fossil Canyon had attracted me at least as much as the practical advantages, and for three days, based on my airdrop camp, I walked and scrambled and climbed and inched my way down and along and then back and along and then across and up and along an endless succession of terraces and ledges and cliffs. Twice I followed tapering cliff-face cracks until I was out in places I should never have been. And there was one talus slope I hope some day to forget. On the third evening I came back to camp exhausted. My left hand was a throbbing pin cushion: in a sudden moment of fear, on a sloping rockledge strewn with rubble, I had grabbed blindly for a handhold and found a prickly pear. And for the third straight day I had failed to find a break in the Redwall cliff that is Fossil Canyon's major barrier.

It was as I lay in my mummy bag waiting for dinner to cook that I realized that by concentrating on the reconnaissance I had lost sight of why I had come down into the Canyon. Once the idea had occurred to me, the stupidity of the mistake became quite clear. And I decided immediately that I would rest for two days beside the large rainpocket at the head of Fossil Bay—the rainpocket that had been the proper alternate drop site—and then strike out along the terrace toward Bass Camp.

That decision was the real turning point.

I do not mean that I discovered at once the things I had come to find. But from then on I moved steadily toward them. Moved closer to rock and sky, to light and shadow, to space and silence. Began to feel their rhythms.

Of course, the change did not appear clear-cut. If you had asked me at almost any time during that week how the journey was progressing I would have answered, I think, with reports on water supply and condition of feet and quantity of food left and distance remaining to the next cache. These were still the things I measured progress by. Most of the time, anyway.

On this important and insistent level, the week was a period of steady and straightforward physical progress. I rested as planned for almost two full days beside the deep rainpocket at the head of Fossil Bay, then struck south. The terrace that led to Bass Camp was four times as long as the one I had barely managed to complete on that first Butchart test day to Sinyala Canyon,[1] and even with my halfway cache at Apache Point it looked as if it would be the toughest leg so far. But now I was ten days better tuned, and the operation went off exactly according to plan.

I left the head of Fossil Bay in the cool of evening, as I usually do when a long day lies ahead. I carried three gallons of water and camped barely two hours out. By six o'clock next evening I had crossed the precipitous head of Forster Canyon—a barrier that wild burros cannot pass, and which marks the eastern limit of the bighorn country, just as the amphitheater under Great Thumb Mesa marks its western limit. At nightfall I camped close under Apache Point, on the first map-marked trail since Supai. This Apache

---

[1]Fletcher had made test runs based on Harvey Butchart's exploratory jaunts, which set the standard Fletcher tried to match.

Trail, though betraying no hint of human use, turned out to be a busy burro turnpike (the burros are the National Park's unpaid trail maintenance crew) and I made good time along it. By noon next day I had reached and found unharmed the five-gallon can of supplies and the four gallons of bottled water that formed my cache at Apache Point. (I arrived with only 65 cc. of water left, but the situation was much less critical than it sounds: before climbing the steep thousand-foot talus slope below the cache I had lightened my load by drinking most of the quite adequate supply left in my canteens.) In the cool of that evening I carried three gallons of water back down to the terrace and camped. Next day I broke the back of the long, zigzag, burro-trail swing around Aztec Amphitheater. And by ten o'clock on the fourth morning after leaving Fossil Bay I was standing on Bass Trail with half a gallon of water left in my canteens and luxuriating in the comfortable knowledge that the Bass Camp cache lay only a thousand vertical feet above. The week's physical progress was as simple and straightforward as that.

The deeper progress of these days was even more satisfying—but neither so simple nor so straightforward. It came erratically and hesitantly, so that later I remembered the week less as a steady stream of events than as a montage of moments.

They often came, these moments, quite unexpectedly.

About ten o'clock on the morning after I had abandoned the Fossil Canyon reconnaissance I was breaking my airdrop camp in leisurely fashion for the move to the head of Fossil Bay when I noticed a small green-speckled lizard move speculatively out from a crack in the red rock. Jerkily, with many interrogatory genuflections, it investigated my toothbrush. Then it strolled across my outspread washcloth, mounted the stone that was holding it down, closed its eyes, and basked. I went quietly about my business. Quarter of an hour, and the lizard opened its eyes. A minute passed before it moved; but when it did it no longer strolled. It flicked forward; halted; inspected the world; riveted its attention on a shrub; rocketed toward it; leaped. The leap carried it a full five inches off the ground. At least, I received the impression of a five-inch jump. But all I really saw was a blur—

and then a re-landed lizard smacking its lips and looking very pleased with itself and obviously more than ready for another fly if one should be so ill-advised as to settle within jumping range.

Now, every sunlit desert morning has a magic moment. It may come at five o'clock, at seven, or at eleven, depending on the weather and the season. But it comes. If you are in the right mood at the right time you are suddenly aware that the desert's countless cogs have meshed. That the world has crystallized into vivid focus. And you respond. You hold your breath or fall into a reverie or spring to your feet, according to the day and the mood.

The leaping lizard heralded such a moment. I do not mean that anything very dramatic happened. A waspish-banded fly took a hovering look at my nylon rope, then snapped away into invisibility. A butterfly landed on one of my red socks. A hummingbird buzzed the sock and the butterfly flickered, vanished. The hummingbird cased the orange parachute, rejected it, up-tailed away to a nearby bush, and perched there with constant nervous quiverings of its violet-banded neck. That was all, I suppose. That, and a sharpening of the sunlight, a thickening of wind-borne scents, or perhaps a deeper vibration somewhere down in the silence. But I know that all at once, standing there on the red rock terrace, still watching the lizard, I was knife-edge alive.

It did not last, of course. They cannot last, these climax moments. In five minutes or ten or thirty the heat begins. Gently at first, then harshly, it clamps down on the desert, stifling the day's vitality. And you sink back from your peak of awareness. In a little while, that sunlit morning on the red rock terrace, I sank slowly and sadly back; but afterward, all through the two days I rested beside the big rainpocket at the head of Fossil Bay, I remained aware of simple things that the trivia had been smothering. I stood in silence beneath the curving harmony of three huge sandstone boulders. I wondered what lived down a tiny vertical shaft in hot red sand. I even found myself listening to birdsong, which is not, I'm afraid to say, my habit. Found myself really listening—to a piercing intermittent blast so like a referee's whistle that it kept stopping me in my tracks; and to a soft, contemplative warble that repeated, endlessly: "Years and years and years and years and years. . . ."

When I saw another bighorn sheep—clear and sharp this time, in sunlight, and quite close—I realized that I had come to understand something about the lives of these graceful and dignified creatures. I am not talking now about hard zoological facts. Nor even about such practical information as that these nimble-footed individualists are mediocre trailmakers. (Their most heavily used highway never amounted to much more than a suggestion that a couple of little bighorns might have passed that way in Indian file about the time of Custer's last stand.) I am thinking of less tangible matters.

During my reconnaissance of Fossil Canyon, cloven tracks in rain-smoothed sand pockets had shown me that bighorns travel by preference along the brinks of precipices. I had discovered too that they choose their hideouts, or at least their habitual lying-down places, far out along perilously inaccessible rockledges. Most of the heavily patrolled precipices and all the hideouts commanded magnificent, sweeping panoramas of the kind that no man can look at unmoved. After a day or two it occurred to me that the bighorns' choice might be no coincidence; and the more I thought about it, the more difficult I found it to avoid the idea that these dignified animals appreciate scenic beauty.

• • •

Sometimes now I found myself thinking, quite specifically, about the longer time spans.

From the earliest planning days I had expected that as I walked I would ponder a great deal about the rock. After all, the Canyon is above everything else a geological phenomenon. But it had not happened this way. The rock had always been there, but by and large my eye had seen only its surface. Had seen only route and obstacle, shape and shadow, or at the most, magnificent sculpture. Back on the Esplanade, even a striking example of a toadstool rock had seemed little more than an oddity, a chance photogenic freak. I had seen, in other words, only static things, not imprints of a flowing process.

For stimulation along the way I had put in my pack a small paperback book on geology, but in the first two weeks there had been no time to do more than glance at it. But now, resting beside the big rainpocket at the head of Fossil Bay, I began to read.

Perhaps the book was one reason why, as I bathed one morning in water from the rainpocket, standing in warm and soothing sunshine, I noticed that I had a shell-patterned bathroom wall. The big white boulder had broken away quite recently, I saw, from the cliffs above. Less than a million years ago, certainly. Probably no more than a few hundred thousand years ago. Perhaps it had even fallen since that yesterday in which García López de Cárdenas and his party stood awestruck on the Rim.[2] And as I stood wet and naked in the sunshine, looking down at the shells that were now fossils (they looked exactly like our modern cockleshells), I found myself understanding, vividly and effortlessly, that they had once been the homes of sentient, breathing creatures that had lived out their lives on a dark and ancient ocean floor and in the end had died there. Slowly, year after year, their empty shells had been buried by the minute specks that are always settling to the floor of any ocean (specks that are themselves often the shells of tiny creatures that have also lived and felt and died). For a moment I could visualize this drama quite clearly, even though what had once been the slowly building ocean floor was now four hundred feet of solid limestone high above my head, gleaming white in the desert sunlight. I could feel the actuality so clearly that the wetness of that ancient ocean was almost as real to me as the wetness of the water on my body. I could not comprehend in any meaningful way *when* all this had happened, for I knew that those shells in my bathroom wall had lived and died 200 million years before I came to wash beside them; and 200 million years, I had to admit, still lay beyond my grasp. But after the moment of understanding had passed, as it soon did, I knew with certainty that in its own good time the Canyon would show me the kind of geology I had hoped to find.

The evening I struck south from Fossil Bay, the look and challenge of

[2]Leader of the first party of Europeans ever to see the canyon, Cárdenas was a captain whom Coronado had sent out on a reconnaissance in 1542. The Spaniards were appalled rather than awestruck to discover the great ditch blocking their way.

the terrace that stretched out ahead, on and on, inevitably screwed my mind back to the present. Two hours out, as night fell, I camped—because it happened at that moment to become too dark to go on—beside a dead juniper tree. "Damn!" my notebook complained. "Back to press, press, press. Back to Butcharting." But by nine o'clock next morning I had covered half the straight-line distance between Fossil and Apache, and the pressure began to ease. Then, as I swung around an outcrop and for the first time that morning came to the very lip of the terrace, I stopped in my tracks.

Since leaving Supai I had glimpsed the Colorado only briefly, a short segment at a time, framed deep in the V of a sidecanyon. It had remained remote, cut off from my terrace world. But now there opened up at my feet a huge and unexpected space. On the floor of this space, three thousand feet below, flowed the river. It flowed directly toward me, uninterrupted, down the long and arrowlike corridor of a tremendous gorge.

The whole colossal scene was filled and studded and almost ignited by the witchery of desert sunlight, and the Gorge no longer looked at all a terrible place. Compared with the gloomy chasm in which I had made my reconnaissance, it seemed broad and open and inviting. Now the Colorado no longer swirled brown and sullen; its bright blue surface shone and sparkled. And although the river lay far below me I found that it no longer existed in a totally different world.

Yet because of the size and the beauty and the brilliance of this magnificently unexpected view I felt in that first moment on the lip of the terrace something of the shock that had overwhelmed me when I first stood, a year earlier, on the Rim of the Canyon. It even seemed that, once again, I was meeting the silence—the silence I thought I had grown accustomed to—as something solid, face to face. And just for a moment I felt once more the same understanding and acceptance of the vast, inevitable sweep of geologic time.

The understanding did not last, of course. I was too firmly embedded that morning in the hours and the minutes (though I stayed for almost an hour, gazing at and then photographing that stupendous corridor, which the map calls Conquistador Aisle). But when I walked on eastward again—

hurrying a little now, to make up for lost time—I remembered that moment of shock when I first saw the corridor open up in front of me. And I knew that, like the shell pattern in my bathroom wall, the moment had been a promise.

There is something of a gap, then, in my montage of moments. For the next two days, in unbroken sunshine and growing heat, it was all yard and mile, minute and hour; zig and then zag and then zig again along terrace and talus, terrace and talus, terrace and talus; a scrambling, sweaty climb to Apache Point; the long swing around Aztec Amphitheater. But the cool of each evening was an intermission.

The first of these nights I camped—again because that was where I happened to run out of daylight—beside a big juniper tree. As I went to sleep, black branches curved up and over against the stars. The next night I once more camped beside a juniper tree. This time, I camped there because it grew on the brink of a precipice that promised magnificent moonlight vistas. I lit no fire, so that nothing would block me off from the night. And before I went to sleep I sat and watched the promised vistas materialize, gloriously, and felt the hours of sweat and effort sink back and away.

The third night I stumbled on one of those strokes of luck that you seem almost able to count on when things are going well.

I had not actually run short of water; but by dusk I was conscious that I would have to drink a little sparingly until I reached my Bass Camp cache, sometime next day. Then, as the burro trail I was following skirted a smooth shelf of rock, I saw out of the corner of my eye what seemed in the failing light to be the glint of dampness. I stopped, took two paces backward. Above the dampness, half-concealed, a tiny pool of water. Nothing more. I drew a finger across the dampness. For a moment there was a causeway of dry rock. Then moisture had welled over again, slowly but without hesitation, and erased it.

I held my breath and listened. A rhythmic rippling of the silence, barely perceptible. I climbed down a few feet of layered rock below the dampness and found, sure enough, a little overhang; and when I put a cooking pot beneath it the metallic and monotonous drip, drip, drip of the single drops of water made beautiful and moving music.

I camped ten feet from the seep, beside a white-flowering bush that overhung a precipice. From my bedside the bush framed with Japanese delicacy an immense blue-black pit that was filled not so much with shapes as with suggestions of shapes—gargantuan shapes that would have been deeply disturbing if I had not known by heart now exactly what they meant.

That night, again, I lit no fire. And as I sat waiting for dinner to cook—cut off from the silence, inside the roaring world of my little stove—I watched the evening sky grow dark. Slowly the darkness deepened. But the blue-black pit below me remained blue-black. Began, even, to ease back from the brink of blackness. For as the last daylight sank away, the moon took over, casting shadows at new angles, constructing new shapes, warding off the blackness with a new and cool and exquisitely delicate blue.

When I took dinner off the stove I found myself looking at the fire ring, shining red-hot out of the darkness. Found myself, unexpectedly, appreciating that it too was a thing of beauty and value. And when I turned off the stove I heard all around me, as always happens, the sudden and surprising silence.

While I ate dinner, with the silent blue-black pit opening up below me, I found myself savoring the sense of newness and expectancy that now came with every step of my journey—the always-moving-forward that now filled each day of my life. Soon, I began to contemplate the clock that measured this daily progress; and all at once I was feeling, as if I had never understood it before, the swing and circle of the sun. Sunrise and sunset; sunrise and sunset; sunrise again; and then sunset. It happened everywhere, of course, all over the earth. But now I could detect in the beat of that rhythm an element I had never felt before. Now I could feel the inevitability of it. An inevitability that was impersonal and terrifying and yet, in the end, comforting. And as I sat looking out over the huge and mysterious blue-black space it occurred to me that the pioneers who crossed the American prairies in their covered wagons must have felt, many days out from sight of mountains, the power of this ceaseless rhythm. For them the understanding would have been generated by the monotony of the plains. For me it had something to do with the colossal sameness of the Canyon; but that was a sameness not of monotony but of endlessly repeated yet endlessly varied pattern. A prodigal repetition of terrace mounting on terrace mounting on terrace, of canyon after canyon after canyon after canyon. All of them, one succeeding the other, almost unknown to man, just existing, existing, existing, existing. There seemed at first no hope of a beginning, no hint of an end. But I knew now, more certainly and more easily, that the regularity and the existence were not really timeless. I knew they were echoing reminders of a time, not so very long ago, before the coming of the noisy animal, when the earth was a quiet place.

When I had finished my dinner I lay still and listened to the silence. To the silence and to the music of the water splashing metronomically down into my cooking pot. Before I fell asleep—warm and comfortable inside my mummy bag, passively at ease now inside the silence and the darkness—I knew that at last I stood on the threshold of the huge natural museum that is Grand Canyon.

You cannot, of course, enter such a museum without preparation. It is not a mere place of knowledge. It is not really a place at all, only a state of understanding. As I lay in the darkness, staring up at the stars and hearing how the silence was magnified by the drip, drip, drip of water, I knew that after all my days of effort and silence and solitude I was almost ready at last to move inside the museum.

• • •

RICHARD BANGS

(b. 1950)

"First Bend on the Baro"

*Adventurers are often eloquent when narrating their close calls and dar-
ing deeds, but in another area they tend to be all but tongue-tied. Every
jaunt into the wilderness carries with it the baggage of interpersonal responsibility, yet few explorers have tried to examine that realm.*

*Richard Bangs would go on from his youthful first descents of
Ethiopian rivers to become one of the most accomplished river rafters
in the world. As recently as 1996, twenty-three years after the tragedy
he chronicles in this essay, Bangs returned to Ethiopia to make the first
descent of the Tekeze, the last major tributary of the Nile to be run. Yet
for all his veteran expertise, the loss of Angus MacLeod on the Baro has
haunted Bangs's life.*

*In this 1984 piece, Bangs asks himself some hard questions. As a
twenty-three-year-old, had he known what he was doing on the Baro?
Had he, with his blithe enthusiasm, encouraged a novice to get in over
his head, with fatal results? The search for Angus MacLeod's body, for*

an understanding of his fate, becomes, thanks to Bangs's honesty, a search for a rationale for adventure itself.

Above, the jungle was a brawl of flora and vines and roots. Colobus monkeys sailed between treetops, issuing washboard cries.

Below, three specially designed inflatable white-water rafts bobbed in a back eddy, looking, from the ridge, like restless water bugs. There were 11 of us, all white-water veterans, save Angus. He was in the raft with me, John Yost, and Karen Greenwald. As the leader and the most experienced river-runner, I was at the oars.

Our raft would go first. At the correct moment we cast off—Angus coiled the painter and gripped for the ride. I adjusted the oars and pulled a deep stroke. For a prolonged instant the boat hung in a current between the eddy and the fast water. Then it snapped into motion with a list that knocked me off my seat.

"This water's faster than I thought," I yelled. Regaining the seat, I straightened the raft, its bow downstream. The banks were a blur of green; water shot into the boat from all sides.

Just minutes after the start of the ride, we approached the rapid. Though we'd been unable to scout it earlier, I had a hunch that it would be best to enter the rapid on its right side. But the river had different notions. Despite frantic pulls on the oars, we were falling over the lip on the far left.

"Oh my God!" someone screamed. The boat was almost vertical, falling free. This wasn't a rapid—this was a waterfall. I dropped the oars and braced against the frame. The raft crashed into a spout, folded in half, and spun. Then, as though reprieved, we straightened and flumped onward. I almost gasped with relief when a lateral wave pealed into an explosion on my left, picking up the raft, slamming it against the nearby cliff wall like a toy, then dumping it and us upside down into the millrace.

I tumbled, like falling down an underwater staircase. Seconds later, I surfaced in the quick water below the rapid, a few feet from the overturned raft. My glasses were gone, but through the billows I could make out another rapid 200 yards downstream, closing in fast. I clutched at a rope and tried to tow the raft toward shore. Behind I heard Karen: "Angus. Go help Angus. He's caught in a rope!"

He was trailing ten feet behind the raft, a piece of the bowline tight across his shoulder, tangled and being pulled through the turbulence. Like the rest of us, he was wearing a sheathed knife on his belt for this very moment— to cut loose from entangling ropes. His arms looked free, yet he didn't reach for his knife. He was paralyzed with fear.

With my left hand I seized the rope at his sternum, and with my right I groped for my own Buck knife. In the roiling water it was a task to slip the blade between Angus's chest and the taut rope. Then, with a jerk, he was free.

"Swim to shore," I yelled.

"Swim to shore, Angus," Karen cried from the edge of the river.

He seemed to respond. He turned and took a stroke toward Karen. I swam back to the runaway raft with the hope of once again trying to pull it in. It was futile: The instant I hooked my hand to the raft it fell into the pit of the next rapid, with me in tow.

I was buffeted and beaten by the underwater currents, then spat to the surface. For the first time, I was really scared. I saw another rapid speeding toward me. Abandoning the raft, I stretched my arms to swim to shore, but my strength was sapped. This time I was shot into an abyss. I was in a whirlpool, and looking up I could see the surface light fade as I was sucked deeper. At first I struggled, but it had no effect, except to further drain my small reserves. My throat began to burn. I went limp and resigned myself to fate. In the last hazy seconds I felt a blow from beneath, and my body was propelled upward. I was swept into a spouting current, and at the last possible instant I broke the surface and gasped. I tried to lift my arms; they felt like barbells. My vision was fuzzy, but I could make out another rapid approaching, and I knew I could never survive it. But neither could I swim a stroke.

Then, somehow, a current pitched me by the right bank. Suddenly branches and leaves were swatting my face as I was borne around a bend.

I reached up, caught a thin branch, and held tight. I crawled to a rock slab and sprawled out. My gut seized, and I retched. A wave of darkness washed through my head, and I passed out.

When my eyes finally focused, I saw figures foraging through the gluey vegetation on the opposite bank. John Yost was one—he was a close friend since high school. Lew Greenwald, another. He had been in the third boat, and seeing him reminded me that there were two boats and seven people behind me. How had they fared?

John paced the bank until he found the calmest stretch of river, then dived in; the water was so swift that he reached my shore 50 yards below his mark. He brought the news: The second raft, piloted by Robbie Paul, had somehow made it through the falls upright. In fact, Robbie was thrown from his seat into the bilge during the first seconds of the plunge, and the raft had continued through captainless. The third boat, handled by Bart Henderson, had flipped. Bart was almost swept under a fallen log, but was snatched from the water by the crew of Robbie's boat.

All were accounted for—except Angus MacLeod.

THE DATE WAS Friday, October 5, 1973. I was 23 years old. The place was Illubabor Province, Ethiopia, and our goal had been to make the first raft descent of the Baro River, a major tributary of the White Nile. We had come here, all of us, at my design: I had graduated from the Colorado River and spent four summers guiding rafts and tourists through the rapids there, all the while dreaming of far-off waters. Inspired by accounts of the British army making a raft descent of Ethiopia's Blue Nile in 1968, I'd set my sights on Africa. But where the British had failed—one of their party, Ian MacLeod, drowned while attempting to cross a swollen tributary—I felt certain I could succeed. It had struck me before that Angus had the same surname as the British fatality, and I even mentioned it to Angus, but neither of us was superstitious.

In February of that year—1973—with a small team of conspirators, I had made the first descent of Ethiopia's Awash River. A month later we repeated our success on the classic Omo, a river famous to the world because of Louis Leakey's fossil discoveries on its lower reaches. Both expeditions pitted us against a litany of obstacles, from hippos and poisonous snakes to crocodiles and deadly microorganisms in the water. It was the crocodiles we feared most, so we named our venture SOBEK Expeditions, after the ancient Egyptian crocodile god of the Nile. I had returned to the Colorado with tales of exotic river-running, and now, along with three Africa veterans, seven newcomers had followed me back to tackle another river—the Baro.

As a fervid river-runner, I felt I understood the reasons for everyone's involvement in the expedition, except Angus's. He was the odd man out. I met him in New Jersey a few weeks before our departure. We were introduced by a neighbor of his, whom I'll call Tom. Tom liked to tell people that he was a "professional adventurer." He'd had a brochure printed up describing himself as "Writer, Scientist, Adventurer, Ecologist." Something about him seemed less than genuine, but he had hinted that he might invest in our Baro expedition, and we desperately needed money. I agreed to hear him out. He flew me from Arizona, where I'd been guiding, to New Jersey. I was impressed—no one had ever offered to pay air fare to hear my plans, and Tom's family certainly had money. In exchange for what seemed like a sizable contribution to our cause, Tom had two requests: that he be allowed to join the expedition, and that I consider letting his friend, Angus MacLeod, come along as well.

I was leery of bringing along anyone outside my tightknit, experienced coterie on an exploratory, but the lure of capital was too strong. Tom, however, would never make it out onto the Baro. He traveled with us to the put-in, took one look at the angry, heaving river, and caught the next bus back to Addis Ababa. He may have been the smartest of the lot.

Angus was altogether different. While Tom smacked of pretension and flamboyance, Angus was taciturn and modest. He confessed immediately to having never run a rapid, yet he exuded an almost irresistible eagerness and carried himself with the fluid bounce of a natural athlete. He was ruggedly handsome and had played professional soccer. After spending a short time with him I could see his quiet intensity, and I believed that—despite his lack of experience—he could handle the trip.

Once in Ethiopia, Angus worked in the preparations for the expedition with a lightheartedness that masked his determination. On the eve of our trip to Illubabor Province—a 17-hour bus ride on slippery, corrugated mountain roads—I told Angus to make sure he was at the bus station at 7 A.M. for the 11 A.M. departure. That way we would all be sure of getting seats in the front of the bus, where the ride wasn't as bumpy or unbearably stuffy. But, come the next morning, Angus didn't show until 10:45. He got the last seat on the bus and endured.

LATER, AFTER THE accident, standing on the bank of the river with John Yost, I wondered if I'd made the right decision about Angus. We searched the side of the river where I'd washed ashore; across the rumble of the rapids we could hear the others searching. "Angus! Are you all right? Where are you?" There was no answer. Just downriver from where I'd last seen him, John found an eight-foot length of rope—the piece I'd cut away from Angus's shoulders.

After an hour John and I gave up and swam back across the river. We gathered the group at the one remaining raft, just below the falls.

"He could be downstream, lying with a broken leg," someone said.

"He could be hanging onto a log in the river."

"He could be wandering in a daze through the jungle."

Nobody suggested that he could be dead, though we all knew it was a possibility. All of us had a very basic, and very difficult, decision to make, the kind of decision you never want to have to make on an expedition: Should we stay and look for Angus, or should we get out while there was still light? Robbie, Bart, and George and Diane Fuller didn't hesitate—they wanted out. Karen Greenwald wanted to continue searching, but she was hysterical and the weakest member of the group. Against her protests, we sent her out with the others.

That left five of us—Lew Greenwald, Gary Mercado, Jim Slade, John Yost, and me. We decided to continue rafting downstream in search of Angus on the one remaining raft. I had mixed feelings about it—suddenly I was scared to death of the river; it had almost killed me. Yet I felt obligated to look for a man missing from a boat I had capsized, on an expedition I had organized. And there was more: I felt I had to show something to the others—that I wasn't scared of the river.

But the river wasn't through with us. When we were ready to go, I climbed into the seat of the raft and yelled for Jim to push off. Immediately we were cascading down the course I'd swum earlier. In the rapid that had nearly drowned me, the raft jolted and reeled, kicking Gary and me into the brawling water.

"Shit—not again," was my only thought as I spilled out of the raft into another whirlpool. But this time I had the bowline in hand, and I managed to pull myself quickly to the surface. I emerged beside the raft, and someone grabbed the back of my life jacket and pulled me in. My right forearm was lacerated and bleeding. Jim jumped to the oars and rowed us to shore.

My injury wasn't bad—a shallow cut. But Gary had dislocated his shoulder; he'd flipped backward over the gunwale while still holding onto the raft. He was in a lot of pain, and it was clear he couldn't go on. Lew—thankful for the opportunity—volunteered to hike him out.

John, Jim, and I relaunched and cautiously rowed down a calmer stretch of the river, periodically calling out for Angus. We were just three degrees north of the equator, where the sun sets promptly at 6 P.M. year-round. It was twilight when we approached another large rapid, so we decided to stop and make camp. It was a bad, uncomfortable night. Between us, we had a two-man A-frame tent, one sleeping bag, and a lunch bag of food. Everything else had been washed into the Baro.

The rude bark of a baboon shook us awake the next morning. The inside of the tent was dripping from condensation, and we were soaked. I crawled outside and looked to the eastern sky, which was beginning to blush. My body ached from the previous day's ordeal. I wanted to be back in Bethesda, at my folks' home, warm, dry, and eating a fine breakfast. Instead, we huddled around a wisp of fire, sipping weak tea and chewing wet bread.

The next morning we eased downriver, stopping every few minutes to scout, hugging the banks, avoiding rapids we wouldn't have hesitated to run were they back in the States. At intervals we called into the rain forest for Angus, but now we didn't expect an answer.

Late in the afternoon we came to another intimidating rapid, one that galloped around a bend and sunk from sight. We took out the one duffel bag containing the tent and sleeping bag and began lining, using ropes to lower the boat along the edge of the rapid. Fifty yards into the rapid, the raft broached perpendicular to the current, and water swarmed in. Slade and I, on the stern line, pulled hard, the rope searing our palms, but the boat ignored us. With the snap of its D-ring (the bowline attachment), it dismissed us to a crumple on the bank and sailed around the corner and out of sight.

There was no way to continue the search. The terrain was too rough, and we were out of food, the last scraps having been lost with the raft. We struck up into the jungle, thrashing through wet, waist-high foliage at a slug's pace. My wound was becoming infected. Finally, at sunset, we cleared a near-level spot, set up the tent, squeezed in, and collapsed. Twice I awoke to the sounds of trucks grumbling past, but dismissed it as jungle fever, or Jim's snoring.

In the morning, however, we soon stumbled onto a road. There we sat, as mist coiled up the tree trunks, waiting. In the distance we could hear the thunder roll of a rapid, but inexplicably the sound became louder and louder. Then we saw what it was: 200 machete-wielding natives marched into sight over the hill. General Goitom, the police commissioner of nearby Motu, hearing of the accident, had organized a search for Angus. Their effort consisted of tramping up and down the highway—the locals, it turned out, were more fearful of the jungle canyon than we were.

I remember very little of the next week. We discovered that Angus had held a United Kingdom passport, and I spent a fair amount of time at the

British embassy in Addis Ababa filling out reports, accounting for personal effects, and communicating with his relatives. John and Jim stayed in Motu with General Goitom and led a series of searches back into the jungle along the river. We posted a $100 reward—more than double what the villagers earned in a year—for information on Angus's whereabouts. With financial assistance from Angus's parents, I secured a Canadian helicopter a few days after the accident and took several passes over the river. Even with the pilot skimming the treetops, it was difficult to see into the river corridor. The canopy seemed like a moldy, moth-eaten army tarpaulin. On one flight, however, I glimpsed a smudge of orange just beneath the surface of the river. We made several passes, but it was impossible to make out what it was. Perhaps, I thought, it was Angus, snagged underwater. We picked as many landmarks as possible, flew in a direct line to the road, landed, cut a marker on a dohm palm tree, and headed to Motu.

A day later John, Jim, and I cut a path back into the tangle and found the smudge—a collection of leaves trapped by a submerged branch. We abandoned the search.

THREE MONTHS LATER I was wandering through the recesses of the spice market in Addis Ababa when a vendor I knew approached me. "Mr. Richard. Did you hear about Mr. Angus? They say he is alive. He was found by villagers on the river, and he is living with them now. It is the talk everywhere. I do not know from where the story comes."

I went to the British and U.S. embassies. People there, too, had heard the rumor. One consul said he'd heard a fanciful embellishment to the story—that Angus was living fine and well as king of a tribe of Amazon-like women. As the story went, Angus had been visited by outside villagers and invited to leave with them, but he declined. He was in Paradise.

Hearing the rumors was hard. I wanted to squelch the sensational gossip, to finish business left undone, to determine beyond all doubt what really happened to Angus. And to cleanse my conscience. So in January of 1974, I made another trip to the upper reaches of the Baro. This time the river was ten vertical feet lower than on our last trip: It was dry season in a drought year. What was before a swollen rampage was now a slow, thin trickle. There were four of us in a single raft: Lew Greenwald, Gary Mercado, Professor Conrad Hirsh of Haile Selassie University, and me.

Again, we reached the first rapid within minutes. This time, though, it was a jumble of bus-size basalt boulders, the bedrock that fashioned the falls during times of flooding. It was unnavigable, so we stood in chest-deep water and wrenched the inflatable boat over and down the rocks, turning it on its side to push it through the tighter passages. A similar configuration constituted the next rapid, and the next, and the next. The routine was quickly established. It was a constant battle against rocks, water, heat, fatigue, and insects. We had naively hoped to run the raft some 150 miles to Gambella, near the Sudanese border, where the river flows wide and flat. We had rations for a week. With all the portaging, we were making less than five miles a day.

Scattered along our course, sometimes in branches high above us where the water once swirled, we found vestiges of the first expedition: five oars, Jim Slade's sleeping bag, a torn poncho, a pack of insect-collecting equipment donated by the Smithsonian, crushed pots and pans, and a ripped sweater that had belonged to Angus, one he had packed in his duffel. But no sign of Angus.

After six days we had made only 30 miles; our bodies were pocked with insect bites, and we had exhausted our food and strength. A trail up the steep slope put an end to our ordeal. We repaired to Addis Ababa with no new answers.

I RETURNED TO the States and graduate school, running few rivers myself but continuing to manage the business of SOBEK (which was growing despite the accident) from my apartment. The following January, Lew Greenwald, my original partner in the business, was drowned on an exploratory run of the Blue Nile in northern Ethiopia. The news shattered me: I burrowed deeper into academia, denounced river-running as selfish and insane, and put SOBEK aside.

Time softened my edges. By summer I had reenlisted and was once again organizing trips to Ethiopia—though I had no intention of ever going back myself. But the mystery of Angus gnawed. Sometimes in the middle of a mundane chore—taking out the trash, doing the laundry—I'd stop and see Angus's frozen features as I cut him loose. In weak moments I would wonder if there just might be a chance that he was still alive. And I'd be pressed with a feeling of guilt, that I hadn't done enough, that I had unhonorably waded in waist deep, then turned back. I wondered how Angus had felt in those last few minutes—about himself, about me.

In November of that year, 1975, I got a call from a friend, a tour operator. A trip he'd organized to the Sahara had been canceled by the Algerian government, and his clients wanted an alternative. Would I be interested in taking them to Ethiopia? Two weeks later I arrived in Addis Ababa, where I met up with John Yost, Jim Slade, and a trainee-guide, Gary Bolton, fresh from a SOBEK raft tour of the Omo River. They were surprised to see me, here where nobody expected I would return.

By late December, after the commercial tour, John, Jim, and I had decided to try the Baro once again. The river pummeled us, as it had before, randomly tossing portages and major rapids in our path. But during the next few days, the trip gradually, almost imperceptively, became easier. On Christmas morning I decorated a bush with my socks and passed out presents of party favors and sweets. Under an ebony sapling I placed a package of confections for Angus. It was a curiously satisfying holiday, being surrounded by primeval beauty and accompanied by three other men with a common quest. No one expected to find Angus alive, but I thought that the journey—at least for me—might expunge all doubt, exorcise guilt. I wanted to think that I had done all that was humanly possible to explore a death I was partly responsible for. And somehow I wanted him to know this.

As we tumbled off the Abyssinian plateau into the Great Rift Valley of Africa, taking on tributaries every few miles, the river and its rapids grew.

At times we even allowed ourselves to enjoy the experience, to shriek with delight, to throw our heads back in laughter as we bounced through Colorado-style white water and soaked in the scenery. Again, we found remnants of that first trip—a broken oar here, a smashed pan there. Never, though, a hint of Angus.

On New Year's Eve we camped at the confluence of the Baro and the Bir Bir rivers, pulling in at dusk. A lorry track crossed the Baro opposite our camp. It was there that Conrad Hirsh, the professor from the second Baro attempt, had said he would try to meet us with supplies. We couldn't see him, but Jim thought there might be a message waiting for us across the river. "I think I'll go check it out," he said.

"Don't be a fool," John warned. "We're in croc country now. You don't want to swim across this river."

An hour later, just after dark, Jim had not returned. We shouted his name, first individually, then as a chorus. No answer. Jim had become a close friend in the two years since we had shared a tent on the upper Baro; he had been a partner in ordeal and elation, in failure and success. Now John and I swept our weak flashlight beams along the dark river. We gave up. We were tired, and we sat around the low licks of our campfire, ready to accept another loss, mapping out the ramifications in our minds. Suddenly Jim walked in from the shadows and thrust a note at us.

"Conrad arrived three days ago, waited two, and left this morning," he said, his body still dripping from the swim.

"You fool! I knew you couldn't disappear now—you owe me $3.30 in backgammon debts." I said it with all the disciplinary tone I could muster.

The following day we spun from the vortex of the last rapid into the wide, Mississippi-like reaches of the Baro. Where rocks and whirlpools were once the enemy, now there were crocodiles and hippos. We hurled rocks, made threatening gestures, and yelled banshee shrieks to keep them away. Late in the day on January 3, 1976, we glided into the outpost town of Gambella. The villagers there had neither seen nor heard of Angus MacLeod.

• • •

I NEVER TOLD Angus's relatives of our last search; we didn't find what might have given them solace. What I found I kept to myself, hidden like buried treasure in my soul. It lies there still, dusty, but ready to be raised if needed. It is the knowledge of the precious and innate value of endeavor. Both Angus and I tried, and in different ways we both failed.

I hardly knew Angus MacLeod, not as friends and family know one another. But in the years of searching, wondering, I've gotten to know him in other ways. There are things we tell ourselves. I want to believe that when Angus boarded my tiny boat and committed himself, he was sparked with life and light, that his blood raced with the passion of existence—perhaps more than ever before.

On that first Friday in October, almost 11 years ago, ten of us thought we knew what we were doing: another expedition, another raft trip, another river. Only Angus was exploring beyond his being. Maybe his was a senseless death, moments after launching, in the very first rapid. I will never forget that look of horror in his eyes as he struggled there in the water. But there are other ways to think about it. He took the dare and contacted the outermost boundaries. He lost, but so do we all, eventually. The difference—and it is an enormous one—is that he reached for it, wholly.

Finally, though it took years, I believe I did the same.

JON KRAKAUER

(b. 1954)

"The Devils Thumb"

From *Eiger Dreams*

An obvious choice for this anthology would have been an excerpt from Jon Krakauer's already classic account of the 1996 Everest disaster, Into Thin Air. *Equally fine, however, and less well known is Krakauer's earlier essay, "The Devils Thumb," which first appeared (in a shorter version) in* Climbing *magazine in 1990.*

"The Devils Thumb" recounts an extremely nervy solo attempt by a new route on one of North America's most daunting mountains. What gives the piece its special resonance, however, is how it accomplishes that rare thing in adventure writing: youthful passion and folly recollected and sifted through in maturity.

B y the time I reached the interstate I was having trouble keeping my eyes open. I'd been okay on the twisting two-lane blacktop between Fort Collins and Laramie, but when the Pontiac eased onto the smooth, unswerving pavement of I-80, the soporific hiss of the tires began to gnaw at my wakefulness like ants in a dead tree.

That afternoon, after nine hours of humping 2×10s and pounding recalcitrant nails, I'd told my boss I was quitting: "No, not in a couple of weeks, Steve; right now was more like what I had in mind." It took me three more hours to clear my tools and other belongings out of the rust-stained construction trailer that had served as my home in Boulder. I loaded everything into the car, drove up Pearl Street to Tom's Tavern, and downed a ceremonial beer. Then I was gone.

At 1 A.M., thirty miles east of Rawlins, the strain of the day caught up to me. The euphoria that had flowed so freely in the wake of my quick escape gave way to overpowering fatigue; suddenly I felt tired to the bone. The highway stretched straight and empty to the horizon and beyond. Outside the car the night air was cold, and the stark Wyoming plains glowed in the moonlight like Rousseau's painting of the sleeping gypsy. I wanted very badly just then to be that gypsy, conked out on my back beneath the stars. I shut my eyes—just for a second, but it was a second of bliss. It seemed to revive me, if only briefly. The Pontiac, a sturdy behemoth from the Eisenhower years, floated down the road on its long-gone shocks like a raft on an ocean swell. The lights of an oil rig twinkled reassuringly in the distance. I closed my eyes a second time, and kept them closed a few moments longer. The sensation was sweeter than sex.

A few minutes later I let my eyelids fall again. I'm not sure how long I nodded off this time—it might have been for five seconds, it might have been for thirty—but when I awoke it was to the rude sensation of the Pontiac bucking violently along the dirt shoulder at seventy miles per hour. By all rights, the car should have sailed off into the rabbitbrush and rolled. The rear wheels fishtailed wildly six or seven times, but I eventually managed to guide the unruly machine back onto the pavement without so much as blowing a tire, and let it coast gradually to a stop. I loosened my death grip on the wheel, took several deep breaths to quiet the pounding in my chest, then slipped the shifter back into drive and continued down the highway.

Pulling over to sleep would have been the sensible thing to do, but I was on my way to Alaska to change my life, and patience was a concept well beyond my twenty-three-year-old ken.

Sixteen months earlier I'd graduated from college with little distinction and even less in the way of marketable skills. In the interim an off-again, on-again four-year relationship—the first serious romance of my life—had come to a messy, long-overdue end; nearly a year later, my love life was still zip. To support myself I worked on a house-framing crew, grunting under crippling loads of plywood, counting the minutes until the next coffee break, scratching in vain at the sawdust stuck *in perpetuum* to the sweat on the back of my neck. Somehow, blighting the Colorado landscape with condominiums and tract houses for three-fifty an hour wasn't the sort of career I'd dreamed of as a boy.

Late one evening I was mulling all this over on a barstool at Tom's, picking unhappily at my existential scabs, when an idea came to me, a scheme for righting what was wrong in my life. It was wonderfully uncomplicated, and the more I thought about it, the better the plan sounded. By the bottom of the pitcher its merits seemed unassailable. The plan consisted, in its entirety, of climbing a mountain in Alaska called the Devils Thumb.

The Devils Thumb is a prong of exfoliated diorite that presents an imposing profile from any point of the compass, but especially so from the north: its great north wall, which had never been climbed, rises sheer and clean for six thousand vertical feet from the glacier at its base. Twice the height of Yosemite's El Capitan, the north face of the Thumb is one of the biggest granitic walls on the continent; it may well be one of the biggest in the world. I would go to Alaska, ski across the Stikine Icecap to the Devils Thumb, and make the first ascent of its notorious nordwand. It seemed, midway through the second pitcher, like a particularly good idea to do all of this solo.

Writing these words more than a dozen years later, it's no longer entirely clear just *how* I thought soloing the Devils Thumb would transform my life. It had something to do with the fact that climbing was the first and only thing I'd ever been good at. My reasoning, such as it was, was fueled by the scattershot passions of youth, and a literary diet overly rich in the works of Nietzsche, Kerouac, and John Menlove Edwards—the latter a deeply troubled writer/psychiatrist who, before putting an end to his life with a cyanide capsule in 1958, had been one of the preeminent British rock climbers of the day.

Dr. Edwards regarded climbing as a "psycho-neurotic tendency" rather than sport; he climbed not for fun but to find refuge from the inner torment that characterized his existence. I remember, that spring of 1977, being especially taken by a passage from an Edwards short story titled "Letter From a Man":

> So, as you would imagine, I grew up exuberant in body but with a nervy, craving mind. It was wanting something more, something tangible. It sought for reality intensely, always if it were not there . . .
> But you see at once what I do. I climb.

To one enamored of this sort of prose, the Thumb beckoned like a beacon. My belief in the plan became unshakeable. I was dimly aware that I might be getting in over my head, but if I could somehow get to the top of the Devils Thumb, I was convinced, everything that followed would turn out all right. And thus did I push the accelerator a little closer to the floor and, buoyed by the jolt of adrenaline that followed the Pontiac's brush with destruction, speed west into the night.

YOU CAN'T ACTUALLY get very close to the Devils Thumb by car. The peak stands in the Boundary Ranges on the Alaska–British Columbia border, not far from the fishing village of Petersburg, a place accessible only by boat or plane. There is regular jet service to Petersburg, but the sum of my liquid assets amounted to the Pontiac and two hundred dollars in cash, not even enough for one-way airfare, so I took the car as far as Gig Harbor, Washington, then hitched a ride on a northbound seine boat that was short on crew. Five days out, when the *Ocean Queen* pulled into Petersburg to take on fuel and water, I jumped ship, shouldered my backpack, and walked down the dock in a steady Alaskan rain.

Back in Boulder, without exception, every person with whom I'd shared my plans about the Thumb had been blunt and to the point: I'd been smoking too much pot, they said; it was a monumentally bad idea. I was grossly overestimating my abilities as a climber, I'd never be able to hack a month completely by myself, I would fall into a crevasse and die.

The residents of Petersburg reacted differently. Being Alaskans, they were accustomed to people with screwball ideas; a sizeable percentage of the state's population, after all, was sitting on half-baked schemes to mine uranium in the Brooks Range, or sell icebergs to the Japanese, or market mail-order moose droppings. Most of the Alaskans I met, if they reacted at all, simply asked how much money there was in climbing a mountain like the Devils Thumb.

In any case, one of the appealing things about climbing the Thumb — and one of the appealing things about the sport of mountain climbing in general — was that it didn't matter a rat's ass what anyone else thought. Getting the scheme off the ground didn't hinge on winning the approval of some personnel director, admissions committee, licensing board, or panel of stern-faced judges; if I felt like taking a shot at some unclimbed alpine wall, all I had to do was get myself to the foot of the mountain and start swinging my ice axes.

Petersburg sits on an island, the Devils Thumb rises from the mainland. To get myself to the foot of the Thumb it was first necessary to cross twenty-five miles of salt water. For most of a day I walked the docks, trying without success to hire a boat to ferry me across Frederick Sound. Then I bumped into Bart and Benjamin.

Bart and Benjamin were ponytailed constituents of a Woodstock Nation tree-planting collective called the Hodads. We struck up a conversation. I mentioned that I, too, had once worked as a tree planter. The Hodads allowed that they had chartered a floatplane to fly them to their camp on the mainland the next morning. "It's your lucky day, kid," Bart told me. "For twenty bucks you can ride over with us. Get you to your fuckin' mountain in style." On May 3, a day and a half after arriving in Petersburg, I stepped off the Hodads' Cessna, waded onto the tidal flats at the head of Thomas Bay, and began the long trudge inland.

THE DEVILS THUMB pokes up out of the Stikine Icecap, an immense, labyrinthine network of glaciers that hugs the crest of the Alaskan panhandle like an octopus, with myriad tentacles that snake down, down to the sea from the craggy uplands along the Canadian frontier. In putting ashore at Thomas Bay I was gambling that one of these frozen arms, the Baird Glacier, would lead me safely to the bottom of the Thumb, thirty miles distant.

An hour of gravel beach led to the tortured blue tongue of the Baird. A logger in Petersburg had suggested I keep an eye out for grizzlies along this stretch of shore. "Them bears over there is just waking up this time of year," he smiled. "Tend to be kinda cantankerous after not eatin' all winter. But you keep your gun handy, you shouldn't have no problem." Problem was, I didn't have a gun. As it turned out, my only encounter with hostile wildlife involved a flock of gulls who dive-bombed my head with Hitchcockian fury. Between the avian assault and my ursine anxiety, it was with no small amount of relief that I turned my back to the beach, donned crampons, and scrambled up onto the glacier's broad, lifeless snout.

After three or four miles I came to the snow line, where I exchanged crampons for skis. Putting the boards on my feet cut fifteen pounds from the awful load on my back and made the going much faster besides. But now that the ice was covered with snow, many of the glacier's crevasses were hidden, making solitary travel extremely dangerous.

In Seattle, anticipating this hazard, I'd stopped at a hardware store and purchased a pair of stout aluminum curtain rods, each ten feet long. Upon reaching the snowline, I lashed the rods together at right angles, then strapped the arrangement to the hip belt on my backpack so the poles extended horizontally over the snow. Staggering slowly up the glacier with my overloaded backpack, bearing the queer tin cross, I felt like some kind of strange *Penitente*. Were I to break through the veneer of snow over a hidden crevasse, though, the curtain rods would—I hoped mightily—span the slot and keep me from dropping into the chilly bowels of the Baird.

The first climbers to venture onto the Stikine Icecap were Bestor Robinson and Fritz Wiessner, the legendary German-American alpinist, who spent a stormy month in the Boundary Ranges in 1937 but failed to reach any major summits. Wiessner returned in 1946 with Donald Brown and Fred Beckey to attempt the Devils Thumb, the nastiest looking peak in the Stikine. On that trip Fritz mangled a knee during a fall on the hike in and limped home in disgust, but Beckey went back that same summer with Bob Craig and Cliff Schmidtke. On August 25, after several aborted tries and some exceedingly hairy climbing on the peak's east ridge, Beckey and company sat on the Thumb's wafer-thin summit tower in a tired, giddy daze. It was far and away the most technical ascent ever done in Alaska, an important milestone in the history of American mountaineering.

In the ensuing decades three other teams also made it to the top of the Thumb, but all steered clear of the big north face. Reading accounts of these expeditions, I had wondered why none of them had approached the peak by what appeared, from the map at least, to be the easiest and most logical route, the Baird. I wondered a little less after coming across an article by Beckey in which the distinguished mountaineer cautioned, "Long, steep icefalls block the route from the Baird Glacier to the icecap near Devils Thumb," but after studying aerial photographs I decided that Beckey was mistaken, that the icefalls weren't so big or so bad. The Baird, I was certain, really was the best way to reach the mountain.

For two days I slogged steadily up the glacier without incident, congratulating myself for discovering such a clever path to the Thumb. On the third day, I arrived beneath the Stikine Icecap proper, where the long arm of the Baird joins the main body of ice. Here, the glacier spills abruptly over the edge of a high plateau, dropping seaward through the gap between two peaks in a phantasmagoria of shattered ice. Seeing the icefall in the flesh left a different impression than the photos had. As I stared at the tumult from a mile away, for the first time since leaving Colorado the thought crossed my mind that maybe this Devils Thumb trip wasn't the best idea I'd ever had.

The icefall was a maze of crevasses and teetering seracs. From afar it brought to mind a bad train wreck, as if scores of ghostly white boxcars had derailed at the lip of the icecap and tumbled down the slope willy-nilly. The closer I got, the more unpleasant it looked. My ten-foot curtain rods seemed a poor defense against crevasses that were forty feet across and two hundred fifty feet deep. Before I could finish figuring out a course through the ice-fall, the wind came up and snow began to slant hard out of the clouds, stinging my face and reducing visibility to almost nothing.

In my impetuosity, I decided to carry on anyway. For the better part of the day I groped blindly through the labyrinth in the whiteout, retracing my steps from one dead end to another. Time after time I'd think I'd found a way out, only to wind up in a deep blue cul de sac, or stranded atop a detached pillar of ice. My efforts were lent a sense of urgency by the noises emanating underfoot. A madrigal of creaks and sharp reports—the sort of protests a large fir limb makes when it's slowly bent to the breaking point—served as a reminder that it is the nature of glaciers to move, the habit of seracs to topple.

As much as I feared being flattened by a wall of collapsing ice, I was even more afraid of falling into a crevasse, a fear that intensified when I put a foot through a snow bridge over a slot so deep I couldn't see the bottom of it. A little later I broke through another bridge to my waist; the poles kept me out of the hundred-foot hole, but after I extricated myself I was bent double with dry heaves thinking about what it would be like to be lying in a pile at the bottom of the crevasse, waiting for death to come, with nobody even aware of how or where I'd met my end.

Night had nearly fallen by the time I emerged from the top of the serac slope onto the empty, wind-scoured expanse of the high glacial plateau. In shock and chilled to the core, I skied far enough past the icefall to put its rumblings out of earshot, pitched the tent, crawled into my sleeping bag, and shivered myself to a fitful sleep.

•••

ALTHOUGH MY PLAN to climb the Devils Thumb wasn't fully hatched until the spring of 1977, the mountain had been lurking in the recesses of my mind for about fifteen years—since April 12, 1962, to be exact. The occasion was my eighth birthday. When it came time to open birthday presents, my parents announced that they were offering me a choice of gifts: According to my wishes, they would either escort me to the new Seattle World's Fair to ride the Monorail and see the Space Needle, or give me an introductory taste of mountain climbing by taking me up the third highest peak in Oregon, a long-dormant volcano called the South Sister that, on clear days, was visible from my bedroom window. It was a tough call. I thought the matter over at length, then settled on the climb.

To prepare me for the rigors of the ascent, my father handed over a copy of *Mountaineering: The Freedom of the Hills*, the leading how-to manual of the day, a thick tome that weighed only slightly less than a bowling ball. Thenceforth I spent most of my waking hours poring over its pages, memorizing the intricacies of pitoncraft and bolt placement, the shoulder stand and the tension traverse. None of which, as it happened, was of any use on my inaugural ascent, for the South Sister turned out to be a decidedly less than extreme climb that demanded nothing more in the way of technical skill than energetic walking, and was in fact ascended by hundreds of farmers, house pets, and small children every summer.

Which is not to suggest that my parents and I conquered the mighty volcano: From the pages and pages of perilous situations depicted in *Mountaineering: The Freedom of the Hills*, I had concluded that climbing was a life-and-death matter, always. Halfway up the South Sister I suddenly remembered this. In the middle of a twenty-degree snow slope that would be impossible to fall from if you tried, I decided that I was in mortal jeopardy and burst into tears, bringing the ascent to a halt.

Perversely, after the South Sister debacle my interest in climbing only intensified. I resumed my obsessive studies of *Mountaineering*. There was something about the scariness of the activities portrayed in those pages that just wouldn't leave me alone. In addition to the scores of line drawings—most of them cartoons of a little man in a jaunty Tyrolean cap—employed to illustrate arcana like the boot-axe belay and the Bilgeri rescue, the book contained sixteen black-and-white plates of notable peaks in the Pacific Northwest and Alaska. All the photographs were striking, but the one on page 147 was much, much more than that: it made my skin crawl. An aerial photo by glaciologist Maynard Miller, it showed a singularly sinister tower of ice-plastered black rock. There wasn't a place on the entire mountain that looked safe or secure; I couldn't imagine anyone climbing it. At the bottom of the page the mountain was identified as the Devils Thumb.

From the first time I saw it, the picture—a portrait of the Thumb's north wall—held an almost pornographic fascination for me. On hundreds—no, make that thousands—of occasions over the decade and a half that followed I took my copy of *Mountaineering* down from the shelf, opened it to page 147, and quietly stared. How would it feel, I wondered over and over, to be on that thumbnail-thin summit ridge, worrying over the storm clouds building on the horizon, hunched against the wind and dunning cold, contemplating the horrible drop on either side? How could anyone keep it together? Would I, if I found myself high on the north wall, clinging to that frozen rock, even attempt to keep it together? Or would I simply decide to surrender to the inevitable straight away, and jump?

I HAD PLANNED on spending between three weeks and a month on the Stikine Icecap. Not relishing the prospect of carrying a four-week load of food, heavy winter camping gear, and a small mountain of climbing hardware all the way up the Baird on my back, before leaving Petersburg I paid a bush pilot a hundred and fifty dollars—the last of my cash—to have six cardboard cartons of supplies dropped from an airplane when I reached the foot of the Thumb. I showed the pilot exactly where, on his map, I intended to be, and told him to give me three days to get there; he promised to fly over and make the drop as soon thereafter as the weather permitted.

On May 6 I set up a base camp on the Icecap just northeast of the Thumb and waited for the airdrop. For the next four days it snowed, nixing any chance for a flight. Too terrified of crevasses to wander far from camp, I occasionally went out for a short ski to kill time, but mostly I lay silently in the tent—the ceiling was too low to sit upright—with my thoughts, fighting a rising chorus of doubts.

As the days passed, I grew increasingly anxious. I had no radio, nor any other means of communicating with the outside world. It had been many years since anyone had visited this part of the Stikine Icecap, and many more would likely pass before anyone did so again. I was nearly out of stove fuel, and down to a single chunk of cheese, my last package of ramen noodles, and half a box of Cocoa Puffs. This, I figured, could sustain me for three or four more days if need be, but then what would I do? It would only take two days to ski back down the Baird to Thomas Bay, but then a week or more might easily pass before a fisherman happened by who could give me a lift back to Petersburg (the Hodads with whom I'd ridden over were camped fifteen miles down the impassable, headland-studded coast, and could be reached only by boat or plane).

When I went to bed on the evening of May 10 it was still snowing and blowing hard. I was going back and forth on whether to head for the coast in the morning or stick it out on the icecap, gambling that the pilot would show before I starved or died of thirst, when, just for a moment, I heard a faint whine, like a mosquito. I tore open the tent door. Most of the clouds had lifted, but there was no airplane in sight. The whine returned, louder this time. Then I saw it: a tiny red-and-white speck, high in the western sky, droning my way.

A few minutes later the plane passed directly overhead. The pilot, however, was unaccustomed to glacier flying and he'd badly misjudged the scale of the terrain. Worried about winding up too low and getting nailed by unexpected turbulence, he flew a good thousand feet above me—believing all the while he was just off the deck—and never saw my tent in the flat evening light. My waving and screaming were to no avail; from that altitude I was indistinguishable from a pile of rocks. For the next hour he circled the icecap, scanning its barren contours without success. But the pilot, to his credit, appreciated the gravity of my predicament and didn't give up. Frantic, I tied my sleeping bag to the end of one of the crevasse poles and waved it for all I was worth. When the plane banked sharply and began to fly straight at me, I felt tears of joy well in my eyes.

The pilot buzzed my tent three times in quick succession, dropping two boxes on each pass, then the airplane disappeared over a ridge and I was alone. As silence again settled over the glacier I felt abandoned, vulnerable, lost. I realized that I was sobbing. Embarrassed, I halted the blubbering by screaming obscenities until I grew hoarse.

I awoke early on May 11 to clear skies and the relatively warm temperature of twenty degrees Fahrenheit. Startled by the good weather, mentally unprepared to commence the actual climb, I hurriedly packed up a rucksack nonetheless, and began skiing toward the base of the Thumb. Two previous Alaskan expeditions had taught me that, ready or not, you simply can't afford to waste a day of perfect weather if you expect to get up anything.

A small hanging glacier extends out from the lip of the icecap, leading up and across the north face of the Thumb like a catwalk. My plan was to follow this catwalk to a prominent rock prow in the center of the wall, and thereby execute an end run around the ugly, avalanche-swept lower half of the face.

The catwalk turned out to be a series of fifty-degree ice fields blanketed with knee-deep powder snow and riddled with crevasses. The depth of the snow made the going slow and exhausting; by the time I front-pointed up the overhanging wall of the uppermost *bergschrund*,[1] some three or four hours after leaving camp, I was whipped. And I hadn't even gotten to the "real" climbing yet. That would begin immediately above, where the hanging glacier gave way to vertical rock.

The rock, exhibiting a dearth of holds and coated with six inches of crumbly rime, did not look promising, but just left of the main prow was an inside corner—what climbers call an open book—glazed with frozen

---

[1] A crevasse that separates the mountain proper from the glacier beneath it.

melt water. This ribbon of ice led straight up for two or three hundred feet, and if the ice proved substantial enough to support the picks of my ice axes, the line might go. I hacked out a small platform in the snow slope, the last flat ground I expected to feel underfoot for some time, and stopped to eat a candy bar and collect my thoughts. Fifteen minutes later I shouldered my pack and inched over to the bottom of the corner. Gingerly, I swung my right axe into the two-inch-thick ice. It was solid, plastic—a little thinner than I would have liked but otherwise perfect. I was on my way.

The climbing was steep and spectacular, so exposed it made my head spin. Beneath my boot soles, the wall fell away for three thousand feet to the dirty, avalanche-scarred cirque of the Witches Cauldron Glacier. Above, the prow soared with authority toward the summit ridge, a vertical half-mile above. Each time I planted one of my ice axes, that distance shrank by another twenty inches.

The higher I climbed, the more comfortable I became. All that held me to the mountainside, all that held me to the world, were six thin spikes of chrome-molybdenum stuck half an inch into a smear of frozen water, yet I began to feel invincible, weightless, like those lizards that live on the ceilings of cheap Mexican hotels. Early on a difficult climb, especially a difficult solo climb, you're hyperaware of the abyss pulling at your back. You constantly feel its call, its immense hunger. To resist takes a tremendous conscious effort; you don't dare let your guard down for an instant. The siren song of the void puts you on edge, it makes your movements tentative, clumsy, herky-jerky. But as the climb goes on, you grow accustomed to the exposure, you get used to rubbing shoulders with doom, you come to believe in the reliability of your hands and feet and head. You learn to trust your self-control.

By and by, your attention becomes so intensely focused that you no longer notice the raw knuckles, the cramping thighs, the strain of maintaining nonstop concentration. A trance-like state settles over your efforts, the climb becomes a clear-eyed dream. Hours slide by like minutes. The accrued guilt and clutter of day-to-day existence—the lapses of conscience, the unpaid bills, the bungled opportunities, the dust under the couch, the festering familial sores, the inescapable prison of your genes—all of it is temporarily forgotten, crowded from your thoughts by an overpowering clarity of purpose, and by the seriousness of the task at hand.

At such moments, something like happiness actually stirs in your chest, but it isn't the sort of emotion you want to lean on very hard. In solo climbing, the whole enterprise is held together with little more than chutzpa, not the most reliable adhesive. Late in the day on the north face of the Thumb, I felt the glue disintegrate with a single swing of an ice axe.

I'd gained nearly seven hundred feet of altitude since stepping off the hanging glacier, all of it on crampon front-points and the picks of my axes. The ribbon of frozen melt water had ended three hundred feet up, and was followed by a crumbly armor of frost feathers. Though just barely substantial enough to support body weight, the rime was plastered over the rock to a thickness of two or three feet, so I kept plugging upward. The wall, however, had been growing imperceptibly steeper, and as it did so the frost feathers became thinner. I'd fallen into a slow, hypnotic rhythm—swing, swing; kick, kick; swing, swing; kick, kick—when my left ice axe slammed into a slab of diorite a few inches beneath the rime.

I tried left, then right, but kept striking rock. The frost feathers holding me up, it became apparent, were maybe five inches thick and had the structural integrity of stale cornbread. Below was thirty-seven hundred feet of air, and I was balanced atop a house of cards. Waves of panic rose in my throat. My eyesight blurred, I began to hyperventilate, my calves started to vibrate. I shuffled a few feet farther to the right, hoping to find thicker ice, but managed only to bend an ice axe on the rock.

Awkwardly, stiff with fear, I started working my way back down. The rime gradually thickened, and after descending about eighty feet I got back on reasonably solid ground. I stopped for a long time to let my nerves settle, then leaned back from my tools and stared up at the face above, searching for a hint of solid ice, for some variation in the underlying rock strata, for anything that would allow passage over the frosted slabs. I looked until my neck ached, but nothing appeared. The climb was over. The only place to go was down.

...

HEAVY SNOW AND incessant winds kept me inside the tent for most of the next three days. The hours passed slowly. In the attempt to hurry them along I chain-smoked for as long as my supply of cigarettes held out, and read. I'd made a number of bad decisions on the trip, there was no getting around it, and one of them concerned the reading matter I'd chosen to pack along: three back issues of *The Village Voice*, and Joan Didion's latest novel, *A Book of Common Prayer*. The *Voice* was amusing enough—there on the icecap, the subject matter took on an edge, a certain sense of the absurd, from which the paper (through no fault of its own) benefited greatly—but in that tent, under those circumstances, Didion's necrotic take on the world hit a little too close to home.

Near the end of *Common Prayer*, one of Didion's characters says to another, "You don't get any real points for staying here, Charlotte." Charlotte replies, "I can't seem to tell what you do get real points for, so I guess I'll stick around here for awhile."

When I ran out of things to read, I was reduced to studying the ripstop pattern woven into the tent ceiling. This I did for hours on end, flat on my back, while engaging in an extended and very heated self-debate: Should I leave for the coast as soon as the weather broke, or stay put long enough to make another attempt on the mountain? In truth, my little escapade on the north face had left me badly shaken, and I didn't want to go up on the Thumb again at all. On the other hand, the thought of returning to Boulder in defeat—of parking the Pontiac behind the trailer, buckling on my tool belt, and going back to the same brain-dead drill I'd so triumphantly walked away from just a month before—that wasn't very appealing, either. Most of all, I couldn't stomach the thought of having to endure the smug expressions of condolence from all the chumps and nimrods who were certain I'd fail right from the get-go.

By the third afternoon of the storm I couldn't stand it any longer: the lumps of frozen snow poking me in the back, the clammy nylon walls brushing against my face, the incredible smell drifting up from the depths of my sleeping bag. I pawed through the mess at my feet until I located a small green stuff sack, in which there was a metal film can containing the makings of what I'd hoped would be a sort of victory cigar. I'd intended to save it for my return from the summit, but what the hey, it wasn't looking like I'd be visiting the top any time soon. I poured most of the can's contents onto a leaf of cigarette paper, rolled it into a crooked, sorry looking joint, and promptly smoked it down to the roach.

The reefer, of course, only made the tent seem even more cramped, more suffocating, more impossible to bear. It also made me terribly hungry. I decided a little oatmeal would put things right. Making it, however, was a long, ridiculously involved process: a potful of snow had to be gathered outside in the tempest, the stove assembled and lit, the oatmeal and sugar located, the remnants of yesterday's dinner scraped from my bowl. I'd gotten the stove going and was melting the snow when I smelled something burning. A thorough check of the stove and its environs revealed nothing. Mystified, I was ready to chalk it up to my chemically enhanced imagination when I heard something crackle directly behind me.

I whirled around in time to see a bag of garbage, into which I'd tossed the match I'd used to light the stove, flare up into a conflagration. Beating on the fire with my hands, I had it out in a few seconds, but not before a large section of the tent's inner wall vaporized before my eyes. The tent's built-in rainfly escaped the flames, so the shelter was still more or less weatherproof; now, however, it was approximately thirty degrees cooler inside. My left palm began to sting. Examining it, I noticed the pink welt of a burn. What troubled me most, though, was that the tent wasn't even mine—I'd borrowed the shelter from my father. An expensive Early Winters OmnipoTent, it had been brand new before my trip—the hang-tags were still attached—and had been loaned reluctantly. For several minutes I sat dumbstruck, staring at the wreckage of the shelter's once-graceful form amid the acrid scent of singed hair and melted nylon. You had to hand it to me, I thought: I had a real knack for living up to the old man's worst expectations.

The fire sent me into a funk that no drug known to man could have alleviated. By the time I'd finished cooking the oatmeal my mind was made up: the moment the storm was over, I was breaking camp and booking for Thomas Bay.

TWENTY-FOUR HOURS LATER, I was huddled inside a bivouac sack under the lip of the *bergschrund* on the Thumb's north face. The weather was as bad as I'd seen it. It was snowing hard, probably an inch every hour. Spindrift avalanches hissed down from the wall above and washed over me like surf, completely burying the sack every twenty minutes.

The day had begun well enough. When I emerged from the tent, clouds still clung to the ridge tops but the wind was down and the icecap was speckled with sunbreaks. A patch of sunlight, almost blinding in its brilliance, slid lazily over the camp. I put down a foam sleeping mat and sprawled on the glacier in my long johns. Wallowing in the radiant heat, I felt the gratitude of a prisoner whose sentence has just been commuted.

As I lay there, a narrow chimney that curved up the east half of the Thumb's north face, well to the left of the route I'd tried before the storm, caught my eye. I twisted a telephoto lens onto my camera. Through it I could make out a smear of shiny gray ice—solid, trustworthy, hard-frozen ice—plastered to the back of the cleft. The alignment of the chimney made it impossible to discern if the ice continued in an unbroken line from top to bottom. If it did, the chimney might well provide passage over the rime-covered slabs that had foiled my first attempt. Lying there in the sun, I began to think about how much I'd hate myself a month hence if I threw in the towel after a single try, if I scrapped the whole expedition on account of a little bad weather. Within the hour I had assembled my gear and was skiing toward the base of the wall.

The ice in the chimney did in fact prove to be continuous, but it was very, very thin—just a gossamer film of verglas. Additionally, the cleft was a natural funnel for any debris that happened to slough off the wall; as I scratched my way up the chimney I was hosed by a continuous stream of powder snow, ice chips, and small stones. One hundred twenty feet up the groove the last remnants of my composure flaked away like old plaster, and I turned around.

Instead of descending all the way to base camp, I decided to spend the night in the 'schrund beneath the chimney, on the off chance that my head would be more together the next morning. The fair skies that had ushered in the day, however, turned out to be but a momentary lull in a five-day gale. By midafternoon the storm was back in all its glory, and my bivouac site became a less than pleasant place to hang around. The ledge on which I crouched was continually swept by small spindrift avalanches. Five times my bivy sack—a thin nylon envelope, shaped exactly like a Baggies brand sandwich bag, only bigger—was buried up to the level of the breathing slit. After digging myself out the fifth time, I decided I'd had enough. I threw all my gear in my pack and made a break for base camp.

The descent was terrifying. Between the clouds, the ground blizzard, and the flat, fading light, I couldn't tell snow from sky, nor whether a slope went up or down. I worried, with ample reason, that I might step blindly off the top of a serac and end up at the bottom of the Witches Cauldron, a half-mile below. When I finally arrived on the frozen plain of the icecap, I found that my tracks had long since drifted over. I didn't have a clue how to locate the tent on the featureless glacial plateau. I skied in circles for an hour or so, hoping I'd get lucky and stumble across camp, until I put a foot into a small crevasse and realized I was acting like an idiot—that I should hunker down right where I was and wait out the storm.

I dug a shallow hole, wrapped myself in the bivvy bag, and sat on my pack in the swirling snow. Drifts piled up around me. My feet became numb. A damp chill crept down my chest from the base of my neck, where spindrift had gotten inside my parka and soaked my shirt. If only I had a cigarette, I thought, a single cigarette, I could summon the strength of character to put a good face on this fucked-up situation, on the whole fucked-up trip. "If we had some ham, we could have ham and eggs, if we had some eggs." I remembered my friend Nate uttering that line in a similar storm, two years before, high on another Alaskan peak, the Mooses

Tooth. It had struck me as hilarious at the time; I'd actually laughed out loud. Recalling the line now, it no longer seemed funny. I pulled the bivvy sack tighter around my shoulders. The wind ripped at my back. Beyond shame, I cradled my head in my arms and embarked on an orgy of self-pity.

I KNEW THAT people sometimes died climbing mountains. But at the age of twenty-three personal mortality—the idea of my own death—was still largely outside my conceptual grasp; it was as abstract a notion as non-Euclidian geometry or marriage. When I decamped from Boulder in April, 1977, my head swimming with visions of glory and redemption on the Devils Thumb, it didn't occur to me that I might be bound by the same cause-effect relationships that governed the actions of others. I'd never heard of hubris. Because I wanted to climb the mountain so badly, because I had thought about the Thumb so intensely for so long, it seemed beyond the realm of possibility that some minor obstacle like the weather or crevasses or rime-covered rock might ultimately thwart my will.

At sunset the wind died and the ceiling lifted 150 feet off the glacier, enabling me to locate base camp. I made it back to the tent intact, but it was no longer possible to ignore the fact that the Thumb had made hash of my plans. I was forced to acknowledge that volition alone, however powerful, was not going to get me up the north wall. I saw, finally, that nothing was.

There still existed an opportunity for salvaging the expedition, however. A week earlier I'd skied over to the southeast side of the mountain to take a look at the route Fred Beckey had pioneered in 1946—the route by which I'd intended to descend the peak after climbing the north wall. During that reconnaissance I'd noticed an obvious unclimbed line to the left of the Beckey route—a patchy network of ice angling across the southeast face— that struck me as a relatively easy way to achieve the summit. At the time, I'd considered this route unworthy of my attentions. Now, on the rebound from my calamitous entanglement with the nordwand, I was prepared to lower my sights.

On the afternoon of May 15, when the blizzard finally petered out, I returned to the southeast face and climbed to the top of a slender ridge that abutted the upper peak like a flying buttress on a Gothic cathedral. I decided to spend the night there, on the airy, knife-edged ridge crest, sixteen hundred feet below the summit. The evening sky was cold and cloudless. I could see all the way to tidewater and beyond. At dusk I watched, transfixed, as the house lights of Petersburg blinked on in the west. The closest thing I'd had to human contact since the airdrop, the distant lights set off a flood of emotion that caught me completely off guard. I imagined people watching the Red Sox on the tube, eating fried chicken in brightly lit kitchens, drinking beer, making love. When I lay down to sleep I was overcome by a soul-wrenching loneliness. I'd never felt so alone, ever.

That night I had troubled dreams, of cops and vampires and a gangland-style execution. I heard someone whisper, "He's in there. As soon as he comes out, waste him." I sat bolt upright and opened my eyes. The sun was about to rise. The entire sky was scarlet. It was still clear, but wisps of high cirrus were streaming in from the southwest, and a dark line was visible just above the horizon. I pulled on my boots and hurriedly strapped on my crampons. Five minutes after waking up, I was front-pointing away from the bivouac.

I carried no rope, no tent or bivouac gear, no hardware save my ice axes. My plan was to go ultralight and ultrafast, to hit the summit and make it back down before the weather turned. Pushing myself, continually out of breath, I scurried up and to the left across small snowfields linked by narrow runnels of verglas and short rock bands. The climbing was almost fun—the rock was covered with large, in-cut holds, and the ice, though thin, never got steep enough to feel extreme—but I was anxious about the bands of clouds racing in from the Pacific, covering the sky.

In what seemed like no time (I didn't have a watch on the trip) I was on the distinctive final ice field. By now the sky was completely overcast. It looked easier to keep angling to the left, but quicker to go straight for the top. Paranoid about being caught by a storm high on the peak without any kind of shelter, I opted for the direct route. The ice steepened, then steepened some more, and as it did so it grew thin. I swung my left ice axe and

struck rock. I aimed for another spot, and once again it glanced off unyielding diorite with a dull, sickening clank. And again, and again: It was a
reprise of my first attempt on the north face. Looking between my legs, I
stole a glance at the glacier, more than two thousand feet below. My stomach churned. I felt my poise slipping away like smoke in the wind.

Forty-five feet above the wall eased back onto the sloping summit shoulder. Forty-five more feet, half the distance between third base and home
plate, and the mountain would be mine. I clung stiffly to my axes, un-
moving, paralyzed with fear and indecision. I looked down at the dizzying
drop to the glacier again, then up, then scraped away the film of ice above
my head. I hooked the pick of my left axe on a nickel-thin lip of rock, and
weighted it. It held. I pulled my right axe from the ice, reached up, and
twisted the pick into a crooked half-inch crack until it jammed. Barely
breathing now, I moved my feet up, scrabbling my crampon points across
the verglas. Reaching as high as I could with my left arm, I swung the axe
gently at the shiny, opaque surface, not knowing what I'd hit beneath it. The
pick went in with a heartening *THUNK!* A few minutes later I was standing on a broad, rounded ledge. The summit proper, a series of slender fins
sprouting a grotesque meringue of atmospheric ice, stood twenty feet directly above.

The insubstantial frost feathers ensured that those last twenty feet remained hard, scary, onerous. But then, suddenly, there was no place higher
to go. It wasn't possible, I couldn't believe it. I felt my cracked lips stretch
into a huge, painful grin. I was on top of the Devils Thumb.

Fittingly, the summit was a surreal, malevolent place, an improbably
slender fan of rock and rime no wider than a filing cabinet. It did not encourage loitering. As I straddled the highest point, the north face fell away
beneath my left boot for six thousand feet; beneath my right boot the south
face dropped off for twenty-five hundred. I took some pictures to prove I'd
been there, and spent a few minutes trying to straighten a bent pick. Then
I stood up, carefully turned around, and headed for home.

• • •

FIVE DAYS LATER I was camped in the rain beside the sea, marveling at the sight of moss, willows, mosquitoes. Two days after that, a small skiff motored into Thomas Bay and pulled up on the beach not far from my tent. The man driving the boat introduced himself as Jim Freeman, a timber faller from Petersburg. It was his day off, he said, and he'd made the trip to show his family the glacier, and to look for bears. He asked me if I'd "been huntin', or what?"

"No," I replied sheepishly. "Actually, I just climbed the Devils Thumb. I've been over here twenty days."

Freeman kept fiddling with a cleat on the boat, and didn't say anything for a while. Then he looked at me real hard and spat, "You wouldn't be givin' me double talk now, wouldja, friend?" Taken aback, I stammered out a denial. Freeman, it was obvious, didn't believe me for a minute. Nor did he seem wild about my snarled shoulder-length hair or the way I smelled. When I asked if he could give me a lift back to town, however, he offered a grudging, "I don't see why not."

The water was choppy, and the ride across Frederick Sound took two hours. The more we talked, the more Freeman warmed up. He still didn't believe I'd climbed the Thumb, but by the time he steered the skiff into Wrangell Narrows he pretended to. When we got off the boat, he insisted on buying me a cheeseburger. That night he even let me sleep in a derelict step-van parked in his backyard.

I lay down in the rear of the old truck for a while but couldn't sleep, so I got up and walked to a bar called Kito's Kave. The euphoria, the overwhelming sense of relief, that had initially accompanied my return to Petersburg faded, and an unexpected melancholy took its place. The people I chatted with in Kito's didn't seem to doubt that I'd been to the top of the Thumb, they just didn't much care. As the night wore on the place emptied except for me and an Indian at a back table. I drank alone, putting quarters in the jukebox, playing the same five songs over and over, until the barmaid yelled angrily, "Hey! Give it a fucking rest, kid! If I hear 'Fifty Ways to Lose Your Lover' one more time, *I'm* gonna be the one who loses it." I mumbled an apology, quickly headed for the door, and lurched back to

Freeman's step-van. There, surrounded by the sweet scent of old motor oil, I lay down on the floorboards next to a gutted transmission and passed out.

It is easy, when you are young, to believe that what you desire is no less than what you deserve, to assume that if you want something badly enough it is your God-given right to have it. Less than a month after sitting on the summit of the Thumb I was back in Boulder, nailing up siding on the Spruce Street Townhouses, the same condos I'd been framing when I left for Alaska. I got a raise, to four dollars an hour, and at the end of the summer moved out of the job-site trailer to a studio apartment on West Pearl, but little else in my life seemed to change. Somehow, it didn't add up to the glorious transformation I'd imagined in April.

Climbing the Devils Thumb, however, had nudged me a little further away from the obdurate innocence of childhood. It taught me something about what mountains can and can't do, about the limits of dreams. I didn't recognize that at the time, of course, but I'm grateful for it now.

PART II

Idylls

JOSHUA SLOCUM

(1844–c. 1909)

From *Sailing Alone Around the World*

It is fudging a bit to include Joshua Slocum in an anthology of great adventure writing of the twentieth century, for his Sailing Alone Around the World *was published in 1899. Yet Slocum deserves a place here, so forward-thinking was the conception of his journey: to make the first solo circumnavigation of the globe, not for any ulterior motive, but just because it had never been done.*

In contrast to modern single-handers racing around the world, out of sight of land for weeks at a time, Slocum took his sweet time, laying over wherever it struck his fancy for as long as he felt like it. The journey in all lasted more than three years, from April 1895 to June 1898. Slocum's shore passages, full of curious incidents and strange people, give much of the flavor of blithe Yankee humor to this sailing classic. Reading the narrative, in fact, one has little sense of any loneliness on the skipper's part. Slocum turns the superbly seaworthy Spray, which he had built with his own hands, into a veritable character. And the author's unflappable optimism informs the book's central conceit: that the whole incredible voyage, navigating often by dead reckoning, was a piece of cake.

In this passage, Slocum tarries on the tiny island of Juan Fernández, off the west coast of Chile, where the Scottish sailor Alexander Selkirk had been put ashore in 1704 after a quarrel with his captain. Rescued more than four years later, Selkirk furnished the story that Daniel Defoe used as the basis for Robinson Crusoe.

After several years in dry dock, when he tried to turn the Spray *into a waterfront museum, Slocum set sail once more, in 1909, in his beloved boat—only to vanish at sea.*

The *Spray* being secured, the islanders returned to the coffee and doughnuts, and I was more than flattered when they did not slight my buns, as the professor had done in the Strait of Magellan.[1] Between buns and doughnuts there was little difference except in name. Both had been fried in tallow, which was the strong point in both, for there was nothing on the island fatter than a goat, and a goat is but a lean beast, to make the best of it. So with a view to business I hooked my steelyards to the boom at once, ready to weigh out tallow, there being no customs officer to say, "Why do you do so?" and before the sun went down the islanders had learned the art of making buns and doughnuts. I did not charge a high price for what I sold, but the ancient and curious coins I got in payment, some of them from the wreck of a galleon sunk in the bay no one knows when, I sold afterward to antiquarians for more than face-value. In this way I made a reasonable profit. I brought away money of all denominations from the island, and nearly all there was, so far as I could find out.

Juan Fernández, as a place of call, is a lovely spot. The hills are well

---

[1] "The professor" was an unfriendly Swedish scientist whose path Slocum crossed when he stopped at Port Angosto to fill his water casks. The scientist, Slocum insisted, was studying varieties of moss.

wooded, the valleys fertile, and pouring down through many ravines are streams of pure water. There are no serpents on the island, and no wild beasts other than pigs and goats, of which I saw a number, with possibly a dog or two. The people lived without the use of rum or beer of any sort. There was not a police officer or a lawyer among them. The domestic economy of the island was simplicity itself. The fashions of Paris did not affect the inhabitants; each dressed according to his own taste. Although there was no doctor, the people were all healthy, and the children were all beautiful. There were about forty-five souls on the island all told. The adults were mostly from the mainland of South America. One lady there, from Chile, who made a flying-jib for the *Spray*, taking her pay in tallow, would be called a belle at Newport. Blessed island of Juan Fernández! Why Alexander Selkirk ever left you was more than I could make out.

A large ship which had arrived some time before, on fire, had been stranded at the head of the bay, and as the sea smashed her to pieces on the rocks, after the fire was drowned, the islanders picked up the timbers and utilized them in the construction of houses, which naturally presented a ship-like appearance. The house of the king of Juan Fernández, Manuel Carroza by name, besides resembling the ark, wore a polished brass knocker on its only door, which was painted green. In front of this gorgeous entrance was a flag-mast all ataunto, and near it a smart whale-boat painted red and blue, the delight of the king's old age.

I of course made a pilgrimage to the old lookout place at the top of the mountain, where Selkirk spent many days peering into the distance for the ship which came at last. From a tablet fixed into the face of the rock I copied these words, inscribed in Arabic capitals:

IN MEMORY

OF

ALEXANDER SELKIRK,

MARINER,

A native of Largo, in the county of Fife, Scotland, who lived on this island in complete solitude for four years and four months. He was landed from the *Cinque Ports* galley, 96 tons, 18 guns, A.D. 1704, and was taken off in the *Duke*, privateer, 12th February, 1709. He died Lieutenant of H. M. S. *Weymouth*, A.D. 1723,[2] aged 47. This tablet is erected near Selkirk's lookout, by Commodore Powell and the officers of H. M. S. *Topaze*, A.D. 1868.

The cave in which Selkirk dwelt while on the island is at the head of the bay now called Robinson Crusoe Bay. It is around a bold headland west of the present anchorage and landing. Ships have anchored there, but it affords a very indifferent berth. Both of these anchorages are exposed to north winds, which, however, do not reach home with much violence. The holding-ground being good in the first-named bay to the eastward, the anchorage there may be considered safe, although the undertow at times makes it wild riding.

I visited Robinson Crusoe Bay in a boat, and with some difficulty landed through the surf near the cave, which I entered. I found it dry and inhabitable. It is located in a beautiful nook sheltered by high mountains from all the severe storms that sweep over the island, which are not many; for it lies near the limits of the trade-wind regions, being in latitude 35½°S. The island is about fourteen miles in length, east and west, and eight miles in width; its height is over three thousand feet. Its distance from Chile, to which country it belongs, is about three hundred and forty miles.

Juan Fernández was once a convict station. A number of caves in which the prisoners were kept, damp, unwholesome dens, are no longer in use, and no more prisoners are sent to the island.

The pleasantest day I spent on the island, if not the pleasantest on my whole voyage, was my last day on shore, — but by no means because it was the last, — when the children of the little community, one and all, went out with me to gather wild fruits for the voyage. We found quinces, peaches, and figs, and the children gathered a basket of each. It takes very little to please children, and these little ones, never hearing a word in their lives

[2]Selkirk actually died in 1721.

except Spanish, made the hills ring with mirth at the sound of words in English. They asked me the names of all manner of things on the island. We came to a wild fig-tree loaded with fruit, of which I gave them the English name. "Figgies, figgies!" they cried, while they picked till their baskets were full. But when I told them that the *cabra* they pointed out was only a goat, they screamed with laughter, and rolled on the grass in wild delight to think that a man had come to their island who would call a cabra a goat.

The first child born on Juan Fernández, I was told, had become a beautiful woman and was now a mother. Manuel Carroza and the good soul who followed him here from Brazil had laid away their only child, a girl, at the age of seven, in the little churchyard on the point. In the same half-acre were other mounds among the rough lava rocks, some marking the burial-place of native-born children, some the resting-places of seamen from passing ships, landed here to end days of sickness and get into a sailors' heaven.

The greatest drawback I saw in the island was the want of a school. A class there would necessarily be small, but to some kind soul who loved teaching and quietude life on Juan Fernández would, for a limited time, be one of delight.

On the morning of May 5, 1896, I sailed from Juan Fernández, having feasted on many things, but on nothing sweeter than the adventure itself of a visit to the home and to the very cave of Robinson Crusoe. From the island the *Spray* bore away to the north, passing the island of St. Felix before she gained the trade-winds, which seemed slow in reaching their limits.

If the trades were tardy, however, when they did come they came with a bang, and made up for lost time; and the *Spray*, under reefs, sometimes one, sometimes two, flew before a gale for a great many days, with a bone in her mouth, toward the Marquesas, in the west, which she made on the forty-third day out, and still kept on sailing. My time was all taken up those days—not by standing at the helm; no man, I think, could stand or sit and steer a vessel round the world: I did better than that; for I sat and read my books, mended my clothes, or cooked my meals and ate them in peace. I had already found that it was not good to be alone, and so I made companionship with what there was around me, sometimes with the universe and sometimes with my own insignificant self; but my books were always my friends, let fail all else. Nothing could be easier or more restful than my voyage in the trade-winds.

I sailed with a free wind day after day, marking the position of my ship on the chart with considerable precision; but this was done by intuition, I think, more than by slavish calculations. For one whole month my vessel held her course true; I had not, the while, so much as a light in the binnacle. The Southern Cross I saw every night abeam. The sun every morning came up astern; every evening it went down ahead. I wished for no other compass to guide me, for these were true. If I doubted my reckoning after a long time at sea I verified it by reading the clock aloft made by the Great Architect, and it was right.

There was no denying that the comical side of the strange life appeared. I awoke, sometimes, to find the sun already shining into my cabin. I heard water rushing by, with only a thin plank between me and the depths, and I said, "How is this!" But it was all right; it was my ship on her course, sailing as no other ship had ever sailed before in the world. The rushing water along her side told me that she was sailing at full speed. I knew that no human hand was at the helm; I knew that all was well with "the hands" forward, and that there was no mutiny on board.

The phenomena of ocean meteorology were interesting studies even here in the trade-winds. I observed that about every seven days the wind freshened and drew several points farther than usual from the direction of the pole; that is, it went round from east-southeast to south-southeast, while at the same time a heavy swell rolled up from the southwest. All this indicated that gales were going on in the anti-trades. The wind then hauled day after day as it moderated, till it stood again at the normal point, east-southeast. This is more or less the constant state of the winter trades in latitude 12° S., where I "ran down the longitude" for weeks. The sun, we all know, is the creator of the trade-winds and of the wind system over all the earth. But ocean meteorology is, I think, the most fascinating of all. From Juan Fernández to the Marquesas I experienced six changes of these great palpitations of sea-winds and of the sea itself, the effect of far-off gales. To know the laws that govern the winds, and to know that you know them, will give you an easy mind on your voyage round the world; otherwise you may tremble at the appearance of every cloud. What is true of this in the trade-winds is much more so in the variables, where changes run more to extremes.

To cross the Pacific Ocean, even under the most favorable circumstances, brings you for many days close to nature, and you realize the vastness of the sea. Slowly but surely the mark of my little ship's course on the track-chart reached out on the ocean and across it, while at her utmost speed she marked with her keel still slowly the sea that carried her. On the forty-third day from land, —a long time to be at sea alone, —the sky being beautifully clear and the moon being "in distance" with the sun, I threw up my sextant for sights. I found from the result of three observations, after long wrestling with lunar tables, that her longitude by observation agreed within five miles of that by dead-reckoning.

This was wonderful; both, however, might be in error, but somehow I felt confident that both were nearly true, and that in a few hours more I should see land; and so it happened, for then I made the island of Nukahiva, the southernmost of the Marquesas group, clear-cut and lofty. The verified longitude when abreast was somewhere between the two reckonings; this was extraordinary. All navigators will tell you that from one day to another a ship may lose or gain more than five miles in her sailing-account, and again, in the matter of lunars, even expert lunarians are considered as doing clever work when they average within eight miles of the truth.

I hope I am making it clear that I do not lay claim to cleverness or to slavish calculations in my reckonings. I think I have already stated that I kept my longitude, at least, mostly by intuition. A rotator log always towed astern, but so much has to be allowed for currents and for drift, which the log never shows, that it is only an approximation, after all, to be corrected by one's own judgment from data of a thousand voyages; and even then the master of the ship, if he be wise, cries out for the lead and the lookout.

Unique was my experience in nautical astronomy from the deck of the Spray—so much so that I feel justified in briefly telling it here. The first set of sights, just spoken of, put her many hundred miles west of my reckoning by account. I knew that this could not be correct. In about an hour's time I took another set of observations with the utmost care; the mean result of these was about the same as that of the first set. I asked myself why, with my boasted self-dependence, I had not done at least better than this. Then I went in search of a discrepancy in the tables, and I found it. In the tables I found that the column of figures from which I had got an important logarithm was in error. It was a matter I could prove beyond a doubt, and it made the difference as already stated. The tables being corrected, I sailed on with self-reliance unshaken, and with my tin clock fast asleep. The result of these observations naturally tickled my vanity, for I knew that it was something to stand on a great ship's deck and with two assistants take lunar observations approximately near the truth. As one of the poorest of American sailors, I was proud of the little achievement alone on the sloop, even by chance though it may have been.

I was *en rapport* now with my surroundings, and was carried on a vast stream where I felt the buoyancy of His hand who made all the worlds. I realized the mathematical truth of their motions, so well known that astronomers compile tables of their positions through the years and the days, and the minutes of a day, with such precision that one coming along over the sea even five years later may, by their aid, find the standard time of any given meridian on the earth.

To find local time is a simpler matter. The difference between local and standard time is longitude expressed in time—four minutes, we all know, representing one degree. This, briefly, is the principle on which longitude is found independent of chronometers. The work of the lunarian, though seldom practised in these days of chronometers, is beautifully edifying, and there is nothing in the realm of navigation that lifts one's heart up more in adoration.

ROBERT DUNN

(1877–1955)

From *The Shameless Diary of an Explorer*

$\oplus$

Dr. Frederick A. Cook would become an infamous and ultimately tragic figure in exploration history, after he faked the first ascent of Mount McKinley in 1906 and the first attainment of the North Pole two years later. By 1903, however, he was a thirty-eight-year-old adventurer with a solid record on five previous expeditions to the Arctic and the Antarctic.

That year, he led an epic three-month circumnavigation of Mount McKinley, a feat not repeated until 1978. On August 30, attempting the summit, the party reached eleven thousand feet on the mountain's northwest ridge, a route that would not be successfully climbed for another fifty-one years.

Cook's misfortune was to have Robert Dunn among his teammates. A protégé of the muckraking journalist Lincoln Steffens, Dunn talked his way onto the expedition, secretly determined to write a no-holds-barred account of the adventure, with all its personality clashes, bunglings, and dirty laundry in full view. In 1907, The Shameless Diary of an Explorer appeared. Archbishop Hudson Stuck, later to make the first ascent of McKinley, spoke for many other expedition veterans when he wrote: "The book has a curious, undeniable power, despite its brutal frankness. . . . One is thankful, however, that it is unique in the literature of travel."

So scurrilous were the vignettes Dunn offered that he felt compelled to change the names and disguise the identities of his comrades. Cook is "the Professor." Fred Printz, Montana horse packer and the expedition's strongest performer, becomes "King"—and so forth.

The Shameless Diary's portrait of Cook as a pompous, childlike incompetent is blatantly unfair to the man, and Dunn's anti-Semitism runs rampant as he lampoons "Simon," a wealthy New Yorker named Ralph Shainwald. Yet for all that, the book captures the texture—the strains, squabbles, tedium, and occasional joys—of day-to-day life in camp and on the trail as well as any chronicle ever written.

*J*uly 15.—We woke gasping for air, like trout on a bank, for the rain glazes a tent's pores, and makes it air-tight, but never mosquito-proof. At three o'clock, I moved under the Professor's silk, which was black with the vampires. They'd driven him into the open, mummied in blankets, but didn't faze me.

Miller helped at breakfast. Fred and I were ages adjusting packs, while the Professor vanished, writing to his wife, I guess. I scrawled a few lines home, and gave it to the Indian boys, who dropped down the river with a little grub and some of our superfluities, in the folding kettle and night-lamp style, bound for the trading-post on Sushitna River. Simon delayed us by the school-girl trick of cutting birch bark to write home on.

We started at ten-thirty, cutting trail west, straight up the river-bank, with all the world holds for us gathered together at last, and overburdening the poor, tuckered, fourteen hairless brutes. Jack and King chopped trail ahead, the Professor leading the train with the big bay branded L. C. groaning under the junk boxes, which are a crime to pack on a horse. He has the easiest job—no brutes to drive, unmuck and recinch—but it looks important. Then come four horses, then Simon lazily moving his fat little legs, shouting when they're stuck, just in time to drive them off the trail; then four more beasts, then Miller, tall and silent in khaki; then five, and yours truly, the peevish rear-guard.

The going was better, through willow slews and spruce flats, but the 'skeet sparks swept our necks, the poison of the squashed and dead irritating the raw far worse in the wet. The Alaska 'skeet carries a whetstone, and flies sharpening his stinger. . . .

To-night, the Professor is sitting behind the blanket-wall of Jack's fire, asking such questions as, "What trees are those across the river?" (Cottonwoods, of course.) And about distances and directions which any child with a map of Alaska could answer. He shows his gold front tooth as he smiles so slowly. Miller is reading Jack's "Pelham." Jack is laying down the law—and all wrong—about the difference between blueberries and huckleberries. Simon is putting a new ventilator into the tent, making Fred very sore by thus keeping him from going to bed. The wind's cool and from the North. Well, I must water the beans. . . .

I scent trouble with the horses. They're playing out, and no denying it. We eased the loads of the Whiteface and Brown mare while crossing to the Skwentna, for one had got very thin, and the other lay down in the trail wherever she could. All are losing flesh fast, and the hair that the flies dug out isn't growing again, and more's falling. They stand around near camp, staring dazedly at us instead of rustling grass. Worst of all, their legs are swollen to double natural size.

"Just you see," said Jack in the Professor's hearing to-day, "another day in these snags and mud-holes, and good-bye to this pack train." King assented, but not before the Professor. In his hearing, Fred only shook his head, and said that the beasts did look mighty poorly. I know that what he *thought* was worse. He's the greatest diplomat I've ever known. It's impossible for him in all this stress to offend, even to disagree with any one to his face—except Simon, whom he joshes.

July 16.—It's happened—the expected! But prefaced by the Professor's funniest shine yet.

Fording a tributary to-day, Big Buck, behind whose pack he'd jumped, dumped him sprawling in midstream. Away floated his mosquito hat (which we haven't dared burn) and he after it, jounced along on the bottom bowlders. He's sure a peach. "When do we cross the Keechatna again?" he gurgled to King, crawling ashore. He thought that the creek was the main river, and he on a scientific expedition to map the wilderness. But I suppose it was a great loss, that mosquito hat, and he was dazed. So he tied a red bandanna handkerchief over his ears, and now looks like a Bashibazouk.[1]

We climbed a ridge hinting of foot-hills hid in the rain, and nooned in a tundra. Again exotic park lands silenced us, luxuriant birches drooped, uncanny lush meadows waved deserted and unscarred, neck-deep with red-top. We drove on. Tundra suddenly. I was thinking how the swamp smell of Labrador tea oppressed me—suggesting, somehow, dead flesh—when ahead I heard Miller shout and shout to the Skinny Bay horse—the Moth-eaten Bay, we call him, he has lost so much hair. I saw Miller stop, but keep on beating the brute. No use. He wouldn't move. I ran up. I jabbed him with my stick. It only peeled off chunks of skin and hair. He had played out; now he spread his legs, trembled, lowered his head and blinked stupidly. I got Jack and King, and we unpacked him, carried his load, and led him to camp by the swamp-side.

Fred said, "He wouldn't have played out if I'd done with the horses as I wanted." I reminded him that on the fourth day out from Tyonek I had suggested laying over, and said that I never used to travel in the rain. To which he had replied, "It won't hurt them to travel every day, even a little, so long as you keep going"; which was characteristically meaningless. He says now that the horses have been worked too hard in a very bad country.

I repeated all this to the Professor, adding that a rest of two or three days here was imperative, as the Whiteface, Dark Buckskin, and Bridget, the

[1] A mounted irregular soldier in a Turkish troop.

white cook-horse (Miller named her) are on the verge of collapse. The Professor sighed, "Um!—de-um-de-ay!"

King says that if we keep on to-morrow, we'll never make the pass. I asked him what he'd do if this were his outfit. He answered: "Rest here a few days, and go on slowly, making short hour travels, adding a half-hour each day, if the horses pick up." I said, "Tell the Professor that. He expects you to. That's why you're along." He said, "I won't unless he asks me what I think. I'm only hired." I said that I'd tell the Professor all this, in that case. "Of course, it 'ud be different," added King, "if he'd put getting the horses through safe entirely in my hands." "I thought he had," said I, surprised. "He never said nothin' about it," answered Fred. "What I said about the horses with the Government last year, went. No one ever said, 'Isn't the' a better place a little further on?' when I said we had to stop to rest the horses, the way the Professor did last night."

The Professor says that we'll pull on to-morrow. I've promised the crowd that we shan't. The man hasn't the least idea of a horse's needs, nor of Alaskan travel. King is so afraid of giving offense, he won't express any more opinions at all. Yet he's anything but mild when it comes to grub, or dulling the axe. . . .

July 17.—Sixth day of rain—and we haven't moved. I asked the Professor to come out and look at the horses with me, but he wouldn't. What do you think of that? His pack train is going to the devil, and he doesn't pay the least attention. Still just packs and unpacks his instruments. I wonder if he can use a theodolite, after all.[2]

King and I went out to the beasts, he knocking the Professor and the outfit, saying that the horses were never fit for Alaska, anyway. "I wouldn't have looked twice at that bay mare for this country, if I'd had the picking of this train," he said. "Yes, sir, we'll be lucky to get to the pass at all." But you can't

---

[2] The suspicion that Cook was incapable of using the theodolite (a surveying device used to ascertain latitude) became a critical argument against his claim to have reached the North Pole in 1908.

always take men like Fred at their forecasts. Facts, which they're always swearing by, often turn out to be only what ought-to-be, or they fear-may-be.

The brutes' legs were still very swollen. That's the chief trouble, caused by snags on that first wet hike up-river. They seemed dazed, too. So are we. We're all depressed and grate on one another—and perhaps I do nag Simon too much.

The Professor has just observed that we may expect steady rain till we cross the pass. "Yes, and steady rain on the other side, too," snapped back Jack. He has never a word to say now about our troubles, quite dropping out as a factor in the outfit. Sometimes he and King have long whispered talks. Plots of mutiny! 'Sdeath! I had silly words with Jack at supper. Proud of his camp craft, he advises you how to do everything about it, as if he were commanding. I was adjusting the doughfull reflector in a hole before the camp-fire, when he said, "You'll have a —— of a time baking bread there." "Why, no," said I, "the reflector 'll tip forward and give the biscuits a better crust." He contradicted violently, so in my most exasperating way I faked a "scientific reason"—something about radiating angles of heat— to support me. He assailed me violently for "all your —— scientific views" (as if I ever had any). The reflector was burning my fingers, and I said, to get rid of him, "Haven't you any blankets to dry to-night?" "That's none of your —————— business!" he yelled, before the whole hungry crowd of us.

Blanket-drying is a sore point with Jack. He and King steal away from camp work these rainy nights to their drying-fires, excluding Simon. Once, after dish-washing, I built a big one. "What yer doing that for? There's plenty of fire over here for you," called Jack. "It's no trouble to build a fire," I answered. (It was, though, in the wet, and I lied.) "Now, everybody come here to dry his blankets," I said. Jack growled something about my getting huffy when he'd invited me to his fire. I answered sweetly. A gentle answer does turn away wrath, except from Jack. He has hardly spoken to me since. Silly, aren't we? But he has worse tiffs all the time with Miller and Simon, which are none of my business. He and the Professor hardly ever speak. . . .

Clearing mists are lifting threadily over the strange green hills northward. The Professor is lisping about eating seal and penguin and killing pelican in the Antarctic. Miller is crouching low out on the tundra, stalking what yells like a raven, but he calls a goose. "I'll eat it raw if it ain't a duck," said Fred. Simon is everywhere. We bore one another, I'm thinking, "Next trip, I'll avoid such a human combination as this." Suppose all the rest have said that to themselves, too. . . .

Shall we move to-morrow? The Professor hasn't peeped about it. King still agrees that the only thing to do is to rest here a while to let the horses pick up, and then drive only two or three hours a day. Otherwise, the whole jig is up. I've told Miller, who has been ordered to build the fire these mornings—the first command yet given—not to be too hasty about getting up to-morrow. The Professor may find his mind in the night. I'm determined we shan't travel yet. . . .

Oh! the silent reaches of wavy grass in this overnourished region; it's like the parks of carefully gardened English manors—but vacant, tragic. The immense drooping birches peel off great scrolls of bark; huge dead trunks waste away in the rainy luxuriance. For years they rot whitely before no human eyes. The dead spruce falls and is buried in moss, but the birch's ghost is imperishable. . . .

July 18. —Seventh day of rain. We count as Noah must have. The Professor said nothing about moving, so here we are still. Again he wouldn't look at the horses. He doesn't seem to give a darn. Their legs are less swollen, and five galloped off when they saw me. They haven't done that for days, so they're better, except the Moth-eaten Bay, who was caught in an alder thicket, and couldn't eat till I turned him out.

Pull out to-morrow? No one knows. The Professor says we'll "try it, and see how it goes." The devil of a principle! We've got to run this team on some system, or we're done for. The Professor won't tell if we're going to travel two hours or twenty. He can't make up his mind. Can't seem to grasp the situation. I protested that we shouldn't hike for more than three hours, anyway. "If we do that, we might as well stay here," said he. Logic, eh?

Simon is ordered to help Miller cook breakfast every day, Jack and King to get supper. Jack growls at having to eat Simon's cooking; says that the kid doesn't wash himself enough. We should be more cheerful, but we're not. We have no common sense of humor. Jack and the Professor have none at all; King's is rooted in queer little repartees and rhymes, and Simon's in bad puns. I've been told mine is pretty badly distorted, too. But I'd like to hear a good, hearty laugh, even my own. . . . Miller is playing checkers with Simon on a pencil-marked board on the kerosene can. Jack is reading a Government Survey report. The Professor, having just broached a scheme to cut off distance by finding a pass north of Brooks', is fussing, fussing, fussing——![3]

July 19. — So we started. Bridget, the cook-horse, was down on his knees before we'd gone three hundred yards, not mired in the swamp, but played out. I shouted, and ran forward, suggesting we return. The Professor, who was 'way ahead of his train, wouldn't hear of it. He and Simon tried to bat the brute up. I wouldn't hit him, nor would Jack or Fred. When a horse knees down, he's failed, and no amount of banging his skull with a club does any good. I hate the cayuse for a mean, sly, contrary beast, but I won't stand by and see any warm-blooded animal tortured when it's at the end of its rope.

I could hear Simon's monotonous "git up"—he's mighty handy at beating horses to show off to the Professor—and Miller curse him for hitting the poor brute on his head with the butt of a pole. At last they seemed to have got him up.

Twenty yards on, a flooded creek flowed through willows. Bridget and three others went down. This time, Miller refused to help; and Jack and I held off till we saw the beasts would suffer worse in the mud. "No one seems inclined to aid," said the Professor. We pulled them out without beating, and King filled the worst mud-holes with brush, complaining the while to me of Simon's and the Professor's brutality. Somehow we got across, but

[3]In 1902, Alfred H. Brooks had led a pioneering eight-hundred-mile trek that culminated nine miles from McKinley's summit, the closest to the mountain any non-Indians had yet got.

had more mirings. In three hours the order was given to camp. So what I suggested does go. I think the Professor really intended to go only three hours, but pig-headedly wouldn't say so, not to appear to be taking orders from me. I hope he's beginning to realize the nature of a pack horse, and what we're up against in Alaska. I'd like to call this camp the Camp of the Dawn of Reason.

We're brighter. Yet hardly a third of the distance to McKinley has been covered, and we must reach the mountain by August 15th. After that, it will be too cold to climb, and grub will run out. Sack after sack of flour disappears, one each week, and one should last ten days. And the pass found by Herron and lost by Brooks is still ahead. . . .[4]

We've been arguing about the fable of the ant and the grasshopper. I took the cicada's side, and put it all over the ant as a mean, crusty beast, who had lost all capacity for enjoyment through blind, hard work, and therefore boiled at pleasure got by others. Somehow Jack was peevish, because Simon and I said we thought it a joke to call the white gelding "Bridget," and "she." Now he is reading Tom Sawyer, and the Professor the *Fortnightly Review*— for the first time in his life, I guess.

So at last it has cleared in the windless, nerveless, Alaskan way. Clouds form here without motion in the glittery white sky; it rains a month; suddenly, still without wind or mist movement—it magically clears.

[4]In 1899, Joseph S. Herron had traversed the Alaska Range and explored the terrain northwest of McKinley. His Indian guides deserted, and Herron's men nearly starved before other Indians rescued them.

ROBERT MARSHALL

(1901–1939)

From *Alaska Wilderness: Exploring the Central Brooks Range*

Despite the close call narrated in this excerpt, Robert Marshall's Alaska Wilderness is a sustained panegyric on the Brooks Range, which the author and a series of cronies explored through several summers beginning in 1929. A visionary forester and ecologist, Marshall died of a heart attack at only thirty-eight. (The Bob Marshall Wilderness in Montana is named after him.) Alaska Wilderness was published posthumously in 1956.

On the North Fork of the Koyukuk River with prospector Al Retzlaf, Marshall began his prowling in August 1929. Throughout his extended idyll in the Brooks Range, he never tired of reflecting on the contrast between his carefree vagabondage and the misery of his fellow Americans "Outside" (as Alaskans refer to the contiguous forty-eight states), mired in the Great Depression. Everywhere Marshall went, he bagged unclimbed mountains and hiked up valleys known only to the Inuit, who had moved from the Brooks Range to the coast fifty years before.

On either side of Mount Doonerak were deep gorges. The upper—between it and Wien Mountain—had a fair-sized creek which broke into a great silver plunge of several hundred feet. The lower gorge was a narrow cleft which divided Mount Doonerak from Hanging Glacier Mountain. This cleft I determined to explore. A quarter-mile climb up the bottom of the U-valley brought me to the mouth of the cleft. This I followed for a mile and a half between frowning, almost overhanging walls till I came to an enforced halt when precipices rose on every side. Marvelous waterfalls were plunging down on every side. I was continuously in their spray, so narrow was the chasm. Some were just small trickles of water, others were good-sized streams. In this mile and a half I counted thirteen falls with an estimated drop of 200 feet or more, and innumerable smaller cascades. This, to be sure, was an abnormal condition caused by the rains of the past few days and their melting effect on the two hanging glaciers. I returned to camp at the North Fork–Ernie Creek junction still with the overwhelming impression of that unique experience in my mind.

When we started downstream next morning we found that the heavy rains of the past few days had so swollen the upper North Fork that it had cut a new channel. Instead of joining Ernie Creek about three-quarters of a mile south of our camp, as it had done on the way up, only a small slough now entered at this point, while the main stream came in three miles farther down.

It was cold, damp, and completely overcast during lunch, and about as dreary as one could imagine with the black, frowning Gates[1] and the barren bars surrounding us. As we started again, the rain commenced and continued the rest of the day. It hardly mattered because the afternoon was just one river-wading after another. We must have waded up to our thighs half a dozen times and to our knees twenty-five or thirty times. Part of the way we followed side sloughs. The North Fork was so deep and swift that the risk of drowning was very real. Since we could not get across, wherever the

---

[1]Gates of the Arctic, named by Marshall, is a vast region in the central Brooks Range, today a national park.

river cut against the east bank we had to take to the hills and tug the horses through the soggy moss. This made a lot nastier going than even the continual river wading. At some places we had to follow perilous side slopes almost too steep for horses. At one point Al, returning from an inspection of a game trail, reported "some of the moose went ahead and most didn't, but we'll try it." We emulated the minority and got through. Thus, between soakings in the river and fatiguings in the moss we covered ten miles until wet to the skin, tired, but in excellent spirits, we pitched our camp in pouring rain in the very spot we had pitched it at two o'clock in the morning after our all-night march. It was so wet that we had to split logs to get dry wood, and we were forced to start the fire under the shelter of a tarpaulin; but we had a wonderful supper, wrung out our clothes, and retired for a comfortable rest. It poured all night, but the tent was dry and the sleeping bags warm.

Next morning, the rain stopped just long enough for us to cook breakfast and break camp; but by the time we resumed our march, the rain resumed too. We struck two miles of easy going along river bars, then took to the hills for six miles, and kept high up above the river on ridges covered principally with reindeer moss, sphagnum, Labrador tea, sedge, and dwarf birch. We had frequent fine views of the winding river; but of the mountains we saw only their bases.

We stopped for lunch in a queer pit, the basin of a dried-up miniature lake, about two hundred yards across. The shoreline was plainly apparent all the way around. In the center were large stones so evenly sorted by size that, as Al remarked, they looked as though someone had been there with a sifter.

Shortly after resuming our travels we passed three lakes, one with a large flock of ducks. A hundred yards beyond, we came out on the river which we followed near its edge through spruce, cottonwood, and willow to our island camp of twelve days before at the junction of Clear River and the North Fork.

We found the island camp an island indeed. We reached it by wading through what formerly was the shallow slough which separated it from the peninsula between the North Fork and Clear River and had now become a good-sized, though shallow, pond. The North Fork, easily fordable on our trip north, was now a wild river, uncrossable except by boat or raft. Clear River had risen three feet, and was now a raging torrent. We wondered how we could get across. Our old ford had become impossible.

The streams had become so high and dirty that we could not fish any more. Fortunately we found our cache intact. After supper Al reconnoitered up Clear River for about a mile to find a possible ford. He reported that wading was absolutely out of the question. A raft would be the only possibility. We could take ourselves and our equipment over that way and drive the horses across, but it would be risky at best. Our only other possibility would be to wait two months for cold weather, when the river would go down and we could ford it; but we had only five days of normal rations and only a fighting chance to get a moose. Of course, we could barbecue the horses!

Our nearest neighbor was forty-nine miles away. Gloomily we went to bed.

At three in the morning I awoke from the noise of rushing water. It was raining hard when I looked outside and, much to my surprise, I discovered that the water in the quiet slough next to camp had risen almost to the fire, and had become a strong, churning current. I moved the cooking pots back to what I thought was a safe place, commented casually to Al on the phenomenal rise of the water, and hurried back to bed. Moved by my report, Al took one sleepy look out of the tent and immediately was all consternation.

"Hurry, get up," he shouted, "we've got to get out of here quick. The main river's cutting back of our island and if we're not damn fast we'll be cut off from everything."

I thought he was exaggerating, but one look at his grim countenance and feverish haste in dressing made me change my mind, and I started putting on my clothes with all speed. It was now about three-thirty. Al, dressed first, grabbed the halters and started after the horses, calling for me to hurry and pack things. In a few minutes he was back, even more agitated.

"It's too late to pack the horses. It may be too late even if we carry the stuff ourselves, but we've just a chance. Water's up to my thighs already and cutting out the bottom. We've got a few minutes at best. Never mind the little things. Just pack up the tent and bed rolls, but for heaven's sake hurry. I'll take this box."

And away he went with his little packsack on his back, a heavy box of food on one shoulder, and the ax.

I continued the packing at breakneck speed, appreciating the danger, but strangely enough I felt quite calm. Al was back again before I had finished with the tent. He started across again with my big packsack, the gun, and the extra harness. When he returned a third time I had the tent done up.

"Just about time for one more load," he shouted, taking up the other box of food and the tent. But the load was too big and he had to drop the tent. I followed with his bed roll which also contained many stray items. We got across safely, though the water was nearly to our waists and just about as swift as we could stand. We immediately turned back, Al to pick up what was left around the camp and I to pick up the tent. I recovered it, deposited it on shore, and returned halfway into the water to relieve Al, staggering under a clumsy load, of his bed and some pots while he continued with the saddles, tarps, and shovels. It was four o'clock when we had led the horses across too and reached the safe shore for the last time, just thirty minutes after Al's alarm. Ten minutes later the channel was absolutely impassable for any human being. Had we slept even a little longer, we would have been caught on a tiny island covered only with willows and half a dozen slender cottonwoods, with no game, and food for only five days.

Some time during the excitement it had stopped raining. We set up camp again at what we believed to be a safe distance from the river on the highest spot of ground we could find, but it barely gave us a four-foot margin. I walked down once more to the edge of the river in the grim, gray light of a cloudy morning, and watched the mad torrent raging. Man may be taming nature, but no one standing on the bank of the North Fork of the Koyukuk on this gray morning would have claimed that nature is conquered.

We went back to sleep for three hours, then, before breakfast, back-tracked up the North Fork half a mile to where the day before we had seen some felled spruce logs by the ruins of a very old cabin. We found, to our delight, that these logs were sound enough for a raft. This helped us decide that our only hope of escape from our trap between the unfordable North Fork on one side and Clear River on the other was by raft.

We returned to our refugee camp for breakfast. It had definitely started to clear, which made the situation a little more cheering. After breakfast we reconnoitered two miles up Clear River for a possible place to drive the horses across. There was none, and the river had run completely wild. It was split into three or four different channels, each impassable. It seemed almost as big as the North Fork, and much swifter. We estimated its speed as fifteen miles an hour, the North Fork's as about twelve. On the way back to camp we scared up a moose cow and calf. Al did not have quite enough time to get a shot and felt badly about it.

We now set out for the old logs which we were going to use, and started the construction of a raft. "We" means really Al, for his was the plan, the skill, and half of the unskilled labor. He was very much a hero today, because of the morning dash to safety, where perhaps he saved both our lives, and because of his ready plan for a vessel, which we hoped would free us from our dilemma.

We first cleared out the brush and small trees from the area in which we planned to build our raft. Then we cut two skids sloping to the edge of the water and laid nine 16-foot logs across these, alternating big and small ends at each side. They formed the foundation for the raft. Al deftly notched each log so that there were four grooves running the width of the raft, one above and one below at each end of the logs. Into these grooves we fitted stout, green spruce poles, two on top and two below, and by lashing them firmly together with rope we hoped to provide a firm binding for the raft. The upper two poles were augmented by two shorter, parallel poles holding the center, attached by six 6-inch spikes which we found at the old cabin, and by additional rope.

We laid a platform of smaller logs on top of the last two shorter poles in order to provide a dry place for our goods, bound these in place with three more poles at right angles to the smaller logs of the platform; finally we lashed two more logs across the front and back ends of the three poles, in order to have something to brace ourselves against when poling the raft. We also cut three slender 15-foot poles to use for guiding the raft. For lashing the raft together, we used both sling ropes, five tent ropes, and one strong extra rope. For mooring it, we used two lash ropes.

We completed the raft the following noon after a final two hours of high-tension work. She seemed strong enough to hold together against the buffeting of an ocean, but one unavoided submerged tree or rock would inevitably tip her over in that terrific current, and our chances of swimming out would be slight indeed.

How I felt can be seen by the following entry in my journal: "August 13, 1929. Yesterday's beautiful weather is gone, and it is pouring once more. It is a case of now or never while the relatively low water due to yesterday's dryness still holds. We will shove off the raft as soon as we can. This may be the last thing I ever write."

However, everything turned out differently than expected.

As soon as the raft was finished, we took the horses to the tip of the peninsula between Clear River and the North Fork and tried to make them swim Clear River to the mainland on the east side of the North Fork, but they refused, returning to us in great terror.

This entirely upset our plans, for our only other choices were (1) to leave the horses, (2) to wait for a lowering of Clear River despite the fact that our rations were now reduced to four days, (3) to tow the horses behind the raft, which in that shallow water and terrific current would have augmented the already great hazards of our voyage.

We started back up Clear River in a desolate way, still harboring the hope that we might by some hundred-to-one chance find a ford for the horses. And actually we did. About a quarter of a mile from the mouth, the terrific current of Clear River was cutting a new channel and filling up the old one with a wall of boulders so that it looked as if we could, with difficulty, cross it. Meanwhile the new channel was not quite deep enough to bar us.

Al tried the crossing, found it just passable, and decided that if we rushed we could still make it before the new channel was too deep. We ran with the horses most of the way back to the raft, to which we had transported our entire equipment in the morning. It was all ready for loading. In a great rush we unlashed the ropes from the raft, reassembled the packing outfit, and packed the two horses. Within an hour we were back at our ford. We crossed the torrent in a great semicircle of about two hundred yards. At the worst place the new channel was three feet deep and raced along at about eight miles an hour. By walking with the current, bracing ourselves for all we were worth, and using the horses for support, we barely managed to get across. Several times we were swept off our feet, but by clinging to the halters were able to regain our footing. Within five minutes we stood on the far shore, miraculously escaped from our flood-lined trap. An hour later we would in all probability have been too late; an hour sooner, we would have been too early.

We proceeded downstream two and a half miles along a high beach and pitched camp in the rain, which had continued since morning, on a flat, three feet above the river. It was a cold, soggy night and a wild camp still many miles from our nearest neighbor; there were hardships ahead, but freed from our nerve-wracking plight we felt cozier and jollier than if we had been housed in a modern steam-heated apartment.

The rest of our return trip to Wiseman[2] we continued following approximately the same route which we had taken on our way out. On one occasion we heard part of a mountain across the river tumbling with a thunderous noise—the effect of the only recently receded glaciation in this geologically young country. At Jack Delay Pass we saw two moose—a lone cow, and a calf. They were quite close and tame and we could have shot them easily, but we did not want to waste a moose just for the one or two meals we still had ahead of us. During the last night I was awakened by splashing and looked out of the tent to see a moose calf crossing Glacier River.

Opposite Yale's cabin, Al caught the first fish since the flood. After our meal, we checked our food supply and found that after twenty-three days all we had left was eight ounces of salt and four ounces of tea!

---

[2] The small ex-gold-rush town south of the Brooks Range, from which the men had set out.

When we struck the Nolan–Wiseman road late that afternoon, the last real hardship was over. At the top of the long grade from Wiseman Creek to the Middle Fork we saw our first human being in twenty-two days. Pete Dow, a hard-bitten cynical sourdough of thirty-two arctic winters, was standing beside his tent and greeted us enthusiastically. He told us there had been speculation during the past few days whether we would come back.

At seven-thirty in the evening, on August 16, we drew up in front of the roadhouse at Wiseman. A whole mob of people came out and welcomed us warmly, held the horses, and helped us unpack. Jack Hood, the owner of Brownie and Bronco, was there, too, grinning from ear to ear. They had been kidding him and saying that we had probably crossed over to Point Barrow and run off with the horses. Martin Slisco, the roadhouse proprietor, was more warm-hearted than ever; he kept slapping us on the back and laughing, and reiterating how relieved he was that we were back. There were many questions about the mysterious upper North Fork, which were very pleasant to answer. Martin soon had a delicious dinner ready, with caribou liver the *pièce de résistance*. We gorged ourselves, but then we had been traveling on pretty light rations for several days.

Adventure is wonderful, but there is no doubt that one of its joys is its end. That night, sitting in a dry room by a warm fire, we felt a pleasure unknown to anyone who has not experienced days on end of cold and soggy travel. Later, lying in bed with no rising rivers, no straying horses, no morrow's route to worry about, we enjoyed a delightful peacefulness.

CLYDE KLUCKHOHN

(1905–1960)

From *Beyond the Rainbow*

Clyde Kluckhohn would go on to become the outstanding Navajo ethnographer of his generation. In 1926, however, he was an undergraduate at the University of Wisconsin, consumed with a passion to explore blanks on the map. A National Geographic article fired his ambition to make his way to the top of fifty-mile-long Wild Horse Mesa (known today as Kaiparowits Plateau), located in an exceedingly remote part of southern Utah. No Anglos, Kluckhohn thought, had ever climbed the mesa, but the Anasazi, who had abandoned the region at the end of the thirteenth century, might well have built great cliff dwellings like the ones at Mesa Verde on top of the inaccessible plateau.

It took Kluckhohn and his young comrades three summers to realize their dream. Finally, on their third expedition, at the end of July 1928, after hazardous fords of the San Juan and Colorado Rivers, Kluckhohn, accompanied by pals Jim Hanks, Bill Gernon, Lauri Sharp, and Nel Hagan, as well as a Navajo guide, Hosteen Dogi, and assorted

mules and horses, reached the top of Wild Horse Mesa. The team
spent the next month exploring the plateau.

Failing to find any Cliff Palaces on Wild Horse, stunned to come
across the signatures of Mormon ranchers who had preceded them, the
Filthy Five (as they called themselves) almost abandoned their journey.
Yet as they lingered among the pines and junipers, making one quiet
discovery after another, the young explorers saw their adventure turn
into the idyll recounted in this excerpt. Kluckhohn's closing meditation,
in which he ponders the drawbacks of including the region in a proposed
national park, seems remarkably prescient: the top of Kaiparowits
Plateau today remains nearly as wild as it was in 1928.

Here in the cool sunlight and cold nights of a high altitude, under such stars and such a full moon as only the Southwestern heavens can hold, we spent wonderful weeks. Only after the tribulations of trail life can the joys of a permanent camp be fully appreciated. Here there was no longer the daily chore of packing and unpacking. No longer the struggle with pack animals under a dessicating sun. Our beds had their places. Our supplies remained in our kitchen under the trees. The spring, which the sun never reached, served as an ice-box. A rice pudding, heavy with raisins and flavored with lemon powder, placed there when we left camp in the morning was deliciously cold when we returned at night. Sometimes when we were a little tired after climbing into cliff dwellings we refreshed ourselves with lemonade—"like a bunch of softies," to use Bill's phrase.

In the best climactic tradition of moving picture plot development the Mesa revealed to us progressively and slowly, her antiquities. After discovering the archaic stone steps immediately upon our arrival, we expected that first day to find a ruin as great as Cliff Palace on Mesa Verde. In this we were disappointed. In our first rambles about camp we found no further evidence of prehistoric occupation. This must have been because we were too excited, for in covering the same ground the second day we found many flint chips and arrowheads. That, however, proved only that the Mesa had long been a hunting ground. But the third day I found one potsherd, and the fourth day we found many potsherds in a valley not far from the camp.

Our fifth day on the Mesa was a day of jubilation. Jim and I were working our way along through a particularly heavy growth of scrub oak and maple just under the Mesa's top cliff. We were looking for other springs like the one near our camp. Below a cave we came upon what were clearly, on close examination, another set of rude stone footholds. I said to Jim, "Boost me up." On the cave wall there was painted a huge turtle and two human figures. I shouted wildly to Jim, and gave him a hand. There were indications that there had been more pictographs which had been destroyed by exfoliation, but there was no evidence that the cave had been lived in. It was possible that these pictures represented only the surplus energy of a hunter whom bad weather had driven to the cave's shelter. But they were not the work of recent Navajo or Pahute hunters, for they were unlike the drawings which Navajoes occasionally scratch on the rocks, while they resembled the pictographs in Antelope Cave in Canyon del Muerto.[1] Moreover, the cave was directly beneath the valley where we had seen the fragments of old pottery.

Jim and I continued our search at this level under the Mesa rim, and not more than an hour later the same magic formula "Boost me up" resulted in another shout of joy and triumph. Here in the corner of a cave was a small storage cist built of large rock slabs and plastered with mud. But there was no other evidence of building in the cave. What did this lonely cist mean? Could it have been a storage place for piñon nuts, used by men who did not live on the Mesa but came here in the autumn to hunt and gather nuts? Against this hypothesis was the fact that the cave was too difficult of access from the top of the Mesa. A cache could have been more conveniently, and as securely, hidden on the Mesa's surface. Imagination advanced the theory that here for a time lived a lone outcast from his people. The roof

[1]The north branch of Canyon de Chelly, in northeast Arizona—full of Anasazi ruins.

of the cave showed no evidence of smoke. But that might well have been destroyed by weathering of the rock. Far back in the cave we found many cut sticks. None of us had even a theory which would plausibly explain their presence in such numbers.

Still we had found no dwelling. That came two days later on. All of us together were continuing the survey under the rim. We had seen evidence of occupation in many caves. Wedged in one rock fissure were shriveled corncobs and corn grains black with age. All along this ledge there was a slow seep which had once no doubt been a copious spring and the source of water supply to a whole community. Now we had to squeeze the moss which grew along the wall for our cold drink. Great piles of dung proved coyotes and other animals to be present occupants of these caves, but the indications were that once there had been an almost continuous village built along the ledge.

We had turned a bend—as always in the Southwest—when suddenly we saw high above us a most striking pictograph. In the same glance our eyes took in three fine buildings: the first irrefutable evidence of the ancient habitation of our Mesa. By the cold water seep below, among the lilies, wild honeysuckles, and blueberries were many pottery fragments, a few pieces almost whole.

The lone pictograph held us staring. It was in brilliant red, a color made from hematite iron, like that in the first pictograph we had found. But this was painted in a completely different style. To us then it suggested a great female goddess with a plumed helmet cap. We thought of the old tales in Navajo legend of "the white warrior woman who came up from the south" and "the Bride of the Sun on whom no other man ever looked."

The ruin was a clear forty feet above us. The builders must have had ladders which they carried up after them. Jim said "That climb doesn't look good to father." I tried it and decided it didn't look good to me either. After many a trial and some breathless climbing Lauri did get up to the houses, but the rest of us were content to examine from below. The buildings were small but sturdily and skilfully constructed. One was round and built into the rock wall, like a castle tower of Carcassonne.[2] This may well have been the fortress look-out for a whole community, or for a large pueblo on the Mesa surface. It had an outlook over an enormous range of country, and it could only have been approached to the attacker's disadvantage—from below. From the Mesa's surface no direct descent was possible. Indeed the site was invisible from above. More than once we had sat on the Mesa's point above these ruins and never dreamed of either caves or dwellings beneath.

If our favorite occupation was hunting cliff houses, Dogi's was stalking deer. The afternoon of our second day on Wild Horse Mesa, he and Jim had gone rabbit hunting with the shotgun and saw a deer. They came back in great excitement, and the next morning we all got up at dawn and went off deer hunting. Dogi was thoroughly disgusted because we insisted that the moving picture camera had to take precedence over the gun. Such depravity he couldn't understand. In any case there was small chance of violation of the game laws, for our 30-30 had had a share in the San Juan débacle, and the stock was so warped that one had to aim ten yards, more or less, to the right of the object one wanted to hit. Dogi never did get a deer, though he often came back with hunter's tales of how narrowly he had missed. Nor, in point of fact, did I ever get a moving picture of a deer. Whenever we saw deer, the machine had been left in camp—just as it was when I saw three coyotes slinking along a ledge, not twenty yards away. So I suppose it was, has ever been, and shall eternally be with cameras.

Dogi's interest in deer was partly caused by his craving for meat. We had only a limited supply of but two kinds—a cheap bacon called Saltside which Dogi devoured ravenously, and dried chunks of beef which had to be chipped and chopped with the axe like firewood, and could only be masticated after being stewed at least all night. Dogi enriched our larder by bringing in rabbits daily. His longing for meat was increasing, as we surmised one evening when he ate three rabbits before the rest of us could fin-

[2]A fortified town in southwestern France, one of the pivotal battlefields of the Albigensian Crusade.

ish two. So we were not surprised when he announced, after just a week on the Mesa, that he must return home to care for his horses and his little field of corn. He was clearly hungry for a proper diet and for people who spoke decent Navajo.

A day or two before his departure there was a big hocuspocus about signal fires. Down on the far north end of the Mesa he lit whole trees until we protested that he would be starting a forest fire. He said it was necessary to let his wives know he was leaving, and he claimed to see an answering smoke which we couldn't perceive at all. He was in high good humor the final evening because we had given him the useless 30-30, and as a proof of his friendliness and favor he allowed us to take flashlight pictures of him sitting in the family group around the campfire. The next morning, after we had given him flour, oatmeal, and rice for his return journey, he left us, benevolently calling "*Ah ha lani siccis*," "may all be well with you, my friends."

Dogi was a typical Navajo of the old school. His psychology was that of a child. Suspicious of the white man, he was as afraid of being cheated as a child might be who had had an unpleasant experience. His happiness was in song and dance. His hopes, like those of a small boy, fixed on the immediate possession of a horse, a gun. When we had thrown away some horseshoes, and some forks, which our table etiquette rendered useless, he had carefully cached them at Hole-in-the-Rock. He was curious about everything—about our reading Shakespeare aloud, about our writing in our journals, about our picture-taking. Like most conservative Navajoes, he thoroughly objected to being photographed himself. Thinking to capture his interest, I explained to him that the pictures I took were not ordinary still photographs, but that the subjects moved in them as in real life. Finally he understood. Then he was horrified:

"You take such a picture. You say you see me there—then a part of me must go on that picture," he said. "Then sometimes at night when the real I is asleep in my house, you show me to your friends at your house in the picture. I walk all the night in the picture. Next morning when I wake up at my house, I am all tired out. I die sooner because part of my strength works in your picture all the time. — *Tschindi!* The devil with that!"[3]

Dogi nevertheless was good-natured and he had a keen sense of humor. I think it was his delight in horse play which bound him to Hanks. They had a very special friendship. Jim's Navajo was limited, but he and Dogi used to sit for long hours about the campfire in earnest conversation, and the degree to which they understood each other was remarkable. Dogi told Jim all the intimate details about his two wives, one of whom was a Pahute. He seemed shocked that a healthy young fellow like Jim was unmarried and — reiterated again and again his opinion: "*Atin assan do ya shonde*," "No woman, no good." To Jim he repeated his other simple and direct strictures about life: "*O'l ta dah ai gissi do ya shonde*, Schoolboys are absolutely worthless; *Bah, bisoti, ya ta hey*, Bread and meat is the diet for any man."

Dogi left us, the only human beings within a radius of we didn't know how many miles. But honesty compels the admission that we found evidence of modern as well as ancient man. Near the spring by our own camp there were initials and dates carved on a basswood tree. Later we found the same initials in other spots. The fact that initials were carved proved how remote the Mesa was considered. Most of the dates were from 1925 and 1926. There was one from 1918. It is likely that about that time some cow outfit in Utah began pushing its cattle down toward this region, and some 'punchers followed stray cattle up on the Mesa.

One of them must have had archaeological interests, for we found the name "Ken Porter" scratched on the walls of Pictograph Cave and in several other sites on the east rim. Great was our disappointment, when Lauri found carved in the cliff dwelling of the Red Goddess: Tillman Felix, Arden Woolsey; February, 1928. We were just six months too late. Had only our 1927 try been successful! I have little doubt that the unknown Messrs. Felix

---

[3] This disquisition on Navajo temperament is the work of an adventurer in his twenties. Kluckhohn the anthropologist would later come to a far more sophisticated and less condescending grasp of Navajo culture.

and Woolsey were the first two white men on the north rim of Wild Horse
Mesa. Later on the west rim we found many ruins where there was no sign
that anyone had ever been since their owners had deserted them.

Over most of the surface of the Mesa where it was possible, and—as Lauri
maintained—in some places where it wasn't, there were cattle trails. We
often had cause to wish that cattle stood as tall as men, or that these had
been John Bunyan's oxen, or—best of all—that our skins were as tough as
cowhide. Cattle trails where one has to duck or be swept aside by jutting
branches are disastrous to naked hide and to temper.

Droopy,[4] whom we now occasionally rode, used perversely to head
straight for the obstacles, increasing her speed as she went. Our bronzed
backs were always streaked with red. We found no cow trails immediately
beneath the rim, but Jim and Lauri reported a few cows out on one Mesa
buttress, miles apparently, from the nearest water. We saw few cattle. All of
them were very wild. They probably saw a man only once yearly, at roundup time, if that often.

Those weeks of ours on Wild Horse Mesa were so strange and precious
an interlude in ordinary humdrum life partly because no other human beings were near. Once at night Dogi had pointed to a tiny gleam on a far
far horizon to the north and said "*Gomollon bi kon*, Mormon, his fire." But
otherwise we saw no signs of human life. And so we minded curiously little that others had been there before us. Had we known two years earlier
that the Mesa had already been visited, I think we should all have been less
eager. We should probably have decided to explore the Arizona strip or some
other locality where we were sure no white man had been. But now that
we were here the Mesa was so perfect, so absolute a thing in itself that
whether others had been here or not mattered no longer.

Had our introduction to this region been from the Utah side, we should
doubtless have heard of the cow outfits. The Mesa must be better known
in Utah. The next summer Lauri's mother and father looked from Bryce
Canyon and saw the Mesa dominating the eastern prospect. But, though

---

[4]One of the mules, also known as Ush Kush, Navajo for "sleepy."

the trading posts of the northern Navajo Reservation are as close in miles to the Utah ranches as they are to Flagstaff, the Colorado severs Utah and Arizona so completely that there is no exchange of news between north and south. We had been so long steeped in the Arizona beliefs about the Mesa that the finding of dates, initials, and cattle altered our fundamental attitudes but little. Psychologically, Wild Horse Mesa was still the one virgin outpost of the vanishing frontier. Psychologically we claimed the Mesa as our domain by right of discovery, and we had all the thrill in getting to know it that a Spanish Grandee or an English Cavalier must have had in exploring the unknown slice of New Spain or Virginia granted him by his King.

Establishing the geography of Wild Horse Mesa was as much fun as putting together a picture puzzle. At the end of ten days we had a fair idea of the general forms and topography north of our camp, but it was not until our explorations began to reach out west and south that the immensity of the Mesa acquired imaginative reality for us. Jim came back one day from a trip to the west rim and said "Buddy, you ain't seen the half of this mesa yet."

Wild Horse Mesa is remarkably architectural in design. It has roughly the form of a Gothic Cathedral fifty miles long and four thousand feet high, with enormous flying buttresses radiating out at extraordinarily regular intervals from the bench which encircles the Mesa like a wide even ribbon of drab gray-green. One can imagine this cathedral as lying squarely north and south with the apse overlooking the Colorado and directly facing Navajo Mountain. The end of the Mesa is a series of terraced blocks, broken by V-shaped valleys, the points of which define the apse chapels. Our camp was at the southeast point of the choir, the narrowest part of the Mesa. Since the choir has been formed by the erosion of the top rock formation, we from our camp could look down the Mesa, the full length of the choir, to where the east transept rose and lunged out. Apse and choir, and to a lesser extent the transepts, are broken into low valleys by drainage lines which to the west deepen into canyons. These canyons converge in a tremendous abyss, the great cliff of which marks the west transept. Our knowledge of the Mesa never extended beyond the transepts. Once we stood on a high point of the west transept and saw the nave — its line broken by a series of burnt-sienna cliffs rising steadily to the north and, far beyond on the skyline—far, far north in Utah . . . colossal plateaus.

To cover the more ground, we often divided into parties, one or more working the surface on horseback, while others climbed below the rim on foot. Jim and Lauri were specialists on the bench below our camp and on the Buttresses. Gothic Buttress, jutting out over the Colorado, was an excellent place for photography. Bridge Buttress (just below our camp) presented many geological problems. Its surface was like an ancient sea beach with shells, with bright-colored, rounded pebbles, with petrified logs and stumps and with hollow rocks which looked as if they had been blown up with gas so that they seemed like egg shells. The petrified logs were not so thoroughly agatized as those in the famous Arizona Forest.[5] They could be broken into small slivers. The outcrop on the side of the buttress showed brittle blocks of conglomerate, containing petrified wood, sponges, algae colonies and more sea-worn rocks and pebbles—the whole cemented together with sand which was sometimes coarse, sometimes fine. The natural bridge from which it got its name was formed by the falling away of conglomerate blocks. From our camp the bridge looked small as a needle's eye, but Lauri and Jim reported it twenty feet high and forty feet wide.

Each region had its own attractions. Indeed in all the Southwest no single spot is quite so rich and varied as Wild Horse Mesa. The Mesa might well be described as the Southwestern synthesis. It has its own natural bridge, petrified forest, painted desert, cliff ruins, and canyons. Piñon, cedar, pine, poplar, basswood, oak, maple; a plant like English ivy and many other plants and shrubs grew in the undergrowth beneath the rim; spiny, ground-clinging cacti and their antlered Brobdingnagian cousins, feathery chamiza, sage, greasewood, and mesquite—these supply the incredibly numerous nuances of green characteristic of the Southwest at various altitudes.

There is already a project on foot, agitated by Bernheimer, John Wetherill and others,[6] to turn the Rainbow Bridge region with Pahute and Segi

---

[5]Today Petrified Forest National Park, just east of Holbrook.

[6]At the time John Wetherill, of Kayenta, Arizona—the first white trader in the heart of the Navajo Reservation—knew the canyon country better than any other Anglo. His patron,

Canyons into a National Park. Department of the Interior officials have already made visits and studied the situation. In the proposed National Park, Wild Horse Mesa and a strip of encircling country ought certainly to be included.

Indeed, quite by itself, Wild Horse Mesa would offer a variety which no present park could surpass. For forest beauties it could not be compared with Yosemite or Glacier, for lyric beauty, with Rainier, for wild life with Yellowstone. If one were to compare it with any existing National Park, Mesa Verde is the obvious parallel. Its discovered antiquities are not so grand, it is true, but they seem to be as numerous. Wild Horse Mesa's general shape and contours, its rock formations, its canyons, its general geology and its outlook over the surrounding country, resemble Mesa Verde closely. But it is Mesa Verde on an exaggerated scale. The panoramas from the rim are more magnificent. Indeed for sublimity of scenery Wild Horse Mesa surpasses even Grand Canyon.

It must also be remembered that this is not a cheap scenery; it must be bought with time and sweat. But at Grand Canyon one does get cheap scenery in this sense. One can look down into Grand Canyon without having abandoned a single comfort or luxury, while the view from the rims of Wild Horse Mesa is purchased at high price, and perhaps is therefore understood and appreciated the more.

That is why I wonder if we want to make Wild Horse Mesa into a National Park, after all. At least I doubt if "Park" is the word. It suggests too much carefully built roads and elaborate regulations. Simply turn the Mesa into a national preserve denied to settlement. That is not a fantastic suggestion. The area of land involved is large, but is economically not of great value. Since there are, of course, no settlers on it now, there would be no question of land rights to be bought. All that would be necessary would be an Act of Congress withdrawing these public lands from the areas that may be homesteaded, and forbidding the building of roads. The last thing wanted is an appropriation for "developing" the area and for upkeep. To avoid later complications the boundaries ought doubtless to be surveyed, but other-

Manhattan businessman Charles Bernheimer, bankrolled a number of Wetherill expeditions and wrote a lyrical book called *Rainbow Bridge* about these outings.

wise let the surveyor and trail builder keep out. The one regulation that would be necessary would be: NO ROADS, NO BUILT TRAILS.

The Mesa ought also to be perpetually forbidden to airplane traffic. Jim used to horrify us by mapping out landing fields. Airplanes are very marvelous and very useful, but they and the other instruments of our technical civilization are destroying all too quickly the type of conditions out of which American character developed. Let us leave for coming generations this one corner where they can approach the feelings their ancestors had during the winning of the West. How else can we draw near to those who shaped America? . . .

No one would deny that our present system of National Parks is a fine achievement and a precious possession. The idea is one of the best and most American contributions to general culture. One may well admire the means by which natural glories have been made accessible to so large a number of citizens. But there are some Americans for whom smartly uniformed, courteous, intelligent rangers and well-built, well-marked roads and trails hold small attraction. We may rejoice that the Parks are so popular with the American people as recreation centers, and yet we may ourselves be frightened away by the statistics of how many hundred thousand visit a park every season. The Parks seem a little too near commercialized wilderness.

Wild Horse Mesa, if protected against the encroachment of civilization, would not merely be a dynamic and creative memorial of the old West. Its prehistoric remains would attract the archaeologist. For comparative study the botanist would have here, a cross-section of the vegetation of semi-arid regions. The geologist would find petrified forests, faults, coal seams, and a 4,000-foot outcrop presenting unusual structural problems. He would be able to observe from a new point of vantage one of the greatest geographical phenomena in the whole world—the erosional work of the Colorado River system. The naturalist, amateur or professional, could occupy himself with rabbits, coyotes, wildcats, deer, mountain sheep, uncommon varieties of chipmunk and squirrel; eagles, hawks, wild duck, snipe and other water birds, wrens, flickers, humming birds, piñon jays, bluebirds, goldfinches, mourning doves, swallows, owls, thrushes. The ruins, the fine springs and cool caves, the delightful climate, the fair timbered valleys would charm every wanderer.

H. M. TOMLINSON

(1873–1958)

From *The Sea and the Jungle*

One of the consultants for this anthology, Randy Wayne White, felt so
passionate about The Sea and the Jungle *that he volunteered to write
his own introductory note.*

   "Although Henry Major Tomlinson died in 1958 at the age of eighty-
five, I owe this English journalist, war correspondent, and gentleman
a debt of gratitude. Over the years, he's introduced me to two of my most
trusted friends as well as a half dozen like-minded traveling companions. How? When writers, wanderers, and other undependable types
meet, our conversations follow predictable paths: exchange rates, good
billets, unpleasant border guards, beers of choice, and travel books we
admire. On the rare, rare occasion when someone tells me that Tomlinson's The Sea and the Jungle *is among his or her favorite travel books,
then I know I have met a kindred soul. I know that the person will have
a linear appreciation of natural history and a sense of humor. I know
that he or she has an eye for detail and a love of unsentimental prose.*

I also know that he or she will be something else that is rare indeed: a first-rate travel partner.

"The Sea and the Jungle *is Tomlinson's brilliant narrative of a voyage he took during the years 1909 and 1910. It is the story of the tramp steamer* Capella *and her crew on a journey from Swansea, England, to Brazil, and then two thousand miles through the forests of the Amazon (here called Orellana) and Madeira Rivers to the San Antonio falls before returning to Tampa, Florida, by way of Jamaica. The excerpt that follows, in which the* Capella *ports at Belém, capital of the region Pará, in Brazil, demonstrates the writer's gifts for description and for capturing odd characters, and his love of irony.*

"*It's my guess that Tomlinson must have been a fine travel companion, though he was an unlikely choice with whom to bushwhack the rain forest. For one thing, he was British to his bones, so much so that it is written the man never went outside without his black bowler hat. Also, he was deaf. Perhaps that is why he writes so vividly about textures of light and odor.*

"*Tomlinson grew up in the East End of London where he spent his life working as a shipping clerk, a journalist, a war correspondent, a newspaper editor, and then as a travel writer and novelist. His first books were largely ignored at the time of their printing, but his travel books have always maintained a devoted audience. There are not many of us, which is why I am so pleased to play a small role in introducing them to the readers of this new century. On winter nights, when an Arctic wind blows down out of the stars, I still delight in sitting by the fire in my old Florida home and rereading tales of the tramp steamer* Capella. *Tomlinson is dead, but his prose has not aged.*"

At eight this morning we crossed the equator. I paid my footing in whisky, and forgot all about the equator. Soon after that, while idling under the poop awning, I picked up the Doctor's book from his vacant chair. I took the essays of Emerson carelessly and read at once—

the sage plainly had set a trap for me — "Why covet a knowledge of new facts? Day and night, a house and garden, a few books, a few actions, serve as well as all trades and spectacles." So —— At this very moment the first mate crossed my light, and presently I heard the sounding machine whir, and then stop. There was a pause, and then the mate's uplifted but unimportant voice, "Twenty-five fathoms, sir, grey sand!"

Emerson went sprawling. I stood up. Twenty-five fathoms! Then that grey sand stuck to the tallow of the weight was the first of the Brazils. The circle of waters was still complete about us, but over the bows, at a great distance, were thunder clouds and wild lights. The oceanic swell had decreased to a languid and glassy beat, and the water had become jade green in colour, shot with turquoise gleams. The Skipper, himself interested and almost jolly, announced a pound of tobacco to the first man who sighted the coast. We were nearing it at last. Those far clouds canopied the forests of the Amazon. We stood in at slow speed.

I know those forests. I mean I have often navigated their obscure waterways, rafting through the wilds on a map, in my slippers, at night. Now those forests soon were to loom on a veritable skyline. I should see them where they stood, their roots in the unfrequented floods. I should see Santa Maria de Belém, its aerial foliage over its shipping and squalor. It was quite near now. I should see Santarem and Obydos, and Ita-coatiara; and then, turning from the King of Rivers to his tributary, the Madeira, follow the Madeira to the San Antonio falls in the heart of the South American continent. We draw over 23 feet, with this *Capella*. We are going to try what has never before been attempted by an ocean steamer. This, too, was pioneering. I also was on an adventure, going two thousand miles under those clouds of the equatorial rains, to live for a while in the forests of the Orellana. And our vessel's rigging, so they tell me, sometimes shall drag the foliage in showers to our decks, and where we anchor at night the creatures of the jungle will call.

Our nearness to land stirs up some old dreads in our minds also. We discuss those dreads again, though with more concern than we did at Swansea. Over the bows is now the prelude. We have heard many unsettling legends of yellow fever, malaria, blackwater fever, dysentery and beri-beri. The mates, looking for land, swear they were fools to come a voyage like this. They ought to have known better. The Doctor, who does not always smile when he is amused, advises us not to buy a white sun umbrella at Para, but a black one; then it will do for the funerals.

"Land Ho!" That was the Skipper's own perfunctory cry. He had saved his pound of tobacco.

It was two in the afternoon. There was America. I rediscovered it with some difficulty. All I could see was a mere local thickening of the horizon, as though the pen which drew the faint line dividing the world ahead into an upper and a nether opalescence had run a little freely at one point. That thickening of the horizon was the island of Monjui. Soon, though, there was a palpable something athwart our course. The skyline heightened into a bluish barrier, which, as we approached it, broke into sections. The chart told us that a chain of low wooded islands skirt the mainland. Yet it was hard to believe we were approaching land again. What showed as land was of too unsubstantial a quality, too thin and broken a rind on that vast area of water to be of any use as a foothold. Where luminous sky was behind an island groups of diminutive palms were seen, as tiny and distinct as the forms of mildew under a magnifying glass, delicate black pencillings along the foot of the sky-wall. Often that hair-like tracery seemed to rest upon the sea. The *Capella* continued to stand in, till America was more than a frail and tinted illusion which sometimes faded the more the eye sought it. Presently it cast reflections. The islands grew into cobalt layers, with vistas of silver water between them; they acquired body. The course was changed to west, and we cruised along for Atalaia Point, towards the pilot station. Over the thin and futile rind of land which topped the sea—it was thin enough to undulate on the low swell—ponderous thunder clouds towered, continents of night in the sky, with translucent areas dividing them which were brightly illuminated from the hither side. Curtains as black as bitumen draped to the waters from great heights. Two of these appalling curtains, trailing over America, were drawn a little apart. We could see beyond them to a diminishing array of glowing cloud summits; far through those parted black curtains of storm we saw an accidental revelation of a secret and wonderful region with a sun of its own. And all, gigantic clouds, the sea, the far and frail coast, were serene and still. The air had ceased to breathe. I thought this new lucent world we had found might prove but a lucky dream after all, to be seen but not to be entered, and that some noise would presently shatter it and wake me. But we came alongside the white pilot schooner, and the pilot put off in a boat manned by such a crowd of grinning, ragged, and cinnamon skinned pirates as would have broken the fragile wonder of any spell. Ours, though, did not break, and I was able to believe we had arrived. At sunset the great clouds were full of explosions of electric fire, and there were momentary revelations above us of huge impending shapes. We went slowly over a lower world obscurely lighted by phosphorescent waves.

IT WAS NOT easy to make out, before sunrise, what it was we had come to. I saw a phantom and indeterminate country; but as though we had guessed that it was suspicious and observant, and its stillness a device, we moved forward slowly and noiselessly, as a thief at an entrance. Low level cliffs were near to either beam. The cliffs might have been the dense residue of the night. The night had been precipitated from the sky, which was clearing and brightening. Our steamer was between banks of these iron shades.

Suddenly the sunrise ran a long band of glowing saffron over the shadow to port, and the vague summit became remarkable with a parapet of black filigree, crowns and fronds of palms and strange trees showing in rigid patterns of ebony. A faint air then moved from off shore as though under the impulse of the pouring light. It was heated and humid, and bore a curious odour, at once foreign but familiar, the smell of damp earth, yet not of the earth I knew, and of vegetation, but of vegetation exotic and wild. For a time it puzzled me that I knew the smell; and then I remembered where we had met before. It was in the palm house at Kew Gardens. At Kew that odour once made a deeper impression on me than the extraordinary vegetation itself, for as a boy I thought that I inhaled the very spirit of the tropics of which it was born. After the first minute on the Para River that smell went, and I never noticed it again.

Full day came quickly to show me the reality of one of my early visions, and I suppose I may not expect many more such minutes as I spent when watching from the *Capella's* bridge the forest of the Amazon take shape. It was soon over. The morning light brimmed at the forest top, and spilled into the river. The channel filled with sunshine. There it was then. In the cliff to starboard I could see even the boughs and trunks; they were veins of silver in a mass of solid chrysolite. This forest had not the rounded and dull verdure of our own woods in midsummer, with deep bays of shadow. It was a sheer front, uniform, shadowless, and astonishingly vivid. I thought then the appearance of the forest was but a local feature, and so gazed at it for what it would show next. It had nothing else to show me. Clumps of palms threw their fronds above the roof of the forest in some places, or a giant exogen raised a dome; but that was all. Those strong characters in the growth were seen only in passing. They did not change that outlook ahead of converging lines of level green heights rising directly from a brownish flood. Occasionally the river narrowed, or we passed close to one wall, and then we could see the texture of the forest surface, though we could never see into it for more than a few yards, except where, in some places, habitations were thrust into the base of the woods, as in lower caverns. An exuberant wealth of forms built up that forest which was so featureless from a little distance. The numerous palms gave grace and life to the façade, for their plumes flung in noble arcs from tall and slender columns, or sprayed directly from the ground in emerald fountains. The rest was inextricable confusion. Vines looped across the front of green, binding the forest with cordage, and the roots of epiphytes hung from upper boughs like hanks of twine.

At times the river widened into lagoons, and we might have been in a maze of islands. Canoes shot across the waterways, and river schooners, shaped very like junks, with high poops and blue and red sails, were diminished beneath the verdure, and betrayed the great height of the woods.

The lines of the forest, contracting in a long vista, did not suggest its great height until you saw a ship beneath a near wall of the woods. The scene was so luminous, still, and voiceless, it was so like a radiant mirage, or a vivid remembrance of an emotional dream got from books read and read again, that only the unquestionable verity of our iron steamer, present with her smoke and prosaic gear, convinced me that what was outside us was there. Across a hatch a large butterfly hovered and flickered like a flame. Dragonflies were suspended over our awning, jewels in shimmering enamels.

WE ANCHORED JUST before breakfast, and a small launch flying a large Brazilian flag was soon fussing at our gangway. The Brazilian customs men boarded us, and the official who was left in charge to overlook the *Capella* while we were anchored off Para was a tall and majestic Latin with dark eyes of such nobility and brooding melancholy that I considered our doctor, who has travelled much, was a fellow with a dull Anglo-Saxon mind when he removed some loose property to his cabin and locked his door, before he went ashore. So I left my field-glasses on the ice-chest; and that was the last I saw of them. Yet that fellow had such lovely hair, as the ladies would say, and his smile and his courtesy were right for a prince. He carried a scented pink handkerchief and wore patent leather boots. Our surgeon had but a faint laugh when these explanations were made to him, taking my hand fondly, and saying he loved little children.

Para, a flat congestion of white buildings and red roofs in the sun, was about a mile beyond our anchorage, over the port bow; and as its name has been to me one that had the appeal of the world not ours, like Tripolo of Barbary, Macassar, the Marquesas and the Río Madre de Díos, the agent's launch, as it took us towards the small craft lying immediately before the front of that spread of houses between the river and the forest, was so momentous an occasion that the small talk of the dainty Englishmen in linen suits, a gossiping group around the agent and the Skipper, hardly came into the picture, to my mind. The launch rudely hustled through a cluster of gaily painted native boats, the dingiest of them bearing some sonorous name, and I landed in Brazil.

There was an esplanade, shadowed by an avenue of mangoes. We crossed that, and went along hot narrow streets, by blotched and shabby walls, to the office to which our ship was consigned. We met a fisherman carrying a large turtle by a flipper. We came to a dim cool warehouse. There, some negroes and half-breeds were lazily hauling packages in the shadows. It had an office railed off where a few English clerks, in immaculate white, over-looked a staff of natives. The warehouse had a strange and memorable odour, evasive, sweet, and pungent, as barbaric a note as I found in Para, and I understood at once I had come to a place where there were things I did not know. I felt almost timorous and yet compelled when I sniffed at those shadows; though what the eye saw in the squalid streets of the river-side, where brown folk stood regarding us carelessly from openings in the walls, I had thought no more than a little interesting.

What length of time we should have in Belém was uncertain, but presently the Skipper, looking most morose, came away from his discussion with the agent and told us, at some length, what he thought of people who kept a ship waiting because of a few unimportant papers. Then he mumbled, very reluctantly, that we had plenty of time to see all Para. The Doctor and I were out of that office before the Skipper had time to change his mind. Our captain is a very excellent master mariner, but occasionally he likes to test the security of his absolute autocracy, to learn whether it is still sound. I never knew it when it was not; but yet he must, to assure himself of a certainty, or to exercise some devilish choler in his nature, sometimes beat our poor weak bodies against the adamant thing, to see which first will break. I will say for him that he is always polite when handing back to us our bruised fragments. Here he was giving us a day's freedom, and one's first city of the tropics in which to spend it; and we agreed with him that such a waste of time was almost unbearable, and left hurriedly.

Outside the office was a small public square where grew palms which ran flexible boles, swaying with the weight of their crowns, clear above the surrounding buildings, overshadowing them, except in one place, where the front of a ruinous church showed, topped by a crucifix. The church, a white and dilapidated structure, was hoary with ficus and other plants which grew from ledges and crevices. Through the crowns of the palms the sunlight fell in dazzling lathes and partitions, chequering the stones. An ox-cart stood beneath.

The Paraenses, passing by at a lazy gait—which I was soon compelled to imitate—in the heat, were puzzling folk to one used to the features of a race of pure blood, like ourselves. Portuguese, negro, and Indian were there, but rarely a true type of one. Except where the black was the predominant factor the men were impoverished bodies, sallow, meagre, and listless; though there were some brown and brawny ruffians by the foreshore. But the women often were very showy creatures, certainly indolent in movement, but not listless, and built in notable curves. They were usually of a richer colour than their mates, and moved as though their blood were of a quicker temper. They had slow and insolent eyes. The Indian has given them the black hair and brown skin, the negro the figure, and Portugal their features and eyes. Of course, the ladies of Para society, boasting their straight Portuguese descent, are not included in this insulting description; and I do not think I saw them. Unless, indeed, they were the ladies who boldly eyed us in the fashionable Para hotel, where we lunched, at a great price, off imported potatoes, tinned peas, and beef which in England would be sold to a glue factory; I mean the women in those Parisian costumes erring something on the side of emphasis, and whose remarkable pallor was even a little greenish in the throat shadows.

After lunch some disappointment and irresolution crept into our holiday. There had been a time—but that was when Para was only in a book; that was when its mere printed name was to me a token of the tropics. You know the place I mean. You can picture it. Paths that go at noon but a little way into the jungle which overshadows an isolated community of strange but kindly folk, paths that end in a twilight stillness; ardent hues, flowers of vanilla, warm rain, a luscious and generative earth, fireflies in the scented dusk of gardens; and mystery, every outlook disappearing in the dark of the unknown.

Well, here I was, placed by the ordinary moves of circumstance in the very place the name of which once had been to me like a chord of that music none hears but oneself. I stood in Para, outside a picture postcard shop. Electric cars were bumping down a narrow street. The glitter of a cheap jeweller's was next to a stationer's; and on the other side was a vendor of American and Parisian boots. There have been changes in Para since Bates[1] wrote his idylls of the forest. We two travellers, after ordering some red earthenware chatties, went to find Bates' village of Nazareth. In 1850 it was a mile from the town. It is part of the town now, and an electric tram took us there, a tram which drove vultures off the line as it bumped along. The heat was a serious burden. The many dogs, which found energy enough to limp out of the way of the car only when at the point of death, were thin and diseased, and most unfortunate to our nice eyes. The Brazilian men of better quality we passed were dressed in black suits, and one mocked the equator with a silk hat and yellow boots. I set down these things as the tram showed them. The evident pride and haughtiness, too, of these Latins, surprised one of a stronger race. We stopped at a street corner, and this was Nazareth. Bates' pleasant hamlet is now the place of Para's fashionable homes—pleasant still, though the overhead tram cables, and the electric light standards which interrupt the avenues of trees, place you there, now your own turn comes to look for the romance of the tropics, in another century. But the walls of the villas are in heliotrope, primrose, azure, and rose, and are bowered in extravagant arbors of papaws, mangoes, bananas, and palms, with shrubberies beneath of feathery mimosas, and cassias with orange and crimson blooms. And my last walk ashore was in Swansea High Street in the winter rain! From Nazareth's main street the side turnings go down to the forest. For, in spite of its quays, its steamers, and its electric trams, Para is built in but a larger clearing of the wilderness. The jungle stood at the bottom of all the suburban streets, a definite city wall. The spontaneity and savage freedom of the plant life in this land of alternate hot sun and warm showers at last blurred and made insignificant to me the men who braved it in silk hats and broadcloth there, and the trams, and the jew-

[1] Henry Walter Bates (1825–1892), author of *The Naturalist on the River Amazon*.

ellers' shops, for my experience of vegetation was got on my knees in a London suburb, praying things to come out of the cold mud. Here, I began to suspect, they besieged us, quick and turbulent, an exhaustible army, ready to reconquer the foothold man had hardly won, and to obliterate his works.

We passed through byways, where naked brown babies played before the doors. We happened upon the cathedral, and went on to the little dock where native vessels rested on garbage, the tide being out. Vultures pulled at stuff beneath the bilges. The crews, more Indian than anything, and men of better body than the sallow fellows in the town, sprawled on the hot stones of the quays and about the decks. There was a huge negress, arms akimbo, a shapeless monument in black india rubber draped in cotton print, who talked loudly with a red boneless mouth to two disregarding Indians sitting with their backs to a wall. She had a hare's foot, mounted in silver, hanging between her dugs. The schooners, ranged in an arcade, were rigged for lateen sails, very like Mediterranean craft. The forest was a narrow neutral-tinted ribbon far beyond. The sky was blue, the texture of porcelain. The river was yellow. And I was grievously disappointed; yet if you put it to me I cannot say why. There was something missing, and I don't know what. There was something I could not find; but as it is too intangible a matter for me to describe even now, you may say, if you like, that the fault was with me, and not with Para. We stood in a shady place, and the Doctor was looking down at his hand, and suddenly he struck it. "Let us go," he said. He showed me the corpse of a mosquito. "Have you ever seen the yellow fever chap?" the Doctor asked. "That is he." We left.

Near the agent's office we met an English shipping clerk, and he took us into a drink shop, and sat us at a marble-topped table that had gilded iron legs, and he called for gin tonics. We began to tell him what we thought of Para. It did not seem much of a place. It was neither here nor there.

He was a pallid fellow with a contemplative smile, and with weary eyes and tired movements. "I know all that," he said. "It's a bit of a hole. Still—you'd be surprised. There's a lot here you don't see at first. It's big. All out there"—he waved his arm west inclusively—"it's a world with no light yet. You get lost in it. But you're going up. You'll see. The other end of the forest is as far from the people in the streets here as London is—it's farther—and they know no more about it. I was like you when I first came. I gave the place a week, and then reckoned I knew it near enough. Now, I'm—well, I'm half afraid of it . . . not afraid of anything I can see . . . I don't know. There's something damn strange about it. Something you can never find out. It's something that's been here since the beginning, and it's too big and strong for us. It waits its time. I can feel it now. Look at those palm trees, outside. Don't they look as if they're waiting? What are they waiting for? You get that feeling here in the afternoon when you can't get air, and the rain clouds are banking up round the woods, and nothing moves. 'Lord,' said a fellow to me when I first came, 'tell us about Peckham.[2] But for the spicy talk about yellow fever I'd think I was dead and waiting wide awake for the judgment day.' That's just the feeling. As if something dark was coming and you couldn't move. There the forest is, all round us. Nobody knows what's at the back of it. Men leave Para, and go up river. We have a drink in here, and they go up river, and don't come back.

"Down by the square one day I saw an old boy in white ducks and a sun helmet having a shindy with the sentry at the barracks. The old fellow was kicking up a dust. He was English, and I suppose he thought the sentry would understand him, if he shouted. English and Americans do.

"You have to get into the road here, when you approach the barracks. It's the custom. The sentry always sends you off the pavement. The old chap was quite red in the face about it. And the things he was saying! Lucky for him the soldier didn't know what he meant. So I went over, as he was an Englishman, and told him what the sentry wanted. 'What,' said the man, 'walk in the road? Not me. I'd sooner go back.'

"Go back he did, too. I walked with him and we got rather pally. We came in here. We sat at that table in the corner. He said he was Captain Davis, of Barry. Ever heard of him? He said he had brought out a shallow-draught river boat, and he was taking her up the Rio Japura. The way he talked! Do you know the Japura? Well, it's a deuce of a way from here. But that old

[2]A district in London.

captain talked—he talked like a child. He was so obstinate about it. He was going to take that boat up the Japura and you'd have thought it was above Boulter's Lock.[3] Then he began to swear about the Dagoes.

"The old chap got quite wild again when he thought of that soldier. He was a little man, nothing of him, and his face was screwed up as if he was always annoyed about something. You have to take things as they come, here, and let it go. But this Davis man was an irritable old boy, and most of his talk was about money. He said he was through with the boat running jobs. No more of 'em. It was as bare as boards. Nothing to be made at the game, he said. Over his left eye he had a funny hairy wart, a sort of knob, and whenever he got excited it turned red. I may say he let me pay for all the drinks. I reckon he was pretty close with his money.

"He told me he knew a man in Barry who'd got a fine pub—a little gold-mine. He said there was a stuffed bear at the pub and it brought lots of customers. Seemed to think I must know the place. He said he was going to try to get an alligator for the chap who kept the pub. The alligator could stand on its hind legs at the other side of the door, with an electric bulb in its mouth, like a lemon. That was his fine idea. He reckoned that would bring customers. Then old Davis started to fidget about. I began to think he wanted to tell me something, and I wondered what the deuce it was. I thought it was money. It generally is. At last he told me. He wanted one of those dried Indian heads for that pub. 'You know what I mean,' he said. 'The Indians kill somebody, and make his head smaller than a baby's, and the hair hangs down all round.'

"Have you ever seen one of those heads? The Indians bone 'em, and stuff 'em with spice and gums, and let 'em dry in the sun. They don't look nice. I've seen one or two.

"But I tried to persuade him to let the head go. The Government has stopped that business, you know. Got a bit too thick. If you ordered a head, the Johnnies would just go out and have somebody's napper.

"I missed old Davis after that. I was transferred to Manaos, up river. I don't

[3]On the River Thames, in Maidenhead, England.

know what became of him. It was nearly a year when I came back to Para. Our people had had the clearing of that boat old Davis brought out, and I found some of his papers, still unsettled. I asked about him, in a general way, and found he hadn't arrived. His tug had been back twice. When it was here last it seemed the native skipper explained that Davis went ashore, when returning, at a place where they touched for rubber. He went into the village and didn't come back. Well, it seems the Skipper waited. No Davis. So he tootled his whistle and went on up stream, because the river was falling, and he had some more stations to do in the season. He was at the village again in a few days, though, and Davis wasn't there then. The tug captain said the village was deserted, and he supposed the old chap had gone down river in another boat. But he's not back yet. The boss said the fever had got him, somewhere. That's the way things go here.

"A month ago an American civil engineer touched here, and had to wait for a boat for New York. He'd been right up country surveying for some job or another, Peru way. I went up to his hotel with the fellows to see him one evening. He was on his knees packing his trunks. 'Say, boys,' he said, sitting on the floor, 'I brought a whole lot of truck from way up river, and now I don't know why.' He offered us his collection of butterflies. Then the Yankee picked up a ball of newspaper off the floor, and began to peel it. 'This goes home,' he said. 'Have you seen anything like that? I bet you haven't.' He held out the opened packet in his hand, and there was a brown core to it. 'I reckon that is thousands of years old,' said the American.

"It was a little dried head, no bigger than a cricket ball, and about the same colour. Very like an Indian's too. The features were quite plain, and there was a tiny wart over the left eyebrow. 'I bet you that's thousands of years old,' said the American. 'I'll bet you it isn't two,' I said."

• • •

ERIC HANSEN

(b. 1948)

"On Foot Towards the Highlands"

From *Stranger in the Forest: On Foot Across Borneo*

By heading alone, with very little gear, into the rain forest of Borneo in 1982, American vagabond Eric Hansen submitted to an experience that used to be the fate more often of field anthropologists than of adventurers. Hansen's goal was not so much to get anywhere in particular as to learn his way around this daunting wilderness by becoming the helpless protégé of the Penan—reclusive nomads who had fought the hardest of all Borneo indigenes against civilization and Christian missionaries.

It is Hansen's gift not to let the odd touches of acculturation—such as the Penan man he finds wearing a Beatles T-shirt—obscure the profound cultural exchange he underwent by agreeing to be led and taught by these forest dwellers. Robyn Davidson, who had undertaken a similar solo trek by camel across the western desert of Australia, said of Hansen: "Only a consummate traveler or lunatic would set off alone across Borneo with nothing but a pair of ratty sand shoes and a knapsack full of trading goods."

T hat morning I decided to put away my map. With maximum views of about fifty feet beneath the jungle canopy, it wasn't much use. In eight to ten hours of walking each day, we were covering fewer than four miles; on the map that was represented by about one-quarter inch. John Bong said he could tell direction by the network of streams, by where on the tree a certain vine grew, and from brief views of the sun.[1] All the vines looked the same to me, and since I spent most of my time looking at the ground immediately in front of my feet, I simply followed as best I could.

The morning tea began to boil in its bamboo kettle. Seated by the fire, we could glimpse a rare, distant view between the trees. Thick clouds of steam were rising from the jungle valleys five hundred feet below. Silhouetted against this sea of white billowing clouds a pair of black Brahminy kites (*Halastur indus*) circled briefly then drifted from sight. For a moment their shrill cries continued to hang in the air, then it was again silent. I finished mending a tear in my running shoes with nylon fishing line, removed two leeches and flicked them into the fire, and handed out shotgun shells for the day's hunting.

Our plan for this day, as with every other, was to walk for about eight hours; yet no one was in any hurry to get started. We joked about the previous night's rainstorm, which had left us cold and shivering throughout the night. By contrast, the early morning hours seemed especially pleasant. Our bedsheets were spread out to dry in three different patches of sunlight. Tingang Na cracked open the section of charred bamboo filled with a leaf-wrapped tube of rice and succulent morsels of fatty pig meat.[2] He tapped this mixture onto a broad communal leaf, and we squatted in a circle, eating with our fingers.

The week we had spent in each other's company made me realize how helpless and dependent I was: I had no jungle skills, and as a result, my ad-

---

[1]John Bong is a relatively acculturated, village-dwelling Penan man whom Hansen hires to guide him into the rain forest to make contact with the truly nomadic Penan.

[2]Like John Bong, Tingang Na is another village-dwelling Penan whom Hansen hires as his second guide.

miration for John and Tingang Na grew each day. Their uncanny and seemingly effortless ability to live off the jungle filled me with excitement and wonder. This was a feeling that would never leave me. A piece of thin bark placed between two small river rocks became a drinking fountain; a leaf plucked off a certain tree, folded double, and sucked on to create a vibrating sound, would call the inquisitive barking deer (*Muntiacus muntjak*) to within shotgun range; a vine known as *kulit elang*, when pounded and dipped in water and scrubbed on our ankles, would keep leeches from climbing up our legs. As we advanced through the rain forest, fruit trees laden with loquats, giant grapefruit, durians, mangosteens, guavas, rambutans, and jackfruit appeared at regular intervals, and it rarely took more than an hour to set up camp and collect food. It was so easy—in the company of experts. On my own I would have died of hunger.

The jungle was vibrant and dynamic with a pulse of its own. For those who were sensitive to that rhythm, the jungle was bountiful and kind; for me, it remained a maze of obstacles for months. I didn't know how to blend in. I was charmed, but at the same time overwhelmed by the complex struggle of simply surviving on a day-to-day basis.

About an hour after sunrise we shouldered our packs and started off. The weight of the rice we had consumed was offset by the addition of dried fish, smoked meat, and a growing collection of plants. Certain varieties had medicinal value and could be used in trade. I was planning on paying for part of my journey by collecting these plants and selling them.

At midmorning, as we traversed a steep slope covered with waist-high brachiated ferns, John pointed to a jungle creeper that he called, in Penan, *tawan-turok*. Also, he referred to the vine as *obat ular*, Malay for "the snake medicine." When the vine was pounded to a pulp and applied to the bite, it acted as a general antivenin. Powdered gramophone records were another common remedy. For snakebites we carried a more popular cure, wooden matches, which could be ignited and plunged into the puncture wounds to "kill" the poison.

Climbing to the top of the slope, at about four thousand feet, we entered a fine example of moss forest. Gigantic epiphytes—clinging plants such as orchids, ferns, and mosses that attach themselves to other plants—had covered every branch and tree trunk with a thick, shaggy coat of green. John uprooted a plant and brought it to me. It was *gerangau mereh* (*Boesenbergia*, an unidentified species of grass), one of the most valuable medicinal plants in the rain forest. It is chewed or mashed and brewed into a sweet-smelling but bitter-tasting tea. A mild stimulant, it is used for upset stomach, nausea, headache, and lower-back pain. *Gerangau mereh* is collected mainly because it is the only known cure for a rice-wine hangover. During the two- to three-day nonstop rice-harvest parties, *gerangau mereh* becomes fantastically expensive: two finger lengths of dried root can be sold for a price equivalent to one day's labor. Where we were standing, the plant grew abundantly. We removed our packs and set about collecting twenty pounds of roots, roughly equivalent to six months' wages when sold by the piece.

We rinsed the roots in a narrow, leaf-choked stream and continued walking while John told me about *kayu hujan panas* (literally, hot rainwater wood). I was cautioned not to step over a fallen stick of this wood on the trail. When I asked why, John replied, "Your balls will become painfully swollen, and you won't be able to walk."

The antidote for swollen balls, I learned, was to drink a tea made from the scraped bark. There were other uses for the wood too: a piece of *kayu hujan panas* placed in the attic of a new longhouse would ward off evil spirits, and a small piece carried as a charm would keep poisonous snakes away. Until recently this wood was commonly used to prevent paralysis that comes as a result of being caught in a daylight rain shower during a rainbow. The tea is still given to Malay women after childbirth. To collect *kayu hujan panas*, you turn your back to the plant—being careful to shade it from the sun with your body—then grasp it with both hands and uproot it. Later that day I was handed a small piece of root, which I kept in my pack until I left the rain forest five months later.

Before Christian burials became common in the highlands at the end of World War II, the dead were placed in wooden coffins and allowed to rot on the longhouse porch. Holes were punched in the bottom of the coffins and bamboo poles inserted to allow for drainage. It was considered an expression of love and respect to put up with the stench of putrefying flesh. Each day at noon *kayu udjung panas* would be burned to scare away the spirit, the departed soul, and, it was hoped, some of the frightful smell.

We would often walk for hours without speaking, except to make brief comments on the terrain or the number of leeches. One day I removed more than one hundred leeches from my right leg; I didn't even bother to count those on my left. The best way I found to get rid of leeches was to pull them off and roll them between my fingertips for a few moments. They became disoriented, released their grip, and could be easily flicked off. Otherwise they were like trying to get adhesive tape off my fingers.

When the walking became really rough, both John and Tingang Na would encourage me by repeating the words *hati, hati.* In my dictionary *hati* meant liver. What sort of message, I asked myself, were they trying to convey with the expression "liver, liver." Later I discovered that in Malaysia and Indonesia the liver is considered to be the emotional center of the body, as the heart is for Westerners. "*Hati, hati*" meant "Take courage, have a strong heart." There were other uses for the word *hati.* I once heard a woman referred to as *bagus dan murah hati* (good and inexpensive liver), which meant she gave of her emotions freely—a warm, generous person. If a person had *sakit hati* (sick liver), he or she was cruel and conniving. Practitioners of black magic have very sick livers.

Despite total concentration I managed to stumble and fall heavily on my face and backside at least ten times each day. My shins, knees, elbows, and shoulders soon became battered from many falls. Although I usually walked between my guides, watching their footsteps, it took weeks to recognize footholds properly. Innocent-looking river rocks were treacherously unstable and covered with a slippery invisible film. Eventually I assumed every step of the way was unsafe until proven otherwise. On the steep, clay slopes it was important to learn how to use the tangled, exposed tree roots to improve my footholds; edging my shoes and skidding down mud slopes was like skiing, except for the total lack of control. I slid down muddy trails, hands grabbing the air, as long trailing vines reached out to trip and choke me as well as to rip my clothing and skin with one-way barbs that acted like fishhooks. More than once I careened to a halt at the edge of the trail so entangled and bloodied by the rattan tendrils that John and Tingang Na had to come back and cut me loose. They treated the superficial cuts with *sakali-olo,* a leaf chewed to a paste and smeared on the skin to stanch the flow of blood and prevent infection. Sometimes moss was used. The deeper ragged cuts were treated with a root that was first roasted on fire for five minutes then frayed with the edge of a knife. The resulting fibrous mass looked like grated ginger and had a similar smell. This preparation was placed on the cut with a leaf and held in place with thin strips of bark. These cuts healed quickly and left very little scar tissue.

The six-inch diameter, single-log bridges were the most trying obstacles of all: inclined, no handrails, slippery, and often rotten. They seemed to be designed to bear a maximum load of about 150 pounds. I weighed 175 without a pack, and at nearly two meters tall I was constantly confronted with a world designed for small people. Three times in the same day I watched my two guides with full packs safely file across one of those precarious affairs. In each case, when I arrived at midspan, the log gave way with a sharp crack, sending me headlong into the stinking mud and thorn bushes. Each time John and Tingang Na had to follow my cries as they cut a path to where they could extricate me from the network of bushes and snags.

"*Tidak apa*" (it doesn't matter), they said, laughing at my predicament. As long as I wasn't hurting myself seriously, my poor balance and bad luck on the trail were a continual source of amusement to them. *Tidak apa* is more than an expression. In a world filled with so many uncertainties and difficulties, *tidak apa* has become a philosophy of life in Borneo—the universal "It's all right."

"*Tidak apa,*" I mumbled through clenched teeth as I got to my feet. Humility was the first jungle skill I acquired.

As consolation I conjured up the image of these two men seated behind the wheel of an automobile for the first time. With a line of honking vehicles backed up behind them, they were trying to merge into rush-hour traffic on the Santa Monica Freeway in Los Angeles. Also, I decided to grow a mustache to boost my self-esteem. It was one thing I could do that they could not. Compared to their hairless, baby-smooth complexions, I could grow the whiskers of a lifetime in a matter of weeks. I used the whiskers as a means of discovering what John and Tingang Na thought of me and my journey. Each morning they ran their fingers over the lengthening whiskers and asked if I used *obat* (medicine/magic) to make them grow. They were always asking about my *obat*. What magic had I brought with me? White people are clever enough to build airplanes; surely they must have powerful potions or magic to help them? John and Tingang Na began to enjoy my company and sense of humor, but they were totally mystified by the amount of pain I was willing to endure for the sake of collecting plants, taking pictures of trees, and listening to their stories. Was I hiding some secret purpose, they wondered? Why did I want to find the jungle Penan? Couldn't I just fly to the other side of the island? They would be terrified to travel alone into other tribal territory. Why wasn't I afraid of going into areas where I didn't know the spirits? We had become friends, but my journey remained a mystery to them.

At midday we heard the sounds of flapping wings somewhere above the green canopy of leaves and branches one hundred feet overhead. John and Tingang Na paused, smiled knowingly, and after identifying the unseen birds as *belingan* (*Buceros rhinoceros* — the rhinoceros hornbill), they asked whether I would like to try one for lunch. Feeling slightly incredulous, I said, "Yes, certainly." We squatted comfortably, and Tingang Na began to call to the birds with a loud "Kock . . . kock . . . kock" sound. Within a few minutes two large, black birds were perched overhead.

There was a slight click as the thumb hammer of the shotgun was pulled back, followed by a pause just before the straining inner tube that ran the length of the barrel was finally unleashed to drive the firing pin home. There was a loud explosion, the smoke cleared, and one of the birds (last seen perched inquisitively on the branch) plummeted to earth not more than twenty feet away with a dull, feathery thump. We plucked the feathers from the warm bird, and a swarm of lice covered our hands and forearms. An hour later we were picking the last of the bones and finishing the steamed rice before setting off once again.

During this first foray into the rain forest, I learned to adapt my appetite and tastes to such foods as bee larvae and rice soup, roasted rattan shoots, boa constrictors, lizards, monkeys, bats, and the large animals—pigs and deer. I drank the river water and ate whatever my guides could find. I never got sick. I believed that by eating the local foods I would build up a natural resistance to the common jungle diseases: cholera, amoebic dysentery, typhoid fever, and malaria. My primary concern in this climate was septicemia. I was careful to treat every cut immediately. I knew from previous travels in Asia that even a small scratch could quickly develop into a festering tropical ulcer.

I began to learn about edible jungle plants. Many species of rattan can be eaten, but not all. After lunch one day I stopped to collect a large shoot for dinner. John and Tingang Na patiently watched as I avoided the barbed tendrils and removed the delicate yellow inner shoot with my knife the way they had shown me earlier.

"Not that one," they explained, "that is called *mato tagaro*, it will make your throat swell up, and you will die."

They conceded, however, that my knife work was improving. Later I pointed to some mushrooms and asked if they were edible. Tingang Na said they were, but the mushrooms would make me dream too much, and I would get lazy for many hours.

During the afternoons, as we tired from the river crossings, the terrain of the mountains, and the constant leech removal, our pace gradually slackened and more conversation developed. There were more frequent stops, and soon the talk turned to where we would camp for the night. This always depended on the availability of water and suitable fan palm leaves to make a watertight roof for the sleeping shelter in anticipation of the nightly downpour. Because of the winds, it was important not to sleep under trees with any deadwood or signs of termite activity. There are three types of wind to watch for in the jungle: storm winds, whirlwinds, and sudden direct blasts. The first two can bring down a lethal shower of dead branches and the occasional tree. The sudden blast of wind is much more dangerous. It can set off a chain reaction, toppling trees that may level a quarter square mile of rain forest. The only protection from the falling trees is to hide between the buttressed roots and hope your tree doesn't get pulled down. Falling branches and trees and a fuzzy red caterpillar are the most dangerous things in the jungle. John Bong was always chopping up caterpillars on the trail with his jungle knife, and when I asked him why, he showed me a hole in his foot where he had stepped on a red caterpillar ten months earlier. The invisible, fine hairs had painlessly entered the sole of his foot and had developed into a crippling septic wound that was just beginning to heal.

Once we found an ideal spot to set up camp, it took less than an hour to lash together a sturdy ten-foot-by-ten-foot sloped roof shelter with a triple layer of palm leaves on the roof.

The sunset and night air were filled with strange and thrilling insect sounds that variously buzzed, whistled, rasped, pulsated, and occasionally burst out in unison at such volume that conversation was barely possible. There were muffled animal screams in the distance, and one evening in the confusion of noises my ears deceived me and I was struck by a moment of nostalgia. I distinctly heard the ringing of my grammar school bell that had marked the end of playtime each afternoon.

Fireflies dotted the night like a blinking Milky Way punctuated with erratic miniature comets. Mushrooms (Mycena cyanophos) glowed in the dark, and splattered patches of yellow-green phosphorescence clung to the tree trunks. By early evening I would have completed my notes and we could enjoy some leisure time, which was always spent in the same way: storytelling.

One night we lay back on the irregular sapling floor, side by side beneath our blankets, adjusting our positions for greater comfort. The smell of smoke from the fire lingered as the first heavy raindrops began to fall, marking the steady patter of rain that would often continue throughout the night. Flashes of lightning briefly lit up the jungle, and I listened to traditional Borneo animal fables. Tingang Na and John often talked about the clever mouse deer, *plandok*, and the strange and frightening spirit *Pehnako*, who lives in the jungle. We could hear his cry: a loud "Kong-ka-ka . . . EEE-gut-gut!" I never discovered what made the sound. With only the dying fire to illuminate the scene, their stories created a very haunting mood.

Tingang Na would sit up to add sticks of green wood to the fire to keep the mosquitoes away. When I asked where the first Penan came from, John told me the story of "The Hole in the Tree."

There was a tree in the deep jungle that had a big hole in the trunk far above the ground. Nearby was another tree that had a thick branch that grew at the same height as the hole and pointed towards it. In the same part of the jungle were a man and a woman who lived alone and didn't know about reproduction or sex. During a big storm the man and woman watched as the two trees were blown about by the wind. Eventually the two trees were blown against each other, and the branch entered the hole. The force of the wind made the branch move in and out of the hole for a long time, and this gave the man an idea. The man and the woman imitated the trees, and their children were the beginning of the Penan people.

Delighted with their story, I asked them whether they believed it. They were uncertain, but said it was common to joke about the groaning sounds of trees rubbing against each other.

One of the most popular stories I told was my special abridged version of *Cinderella*, with Cinderella working hard for her big, ugly, unmarried sisters—washing clothes in the river, cutting up tapioca for the pigs, and chopping firewood in the jungle. Along came the headman's son, who met her at an all-night rice-wine party and dance. Unfortunately Cinderella had to return to her village before midnight; otherwise her exquisitely carved and painted longboat would turn back into a banana (I didn't know the Malay word for pumpkin). The headman's son married Cinderella and took her away to the mouth of the river, where there were lots of fish and fat pigs. They lived happily ever after, of course. *Little Red Riding Hood* and *The Three Little Pigs* were told in similar fashion to my captive audience. As I developed fluency, my evening stories became more animated and absurd. The storytelling helped me remain optimistic during this first walk in the jungle. If I could fall asleep laughing, I would be fine for the next day. I could do without a map, but a sense of humor was essential.

The morning of the tenth day we waded through a thick ground mist that carpeted the surrounding fern forest. The air was damp, and each time we brushed against any of the giant ferns we were deluged by a shower of cold water. Before our morning tea stop we came across two freshly whittled Penan message sticks. They were four feet long and stuck obliquely into the ground. Notches and clefts along the sticks were embellished with pieces of rattan, leaves, and twigs. Message sticks usually give hunting or trail directions. Tingang Na "read" the sticks for me. One of them said, "We are hungry. Went hunting with blowpipe for pig. This way." The second stick (known as *Bata'Oro*) said in Penan, "There are three strangers in the forest."

These sticks were placed where we could see them. This was the first time the nomadic Penan had acknowledged our presence. Where were they? We continued to see their message sticks for the rest of the day, but they would not answer our calls. Tingang Na said that they were shy and probably suspicious of me. He called out like an owl—"OOOOH-OOOOH!"—but there was no answer. We suspected the Penan were watching and sat down to wait. To encourage them we made it obvious that we had brought tobacco, tea, ammunition, and guns.

Jungle talk—similar to bird and insect calls of the area—is used by the Penan to avoid scaring the wildlife and to conceal messages from strangers. Here in the montane faunal area (four thousand feet) my lowland guides were unfamiliar with many of the natural sounds that could have been people talking to one another. I had been taught to use a soft, high-pitched "oooh" call or a quiet whistle if I wanted to attract someone's attention when we were hunting or walking. The tremor set off by a human voice quickly disrupts the tranquillity of the rain forest. A ripple of warning by the wildlife, inaudible to the untrained ear, radiates for hundreds of yards in all directions.

By sunset no one had responded to our calls, so after dinner John announced that he was going out to shoot a mouse deer. He walked into the pitch-black night with a tree-resin torch and his gun. Five minutes later there was the sound of a distant shot. John returned with what looked like an overgrown rat with long legs and tiny cloven hooves. The body was riddled with pellet holes.

"*Plandok*" (mouse deer), he said.

Without disemboweling it he threw the carcass onto the fire, and the fur began to burn. It smelled horrible. He scraped off most of the hair and left the singed body on the wooden drying rack above the fire for the night. By morning the mouse deer was black and bloated, and the eyes were bulging in their sockets. We chopped up the body and boiled it in a pot with river water and salt. My anxiety mounted as the stench from the bubbling pot increased. Our morning's repast was dumped onto a bed of steamed white rice, and we began to eat. Tingang Na pointed out the delicacies—the stomach, lungs, liver, head, and what looked like the aorta. He handed me the head and told me how to eat it, "First the lips, then the tongue, then the eyes . . ."

My appetite faltered as I looked into the mouse deer's eyes. They had glazed over, and there were singed whiskers around the mouth. A meal with stubble was too much for me. I politely returned the avocado-size head to Tingang Na, who was touched by the generosity of my offer. He split the skull neatly in two with his parang and handed half to John. They scooped out the brains with their index fingers as I attempted to savor the aroma of burnt fur. I tried a lung; it was the texture of an old sink sponge.

As we were packing up, a hornbill's raucous call broke the jungle silence then drifted off into the surrounding vegetation. I was unconcerned and hoped only that we were creating enough interest for the forest people to show themselves.

That morning we finally got a response to our calls.

"OOOOH-OOOOH," someone called back.

We replied with the customary, "*My ke put koo*" (don't shoot us with your blowpipe).

In a sing-song manner the voice said, "*Tek-kenay?*" (who are you).

"*Ak-O ee-to*" (it is I), I responded. "*Jee-an ako ee-too*" (I am a good person), I added.

"*Ma-hat ku koo-ee*" (let us know where you are), called out Tingang Na.

The response was a vague, "I am here."

The exchanges continued until finally, and silently, a powerfully built jungle man appeared beside a nearby wall of leaves. I was startled by how close he was to us. His earlobes were distended, and he wore his hair in a ponytail that hung to his waist. The hair on his forehead was cut in a perfectly straight line, and there wasn't a trace of facial hair on his copper-colored cheeks. He was dressed in a loincloth and a very worn Western T-shirt that read, "Sgt. Pepper's Lonely Hearts Club Band." The incongruity of his T-shirt didn't detract a bit from his mesmerizing presence. Half-concealed by the undergrowth, he stood perfectly still, staring at us cautiously. In his hand was a seven-foot-long blowpipe. A spear tip was attached to the end with thin strips of carefully knotted rattan. At his waist was a bamboo quiver of poison darts and a 24-inch-long parang in a hardwood sheath. He continued gazing at us, and for the first few moments we returned his wordless stare. Tingang Na spoke a few words; then the Penan turned and motioned us to follow. As we walked, he removed the dart from his blowpipe and replaced it in his quiver. He was the first nomadic Penan I had met. Walking in this man's scent trail, I picked up a very distinct acrid smell of smoke and unwashed skin. The man's body odor wasn't unpleasant—it was animallike, a primeval, natural smell.

The camp was so well hidden that we arrived before I had any idea we were even getting close. There were five open-air sapling shelters laid out at random on a low ridge between two small streams. The shelters were similar to our nightly *pondoks*, but had permanent cooking areas and slat shelves for overhead storage. A special raised platform bed near the fire was for the favorite hunting dogs. The sapling floors were built two or more feet off the ground, to provide ventilation and to avoid snakes, leeches, and fire ants. Woven mats helped make sitting and sleeping more comfortable.

Two dozen people lived in Ba 'Talun camp, but there were only two old women and a few children in sight when we arrived. They looked ready to bolt for the jungle at a moment's notice. Jangang, the man who had met us, was watching the camp while the other men and women were out collecting sago shoots, gathering firewood, or hunting.

I handed Jangang and the women large pinches of powerful red Thai tobacco. They rolled four-inch-long conical cigarettes with pieces of dried banana leaf and put the rest in waterproof bamboo containers where they stored their flint and steel.

The children were terrified of me, and the women feigned disinterest. In typical Borneo fashion everyone waited for "the mood to be right." There were no frantic handshaking introductions, nor was there an urgency to establish who we were or why we were in the jungle. Eventually Tingang Na told Jangang that I had come to collect plants and stories from the forest. He emphasized the fact that I had plenty of tobacco and ammunition with me. This comment was followed by an hour of "sharing news" about our journey from Long Seridan.[3] Tingang Na and John spoke a Penan dialect that I didn't understand, but by following their movements and excited patterns of speech I knew what they were talking about. Watching them, I was amazed by how they remembered every incident in detail. In great dramatic style they took extreme pleasure in embellishing their favorite moments. They took turns performing merciless imitations of my falling off the log bridges.

Satisfied with the stories and the tobacco, Jangang pointed to an area of ground next to a small clearing and said, "You can build your shelter there, but first we will eat."

We were served a dish that was described as "Penan cake," which consisted of smoked wild sago flour moistened in pig blood then dumped into a great cast-iron wok of sizzling pig fat. Stirred constantly over high heat, the mixture eventually attained a chewy granular texture. The cake had a pleasant nutty, animal taste and wasn't nearly as greasy as I had expected. We ate with our hands, and before we were through the ever-present camp flies were thick on our fingers. We wiped our hands on the trees to get rid of the flies; then John Bong, Tingang Na, and I went into the jungle to collect poles and rattan for our sleeping shelter. For the sake of the Penan, Tingang Na and John displayed their skill by spending more time than usual

---

[3]The town in Sarawak from which Hansen sets out on his jungle odyssey.

on the construction. The vine lashings were more decorative, and every sapling that pointed towards the clearing was neatly cut to a four-cornered point.

People began returning to camp in the late afternoon, and introductions were made. I handed out more tobacco to the adults and some brightly colored balloons to the children. Abat, a diminutive childlike mother of five children, was without doubt the most beautiful and graceful woman I met in the rain forest. Her husband, Tevaoun, I soon learned, was the most skilled hunter. They lived in the shelter next to ours.

At first the men were shy, but the prospect of borrowing a shotgun helped them get over their hesitation. The next morning I lent one of the guns to Tevaoun and offered him a handful of shotgun shells. He took one and disappeared into the jungle.

Three hours later Tevaoun's whistle call was picked up by people in the surrounding forest. His message was quickly relayed to camp by more excited whistles. The message was: "Tevaoun returning with pig . . . *big pig!*"

Tevaoun must still have been half a mile away when the first ripple of excitement passed through Ba 'Talun camp. By the time he arrived everyone was waiting. Tevaoun stepped out of the forest with a wild pig lashed to his back. The dead animal was beautifully trussed up on a five-foot stick and supported with a tumpline and shoulder straps of fibrous bark that passed through the carcass. The pig must have weighed well over three hundred pounds. The rump hung down below Tevaoun's knees, and the snout was at least eighteen inches above his head. I tried to lift the pig off the ground by grasping it around the midsection with both arms and lifting with my legs. I strained—nothing happened—and there were a few snickers. Attempt number two was more successful, and I managed to budge the pig slightly. Tevaoun looked ill. He had carried the pig for hours and was utterly exhausted. He climbed into his shelter and fell asleep immediately.

The animal was butchered, and equal portions were given to each of the six family groups. The liver was placed directly on the coals and consumed immediately. The families took turns receiving the head. That night I helped cube the meat and force it onto 18-inch skewers that were smoked over the fire. The women rendered the fat in a wok 2½ feet wide. The fat was more valuable than the meat because it could be used in trade. It would be carried to Bario in sealed, 3-foot lengths of bamboo 5 inches in diameter and traded for salt and shotgun shells.

The Penan do not practice any form of meat preservation other than heat smoking. When there is food, they eat; when there is none, they search for it.

Every family brought leaf bundle after leaf bundle of barbecued, boiled, burned, fried, mashed, and skewered pig meat to us. It was an amount impossible to consume, but since we had provided the gun we kept receiving a large share of the meat. Every man wanted to use the gun, so for the next week we continued to eat, cook, tell stories, sleep, and eat again. Ba 'Talun camp took on a holiday spirit.

Sago is the Penan's staple food, and one day I went to the river with Tevaoun and Abat to learn how to make sago flour. We had no language in common. They handed me a tool that looked like a croquet mallet, and I tried to imitate their effortless movements. Straddling the logs that Tevaoun had split with a short-handled ax, we worked our way forward—striking rhythmically at the soft inner pith with our sago mallets. The damp fibrous pulp fluffed up between my ankles as the sweat ran down my nose. I hit my toes a few times. The pulp was placed in a low 4-foot-by-4-foot sapling frame that held two finely woven rattan mats—one above the other. The sago pulp was mixed with water in the top mat and kneaded by Abat's bare feet. This action extracted a fine brown sludge, which was caught in the lower mat. The pulp was discarded and the process repeated. The sludge in the lower mat was allowed to drain. Back at camp it would be smoked to remove excess moisture and would become sago flour. In one day we made enough sago flour to last four or five days.

We relaxed on the gravel beach after we finished the last of the logs, and I washed the blood off my toes where I had walloped them twice with the sago mallet. Tevaoun waded into the stream and rinsed out his shorts. Abat sat on a discarded sago log and began to sing a quiet song. She stopped occasionally and then continued. Her song was sung very sweetly to no one in particular. Then Tevaoun began to sing back. I watched the two of them in their totally natural and spontaneous interaction. They stopped to tease each other then sat at the water's edge. They continued singing until Abat reached between her husband's legs and gave him a friendly squeeze and a tug. It was her way of telling him it was time to get the sago back to camp.

After dinner that evening a small *damar* (tree resin) fire flickered to life in the clearing in front of our shelter. As I relaxed in the shelter, I began to notice rapidly moving orange-red bars of light in the darkness. They came from different directions. As the lights grew closer, people appeared from between trees waving small bundles of glowing sticks in front of their feet to find the way. They placed the sticks on the *damar* fire and sat down at the edge of the firelight. The men and women sat separately. A dulcimer-like three-stringed *sapeh* was quietly tuned as people warmed up with bamboo nose flutes and a bamboo Jew's harp. A bright half moon cast an eerie glow on the clearing through the opening in the forest canopy. Jangang stood up and performed a solo dance—*ngajat* (traditional dancing). Tevaoun got up next; then one by one the other men took their turns. Each dancer changed into a special red-white-and-blue loincloth. The dances began with blood-curdling screams into the night, hot-blooded challenges to imaginary foes. Those were followed by rhythmic circling and twisting movements of arms, legs, and hands. Some of the better dancers used a parang in mock combat; others danced just for fun. Every man did his best to impress the women, who watched carefully out of the corners of their eyes. After some good-natured urging and serious tugging by strong girlish hands, I was persuaded to put on the loincloth. As Jangang helped adjust the back, I let out a scream (in imitation of their war cry), as if he were trying to goose me.

Dressed in the loincloth with a headhunting sword in my hand, I stepped into the moonlight at the edge of the clearing. I wasn't quite sure what I would do. The women were far less uncertain; they took one look at me and collapsed in laughter.

I let out a savage cry as the music started then stepped back and caught my heel on a root. A terrific crunching and snapping of twigs followed as

I lost my balance and disappeared backwards into the darkness. There were more shrieks of laughter as I reentered the *damar*-lit dancing ground. I performed a sword dance, pretending I couldn't get the blade out of the sheath as an imaginary foe pursued me around the clearing. Flapping the loincloth at the women and waving the now unsheathed sword over their heads, I sang out one of my few Penan phrases: "*My ke medai, my ke medai*" (don't be afraid, don't be afraid). They remained unconvinced until I was safely seated with sword in sheath. We were all laughing, and from behind me I could hear Tingang Na giggling uncontrollably, "They are liking too much . . . they are really liking too much!"

The women began to dance. They got up one at a time. It was a basic side-to-side step—arms waving alternately in front and back. Compared to the sinuous movements of the men, these dances were quite plain. The women danced with their backs to the fire out of shyness, and all that I could see from the men's side of the fire was the dancer's black hair against a brown back and swaying hips. Then one of the younger unmarried women—bare breasted and dressed in a brand-new sarong (with paper label still attached)—performed an astonishing dance. Keeping time to the music, she turned to face the fire and the men. She began rubbing her hips, crotch, and thighs in such a blatant manner that I was uncertain how to interpret her gestures. When I asked the man next to me what her dance meant, he nearly rolled over backwards in amusement before he said mockingly in Malay, "Well, what do you think it means?"

Some of the later dances were even more graphic. One older man did an absurdly exaggerated version of lovemaking. He leapt about trying to copulate with an imaginary, elusive lover. First he pretended his penis was too small, then too soft, then much too big—he staggered around the fire under the weight of it. Men, women, and children were laid out on the ground shaking with laughter.

The dancing continued until the moon was lost in the trees. We danced in groups, and in the end the best mimics got up and improvised variations on recent events: Tevaoun's big pig, a child chased by tiger hornets, Jangang's being bit on the end of his penis by a deerfly, and a white man pounding his toes with a sago mallet. The dancing served as a catharsis; it helped people shed their burdens and reinforced the fact that life in the jungle was good—the very best.

The music finally stopped, and people began to leave the dance ground. Singly and in small groups people took glowing sticks from the fire to find the way back to their shelters. As I lay beneath my mosquito net, my sides were sore from laughing. I fell asleep feeling euphoric.

At dawn I was awakened by the thud of a parang blade and the splitting of firewood. Rain had fallen lightly for most of the night, and fine droplets of water still clung to each leaf tip and spider web. Snug under my bed-sheet in a sarong and sweater, I woke up realizing that all my doubts and misgivings about being in the jungle had vanished. I felt accepted. By making a complete fool of myself the night before I had shown trust in the good nature of these people. I had made myself vulnerable to ridicule, and they had loved it. The only white men these people knew were either Christian missionaries or European geologists. I was something else.

One of the men had an ancient transistor radio. He warmed the batteries by the fire to strengthen them, and, using a shotgun barrel as an antenna, we tuned in to a "Voice of America" broadcast from Singapore. Over the static we listened to the Beach Boys singing "In My Room." There was some twangy Don Ho–type Hawaiian ukelele music, and finally "This Old Man" was sung by a group of Australian preschoolers. Then the radio went dead. When I was asked about the songs I said that they were for traditional dancing in my village in America.

Ten days had passed since we had arrived in Ba 'Talun camp. On the other side of the Tamabo Mountains was the Kelabit highland community of Bario, my destination. I was fascinated by this first group of jungle people. I felt like one of the family and had a difficult time deciding when I should leave. John Bong and Tingang Na were happy to stay as long as I wanted. They were delighted with how the journey was developing, and they continued to earn their wage each day. There were some practical con-

siderations. We had run out of our own food days before, but when I asked
my guides to mention this to Tevaoun, he replied, "We have food, and therefore we can share."

While I was trying to think of a way to repay them for their hospitality,
I came upon a shredded *jala* (cast net). Ten years earlier I had worked on
an Australian prawn trawler off the coast of Arnhem Land patching the shark
holes in the nets. I could remember the sequence of knots and diamond
patterns, so I spent an afternoon repairing their net with nylon fishing line
and a hardwood mending needle.

As I worked on the net, Abat sang a song for me as Tevaoun and his sister played a nose flute and bamboo Jew's harp. Abat sang about my arrival
in the camp, what had happened during my stay, and how I would be leaving them soon to "go to the mouth of the river." "You will be leaving us in
the jungle and will fly through the sky like a bird to your home. We would
like to go with you, but we are lower people. We have no money and must
stay here in the forest. Be careful at the mouth of the river." The mouth of
the river is the farthest point in the Penan universe. No one at Ba 'Talun
had ever seen the ocean.

The next day I left the camp. The Ba 'Talun Penan walked with me as
far as the river, stroking the hair on my arms and holding my hands warmly.
They loaded us up with skewers of smoked pig meat and a large sack of sago
flour. I gave them tobacco and five shotgun shells—for the next time they
borrowed a gun. I crossed the shallow, slow-moving river with a walking staff
that Tevaoun had cut for me. Before reentering the jungle on the far side
of the river, I turned to wave. Everyone was lined up holding their children
and smiling. As long as we were within calling distance I could hear their
sing-song voices:

"*Dawai-dawai . . . dawai-dawai*" (go slow, be careful . . . don't fall down,
don't cut yourself with your parang).

That day we joined a major highland footpath and passed abandoned
longhouses and old fields that had been reclaimed by the jungle. On the
third day we stopped to rest at a pass called Punga Pawan. The clouds to
the east parted, and for the first time we could see the Plains of Bah in

Kelabit country. We descended the eastern slope of the Tamabo Mountains through heavy rain forest and emerged onto a wide plain of shimmering emerald green rice padis. I could see the great dividing range that marked Indonesian Borneo ten miles to the east. It was thrilling to be out of the jungle. I could see the sky, clouds, people working in the distance; and the ground was flat. The trails were three feet wide and seemed like super expressways. I could walk with my head up and stretch out with a normal stride. I was beaming as we approached Bario longhouse just before midday. We had been in the rain forest nearly a month.

REDMOND O'HANLON

(b. 1947)

From *Into the Heart of Borneo*

Redmond O'Hanlon's account of a two-month exploration in the Borneo state of Sarawak is a classic in the genre of "Bunglers Abroad."
Unlike Eric Hansen's far more seriously conceived immersion in another
part of Borneo, the sojourn of O'Hanlon and his friend James Fenton
up jungle rivers toward a little-known mountain range never gradu-
ates to the sophistication of a true ethnographic encounter. The two
Englishmen remain staunchly British throughout, and much of the delicious humor of Into the Heart of Borneo *derives from the constant
conceit that their Iban guides treat the men as not very promising children who would never survive on their own in the rain forest.*

O'Hanlon thus camouflages the fact that he is an accomplished and
curious natural historian. Indeed, on the opening page he jocularly
feigns a certain terror as he bones up for the journey (which was Fenton's idea): "As a former academic and a natural history book reviewer
I was astonished to discover, on being threatened with a two-month exile

to the primary jungles of Borneo, just how fast a man can read." In fact, the 1983 outing, which covered some four hundred miles of wilderness (mostly by river), was a remarkable expedition for untrained Europeans to have achieved.

I awoke at dawn, to the *dididididi* call of the Grey drongo (probably); the chatterings and mutterings and babblings of unseen Babblers (perhaps); the flutings and whistlings and cat-calls of hidden pittas or bulbuls or cuckoo-shrikes or laughing-thrushes (maybe); and the distant hoot of a gibbon (certainly).

Dana, Leon and Inghai were already up,[1] packing the supplies into Iban carrying baskets.

"Empliau!" I said. "Gibbons!"

The Iban laughed. "No, no my friend," said Leon with a grin, "you tell that Mr Smythies in the book,[2] it's not empliau, it's a bird. The empliau—they called when you asleeps."

"A bird?"

"Ruai. He very smarts. He make a little padi clearing in the jungle and all his wives they come to see his tail."

Checking the Iban against scientific and English names at the back of Smythies, the mystery was soon solved: ruai was *Argusianus* and *Argusianus* was the Great argus pheasant.

After breakfast, I awkwardly manouevred my Bergen on to my back. It always seemed intolerably heavy until it was in position, when the brilliantly designed strapping and cushioning and webbing so balanced its frame on the back that it was possible (on rare occasions) to forget that it was there. I then buckled on my SAS[3] belt with its attached compass-bag, parang, and

---

[1] O'Hanlon and Fenton's Iban guides.

[2] Bertram E. Smythies, author of the classic book *The Birds of Borneo*, which O'Hanlon carried with him.

[3] Special Air Service, an elite English military unit.

two water bottles in their canvas cases designed to fit against either hip. I filled both from the stream and put two water-purifying pills in each before screwing their tops back on and slotting them into their holders.

James was similarly equipped, looking a little mournful, smoking a cigarette, standing on the shingle and studying the stones at his feet. Dana, Leon and Inghai finished hiding the supplies we were to leave behind and securing the dugout well up a small creek, then hoisted long padi-carrying baskets on to their backs, and joined us. We waded across the Baleh and entered the jungle on the southern bank. Dana took the lead, holding his shotgun; I followed, James came behind me, then Inghai and then Leon, also with a shotgun.

"Why are we armed front and rear?" said James.

"For the wild Ukit men, they attack," said Leon. "This their land. They king of the jungle."

"Heck," said James, wheezing slightly under his Bergen.

"No, my very best friend," said Leon after a pause, "I jokes with you. They go away. They not disturb us. We leave messages. Our Tuai Rumah[4]—he know what to do."

The first hill, which I took to be just the river bank, was so steep that it was easiest to go up it on all fours, when not holding on to the saplings or tree trunks or creepers (and I quickly learnt to inspect each hand-hold for thorns or ants and, in general, snakes). The ridge at the top, however, to my great surprise, was only a pace or two across, and Dana's powerful tattooed-black calf muscles, on which my eyes were sweatily focused, suddenly disappeared from view, over the top and down the other side. I followed as best I could, picked up, it seemed, and hurled down the slope by the great weight of the Bergen, which nudged one in the back like a following bull. I slid over on to my chest and negotiated the steeper twists and turns as if descending a ship's rigging, holding on to the convoluted lattice of roots.

The heat seemed insufferable, a very different heat from the dazzling

[4]Longhouse headman.

sunlight of the river-side, an all-enclosing airless clamminess that radiated from the damp leaves, the slippery humus, the great boles of the trees. Three hills in, the sweat towel round my forehead was saturated. My shirt was as wet as if I had worn it for a swim in the river. Dana, just ahead of me, however, appeared unaffected, his own shirt almost dry: and indeed the indigenous peoples of Borneo hardly sweat at all—with a humidity of 98 per cent there is nowhere for sweat to evaporate, no relief by cooling, just an added body-stocking of salt and slime and smell and moisture. I could feel a steady rivulet of sweat running down the centre of my chest, into my belly-button, and on into my pubic hairs, washing the precious crutch powder down my legs.

By hill five, I found it difficult to imagine how I could possibly sustain this pace, carrying this weight. Dana's hugely-muscled little legs were beginning to blur, two mad little pistons pumping up and down through the airless gloom of the forest. There were rare patches of light where a tree had fallen, brief stretches of sunlight on two-hundred-foot-long rotten trunks sprouting with fungi, heavy with moss and lichen, and surrounded by dense, springing vegetation, by thickets of ferns. But otherwise it was a creepered world of apparently endless twilight.

In the warm and scummy bathwater that seemed to slop from skullside to skullside in my head at every step, words of advice from the SAS Major in Hereford suddenly surfaced.[5] It was the kind of comfort which he himself might have needed, I imagined, only after several months rather than several hours of this kind of walk, but it was a comfort, all the same: "In those hills, lads, think of nothing if the going gets tough. Or, if you're young enough [he had seemed dubious], think of sex. Never, ever, think of the mountain that never gets any nearer. Think of nothing, and you'll survive to be a credit to the regiment." I decided, in a *Boys' Own* sort of way, that yes, I very much wanted to be a credit to the regiment. So I thought of sex. But, just as I conjured the first pair of perky breasts and little brown nipples

[5] The unnamed Special Air Service officer in an English military training camp where O'Hanlon and Fenton prepared for their journey.

before my eyes and steamed-up glasses, the gully of the hill stream I was crossing went black with oncoming heatstroke. I dimly realised, with heat-hazy annoyance, that I really must be far too old to do it on the march. Instead, a poem, all of my own, burst before me like a volcanic bubble in a mudpool. It went like this:

Oh, fuck it,
it's an Ukit.
We're going to kick the bucket.

This was so brilliant, so obviously a poem of intrinsic interest, that it kept me amused, one word at a time, on the step, for the next three hills.

From a long, long way back we heard a shout. "Stop!" it said. James had made the right decision.

Dana, looking surprised (and a little annoyed, as if he had expected us to run with him all the way to Bukit Batu Tiban without a break) sat down on a tree trunk on the next ridge. I shed my Bergen, sat on it, indulged in some desperate heavy breathing without once thinking of sex, and then opened a water bottle. Its warm, chlorinated contents were perhaps the best drink I have ever taken.

James appeared, closely followed by Inghai and Leon. James looked very hot. He sat on the tree trunk next to Dana, held his head in his hand—and then bounded up with a yell. There was a leech on his left arm. He pulled it off with his right hand, but the leech looped over and sank its mouthparts into his palm. James began to dance, wriggling convulsively. He made a curious yelping sound. The Iban lay down, and laughed. James pulled the leech out of his right palm with his left hand. The brown-black, tough, rubbery, segmented, inch-long Common ground leech, *Haemadipsa zeylanica*, then twisted over and began to take a drink at the base of James's thumb.

"Shit!" said James.

At this point, Leon obviously decided that the two had got to know each other well enough.

"Ah, my best friend," he said to James, as he pulled the leech out, rubbed it on a tree and cut it in half with his parang, "why you come so far to suffer so? Eh?"

James sat down, trembling a bit, and pulled out a cigarette.

"For bully beef," said Dana suddenly, the English of his army days unexpectedly coming back to him. "For Badas bully beef."

"I don't know about that, but I certainly feel I'm being bullied," said James. "There is *absolutely no need* to treat this as an endurance test. From now on, I shall be in second place and we will all be sensible about it."

James, I decided, was an admirable man in every way, having just saved us from death by heart attack, or an all-in melting of the arteries.

"Okay," I said, shrugging my shoulders as if I had actually been about to suggest that we take the next stage at a sprint. "It's all the same to me."

"Jams, my very best friend," said Leon, "you not be angries. Our Tuai Rumah—he always walk fast. He want to tell us he not an old man. He want to tell us he the strongest in the longhouse."

I looked at my legs. And then I looked again. They were undulating with leeches. In fact James's leech suddenly seemed much less of a joke. They were edging up my trousers, looping up towards my knees with alternate placements of their anterior and posterior suckers, seeming, with each rear attachment, to wave their front ends in the air and take a sniff. They were all over my boots, too, and three particularly brave individuals were trying to make their way in via the air-holes. There were more on the way—in fact they were moving towards us across the jungle floor from every angle, their damp brown bodies half-camouflaged against the rotting leaves.

"Oh God," said James, "*they are really pleased to see us.*"

The Iban were also suffering, and we spent the next few minutes pulling leeches off our persons and wiping them on the trees. The bite of *Haemadipsa zeylanica* is painless (although that of the Borneo tiger-leech is pungent), containing an anaesthetic in its saliva as well as an anti-coagulant, but nonetheless it was unpleasant to watch them fill with blood at great speed, distending, becoming globular and wobbly.

Now that I had become accustomed to leech-spotting I discovered that they were rearing up and sniffing at us from the trees, too, from leaves and creepers at face height. We covered ourselves with Autan jelly, socks and trousers, chests, arms and neck. Dana, Leon and Inghai put on their best (and only) pairs of long trousers, and I lent them pairs of socks (they were desperate). I took the opportunity to sidle off behind a bush and fill my boots and y-fronts with handfuls of zinc powder. Sitting down again, I was pleased to see that chemical warfare works: the leeches looped and flowed towards me and then stopped, in mid-sniff, as disgusted by me as I was by them. They waved their heads about, thought a bit, decided that they really were revolted, and reversed.

We set off at a more gentlemanly pace, a slow climb and descent which give us time to drink one bottleful of water at every third gully from the clear tumbling streams, re-fill it, drop in two water-purifying pills, and drink the second bottle at the next pause, repeating the process. Inspecting every tiny rock-pool in which I submerged my flask, I was grateful for Audy and Harrisson's warning:[6] there was invariably a Thread leech or two stretching itself towards my hand from the rounded tops of adjacent stones, looking, between each bunching movement, exactly like a pale length of cotton thread. It would have been annoying to have gulped one in, to have it swelling in the throat or setting off for a leisurely peek down the windpipe.

We made our laborious way gradually south-eastwards, keeping the Ulu Baleh to our left. For a time we walked above and beside it, at the top of a great ravine, catching glimpses of its foaming white water, far below, between the hanging fronds of Climbing ferns which seemed to ascend every tree. As the sweat washed the Autan off my neck I replenished it, because there were leeches all the way along the route, in the lianas and on the ground. Indeed, if the number of leeches was any indication whatever of the population density of their warm-blooded victims, then the forest must have been swarming with pigs and deer and squirrels and bears and leopard-cats. But James and I on the move, over-laden, unfit, too old, missing our

---

[6] Tom Harrisson was a veteran explorer who had written several books about the Borneo wilderness.

footing, slithering down slopes, crashing into trees, shish-kebab'd by rattan thorns, panting like an engine shed, must have woken every tarsier, coast to coast.

Dana, now well beyond the route he had marked the previous day, began to notch prominent trees we passed and, when it seemed possible to take either of two alleys up a hill or down a valley he would block the one we were not to use with a bent sapling. When we stopped for a brief (and almost speechless) lunch of fish and rice Dana cut a yard-length of sapling and carefully peeled back strips of bark from its centre. He then hacked down a branch, trimmed it altogether clean of bark, spliced its top, set it in the ground, and placed his rod of curlicues on top.

"What's that for?" said James.

"It tells the Ukit man," said Leon, "that we here in peace, five of us, and that we leave soon."

"In that case," said James, with only half a smile, "perhaps you could make a few more? Strew them about the place a bit?"

"We be all right," said Leon with a grin. "The Ukit man—he only want your head. He never seen a head like yours."

On the march again, caressed by ferns, restrained by lianas, pulling ourselves up banks by the bark of trees, each one of which seemed to have a differently shaped and patterned trunk attended by different lichen and fungi, making our way between trees that were pole-like or thickened at the base or equipped with flying buttress, out-jutting walls of wood, it was easy to believe in the astonishing number of tree species in the jungle. But in the permanent and monotonous midday dusk it was less easy to believe that the South-east Asian rain-forest is floristically the richest in the world. There were epiphytic orchids to be seen here and there in the clefts of smaller trees near the river-cliffs, but little sign of the jungle's 25,000 species of flowering plants (Europe has fewer than 6,000). They live in the canopy, by the banks of rivers, in secondary jungle or in clearings, but now and then we did see a very odd idea in flowers: blossom growing straight from the trunks of trees, sometimes no more than three or four feet from the ground. These flowers, often pollinated by bats, produce a seed complete with a large supply of starting-food to give it a chance in the impoverished soil—an enormous, hard, wrinkled nut that would barely fit in my pocket.

Dana stopped every five hundred yards or so to shred the fronds of overhanging ferns into clusters of thin spirals—but whether to mark our passage or to reassure the Ukit I was too exhausted to enquire. After about a thousand hours (or so it seemed) we climbed slowly down to our left, down to the banks of the Ulu Baleh, which had now shrunk to the size of an English river, waded across it, and collapsed on the northern bank. Dana had decided to make camp.

We all went for a swim—or rather the Iban did, swimming underwater to the far bank and back, whilst James and I sat wedged in the rocks in the shallows, letting the current take some of the terrible heat out of our bodies. Then Inghai unpacked his cooking equipment and began to build a fish-smoking hut whilst Dana and Leon helped us put up our bashas. There was not enough flat space anywhere on the steeply-rising bank to build a communal pole-bed hut, so the Iban made do with a rough shelter.

Sitting round Inghai's fire on the shingle, eating our fish and rice, Leon seemed agitated.

"Redmon," he said, "the Tuai Rumah—he want to know if we climb to the tops of the mountain?"

"I certainly hope so. We'll take it slowly."

"No, Redmon. We Christians like you. We Methodists from Kapit. But we not want to disturb the spirits. Very bad lucks for us to go to the very tops. We go most of the way. You go to the tops."

I remembered Hose's problems one hundred years ago:[7] "The more remote and inaccessible the region, the more are the Toh [minor spirits] of it feared; rugged hill tops and especially mountain tops are the abodes of especially dangerous Toh, and it was only with difficulty that parties of men could be induced to accompany us to the summits of any of the mountains." So said my notebook, and with it I had extracted a map.

[7]Charles Hose, turn-of-the-century naturalist and explorer, co-author of the magisterial *The Pagan Tribes of Borneo*.

This map of the soul's journey was drawn for Hose, with pieces of stick and lengths of rattan on the longhouse floor, by a chief of the Madang (a sub-tribe of the Kenyah). With a few minor variations, Hose found its topography to be common to all the inland peoples. The soul of the dead man wanders through the jungle until he comes to the top of a mountain ridge. From here (much as I hoped we would do from the summit of the unnamed mountain in the Tiban range) he looks down into the basin of a great river. There are five different districts within it, five areas of the dead. Those who die by disease or ageing go to Apo Laggan where they live as they did in life. Those who are killed in battle or by an accident go to the basin of a tributary river, Long Julan, to live by the Lake of Blood, Bawang Daha, where they become rich without having to do any work at all and have their pick of all the women who die in childbirth (a great number). There is a special watery home beneath the rivers for those who are drowned, and they inherit all the valuables lost when boats sink or floods overrun a longhouse. The souls of still-born children, fearless because they have not known pain, live in Tenyu Lalu; and suicides (cases do occur, though rarely, the usual method being to drive a parang into the throat) go to Tan Tekkan, where they live miserably and eat only roots, berries and sago.

Standing on the mountain top, the soul feels a little odd and begins to suspect that he has come along without his body. Joined there by his parang soul and tobacco-box soul, say, by his dart-holder soul and his blowpipe soul, by the ghosts of the objects hung about his tomb, he sits and laments (if he is a warrior) or howls (if he is anyone else). He then descends to cross the river of the dead. This is a tricky business because the bridge consists of a single tree trunk laid from bank to bank (no problem in itself for an agile Kayan or Kenyah or Iban or Punan) which is being tipped and rolled from side to side by a guardian, Maligang (no bother only if you are an Ukit). If, in life, the soul has taken a head or even been a member of a fruitful headhunting raid, a distinction which will be marked upon the ghost as clearly as on his former body by the tattoos on his hands, then he crosses without mishap. If not, however, the surplus soul falls into the river and is consumed either by maggots or by a large fish, Patan. In some versions the soul approaches the great dividing ridge, as we had done, by boat.

I opened my notebook at the map and showed it to Dana and Leon and Inghai. Dana scrutinised it and a discussion in Iban took place.

"The Tuai Rumah," said Leon, "he says this is an old man's map. This is how the old men found their way."

"Does he believe it?"

"Yes," said Leon. "It tell of the right country—but the names, they all wrong."

"Do you believe it?"

"At Kapit, I reach the fifth grade. We taught to be Christian at school. The old men, they think like that. They believe in the spirits. Me and Inghai, sometimes we think they right, sometimes we laugh at them. What about you, Redmon? Do you believe it?"

"No, I don't. But I don't believe in Christianity, either. I think that when we die, we rot. And that's the end of it."

"Then I very sorries for you," said Leon, looking immeasurably sad, getting up and collecting his things. "I tired. I sleep now."

EDWARD HOAGLAND

(b. 1932)
From "Hailing the Elusory Mountain Lion"
From *Walking the Dead Diamond River*

One of the masters in our time of the personal essay, Edward Hoagland
has spent a lifetime observing nature and writing unforgettably about
it. An innate modesty curbs any temptation in Hoagland to portray himself as a more doughty adventurer than he knows he is. He also happens to be one of the great listeners: his masterpiece, Notes from the
Century Before, *consists of little more than Hoagland's musings on the
endless gossip of old-timers he met in northern British Columbia.*

*In this characteristic essay, Hoagland begins by telling wonderful sto-
ries from others' lips about spotting mountain lions, before turning to
his own fugitive sighting at age twenty, where we pick up the story. Few
writers could spin such eloquence out of an encounter that—as he ad-
mits—may not have actually happened.*

I, too, cherish the notion that I may have seen a lion. Mine was crouched on an overlook above a grass-grown, steeply pitched wash in the Alberta Rockies—a much more likely setting than anywhere in New England. It was late afternoon on my last day at Maligne Lake, where I had been staying with my father at a national-park chalet. I was twenty; I could walk forever or could climb endlessly in a sanguine scramble, going out every day as far as my legs carried me, swinging around for home before the sun went down. Earlier, in the valley of the Athabasca, I had found several winter-starved or wolf-killed deer, well picked and scattered, and an area with many elk antlers strewn on the ground where the herds had wintered safely, dropping their antlers but not their bones. Here, much higher up, in the bright plenitude of the summer, I had watched two wolves and a stately bull moose in one mountain basin, and had been up on the caribou barrens on the ridge west of the lake and brought back the talons of a hawk I'd found dead on the ground. Whenever I was watching game, a sort of stopwatch in me started running. These were moments of intense importance and intimacy, of new intimations and aptitudes. Time had a jam-packed character, as it does during a mile run.

I was good at moving quietly through the woods and at spotting game, and was appropriately exuberant. The finest, longest day of my stay was the last. Going east, climbing through a luxuriant terrain of up-and-down boulders, brief brilliant glades, sudden potholes fifty feet deep—a forest of moss-hung lodgepole pines and firs and spare, gaunt spruce with the black lower branches broken off—I came upon the remains of a young bear, which had been torn up and shredded. Perhaps wolves had cornered it during some imprudent excursion in the early spring. (Bears often wake up while the snow is still deep, dig themselves out and rummage around in the neighborhood sleepily for a day or two before bedding down again under a fallen tree.) I took the skull along so that I could extract the teeth when I got hold of some tools. Discoveries like this represent a superfluity of wildlife and show how many beasts there are scouting about.

I went higher. The marmots whistled familially; the tall trees wilted to stubs of themselves. A pretty stream led down a defile from a series of openings in front of the ultimate barrier of a vast mountain wall which I had been looking at from a distance each day on my outings. It wasn't too steep to be climbed, but it was a barrier because my energies were not sufficient to scale it and bring me back the same night. Besides, it stretched so majestically, surflike above the lesser ridges, that I liked to think of it as the Continental Divide.

On my left as I went up this wash was an abrupt, grassy slope that enjoyed a southern exposure and was sunny and windblown all winter, which kept it fairly free of snow. The ranger at the lake had told me it served as a wintering ground for a few bighorn sheep and for a band of mountain goats, three of which were in sight. As I approached laboriously, these white, pointy-horned fellows drifted up over a rise, managing to combine their retreat with some nippy good grazing as they went, not to give any pursuer the impression that they had been pushed into flight. I took my time too, climbing to locate the spring in a precipitous cleft of rock where the band did most of its drinking, and finding the shallow, high-ceilinged cave where the goats had sheltered from storms, presumably for generations. The floor was layered with rubbery droppings, tramped down and sprinkled with tufts of shed fur, and the back wall was checkered with footholds where the goats liked to clamber and perch. Here and there was a horn lying loose—a memento for me to add to my collection from an old individual that had died a natural death, secure in the band's winter stronghold. A bold, thriving family of pack rats emerged to observe me. They lived mainly on the nutritives in the droppings, and were used to the goats' tolerance; they seemed astonished when I tossed a stone.

I kept scrabbling along the side of the slope to a section of outcroppings where the going was harder. After perhaps half an hour, crawling around a corner, I found myself faced with a bighorn ram who was taking his ease on several square yards of bare earth between large rocks, a little above the level of my head. Just as surprised as I, he stood up. He must have construed the sounds of my advance to be those of another sheep or goat. His horns had made a complete curl and then some; they were thick, massive and bunched together like a high Roman helmet, and he himself was muscly and military, with a grave-looking nose. A squared-off, middle-aged, trophy-type ram, full of imposing professionalism, he was at the stage of life when rams sometimes stop herding and live as rogues.

He turned and tried a couple of possible exits from the pocket where I had found him, but the ground was badly pitched and would require a reeling gait and loss of dignity. Since we were within a national park and obviously I was unarmed, he simply was not inclined to put himself to so much trouble. He stood fifteen or twenty feet above me, pushing his tongue out through his teeth, shaking his head slightly and dipping it into charging position as I moved closer by a step or two, raising my hand slowly toward him in what I proposed as a friendly greeting. The day had been a banner one since the beginning, so while I recognized immediately that this meeting would be a valued memory, I felt as natural in his company as if he were a friend of mine reincarnated in a shag suit. I saw also that he was going to knock me for a loop, head over heels down the steep slope, if I sidled nearer, because he did not by any means feel as expansive and exuberant at our encounter as I did. That was the chief difference between us. I was talking to him with easy gladness, and beaming; he was not. He was unsettled and on his mettle, waiting for me to move along, the way a bighorn sheep waits for a predator to move on in wildlife movies when each would be evenly matched in a contest of strength and position. Although his warlike nose and high bone helmet, blocky and beautiful as weaponry, kept me from giving in to my sense that we were brothers, I knew I could stand there for a long while. His coat was a down-to-earth brown, edgy with muscle, his head was that of an unsmiling veteran standing to arms, and despite my reluctance to treat him as some sort of boxed-in prize, I might have stayed on for half the afternoon if I hadn't realized that I had other sights to see. It was not a day to dawdle.

I trudged up the wash and continued until, past tree line, the terrain widened and flattened in front of a preliminary ridge that formed an obstacle before the great roaring, silent, surflike mountain wall that I liked to think of as the Continental Divide, although it wasn't. A cirque separated the preliminary ridge from the ultimate divide, which I still hoped to climb to and look over. The opening into this was roomy enough, except for being littered with enormous boulders, and I began trying to make my way across them. Each was boat-sized and rested upon under-boulders; it was like running in place. After tussling with this landscape for an hour or two, I was limp and sweating, pinching my cramped legs. The sun had gone so low that I knew I would be finding my way home by moonlight in any case, and I could see into the cirque, which was big and symmetrical and presented a view of sheer barbarism; everywhere were these cruel boat-sized boulders.

Giving up and descending to the goats' draw again, I had a drink from the stream and bathed before climbing farther downward. The grass was green, sweet-smelling, and I felt safely close to life after that sea of dead boulders. I knew I would never be physically younger or in finer country; even then the wilderness was singing its swan song. I had no other challenges in mind, and though very tired, I liked looking up at the routes where I'd climbed. The trio of goats had not returned, but I could see their wintering cave and the cleft in the rocks where the spring was. Curiously, the bighorn ram had not left; he had only withdrawn upward, shifting away from the outcroppings to an open sweep of space where every avenue of escape was available. He was lying on a carpet of grass and, lonely pirate that he was, had his head turned in my direction.

It was from this same wash that looking up, I spotted the animal I took to be a mountain lion. He was skulking among some outcroppings at a point lower on the mountainside than the ledges where the ram originally had been. A pair of hawks or eagles were swooping at him by turns, as if he were close to a nest. The slant between us was steep, but the light of evening was still more than adequate. I did not really see the wonderful tail—that special medallion—nor was he particularly big for a lion. He was gloriously catlike and slinky, however, and so indifferent to the swooping birds as to seem oblivious of them. There are plenty of creatures he wasn't: he wasn't a marmot, a goat or other grass-eater, a badger, a wolf or coyote or fisher. He *may* have been a big bobcat or a wolverine, although he looked ideally lion-colored. He had a cat's strong collarbone structure for hitting, powerful haunches for vaulting, and the almost mystically small head mountain lions possess, with the gooseberry eyes. Anyway, I believed him to be a mountain lion, and standing quietly I watched him as he inspected in leisurely fashion the ledge that he was on and the one under him savory with every trace of goat—frosty-colored with the white hairs they'd shed. The sight was so dramatic that it seemed to be happening close to me, though in fact he and the hawks or eagles, whatever they were, were miniaturized by distance.

If I'd kept motionless, eventually I could have seen whether he had the proper tail, but such scientific questions had no weight next to my need to essay some kind of communication with him. It had been exactly the same when I'd watched the two wolves playing together a couple of days before. They were above me, absorbed in their game of noses-and-paws. I had recognized that I might never witness such a scene again, yet I couldn't hold myself in. Instead of talking and raising my arm to them, as I had with the ram, I'd shuffled forward impetuously as if to say *Here I am!* Now, with the lion, I tried hard to dampen my impulse and restrained myself as long as I could. Then I stepped toward him, just barely squelching a cry in my throat but lifting my hand—as clumsy as anyone is who is trying to attract attention.

At that, of course, he swerved aside instantly and was gone. Even the two birds vanished. Foolish, triumphant and disappointed, I hiked on down into the lower forests, gargantuanly tangled, another life zone—not one which would exclude a lion but one where he would not be seen. I'd got my second wind and walked lightly and softly, letting the silvery darkness settle around me. The blowdowns were as black as whales; my feet sank in the moss. Clearly this was as crowded a day as I would ever have, and I knew my real problem would not be to make myself believed but rather to make myself understood at all, simply in reporting the story, and that I must at least keep the memory straight for myself. I was so happy that I was unerring in distinguishing the deer trails going my way. The forest's night beauty was supreme in its promise, and I didn't hurry.

• • •

JOHN G. MITCHELL
(b. 1931)
From *The Hunt*

*The modern tendency to separate hunting altogether from other forms
of adventure—few "outdoor" journals would ever run a hunting piece,
and few of the "bait and bullet" magazines would publish an essay
about hiking or ice climbing—obscures the fact that the armed pursuit
of wild animals is the oldest (and arguably the most fundamental)
human adventure of all. Indeed, before the last half of the twentieth
century, the revisionist impulse to see big-game hunting as wanton car-
nage rather than good sport was altogether absent. Only late in life did
Ernest Hemingway's stirring tales of hunting lions in Africa earn him
opprobrium rather than admiration.*

No one in this century—except William Faulkner in Go Down,
Moses, *which is, after all, fiction—has written better in English about
hunting than John Mitchell. On this hunt along the Gallatin Divide
in Montana, Mitchell keeps his eyes peeled not only for bull elk but for
the austere beauty of the landscape, the quirks of his companions, and*

the passions that unite the men he travels with. (This excerpt has been edited somewhat from the original by Mitchell himself.)

A cold wind came down Big Creek Canyon, crossed the valley of the Yellowstone, and flailed the grass where we were sitting with our backs to the Absarokas. The wind promised snow. Already, the ridgelines of the Gallatin Divide, across the valley, were powdered white down to eight thousand feet. Tom Davis said he figured the snow would be better for us than for elk. "It'll bring those bulls off the high ground," he said. "We'll be eating their livers for supper tomorrow night." I said, "If you score that fast, what will you do for the rest of the week?" Davis squinted at the mountains where the snow would be waiting for us in the morning. He said, "I've got a better idea. We'll eat liver for our last supper, coming out."

In the morning we would be going to camp, up Big Creek toward the divide—seven hunters, three wranglers, the outfitter, the cook, the dude with pencil and notebook, and about twice as many horses and mules as there were human fannies to set upon them. Always this time of year, October turning November, the hunters went in on Sunday and came out the following Saturday, so that each man and woman of them could put in a full five-day week, not counting commutation time, at the job of trying to kill an elk. And always this time of year, snow helped; though too much of it, too soon, could work against the hunters. Too much and horses would founder in drifts. Too much and some unlucky nonresident would drift in over his head, obliging the hometown mortician to defer interment until after spring thaw. But too little and the elk would stay high and dispersed on the ridgetops, and nothing to shoot at, and no wild liver for supper, and no horn for the trophy-room wall.

We sat in the grass on a steep slope above the inn at Chico Hot Springs. Davis was one of the hunters. He held an 8-mm. Mauser in the crook of his arm; and from time to time, as his eye ran along the edge of the timber above us, he snapped the rifle to his shoulder and used its telescopic sight for a spyglass. It was a strong-looking rifle. It showed much use. Years ago he had found it between the wallboards of a house his grandfather leased to seasonal tenants in Michigan. The Mauser was a war souvenir. Then, it had a scope with a broken lens and a very long barrel, and Davis supposed that once upon a time, somewhere in North Africa or Europe, it had belonged to a jackbooted sniper whose allegiance ran more or less toward the Third Reich. Davis took six inches off the barrel and had the entire action refitted with a sporter stock. Almost every year after that, he had taken a white-tailed deer in Michigan with the Mauser. And with it, too, he had taken antelope, elk, goat, moose, and mule deer out here in the big-sky, big-game West.

This Montana, in bygone times, was North America's Serengeti — game enough to bury any swaggering tenderfoot under tons of hides and antlers and boned-out meat; then, the time and place of beaver and bison, and of grizzlies scattered wide and saucy on the plains rather than bunched and skulking in parks in the mountains. Yet for all the shrinkage of wild populations and habitats, Montana still offers the widest variety of big-game hunting experiences available in the Lower Forty-eight, though Wyoming might give its neighbor a good fast run for that kind of money. Montana over the years has been able to claim with notable consistency that it is visited by more nonresident hunters than any other state. And, with one of the nation's most alert fish and game agencies manipulating the management tools, the Big Sky State has become known as the kind of place where, almost as often as not, a hunter can find — and kill — what he is hunting for.

"Now, places down in Wyoming," Davis was saying, "elk are so easy they're practically giving them away. That's not for me. I'll take my chances up here, the hard way."

I had already guessed that hard is how Tom Davis would want the hunting to be. He is a wiry man, strong-looking like his rifle, just thirty-six that fall, showing some thinning out of the topknot, with faraway eyes the color of a mountain tarn. In Michigan, he is the proprietor of a concession offering sites for camping, horses for riding, and canoes for paddling. For fifteen dollars, one may paddle a canoe seventeen miles through a chain of lakes in the state-owned Pinckney Recreation Area northwest of Ann Arbor and wind up at Hell Creek Ranch, which is Davis's place. "It's a good living," Davis said. "Not rich, but good enough so that I can afford this."

"Why *Hell* Creek Ranch?"

"Why not?" Davis replied. "It's near Hell, Michigan."

"So, why Hell, Michigan?"

"Because there used to be some hellish mills along the river and because there was a helluva fire."

I told Davis that according to all the maps, this place where the Yellowstone flows is known as Paradise Valley, and that if he was truly from Hell, he'd better tread lightly.

"And what's the name of that little town up the road where we'll meet Neal in the morning?" Davis asked. Duane Neal was our outfitter.

"Pray," I said.

"Why Pray?"

"Why not Pray?" I said, and let it go at that.

THERE IS AN uncommonly large appreciation for natural country among big-game mountain hunters. I do not mean by this to belittle the relative importance of landscape to flatland gunners of critters with low profiles. I know waterfowlers who are filled with joy to behold no ducks against a horizon of unbroken spartina grass, and squirrelers who would measure paradise not by its capacity to grow bushy tails but rather oak, beech, and hickory along the same creek bottom. I suspect country gets under the skin of most hunters, whatever the quarry or the angle of the slope. But I suspect, too, that mountains somehow hone the appreciation a little sharper. In however large or small a hunter's measure of caring for country may be, there one can probably size up the worth of the hunter himself, and know why it is he hunts, and possibly begin to understand what he is seeking beyond the treasured horn or the tender flesh.

Sitting with Tom Davis in the grass above Chico, I was struck immediately by the man's involvement with the physical environment—the intense way he stared appraisingly at the snow-dusted mountains across the valley;

the occasional quiver of his nostrils, testing the wind like a dog's; the per-sistence with which his perception of country kept cropping out like bedrock from accounts of other hunts and other places. "I just love those mountains," Davis at one point was saying of the Montana-Idaho Bitterroots, where he had killed a mountain goat several years earlier. "You feel like you're on top of the world. There's no way you can't love it." It was as though he were speaking of a woman. I knew then Tom Davis had already fallen head over heels for country.

For a while, then, we talked about the one aspect of hunting with which most hunters do not often care to grapple—the kill, and to what extent it might figure as the essential goal of the whole hunting experience. Neither of us arrived at any profound conclusion. I found my own mind wander-ing in and out of the philosophies of the Spaniard José Ortega y Gasset, whose views of the blood sport had struck me as somewhat romantic, if not slightly askew, when I first read them in his classic treatise, *Meditations on Hunting*. Though now, having met Tom Davis, I wasn't all *that* sure that the old philosopher was off the mark. "To the sportsman," according to Ortega y Gasset, "the death of the game is not what interests him; that is not his purpose. What interests him is everything he had to do to achieve that death—that is, the hunt. . . . Death is essential because without it there is no authentic hunting: the killing of the animal is the natural end of the hunt and the goal of hunting itself, *not* of the hunter. . . . To sum up, one does not hunt in order to kill; on the contrary, one kills in order to have hunted."

I told Davis that I had heard a number of variations on this theme, and that possibly the most interesting had come my way from the mouth of a neurologist in New York City named Mortimer Shapiro, who hunts big game wherever he can, but mostly in Africa. Shapiro had said that for him, after all of the other things that go into a hunt, pulling the trigger has no more significance than putting a period at the end of a sentence.

"Maybe there are times when you don't need a period," Davis said. "You don't have to kill every time. Sometimes you can't kill because you don't get the chance. But still you have hunted."

And sometimes, I supposed, there were times when the hunter faced doubts. Ortega y Gasset had an opinion on that, too. "Every good hunter," he wrote, "is uneasy in the depths of his conscience when faced with the death he is about to inflict on the enchanting animal. He does not have the final and firm conviction that his conduct is correct. But neither, it should be understood, is he certain of the opposite."

Davis said, "I didn't have those doubts when I was younger. I think they grow on you the more you hunt."

"That, or you're slowing down. And besides, you've already taken every kind of animal worth taking in these mountains."

"No, I haven't," said Davis. "There's still the bighorn. I don't have a sheep yet."

"Does that bother you?"

"Not really," he said. "Maybe if I draw a permit someday. Or maybe not. It really doesn't matter much one way or another. But I sure would like to get up there and see where they're at."

WHAT HAD STARTED as sleet as we rode away from the trailhead, Sunday morning, was snow by the time we arrived in camp. It was a wet clumping snow that settled heavily on the lodgepole pine, Douglas fir, and Engelmann spruce, and there was much slipping of hooves on the trail going in. The camp was set up on a natural bench at the confluence of Big and Bark Cabin creeks, at about 6,500 feet of elevation, with plenty of open meadow round about for the pasturing stock. On the bench were five wall tents, a makeshift corral, and one latrine. The first tent on the left was reserved for occasional visitors and surplus gear. Our occasional visitor was Joe Gaab of Livingston, recently retired as supervisor of outfitters for the Montana Department of Fish and Game. In the second tent on the left was the boss, Duane Neal, and his three wranglers, Stan Broughtan, Perry Frost, and Lynn Simon. Next, in the middle, was the cook tent. In addition to the obvious culinary things, it was occupied by Juli Kane, the cook, from a suburb of Washington, D.C. The hunters took the two tents on the right.

There was the Midwest tent, occupied by Tom Davis, his hunting partner from Hillman, Michigan, Earle Duffy, and the two gentlemen from Fond du Lac, Wisconsin, Louis H. Lange, Jr., and Daniel Edgarton. And, finally, there was the tent of the East, sheltering Jim Hare, Ed Sahrle, and Sid Wiedrick, all of Rochester, New York, and the dude with the notebook, from Connecticut.

When I first met Duane Neal, at Chico Hot Springs, I thought that here surely was a man to match these mountains—tall and craggy and tough. He had come out from Nebraska, maybe twenty years ago, had tried his luck with cattle and sheep, and then had bought Black Otter Guide Service from his brother. This was his eleventh season outfitting elk hunters. By arrangement with the U.S. Forest Service, he maintained two separate camps in Gallatin National Forest—the one here at Big Creek, the other across the Yellowstone Valley in the Absarokas, at Hellroaring Creek; and then he crossed over to the Gallatin Range for five weeks of hunting here. Here, Neal had set up spike camps—one or two tents only—at the heads of Bear and Bark Cabin creeks, high up near the divide; and some hunters, weather permitting, used these to avoid a long ride up from base camp in the morning. Between Bear and Bark Cabin, the other drainages had good trails leading up through stands of lodgepole and spruce to untimbered heights at nine to ten thousand feet. From the vantage of the divide, as I would presently discover, one could see twenty miles south into Yellowstone National Park, north almost to Bozeman, and west across the Gallatin River to the wilder shores of the Spanish Peaks. All of it from Big Creek to the divide was roadless, much of it had never been touched by an ax, and some of it, at the time, was being reviewed for possible addition to the National Wilderness Preservation System.

"I guess I like it better over at Hellroaring," Duane Neal was saying that first afternoon in camp. "The Absarokas are wilder and they're diverse and the fishing's better, and maybe the scenery's better, too. But for elk I'd rather be here."

Sid Wiedrick asked how, for elk, the Gallatins could be that different from the Absarokas, and Neal replied, "Lot of elk over there come out of

Yellowstone Park tame. Ones over here run wild and native. You get an elk over here, you've really *done* something."

DURING THE NIGHT the snow stopped, and in the tent of the East Jim Hare kept waking to feed the stove. Stan Broughtan barked "Let's go!" through the flaps of the tent at six o'clock. Sid Wiedrick lighted a Coleman lantern and, shivering out of our sleeping bags, we dressed quickly. Ed Sahrle said, if no one minded, he would stay *in* his bag and wear it to breakfast. The men from the Midwest were already up. They stood outside the cook tent waiting for Juli Kane to summon them in. And she did that, telling the hunters "Let's eat!" with a bark as authoritative as Broughtan's.

On the stove were eggs and bacon and thick slices of French toast, and there was Duane Neal saying, between sips of coffee, that he would be going with Davis and Duffy to the Triangle, a big swatch of meadow high on the mountain in back of camp. Meanwhile, Joe Gaab, Juli Kane, and I—the three noncombatants—would ride up Bark Cabin Creek to see what kind of sign had been left in the fresh snow. "Now remember," I said to Tom Davis after breakfast as he swung into his saddle, "don't spoil it by getting your elk on the first day."

According to the record books, some mighty big elk had been taken in this mountain country over the years. I mean in the generous sense of a day or two's ride from Pray. And by "big elk" I mean big enough to rate a listing by the Boone and Crockett Club, the official judge of big-game trophy pecking orders in North America. Certainly, these would be animals larger than the seven-hundred-pound live-weight average for Rocky Mountain bull elk. And as I watched Tom Davis ride away that morning, I was startled to find myself wishing him the kind of luck that would bring down a truly big one, even at the risk of leaving the hunter spoiled and sedentary for the rest of the week.

One can learn much from the record books. I suspect more people buy and use them as tip sheets on where to go for the biggest game than for any other reason. If, indeed, there *is* any other reason to wallow through pages of names and measurements. One runs the eye down the long columns and soon discovers, for example, that if it's a trophy grizzly you want, then your best bet is out of Bella Coola, British Columbia. Or was, when the big ones were toppling round about. An Alaskan brown? Taxonomically, grizz and brown are the same critter. But Boone and Crockett types are not slavishly concerned with taxonomy. They play it by size as conditioned by geography, placing the browns along the robust shores of Alaska, where the bears grow tall and fat feasting on salmon; while the grizz is held to the interior, where size diminishes as a factor of sparser diet. Overall, the books list thirty-one categories of North American big game. These include three kinds of moose, though, biologically, there is only one species. A dead moose in Ontario may therefore vie with one from Maine for the honor of being listed as the biggest "Canada moose," but not with a moose from Wyoming, which is a category unto itself, nor with a moose from the Yukon-Alaska region, which is likewise gerrymandered as the range of a separate "subspecies."

Someone was mentioning browns. Want a big one? Get thee to Kodiak Island. Want a polar bear? Can't have one. Not now in Alaska. But when you could have had one, you would have safaried north from Kotzebue along the frozen shore of the Chukchi Sea. Can't have a jaguar now, either. At least, you can't bring the skin or head into this country; so why bother? But when you could have bothered, you would have headed for Nayarit, Mexico, probably. Want an elk? They grow big in Colorado and Utah, scattered all over the mountains. But they grow big here, too, in Park and Gallatin counties, Montana. . . .

In the afternoon, I went out from camp across a meadow to a large lichened rock and waited there for the echo of a gunshot to roll down the mountains. It never came. Only the hunters came on horseback, one by one, slumped in their saddles, showing fatigue and, it seemed to me, a measure of surprise that all had shared this smallest of humiliations—being skunked the first day. Except for Tom Davis. He was the last man out. And the last chance left for liver, to bring them all better luck the next morning.

Whatever Davis's own luck this day or tomorrow, he was not in the record-book league, and I supposed he never would be. Not that there weren't any number of regular-Joe-and-Josephine hunters in the record books, men and women who had just lucked into the big one without really trying. But as I was ruminating not long ago, one can learn much reading the scores; and it is downright surprising how often a few names keep turning up on the lists in a way that suggests that they really *were* trying. I mean names such as Herb Klein and Bert Klineburger. The late Herb Klein came out of Dallas with money in oil and Weatherby rifles. Bert Klineburger for many years was proprietor of Jonas Brothers, the Seattle taxidermy emporium with sideline safari service to exotic places. Neither of these men was or is a member of the exclusive Boone and Crockett Club. It is their names only that are admitted to the lists of the club's North American big-game trophy program.

For many years, too, it might have appeared to anyone studying the records that Herb Klein and Bert Klineburger were in some kind of fierce contest to see who could get his name more often into the lists and at a higher level of achievement. I do not mean to suggest here that either man threw a gauntlet to the boot of the other. I guess only that each knew the other was trying to excel at hunting and killing and mounting the largest specimens of game animals on this continent, and that the presence of one runaway performer must certainly have put the spur to the other's quest. Both did most of their high-score shooting in the 1960s, though one of Klein's standing records, for goat, goes back to 1934.

I cannot begin to call the winner of this contest. Klein had 41 recognized entries spread over 21 categories of game in the 1976 record book; Klineburger had 14 spread over 10—an entry being any individual specimen exceeding the minimum size set by the Boone and Crockett Club for each of the 31 game categories. So, in terms of trophy numbers only, Klein had it. And Klein got it through dogged persistence, as in the case of the Barren Ground caribou. In 1955 Klein entered the lists by killing a Barren Ground caribou that would qualify for the rank of 299th; that is, as of publication of the 1976 records, there were only 298 sets of caribou antlers recognized officially as being superior to Klein's 1955 entry. In 1960, Klein killed another Barren Ground caribou—ranked 286th—and thereby moved 13 places closer to *numero uno.* But that wasn't good enough for Klein. In 1964, he killed two more Barren Ground caribou, moving to 170th place with one animal and to 61st with the other. And in 1967, he killed three more, losing considerable ground with two of these animals, but progressing to 41st place with the third. Yet when Klein arrived proudly at 41st place, who do you suppose was already 20 steps ahead of him, in 21st place? None other than Bert Klineburger.

That was Klineburger's style—not so many animals as good ones almost every time, or at least ones that might often be better than Klein's. Running down the 1976 lists, one sees that, for grizzly, Klein and Klineburger were tied in 33rd place; for brown bear, Klein's 48th topped Klineburger's 118th; for polar bear, Klein's 81st beat Klineburger's 95th; but that Klineburger then turned the tables on Klein in six other categories, beating him at Pacific walrus (37th to 54th), at mountain caribou (28th to 36th), at Barren Ground caribou, at bison (9th to 72nd), at musk-ox (12th to 79th), and at Alaska-Yukon moose (1st to 66th). A counterattack by Klein in the Canada moose category managed to edge out Klineburger, 18th to 19th. So, counting rank as well as numbers, who knows? Having the biggest Alaska-Yukon moose is an impressive accomplishment (for Klineburger). But so is having the 9th largest desert sheep, the 10th largest Stone's sheep, and the 13th largest bighorn sheep (for Klein). Not that it matters at all to me. Nor much, I'd guess, to the elk hunter from Hell, Tom Davis.

They were waiting for Davis in the Midwest tent with a bottle of Irish Mist. Duffy was pouring when the tent flaps snapped open and there, silhouetted against the dusky sky, stood Davis, cradling his Mauser.

"Where you been, Tommie?" said Duffy.

"In the wrong place at the wrong time," Davis replied. "Came off the ridge above the Triangle and saw where they had bedded down in the meadow. Two bulls and four cows. They crossed over Bear Creek and went up the other side and that's where I scoped them. Big bulls."

"What the hell good is that?" someone said. "Why didn't you shoot one?"

Davis was under the light from the Coleman now, and he looked tired. "Shoot one?" he said softly. "At over a thousand yards?"

In the morning we rode up the ridge between Big and Bear creeks and, looking from a switchback across the valley at the great open scar of the Triangle, saw eight elk grazing there. "That figures," said Davis. "Now they're over there, where I scoped them from yesterday, and we're over here, where they ought to have stayed. And there's a mile between us." It was the second day of the hunt. For supper that evening we ate beefsteaks and boiled potatoes. And no liver.

WEDNESDAY MORNING — TWO days down and three to go — Tom Davis and I watched the others ride out to give the Triangle another working over, then pointed our own horses up the winding trail to the spike camp at the head of Bark Cabin Creek. It was a pleasant ride through lodgepole forest first; past a couple of meadow ponds looking productive of moose, but no sign of any; past the bleached, slivered ruins of a trapper's cabin, but no sign of any wolfskins, no more the rendezvous of mountain men with Hawken rifles; and at last, steeply, through spruce into open parkland with islands of whitebark pine and alpine fir at 8,500 feet. We had come out onto the floor of a bowl. West a scant mile, the final upthrust of the Gallatin Divide rose sharply another 1,300 feet to the dome-shaped prominence of the Sentinel, where the divide trail swung in from Windy Pass. North and south, rimrock ledges ran out from the main divide and tumbled into talus slopes, while to the east, the canyon of the creek we had ascended opened just wide enough to frame the smoky-blue maze of the Absarokas beyond the Yellowstone. Smiling, Davis turned slowly in his saddle and said that this was where he would take his trophy elk.

Two hunters, not of our party but friends of Neal's, were already ensconced in the one-tent spike camp when we arrived. They appeared at the open flaps in blaze orange jackets and introduced themselves as Dexter and Lee. We unsaddled, tied up the horses, stashed our meager gear, drank some coffee, asked about elk, heard there were fresh tracks just below the divide. The four of us walked then across the bowl with loud crunching underfoot in the crusted snow. "We better split up here," Lee said. Lee was a retired

Air Force major and sometime rodeo cowboy. His home was in Livingston. He said, "Just poke along nice and easy and remember to look behind you as often as in front. I learned that cowboying. Same as cows, elk'll pussyfoot out behind you after you've passed."

For an hour or so, we tried to pussyfoot ourselves, poking around the edges of conifer islands, Davis with the Mauser unslung, at the ready, and I staying a fair distance behind so as not to be in the way. Presently we came to an old upended fir and stopped to lean against its trunk, and we talked for a while about the good feeling one gets being high in the mountains, away from the road hunters and the constant crackle of gunfire one hears so often at hunting times in eastern woods. Davis said he figured it was getting awfully crowded for hunters in Michigan, and that next year he might put the Mauser aside during the regular deer season and try hunting instead with a bow. He said with the earlier bow season falling in October, the woods were prettier then, and with fewer hunters, less busy, too. Davis didn't like busy places. The country around Hell Creek Ranch was going that way. Most of southern Michigan had gone that way long ago. Near Gunnison, Colorado, he had bought a small piece of land some years ago, figuring one day it might be a place to retire. Now, he might not wait that long. Maybe he would move out to Colorado and start outfitting for hunters, like Duane Neal here in Montana. Or maybe he would run summer pack trips just for people who liked going high and wild. Neal did that here, too. "One of these years," he said. "But then, I don't know. Even Colorado's getting crowded. Seems everyone in Texas wants to go to the mountains."

I asked Davis how long he figured it would be before the mountains here got so busy there would be only one place left, called Alaska. Davis said, "Country like this should last forever, but nothing ever does. I've got two boys at home, both under ten. I like to think a place like this will still be here for them. I don't know if they'll ever hunt. But if they do, there's sure got to be something a whole lot better than Big Louie's." Big Louie's is an outdoor shooting gallery in southern Michigan—game animals are the targets—and not unlike some of the exotic game ranches in Texas. "It's not hunting," Davis added, "if you and the animal are inside a wire fence."

We saw good elk sign later that day. One cleft print in the snow was the size of my fist, and Davis said that its maker might be pushing nine hundred pounds. But we saw no elk, heard none bugling. Nor did Dexter and Lee. As we headed back across the bowl toward the spike camp, I kept watching Davis for some signal that his confidence might at last be eroding. We were three days down and two to go, the weather was warming up, and new snow was nowhere in prospect. Conditions were running to favor the elk. Yet here was Davis as jauntily full of great expectations as a country boy on Opening Day of his first hunting season.

In the tent, after supper, Lee told us about his cowboying years in the West, Dexter spoke nostalgically of the wild hunting country that no longer abides in his homeland of southern California, and Davis said that he hoped someday to hunt in Alaska. It occurred to me as we were turning in for the night that no one had mentioned Africa. I expect the omission struck me because I had packed along with my gear a copy of Ernest Hemingway's *Green Hills of Africa*, a dog-eared schoolboy edition of Papa's 1935 epic of a safari through Masai country. In the tent now, with the others zipped into their sleeping bags, and the lantern dying, and a flashlight to carry on, I read through the first chapter to the part in which Hemingway described his own expectations as a hunter. They had been seeking greater kudu for ten days, had not yet seen a mature bull, and had only three days more before heavy rains moving north from Rhodesia would spoil it all. So Hemingway wrote:

"Now it is pleasant to hunt something that you want very much over a long period of time, being outwitted, out-maneuvered, and failing at the end of each day, but having the hunt and knowing every time you are out that, sooner or later, your luck will change and that you will get the chance that you are seeking. But it is not pleasant to have a time limit by which you must get your kudu or perhaps never get it, or even see one. It is not the way hunting should be."

I closed the book and lay in the dark, cold, hearing the wind and the occasional stomp and whinny of a tethered horse; and I thought how differently—how more gracious, though deprived—Tom Davis might have felt with ten days down and three to go, and no kudu, on the hot, dry plains beneath the snows of Kilimanjaro.

Davis did not get his elk the next day in the bowl at the head of Bark Cabin Creek. In fact, we saw no elk, though we heard one bugling late that morning across the bowl. In the afternoon we rode up to the Sentinel with Lee, and down again, and Davis said he'd stay another night at spike, and I said I wouldn't, and everyone said goodbye as I headed down the trail to the main camp at Big Creek. I was past the ruined trapper's cabin, watching dusk come on, when I heard a horseman coming down behind me. It was Davis.

"I thought you were staying up there."

"I changed my mind," he said. "Tomorrow's the last day. I want to see how Duffy's making out, and in the morning I've got a date with an elk at the Triangle."

At the edge of a meadow near camp, a great horned owl watched us approach from its perch high on a branch of a skeleton spruce. Silhouetted against the sky, its head swiveled slowly as we passed. A small animal, a rodent of a kind we could not identify in the half-light, hung slack from the owl's talons. Saluting the owl with a tip of his hat, Davis said, "Some guys have all the luck."

FOUR DOWN AND one to go. And the air space under the meat pole was empty when we rode into camp. After supper, everyone retired, a bit earlier than usual and, it seemed to me, with a curious lack of interest in snooze-off palaver.

There was little talk, too, in the morning at breakfast, and less as the hunters saddled up and rode out toward their appointed beats. Davis turned in his saddle and tipped his hat, going down to the creek, and I guessed from the faraway look on his face that he already knew how the day might be ending. . . .

The hunters sat in silence at the table in the cook tent, waiting for Ed Sahrle to return. He was the last man out and it was already after six, and dark. Sahrle had gone off to circle the Triangle, solo; and Davis had waited for him a half hour and then come in, thinking that Sahrle had misunderstood about a rendezvous and soloed to camp instead. But Sahrle was still up on the mountain somewhere. Our last hope.

Stan Broughtan said at last, "I can't understand it. I was in elk all afternoon, but all I could see were cows and calves."

"I say the elk ran it up on us," said Louie Lange.

"And it wasn't even fair," said Dan Edgarton. "They had *all* the advantages."

From the hay bales, Joe Gaab put in, "Come on down through Livingston, boys, and I'll sell you a couple of fine steers."

Then Sahrle burst through the tent flaps. His face was flushed. For a moment, he looked along the two rows of hunters until his eyes fixed on Davis. "You *turkey!*" he shouted. "I've been busting down through the blowdowns feeling guilty for leaving you up there alone in the dark."

"I thought you'd already come in," Davis said evenly. "Welcome to the last supper."

We packed our gear, cinched up the duffels and panniers, and rode out in the morning with a warm wind blowing down on our backs from the Gallatin Divide. At a stream crossing along the way, Davis stopped for a while to water his horse. I reined in beside him.

"Was it a good hunt?" I asked. "I mean, for you."

Davis looked back over his shoulder in the direction of camp. "Good?" he said. "You better believe it was good." Then he twisted around in the saddle and tipped his hat toward the unseen divide. "There's still next year," he said, staring up the riderless trail. "And there's still that big bull elk up there at the Triangle, waiting for *me*."

Next year? Yes, and the year after that, I supposed. And all the years after, for as long as there would ever be country like this, and men like Davis with ancient yearnings to prowl high and wild. Or at least until such time as there might be, one way or another, an end to the game.

FREYA STARK

(1893–1993)

From "The Hidden Treasure"

From *The Valleys of the Assassins and Other Persian Travels*

Freya Stark, one of the most inveterate travelers of our century, made a specialty of the Near East. In 1930, she set off for Persia (present-day Iran) with a vague intention of exploring a remote region called Luristan, the country of the Lurs. At a party in Baghdad one evening, however, her quest was sharpened when a friend mentioned a tale of hidden treasure in Luristan. Initially skeptical, Stark was introduced to Hasan, an eighteen-year-old Lur youth to whom a tribesman had once told a story of stumbling across "twenty cases of gold ornaments, daggers, coins and idols" hidden in a cave. Hasan had never been to the cave, but he knew where it was and agreed to guide Stark to the site.

Implicit in her mission was Stark's plan to smuggle some of the loot past policemen and customs officials, interest a museum or archaeologists in her find, and thus preserve it from Persian profiteers. It is characteristic of this blithe traveler's writing that even at her most engaged in the quest, she preserves a healthy irony about her wild-goose chase.

That night, while the cows came and nibbled at my roof in the darkness, I tried to make my plans.

Hasan had not turned up from Baghdad. He was in prison, put there by his enemy, the vizier, to prevent his leaving the country, but I could not guess this at the time. It was clear that I should have to do what I could without him.

The first thing was to go up into the treasure mountain and see if the map was correct. The second was to shake off the police, if possible, and get across the river to Lakistan. I decided that the first was the more important of these objectives and the second must, if necessary, be sacrificed to it, since it is an axiom that one cannot be sure of getting more than one thing at a time. The police would probably refuse to be shaken off: already they had spoken of accompanying me to Husainabad next day, and only the assurance that I was far too tired to start on a two days' journey had put an extinguisher on the lieutenant's plans.

By the morning my tactics were ready. When the *kadkhuda* came,[1] sent by the enemy to question me, I made, as it were, a reconnaissance by saying that I had decided to cross the river, to spend ten days or so in Lakistan, and then return by way of Husainabad and call on the Governor on my way home. I waited to see what would happen. There was an ominous nodding of heads between the *kadkhuda* and the chiefs of the Musi[2] over this statement. Mahmud,[3] his face very serious, sat looking at the ground. A little later, when all had been duly reported, the lieutenant came to call, sat on the carpet, talked about religion in the most elevating way, and asked if it was true that I meant to cross the river.

"I had thought of it," said I. "My plans are quite vague. So long as I can visit interesting ruins in this country, I am content wherever I go. What do you recommend?"

The lieutenant shrugged his shoulders. "Anything you please," said he. "I only desire to serve you. You can go where you like best."

[1] The tribal headman.
[2] A local tribe.
[3] Cousin of Shah Riza (see n. 4, below).

My heart rose. For a few hours I hoped that after all I might visit the treasure valley and cross the river too. I told Shah Riza[4] to have the horses ready next morning. After a decent interval, Shah Riza came to tell me that there were no horses left among the tribe.

"No horses?" said I, outraged at my old Philosopher's sanctimonious duplicity. "What has happened to those we were riding yesterday?"

"They had to be sent off early this morning."

I was on the way back from a visit to my small patient, and caught up with Mahmud behind his tent.

"What is this about the horses?" I asked.

"What about the horses?" said he.

"I have been telling her that there are no horses left here," said Shah Riza in obvious discomfort.

Mahmud looked down at me from his great height and stooping shoulders. He seemed to be making up his mind.

"You shall have as many horses as you like," said he. "They are my horses, after all. And we will take you to Tarhan to-morrow if you wish, whatever anyone may say."

This truly courageous offer touched me very much. I thanked Mahmud.

"I knew Shah Riza was lying," I said. The Philosopher looked unhappy.

"I did it for the good of my people," he explained. "The lieutenant tells you one thing, but he threatens us with punishment if we let you have a horse, or guide you where you want to go. Mahmud is reckless: he will do anything: but it is he who will have to pay, and you will be far away."

This was true enough, and I gave up there and then any thought of crossing the river that time. I decided not to take risks that other people would have to pay for, and by giving way gracefully to improve my chances of a day in the treasure valley. When next we sat at tea round the fire, I said that I had changed my mind: if the lieutenant would wait a day for me, I would take advantage of the fortunate chance of his company and guidance and

[4]A maker of quilts and Stark's guide from Baghdad to Luristan, whom she nicknames "the Philosopher."

go to Husainabad *first*, and thence if possible to Tarhan, after having visited the Governor. I only required one day more here, to look at some old
ruins I had heard of in the neighbourhood, and then I would be ready to
start. The lieutenant was charmed. No doubt he was pleasantly surprised
to find that his desires and mine coincided so happily. The day's delay was
nothing to him; he did not even take the trouble to insist on escorting me
to my ruins.

But now another difficulty threatened.

I sent a message to Sa'id Ja'far[5] to ask if he would guide us up next day,
and Sa'id Ja'far, when he heard the direction in which I intended to go, declared that he would not risk it, not with five tribesmen behind him.

"There is a track," he said, "which runs along the level ground up there.
It is hidden from sight between two hills, and there are no tents for miles
on any side. And always there are brigands: they come up from the river
and lie in ambush. You know that we are disarmed. If I had a weapon, I
would not care."

"Providence has attended to this matter," said I. "We will ask the lieutenant to lend us a policeman. Then we shall be safe against anything."

I wrote a little note and sent it to the *kadkhuda*'s tent. The reply came
back in the hands of a young policeman who was himself to accompany
us. I begged Shah Riza to make his prayers next morning short and early;
and feeling that I had done all that circumstances allowed, I left the party
and went to think out in my sleeping-sack the details of the adventure, of
which the most difficult day lay before me.

Next morning I dressed as usual before it was light, and made a few al-
terations to my costume. I emptied the map case I carried round my waist,
and substituted for its ordinary contents an electric torch, a candle and box
of matches, and a strong knife, suitable for opening treasure chests if any
such were found. I pinned a small pillow-case, which happened to be travelling with me, round my waist under my skirt. And I looked again at the
pencilled map, memorizing it thoroughly. If fortune were kind and I man-

[5]Another cousin of Mahmud and Shah Riza.

aged to throw off both the police escort and the tribesmen, and then to find the cave, I would be ready to take away some specimens of the treasure undetected. They would be sufficient to interest any museum or connoisseur; and the next step might be taken in a more orthodox way, with the help of proper antiquarians. So, full of hope, and with the excitement of action upon me, I went out to see my party.

Shah Riza, I decided, must stay at home. His sense of responsibility was so great that I would never shake him off. His ardour for archæology had worn rather thinner during the last days, and I had no difficulty in making him see that a quiet rest was good for his health.

"The *Khanum*,[6] she thinks of everything: better than I do for myself." I let the undeserved praise pass, and waited to see with some anxiety who else was coming with me.

Sa'id Ja'far was there, with black cotton trousers reaching half-way down his legs and *givas*[7] on his bare feet, ready for walking. He had the heavy metal-headed stick of the country in his hand as a weapon. Husein and Ali, two of Mahmud's retainers, one dressed in black cotton, the other in white felt, completed the party, together with the policeman, whom we sent for as soon as we were ready. All were on foot, for the road was said to be difficult. The grey mare was there for me alone, with a water-skin looped over the pommel to last us for the day.

I had prepared the tribesmen by saying that I expected to find on the hill the ruins of a fortification of the time of Nushirvan,[8] so that even if I could not escape from them, they would, I thought, be looking for ruins while I was looking for the cave, and something might yet be accomplished. For the rest, I left my tactics to time and circumstance, and watched, as I went along, how the landscape fitted in with my map.

We went up the valley, retracing the steps of our coming until, after half

[6]Lady.

[7]A type of handmade shoes.

[8]Khosrow I (also Khusrau or Chosroes), titled Nushirvan, or Anushirvan ("of immortal soul"), king of Persia 531–79; he was the most famous of the Sasanian rulers, and pre-Islamic ruins in Iran are traditionally attributed to his rule.

an hour, we came, as Hasan had said, to a path which tilted itself up the slope of the mountain through patches of white limestone like salt. The pony found difficulties here; the white rock crumbled under its hooves like powder, and the path had no thoughts for gradients. Under ordinary circumstances I should have walked. But I was making a plan, which involved fatiguing my escort while I myself kept fresh, and so I remained seated, watching the men climbing with easy mountaineering strides ahead. It was full morning and the sun was hot: the white slope, dotted with broom bushes and small shrubs, glistened in the sun: we were being lifted up again into the joyful loneliness of hills. At the top of the mountain's long torpedo ridge runs an important track from an *Imamzadeh*[9] on the Saidmarreh banks, along the level height, and down into the plain of Shirwan on the north-west. The track keeps a little north of the ridge up to a point where that dips and rises again to another ridge, parallel, higher, and equally long; so that for a lonely stretch the road lies, as it were, in a hammock elevated between the two hills, out of sight of everything except their solitary summits. This, Sa'id Ja'far said to me, was a place almost always infested by thieves. As we emerged on to it, a man leaped out from a small gully below us, and sped over the rocks. Our policeman swung his gun and shot at him.

This was the first time in my life that I saw, as I thought, a brigand, and I cannot say that I felt anything except a pleasant exhilaration. There was a little band of them down the road, and our policeman, Sa'id Ja'far, and Ali were bearing down upon them, fast but cautiously, as if they expected to be shot at. Beyond, making downhill as fast as their legs would carry them, were two men with some goats. It went through my mind in a flash that this was curious impedimenta for a robber band to be burdened with, but I was too much absorbed in our own party to trouble with inferences. I stopped my horse under a little thorn tree, and watched the operations, like the damsel in a medieval romance, hoping for a battle.

The brigands, after wavering a moment or two, decided not to wait for our advance, and turned downhill, leaping like gazelles. Sa'id Ja'far and the

---

[9]Shrine.

policeman shouted to me: I hurried up to them, dismounted, snatched the extra weight of the water-skin off the saddle, while the policeman leaped into it and pursued over the long grassy shoulder of the mountain. Husein went running after: the other two stood by me, watching them out of sight.

They were away for over forty minutes, and a beautiful peace, an unbroken solitude, lay around us again. I began to fear that our policeman had been killed. Sa'id Ja'far thought not. The fugitives, he considered, were amateurs. Professional bandits, he said, wore white, which made them inconspicuous in the rocks: but quite a number of honest tribesmen might turn to a bit of robbery on a track as lonely and as notorious as this, especially now when they would hardly ever meet an armed opponent. One need never fear a sudden attack in force, Sa'id Ja'far explained. What happens is, that as you ascend towards the pass one man will step out as this man did from some gully, and ask you to allow yourself to be looted. If you comply, you can go on, denuded but not molested. If you resist, the robber will turn and usually get away in the rough ground. You and your caravan will continue in apparent safety until you reach the pass: this is usually a narrow passage between rocks: and here an enfilading fire from either side will make an end of you and your obstinacy.

Sa'id Ja'far had just finished his exposition of the technique of the national pastime in Luristan, when two wayfarers appeared, coming towards us along the lonely level of the track. One was an oldish, the other a young, man, and both had the heavy-headed metal stave in their hand. Sa'id Ja'far and Ali went to meet them before they came too close to me. It was amusing to watch the approach, for each side evidently had the blackest suspicions of the other. From a safe distance they called a greeting; then gingerly drew near, sticks held ready. They asked each other the names of their tribes, and where they were travelling. As the explanations appeared satisfactory, the grip on the sticks relaxed, the distance became less carefully maintained, and I was allowed to draw into the radius of conversation.

The two travellers said that they had seen the men who caused all the commotion. They were not robbers at all. They were Hindimini tribesmen.

"Why did they leap out at us from the rocks?" said I.

The party seemed to think this quite natural.

"Either they thought *we* were robbers, and wanted to be in the best position to begin with," said Sa'id Ja'far, "or they may have hoped that we were unarmed, and then of course they might have robbed us whether they were robbers or no."

"It just shows," said I, "that when one goes about with a policeman one can always find somebody to shoot. How lucky to have missed the man."

"Well," said Sa'id Ja'far, "it was his fault. He ought to have stopped when he saw a policeman, and not made him gallop like this for miles. Here they come back."

The policeman was trotting towards us, with Husein jogging at his stirrup leather, and the old mare tossing her mane as if she felt that it had been a holiday.

He was very cross with the Hindimini. They had made him gallop halfway over the hill before he rode them down, and then they had turned out to be most disappointingly respectable quiet people.

"And the Naib (lieutenant), will think that I wasted a cartridge for nothing," he added.

"Never mind," said I, "it was an excellent tamasha."[10]

On this we were all agreed, and set off again in the best of spirits on our delayed expedition.

The summit of the ridge, when we came to it, was a delightful place. Oak trees, well grown and round as cabbages, spaced singly here and there, threw shady patterns on the grass like splashes of Chinese embroidery on a tablecloth. The yellow lawns spread more or less on a level with gentle ups and downs. From the edge on the right one had only a monotonous ridge in sight across the dip we had skirted that morning: but the other edge jutted on to space. It went steeply down like a wave just gathering, and looked on the Saidmarreh River, green as paint in the valley below. Behind us the wave continued, descending in tree-dotted slopes to the plain of Shirwan, visible with cultivation: that part of the mountain backbone was Waraq

---

[10]Entertainment.

Husil; we had seen its other face from the pass of Milawur. From north-west, along the plain, the river came winding in a ribbon of flat land where the wintering tribes sow their corn: there it had eaten itself a bed between low cliffs filled with thickets of tamarisk.

At present, but for a small cultivated patch of Rudbar Arabs on our right, the land was empty. One beyond another, long hills, cuirassed with flat slabs, lay behind the river like a fleet at anchor, motionless and stripped for battle. Facing us there, was a wall of a ridge called Barkus; not a blade of grass appeared to grow upon it: its rusty boiler-plates of rocks were cleft into shallow cracks for water, and its base was decorated with a series of very regular pinky-white triangles, where small streams, descending in parallel gullies, had laid bare in so amusingly symmetrical a fashion the lower strata of limestone in the soil. The foothills between Barkus and the flat river-land, were all salty, and nothing, Sa'id Ja'far said, would grow upon them: but they had here and there traces of low mud walls which serve to surround and protect the tents of the Lurs in winter, for the tribes live on that higher ground above their riverain fields. The track from Lakistan, along which they would be migrating in a month or so, ran over these foothills from the country of Tarhan. We saw how it kept to the higher ground, avoiding the dangerous recess of the Berinjan defile, into which we could look straight down. Another black cut in the landscape showed the Tang Siah beyond, the Black Narrows, which, they told me, must be negotiated before one can emerge into Tarhan, a far, romantic landscape lost in mists of sunlight.

We sat down where we could look at all this. I feared now that I should never cross the river, but it was something to gaze at its unknown course, and see the way upon its farther side. No doubt was left in my mind that somewhere along this water highroad the old civilizations must be looked for; a natural law links its fertile plains together in a chain which probably continues unbroken between Kermenshah in the north and Susa in the south.

I had brought lunch on my own account, foreseeing that a folded piece of bread stowed away in their waistbands was all that my escort would think of in the way of food. Sa'id Ja'far, however, had been additionally inspired by two pomegranates. Apart from everything else, I was anxious that my people should feel as happy and somnolent as possible for reasons of my own. I fed them with sheep's-tongue in a tin, jam, bread, and tea, to which the goatskin water gave rather a depressing taste. I had asked whether the sheep's-tongue was safe for Moslems when I bought it, and having satisfied their religious doubts, I watched them take to it with enthusiasm. After we had eaten, and drunk our tea, I handed over a packet of cigarettes and remarked that, as they had walked while I had ridden, I might perhaps wander by myself and look for ruins while they rested: they could follow when they felt so inclined.

All went well. No one showed any inclination to move. Husein offered to come if I felt any alarm, but was obviously relieved when I remarked that, as the landscape would be clear of brigands for a week after the morning's doings, I would go alone. I strolled away slowly till I was out of sight: then I started to hurry as fast as I could, north-west to the *wadi* of the treasure.

For twenty minutes the ridge continued its broad and park-like symmetry, in a solitude so great that six ibex, standing on their hind legs to reach the lower branches of an oak tree, were frightened away by my approach. It was two-thirty when I left my party: two hours was the utmost I could allow myself before our return, and the men might begin to search for me sooner: and yet no *wadi* was in sight.

I was beginning to doubt the map after all, when a cleft appeared descending on the northern side of the hill to the river, and therefore invisible from the south as we came up. Here, by rights, should be the treasure. A black rock should overhang on the left side as one climbed down; four wan trees and an oak should make a group before it; and between the rock and the trees I ought to find the entrance to the cave.

Partly with the haste of my walk, and partly with excitement, my heart was now beating, my knees and hands shaking. I began to descend in a great hurry, pausing at every group of rocks to see if the cave could be there. The ravine, from a shallow grassy basin, quickly turned into a sort of funnel with overhanging rocks, a series of small granite amphitheatres descending in tiers, and every one of them capable of containing half a dozen caves or more. And trees, wan and oak, grew everywhere. In five minutes I had descended what would take me four times as long to climb up again. And the ravine grew more and more difficult. Black rocks were all about it, mocking me with little openings of possible caves.

I remembered a fairy story of my childhood. The Prince's Beloved had been carried off by a witch to Lapland and turned into a plant of heather: she would be frozen by the winter night if the word to disenchant her were not recalled: the word was forgotten: alone on the moor in the dusk, with the deadly night coming, the Prince could not distinguish, among so many like her, the little plant he loved: he tried word after word: only at the very last the right one came, and the figure of his love rose up in the twilight.

But my word did not come. Whether I had not descended far enough, or whether I missed the right place in that chaos of rocks, I do not know. But the very last of my time was up, and I dared not seek further. Somehow or other I must scramble back up the ravine and try not to arouse suspicion. So much time had gone already, that even if I now found the cave, I should not be able to explore it. I turned to hurry again, faster than ever I had climbed before, up the steep sides of the ravine.

The two hours were up before I reached the grass of the higher hollow. I saw Husein pass along the skyline, looking for me, and squatted down a moment among the rocks while he went by. Then I continued to race up, my ears filled with the drumming of my heart and every step feeling like the last effort of which I was capable. A little swarm of flies which travelled with me, buzzing round my head, was almost more than I could bear: they settled on my lips and rushed down my throat whenever I opened my mouth in the effort to breathe: I was too incapable of extra effort to brush them away: I came to the conclusion that the want of moisture in the neighbourhood made them such a nuisance: my lips were the only moist objects thereabout, and they tried to settle on them in crowds.

When I reached the top of the ridge again, I devoted five more minutes to a last survey. I reached a high point whence I could see how the end of the mountain dipped down to the Saidmarreh on one side and the plain of Shirwan on the other. In the east was the northern wall of the Unbelievers' Defile where we had travelled: the upper edge of that precipice was just visible. I made a careful note of the landscape and position, and with a little breath again in my body, started to race back along the ridge as I had come. A hare leaped out and scuttered from under my feet. A jay screeched in the trees. I could not think, but went counting my steps mechanically to make myself keep on. And after hours as it seemed, I saw the policeman and Sa'id Ja'far, still placidly resting under the oak tree, and the grey mare browsing near-by.

That was the end of the treasure hunt. And what there may be in the cave of the mountain still remains a mystery.

Sa'id Ja'far and the policeman had been getting anxious. Husein soon returned and showed great joy and surprise at finding me: he could not think how he had missed me on the ridge. As quickly as we could, for we had no time to lose, we started homeward; and had descended, and reached again the track to Shirwan, when we saw Ali and another man, a policeman, coming to meet us, with the lieutenant's fine bay and a second water-skin, a thoughtful offering on his part.

The rest of the descent was a long affair, and the white limestone as bad downhill as up for the horse's feet. Between one skid and another, the day's adventure with the brigands was recounted. Our own policeman, a pleasant healthy peasant lad from Kermenshah, showed his cartridge-belt with the cartridge missing: he was pleased and relieved because the lieutenant had sent words of praise. I took little part in all this, for my heart still seemed to be pounding my ribs after that hectic race. But presently I was roused by the man who came with Ali, who asked if I had seen the cave.

"What cave?" said I. "I am interested in caves."

"Far on the other side, a big cave near the river."

"Some day," said I, "I will come again, and you shall take me to see it. Have you been inside?"

"Yes, indeed," said he. "It is a big cave, but with nothing inside it."

And that is the last I heard about the place of the treasure, until I returned to Baghdad.

• • •

TOM PATEY

(1932–1970)

"A Short Walk with Whillans"

From *One Man's Mountains*

*Tom Patey, a top Scottish ice climber who was killed in a rappel acci-
dent in 1970, was the finest satirist in a long line of superb British
mountaineer-writers who undercut their bold deeds in whimsical and
ironic journal articles. In this classic account of a 1963 attempt on the
north face of the Eiger—the deadliest wall in the Alps—Patey captures
the morbid fatalism of his legendary compatriot Don Whillans, thereby
conveying more of the paradoxical essence of mountaineering than any
number of more earnest narratives.*

"Did you spot that great long streak of blood on the road over
from Chamonix? Twenty yards long, I'd say."

The speaker was Don Whillans. We were seated in the
little inn at Alpiglen and Don's aggressive profile was framed against an
awe-inspiring backdrop of the Eiger-Nordwand. I reflected that the conversation had become attuned to the environment.

"Probably some unfortunate animal," I ventured without much conviction.

Whillans' eyes narrowed. "Human blood," he said. "Remember—lass?" (appealing to his wife Audrey), "I told you to stop the car for a better look. Really turned her stomach, it did. Just when she was getting over the funeral."

I felt an urge to inquire whose funeral they had attended. There had been several. Every time we went up on the Montenvers train we passed a corpse going down. I let the question go. It seemed irrelevant, possibly even irreverent.

"Ay, it's a good life," he mused, "providing you don't weaken."

"What happens if you do?"

"They bury you," he growled, and finished his pint.

Don has that rarest of gifts, the ability to condense a whole paragraph into a single, terse, uncompromising sentence. But there are also occasions when he can become almost lyrical in a macabre sort of way. It depends on the environment.

We occupied a window table in the inn. There were several other tables, and hunched round each of these were groups of shadowy men draped in black cagoules[1]—lean-jawed, grim, uncommunicative characters who spoke in guttural monosyllables and gazed steadfastly towards the window. You only had to glimpse their earnest faces to realise that these men were Eiger Candidates—martyrs for the "Mordwand."[†]

"Look at that big black bastard up there," Whillans chuckled dryly, gesturing with his thumb. "Just waiting to get its claws into you. And think of all the young lads who've sat just where you're sitting now, and come back all tied up in sacks. It makes you think."

It certainly did. I was beginning to wish I had stayed at Chamonix, funerals or no funerals.

"Take that young blonde over there," he pointed towards the sturdy

---

[†]Eiger pseudonym coined by German Press—literally "Murder Wall." [Footnotes preceded by symbols are the author's.]

---

[1]Rain jackets.

Aryan barmaid, who had just replenished his glass. "I wonder how many dead men she's danced with? All the same," he concluded after a minute's reflection, "t'wouldn't be a bad way to spend your last night."

I licked my lips nervously. Don's philosophic discourses are not for the faint hearted.

One of the Eiger Candidates detached himself from a neighbouring group and approached us with obvious intent. He was red haired, small and compact and he looked like a Neanderthal man. This likeness derived from his hunched shoulders, and the way he craned his head forwards like a man who had been struck repeatedly on the crown by a heavy hammer, and through time developed a protective over-growth of skull. His name proved to be Eckhart, and he was a German. Most of them still are.

The odd thing about him was his laugh. It had an uncanny hollow quality. He laughed quite a lot without generating a great deal of warmth, and he wore a twisted grin which seemed to be permanently frozen onto his face. Even Whillans was moved.

"You—going—up?" he inquired.

"Nein," said Eckhart. "Nix gutt! . . . You wait here little time, I think. . . . Now there is much vatter." He turned up his coat collar ruefully and laughed. "Many, many stein fall. . . . All day, all night. . . . Stein, stein." He tapped his head significantly and laughed uproariously. "Two nights we wait at *Tod Bivouac*." He repeated the name as if relishing its sinister undertones. ("It means Dead Man," I said to Whillans in a hushed whisper.) "Always it is nix gutt. . . . Vatter, stein. . . . Stein, vatter . . . so we go down. It is very funny."

We nodded sympathetically. It was all a huge joke.

"Our two Kameraden, they go on. They are saying at the telescopes, one man he has fallen fifty metres. Me? I do not believe this." (Loud and prolonged laughter from the company.)

"You have looked through the telescope?" I inquired anxiously.

"Nein," he grinned, "Not necessary . . . tonight they gain summit . . . tomorrow they descend. And now we will have another beer."

Eckhart was nineteen. He had already accounted for the North Face of the Matterhorn as a training climb and he intended to camp at the foot of the Eigerwand until the right conditions prevailed. If necessary, he could wait until October. Like most of his countrymen he was nothing if not thorough, and finding his bivouac-tent did not measure up to his expectations he had hitchhiked all the way back to Munich to secure another one. As a result of this, he had missed the settled spell of weather that had allowed several rivals to complete the route, including the second successful British team, Baillie and Haston, and also the lone Swiss climber, Darbellay, who had thus made the first solo ascent.[2]

"Made of the right stuff, that youngster," observed Don.

"If you ask me I think he was trying to scare us off," I suggested. "Psychological warfare that's all it is."

"Wait till we get on the face tomorrow," said Whillans. "We'll hear your piece then."

SHORTLY AFTER NOON the next day we left Audrey behind at Alpiglen, and the two of us set off up the green meadows which girdle the foot of the Eigerwand. Before leaving, Don had disposed of his Last Will and Testament. "You've got the car-key, lass, and you know where to find the house-key. That's all you need to know. Ta, for now."

Audrey smiled wanly. She had my profound sympathy.

The heat was oppressive, the atmosphere heavy with menace. How many Munich Bergsteigers had trod this very turf on their upward path never to return to their native Klettergarten?[3] I was humming Wagner's *Valkyrie* theme music as we reached the lowest rocks of the Face.

Then a most unexpected thing happened. From an alcove in the wall emerged a very ordinary Swiss tourist, followed by his very ordinary wife, five small children and a poodle dog. I stopped humming immediately. I

[2]Rusty Baillie and Dougal Haston, two first-rate British climbers. Michel Darbellay, who soloed the face in two days in 1963.

[3]*Bergsteigers*: German for "mountain climbers." *Klettergarten*: "climbing garden"—i.e., a local cliff used as a training area.

had read of tearful farewells with wives and sweethearts calling plaintively, but this was ridiculous. What an undignified send-off! The five children accompanied us up the first snow slope scrambling happily in our wake, and prodding our rucksacks with inquisitive fingers. "Go away," said Whillans irritably, but ineffectively. We were quite relieved when, ultimately, they were recalled to base and we stopped playing Pied Pipers. The dog held on a bit longer until some well directed stones sent it on its way. "Charming, I must say," remarked Don. I wondered whether Hermann Buhl[4] would have given up on the spot—a most irregular start to an Eiger Epic and probably a bad omen.

We started climbing up the left side of the shattered pillar, a variant of the normal route which had been perfected by Don in the course of several earlier attempts. He was well on his way to becoming the Grand Old Man of Grindelwald, though not through any fault of his own. This was his fourth attempt at the climb and on every previous occasion he had been turned back by bad weather or by having to rescue his rivals. As a result of this he must have spent more hours on the Face than any other British climber.

Don's preparations for the Eiger—meticulous in every other respect— had not included unnecessary physical exertion. While I dragged my weary muscles from Breuil to Zermatt via the Matterhorn he whiled away the days at Chamonix sun bathing at the Plage until opening time. At the Bar National he nightly sank five or six pints of "heavy," smoked forty cigarettes, persuaded other layabouts to feed the juke box with their last few francs and amassed a considerable reputation as an exponent of "Baby Foot," the table football game which is the national sport of France. One day the heat had been sufficiently intense to cause a rush of blood to the head because he had walked four miles up to the Montenvers following the railway track, and had acquired such enormous blisters that he had to make the return journey by train. He was nevertheless just as fit as he wanted to be, or indeed needed to be.

---

[4]The great Austrian mountaineer, who spearheaded an epic early ascent of the Eiger in 1952 and who made the solo first ascent of Nanga Parbat in the Himalaya the next year.

First impressions of the Eigerwand belied its evil reputation. This was good climbing rock with excellent friction and lots of small incuts. We climbed unroped, making height rapidly. In fact I was just starting to enjoy myself, when I found the boot. . . .

"Somebody's left a boot here," I shouted to Don.

He pricked up his ears. "Look and see if there's a foot in it," he said.

I had picked it up: I put it down again hurriedly.

"Ha! Here's something else—a torn rucksack," he hissed. "And here's his waterbottle—squashed flat."

I had lost my new-found enthusiasm and decided to ignore future foreign bodies. (I even ignored the pun.)

"You might as well start getting used to them now," advised Whillans. "This is where they usually glance off, before they hit the bottom."

He's a cheery character I thought to myself. To Don, a spade is just a spade—a simple trenching tool used by gravediggers.

At the top of the Pillar we donned our safety helmets. "One thing to remember on the Eiger," said Don, "never look up, or you may need a plastic surgeon."

His advice seemed superfluous that evening, as we did not hear a single ricochet. We climbed on up, past the Second Pillar and roped up for the traverse across to the Difficult Crack. At this late hour the Crack was streaming with water so we decided to bivouac while we were still dry. There was an excellent bivouac cave near the foot of the crack.

"I'LL HAVE ONE of your cigarettes," said Don. "I've only brought Gauloises." This was a statement of fact, not a question. There is something about Don's proverbial bluntness that arouses one's admiration. Of such stuff are generals made. We had a short discussion about bivouacking, but eventually I had to agree with his arguments and occupy the outer berth. It would be less likely to induce claustrophobia, or so I gathered.

I was even more aware of the sudden fall in temperature. My ultra-warm Terray *duvet* failed by a single critical inch to meet the convertible bivvy-rucksack[5] which I had borrowed from Joe Brown. It had been designed, so the manufacturers announced, to Joe's personal specifications, and as far as I could judge, to his personal dimensions as well.

Insidiously and from nowhere it seemed, a mighty thunderstorm built up in the valley less than a mile away. Flashes of lightning lit up the whole Face and grey tentacles of mist crept out of the dusk threatening to envelop our lofty eyrie.

"The girl in the Tourist Office said that a ridge of high pressure occupying the whole of central Europe would last for at least another three days."

"Charming," growled Whillans. "I could give you a better forecast without raising my head."

"We should be singing Bavarian drinking songs to keep our spirits up," I suggested. "How about some Austrian yodelling."

"They're too fond of dipping in glacier streams . . . that's what does it," he muttered sleepily.

"Does what?"

"Makes them yodel. All the same, these bloody Austrians."

THE DAY DAWNED clear. For once it seemed that a miracle had happened and a major thunderstorm had cleared the Eiger, without lodging on the Face. Don remained inscrutable and cautious as ever. Although we were sheltered from any prevailing wind we would have no advance warning of the weather, as our horizons were limited by the Face itself.

There was still a trickle of water coming down the Difficult Crack as Don launched himself stiffly at the first obstacle. Because of our uncertainty about the weather and an argument about who should make breakfast, we had started late. It was 6.30 A.M. and we would have to hurry. He made a bad start by clipping both strands of the double rope to each of the three

---

[5]A pack that doubles as a bivouac sack when the climber thrusts his lower torso inside. *Duvet:* down jacket.

pitons he found in position. The rope jammed continuously and this was even more disconcerting for me, when I followed carrying both rucksacks. Hanging down the middle of the pitch was an old frayed rope, said to have been abandoned by Mlle Loulou Boulaz,[6] and this kept getting entangled with the ice-axes. By the time I had joined Don at this stance I was breathing heavily and more than usually irritated. We used the excuse to unrope and get back into normal rhythm before tackling the Hinterstoisser.[7] It was easy to find the route hereabouts: you merely followed the pitons. They were planted everywhere with rotting rope loops (apparently used for *abseils*)[8] attached to most of them. It is a significant insight into human psychology that nobody ever stops to remove superfluous pegs on the Eiger. If nothing else they help to alleviate the sense of utter isolation that fills this vast Face, but they also act as constant reminders of man's ultimate destiny and the pageant of history written into the rock. Other reminders were there in plenty—gloves, socks, ropes, crampons and boots. None of them appeared to have been abandoned with the owners' consent.

The Hinterstoisser Traverse, despite the illustrations of pre-war heroes traversing "a la Dulfer,"[9] is nothing to get excited about. With two fixed ropes of unknown vintage as an emergency handrail, you can walk across it in three minutes. Stripped of scaffolding, it would probably qualify as Severe by contemporary British standards. The fixed ropes continued without a break as far as the Swallow's Nest—another bivouac site hallowed by tra-

---

[6]A Swiss, one of the first two women seriously to attempt the Eiger, in 1962.

[7]The German Andreas Hinterstoisser, member of the same party that included Toni Kurz, fell to his death in 1936 trying to climb down a delicate traverse he had led. Named after Hinterstoisser, the traverse is now routinely equipped with a fixed rope to preclude such a disaster.

[8]Rappels.

[9]The visionary German climber Hans Dülfer, who also invented the rappel, had shortly after the turn of the century devised a method of crossing unclimbable ground on traverses by using the rope to create critical tension.

dition. Thus far I could well have been climbing the Italian Ridge of the Matterhorn.

We skirted the first ice-field on the right, scrambling up easy rubble where we had expected to find black ice. It was certainly abnormally warm, but if the weather held we had definite grounds for assuming that we could complete the climb in one day—our original intention. The Ice Hose which breaches the rocky barrier between the First and Second Ice-fields no longer merited the name because the ice had all gone. It seemed to offer an easy alley but Don preferred to stick to known alternatives and advanced upon an improbable looking wall some distance across to the left. By the time I had confirmed our position on Hiebeler's route description,[10] he had completed the pitch and was shouting for me to come on. He was well into his stride, but still did not seem to share my optimism.

His doubts were well founded. Ten minutes later, we were crossing the waterworn slabs leading on to the Second Ice-field when we saw the first falling stones. To be exact we did not see the stones, but merely the puff of smoke each one left behind at the point of impact. They did not come bouncing down the cliff with a noisy clatter as stones usually do. In fact they were only audible after they had gone past—WROUFF!—a nasty sort of sound half-way between a suck and a blow.

"It's the small ones that make that sort of noise," explained Whillans. "Wait till you hear the really big ones!"

The blue print for a successful Eiger ascent seems to involve being at the right place at the right time. According to our calculations the Face should have been immune to stonefall at this hour of the morning.

Unfortunately the Eiger makes its own rules. An enormous black cloud had taken shape out of what ought to have been a clear blue sky, and had come to rest on the summit ice-field. It reminded me of a gigantic black

---

[10] Toni Hiebeler, a German climber who had recorded the best pitch-by-pitch description of the classic route on the Eiger north face.

vulture spreading its wings before dropping like lightning on unsuspecting prey.

Down there at the foot of the Second Ice-field, it was suddenly very cold and lonely. Away across to the left was the Ramp; a possible hideaway to sit out the storm. It seemed little more than a stone's throw, but I knew as well as Don did that we had almost 1,500 feet of steep snow-ice to cross before we could get any sort of shelter from stones.

There was no question of finding adequate cover in the immediate vicinity. On either side of us steep ice slopes, peppered with fallen debris, dropped away into the void. Simultaneously with Whillans' arrival at the stance the first flash of lightning struck the White Spider.

"That settles it," said he, clipping the spare rope through my belay karabiner.

"What's going on?" I demanded, finding it hard to credit that such a crucial decision could be reached on the spur of the moment.

"I'm going down," he said. "That's what's going on."

"Wait a minute! Let's discuss the whole situation calmly." I stretched out one hand to flick the ash off my cigarette. Then a most unusual thing happened. There was a higher pitched "WROUFF" than usual and the end of my cigarette disappeared! It was the sort of subtle touch that Hollywood film directors dream about.

"I see what you mean," I said. "I'm going down too."

I cannot recall coming off a climb so quickly. As a result of a long acquaintance Don knew the location of every *abseil* point and this enabled us to bypass the complete section of the climb which includes the Hinterstoisser Traverse and the Chimney leading up to the Swallow's Nest. To do this, you merely *rappel* directly downwards from the last *abseil* point above the Swallow's Nest and so reach a key piton at the top of the wall overlooking the start of the Hinterstoisser Traverse. From here a straightforward *rappel* of 140 feet goes vertically down the wall to the large ledge at the start of the Traverse. If Hinterstoisser had realised that he would probably not now have a Traverse named after him, and the Eigerwand would not enjoy one half its present notoriety. The idea of "a Point of No Return" always captures the imagination, and until very recent times, it was still the fashion to abandon a fixed rope at the Hinterstoisser in order to safeguard a possible retreat.

The unrelenting bombardment, which had kept us hopping from one *abseil* to the next like demented fleas, began to slacken off as we came into the lee of the "Rote Fluh." The weather had obviously broken down completely and it was raining heavily. We followed separate ways down the easy lower section of the Face, sending down volleys of loose scree in front of us. Every now and again we heard strange noises, like a series of muffled yelps, but since we appeared to have the mountain to ourselves, this did not provoke comment. Whillans had just disappeared round a nearby corner when I heard a loud ejaculation.

"God Almighty," he said (or words to that effect). "Japs! Come and see for yourself!"

Sure enough, there they were. Two identical little men in identical climbing uniforms, sitting side by side underneath an overhang. They had been crouching there for an hour, waiting for the bombardment to slacken. I estimated that we must have scored several near misses.

"You—Japs?" grunted Don. It seemed an unnecessary question.

"Yes, yes," they grinned happily, displaying a full set of teeth. "We are Japanese."

"Going—up," queried Whillans. He pointed meaningfully at the grey holocaust sweeping down from the White Spider.

"Yes, yes," they chorused in unison. "Up. Always upwards. First Japanese Ascent."

"You-may-be-going-up-Mate," said Whillans, giving every syllable unnecessary emphasis, "but-a-lot-'igher-than-you-think!"

They did not know what to make of this, so they wrung his hand several times, and thanked him profusely for the advice.

" 'Appy little pair!" said Don. "I don't imagine we'll ever see them again."

He was mistaken. They came back seven days later after several feet of new snow had fallen. They had survived a full-scale Eiger blizzard and had reached our highest point on the Second Ice-field. If they did not receive a medal for valour they had certainly earned one. They were the fore-runners of the climbing élite of Japan, whose members now climb Mount Everest for the purpose of skiing back down again.

We got back to the Alpiglen in time for late lunch. The telescope stood forlorn and deserted in the rain. The Eiger had retired into its misty obliv-ion, as Don Whillans retired to his favourite corner seat by the window.

ERIC NEWBY

(b. 1919)

From *A Short Walk in the Hindu Kush*

One of the finest travel writers and memoirists of our day, Eric Newby has produced no book more blithe than A Short Walk in the Hindu Kush. *A minor comic masterpiece, this account of an impulsive expedition to climb Mir Samir, one of the Hindu Kush mountains of eastern Afghanistan, in 1956 subscribes to a convention that might be called "Bunglers Abroad." Fed up with his job as a London fashion designer, Newby telegraphs his old friend in Rio de Janeiro, Hugh Carless, who for years had regaled Newby with tales of his travels in Nuristan—the region in Afghanistan that centers upon the mountain range of the Hindu Kush. Four years earlier, Carless had made a half-hearted attempt on Mir Samir, a 19,880-foot peak that was still unclimbed in 1956.*

Carless agrees to Newby's whim at once. On reuniting in England, the friends realize that their assault on the distant mountain may be compromised by the fact that neither knows anything about technical climbing. In this passage, only two weeks before heading off to the Hindu Kush, the pair sets out for Wales to acquire the rudiments of the mountaineering art.

When Hugh arrived from New York ten days later I went to meet him at London Airport. Sitting in those sheds on the north side which still, twelve years after the war, give the incoming traveller the feeling that he is entering a beleaguered fortress, I wondered what surprises he had in store for me.

His first words after we had greeted one another were to ask if there was any news from Arnold Brown.[1]

"Not a thing."

"That's bad," he said.

"It's not so disastrous. After all, you have done some climbing. I'll soon pick it up. We'll just have to be careful."

He looked pale. I put it down to the journey. Then he said: "You know I've never done any *real* climbing."

It took me some time to assimilate this.

"But all that stuff about the mountain. You and Dreesen . . ."[2]

"Well, that was more or less a reconnaissance."

"But all this gear. How did you know what to order?"

"I've been doing a lot of reading."

"But you said you had porters."

"Not porters—drivers. It's not like the Himalayas. There aren't any 'tigers' in Afghanistan.[3] No one knows anything about mountaineering."

---

[1] A mountaineer teaching in India whom Carless and Newby had hoped to recruit for their expedition.

[2] Bob Dreesen, an American who had been Carless's partner on his previous attempt on Mir Samir.

[3] On the 1922 Everest expedition, the appellation "tigers" was given to the strongest Sherpas; it has stuck ever since.

There was a long silence as we drove down the Great West Road.

"Perhaps we should postpone it for a year," he said.

"Ha-ha. I've just given up my job!"

Hugh stuck out his jaw. Normally a determined-looking man, the effect was almost overwhelming.

"There's nothing for it," he said. "We must have some lessons."

Wanda[4] and I were leaving England for Istanbul on June 1st. Hugh and I had just four days to learn about climbing.

THE FOLLOWING NIGHT after some brisk telephoning we left for Wales to learn about climbing, in the brand new station wagon Hugh had ordered by post from South America. He had gone to Brighton to fetch it. Painted in light tropical colours it had proved to be rather conspicuous in Hammersmith. Soon it had been covered with swarms of little boys and girls whose mothers stood with folded arms silently regarding it.

We had removed all the furniture from the drawing-room to make room for the equipment and stores. Our three-piece suite was standing in the garden under a tarpaulin. The drawing-room looked like the quartermaster's store of some clandestine force. It was obvious that Hugh was deeply impressed.

"How long have you been living like this?"

"Ever since we can remember. It's not all here yet. There's still the food."

"What food?" He looked quite alarmed.

"Six cases of Army ration, compo.[5] in fibre boxes. It's arriving tomorrow."

"We can always leave it in England. I don't know about you but food doesn't interest me. We can always live off the country."

I remembered von Dückelmann, that hardy Austrian forester without an ounce of spare flesh on him, who had lost twelve pounds in a fortnight in Nuristan.

"Whatever else we leave behind it won't be the food."

[4]Newby's wife.
[5]Components.

"Well, I suppose we can always give it away." He sounded almost shocked, as if for the first time he had detected in me a grave moral defect. It was an historic moment.

With unconcealed joy my wife watched us load some of the mountaineering equipment into the machine.

"We'd better not take all of it," Hugh said. "They might wonder why we've got so much stuff if we don't know how to use it."

Over the last weeks the same thought had occurred to me constantly.

"What about the tent?"

The tent had arrived that morning. It had been described to me by the makers as being suitable for what they called "the final assault." With its sewn-in ground-sheet, special flaps so that it could be weighed down with boulders, it convinced me, more than any other single item of equipment, that we were going, as the books have it, "high." It had been specially constructed for the curious climatic conditions we were likely to encounter in the Hindu Kush.

"I shouldn't take *that*, if I were you," said my wife with sinister emphasis. "The children tried to put it up in the garden after lunch. Whoever made it forgot to make holes for the poles."

"Are you sure?"

"Quite sure. You know it's got those poles shaped like a V, that you slip into a sort of pocket in the material. Well, they haven't made any pockets, so you can't put it up."

"It's lucky you found out. We should have looked pretty silly on Mir Samir."

"You're going to look pretty silly at any rate. I shouldn't be surprised if they've done the same thing to your sleeping-bags."

"Have you telephoned the makers?"

"That's no use. If you send it back to them, you'll never see it again. I've sent for the little woman who makes my dresses. She's coming tomorrow morning."

We continued to discuss what we should take to Wales.

"I should take your Folboat,"[6] said Hugh. "There's bound to be a lake

[6]A collapsible kayak made of wood frame and canvas and rubber skin.

near the inn. It will be a good chance of testing it BEFORE YOU PASS THROUGH THE GORGES. The current is tremendously swift."

I had never had any intention of being either drowned or ritually mutilated in Mahsud Territory.[7] I told him that I hadn't got a Folboat.

"I was almost certain I wrote to you about getting a Folboat. It's a pity. There's not much time now."

"No," I said, "there isn't."

It was nearly midnight when we left London. Our destination was an inn situated in the wilds of Caernarvonshire. Hugh had telephoned the proprietor and explained to him the peculiar state of ignorance in which we found ourselves. It was useless to dissemble: Hugh had told him everything. He was not only an experienced mountaineer, but was also the head of the mountain rescue service. It is to his eternal credit that he agreed to help us rather than tell us, as a more conventional man might have done, that his rooms were all booked.

We arrived at six o'clock the following morning, having driven all night, but already a spiral of smoke was issuing from a chimney at the back of the premises.

The first thing that confronted us when we entered the hotel was a door on the left. On it was written EVEREST ROOM. Inside it was a facsimile of an Alpine hut, done out in pine wood, with massive benches round the walls. On every side was evidence of the presence of the great ones of the mountain world. Their belongings in the shape of ropes, rucksacks, favourite jackets and boots were everywhere, ready for the off. It was not a museum. It was more like the Royal Enclosure.[8] Sir John and Sir Edmund might appear at any moment.[9] They were probably on the premises.

---

[7]The Mahsud are a frontier tribe that occupies a particular territory around the Afghanistan-Pakistan border. The frontier tribesmen fiercely resisted British control and were known for their savagery in battle and strong independence.

[8]Royal Ascot Enclosure, the queen's glass-fronted box at England's premier horse racing event of the year, Ascot week.

[9]Sir John Hunt and Sir Edmund Hillary, respectively leader and summit climber on the 1953 first ascent of Everest.

"Whatever else we do I don't think we shall spend much time in the *Everest Room*," said Hugh, as we reverently closed the door. "For the first time I'm beginning to feel that we really do know damn all."

"EXACTLY."

At this moment we were confronted by a remarkably healthy-looking girl.

"Most people have had breakfast but it's still going on," she said.

The only other occupant of the breakfast room was a compact man of about forty-five, who was eating his way through the sort of breakfast I hadn't been able to stomach for ten years. He was wearing a magnificent sweater that was the product of peasant industry. He was obviously a climber. With an hysterical attempt at humour, like soldiers before an attack, we tried to turn him into a figure of fun, speaking in whispers. This proved difficult, as he wasn't at all comic, just plainly competent.

"He looks desperately healthy." (His face was the colour of old furniture.)

"Everyone looks healthy here, except us."

"I don't think it's real tan."

"Perhaps he's making a film about mountain rescue."

"How very appropriate."

"Perhaps he'll let us stand-in, as corpses."

After breakfast the proprietor introduced us to the mystery man. We immediately felt ashamed of ourselves.

"This is Dr. Richardson," he said. "He's very kindly agreed to take you out and teach you the rudiments of climbing."

"Have you ever done any?" asked the Doctor.

It seemed no time to bring up my scrambles in the Dolomites, nor even Hugh's adventures at the base of Mir Samir.

"No," I said firmly, "neither of us knows the first thing about it."

We had arrived at seven; by nine o'clock we were back in the station wagon, this time bound for the north face of the mountain called Tryfan.

"Stop here," said the Doctor. Hugh parked the car by a milestone that read "Bangor X Miles." Rearing up above the road was a formidable-looking chunk of rock, the *Milestone Buttress*.

"That's what you're going to climb," said the Doctor. "It's got practically everything you need at this stage."

It seemed impossible. In a daze we followed him over a rough wall and into the bracken. A flock of mountain sheep watched us go, making noises that sounded suspiciously like laughter.

Finally we reached the foot of it. Close-to it didn't seem so formidable. The whole face was scarred by the nailed boots of countless climbers.

"This thing is like a by-pass," said the Doctor. "Later in the season you'd have to queue up to climb it. We're lucky to have it to ourselves."

"If there's one thing we don't need it's an audience."

"First of all you've got to learn about the rope. Without a rope, climbing is suicide. It's the only thing that justifies it. Chris told me what you're planning to do. If anything happens on that mountain, it may not get into the papers, and at least no one else will have to risk their necks to get you off if anything goes wrong. If I thought that you were the sort of people who would take risks, I wouldn't have come with you today."

He showed us how to rope ourselves together, using the proper knots; the bowline for the leader and the end man; the butterfly noose, a beautifully symmetrical knot, for the middleman; how to hold it and how to coil it so that it would pay out without snarling up, and how to belay.

"You never move without a proper belay. I start to climb and I go on until I reach a knob of rock on to which I can belay. I take a *karabiner*" (he produced one of the D-shaped steel rings with a spring-loaded clip) "and attach a sling to the loop of rope round my waist. Then all I have to do is to put the sling over the knob of rock, and pass the rope under one shoulder and over the other. If possible, you brace your feet against a solid block. Like that you can take the really big strain if the next man comes off.

"When the second man reaches the leader, the leader unclips the *karabiner* with the sling on it, and the second man attaches it to *his* waist. He's now belayed. The second man gives his own sling to the leader who goes on to the next pitch. Like this."

"What I don't see," I whispered to Hugh, "is what happens if the leader falls on the first pitch. According to this he's done for."

"The leader just mustn't fall off."

"Remind me to let you be leader."

The Doctor now showed what I thought was a misplaced trust in us. He sent us to the top of a little cliff, not more than twenty feet high, with a battered-looking holly tree growing on it. "I want you to pretend that you're the leader," he said to Hugh. "I want you to belay yourself with a sling and a *karabiner* to the holly tree. On the way up I am going to fall off backwards and I shan't tell you when I'm going to do it. You've got to hold me." He began to climb.

He reached the top and was just about to step over the edge when, without warning, he launched himself backwards into space. And then the promised miracle happened, for the rope was taut and Hugh was holding him, not by the belay but simply with the rope passed under one shoulder and over the other. There was no strain on the sling round Hugh's waist at all, his body was like a spring. I was very impressed — for the first time I began to understand the trust that climbers must be able to have in one another.

"Now it's your turn," said the Doctor.

It was like a memorable day in 1939 when I fell backwards off the fore upper topsail yard of a four-masted barque, only this time I expected Hugh to save me. And he did. Elated we practised this new game for some time until the Doctor looked at his watch. It was 11.30.

"We'd better get on to the rock. We wouldn't normally but there's so little time and you seem to be catching on to the roping part. Let's go. We'll take the *Ordinary Route*. You may think it isn't much but don't just go bald-headed at it. I'm going to lead. It's about two hundred feet altogether. We start in this chimney." He indicated an inadequate-looking cleft in the rock face.

It seemed too small to contain a human being at all but the Doctor vanished into it easily enough. Like me, he was wearing nailed boots, not the new-fangled ones with rubber vibram soles. I could hear them screeching on the rock as he scrabbled for a foothold. There was a lot of grunting and groaning then he vanished from sight.

Hugh went next. It was easier for him as he was very slim.

Then it was my turn. Like a boa-constrictor swallowing a live chicken, I wriggled up it, with hideous wear and tear to my knees, until I emerged on a boulder slope.

"Now we begin," said the Doctor.

"What was that, if it wasn't the beginning?"

"The start. This is the beginning."

"How very confusing."

The worst part was what he called "Over the garden wall," which entailed swinging round a projection, hanging over a void and then traversing along a ledge into a cave.

"I wish he'd wear rubbers," I said to Hugh, as the Doctor vanished over the wall with a terrible screeching of tricounis.[10]

"It's not the climbing I object to, it's the noise."

There was still a twenty-foot chimney with a tree in it up which we fought our way and, at last, we lay on the top panting and admiring the view which was breathtaking. I was very impressed and proud. It wasn't much but I had done my first climb.

"What do you call this?" Hugh said, warily. "Easy, difficult or something in between?"

"Moderate."

"How do they go? I've forgotten."

"Easy, moderate, difficult, very difficult, severe, very severe, exceptionally severe, and excessively severe."

"Oh."

While we were eating our sandwiches the Doctor began to describe what he called "The Rappel." More than a year has passed since, for the first and last time, I practised this excruciatingly painful method of descending the face of a mountain. Even now I am unable to remember it without a shudder. Like the use of the bayonet, it was something to be learned and, if possible, forgotten for ever.

"You first," said the Doctor. In dealing with him we suffered the disadvantage that he wasn't retained at some handsome fee to teach us all this. He was in fact ruining his holiday, in order to give us a slightly more than even chance of surviving.

---

[10]Nails affixed to boot soles to give better purchase on ice and wet rock (now obsolete).

"Put a sling round the tree and run the double rope through it; now pass it round your right thigh, between your legs; now up the back and sling it over your left shoulder so that it falls down in front. That's right. Now walk backwards to the edge, keep the rope taut. Now keep your legs horizontal and walk down."

I walked down. It would have been perfect if only the face of the cliff had been smooth; unfortunately it was slightly concave, which made it difficult to keep my legs at right angles to the face. I failed to do so, slipped and went swinging backwards and forwards across the face like a pendulum, with the rope biting into my groin.

"Well, you've learned one lesson," Hugh said cheerfully, when I reached the bottom after disengaging myself from the rope and swarming down in a more conventional manner.

"If it's a question of doing that again or being castrated by Mohmands, I'll take the Mohmands.[11] My groin won't stand up to much more of this."

"You must be very sensitive," Hugh said. "Lots of girls do it."

"I'm not a girl. There must be some other way. It's impossible in thin trousers."

After a large, old-fashioned tea at the inn with crumpets and boiled eggs, we were taken off to the *Eckenstein Boulder*. Oscar Eckenstein was a renowned climber at the end of the nineteenth century, whose principal claim to fame was that he had been the first man in this or any other country to study the technique of holds and balance on rock. He had spent his formative years crawling over the boulder that now bore his name. Although it was quite small, about the size of a delivery van, his boulder was said to apparently embody all the fundamental problems that are such a joy to mountaineers and were proving such a nightmare to us.

For this treat we were allowed to wear gym shoes.

Full of boiled egg and crumpet, we clung upside down to the boulder like bluebottles, while the Doctor shouted encouragement to us from a safe

[11]Another frontier tribe.

distance. Occasionally one of us would fall off and land with a painful thump on the back of his head.

"YOU MUST NOT FALL OFF. Imagine that there is a thousand-foot drop under you."

"I am imagining it but I still can't stay on."

Back at the inn we had hot baths, several pints of beer, an enormous dinner and immediately sank into a coma. For more than forty hours we had had hardly any sleep. "Good training," was Hugh's last muffled comment.

By this time the waitresses at the inn had become interested in this artificial forcing process. All three of them were experienced climbers who had taken the job in the first place in order to be able to combine business with pleasure. Now they continued our climbing education.

They worked in shifts, morning and afternoon, so that we were climbing all the time. We had never encountered anything quite like them before. At breakfast on the last day, Judith, a splendid girl with auburn hair whose father had been on Everest in 1933, told us what she had in mind. "Pamela and I are free this afternoon; we're going to do the *Spiral Stairs* on Dinas Cromlech. It's an interesting climb."

As soon as we could get through our breakfast we looked it up in the Climbing Guide to the Snowdon District, Part 6.

"Dinas Cromlech," said the book, "is perhaps the most impressive cliff on the north side of the Llanberis Pass, its massive rhyolite pillars giving it the appearance of some grim castle . . . all routes have surprising steepness . . . on the whole the rock is sound, although *on first acquaintance it may not appear to be so.*"

Spiral Stairs was described as "Very difficult" and as having "an impressive first pitch with good exposure." At the back was a nasty picture of the Cromlech with the routes marked on it. Besides *Spiral Stairs* there was *Cenotaph Corner, Ivy Sepulchre* and the *Sexton's Route.* It sounded a jolly spot.

"I wish we were doing *Castle Gully.* It says here, 'a pleasant vegetable route.'"

"They might have decided on *Ivy Sepulchre*," said Hugh. "Just listen to this. 'Two hundred feet. Exceptionally severe. A very serious and difficult climb . . . loose rock overhangs . . . progress is made by a bridging type of lay-back movement, an occasional hold of a doubtful nature appearing *now* and *then*.' He doesn't say what you do when it doesn't."

"What's a lay-back?"

"You were doing a lay-back when you fell off the Eckenstein Boulder."

"This is only the beginning, it gets worse. 'At this point the angle relents . . .' "

"Relents is good," I said.

" ' . . . to a small niche below the conspicuous overhang; no belay. Start the overhang by bridging. The climbing at this point is exceptionally severe, strenuous and in a very exposed position.' It goes on and on! 'A short groove leads to the foot of an old rickety holly tree and after a struggle with this and the crack behind it, a good hold can be reached on the left wall.' "

"I wonder why everything seems to end with a rickety old holly tree."

We decided to have a quiet morning. Just then the other two girls appeared loaded with gear.

"Hurry up," they said, "we've got to be back by half-past twelve. We're going to take you up *The Gauge*. You made a nonsense of it, the Doctor said. And you've both got to lead."

THAT AFTERNOON, AS Judith led the way up the scree from the road towards the base of Dinas Cromlech, we felt that if anything the guide book, in spite of its sombre warnings, had not prepared us for the reality. It was as if a giant had been smoothing off the sides of a heap of cement with a trowel and had then lost patience and left it half finished. Its most impressive feature was a vast, right-angled wall, shiny with water and apparently smooth.

"*Cenotaph Corner*," said Judith. "Hundred and twenty feet. When you can do that you really will be climbers."

It seemed impossible.

"Joe Brown led it in 1952, with Belshaw. Joe's a plumber in Manchester. He spends every moment he can here. You remember how awful it was last winter when everyone's pipes were bursting? In the middle of it he left a note on the door of his house: 'Gone climbing. Joe Brown.' People nearly went mad."

"Where is he now?"

"In the Himalayas."

We looked at what he had climbed with awe.

There were already three people on *Spiral Stairs*. I could see what the book meant by "good exposure." At that moment one of them was edging his way round the vertical left-hand edge of *Cenotaph Corner*.

"That's the part that always gives me a thrill," said Pamela, the other girl. "Pity. Let's not wait, let's do *Ivy Sepulchre* instead."

"Oh, Pamela, do you think we ought to? It may be too much for them."

She made us sound like a couple of invalids out on the pier for an airing. Nevertheless, this was no time for stubborn pride. I asked Hugh if that was the climb we had been reading about at breakfast. He said it was.

"I think Judith's right," I said. "It may be too much for us."

As we waited in the cold shadow under the lee of the *Cenotaph*, Judith explained what we were going to do.

"The beginning's rather nasty because of that puddle. It makes your feet slippery just when they need to be dry. We'll climb in two parties. Pamela will lead Hugh, I'll lead you. The first part's seventy feet; round the edge of the *Cenotaph* it's very exposed and you'll feel the wind. Don't come on until I shout and you feel pressure on the rope. I'll be belayed then. Even if you come off you won't fall far."

"What happens if someone does come off? You can't just leave them hanging."

"Send for the fire brigade," said Judith.

Both girls were shuffling their boots on the rock like featherweight boxers.

Then Pamela was gone, soon to be followed by Hugh.

After what seemed an eternity it was Judith's turn. I had her belayed but at this stage it wasn't much use: I remembered the Doctor's warning. "The leader must not fall off." Then she vanished. I continued to pay out the rope. There was a long interval and I heard her shout very distantly to come on and the rope tautened.

It was impossible to get on to the rock without getting at least one foot wet.

Very slowly I worked my way out to the corner of the *Sepulchre*. As I edged round it into what seemed to be empty space I came on to the part with good exposure, the part that always gave Pamela a thrill. Below me was a huge drop to the rocks and as I came round the wind blew my hair into my eyes.

Two more pitches and we were on the top. I felt a tremendous exaltation. Sitting there on a boulder was a man in a bowler hat and white collar smoking a pipe.

"Early closing in Caernarvon," Judith said.

"He looks like an undertaker to me."

"We shall have to hurry, it's Pamela's day to serve tea." We went down a wide gully, then raced down the scree to the car. The others were waiting for us. The girls were pleased, so were we. Only the man with the bowler hat weighed on my mind. I asked Hugh if he had seen him.

"Which man? We didn't see a man."

"Now you're making me feel like one of those schoolteachers at Versailles."[12]

"We saw the other party, but we didn't see a man in a bowler hat."

AS WE WERE leaving for London, Judith gave me a little pamphlet costing sixpence. It showed, with the aid of pictures, the right and wrong ways of climbing a mountain.

[12]A reference to the story of two English schoolteachers who, when visiting Versailles on vacation in August 1901, saw some odd characters dressed in eighteenth-century garb. They later determined that they had traveled back in time to 1792. The two women, Anne Moberly and Eleanor Jourdain, went on to write a book about their experience.

"We haven't been able to teach you anything about snow and ice," she said, "but this shows you how to do it. If you find anything on the journey out with snow on it, I should climb it if you get the chance."

"I wish we were coming with you," she added, "to keep you out of trouble."

"So do we," we said, and we really meant it. Everyone turned out to say goodbye. It was very heart-warming.

"You know that elderly gentleman who lent you a pair of climbing boots," Hugh said, as we drove through the evening sunshine towards Capel Curig.

"You mean Mr. Bartrum?"

"Did you know he's a past President of the Alpine Club? He's written a letter about us to the Everest Foundation. He showed it to me."

I asked him what it said.

"He wrote, 'I have formed a high opinion of the character and determination of Carless and Newby and suggest that they should be given a grant towards the cost of their expedition to the Hindu Kush.' "

TOM WOLFE
(b. 1930)

From *The Right Stuff*

On rereading Tom Wolfe's celebrated 1979 best-seller, The Right Stuff, *it is hard to know whether Wolfe merely captured the essence of a legendary character—test pilot Chuck Yeager, the first man to break the sound barrier—or whether, with his considerable fictive gifts, Wolfe created that character, with his "poker-hollow West Virginia drawl." No matter: the conceit that the best pilots in the world in the late 1940s, holed up at Muroc Field in the Mojave Desert of California, were a gang of seat-of-the-pants cowboys devoted to "Flying & Drinking and Drinking & Driving," placing all their trust in the feel of the plane at 760 mph rather than in the solemn prognostications of physicists, is too satisfying to quibble with.*

At the end of the war the Army had discovered that the Germans not only had the world's first jet fighter but also a rocket plane that had gone 596 miles an hour in tests. Just after the war a British jet, the Gloster Meteor, jumped the official world speed record from 469 to 606 in a single day. The next great plateau would be Mach 1, the speed of sound, and the Army Air Force considered it crucial to achieve it first.

The speed of sound, Mach 1, was known (thanks to the work of the physicist Ernst Mach) to vary at different altitudes, temperatures, and wind speeds. On a calm 60-degree day at sea level it was about 760 miles an hour, while at 40,000 feet, where the temperature would be at least sixty below, it was about 660 miles an hour. Evil and baffling things happened in the transonic zone, which began at about .7 Mach. Wind tunnels choked out at such velocities. Pilots who approached the speed of sound in dives reported that the controls would lock or "freeze" or even alter their normal functions. Pilots had crashed and died because they couldn't budge the stick. Just last year[1] Geoffrey de Havilland, son of the famous British aircraft designer and builder, had tried to take one of his father's DH 108s to Mach 1. The ship started buffeting and then disintegrated, and he was killed. This led engineers to speculate that the g-forces became infinite at Mach 1, causing the aircraft to implode. They started talking about "the sonic wall" and "the sound barrier."

So this was the task that a handful of pilots, engineers, and mechanics had at Muroc. The place was utterly primitive, nothing but bare bones, bleached tarpaulins, and corrugated tin rippling in the heat with caloric waves; and for an ambitious young pilot it was perfect. Muroc seemed like an outpost on the dome of the world, open only to a righteous few, closed off to the rest of humanity, including even the Army Air Force brass of command control, which was at Wright Field.[2] The commanding officer at Muroc was only a colonel, and his superiors at Wright did not relish junkets to the Muroc rat shacks in the first place. But to pilots this prehistoric

[1] 1946.
[2] In Dayton, Ohio.

throwback of an airfield became . . . shrimp heaven! the rat-shack plains of Olympus!

Low Rent Septic Tank Perfection . . . yes; and not excluding those traditional essentials for the blissful hot young pilot: Flying & Drinking and Drinking & Driving.

Just beyond the base, to the southwest, there was a rickety wind-blown 1930's-style establishment called Pancho's Fly Inn, owned, run, and bartended by a woman named Pancho Barnes. Pancho Barnes wore tight white sweaters and tight pants, after the mode of Barbara Stanwyck in *Double Indemnity*. She was only forty-one when Yeager arrived at Muroc, but her face was so weatherbeaten, had so many hard miles on it, that she looked older, especially to the young pilots at the base. She also shocked the pants off them with her vulcanized tongue. Everybody she didn't like was an old bastard or a sonofabitch. People she liked were old bastards and sonsabitches, too. "I tol' 'at ol' bastard to get 'is ass on over here and I'd g'im a drink." But Pancho Barnes was anything but Low Rent. She was the granddaughter of the man who designed the old Mount Lowe cable-car system, Thaddeus S. C. Lowe. Her maiden name was Florence Leontine Lowe. She was brought up in San Marino, which adjoined Pasadena and was one of Los Angeles' wealthiest suburbs, and her first husband—she was married four times—was the pastor of the Pasadena Episcopal Church, the Rev. C. Rankin Barnes. Mrs. Barnes seemed to have few of the conventional community interests of a Pasadena matron. In the late 1920's, by boat and plane, she ran guns for Mexican revolutionaries and picked up the nickname Pancho. In 1930 she broke Amelia Earhart's airspeed record for women. Then she barnstormed around the country as the featured performer of "Pancho Barnes's Mystery Circus of the Air." She always greeted her public in jodhpurs and riding boots, a flight jacket, a white scarf, and a white sweater that showed off her terrific Barbara Stanwyck chest. Pancho's desert Fly Inn had an airstrip, a swimming pool, a dude ranch corral, plenty of acreage for horseback riding, a big old guest house for the lodgers, and a connecting building that was the bar and restaurant. In the barroom the floors, the tables, the chairs, the walls, the beams, the bar were of the sort known as extremely weatherbeaten, and the screen doors kept banging. No-body putting together such a place for a movie about flying in the old days would ever dare make it as dilapidated and generally go-to-hell as it actually was. Behind the bar were many pictures of airplanes and pilots, lavishly autographed and inscribed, badly framed and crookedly hung. There was an old piano that had been dried out and cracked to the point of hopeless desiccation. On a good night a huddle of drunken aviators could be heard trying to bang, slosh, and navigate their way through old Cole Porter tunes. On average nights the tunes were not that good to start with. When the screen door banged and a man walked through the door into the saloon, every eye in the place checked him out. If he wasn't known as somebody who had something to do with flying at Muroc, he would be eyed like some lame goddamned mouseshit sheepherder from *Shane*.

The plane the Air Force wanted to break the sound barrier with was called the X-1. The Bell Aircraft Corporation had built it under an Army contract. The core of the ship was a rocket of the type first developed by a young Navy inventor, Robert Truax, during the war. The fuselage was shaped like a 50-caliber bullet—an object that was known to go supersonic smoothly. Military pilots seldom drew major test assignments; they went to highly paid civilians working for the aircraft corporations. The prime pilot for the X-1 was a man whom Bell regarded as the best of the breed. This man looked like a movie star. He looked like a pilot from out of *Hell's Angels*. And on top of everything else there was his name: Slick Goodlin.

The idea in testing the X-1 was to nurse it carefully into the transonic zone, up to seven-tenths, eight-tenths, nine-tenths the speed of sound (.7 Mach, .8 Mach, .9 Mach) before attempting the speed of sound itself, Mach 1, even though Bell and the Army already knew the X-1 had the rocket power to go to Mach 1 and beyond, if there *was* any *beyond*. The consensus of aviators and engineers, after Geoffrey de Havilland's death, was that the speed of sound was an absolute, like the firmness of the earth. The sound barrier was a farm you could buy in the sky. So Slick Goodlin began to probe the transonic zone in the X-1, going up to .8 Mach. Every time he came down he'd have a riveting tale to tell. The buffeting, it was so fierce—and the listeners, their imaginations aflame, could practically see poor Geoffrey de Havilland disintegrating in midair. And the goddamned aerodynamics—and the listeners got a picture of a man in ballroom pumps skidding across a sheet of ice, pursued by bears. A controversy arose over just how much bonus Slick Goodlin should receive for assaulting the dread Mach 1 itself. Bonuses for contract test pilots were not unusual; but the figure of $150,000 was now bruited about. The Army balked, and Yeager got the job. He took it for $283 a month, or $3,396 a year; which is to say, his regular Army captain's pay.

The only trouble they had with Yeager was in holding him back. On his first powered flight in the X-1 he immediately executed an unauthorized zero-g roll with a full load of rocket fuel, then stood the ship on its tail and went up to .85 Mach in a vertical climb, also unauthorized. On subsequent flights, at speeds between .85 Mach and .9 Mach, Yeager ran into most known airfoil problems—loss of elevator, aileron, and rudder control, heavy trim pressures, Dutch rolls, pitching and buffeting, the lot—yet was convinced, after edging over .9 Mach, that this would all get better, not worse, as you reached Mach 1. The attempt to push beyond Mach 1—"breaking the sound barrier"—was set for October 14, 1947. Not being an engineer, Yeager didn't believe the "barrier" existed.

OCTOBER 14 WAS a Tuesday. On Sunday evening, October 12, Chuck Yeager dropped in at Pancho's, along with his wife. She was a brunette named Glennis, whom he had met in California while he was in training, and she was such a number, so striking, he had the inscription "Glamorous Glennis" written on the nose of his P-51 in Europe and, just a few weeks back, on the X-1 itself. Yeager didn't go to Pancho's and knock back a few because two days later the big test was coming up. Nor did he knock back a few because it was the weekend. No, he knocked back a few because night had come and he was a pilot at Muroc. In keeping with the military tradition of Flying & Drinking, that was what you did, for no other reason than that the sun had gone down. You went to Pancho's and knocked back a few and listened to the screen doors banging and to other aviators torturing the piano and the nation's repertoire of Familiar Favorites and to lonesome mouse-turd strangers wandering in through the banging doors and to Pancho classifying the whole bunch of them as old bastards and miserable peckerwoods. That was what you did if you were a pilot at Muroc and the sun went down.

So about eleven Yeager got the idea that it would be a hell of a kick if he and Glennis saddled up a couple of Pancho's dude-ranch horses and went for a romp, a little rat race, in the moonlight. This was in keeping with the military tradition of Flying & Drinking and Drinking & Driving, except that this was prehistoric Muroc and you rode horses. So Yeager and his wife set off on a little proficiency run at full gallop through the desert in the moonlight amid the arthritic silhouettes of the Joshua trees. Then they start racing back to the corral, with Yeager in the lead and heading for the gateway. Given the prevailing conditions, it being nighttime, at Pancho's, and his head being filled with a black sandstorm of many badly bawled songs and vulcanized oaths, he sees too late that the gate has been closed. Like many a hard-driving midnight pilot before him, he does not realize that he is not equally gifted in the control of all forms of locomotion. He and the horse hit the gate, and he goes flying off and lands on his right side. His side hurts like hell.

The next day, Monday, his side still hurts like hell. It hurts every time he moves. It hurts every time he breathes deep. It hurts every time he moves his right arm. He knows that if he goes to a doctor at Muroc or says anything to anybody even remotely connected with his superiors, he will be scrubbed from the flight on Tuesday. They might even go so far as to put some other miserable peckerwood in his place. So he gets on his motorcycle, an old junker that Pancho had given him, and rides over to see a doctor in the town of Rosamond, near where he lives. Every time the goddamned motorcycle hits a pebble in the road, his side hurts like a sonofabitch. The doctor in Rosamond informs him he has two broken ribs and he tapes them up and tells him that if he'll just keep his right arm immobilized for a couple of weeks and avoid any physical exertion or sudden movements, he should be all right.

Yeager gets up before daybreak on Tuesday morning—which is supposed to be the day he tries to break the sound barrier—and his ribs still hurt like a sonofabitch. He gets his wife to drive him over to the field, and he has to keep his right arm pinned down to his side to keep his ribs from hurting so much. At dawn, on the day of a flight, you could hear the X-1 screaming long before you got there. The fuel for the X-1 was alcohol and liquid oxygen, oxygen converted from a gas to a liquid by lowering its temperature to 297 degrees below zero. And when the lox, as it was called, rolled out of the hoses and into the belly of the X-1, it started boiling off and the X-1 started steaming and screaming like a teakettle. There's quite a crowd on hand, by Muroc standards . . . perhaps nine or ten souls. They're still fueling the X-1 with the lox, and the beast is wailing.

The X-1 looked like a fat orange swallow with white markings. But it was really just a length of pipe with four rocket chambers in it. It had a tiny cockpit and a needle nose, two little straight blades (only three and a half inches thick at the thickest part) for wings, and a tail assembly set up high to avoid the "sonic wash" from the wings. Even though his side was throbbing and his right arm felt practically useless, Yeager figured he could grit his teeth and get through the flight—except for one specific move he had to make. In the rocket launches, the X-1, which held only two and a half minutes' worth of fuel, was carried up to twenty-six thousand feet underneath the wings of a B-29. At seven thousand feet, Yeager was to climb down a ladder from the bomb bay of the B-29 to the open doorway of the X-1, hook up to the oxygen system and the radio microphone and earphones, and put his crash helmet on and prepare for the launch, which would come at twenty-five thousand feet. This helmet was a homemade number. There had never been any such thing as a crash helmet before. Throughout the war pilots had used the old skin-tight leather helmet-and-goggles. But the X-1 had a way of throwing the pilot around so violently that there was danger of getting knocked out against the walls of the cockpit. So Yeager had bought a big leather football helmet—there were no plastic ones at the time—and he butchered it with a hunting knife until he carved the right kind of holes in it, so that it would fit down over his regular flying helmet and the earphones and the oxygen rig. Anyway, then his flight engineer, Jack Ridley, would climb down the ladder, out in the breeze, and shove into place the cockpit door, which had to be lowered out of the belly of the B-29 on a chain. Then Yeager had to push a handle to lock the door airtight. Since the X-1's cockpit was minute, you had to push the handle with your right hand. It took quite a shove. There was no way you could move into position to get enough leverage with your left hand.

Out in the hangar Yeager makes a few test shoves on the sly, and the pain is so incredible he realizes that there is no way a man with two broken ribs is going to get the door closed. It is time to confide in somebody, and the logical man is Jack Ridley. Ridley is not only the flight engineer but a pilot himself and a good old boy from Oklahoma to boot. He will understand about Flying & Drinking and Drinking & Driving through the goddamned Joshua trees. So Yeager takes Ridley off to the side in the tin hangar and says: Jack, I got me a little ol' problem here. Over at Pancho's the other night I sorta . . . dinged my goddamned ribs. Ridley says, Whattya mean . . . *dinged?* Yeager says, Well, I guess you might say I damned near like to . . . *broke* a coupla the sonsabitches. Whereupon Yeager sketches out the problem he foresees.

Not for nothing is Ridley the engineer on this project. He has an inspiration. He tells a janitor named Sam to cut him about nine inches off a broom handle. When nobody's looking, he slips the broomstick into the cockpit of the X-1 and gives Yeager a little advice and counsel.

So with that added bit of supersonic flight gear Yeager went aloft.

At seven thousand feet he climbed down the ladder into the X-1's cockpit, clipped on his hoses and lines, and managed to pull the pumpkin football helmet over his head. Then Ridley came down the ladder and lowered the door into place. As Ridley had instructed, Yeager now took the nine inches of broomstick and slipped it between the handle and the door. This gave him just enough mechanical advantage to reach over with his left hand and whang the thing shut. So he whanged the door shut with Ridley's broomstick and was ready to fly.

At 26,000 feet the B-29 went into a shallow dive, then pulled up and released Yeager and the X-1 as if it were a bomb. Like a bomb it dropped and shot forward (at the speed of the mother ship) at the same time. Yeager had been launched straight into the sun. It seemed to be no more than six feet in front of him, filling up the sky and blinding him. But he managed to get his bearings and set off the four rocket chambers one after the other. He then experienced something that became known as the ultimate sensation in flying: "booming and zooming." The surge of the rockets was so tremendous, forced him back into his seat so violently, he could hardly move his hands forward the few inches necessary to reach the controls. The X-1 seemed to shoot straight up in an absolutely perpendicular trajectory, as if determined to snap the hold of gravity via the most direct route possible. In fact, he was only climbing at the 45-degree angle called for in the flight plan. At about .87 Mach the buffeting started.

On the ground the engineers could no longer see Yeager. They could only hear . . . that poker-hollow West Virginia drawl.

"Had a mild buffet there . . . jes the usual instability. . . ."

Jes the usual instability?

Then the X-1 reached the speed of .96 Mach, and that incredible caint-hardlyin' aw-shuckin' drawl said:

"Say, Ridley . . . make a note here, will ya?" *(if you ain't got nothin' better to do)* ". . . elevator effectiveness *regained*."

Just as Yeager had predicted, as the X-1 approached Mach 1, the stability improved. Yeager had his eyes pinned on the machometer. The needle reached .96, fluctuated, and went off the scale.

And on the ground they heard . . . that voice:

"Say, Ridley . . . make another note, will ya?" *(if you ain't too bored yet)* ". . . there's somethin' wrong with this ol' machometer . . ." (faint chuckle) ". . . it's gone kinda screwy on me. . . ."

And in that moment, on the ground, they heard a boom rock over the desert floor—just as the physicist Theodore von Kármán had predicted many years before.

Then they heard Ridley back in the B-29: "If it is, Chuck, we'll fix it. Personally I think you're seeing things."

Then they heard Yeager's poker-hollow drawl again:

"Well, I guess I am, Jack. . . . And I'm still goin' upstairs like a bat."

The X-1 had gone through "the sonic wall" without so much as a bump. As the speed topped out at Mach 1.05, Yeager had the sensation of shooting straight through the top of the sky. The sky turned a deep purple and all at once the stars and the moon came out—and the sun shone at the same time. He had reached a layer of the upper atmosphere where the air was too thin to contain reflecting dust particles. He was simply looking out into space. As the X-1 nosed over at the top of the climb, Yeager now had seven minutes of . . . Pilot Heaven . . . ahead of him. He was going faster than any man in history, and it was almost silent up here, since he had exhausted his rocket fuel, and he was so high in such a vast space that there was no sensation of motion. He was master of the sky. His was a king's solitude, unique and inviolate, above the dome of the world. It would take him seven minutes to glide back down and land at Muroc. He spent the time doing victory rolls and wing-over-wing aerobatics while Rogers Lake and the High Sierras spun around below.

• • •

TIM CAHILL

(b. 1944)

"Caving in Kentucky"

From *Jaguars Ripped My Flesh*

One of the finest adventure writers of the last thirty years, Tim Cahill has, by his own admission, carved out a career by cadging his way, as an unrepentant amateur, beginner, or even skeptic, along on other adventurers' serious trips. Out of the resultant tension, Cahill has milked a virtually limitless stream of delightful essays about sometimes terrifying experiences. This whimsical account of a subterranean jaunt in the South is a classic example.

Anyone who has ever tried to crowbar a little subterranean information out of people who habitually stumble around in caves—cavers—knows that these people are, by and large, a closed-mouthed, introverted, even slightly hostile group. I was thinking about this late one Sunday evening recently while I was standing waist-deep in a slate-green body of water called Dread Pool, which is two hours deep into a twenty-three-mile-long cave network in central Kentucky. The waters were thick, glassy, ghostly, and cold. To get to some interesting caverns deeper down, one must wade through Dread Pool, and, in certain seasons, the water may reach up to one's chest. About an hour into the cave you start thinking about how cold the water is going to be and you spend the following sixty minutes dreading the pool. Hence the name.

Bad enough to wade through the pool. Worse to stand there, motionless. Posing for a photograph.

Some months previous, a set of remarkable photographs had come into the office. Taken in the same Kentucky cave by a young Ohio businessman and commercial photographer named Jeff Thompson, they were unlike anything I had ever seen. The images were weirdly striking, contorted, vast. They looked the way the Viking's photos of Mars *should* have looked.

I called Jeff, and we made arrangements to see the cave. Thompson described himself as a "soft-core, weekend caver," then launched into a series of relatively hard-core conditions. According to Jeff's instructions, I spent three days at Yosemite sharpening my rock-climbing skills, and a day practicing rappels—a method of descent using a rope with mechanical aids.

I read the books he recommended. I figured I knew every esoteric cave danger encountered by man from time immemorial. Lightning, for instance, can strike deep into a cave, and when such a bolt hits an accumulation of bat excrement—guano—an enormous explosion can result.

Exploding bat shit I was prepared for. Cave photography was another thing altogether. It is, of course, totally dark inside a cave. This means you can leave the shutter open on a camera, then strobe-light dozens of different specific areas around your central subject. It takes time to effect such stygian chiaroscuro. The human subject in such a photo must stand stock still. When the human subject is waist deep in the frigid waters of Dread Pool, he tends to become cranky. He wonders why cavers, as a whole, treasure these experiences, and why they are so secretive. Jeff, for instance, didn't want me to mention the name of the cave in my article. Did he really expect one day to crawl, creepy-damp, through this cave, and find seventy or eighty people lolling around in Dread Pool?

THEY BREATHE, CAVES do, and, depending on the barometric pressure, they inhale or exhale. When we approached Minton Hollow—one of sixteen entrances to this cave, which is one of the twenty longest in the world—I could feel that cold, dark breath on me at fifty yards. The entrance, positioned on the side of a knoll, was surrounded by ferns and looked like a huge, baronial limestone hearth.

We walked, for the first few minutes, through spacious passages, well lit by the miners' lamps we wore. There were five of us: Jeff; myself; Jeff's business associate, Chip Northrup; Mike Davis, a media specialist; and Jon Luzio, a dog warden. Jon, with distressing regularity, kept pointing out wet green leaves stuck in the overhangs at the top of the cave. The cave had been completely flooded, recently, and Jon had read that this low section near Minton Hollow could fill within forty-five minutes.

Twenty yards into the cave, there was no way to know what was going on outside, whether, in fact, a freak rainstorm had burst out of a clear blue sky. If the water began to rise around our feet, we would have to go back the way we came, likely bucking a stream growing geometrically in power. If the water began to rise when we were several hours in, we'd have to look for a high, dry dome—some rise one hundred feet, and more—and climb to a safe spot. If the walls could not be scaled, we'd have to wait in a high room and tread water until it rose to a climbable section of wall.

Experienced cavers have died during unexpected floods. They retreated to the highest rooms, and the water simply continued to rise: to their waists, to their chests, to their necks. In the end—the idea is horrifying—they must have lain back in the water, lips against the cold rock ceiling, and taken one last breath before the room filled completely.

Because of the danger of flooding, Jeff marked the location of the highest dry domes on his map.

Twenty minutes or so in from the entrance, the ceilings began to drop and we adapted a variety of stoop walks. In a passage five feet seven inches high, a six-footer like myself can walk with slightly bended knees. But this is very tiring. Better to tilt the head so that the ear rests very nearly on one's shoulder. A person walking rapidly in this position tends to look slightly psychotic, like Terence Stamp in *The Collector*.

In shallower passages, cavers are obliged to double over, bowing from the waist. One cannot, however, stare only at the passing floor because a slight irregularity in the ceiling can cause a concussion. So one tilts the head up in a comical, neck-straining posture. Technically, such passages are referred to as "Groucho walks."

Passages can get considerably tighter, but only once in twenty hours of heavy caving did I get seriously stuck. There was a narrow hole in the ceiling of a passage leading to a higher room. A slick pile of mud with a single foothold led to the hole. My arms went through first, like a diver's, but just as I pushed my triceps through, I lost the foothold and hung there, absurdly, with my feet dangling below and my arms pinned over my head.

I tried to deal with the panic in a rational manner. I am not, ordinarily, a claustrophobic person, but it seemed to me that I would remain stuck for, oh, ten days at the most, by which time I'd have lost enough weight to slide out of the hole. Of course, there was always the danger of flood during those ten days. The idea of an earthquake—shit, even a minor settling of the stone—was terrifying. I'd end up all bulgy-eyed with my swollen tongue sticking out of my mouth, looking like a gruesome photo in some sleazy tabloid captioned: "Garbage Man Crushed to Death in Own Truck!"

Mike pointed out, in an excessively calm voice, that there was a handhold to my immediate right and that, if I so desired, perhaps I could reach over and pull myself up. Unless, of course, I wanted to rest some more. There was no hurry. This process is called "talking through," and even veteran cavers sometimes catch the fear and have to be talked through tough spots.

For every tight spot, there are dozens of crawlways: nearly oval tubes with fluted walls and ceilings. It was Jon's contention that certain crawls resembled birth canals. Sometimes, so Jon says, the Earth Mother is good, and the floor is sandy. Sometimes she is a bitch, and the floor is covered with sharp baseball-sized rocks that bite right through your mandatory basketball kneepads.

For some reason, the birth-canal analogy offends me, but even more repulsive is the phrase "bowels of the earth." If you consider a certain passage to be a section of bowel, and carry the metaphor to its unfortunate conclusion, then cavers, moving as they do through the bowels, become . . .

Enough.

Jeff says caving scratches his explorer's itch. Where he lives, the land has been given over to farms for more than a century. But precious few people have ever set foot deep into the caverns he loves; and, amazingly, new, virgin caves are being discovered every year.

While Jeff is pragmatic about his romanticism—Stanley and Livingstone in the netherworld—I prefer to let my imagination take control. We had, for instance, been following the sound of falling water for some time when we came to an unnamed waterfall. The dark green river erupted out of an upper passage and tumbled down a twenty-foot pit. It shone green, then silver in our lights. The walls of the pit were striated in browns and greens and ghostly whites. Two smaller streams poured out of a lower passage through formations that looked like nothing so much as balcony windows. On either side of the windows strange, twisted gargoyle shapes stood patient guard. Opposite the falls there was a gnarled, pulpitlike affair, and one could imagine foul rituals, and obscene sermons shrieked through the silent canyons.

The formations had the look of something otherworldly, yet man-made, elegant relics of some twisted culture predating the Ice Age: a culture that had flourished, and decayed. I wanted to imagine a people given to the worship of dark things: cruel dwarf gods and evil warlocks could be seen in the flawed and contorted sculptures before us.

Sitting in front of that waterfall, I got as goofy as I've ever been, dead sober. I had just run through a fantasy about ebony and albino warriors and their revolt against the evil king and his necromaniac rituals, and was working on the one about the torchlit masked ball in the Thunder Room; sautéed eyeless fish, batwing soup, a weird, discordant melody echoing off cold stone, when it occurred to me that this was a very vulnerable fantasy. None of it would be any good if there were some old candy-bar wrappers and a broken RC Cola bottle on the floor.

And I got my first dim glimmering of why cavers are not evangelistic about their sport.

MILLIONS OF YEARS ago this area of Kentucky lay submerged beneath a shallow sea. Uncounted billions of marine plants and animals lived, absorbed calcium compounds from the sea, died, sank to the bottom, and formed thick beds of limestone. The sea retreated and, to the east, the Appalachian Mountains punched up out of the earth, wrinkling the landscape of Kentucky, forming ridges and low, rolling hills. Many of the valleys here have no surface drainage system: no rivers or creeks.

The water goes underground, and, in so doing, it carves out caves. Rainwater percolating through topsoil absorbs carbon dioxide and becomes carbonic acid. Limestone is soluble in carbonic acid. The weakly acidic water finds cracks and fissures in the stone. Sometimes it carves out huge vertical shafts, pits, and chimneys. Then again, the water may flow horizontally, hollowing out oval tubes, some the size of a straw, some eighty feet in diameter.

As the water table sinks—because of drought, or the shifting of the earth's crust, or simply because the nearby river has carved itself a deeper valley—the tubes and pits are left relatively dry. In the rainy season, water, seeking its own level, roars abrasively through the tubes, carving out canyons. Eventually, most of the water makes its way through the maze of underground caverns and empties into a major surface lake or river.

Meanwhile, especially in the big rooms, water is still seeping through small fissures. It may enter the room through a drop-sized crack in the ceiling. Because cave air is almost devoid of carbon dioxide, the acidic water wants to reach chemical equilibrium by giving off CO_2. The water loses its carbonic acid and the dissolved limestone it carries will solidify. Over hundreds of years, limestone deposits, released from a single-drop fissure, can form a spectacular stalactite (these icicle-shaped formations hang *tight* to the ceiling). Water dropping from the tip of a stalactite may form a corresponding formation on the floor (you *might* walk into a stalagmite).

When water runs down the side wall of a big room, it can form fantastic draperies; and when a thin sheet of water runs along the floor of a cave, it forms flowstone, which looks very much like a river frozen into stone. Permanent pools often contain thin stone "lilypads" held on the surface by water tension.

Sometimes passages containing no formations at all have a special beauty. The ceiling may often be covered with closely spaced hanging water drops that, in miners' lights, look like molten silver studs. A bat, hanging upside down in sleep there, may be covered with drops, shining silver in your light.

In certain rooms, bats congregate by the thousands, and they hang there in one vast furry silver gray colony. At dusk, they leave the cave to feed outside, belching up out of the earth like a mass of swooping, swirling refugees from some Baptist preacher's hellfire sermon.

Chip and Mike and Jeff like to tell a bat story on Jon, who was a biology major in college. It seems they were making their way through a narrow passage when a number of bats in exit swooped by. Jon told everyone to remain still. Bats, he explained, send out high-pitched squeaks—inaudible to the human ear—receive the echoes, and fly by an amazingly accurate sonar system. No way could one hit you. At this point, a bat flew directly into Jon's neck and fluttered there, frantically. The bat screeched, audibly. So did Jon. It was hard to tell which was which.

Bats, Jon found out later, switch off most of their sonar in the familiar confines of their home cave and fly by memory. Unfamiliar objects, like cavers, confuse them. The audible sound the bat made, like the audible sound Jon made, was an expression of surprise and horror.

Bats have precious little company in caves. Near the entrances you may find common spiders and salamanders and some nesting birds. In the deeper caverns, far from the twilight world of the entrances, we saw white, eyeless crickets. They had antennae longer than their bodies and they moved surely, in braille. A number of pools contained eyeless, albino crayfish. There are also albino fish in some of the lakes, and where the eyes would be on these fish, there is only smooth, white flesh.

On the whole, however, nothing much lived deep in the limestone caverns we explored, and the air there was cool, sterile. It was without the scent and stench of life and death. There was no mustiness, no dankness. It was unexpectedly fresh and pleasant and primitive, and it tasted, I imagined, much the way the atmosphere of the earth must have when it was newly formed.

THE SAGA OF the West Virginia Death Cave is not something Jeff Thompson likes to talk about, but the tale does have its cautionary aspects. "It was about four years ago," Jeff told me. "We were beginners—a real buncha nerds." In a retarded-sounding drawl he added, "Well, shit-fire buddy, we read two whole books. We figured we knew it all."

Jeff and Jon and Jon's wife, Ronnie—who wrote up an account of the ordeal for me—had entered the cave about noon on a Saturday. The only smart thing they did that day was to tell some fellow cavers they would see them for a party that night around eight.

The first few hours were pretty routine: Groucho walks, crawls, careful climbs over breakdowns, where the ceiling of a big room had caved in. No one thing was very difficult in itself; but, in total, it was exhausting work, especially when done with little rest and at the impatient pace Jeff and Jon cultivated in those days. Fatigue colored their judgment and they began to make mistakes, deadly mistakes.

Five hours in, at the point they should have turned back, they met another group of cavers, coming the other way. That meant there was a connection to be made from where they were, a way out without retracing their steps. They didn't carry maps or compasses at that time, so they listened to a complicated series of instructions, then started off to make the connection. "We thought we had come through the worst of it," Ronnie wrote, "and that it would only get easier. We didn't recognize that the other cavers were very tired."

They stepped up the pace a bit. The party was scheduled for eight. A low, two-foot crawl dropped to one foot. They had to remove their helmets and push them along ahead. Feet wouldn't fit unless they were splayed out sideways. It was a real nose-to-the-limestone, three-hundred-foot squashed bellycrawl over sharp rocks. And now they were lost.

There was a hands-and-knees grotto at the end and two passages leading off from that. "One was an easy crawl over a soft mud floor," Jon said, "and the other was much lower. That easy passage just sucked us in." Jeff tried the passage to see if it would go, returned, and then Jon pushed it for forty-five minutes, while Jeff and Ronnie knelt in the windy grotto. Jon returned and said that he had taken the passage to a series of short climbs that would probably take them to the surface. Ronnie noticed that Jon was very wet. She remembered the other cavers being dry.

Jeff led the wet, muddy crawl, then pushed over the short climbs through a small hole that should have led to the surface. "Oh no," Ronnie heard him moan. Her heart sank. She emerged into a pit surrounded by un-climbable twenty-foot walls.

It was now 6:30. They were scared, lost, exhausted, and freezing to death. The temperature in the cave was perhaps fifty-two degrees, and there was a slight breeze, say five miles per hour, which put the wind-chill factor at about twenty degrees. Worse, they were wet, and water chill is an even more efficient killer than wind chill. Jeff, who had been a medic in the army, diagnosed hypothermia, that deadly dropping of the body's core temperature, sometimes called exposure. In its first stages symptoms of hypothermia include controlled shivering and goose bumps. Then comes uncontrolled shivering, followed by acute confusion and a lowered pulse and heart rate. When the body's core temperature drops below seventy-eight degrees, death comes quickly.

There was no good rest in that pit. Lying on the rocks was suicide: the cold wetness of the stone sucked the heat from their bodies. So they formed a standing tripod. "I never believed I could sleep on my feet," Jon said. But he did and almost instantly rescuers were there and he was whisked out of the cave and into a grassy West Virginia field under the warm West Virginia sun, drinking a nice warm cup of soup. Suddenly his knees buckled and he woke from his dream into a cold, dark, living nightmare. Jon was shivering uncontrollably; shivering so badly, in fact, that he pulled a muscle in his stomach.

Jon and Jeff, who had twice tried to make connections by crawling through half a foot of water, were the worst off. Jeff figured the two of them had about thirty hours to live. Ronnie, who was drier, might go forty-eight. Maybe the cavers they had talked to would notice that they hadn't turned up for the party. Maybe. But more likely their absence wouldn't be noted until they didn't show up for work on Monday, thirty-six hours in the future.

At half-hour intervals they did five minutes of jumping jacks in order to maintain their temperature. Jon's pulse never rose above an ominous sixty-two. They were dead. It was absurd. Here they were, young and in the best of shape, and they could expect death in a day and a half.

Jon switched on his miner's lamp, the only functioning light they had left, and Jeff saw a sad, bitter thing in the sudden brilliance. The cave was sucking away the heat he built up exercising. Steam rose from his hand; rose in five straight shafts from the tips of his fingers. "I'm watching myself die," he said.

They had been hearing the sounds of running water all night, but now it seemed there was something more than water. If you held your breath and listened hard . . . yes, it was the muffled sounds of voices. They called out. They shouted themselves hoarse, and waited for a reply; but the only sound was the distant mumble of running water.

They slept, woke from pleasant wishful dreams of sunlight into their nightmare of frigid darkness. Again they exercised, and watched the cave suck the life out of them. Jeff found his bank book in one pocket, and that was pretty funny. Pretty goddamn funny. They talked about their values and their lives, and the things they had left undone. They resigned themselves to death.

Ronnie had a Timex watch, and as sunrise approached their spirits lifted.

It had been no use looking for an exit in the dark. In the daytime they could switch off Jon's lamp and look for a shaft of light from above. At dawn, they started back down the agonizing series of crawls that had trapped them. They dead-ended, backtracked, and finally found a series of climbs that brought them to a big ledge.

Jon spotted a daddy-longlegs spider, an entrance dweller. And they could smell air: real living air, humid and heavy with the scent of wildflowers. There had to be an exit nearby, but when Jon snapped off his lamp it was, as before, absolutely black. The final desperate crawl had sapped the last of their strength. They sat down on the cold rocks and waited to die.

Which is when the members of the Monongahela and Pittsburgh grottos (chapters) of the National Speleological Society found them. They were fifty feet from a rabbit-hole exit; but, in their exhaustion, they might never have made the necessary traverse of a thirty-foot pit to find the exit that was hidden behind a large pile of breakdown.

The rescue operation had been launched at midnight after Jeff and Jon and Ronnie failed to show for the party. "They spent eight hours searching for us," Ronnie wrote, "and I want to thank them publicly."

"We were," Jeff said, "literally born again. When they found us and discovered that no one was seriously hurt, we had to listen to a lot of lectures about what a bunch of nerds we were. Well, we were. I mean, that had been proven. But it didn't matter. I was as happy as I've ever been in my life and the feeling lasted for days. I was a nerd, all right, but I was a *living* nerd."

EARLY ONE AFTERNOON we rappelled down a narrow twenty-five-foot-deep hole called the Post Office entrance. What happened that day is a good example of how decisions are made in caves.

We pushed through a tight, muddy, painful crawl to a ten-foot drop into a muddy lower level, then walked for some time through a shallow, flowing stream. We climbed some breakdown before coming to a tight hole Jeff persisted in calling a "whoop-de-do." Imagine a vertical "S" curve of basketball hoops eight feet long. Now imagine squeezing through it feet first.

I would estimate that it took me a three-mile jog's worth of energy to squeeze my 210 pounds through Jeff's whoop-de-do.

We crawled to a waterfall so high we could see it from both an upper and a lower passage. The water fell in a silver circle around a perfectly symmetrical stone column the width of an old redwood tree. The circular waterfall emptied into a placid pool whose edges glittered like a pane of opaque green glass.

After a short rest, we pushed on. Our goal was to connect with either Screamin' Willy's entrance or Scowlin' Tom's. According to the map, we would pass through a big room, a lake room, a massive meeting of passageways called Echo Junction, and finally, Grand Central Spaghetti, a bewildering maze of interconnecting passages on several different levels.

An upward-sloping, tube-type crawl ended at a porthole overlooking the Big Room. We were thirty feet up a sixty-foot wall. There was a rope ladder at the end of the tube, but the rope looked old and there were some awful nasty-looking rocks below, not to mention a dull green lake, and no one was willing to bet his life on the ladder. Jeff drove a new expansion bolt into the rock and we rigged a rappel to a ledge twelve feet below. We pulled our doubled rope down after us and followed the ledge to a pile of breakdown, then climbed over into the main section of the Big Room. We found ourselves facing a flooded passage. A heavy rock tossed into the lake confirmed what we already knew. Deep water.

We were only three hours into the cave. I wanted to see Echo Junction and Grand Central Spaghetti: I had connection fever. It seemed to me that doubling back the way we came would be an admission of defeat.

I proposed a plan: at its narrowest point, the lake was fifty yards across; we had that much rope. Since I was relatively certain that there was nothing in the lake that bit or leeched blood, and since I had spent a dozen years of my life engaged in serious competitive swimming, I offered to swim the rope across. I'd tie it off on my end, they'd tie it off on theirs, and they could hand-over-hand to my side of the drink.

A beautiful plan. Mike and Chip and Jeff and Jon were very patient. They never once called me a nerd. They simply pointed out, quite logically, why it would be dangerous and stupid to push on.

Point one: the map showed that parts of Grand Central Spaghetti were at the same elevation as the Big Room. That meant that essential connecting tubes and crawlways were likely to be completely flooded, top to bottom, and totally impassable without scuba gear.

Point two: inevitably, we'd get lost. If we got seriously lost, it could be deadly. We'd left word on the outside, but would rescuers assume that we swam the lake? There we'd be, soaked to the skin in some windy passage, dying of hypothermia and every few minutes I'd find myself saying, "Gosh, you know I'm really sorry about this, guys."

Point three: our lights and batteries were good for twelve hours. We could, conceivably, push on for three more hours. But then, if we didn't make the connection, we could double back and hit the Post Office entrance in twelve hours even. That left no margin for rest or error.

Point four: we'd already made a minor error. (Most cave accidents seem to be built on a foundation of minor errors.) We had brought the rope down after us. We should have left the rope, climbed the breakdown, and examined the Big Room first. Now we'd have to climb from the ledge to the overlook without the aid of the rope.

Luckily, Mike had fastened his etrier to the expansion bolt and left it hanging from the overlook. An etrier is a long, strong piece of nylon webbing tied into two stirrups, one above the other. Like the rest of us, Mike had figured that we'd make the connection. He left the etrier, a sacrifice to an imaginary emergency that had just developed.

We trekked back over the ledge to the point just below the overlook. Mike tied into the rope and Chip put him on belay. If Mike fell, Chip could hold him easily. But say he fell from the mouth of the tube: he'd plummet twelve feet to the ledge, then probably twelve more feet to the end of the rope. A total of twenty-four feet. A fall like that means nasty cuts and abrasions, perhaps even a broken bone, and would leave poor Mike dangling there in agony. We'd have to hoist him up to the ledge where Jeff could put a splint on him. Someone else would have to climb the etrier. Then we'd have to pull Mike up to the overlook, get him down the tube, through the crawls, up the whoop-de-do, and finally pull him twenty-five feet up to the Post Office entrance.

So it was with some trepidation that we watched Mike make the first move around a large boulder on the ledge. There was room for more than half your foot, and the handholds were good. It's just that the concave shape of the boulder forced one's ass into the abyss and, at this point, the heart refused to beat in a regular fashion. On the second move Mike got hold of the etrier, and on the third he placed his left foot in the lower stirrup. He searched for a high handhold, found one, put his right foot into the upper stirrup and did a pushup into the safety of the tube.

Mike belayed the rest of us from above, and this arrangement limited any potential fall to three or four feet. We each accomplished the climb with relative degrees of ease, and started the three-hour hike, climb, squeeze, crawl back.

IN THE TIGHT crawl between the whoop-de-do and the entrance, we heard the muffled sounds of what seemed to be a child screaming in terror and agony. The screams came from the entrance, the twenty-five-foot drop we had made on rappel. From below, we saw a five-year-old boy halfway up the drop. He was hanging there on a rope which was wrapped painfully around his chest and tied, dangerously, with an ordinary square knot. The rope itself was a wonder: frayed black plastic clothesline. The kid was being hauled out of the pit by an unseen force above and he was thumping against ledges and outcropping with painful regularity.

On the surface, we met the unseen force, who turned out to be the boy's father, a pleasant, sandy-haired thirty-year-old I'll call Bob. It turned out that Bob had done some backpacking and river running, and now he was interested in learning a bit about caving. Clearly, he wasn't the sort of pimple who'd snap off a hundred-year-old stalactite for a souvenir, or go around spray painting his name on walls, or leaving empty tins of Vienna sausage in some pristine grotto. But he was dangerously unprepared, and Jeff had no idea what to say to him.

Bob obviously had no technical rock-climbing experience. Swinging the kid around on that idiot rope was likely to put a permanent end to father-and-son outings. Between the two of them, the boy and the man, they had one source of light, a number that fell five short of minimum safety standards. The kid had no helmet, and since there were rockfalls inside, and because *everybody* cracks his head in a cave, he was risking serious concussion. Bob had no map, no compass. The kid had no coveralls. He'd have to crawl through flowing streams in a thin cotton T-shirt, then stand around in a twenty-degree wind chill while Bob tried to figure out where they were.

Bob chatted pleasantly. Jeff didn't say much. He was thinking: Should I tell them about the West Virginia Death Cave? Can I really give this guy a stiff safety lecture in front of his kid? If he did, Bob would think he was an arrogant, condescending turd.

"What you ought to do," Jeff said, "is join the National Speleological Society. They have a grotto here. . . ."

"I heard about them," Bob said, "but first I want to see if I really like caving. Isn't there an easier entrance around here?"

Chip and Mike and Jon faded away from the conversation and got real busy coiling muddy rope. Jeff hesitated way too long and the fellow looked at him strangely. Someday Bob would tell his friends that cavers are, by and large, closed-mouthed, introverted, even vaguely hostile people.

"My boy really wants to see the cave," Bob prodded.

Jeff worked hard on a smile and gave the two of them directions to a distant, empty, caveless field.

ERIC SHIPTON

(1907–1977)

From *That Untravelled World*

$$\text{[compass rose ornament]}$$

One of the legendary partnerships in twentieth-century expeditioneering was that of Eric Shipton and H. W. ("Bill") Tilman. Between them, the two men stood Himalayan mountaineering on its head in the 1930s, as they turned their backs on the massive logistical style of the early Everest expeditions and perfected a lightweight, mobile, small-party style of penetrating into blanks on the map. Later in life, both men separately turned to a new kind of adventure, sailing small boats into Arctic and Antarctic waters and launching overland explorations from them that sought out yet more terra incognita. Tilman, in fact, was lost at sea in the South Atlantic in his eightieth year, on his way to his last such venture.

Both men also happened to be superb writers, in that dry, whimsical, slightly self-mocking British vein. In this passage from his autobiography, Shipton recounts the forging of his partnership with Tilman on the first traverse of Mount Kenya in 1930.

A brief notice of this climb[1], furnished by a local reporter, appeared in the *East African Standard*. As a result, shortly afterwards I received a letter from a stranger who farmed in Sotik, saying that when he was last in England he had done some rock-climbing in the Lake District with a guide, and asking me to advise him how to set about climbing in Kenya. His name was H. W. Tilman. This was the start of a long and fruitful partnership in many mountain ranges. Our first undertaking together was the ascent of Kilimanjaro, which, despite the fact that the mountain is little short of 20,000 feet high, is nothing but a long and, in the conditions we encountered, somewhat gruelling walk. We also climbed Mawenzi, a smaller peak on the same mountain, which was rather more difficult. I soon realised that my new companion (it was many years before I called him "Bill"), though having virtually no mountaineering experience, was ideally suited to the game. I asked him to join me six months later in an attempt to make a complete traverse of the twin peaks of Mount Kenya by climbing the western ridge of Batian[2] and descending by our old route, a project I had cherished ever since I had first seen that glorious ridge.

I decided again to approach the mountain from the northwest. This route had the advantage that pack-ponies could be hired from a white hunter, Raymond Hook, in Nanyuki, and as these could be sent back from our base camp, it was a great deal cheaper than employing porters. The forest was less spectacular than on the Chogoria side, but the journey through the various zones of vegetation was very beautiful, and in the comparatively open country on the lower slopes we saw many wild animals, including elephant and rhinoceros. The forest, too, was full of strange creatures. One of these was the honey-bird, which flitted from branch to branch, singing loudly, evidently trying to attract our attention. According to the Wanderobo, a tribe of forest dwellers who live by hunting, these birds make a practice of leading them to beehives, expecting to be left a share of the booty once the bees have been smoked out. Unfortunately we had no time to make the experiment.

---

[1]A climb of Mount Kenya, of which Shipton had made the second ascent.

[2]At 17,040 feet, the higher of Mount Kenya's twin summits, by a mere thirty feet.

Reaching the head of the Mackinder Valley on July 29, 1930, we found a comfortable cave which served admirably as a base camp. Though 14,000 feet above sea-level, there was some giant groundsel near by which provided us with the luxury of fires. We spent the following day climbing two sharp granite pinnacles, partly for training and acclimatisation, partly because they both afforded fine views of the northern aspect of the main peaks. Few mountains have such a superb array of ridges and faces. From the summit of Batian a sharp, serrated crest runs northward for some distance before dividing into two main ridges, one plunging steeply to the northeast, the other descending westward in a series of huge steps to a col dividing Batian from a massive peak known as Point Piggot. This was the ridge that we hoped to climb. The largest of the steps appeared to be some 500 feet high and vertical; I called it the Grand Gendarme, a name it still bears. Below was the Petit Gendarme, a pinnacle standing above the col at the foot of the ridge. The west ridge was obviously a formidable proposition; certainly not the place to take a novice for his first serious mountaineering exploit, and it was stupid of me even to think of doing so. I was aware of my responsibility, but for a while I fooled myself with the thought that we might at least "have a look at it." So early the next day we set out for the col at the foot of the ridge. Most of the morning was occupied cutting steps up a steep little glacier, across a bergschrund[3] and on up a gully filled with ice. We would have been saved a great deal of trouble if we had had crampons, but as I had hardly ever used them, I did not regret the lack. Reaching the col, we sat with our legs dangling over the Tyndall Glacier, several hundred feet below. Across the chasm was the great west face of Batian, so close that we might have been suspended from a balloon before its ice-scarred ramparts and hanging glaciers. The upper part of the mountain was in cloud, and we could see little of the west ridge; but this was daunting enough. The Petit Gendarme, towering above us in the swirling mist, looked impregnable. The only way to outflank it was by climbing diagonally up a very steep slope of snow or ice to the right. Snow or ice? It was a matter of considerable im-

[3]A crevasse that separates the mountain proper from the glacier beneath it.

portance, for if it were ice the step-cutting involved would take the best part of a day and, with no protection, a slip would have been impossible to check. Again, no place to take a novice, even one of Bill's calibre. Above and beyond, we could see the vertical flanks of the Grand Gendarme thrusting up into the mist.

I returned to camp in a state of some mental conflict, in which prudence fought a losing battle. Happily for Bill, he had no such doubts; for him the issue was simple: we had come to climb the ridge and, if it were possible, climb it we would. As always, he started preparing breakfast long before the time we had planned to do so. At 3 o'clock we emerged from our warm cave into the frozen silence of a moonlit night. I was too numbed with sleep to heed its beauty. I remembered that it was August 1, my twenty-third birthday, and wondered vaguely what it would bring. When we reached the small glacier we kindled a candle lantern to supplement the light of the moon, roped up and, at last fully awake, began to climb rapidly. Our steps of the previous day were still large and comfortable, so hours of toil now sped beneath us with an effortless rhythm as we climbed towards the dawn. It was getting light when we crossed the bergschrund, and we reached the col with the whole day before us. And what a day! Crisp, sparkling, intoxicating. The western face of Batian caught the reflected light of the newly risen sun, and every detail of ice fretwork and powerful granite column showed hard and clear.

The west ridge, towering above us, looked no less formidable, but we paused barely a minute before traversing to the long slope below the Petit Gendarme. It turned out to be composed of ice covered by a layer, not more than an inch or two thick, of frozen snow. It was very steep and its lower edge hung over a sheer drop to the Tyndall Glacier. It was possible, by kicking toe-holds in the snow and by using the blade of the ice-axe for additional support, to climb diagonally up the slope without cutting steps. Moving one at a time, I felt reasonably confident that, should Bill slip, I could hold him; but since I was in the lead, he could not possibly have held me. The slope was in shadow and would remain so for several hours, but once the sun had reached it the thin layer of snow would melt and no longer afford any purchase. It would perhaps have been more prudent to cut steps into the ice beneath, particularly as we would most probably fail to reach the summit, and so be forced to retreat; but this would have taken far too long. In any case I was fairly sure that we could rope down from the Petit Gendarme to the col, thus avoiding the slope on our descent. So I decided to adopt the quicker method.

Even so, it was slow work, particularly as, in several places near small rock outcrops, the layer of snow was lacking and I was forced to cut steps in the blue ice; so it took us some hours to gain the crest of the ridge behind the Petit Gendarme, where we halted for five minutes to eat some chocolate. By then the mountain was wrapped in cloud, which reduced visibility to a hundred yards or so. For a short distance the ridge was broad and gently inclined, but this section ended abruptly under the Grand Gendarme, which towered above us, smooth and vertical for hundreds of feet, its top hidden by mist. It was clearly impossible for us to climb it direct, and our only chance was to find a way of turning it on the left. So we traversed out on to the north face and presently came to a deep gully which led directly upwards. Pitch by pitch we clambered up its dark recess, never able to see far above us, always expecting to be stopped by an impossible overhang. But after an hour and a half we suddenly emerged on the crest of the ridge above the Grand Gendarme. This was a wonderful surprise, and for the first time I began to believe that we might succeed.

When I looked at the next obstacle, however, my optimism dissolved. This was a step, reddish in colour, 130 feet high, extremely steep and undercut at its base. This time there was no way of turning it: to the right was a giddy drop to the hanging glaciers of the west face; to the left the scoop at the base of the step continued as a groove, running obliquely downwards across the north face, overhung by a continuous line of ice-polished slabs. By standing on Bill's shoulders I could just reach two finger holds; hanging on these, with a final kick off my companion's head, I managed to hoist myself up to grasp a hold higher up, and also to find some purchase with my feet to relieve the strain on my arms. The wall above the scoop was nearly vertical, and the holds were only just large enough for a boot nail; but, though few, they were well spaced and the rock was sound. Half-way up, however, there was a very awkward section, involving a long stride from one nail-hold to another, with only the roughness of the surface for my fingers to maintain my changing centre of balance. I contemplated the stride for a long time before cautiously swinging my right foot to the upper hold. But it felt so precarious that I hastily withdrew it. After repeating this fainthearted manoeuvre several times, prompted by my increasing distaste for the position of my left foot, which was becoming painful, I gradually transferred my weight to my right foot which, to my relief, did not slip, and by clawing at the rock face, I managed to hoist myself up.

After this the holds, though small, became more plentiful. By now, however, there was a new source of anxiety: I realised that the rope was not long enough to allow me to reach the top of the step. It was no use Bill unroping, for he could not possibly climb the initial overhang without it. Luckily there was a little recess some fifteen feet below the top which I just managed to reach as the rope came taut. In this I could wedge myself firmly enough to support his full weight. I hauled up the ice-axes and our small rucksack and sent the end of the rope down again. For all my pulling, Bill had a tremendous struggle to surmount the scoop. When he had succeeded I climbed quickly to the top of the step, and the rest was easy.

After that I was infused with a pleasant sense of abandon. Our rope was not long enough for us to abseil[4] down the red step, and the idea of climbing down it without support from above was not to be contemplated; therefore we just *had* to reach the summit. Time was my chief concern. The steps that followed were much easier than the first, and they became progressively smaller until we reached the junction of the northeast and the west ridges. Eagerly we turned towards the south to discover what was in store; but the mist had thickened, and all we could see was some fifty yards of the narrow arête. We clambered along it; sometimes we could balance on the top, sometimes we had to crawl astride it, sometimes we swung along with our hands on the ridge and our feet on ledges below. It was a thrilling situation:

[4]Rappel.

thrust up infinitely high, isolated by the mist from all save the slender granite crest along which we *must* find a way. Somewhere in the grey depths to
the left was the great rock bulge which had foiled my first attempt to climb
the peak. The white glow below our feet to the right was the upper hanging-
glacier of the west face.

Presently we were confronted by a gap in the ridge, thirty feet deep; we
roped down into it without hesitation, for, our boats having already been
burnt, there was nothing to be lost by cutting off our retreat still further.
One after another pinnacles loomed into view, greatly magnified by the
mist; one after the other we set about the problem presented by each new
obstacle, always hoping that it would be the last. I lost count of time; the
ridge seemed to go on for ever, but at least we were going with it; surely
nothing could stop us now. At last, in place of the sharp spire we had come
to expect, a huge, dark-grey mass appeared before us and my last doubts
vanished. A few steps cut in an icy gully, a breathless scramble up easy rock
and we were standing beside the little cairn which I had helped to build
on the summit of Batian.

It was 4.30 P.M. There was no chance of getting down before dark, but I
was much too happy to be bothered about that. Needless to say, much of
my joy stemmed from sheer relief; for, since climbing the red step, failure
to reach the summit would have placed us in an ugly situation, and the issue
had remained in doubt till the last few minutes. Bill had been magnificent;
he had shown no sign of anxiety throughout the climb, and his stoicism no
less than his innate skill in climbing and handling the rope made a vital
contribution to our success.

The rocks on the southern side of Batian were plastered with snow,
which delayed us; but conditions improved between the Gate of the Mist
and the top of Nelion,[5] which we crossed without a pause and hurried down
the gully beyond. There Bill slipped and came on the rope, dropping his
ice-axe, which vanished out of sight in a single bound. This near-accident
checked our haste. Dusk was falling when we reached the top of the sixty-

[5]The lower of Mount Kenya's twin summits.

foot wall above the head of the south ridge, and it was almost dark by the time we had completed the abseil down it. At this point I was sick, whether because of nervous excitement or something I had eaten during our hurried meal on the summit, I do not know.

The clouds had not cleared at dusk in their usual manner, and it looked as though we would have to remain where we were until morning. Later, however, breaks appeared in the mist and the moon came out, providing sufficient light for us to climb slowly down. I felt tired but pleasantly relaxed; the moonlight, the phantom shapes of ridge and pinnacle, interlaced with wisps of silvered mist, the radiant expanse of the Lewis Glacier plunging into the soundless depths below induced a sense of exquisite fantasy. I experienced that strange illusion, not uncommon in such circumstances, that there was an additional member of the party—three of us instead of two. Having been over the route, up or down, six times before, I remembered every step of the way, and dropping from ledge to ledge required little effort. We took a long time negotiating Mackinder's chimney; but that was the last of our troubles, except the long, weary plod across the saddle at the head of the Lewis Glacier, back to our cave.

The traverse of the twin peaks of Mount Kenya was probably the hardest climb I have ever done; though no doubt the cumulative difficulty was greatly exaggerated in my mind by the fact that the ascent of the west ridge was all over virgin ground. Certainly we were ill-equipped by modern standards; crampons, for example, and above all, a length of abseil line would have added greatly to our security.

We spent another six days based on the cave, and did several more climbs. The last of these provided an adventure which came unpleasantly near to disaster. It was up a beautifully symmetrical spire standing above the lower end of the Lewis Glacier, several hours march from our base camp. Though we started early, the clouds had already enveloped the mountain when we reached it; but as this was almost a daily occurrence, we attached no significance to it and started to tackle the peak. The climbing was difficult, but the rock was sound and dry, and it was most enjoyable. Two-thirds of the way up we climbed into a sort of cave; its only exit

was by way of a narrow, slightly sloping ledge jutting above a massive overhang. Though there was no handhold above, it was not unduly difficult to
stand on the ledge and shuffle along it. It was only three yards long and led
to a comfortable platform at the foot of a steep, narrow gully. From the top
of this, easier climbing led to the summit of the peak.

   We were sitting there, relaxed and content, when suddenly it started to
snow heavily. This put an abrupt end to our complacency, for we realised
that the difficult climbing we had enjoyed on the way up would be anything but pleasant on the way down, with the holds covered in fresh snow.
We started down as fast as we could. The rock was still fairly dry when we
reached the top of the narrow gully, though the snow was beginning to settle. There was a large rock bollard[6] round which I hitched the rope while
Bill climbed down the gully and disappeared. The rope went out for a while
then stopped, and I guessed that he had reached the foot of the gully and
was starting to cross the sloping ledge which would now be wet. Suddenly
there was a violent jerk and the rope stretched down the gully, taut as a vi-
olin string. I waited for a moment, expecting to be told whether to hold fast
or lower away, but there was silence. I shouted, but got no reply; so I assumed that Bill was dangling unconscious. I tried to haul him up, but the
friction of the rope against the rock, added to his weight, made this impossible. Perhaps the best thing would have been to make the rope fast and
climb down to investigate the situation; but it is not wise to leave an unconscious man dangling, as he could suffocate in a short time; so I began
to lower away, hoping that he would come to rest on a ledge within the thirty
feet of slack which still remained. Foot by foot I allowed the rope to slip
round the bollard until there was none left, and still there was no easing of
the weight below. I should, of course, have taken the strain from my shoulder in the first place; but I realised that too late; and now there was nothing for me to do but to remove the rope from around the bollard and start
climbing down with it dragging from my waist. Now the friction of the rope
against the rock helped me by acting as a brake on the downward move-

[6]A lump or spike of rock that can be used for a belay or as a rappel anchor.

ment. On the other hand, whenever I bent my hips or knees I could not straighten them again except by stepping down, and I had to plan each movement very carefully. Luckily the gully was narrow enough for me to brace my arms against the walls, which alone enabled me to retain my balance. By now the rocks were deep in snow.

I had not gone far when suddenly the strain lifted. Hurrying down to the platform below the gully, I fastened the rope to a spike of rock and looked over the edge. Bill was sitting on a ledge about fifty feet below looking up at me. He appeared dazed, but he answered my questions with his usual calm and seemed to be unhurt. I discovered later that he was still only half conscious and had no idea where he was. I asked if he could see a way down from where he was sitting, and he replied quite firmly that he could. So I abseiled down to join him. To my dismay I found that his ledge was, in fact, quite isolated, with no way of climbing from it in any direction, and that the next ledge below was beyond the range of our rope. There was nothing for it but to swarm back up the doubled rope by which I had abseiled. Luckily the wall was not deeply undercut and I found sufficient purchase for my feet to relieve the strain on my arms; even so, I had a desperate struggle to regain the platform. I then knotted the doubled rope round the rock spike, and hauled on the half which was tied to Bill's waist, while he swarmed up the other. In this way he managed to join me, a remarkable achievement in his condition.

We still had to cross the sloping ledge which was now covered by a thick layer of snow. I did not fancy shuffling along it as we had done when it was dry; instead, I placed one foot as far out as I could reach and with a combination of a spring and a dive I leapt forward and landed, sprawling, on the lip of the cave beyond. Bill followed in the same way, and the worst of our troubles were over. It was only then that I realised that he was suffering from concussion, for he was unable to remember the accident or any of the events which followed it. Only after we had reached the cave did his mind begin to clear.

By then the rocks were deeply covered with snow, and we could only proceed down by a series of abseils. For each we had to cut off a yard or two of rope to make a sling, so that by the time we reached the base of the peak, our original 120-foot length was reduced to some forty feet. It was still snowing steadily as we trudged slowly up the Lewis Glacier once more to cross the saddle at its head. It was dark when we reached our camp; I have seldom been so glad to arrive anywhere.

• • •

H. W. TILMAN

(1898–1977)

From *The Ascent of Nanda Devi*

Both Bill Tilman and Eric Shipton led Everest expeditions in the 1930s. Shipton, in fact, was slated to be the leader of the 1953 expedition that finally succeeded on the world's highest mountain, only to be passed over in favor of the more orthodox military man Colonel John Hunt.

Tilman's finest mountaineering deed was the first ascent of 25,645-foot Nanda Devi in India in 1936. On this expedition, four seasoned Britons—Graham Brown, Peter Lloyd, Noel Odell (whose last sighting of Mallory and Irvine on Everest in 1924 is excerpted elsewhere in this volume), and Tilman—made a happy collaboration with four young American climbers from Harvard—Charlie Houston, Adams Carter, Arthur Emmons, and Farney Loomis. Nanda Devi would remain for the next fourteen years the highest mountain climbed anywhere in the world, until the French succeeded on Annapurna in 1950.

In this passage, in his typically understated manner, Tilman narrates the summit dash at the end of August.

The 27th was to be for us at Camp IV another day of idleness. That at least was the plan, but the event was different, and for some of us it was a day of the greatest mental and physical stress that we had yet encountered.

I had been worrying all night over the waste of this day, trying to devise some scheme whereby the second pair could go up at once to the bivouac.[1] The trouble was that a second tent was essential, and having seen something of the extraordinary difficulty of finding a site even for the small tent, to go up there on the slim chance of finding a site for the big one as well was incurring the risk of exhausting the party to no purpose. While we were having breakfast, debating this knotty point and wondering how far the summit party had got, Loomis disclosed the fact that all was not well with his feet, the toes being slightly frost-bitten, and that henceforward we should have to count him out. The loss of carrying power knocked the scheme for a second tent on the head and a few moments later we had something else to think about.

We had just decided they must be well on the way to the top when we were startled to hear Odell's familiar yodel, rather like the braying of an ass. It sounded so close that I thought they must be on the way down, having got the peak the previous day, but it suddenly dawned on us that he was trying to send an S.O.S. Carter, who had the loudest voice, went outside to try and open communications, and a few minutes later came back to the tent to announce that "Charlie is killed"—Charlie being Houston. It was impossible to see anyone on the mountain, but he was certain he had heard correctly. As soon as we had pulled ourselves together, I stuffed some clothes and a bandage into a rucksack and Lloyd and I started off as fast as we could manage, to be followed later by Graham Brown and Carter with a hypodermic syringe.

It was a climb not easily forgotten—trying to go fast and realising that at this height it was impossible to hurry, wondering what we should find, and above all what we could do. The natural assumption was that there had been

---

[1]Houston and Odell had bivouacked above, in preparation for a summit attempt.

a fall, and that since they were sure to be roped, Odell was also hurt, and the chance of getting a helpless man down the mountain was too remote to bear thinking about. As if to confirm this assumption, we could get no answer to repeated calls on the way up.

Remembering our struggles yesterday on the ridge and in the chimney, we took a different line and tackled a band of steep rock directly above us, in between the gully and the ridge. It proved to be much worse than it looked and, when we had hauled ourselves panting on to the snow above, we vowed that the next time we would stick to the gully, which here narrowed and passed through a sort of cleft in the rock band.

The time was now about two o'clock, and traversing up and to the right over snow in the direction of the ridge, the little tent came in sight not thirty yards away. Instinctively we tried almost to break into a run, but it was no use, and we advanced step by step, at a maddening pace, not knowing what we should find in the tent, if indeed anything at all. The sight of an ice-axe was a tremendous relief; evidently Odell had managed to crawl back. But when another was seen, conjecture was at a loss. Then voices were heard talking quietly and next moment we were greeted with, "Hullo, you blokes, have some tea." "Charlie is ill" was the message Odell had tried to convey!

Lloyd and I experienced a curious gamut of emotions; firstly and naturally, of profound relief, then, and I think not unnaturally, disgust at having suffered such unnecessary mental torture, and, of course, deep concern for Houston. While we swallowed tea, tea that reeked of pemmican but which I still remember with thankfulness, we heard what they had done and discussed what we were to do.

They had devoted yesterday to a reconnaissance. Following the ridge up they found, at a height of about 500 ft. above the bivouac, a flat snow platform capable of holding two tents comfortably. Beyond that the climbing became interesting and difficult, but they had reached the foot of a long and easy snow slope leading up to the final rock wall. Here they turned back, having decided to move the bivouac next day to the higher site. Both were going strongly, but early that night Houston became violently ill, and in the cramped quarters of the tent, perched insecurely on an inadequate platform above a steep slope, both had spent a sleepless and miserable night. Houston attributed his trouble to the bully beef which both had eaten; Odell was unaffected, but it is possible that a small portion was tainted and certainly the symptoms pointed to poisoning of some kind.

Houston was still very ill and very weak, but it was he who suggested what should be done, and showed us how evil might be turned to good. It was only possible for two people to stay up here, and his plan was that he should go down that afternoon and that I should stay up with Odell, and thus no time would have been lost. We demurred to this on the ground that he was not fit to move, but he was so insistent on the importance of not losing a day and so confident of being able to get down that we at last consented.

We all four roped up, with Houston in the middle, and started slowly down, taking frequent rests. We struck half-right across the snow and joined the gully above the rock band according to our earlier resolution, and there the two men anchored the party while Lloyd cut steps down the narrow cleft, which was very icy. Houston was steady enough in spite of his helpless state of weakness, and having safely negotiated this awkward bit, we kicked slowly down to the left and found our up-going tracks. Presently Graham Brown and Carter hove in sight, and I imagine their amazement at seeing four people coming down was as great as ours had been at the sight of the two ice-axes. When we met, Lloyd and Houston tied on to their rope and continued the descent, while Odell and I climbed slowly back to the bivouac.

This illness of Houston's was a miserable turn of fortune for him, robbing him as it did of the summit. Bad as he was, his generous determination to go down was of a piece with the rest of his actions.

SCENICALLY THE POSITION of the bivouac was very fine but residentially it was damnable. It was backed on two sides by rock, but on the others the snow slope fell away steeply, and the platform which had been scraped out in the snow was so narrow that the outer edge of the tent overhung for almost a foot, thus reducing considerably both the living space and any feeling one yet had of security. Necessity makes a man bold, and I concluded that necessity had pressed very hard that night when they lit on this spot for their bivouac. Odell, who had had no sleep the previous night, could have slept on a church spire, and, as I had Houston's sleeping bag and the extra clothing I had fortunately brought up, we both had a fair night. Odell, who was the oldest inhabitant and in the position of host, generously conceded to me the outer berth, overhanging space.

The weather on the 28th still held and without regret we packed up our belongings and made the first trip to the upper bivouac. The snow slope was steeper than any we had yet met but, at the early hour we started, the snow was good and in an hour we reached the spacious snow shelf which they had marked down. It was about 20 ft. × 20 ft., so that there was room to move about, but on either side of the ridge on which it stood the slope was precipitous. After a brief rest the increasing heat of the sun warned us to be on the move again and we hurried down for the remaining loads. The snow was softening rapidly under a hot sun nor was this deterioration confined only to the snow. We already knew, and it was to be impressed on us again, that at these altitudes a hot sun is a handicap not to be lightly assessed.

Guessing the height of this camp, aided by the absence of the hypsometer,[2] we put it at about 24,000 ft. Trisul was well below us and even the top of East Nanda Devi (24,379 ft.) began to look less remote. The condition of the wide belt of snow which had to be crossed, the difficulties of the final wall, and the weather were so many large question marks, but we turned in that night full of hope, and determined to give ourselves every chance by an early start.

We were up at five o'clock to begin the grim business of cooking and the more revolting tasks of eating breakfast and getting dressed. That we were up is an exaggeration, we were merely awake, for all these fatigues are carried out from inside one's sleeping bag until it is no longer possible to defer the putting on of boots. One advantage a narrow tent has, that at lower altitudes is overlooked, is that the two sleeping bags are in such close proximity that boots which are rammed into the non-existent space between

[2]Altimeter.

them generally survive the night without being frozen stiff. It worked admirably on this occasion so that we were spared the pangs of wrestling with frozen boots with cold fingers. Frozen boots are a serious matter and may cause much delay, and in order to mitigate this trouble we had, since the start, carefully refrained from oiling our boots. This notion might work well enough on Everest in pre-monsoon conditions where the snow is dry, but we fell between two stools, rejoicing in wet feet down below and frozen boots higher up.

By six o'clock we were ready, and shortly after we crawled outside, roped up, and started. It was bitterly cold, for the sun had not yet risen over the shoulder of East Nanda Devi and there was a thin wind from the west. What mugs we were to be fooling about on this infernal ridge at that hour of the morning! And what was the use of this ridiculous coil of rope, as stiff as a wire hawser, tying me for better or for worse to that dirty-looking ruffian in front! Such, in truth, were the reflections of at least one of us as we topped a snow boss behind the tent, and the tenuous nature of the ridge in front became glaringly obvious in the chill light of dawn. It was comforting to reflect that my companion in misery had already passed this way, and presently as the demands of the climbing became more insistent, grievances seemed less real, and that life was still worth living was a proposition that might conceivably be entertained.

This difficult ridge was about three hundred yards long, and though the general angle appeared slight it rose in a series of abrupt rock and snow steps. On the left was an almost vertical descent to a big ravine, bounded on the far side by the terrific grey cliffs that supported the broad snow shelf for which we were making. The right side also fell away steeply, being part of the great rock cirque running round to East Nanda Devi. The narrow ridge we were on formed a sort of causeway between the lower south face and the upper snow shelf.

One very important factor which, more than anything, tended to promote a happier frame of mind was that the soft crumbly rock had at last yielded to a hard rough schistose-quartzite which was a joy to handle; a change which could not fail to please us as mountaineers and, no doubt, to interest my companion as a geologist.[3] That vile rock, schist is, I believe, the technical term, had endangered our heads and failed to support our feet from the foot of the scree to the last bivouac. It was a wonder our burning anathemas had not caused it to undergo a geological change under our very eyes—metamorphosed it, say, into plutonic rocks. But, as had been said by others, there is good in everything, and, on reflection, this very sameness was not without some saving grace because it meant that we were spared an accumulation of rock samples at every camp. A bag of assorted stones had already been left at the Glacier Camp, and I tremble to think what burdens we might have had to carry down the mountain had the rock been as variegated as our geologist, and indeed any right-minded geologist, would naturally desire.

Thanks to the earlier reconnaissance by him and Houston, Odell led over this ridge at a good pace and in an hour and a half we had reached the snow mound which marked the farthest point they had reached. It was a ridge on which we moved one at a time.

In front was a snow slope set at an angle of about 30 degrees and running right up to the foot of the rock wall, perhaps 600 or 700 ft. above us. To the west this wide snow terrace extended for nearly a quarter of a mile until it ended beneath that same skyline ridge, which below had formed the western boundary of the broad gully. On our right the shelf quickly steepened and merged into the steep rock face of the ridge between East Nanda Devi and our mountain. We were too close under the summit to see where it lay, but there was little doubt about the line we should take, because from a rapid survey there seemed to be only one place where a lodgement could be effected on the final wall. This was well to the west of our present position, where a snow rib crossed the terrace at right angles and, abutting against the wall, formed as it were a ramp.

We began the long snow trudge at eight o'clock and even at that early hour and after a cold night the snow was not good and soon became execrable. The sun was now well up. After it had been at work for a bit we were

[3]Odell was a geologist by profession.

going in over our knees at every step, and in places where the slope was steeper it was not easy to make any upward progress at all. One foot would be lifted and driven hard into the snow and then, on attempting to rise on it, one simply sank down through the snow to the previous level. It was like trying to climb up cotton wool, and a good deal more exhausting, I imagine, than the treadmill. But, like the man on a walking tour in Ireland, who throughout a long day received the same reply of "20 miles" to his repeated inquiries as to the distance he was from his destination, we could at any rate say, "Thank God, we were holding our own."

The exertion was great and every step made good cost six to eight deep breaths. Our hopes of the summit grew faint, but there was no way but to plug on and see how far we could get. This we did, thinking only of the next step, taking our time, and resting frequently. It was at least some comfort that the track we were ploughing might assist a second party. On top of the hard work and the effect of altitude was the languor induced by a sun which beat down relentlessly on the dazzling snow, searing our lips and sapping the energy of mind and body. As an example of how far this mind-sapping process had gone, I need only mention that it was seriously suggested that we should seek the shade of a convenient rock which we were then near, lie up there until evening, and finish the climb in the dark!

It is noteworthy that whilst we were enjoying, or more correctly enduring, this remarkable spell of sunshine, the foothills south and west of the Basin experienced disastrous floods. It was on this day that the Pindar river overflowed sweeping away some houses in the village of Tharali, while on the same day nineteen inches of rain fell at the hill station of Mussoorie west of Ranikhet.

We derived some encouragement from seeing East Nanda Devi sink below us and at one o'clock, rather to our surprise, we found ourselves on top of the snow rib moving at a snail's pace towards the foot of the rocks. There we had a long rest and tried to force some chocolate down our parched throats by eating snow at the same time. Though neither of us said so, I think both felt that now it would take a lot to stop us. There was a difficult piece of rock to climb; Odell led this and appeared to find it stimulating, but it provoked me to exclaim loudly upon its "thinness." Once over that, we were landed fairly on the final slope with the summit ridge a bare 300 ft. above us.

Presently we were confronted with the choice of a short but very steep snow gully and a longer but less drastic route to the left. We took the first and found the snow reasonably hard owing to the very steep angle at which it lay. After a severe struggle I drew myself out of it on to a long and gently sloping corridor, just below and parallel to the summit ridge. I sat down and drove the axe in deep to hold Odell as he finished the gully. He moved up to join me and I had just suggested the corridor as a promising line to take when there was a sudden hiss and, quicker than a thought, a slab of snow, about forty yards long, slid off the corridor and disappeared down the gully, peeling off a foot of snow as it went. At the lower limit of the avalanche, which was where we were sitting, it actually broke away for a depth of a foot all round my axe to which I was holding. At its upper limit, forty yards up the corridor, it broke away to a depth of three or four feet.

The corridor route had somehow lost its attractiveness, so we finished the climb by the ridge without further adventure.

The summit is not the exiguous and precarious spot that usually graces the top of so many Himalayan peaks, but a solid snow ridge nearly two hundred yards long and twenty yards broad. It is seldom that conditions on top of a high peak allow the climber the time or the opportunity to savour the immediate fruits of victory. Too often, when having first carefully probed the snow to make sure he is not standing on a cornice, the climber straightens up preparatory to savouring the situation to the full, he is met by a perishing wind and the interesting view of a cloud at close quarters, and with a muttered imprecation turns in his tracks and begins the descent. Far otherwise was it now. There were no cornices to worry about and room to unrope and walk about. The air was still, the sun shone, and the view was good if not so extensive as we had hoped.

Odell had brought a thermometer, and no doubt sighed for the hypsometer. From it we found that the air temperature was 20 degrees F., but in the absence of wind we could bask gratefully in the friendly rays of our late enemy the sun. It was difficult to realise that we were actually stand-ing on top of the same peak which we had viewed two months ago from Ranikhet, and which had then appeared incredibly remote and inaccessi-ble, and it gave us a curious feeling of exaltation to know that we were above every peak within hundreds of miles on either hand. Dhaulagiri, 1000 ft. higher, and two hundred miles away in Nepal, was our nearest rival. I be-lieve we so far forgot ourselves as to shake hands on it.

. . .

PART III

Ordeals

DAVID HOWARTH

(1912–1991)

From *We Die Alone*

But for the diligent journalistic efforts of the British writer David Howarth, one of the most extraordinary survival stories of World War II would remain unknown to the English-speaking world. On March 29, 1943, a boat carrying twelve Norwegian patriots coasted to a remote shore well north of the Arctic Circle in German-occupied Norway. The surprise attack backfired, and the Nazis killed eleven of the twelve men. The sole survivor, Jan Baalsrud, escaped into the high inland plateaus.

Howarth's account records Baalsrud's epic flight—pursued by German soldiers, covertly aided by Norwegian farmers and fishermen—across almost two hundred miles of wilderness until he at last reached neutral Finland. As Sebastian Junger did in writing The Perfect Storm, *Howarth has so steeped himself in the details of his protagonist's desperate journey that* We Die Alone *(the title is one of Pascal's gloomier* Pensées*) reads almost like a first-person account.*

H e lay between the snow wall and the rock for nearly three weeks. In some ways it was better than the grave:[1] he could see rather more of the sky, although he could not see round him beyond the wall; and there was enough room to move about so far as he was able. But in other ways it was worse: it was more exposed to the wind and weather, and it was much more affected by the change in temperature between night and day. In the grave, it had always been a bit below freezing point. In the open, whenever the sun broke through the clouds it melted his sleeping-bag and the snow around him till he was soaked; and when the sun dipped down at night towards the north horizon, his blankets and clothes froze solid. But although this was extremely uncomfortable it never made him ill. In conditions which were more than enough to give a man pneumonia, he never even caught a cold, because there are no germs of such human diseases on the plateau.

He was well stocked with food when they left him there, and different parties of men came up from the valley every three or four days to keep him supplied. None of it struck him as very nice to eat, especially after it had been thawed and frozen several times, and he had nothing to cook with. But still, one can live without such refinements as cookery and he was grateful for it. There was dried fish, and cod liver oil, and bread. It was a question whether the bread was worse to eat when it was wet or when it was frozen. There was also some powdered milk which had to be mixed with water. It occupied him for long hours to melt the snow between his hands so that it dripped into the cup he had been given, and then to stir the powder into it. Later on, when the thaw began in earnest, an icicle on the rock beside him began to drip. At the full stretch of his arm, he could just reach out to put the cup under the drip, and then he would lie and watch it, counting the slow drops as they fell, and waiting in suspense as each one trembled glistening on the tip. Sometimes when the cup had a little water in the bottom, the drops splashed out and half of each one was lost. When he

---

[1]A four-foot-deep hollow in the snow, sheltered by a boulder, which Baalsrud's helpers dug for him to bivouac in, after he grew too weak to travel on his own.

was feeling weak, this seemed a disaster, and he would swear feebly to himself in vexation. But in the end he invented the idea of putting a lump of snow on top of the cup, so that the drops fell through it without splashing. It took hours to fill the cup. The end result, with the milk powder mixed in it cold, was a horrible drink, but it helped to keep his strength up, and he drank it as a duty.

Sometimes in those solitary days, between the chores which always kept him busy, he still had the strength of mind to laugh at the contrast between himself as he used to be and his present state of elementary existence. Looking back, his life before the war, and even in the army, seemed prim and over-fastidious. There was a certain kind of humour in the thought that he had once taken some pride in his appearance, chosen ties as if they were important, pressed his trousers, kept his hair cut, and even manicured his nails. Grubbing about in the snow for a crust of bread reminded him of a time he had had to complain in an Oslo restaurant because there was a coffee stain on the tablecloth, and of how apologetic the waiter had been when he changed it for a clean one. It had seemed important; in fact, it had been important to him as he was in those days. If the man he had then been could have seen the man he was now, the sight would have made him sick. He had not washed or shaved or combed his hair for weeks, or taken off his clothes. He had reached that stage of filth when one's clothes seem to be part of one's body, and he smelt. But, luckily, what had happened to him in the last few weeks had changed him, and he did not mind his dirt. It had changed him more fundamentally than merely by making him dirty and ill and emaciated and crippling his legs. It had changed him so that it was quite difficult for him to recognise the spark of life which still lingered inside that feeble disgusting body as himself. He knew already that if he lived through it all he would never be the same person again. He would have lost his feet, he supposed, but he would have grown in experience. He felt he would never dare to be impatient again, that he would always be placid and tolerant, and that none of the irritations of civilised life would have the power to annoy him any more. Travel broadens the mind, he thought, and laughed out loud because the plateau was so damnably silent.

When he fell into a doze during those days, he often dreamed of wolves. This was a fear he had been spared during his first week on the plateau, because nobody had told him there were wolves up there; but there are. They sometimes attack the reindeer herds, and the Lapps on skis fight running battles with them. They seldom, if ever, attack a man, even if he is alone; but nobody could say for certain whether they would attack a helpless man if they were hungry, as they often are in the time of the early spring. The Mandal men had taken the danger seriously enough to warn Jan about it and give him a stick to defend himself.[2] Later, when they realised that a stick was no good because he had not enough strength to beat off a rabbit with it, they brought up brushwood and paraffin so that he could fire it if the wolves closed in on him. Of course he had a pistol; but it only had three rounds left in it, and he said he wanted to keep them for bigger game than wolves. Jan felt it was silly to be afraid of an animal, or even a pack of them, which had never actually been known to kill a man, so far as anyone could tell him. Yet the thought of it worked on his nerves. Until he was told of the wolves, he had only the inanimate forces of the plateau to contend with. He had relied on his solitude, feeling as safe from a sudden intrusion as he would in a house with the doors and windows locked. With all the dangers that surrounded him, at least he had not had to keep alert for any sudden crisis. But now, as he lay behind his wall of snow, unable to see what was happening on the snowfield around him, helplessly wrapped in his sleeping-bag, he knew he might see the sharp teeth and the pointed muzzle at any moment within a yard of him, or feel the hot breath on his face when he was sleeping, or hear the baying and know they were watching him and waiting. This, more than anything, made him feel his loneliness.

In the comparatively roomy space behind the snow wall, he could wriggle one leg at a time out of the sleeping-bag and look carefully at his feet, which he had never been able to do inside the grave. They were a very disgusting sight. His toes were still worse than anything else, but the whole of each foot was so bad that it was frost-bitten right through from one side to

[2]Mandal is a town at the foot of the plateau.

the other between the Achilles tendon and the bone. All the way up to his knees there were patches of black and grey. He had quite given up thinking of ever being able to walk on them again. As soon as he got to a hospital, he supposed, somebody would put him straight on an operating table and cut off his feet without thinking twice about it. He was resigned to that, but he still very much wanted not to lose his legs. Apart from the problems of keeping himself alive, he had thought more about his legs than anything else, wondering whether there was anything he could do to help to save them. He had made up his mind some time before about one drastic course of action, but in the grave there had not been enough room to put it into effect. He was still under the impression, rightly or wrongly, that gangrene would go on spreading unless one got rid of it, like dry rot in a house. The source of it all was his toes. They were not part of him any more, although they were still attached to him, and it seemed only common sense that he would be better without them. There was nobody he could expect to help him; but now the time and the chance had come, and he made his preparations to cut off his toes himself.

He still had his pocket-knife, and he still had some brandy. With the brandy as anaesthetic, and the knife as a scalpel, lying curled up on his side in the snow with his leg drawn up so that he could reach it, he began carefully to dissect them one by one.

It would have been best to get it all over quickly, but apart from the pain and the sickening repulsion, it was difficult to cut them; more difficult than he had expected. He had to find the joints. His hands were rather clumsy and very weak, because there had been some frostbite in his fingers too, and the knife was not so sharp as it had been. He grimly persevered, and slowly succeeded. As each one was finally severed, he laid it on a small ledge of rock above him where he could not see it, because he no longer had strength to throw it far away. After each one he had to stop, to get over the nausea and dope himself with brandy. Someone had brought him some cod liver oil ointment, and he smeared a thick slab of it on each wound and tied it in place with a strip of blanket.

This grisly operation was spread out over nearly three days. At the end of it, there were nine toes on the ledge. The little toe on his left foot did not seem so bad as the others, so he kept it. When he had finished, he felt very much better in his mind. Of course, there was no immediate improvement in his legs, but it gave him some satisfaction to have done something which he hoped would help to save them; it was better to know that the rotten revolting things were gone and could not poison him any more. It made him feel cleaner.

After it was all done, he went back with relief to the simple routine of his daily life: feeding himself, collecting ice-water, mixing milk, trying to clean his pistol; once in a while, as seldom as he could, rolling a cigarette with infinite care and finding the box of matches which he kept inside his under-clothes next to his skin; trying to put ointment on the sores on his back without getting too cold; sometimes treating himself to a sip of brandy; and always keeping on the watch for new attacks of frostbite. It was terribly difficult to lie there listening, imagining the sound of skis or the distant snarl of wolves. Sometimes he stopped up his ears to keep out the ghastly silence, and sometimes he talked to himself so that there was something to listen to. When people did come from Mandal, shouting "Hallo, gentleman," from far off, the sudden disturbance of the silence was a shock, and often it took him some time to find his voice to answer.

They paid him faithful visits all those weeks, toiling up the long climb every third or fourth night. When they came, they always brought fresh food, and usually some dry wood to make a fire to heat a drink for him; but lighting fires always made them uneasy in case the smoke or the light was seen. Whenever he heard them coming, he pulled himself together and tried to look as alive as he could, because he had a fear at the back of his mind that they might get depressed and give him up as a bad job and stop coming any more. On their side, they felt they had to cheer him up, so that the meetings were usually happy, although the happiness was forced. Sometimes there was even something to laugh at, like the time when one man forgot the password. The story of how Jan had shot the Gestapo officer had got around, and he had the reputation in Mandal of being trigger-conscious and a deadly shot.[3] So when this man found that the words "Hallo, gentle-man" had quite escaped his mind at the critical moment, he hurriedly dropped on his hands and knees and crawled up to Jan on his stomach, keeping well under cover till he was close enough to talk to him and make perfectly certain that there would not be any unfortunate misunderstanding.

On one of their visits, Jan asked them for something to read. What he really wanted was an English thriller or a French one, because during the last couple of years he had got more used to reading foreign languages than his own. But nobody knew of anything like that in Mandal, and the man he happened to ask could only offer him religious works in Norwegian. He declined that offer, but afterwards the man remembered an annual edition of a weekly magazine which he could borrow. Jan thanked him, and the heavy volume was carried up the mountain. But as a matter of fact, Jan did not read very much of it. He never seemed to have time.

Somebody had the brilliant idea, when Jan had been up there for some time, of bringing up a roll of the kind of thick paper which is used for insulating buildings. They bent this over Jan in an arch, like a miniature Nissen hut, and covered it over with snow, and blocked up one end with a snow wall. It was just big enough for Jan to lie in, and it protected him quite well. In fact, it sometimes seemed warm inside. But it had its drawbacks; whenever it seemed to be going to get tolerably warm, the snow on top of it melted and dripped through on him mercilessly, and made him even wetter than before.

Sometimes his visitors came with high hopes, but more often the news they brought him from the valley was disappointing. On one night soon after they left him there, two men came up full of excitement to say that a Lapp had arrived in Kaafjord and promised to take him either that night or the next, and they waited all night to help Jan when he came. But the morn-

[3]Right after the disastrous landing, as Baalsrud fled up a gully, four German officers pursued him. When they demanded his surrender, he turned and fatally shot one, wounded another, and sent the other two scurrying for safety.

ing came without any sign of him. For the next three successive nights men came from the valley to wait with Jan for the Lapp's arrival, and to make sure he did not miss the place. They kept watch for him hour by hour; but no movement broke the skylines of the plateau. On the fourth day they heard that the Lapp had changed his mind because of a rumour that the Germans had sent out ski-patrols on the frontier.

During the next few days this rumour was confirmed from a good many different sources. Recently, everyone had been so completely absorbed by the problems of Jan's health, and the weather, and the journey across the plateau, that they were well on the way to forgetting about the Germans. It was a long time since the garrison had come to Mandal, and that had been the last German move, so far as anyone knew, which had seemed at the time to be part of a deliberate search. The Mandal men had got used to the garrison and begun to despise it. But now it began to look as if the Germans were still on the hunt for Jan and even had a rough idea of where he was. When Jan was told about it, he reflected that the Germans had got a jump ahead of him for the first time in his flight. In the early days, when he was on the move, they had never done more than bark at his heels; but now, it seemed, they had thrown out a patrol line right on the part of the frontier which one day he would have to cross; and unless he crossed it within a few days, he would have to do it in daylight. If only he had been fit, both he and the Mandal men would have treated the patrol as a joke, because like all Norwegians they had a profound contempt, which may not have been justified, for the Germans' skill on skis. Even as things were, nobody except the Lapp was deterred by this extra danger. If they could only get to the frontier, they were sure they would get across somehow.

But soon after this rumour started, there was an extraordinary event on the plateau which really did make them take the danger of Germans more seriously. The most remarkable thing about life on the plateau had always been that nothing happened whatever. Day after day could pass without any event, even of the most trivial kind; and Jan discovered that most of the events which he seemed to remember were really things he had dreamed or imagined. His commonest dream or hallucination was that he heard someone coming. One day, when he was dozing, he heard voices approaching. It had often happened before; but this time, as they came near him, he realised that they were speaking German. He could not understand what they were saying, and they soon faded away again; and when he was fully awake, he thought no more of what seemed a slight variation of his old familiar dream. But the next night, when a party from Mandal came up to see him, they arrived in consternation, because there were two sets of ski tracks which passed thirty yards from the place where Jan was lying, and none of the Mandal men had made them.

It was one of those utterly mysterious things which start endless speculation. Up till then, they had always regarded the plateau as a sanctuary from the Germans, partly because they had never thought the Germans would venture to go up there, and partly because the job of looking for one man in all those hundreds of miles of snow was so hopeless that they had been sure that the Germans would not waste time in trying it. Nobody could imagine where the small party of men who had made the tracks could have come from, or where they had been going, or what they had meant to do. They were not from the Mandal garrison, because that was always kept under observation, and the place was more than a day's journey from any other German post. They could not have been part of a frontier patrol, because it was much too far from the frontier. Yet if they were searching for Jan, it seemed an incredible coincidence that they should have passed so near him, unless there were hundreds of patrols all over the plateau, or unless they had a very good idea of where he was. Besides, to search in that secretive way was un-German. If they did know where he was, they would know he could not be living up there unless Mandal was looking after him, and their reaction to that would certainly be to use threats and arrests in Mandal in the hope of finding someone who would give him away and save them losing face by having to scour the mountains.

They argued round and round the mystery for a long time on the plateau that night, with a new feeling of insecurity and apprehension. It had been pure luck that the Germans, whatever they were doing, had not seen Jan when they passed him. There had been a snowfall earlier in the day which had covered the trampled snow around his lair and all the old ski tracks which led up to it from Mandal. But if they came again, they would find the new tracks and follow them straight to the spot. Altogether, it was alarming, and the only comforting suggestion that anybody thought of was that the tracks might possibly have been made by German deserters trying to get to Sweden. Nobody ever found out the truth of it. Those voices in the night remained a vague menace in the background ever after.

When the Lapp lost courage and changed his mind, it was only the first of a series of disappointments. Hopeful stories of reindeer sledges expected at any moment kept coming in from Kaafjord and other valleys in the district; but every time the hope was doomed to die. After a fortnight in which all their plans were frustrated and came to nothing, the Mandal men got desperate. Every time they went up to look at Jan they found him a little weaker. He seemed to be dying by very slow degrees. Besides that, the spring thaw was beginning in earnest, and with every day the crossing of the plateau and even the climb out of the valley were getting more difficult. The snow was rotten and sticky already on the southern slopes, and the next week or two would see the last chance of a sledge journey before the following winter. During the thaw every year the plateau becomes a bog, criss-crossed by swollen streams, and nobody can cross it; and after the thaw, when the snow is all gone, the only way to move a helpless man would be to carry him, which would be even slower and more laborious than dragging him on a sledge.

So they decided to make a final attempt to man-haul the sledge to Sweden while there was still time, using a larger party which could work in relays. Accordingly, six men went up on the night of the ninth of May, and dragged Jan out of the paper tent and started off again to the southward. But this attempt achieved nothing except to raise false hopes once more. They had only covered a mile or two when clouds came down so thickly that they could only see a few feet ahead of them. They could not steer a course in those conditions, so they turned round and followed their own tracks back to where they had started, and put Jan into the paper tent again.

After this failure, Jan really began to get despondent. He never lost faith in the Mandal men, and still believed they would get him to Sweden some-how if they went on trying long enough; but he began to doubt if it was worth it. Nobody had told him much about what was going on, but he could see for himself what an enormous effort Mandal and the surrounding dis-trict were making on his behalf. So many different men had come up from the valley by then that he had lost count of them, and he had some vague idea of the organisation which must lie behind such frequent visits. As time went on, it seemed more and more fantastic that the German garrison could go on living down there in the valley, in the midst of all this hectic activity, and remain in happy ignorance of what was happening. Every new man who came up to help him meant a new family more or less involved in his affairs, so that the longer Mandal had to go on looking after him the more awful would be the disaster in the valley if the Germans did find out about it. Jan knew, and so did the Mandal men, the results of the uncon-trolled anger of Germans when they found out that a whole community had deceived them. It had happened on the west coast, and villages had been systematically burnt, all the men in them shipped to Germany and the women and children herded into concentration camps in Norway. There was no doubt this might happen to Mandal, now that so many people were involved, and Jan had to ask himself what the reward of running this risk would be. To save his life was the only objective. When he looked at it coolly, it seemed a very bad bargain. There was no patriotic motive in it any more, no idea of saving a trained soldier to fight again; looking at his legs, and the wasted remains of what had once been such a healthy body, he did not think he would be any use as a soldier any more. If he died, he thought, it would be no loss to the army: he was a dead loss anyway. And it was not as if he were married, or even engaged. Nobody depended entirely on him for their happiness or livelihood. His father had another son and daughter: his brother Nils would be quite grown up by now: and even Bit-ten, his young sister whom he had loved so much, must have learned, he supposed, to get on without him, and perhaps would never depend on him again as much as he had always imagined. He wondered whether they had all given him up for dead already, and whether he would ever see them again even if he did live on. As for his war-time friends of the last two years in England, he knew they would all have assumed he was dead if they knew where he was at all.

This idea only came to him slowly, in the course of about ten lonely days after the last abortive journey. It took him a long time to come to a firm conclusion, because by nature he had such a very strong instinct to live. But inevitably the time came, in the end, when he unwillingly saw one duty left before him. His own life was not of any overriding value to anyone but himself; and to himself, life only meant a few more weeks of suffering and a hideous death, or at best, he believed, a future as a more or less useless cripple. The life of any one of his many helpers, healthy and perhaps the focus and support of a family, outweighed it in the balance. He saw quite clearly that he ought not to let them run any more risks for him, and he knew there was only one way he could possibly stop them. His last duty was to die.

To decide to commit suicide when one's instinct is utterly against it argues great strength of mind. Jan's mind was still active and clear, but his decision had come too late. By the time he reached it, his body was too weak to carry it out. He still had his loaded pistol. Lying alone in his sleeping-bag among the wastes of snow, he dragged it out of its holster and held it in his hands. He had used it to save his life already, and he meant to use it again to end it. Until the last week he had always looked after it with the love he had always had for fine mechanism, but lately he had begun to neglect it, and it grieved him to find it was rusty. He held it in the old familiar grip, to cock it for a final shot, but it was stiff and his fingers were very weak. He struggled feebly with the simple action he had been trained to do in a fraction of a second, but it was not the slightest use. He no longer had the strength in his hands to pull back against the spring. He felt a friend had failed him.

Afterwards he tried to think of other ways of doing away with himself. If he could have got out of the sleeping-bag and crawled away into the snow, he could have let the frost finish the work it had begun. But it was a long time then, over a week, since he had had enough strength to disentangle himself from the blankets or move his body more than an inch or two. He thought of his knife too, and tried its edge; but it had not been sharp when he cut off his toes, and now it was rustier and blunter, and the thought of trying to saw at his own throat or the arteries in his wrists was so horrible that his resolution wavered, and he feebly relaxed and tried to make up his mind anew.

It was absurd really. He felt he had made a fool of himself. He had struggled so long to preserve his own life that now he had not enough strength in his fingers to kill himself. If he had not felt ashamed, he would have laughed.

PIERS PAUL READ

(b. 1941)

From *Alive: The Story of the Andes Survivors*

In October 1972, a plane chartered by a Uruguayan rugby team crashed in the Argentine Andes. The team's subsequent ordeal proved so grim that some of the survivors ended up cannibalizing the bodies of their dead comrades. Aerial searches for the missing plane failed completely. Meanwhile the victims—flatlanders with no experience of the mountains—cherished such misconceptions about the terrain in which they were trapped that week after week they sat awaiting deliverance, afraid to leave the dismal refuge of the plane's broken fuselage. Only after the strongest pair finally hiked out to the nearest settlement were the remaining survivors granted that deliverance.

As rumors about the cannibalism leaked out, a number of quickie books and a bad movie capitalized on the sensational story. That the event also had deep moral complexity eluded these first opportunistic chroniclers. Out of frustration, the survivors chose British author Piers Paul Read to write the authorized version of their story.

By focusing on the details and steering clear of moral judgments,
Read produced a compelling account of the tragedy. A quarter century
later, it remains one of the defining narratives of how a group responds
to a long, downward-spiraling crisis in the wilderness. In this excerpt,
Read sympathetically captures the process by which these Catholic
men and women reconciled themselves to the idea of cannibalism.

They awoke on the morning of Sunday, October 22, to face their tenth day on the mountain. First to leave the plane were Marcelo Pérez and Roy Harley. Roy had found a transistor radio between two seats and by using a modest knowledge of electronics, acquired when helping a friend construct a hi-fi system, he had been able to make it work. It was difficult to receive signals in the deep cleft between the huge mountains, so Roy made an aerial with strands of wire from the plane's electric circuits. While he turned the dial, Marcelo held the aerial and moved it around. They picked up scraps of broadcasts from Chile but no news of the rescue effort. All that came over the radio waves were the strident voices of Chilean politicians embroiled in the strike by the middle classes against the socialist government of President Allende.

Few of the other boys came out into the snow. Starvation was taking its effect. They were becoming weaker and more listless. When they stood up they felt faint and found it difficult to keep their balance. They felt cold, even when the sun rose to warm them, and their skin started to grow wrinkled like that of old men.

Their food supplies were running out. The daily ration of a scrap of chocolate, a capful of wine, and a teaspoonful of jam or canned fish—eaten slowly to make it last—was more torture than sustenance for these healthy, athletic boys; yet the strong shared it with the weak, the healthy with the injured. It was clear to them all that they could not survive much longer. It was not so much that they were consumed with ravenous hunger as that they felt themselves grow weaker each day, and no knowledge of medicine or nutrition was required to predict how it would end.

Their minds turned to other sources of food. It seemed impossible that there should be nothing whatsoever growing in the Andes, for even the meanest form of plant life might provide some nutrition. In the immediate vicinity of the plane there was only snow. The nearest soil was a hundred feet beneath them. The only ground exposed to sun and air was barren mountain rock on which they found nothing but brittle lichens. They scraped some of it off and mixed it into a paste with melted snow, but the taste was bitter and disgusting, and as food it was worthless. Except for lichens there was nothing. Some thought of the cushions, but even these were not stuffed with straw. Nylon and foam rubber would not help them.

For some days several of the boys had realized that if they were to survive they would have to eat the bodies of those who had died in the crash. It was a ghastly prospect. The corpses lay around the plane in the snow, preserved by the intense cold in the state in which they had died. While the thought of cutting flesh from those who had been their friends was deeply repugnant to them all, a lucid appreciation of their predicament led them to consider it.

Gradually the discussion spread as these boys cautiously mentioned it to their friends or to those they thought would be sympathetic. Finally, Canessa brought it out into the open.[1]

He argued forcefully that they were not going to be rescued; that they would have to escape themselves, but that nothing could be done without food; and that the only food was human flesh. He used his knowledge of medicine to describe, in his penetrating, high-pitched voice, how their bodies were using up their reserves. "Every time you move," he said, "you use up part of your own body. Soon we shall be so weak that we won't have the strength even to cut the meat that is lying there before our eyes."

Canessa did not argue just from expediency. He insisted that they had a moral duty to stay alive by any means at their disposal, and because Canessa was earnest about his religious belief, great weight was given to what he said by the more pious among the survivors.

---

[1]A medical student, Roberto Canessa emerged as a leader among the survivors. He would be one of the two who finally hiked out to safety, launching the rescue of the others.

"It is meat," he said. "That's all it is. The souls have left their bodies and are in heaven with God. All that is left here are the carcasses, which are no more human beings than the dead flesh of the cattle we eat at home."

Others joined the discussion. "Didn't you see," said Fito Strauch, "how much energy we needed just to climb a few hundred feet up the mountain? Think how much more we'll need to climb to the top and then down the other side. It can't be done on a sip of wine and a scrap of chocolate."

The truth of what he said was incontestable.

A meeting was called inside the Fairchild, and for the first time all twenty-seven survivors discussed the issue which faced them—whether or not they should eat the bodies of the dead to survive. Canessa, Zerbino, Fernández, and Fito Strauch repeated the arguments they had used before. If they did not they would die. It was their moral obligation to live, for their own sake and for the sake of their families. God wanted them to live, and He had given them the means to do so in the dead bodies of their friends. If God had not wished them to live, they would have been killed in the accident; it would be wrong now to reject this gift of life because they were too squeamish.

"But what have we done," asked Marcelo, "that God now asks us to eat the bodies of our dead friends?"

There was a moment's hesitation. Then Zerbino turned to his captain and said, "But what do you think *they* would have thought?"

Marcelo did not answer.

"I know," Zerbino went on, "that if my dead body could help you to stay alive, then I'd certainly want you to use it. In fact, if I do die, and you don't eat me, then I'll come back from wherever I am and give you a good kick in the ass."

This argument allayed many doubts, for however reluctant each boy might be to eat the flesh of a friend, all of them agreed with Zerbino. There and then they made a pact that if any more of them were to die, their bodies were to be used as food.

Marcelo still shrank from a decision. He and his diminishing party of optimists held onto the hope of rescue, but few of the others any longer shared their faith. Indeed, a few of the younger boys went over to the pessimists—

or the realists, as they considered themselves—with some resentment against Marcelo Pérez and Pancho Delgado. They felt they had been deceived. The rescue they had been promised had not come.

The latter were not without support, however. Coche Inciarte and Numa Turcatti, both strong, tough boys with an inner gentleness, told their companions that while they did not think it would be wrong, they knew that they themselves could not do it. Liliana Methol agreed with them. Her manner was calm as always but, like the others, she grappled with the emotions the issue aroused. Her instinct to survive was strong, her longing for her children was acute, but the thought of eating human flesh horrified her. She did not think it wrong; she could distinguish between sin and physical revulsion, and a social taboo was not a law of God. "But," she said, "as long as there is a chance of rescue, as long as there is *something* left to eat, even if it is only a morsel of chocolate, then I can't do it."

Javier Methol agreed with his wife but would not deter others from doing what they felt must be done. No one suggested that God might want them to choose to die. They all believed that virtue lay in survival and that eating their dead friends would in no way endanger their souls, but it was one thing to decide and another to act.

Their discussions had continued most of the day, and by midafternoon they knew that they must act now or not at all, yet they sat inside the plane in total silence. At last a group of four—Canessa, Maspons, Zerbino, and Fito Strauch—rose and went out into the snow. Few followed them. No one wished to know who was going to cut the meat or from which body it was to be taken.

Most of the bodies were covered by snow, but the buttocks of one protruded a few yards from the plane. With no exchange of words, Canessa knelt, bared the skin, and cut into the flesh with a piece of broken glass. It was frozen hard and difficult to cut, but he persisted until he had cut away twenty slivers the size of matchsticks. He then stood up, went back to the plane, and placed them on the roof.

Inside there was silence. The boys cowered in the Fairchild. Canessa told them that the meat was there on the roof, drying in the sun, and that those who wished to do so should come out and eat it. No one came, and again Canessa took it upon himself to prove his resolution. He prayed to God to help him do what he knew to be right and then took a piece of meat in his hand. He hesitated. Even with his mind so firmly made up, the horror of the act paralyzed him. His hand would neither rise to his mouth nor fall to his side while the revulsion which possessed him struggled with his stubborn will. The will prevailed. The hand rose and pushed the meat into his mouth. He swallowed it.

He felt triumphant. His conscience had overcome a primitive, irrational taboo. He was going to survive.

LATER THAT EVENING, small groups of boys came out of the plane to follow his example. Zerbino took a strip and swallowed it as Canessa had done, but it stuck in his throat. He scooped a handful of snow into his mouth and managed to wash it down. Fito Strauch followed his example, then Maspons and Vizintín and others.

Meanwhile Gustavo Nicolich, the tall, curly-haired boy, only twenty years old, who had done so much to keep up the morale of his young friends, wrote to his *novia*[2] in Montevideo.

Most dear Rosina:

I am writing to you from inside the plane (our *petit hotel* for the moment). It is sunset and has started to be rather cold and windy which it usually does at this hour of the evening. Today the weather was wonderful—a beautiful sun and very hot. It reminded me of the days on the beach with you—the big difference being that then we would be going to have lunch at your place at midday whereas now I'm stuck outside the plane without any food at all.

Today, on top of everything else, it was rather depressing and a lot of the others began to get discouraged (today is the tenth day we have been

[2]Fiancée; girlfriend.

here), but luckily this gloom did not spread to me because I get incredible strength just by thinking that I'm going to see you again. Another of the things leading to the general depression is that in a while the food will run out: we have only got two cans of seafood (small), one bottle of white wine, and a little cherry brandy left, which for twenty-six men (well, there are also boys who want to be men) is nothing.

One thing which will seem incredible to you—it seems unbelievable to me—is that today we started to cut up the dead in order to eat them. There is nothing else to do. I prayed to God from the bottom of my heart that this day would never come, but it has and we have to face it with courage and faith. Faith, because I came to the conclusion that the bodies are there because God put them there and, since the only thing that matters is the soul, I don't have to feel great remorse; and if the day came and I could save someone with my body, I would gladly do it.

I don't know how you, Mama, Papa, or the children can be feeling; you don't know how sad it makes me to think that you are suffering, and I constantly ask God to reassure you and give us courage because that is the only way of getting out of this. I think that soon there will be a happy ending for everyone.

You'll get a shock when you see me. I am dirty, with a beard, and a little thinner, and with a big gash on my head, another one on my chest which has healed now, and one very small cut which I got today working in the cabin of the plane, besides various small cuts in the legs and on the shoulder; but in spite of it all, I'm all right.

THOSE WHO FIRST peered through the portholes of the plane the next morning could see that the sky was overcast but that a little sun shone through the clouds onto the snow. Some darted cautious looks toward Canessa, Zerbino, Maspons, Vizintín, and the Strauch cousins. It was not that they thought that God would have struck them down, but they knew from their *estancias*[3] that one should never eat a steer that dies from nat-

[3]Cattle ranches.

ural causes, and they wondered if it might not be just as unhealthy to do the same with a man.

The ones who had eaten the meat were quite well. None of them had eaten very much and in fact they felt as enfeebled as the others. As always, Marcelo Pérez was the first to raise himself from the cushions.

"Come on," he said to Roy Harley. "We must set up the radio."

"It's so cold," said Roy. "Can't you get someone else?"

"No," said Marcelo. "It's your job. Come on."

Reluctantly Roy took his shoes down from the hat rack and put them on over his two pairs of socks. He squeezed himself out of the line of dozing figures and climbed over those nearest the entrance to follow Marcelo out of the plane. One or two others followed him out.

Marcelo had already taken hold of the aerial and was waiting while Roy picked up the radio, switched it on, and began to turn the dial. He tuned it to a station in Chile which the day before had broadcast nothing but political propaganda; now, however, as he held the radio to his ear, he heard the last words of a news bulletin. "The SAR[4] has requested all commercial and military aircraft overflying the cordillera to check for any sign of the wreckage of the Fairchild Number Five-seventy-one. This follows the cancellation of the search by the SAR for the Uruguayan aircraft because of negative results."

The newscaster moved on to a different topic. Roy took the radio away from his ear. He looked up at Marcelo and told him what he had heard. Marcelo dropped the aerial, covered his face with his hands, and wept with despair. The others who had clustered around Roy, upon hearing the news, began to sob and pray, all except Parrado, who looked calmly up at the mountains which rose to the west.

Gustavo Nicolich came out of the plane and, seeing their faces, knew what they had heard.

"What shall we tell the others?" he asked.

[4]Servicio Aéreo de Rescate, the Aerial Rescue Service.

"We mustn't tell them," said Marcelo. "At least let them go on hoping."

"No," said Nicolich. "We must tell them. They must know the worst."

"I can't, I can't," said Marcelo, still sobbing into his hands.

"I'll tell them," said Nicolich, and he turned back toward the entrance to the plane.

He climbed through the hole in the wall of suitcases and rugby shirts, crouched at the mouth of the dim tunnel, and looked at the mournful faces which were turned toward him.

"Hey, boys," he shouted, "there's some good news! We just heard it on the radio. They've called off the search."

Inside the crowded cabin there was silence. As the hopelessness of their predicament enveloped them, they wept.

"Why the hell is that good news?" Páez shouted angrily at Nicolich.

"Because it means," he said, "that we're going to get out of here on our own."

The courage of this one boy prevented a flood of total despair, but some of the optimists who had counted on rescue were unable to rally. The pessimists, several of them as unhopeful about escape as they had been about rescue, were not shocked; it was what they had expected. But the news broke Marcelo. His role as their leader became empty and automatic, and the life went out of his eyes. Delgado, too, was changed by the news. His eloquent and cheerful optimism evaporated into the thin air of the cordillera. He seemed to have no faith that they would get out by their own efforts and quietly withdrew into the background. Of the old optimists, only Liliana Methol still offered hope and consolation. "Don't worry," she said. "We'll get out of here, all right. They'll find us when the snow melts." Then, as if remembering how little food remained besides the bodies of the dead, she added, "Or we'll walk to the west."

To escape: that was the obsession of the new optimists. It was disconcerting that the valley in which they were trapped ran east, and that to the west there was a solid wall of towering mountains, but this did not deter Parrado. No sooner had he learned of the cancellation of the search than he announced his intention of setting off—on his own, if necessary—to the west. It was only with great difficulty that the others restrained him. Ten days before he had been given up for dead. If anyone was going to climb the mountains, there were others in a much better physical condition to do so. "We must think this out calmly," said Marcelo, "and act together. It's the only way we'll survive."

There was still sufficient respect for Marcelo and enough team discipline in Parrado to accept what the others decided. He was not alone, however, in his insistence that, before they got any weaker, another expedition should set out, either to climb the mountain and see what was on the other side or to find the tail.[5]

It was agreed that a group of the fittest among them should set off at once, and a little more than an hour after they had heard the news on the radio, Zerbino, Turcatti, and Maspons set off up the mountain, watched by their friends.

CANESSA AND FITO Strauch returned to the corpse they had opened the day before and cut more meat off the bone. The strips they had put on the roof of the plane had now all been eaten. Not only were they easier to swallow when dried in the outside air, but the knowledge that they were not going to be rescued had persuaded many of those who had hesitated the day before. For the first time, Parrado ate human flesh. So, too, did Daniel Fernández, though not without the greatest effort of will to overcome his revulsion. One by one, they forced themselves to take and swallow the flesh of their friends. To some, it was merely an unpleasant necessity; to others, it was a conflict of conscience with reason.

Some could not do it: Liliana and Javier Methol, Coche Inciarte, Pancho Delgado. Marcelo Pérez, having made up his mind that he would take this step, used what authority he still possessed to persuade others to do so, but nothing he said had the effect of a short statement from Pedro Algorta. He was one of the two boys who had been dressed more scruffily at the air-

---

[5] They hoped to find gear or food in the tail.

port than the others, as if to show that he despised their bourgeois values. In the crash, he had been hit on the head and suffered total amnesia about what had happened the day before. Algorta watched Canessa and Fito Strauch cutting the meat but said nothing until it came to the moment when he was offered a slice of flesh. He took it and swallowed it and then said, "It's like Holy Communion. When Christ died he gave his body to us so that we could have spiritual life. My friend has given us his body so that we can have physical life."

It was with this thought that Coche Inciarte and Pancho Delgado first swallowed their share, and Marcelo grasped it as a concept which would persuade others to follow his example and survive. One by one they did so until only Liliana and Javier Methol remained.

Now that it was established that they were to live off the dead, a group of stronger boys was organized to cover the corpses with snow, while those who were weaker or injured sat on the seats, holding the aluminum water makers toward the sun, catching the drops of water in empty wine bottles. Others tidied the cabin. Canessa, when he had cut enough meat for their immediate needs, made a tour of inspection of the wounded. He was moderately content with what he saw. Almost all the superficial wounds were continuing to heal, and none showed signs of infection. The swelling around broken bones also was subsiding; Alvaro Mangino and Pancho Delgado, for example, both managed, despite considerable pain, to hobble around outside the plane. Arturo Nogueira was worse off; if he went outside the plane he had to crawl, pulling himself forward with his arms. The state of Rafael Echavarren's leg was growing serious; it showed the first indications of gangrene.

Enrique Platero, the boy who had had the tube of steel removed from his stomach, told Canessa that he was feeling perfectly well but that a piece of his insides still protruded from the wound. The doctor carefully unwound the rugby shirt which Platero continued to use as a bandage and confirmed the patient's observation; the wound was healing well but something stuck out from the skin. Part of this projection had gone dry, and Canessa suggested to Platero that if he cut off the dead matter the rest might be more easily pushed back under the skin.

"But what is it sticking out?" asked Platero.

Canessa shrugged his shoulders. "I don't know," he said. "It's probably part of the lining of the stomach, but if it's the intestine and I cut it open, you've had it. You'll get peritonitis."

Platero did not hesitate. "Do what you have to do," he said, and lay back on the door.

Canessa prepared to operate. As scalpel he had a choice between a piece of broken glass or a razor blade. His sterilizer was the subzero air all around them. He disinfected the area of the wound with eau de cologne and then carefully cut away a small slice of the dead skin with the glass. Platero did not feel it, but the protruding gristle still would not go back under the skin. With even greater caution Canessa now cut yet closer to the living tissue, dreading all the time that he might cut into the intestine, but again he seemed to have done no harm and this time, with a prod from the surgeon's finger, the gut retired into Platero's stomach where it belonged.

"Do you want me to stitch you up?" Canessa asked his patient. "I should warn you that we don't have any surgical thread."

"Don't worry," said Platero, rising on his elbows and looking down at his stomach. "This is fine. Just tie it up again and I'll be on my way."

Canessa retied the rugby shirt as tightly as he could, and Platero swung his legs off the door and got to his feet. "Now I'm ready to go on an expedition," he said, "and when we get back to Montevideo I'll take you on as my doctor. I couldn't possibly hope for a better one."

Outside the plane, following the example of Gustavo Nicolich, Carlitos Páez was writing to his father, his mother, and his sisters. He also wrote to his grandmother:

> You can have no idea how much I have thought about you because I love you, I adore you, because you have already received so many blows in your life, because I don't know how you are going to stand this one.

You, Buba, taught me many things but the most important one was faith in God. That has increased so much now that you cannot conceive of it. . . . I want you to know that you are the kindest grandmother in the world and I shall remember you each moment I am alive.

ZERBINO, TURCATTI, AND Maspons followed the track of the plane up the mountain. Every twenty or twenty-five steps the three were forced to rest, waiting for their hearts to beat normally again. The mountain seemed almost vertical, and they had to clutch at the snow with their bare hands. They had left in such a hurry that they had not thought of how they should equip themselves for the climb. They wore only sneakers or moccasins and shirts, sweaters, and light jackets, with thin trousers covering their legs. All three were strong, for they were players who had been in training, but they had barely eaten for the past eleven days.

The air that afternoon was not so cold. As they climbed, the sun shone on their backs and kept them warm. It was their feet, sodden with freezing snow, which suffered most. In the middle of the afternoon they reached a rock, and Zerbino saw that the snow around it was melting. He threw himself down and sucked at drops of water suspended from the disintegrating crystals. There was also another form of lichen, which he put into his mouth, but it had the taste of soil. They continued to climb but by seven o'clock in the evening found that they were only halfway to the peak. The sun had gone behind the mountain and only a short span of daylight remained. They sat down to discuss what they should do. All agreed that it would get much colder and if they stayed on the mountain the three of them might well die of exposure. On the other hand, if they simply slid back down, the whole climb was for nothing. To get to the top or find the tail with the batteries was the only chance of survival for all twenty-seven. They made up their minds to remain on the mountain for the night and look for an outcrop of rocks which would provide some shelter.

A little farther up they found a small hillock where the snow had been blown away to reveal the rocks underneath. They piled up loose stones to form a windbreak and, as dark was almost upon them, lay down to sleep. With the dark, as always, came the cold, and for all the protection their light clothes afforded them against the subzero wind, they might as well have been naked. There was no question of sleep. They were compelled to hit one another with their fists and feet to keep their circulation going, begging one another to be hit in the face until their mouths were frozen and no words would come from them. Not one of the three thought he would survive the night. When the sun eventually rose in the east, each one was amazed to see it, and as it climbed in the sky it brought a little warmth back to their chilled bodies. Their clothes were soaked through, so they stood and took off their trousers, shirts, and socks and wrung them out. Then the sun went behind a cloud so they dressed again in their wet clothes and set off up the mountain.

Every now and then they stopped to rest and glance back toward the wreck of the Fairchild. By now it was a tiny dot in the snow, indistinguishable from any of the thousand outcrops of rock unless one knew exactly where to look. The red S which some of the boys had painted on the roof was invisible, and it was clear to the three why they had not been rescued: the plane simply could not be seen from the air. Nor was this all that depressed them. The higher they climbed, the more snow-covered mountains came into view. There was nothing to suggest that they were at the edge of the Andes, but they could only see to the north and the east. The mountain they were climbing still blocked their view to the south and west, and they seemed little nearer its summit. Every time they thought they had reached it, they would find that they were only at the top of a ridge; the mountain itself still towered above them.

At last, at the top of one of these ridges, their efforts were rewarded. They noticed that the rocks of an exposed outcrop had been broken, and then they saw scattered all around them the twisted pieces of metal that had once been part of the wingspan. A little farther up the mountain, where the ground fell into a small plateau, they saw a seat face down in the snow. With some difficulty they pulled it upright and found, still strapped to it, the body of one of their friends. His face was black, and it occurred to them that he might have been burned from the fuel escaping from the engine of the plane.

With great care Zerbino took from the body a wallet and identity card and, from around the neck, a chain and holy medals. He did the same when they came across the bodies of the three other Old Christians and the two members of the crew who had fallen out the back of the plane.

The three now made a count of those who were there and those who were below, and the tally came to forty-four. One body was missing. Then they remembered the floundering figure of Valeta, who had disappeared in the snow beneath them on that first afternoon. The count was now correct: six bodies at the top of the mountain, eleven down below, Valeta, twenty-four alive in the Fairchild, and the three of them there. All were accounted for.

They were still not at the summit, but there was no sign of the tail section or any other wreckage above them. They started back down the mountain, again following the track made by the fuselage, and on another shelf on the steep decline they found one of the plane's engines. The view from where they stood was majestic, and the bright sunlight reflecting off the snow made them squint as they observed the daunting panorama around them. They all had sunglasses, but Zerbino's were broken at the bridge, and as he climbed the mountain they had slipped forward so that he found it easier to peer over them. He did the same as they started to slide down again, using cushions they had taken from the seats at the top as makeshift sleds. They zigzagged, stopping at each piece of metal or debris to see if they could find anything useful. They discovered part of the plane's heating system, the lavatory, and fragments of the tail, but not the tail itself. Coming to a point where the track of the fuselage followed too steep a course, they crossed to the side of the mountain. By this time, Zerbino was so blinded by the snow that he could hardly see. He had to grope his way along, guided at times by the others. "I think," said Maspons, as they approached the plane once again, "that we shouldn't tell the others how hopeless it seems."

"No," said Turcatti. "There's no point in depressing them." Then he said, "By the way, what's happened to your shoe?"

Maspons looked down at his foot and saw that his shoe had come off while he was walking. His feet had become so numb with cold that he had not noticed.

The twenty-four other survivors were delighted to see the three return, but they were bitterly disappointed that they had not found the tail and appalled at their physical condition. All three hobbled on frozen feet and looked dreadful after their night out on the mountainside, and Zerbino was practically blind. They were immediately taken into the fuselage on cushions and brought large pieces of meat, which they gobbled down. Next Canessa treated their eyes, all of which were watering, with some drops called Colirio which he had found in a suitcase and thought might do them good. The drops stung but reassured them that something was being done for their condition. Then Zerbino bandaged his eyes with a rugby shirt, keeping it on for the next two days. When he removed his bandage he could still see only light and shadow, and he kept the rugby shirt as a kind of veil, shielding his eyes from the sun. He ate under the veil, and his blindness made him intolerably aggressive and irritable.

Their feet had also suffered. They were red and swollen with the cold, and their friends massaged them gently. It escaped no one's notice, however, that this expedition of a single day had almost killed three of the strongest among them, and morale once again declined.

ON ONE OF the days which followed, the sun disappeared behind clouds, rendering the water-making devices useless, so the boys had to return to the old method of putting the snow in bottles and shaking them. Then it occurred to Roy Harley and Carlitos Páez to make a fire with some empty Coca-Cola crates they had found in the luggage compartment of the plane. They held the aluminum sheets over the fire, and water was soon dripping into the bottles. In a short time they had enough.

The embers of the fire were still hot; it seemed sensible to try cooking a piece of meat on the hot foil. They did not leave it on for long, but the slight browning of the flesh gave it an immeasurably better flavor—softer than beef but with much the same taste.

The aroma soon brought other boys around the fire, and Coche

Inciarte, who had continued to feel the greatest repugnance for the raw flesh, found it quite palatable when cooked. Roy Harley, Numa Turcatti, and Eduardo Strauch also found it easier to overcome their revulsion when the meat was roasted and they could eat it as though it were beef.

Canessa and the Strauch cousins were against the idea of cooking the meat, and since they had gained some authority over the group, their views could not be ignored. "Don't you realize," said Canessa, knowledgeable and assertive as ever, "that proteins begin to die off at temperatures above forty degrees centigrade? If you want to get the most benefit from the meat, you must eat it raw."

"And when you cook it," said Fernández, looking down on the small steaks spitting on the aluminum foil, "the meat shrinks in size. A lot of its food value goes up in smoke or just melts away."

These arguments did not convince Harley or Inciarte, who could hardly derive nutrition from raw meat if they could not bring themselves to eat it, but in any case the limit to cooking was set by the extreme shortage of fuel — there were only three crates — and the high winds which so often made it impossible to light a fire out in the snow.

In the next few days, after Eduardo Strauch became very weak and emaciated, he finally overcame his revulsion to raw meat — forced to by his two cousins. Harley, Inciarte, and Turcatti never did, yet they were committed to survival and managed to consume enough to keep alive. The only ones who still had not eaten human flesh were the two eldest among them, Liliana and Javier Methol, and as the days passed and the twenty-five young men grew stronger on their new diet, the married couple, living on what remained of the wine, chocolate, and jam, grew thinner and more feeble.

The boys watched their growing debility with alarm. Marcelo begged them over and over again to overcome their reluctance and eat the meat. He used every argument, above all those words of Pedro Algorta. "Think of it as Communion. Think of it as the body and blood of Christ, because this is food that God has given us because He wants us to live."

Liliana listened to what he said, but time and again she gently shook her head. "There's nothing wrong with you doing it, Marcelo, but I can't, I just can't." For a time Javier followed her example. He still suffered from the altitude and was cared for by Liliana almost as though he were her child. The days passed slowly and there were moments when they found themselves alone; then they would talk together of their home in Montevideo, wondering what their children were doing at that hour, anxious that little Marie Noel, who was three, might be crying for her mother, or that their ten-year-old daughter, María Laura, might be skipping her homework.

Javier tried to reassure his wife that her parents would have moved into their house and would be looking after the children. They talked about Liliana's mother and father, and Liliana asked whether it would be possible when they returned to have her parents come and live in their house in Carrasco. She looked a little nervously at her husband when she suggested it, knowing that not every husband likes the idea of his parents-in-law living under the same roof, but Javier simply smiled and said, "Of course. Why didn't we think of that before?"

They discussed how they might build an annex onto the house so that Liliana's parents could be more or less independent. Liliana worried that they might not be able to afford it or that an extra wing might spoil the garden, but on every point Javier reassured her. Their conversation, however, weakened his resolution not to eat human meat, and so when Marcelo next offered him a piece of flesh, Javier took it and thrust it down his throat.

There remained only Liliana. Weak though she was, with life ebbing from her body, her mood remained serene. She wrote a short note to her children, saying how dear they were to her. She remained close to her husband, helping him because he was weaker, sometimes even a little irritable with him because the altitude sickness made his movements clumsy and slow, but with death so near, their partnership did not falter. Their life was one, on the mountain as it had been in Montevideo, and in these desperate conditions the bond between them held fast. Even sorrow was a part of the bond, and when they talked together of the four children they might never see again, tears not only of sadness but of joy fell down their cheeks, for what they missed now showed them what they had had.

One evening just before the sun had set, and when the twenty-seven survivors were preparing to take shelter from the cold in the fuselage of the plane, Liliana turned to Javier and told him that when they returned she would like to have another baby. She felt that if she was alive it was because God wanted her to do so.

Javier was delighted. He loved his children and had always wanted to have more, yet when he looked at his wife he could see through the tears in his eyes the poignance of her suggestion. After more then ten days without food the reserves had been drawn from her body. The bones protruded from her cheeks and her eyes were sunk into their sockets; only her smile was the same as before. He said to her, "Liliana, we must face up to it. None of this will happen if we don't survive."

She nodded. "I know."

"God wants us to survive."

"Yes. He wants us to survive."

"And there's only one way."

"Yes. There's only one way."

Slowly, because of their weakness, Javier and Liliana returned to the group of boys as they lined up to climb into the Fairchild.

"I've changed my mind," Liliana said to Marcelo. "I will eat the meat."

Marcelo went to the roof of the plane and brought down a small portion of human flesh which had been drying in the sun. Liliana took a piece and forced it down into her stomach.

FRANCIS CHICHESTER

(1901–1972)

From *Gipsy Moth Circles the World*

By the time Francis Chichester set out in August 1966 to sail alone around the world, the feat had been performed by a number of mariners—though most of them had taken the "easy" route through the Panama Canal, rather than around Cape Horn. What made Chichester's voyage a landmark adventure, galvanizing an international public and stimulating the solo circumnavigation races that continue to take place every few years, was a number of "firsts." With his time of 226 days, Chichester made the fastest circumnavigation to that date by any small vessel (single-handed or not), effectively halving the previous record. His was the first round-the-world sailing voyage to make only one shore layover (in Sydney). And he set all kinds of speed records, for periods ranging from a week to 119 consecutive days. All this at the age of sixty-five!

Chichester's character and the book he wrote about his memorable journey make the strongest possible contrast to Joshua Slocum's and his *book* Sailing Alone Around the World. *Chichester is the dour English hypochondriac to Slocum's blithe Yankee optimist. The boats mirror the sailors: Slocum's* Spray *emerges as a miracle of seaworthiness, virtually sailing itself for long stretches, whereas aboard* Gipsy Moth IV *one thing after another goes wrong or breaks down, and Chichester is beside himself to patch his trip back together.*

Chichester's most perilous episode, recounted here, is every mariner's nightmare: a capsize in the open ocean, which occurred in the Tasman Sea only a day and a half after the Gipsy Moth *had embarked from Sydney. The pragmatic, deadpan prose of the account oddly underscores the terror of the event, while adumbrating the pluck and skill it took to survive it and get on with the lonely journey.*

G iles had to return to Oxford, and I was sorry to see him go.[1] I think both of us were thinking of the uncertainty of life. I badly missed his help, too. I was making every possible effort to get away, feeling that every week's delay could mean more unpleasantness at the Horn. At last the time came when I could give out that I was leaving at 11.00 hrs on Sunday, January 29. When the day came there was a tropical cyclone north east of Sydney, and it would have been advisable to delay my leaving. But I hated to do this. I think I have always sailed when I said I would. Max Hinchliffe advised me to get south as much as I could because of the storm, but foolishly I disregarded this excellent advice.[2]

There was no storm in Sydney itself that morning—it was a fine, sunny day. And so, at 11.00 precisely, *Gipsy Moth IV* slipped her moorings and stood out to sea. Lord Casey, the Governor General, had presented me with three miniature bales of wool to be carried by *Gipsy Moth* to London and I reckoned that they were travelling by the smallest wool clipper that ever

---

[1]Giles is Chichester's son, who had flown to Sydney to greet him.

[2]An ex-captain in the Australian navy, Hinchcliffe offered his dock to Chichester while in Sydney.

left Australia! I had a crack crew, all friends, to sail the boat to Sydney Heads. In spite of her foot, Sheila took the helm, and the ship was worked by Alan Payne, Warwick Hood, Max Hinchliffe and Hugh Eaton.[3] Hugh had been working for several days without a let-up helping to get *Gipsy Moth* ready for sea. At the Heads, my crew transferred by way of a rubber motor boat to Trygve Halvorsen's launch, which was standing by as a tender. Sheila and I parted as if for a day. She has an uncanny foresight in spiritual matters, and had no doubt but that we should meet again. I must confess that I wondered rather sadly if we would as I sailed away from the fleet.

I passed Sydney Heads at 12.15, and at 14.30 the last of the accompanying boats left me. I had trouble with the propeller shaft, which I couldn't stop rotating. The brake would not work, so I had to dive down under the cockpit, head first and feet up, to fix the thing. I didn't enjoy these upside-down antics, and I felt horribly seasick. By 18.00 I was becalmed, but the calm didn't last long. There was a dense roll of clouds above the horizon, and wind began coming in from the south, at first lightly, but soon blowing up. By 19.00 it was coming at me in a series of savage bursts. At first I ran off northwards at 8 knots, then I took down all sail and lay ahull—that is, battened down, without sail, to give completely to the sea like a cork—in a great deluge of rain, reducing visibility to about 50 yards. Soon it got dark, and it was *very* dark—absolutely pitch dark. I was seasick and turned in but didn't get much rest. After about three quarters of an hour I heard the self-steering oar banging about, and went on deck to deal with it. The wind was then about 35 knots, and I thought that *Gipsy Moth* could stand a jib and get moving again. I set a working jib, but it was too much for her. So I replaced it with a storm jib. With this I left her to fight her way slowly east at about 2 knots and turned in again, determined to sleep all night.

I stayed in my bunk until just after 04.00, when the wind began coming still more strongly and I went up to drop the storm jib and lie ahull again.

[3]Assorted Australians and Englishmen who helped refit the *Gipsy Moth*. Sheila was Chichester's wife, also on hand in Sydney to greet him; a few days before, she had sprained her ankle in Sydney.

We stayed like this for most of the day; it was too rough for even a storm jib with the wind blowing at 50 knots or more. In the afternoon I did set a storm jib, reefed to only 60 square feet, a mere rag of sail, chiefly to try to cut down the thumping in the heavy seas. I hoped that the thumping was due to the self-steering gear, and not to the new false keel.

In spite of the storm, radio conditions were good, and at 8 A.M. I had a good radio talk with Sheila which cheered me up. I was still sick from time to time, but slowly began to feel better, and gave myself some brandy, sugar and lemon, which I managed to keep down. The weather forecasts were bad with renewed cyclone warnings. This was Tropical Cyclone Diana, which was reported to be moving SE at about 20 mph. I tried to work out where it was in relation to me, and I reckoned that the worst of it would pass some 270 miles to the east of my noon position. That was something, but the whole area of the Tasman Sea was violently disturbed with winds from 40 to 60 knots, gusting up to 80 knots in squalls. There was nothing I could do about it. I did not worry over much, but just tried to exist until the storm passed.

That Monday night was as foul and black a night as you could meet at sea. Although it was pitch dark, the white breakers showed in the blackness like monstrous beasts charging down on the yacht. They towered high in the sky, I wouldn't blame anyone for being terrified at the sight. My crosstree light showed up the breaking water, white in the black darkness, and now and then a wave caught the hull and, breaking against it, sluiced over the decks. As I worked my way along the deck I thought: "Christ! What must it be like in a 120-knot wind!" I dropped the remaining storm sail, furled and tied it down. *Gipsy Moth* had been doing 8 knots with the little sail set, and I thought she would be less liable to damage lying ahull with no forward speed. As I worked my way aft again after finishing the job on the foredeck, I looked at the retaining net amidships, holding the two big genoas bagged up, and the 1,000 feet of warp in several coils. I knew that I ought to pass a couple of ropes over the net between the eye bolts at each side for storm lashings — I had always done this before on the passage out. But these ropes had not been re-rigged in Sydney and I was feeling ghastly, I thought due to seasickness. (From something which happened later I can only deduce that the chief cause of my trouble was the Australian champagne I had drunk. For some reason this acted like poison on me.) Whatever the cause of my trouble, I weakened, and decided to leave the extra lashing until the morning. When I got below and had stripped off my oilskins I rolled into my bunk and put all the lights out. This was about two hours after dark. The bunk was the only place where one could wait below, for it was difficult to stand up, and I should have been continually thrown off if I had sat on the settee. However, lying on my back in the bunk, I dropped into a fitful sleep after a while.

I think I was awake when the boat began to roll over. If not, I woke immediately she started to do so. Perhaps when the wave hit her I woke. It was pitch dark. As she started rolling I said to myself, "Over she goes!" I was not frightened, but intensely alert and curious. Then a lot of crashing and banging started, and my head and shoulders were being bombarded with crockery and cutlery and bottles. I had an oppressive feeling of the boat being on top of me. I wondered if she would roll over completely, and what the damage would be; but she came up quietly the same side that she had gone down. I reached up and put my bunk light on. It worked, giving me a curious feeling of something normal in a world of utter chaos. I have only a confused idea of what I did for the next hour or so. I had an absolutely hopeless feeling when I looked at the pile of jumbled-up food and gear all along the cabin. Anything that was in my way when I wanted to move I think I put back in its right place, though feeling as I did so that it was a waste of time as she would probably go over again. The cabin was 2 foot deep all along with a jumbled-up pile of hundreds of tins, bottles, tools, shackles, blocks, two sextants and oddments. Every settee locker, the whole starboard bunk, and the three starboard drop lockers had all emptied out when she was upside down. Water was swishing about on the cabin sole beside the chart table, but not much. I looked into the bilge which is 5 feet deep, but it was not quite full, for which I thought, "Thank God."

This made me get cracking with the radio, at forty-five minutes after midnight, and two and a quarter hours after the capsize. I was afraid that the radio telephone would go out of action through water percolating it, and that even if it didn't, if the boat went over again the mass of water in the bilge must inevitably flood the telephone and finish it. I had to try to get a message through to say that I was all right, so that if the telephone went dead people would not think I had foundered because of that. I called up on the distress frequency 2182 and got Sydney Radio straight away. As usual they were most efficient and cooperative. I asked them to give my wife a message in the morning to say that I had capsized, but that I was all right and that if they got no more messages from me it would only be because the telephone had been swamped and packed up, and not because I had foundered. I asked particularly that they should not wake up Sheila in the middle of the night, but call her at seven o'clock in the morning. I said that I did not need any help.

I am not sure when I discovered that the water was pouring in through the forehatch. What had happened was that when the boat was nearly upside down, the heavy forehatch had swung open, and when the boat righted itself the hatch, instead of falling back in place, fell forwards onto the deck, leaving the hatchway wide open to the seas. It may seem strange that my memory is so confused, but it was a really wild night, the movement was horrible and every step was difficult.

I must have got out on deck to pump the water below the level of the batteries. I found the holding net torn from its lashings. One of my 600-foot genoas had gone, a drogue, and 700 feet of inch-and-a-half plaited warp. The other big genoa was still there in its bag pressed against the leeward lifeline wires. I don't remember how I secured it. I found the forehatch open and closed that. A section of the cockpit coaming and a piece of the side of the cockpit had been torn away. I was extremely puzzled at the time to know how this could have happened. The important thing was that the masts were standing, and the rigging appeared undamaged. I think it was then that I said to myself, "To hell with everything," and decided to have a sleep. I emptied my bunk of plates, cutlery and bottles, etc. One serrated-edge cutting knife was embedded close to where my head had been, and I thought how lucky I was. I had only a slightly cut lip; I do not know what caused that.

My bunk was soaking wet, which was no wonder, considering that in the morning I could see daylight through where the side of the cockpit had been torn away just above the bunk. But I did not give a damn how wet it was, turned in, and was soon fast asleep. I slept soundly till daylight.

When I awoke the boat was still being thrown about. All that day it was blowing a gale between 40 and 55 knots. I was still queasy and unable to face eating anything. I had not had a proper meal since leaving Sydney. Now and then I had some honey and water, but even that was an ordeal, for I had not filled up my vacuum flasks with hot water before starting as I always intend to do before a voyage, so that I can have honey and water hot as soon as I feel queasy. And I was faced with this awful mess; it looked like a good week's work to clear up, sort and re-pack everything. I have rarely had less spirit in me. I longed to be back in Sydney Harbour, tied up to the jetty. I hated and dreaded the voyage ahead. Let's face it; I was frightened and had a sick feeling of fear gnawing inside me. If this was what could happen in an ordinary storm, how could a small boat possibly survive in a 100-knot greybearder?

After this I made another tour of inspection, surveying the damage. Some extraordinary things had happened. The long mahogany boathook which had been lashed down at the side of the deck was jammed between the shrouds about 6 feet up in the air. By a great stroke of luck the locker under one of the cockpit seats, which had a flap lid with no fastening at all, was still full of gear, including the reefing handles for the main boom and the mizzen boom. I suppose the jumble of ropes and stuff which filled this locker (so that it was practically impossible to find anything in it) had jammed so tightly when upside down that nothing had spilled out. On the other hand, sundry winch handles, which had been in open-topped boxes specially made for them in the cockpit, had all disappeared.

Down below some queer things had happened. To start with, there was that foul smell. I sniffed the bilges, but it did not come from there. I tried the batteries, but they fortunately had been clamped down securely in the bilge and were perfectly all right. At last I tracked it down to the vitamin pills, pink vitamin C. The bottle had shot across the boat from the cupboard above the galley sink, and had smashed to pieces on the doghouse above my head. The pills had spread all over the windows in the doghouse, where they partly dissolved in seawater. I tried to mop them up but the melting vitamin mixture smeared into the joint between the Perspex and wood of the windows and into every possible crack and cranny. For the time being I had to put up with the stink. The irony of it was that I never used a vitamin pill on the whole passage!

I worked at the pump intermittently, stopping for a rest after every 200 strokes (the water had to be "lifted" 10–11 feet) and doing some other job as a change from pumping. When at last I got to the bottom of the bilge I found an assortment of plates and crockery, and also I found plates beside the motor, and one right aft of the motor. I was much puzzled at the time to know how these plates had got into such extraordinary positions, but realised later what had happened. The motor had a wooden casing covering it in at its forward end in the cabin, and the top of this is a step which hinges upwards. This lid had flown open, so that the plates had shot through the gap and when the boat righted herself, the lid had closed down again. One of the strangest things happened at the forward end of the cabin, where I kept on finding minute particles of razor-sharp, coloured glass. It was a long time before I tracked down the origin of this, but one day I came across a cork stuck into about an inch of the neck of a bottle. This was a long time later, but I mention it here because it provided some valuable evidence. It was the cork and neck of a bottle of Irish whiskey, which Jack Tyrrell of Arklow, who built *Gipsy Moth III*,[4] had sent me as a present at the start of this voyage. I knew exactly where this bottle had been standing, in a hole cut in a sheet of plywood to take the bottle in the wine locker on the starboard side of the cabin. This locker had a flap-down lid. So I knew exactly where

[4]Chichester's previous ship. The one on which he made his circumnavigation was properly styled *Gipsy Moth IV*.

the bottle had come from. I also knew exactly where it had gone to; it had hit a deck beam in the ceiling of the cabin, making a bruise a quarter of an inch deep in the wood. Here it had shattered into a thousand fragments, and it was not till even later in the voyage that I found out where most of these were. At the foot of Sheila's bunk on the port side of the cabin there was a shelf, of which half was boxed in with a flap-down lid. In this case also the lid had flown open when the boat went over, the pieces of glass had shot in, and the lid had closed down again. As I write this, the glass is still there. The last fragment of glass I found was one that had dropped on to the cabin floor from somewhere and lodged in the sole of my foot when I was going barefoot. The point about this glass is that it enabled me to measure the exact path of the bottle, which showed that the boat had turned through 131° when the bottle flew out of its niche; in other words, the mast would have then been 41° below the horizontal. I wondered if the shock of a wave hitting the boat had shot the bottle out of its locker, but there was other evidence which convinced me that this was not the case. On the roof of the doghouse the paintwork was spattered all over with particles of dirt up to a line just like a highwater mark on a beach. This dirt must have come from the floor of the cabin when the hatches above the bilge flew off. The particles were so small they would not have any momentum if a wave had hit the boat with a shock; they would have got on to the roof only by dropping there through gravity. What I have described and other little bits of evidence which I came across during the succeeding months convince me that the yacht rolled over until the mast was between 45 and 60° below the horizontal, and I don't believe it would have made much difference if she had come up the other side after completely rolling over.

But this detective work came later. I must return to the state of things at the time. There was butter everywhere and over everything, for 2 lb of butter had landed at the foot of my bunk, and splashed and spread. Coat hangers in the hanging locker were broken, and the basin was full of my clothes. Also in the basin was a Tupperware box containing my first aid equipment. Both cabin bunks had collapsed, spilling the contents of Tupperware containers on top of the contents of the drop lockers. Tins of food, fruit and milk were jumbled up on the cabin floor with shackles, sextants, biscuits and cushions. All the floor boards had taken to the air when *Gipsy Moth* went over, so everything that could find its way to the bilges had duly got there. My camera stand had broken in two, but the loose half was still lying on deck, up to windward. The main halliard was tangled with the burgee halliard.

Gipsy Moth capsized on the night of Monday, January 30. My log notes briefly: "About 22.30. Capsize." Heavy weather continued throughout Tuesday, January 31, and I spent the day lying ahull, doing what I could to clear up. The electric bilge pump would not work, so I had to pump by hand, trying to repair the electric pump in the intervals of hand pumping. After I had cleaned the impeller the electric pump worked for a few minutes, but then sucked at an air lock. The bilge was still half-full, but gradually I got the water down. I streamed my remaining green warp in the hope that it would keep the yacht headed downwind, but without any sails up the warp seemed to have no effect. So I hauled it back inboard and coiled it. The socket for the vane shaft of the self-steering gear was nearly off, so that had to be repaired, a dirty job which put me under water now and again. Thank God the water was warm! As I dealt with these various jobs one after another, my spirits began to pick up. I had been unbelievably lucky. The masts and rigging were all intact, which I attributed largely to Warwick's rigging.[5] I felt a sense of loss that one of the big genoas had gone overboard, but I could get on without it. I was upset at losing one of my drogues and the 700 feet of drogue warp that went with it, for I had intended to stream a drogue at the end of a long warp to slow down *Gipsy Moth* and to keep her stern to the seas in Cape Horner storms. Later, after I had pondered the details of my capsize for many hours, I completely discarded the warp and drogue idea. So the loss of those items was not as serious as I thought at the time.

As the day wore on I began to feel a little hungry, and I lunched on three slices of bread and butter and marmalade. The bread was pretty mouldy,

[5]Warwick Hood (see note 3, above).

but it was solid food, and went down well. My log for that day notes cheerfully: "18.20. Called Sydney Radio. Told Sheila the tale."

That radio talk with Sheila meant much to me. She was as calm and confident as always, and never for a moment questioned my decision to carry on. I said again that I did not want any help. She was as distressed as I was about the mess in our beautifully tidy boat. I could tell her about everything, because she knew exactly where everything was. I remember telling her about the horrible smell like stale, spilled beer, from wet vitamin tablets sticking to the cabin roof. I told her that I had spares on board for most things, and that in time I should be able to tidy up. I drew strength from her.

STEVEN CALLAHAN

(b. 1952)

From *Adrift: Seventy-six Days Lost at Sea*

Steven Callahan's ordeal in the Atlantic Ocean exemplifies Vilhjalmur
Stefansson's cranky dictum that adventure happens only when some-
thing goes wrong. This is not to say that Callahan was a bungler—
though just thirty at the time of his 1982 nautical disaster, he was an
experienced seaman. Single-handed open-ocean sailing is inevitably
dangerous, and when a sudden storm sank the Solo well to the west of
the Canary Islands, Callahan was in as empty a sector of the mid-
Atlantic as he could have chosen.

In any event, it was his canny pluck at survival that allowed Calla-
han to cling to life through seventy-six days in a five-and-a-half-foot rub-
ber raft. At the time, no other castaway had survived longer than a
month alone in an inflatable raft. It took another kind of pluck to cap-
ture the details of his ordeal in Adrift, *a first book that became an in-*
stant classic. Its hallmark is honesty, for despite his ingenuity and skill,
Callahan never forgets that, as much as anything, he owes his survival
to simple luck.

April 12, Day 67

It is April 12, the date that marked the anniversary of my marriage such a very long time ago. Frisha's life as my wife was not easy. I'd take off on a delivery trip or a passage and leave her behind. Sometimes we wouldn't see each other for months. She thought that it was all a very risky business, despite my reassurances. Not long before I left the States on *Solo*, she told me that she thought I would eventually meet my maker at sea, but that it would not be during this voyage. I wonder how she feels about it now. I wonder if she was right. What is Frisha doing? She must believe that I am dead while she studies to bring life from the soil. One day, perhaps, long after I am drowned and consumed by fish, a fisherman may haul aboard a catch that will find its way to her table. She will take the head, tail, and bones and heap them upon her compost pile, mix them with the soil so green life will sprout. Nature knows no waste.

A flying fish crashes onto the canopy behind the solar still. I am losing my taste for fish, but any change from dorado arouses my appetite. My guts feel like they have fallen right out of me. No amount of fish can fill my vacant stomach. I sit up, grab the flyer, and wonder if it is scared or if it accepts death like another swimming stroke.

Maintaining discipline becomes more difficult each day. My fearsome and fearful crew mutter mutinous misgivings within the fo'c's'le of my head. Their spokesman yells at me.

"Water, Captain! We need more water. Would you have us die here, so close to port? What is a pint or two? We'll soon be in port. We can surely spare a pint—"

"Shut up!" I order. "We don't know how close we are. Might have to last to the Bahamas. Now, get back to work."

"But, Captain—"

"You heard me. You've got to stay on ration."

They gather together, mumbling among themselves, greedily eyeing the bags of water dangling from *Ducky*'s bulwarks.[1] We are shabby, almost done

---

[1] Callahan named his life raft the Rubber Ducky.

for. Legs already collapsed. Torso barely holds head up. Empty as a tin drum. Only arms have any strength left. It is indeed pitiful. Perhaps the loss of a pint would not hurt. No, I must maintain order. "Back to work," I say. "You can make it."

Yet I feel swayed more and more by my body's demands, feel stretched so tight between my body, mind, and spirit that I might snap at any moment. The solar still has another hole in it, and the distillate is more often polluted with salt water. I can detect less and less often when it is reasonably unsalty. I may go mad at any time. Mutiny will mean the end. I know I am close to land. I must be. I must convince us all.

We've been over the continental shelf for four days. One of my small charts shows the shelf about 120 miles to the east of the West Indies. I should see the tall, green slopes of an island, if my sextant is correct. I should hit Antigua—ironically, my original destination. But who knows? I could be hundreds of miles off. This triangle of pencils may be a foolish bit of junk. The chart could be grossly inaccurate. I spend endless hours scanning the horizon for a cloud shape that does not move, searching the sky for a long wisp of cloud that might suggest human flight. Nothing. I feel like a watch slowly winding down, a Timex thrown out of an airplane just once too often. I've overestimated my speed, or perhaps I'm drifting diagonally across the shelf. If there was only some way to measure the current. I'm assuming that I'm within two hundred miles of my calculated position, but if I've been off by as little as five miles a day, I could be four hundred miles away from where I hope I am—another eight or even fifteen days. "Water, Captain. Please? Water." Tick, tick, slower and slower. When will it stop? Can I wind it up until the end of the month without breaking the spring?

The next afternoon's sun is scorching. The solar still keeps passing out and looks as if it may not last much longer. By mid–bake-off I can feel myself begin to panic and shiver.

"More water, Captain. We must have more."

"No! No! Well, maybe. No! You can't have any. Not a drop."

The heat pours down. My flesh feels as if it is turning to desert sand. I cannot sit upright without having trouble focusing. Everything is foggy.

"Please, Captain. Water. Now, before it's too late."

"O.K. The tainted water. You can drink as much of it as you want. But the clear water remains. One pint of it a day. That's the limit. It's the limit until we see aircraft or land. Agreed?"

I hesitate. "Yes, all right."

A sludge of orange particles sits in the bottom of the plastic tube in which the wretched canopy water rests. I triple layer my T-shirt and strain the water through it into a tin again and again. The result is a pint of cloudy liquid. It is bitter. I can just keep it down.

My thirst becomes stronger. Within an hour I must drink more. In another hour more still. Soon the bitter pint is gone. It is as if my whole body has turned to ash. I must drink even more.

"No. Can't. No more until tomorrow."

"But we must. You've poisoned us now and we must."

"Stop it!" I must keep command. But my eyes are wild, my limbs shaking in an effort to hold back the panic.

My torso screams out. "Take it!" Limbs reach out for a sack of water.

"No!" I scramble to my knees, almost in tears. I get to my feet and look aft for a moment. I can't stand forever but for now the breeze cools me off.

There, in the sky—a jet! Not just a contrail or the faintest hint of a jet, but a silver-bodied bird streaking to Brazil! Quick, man, the EPIRB![2] Battery is probably shot. Well, the light's on at least and he can't be more than ten miles away. I'll leave it on for twelve hours. The jet looks small. It may not be a commercial flight. Regardless, it couldn't have come at a better time. We must be close. I fulfill my promise. I hand out a pint of clean, sweet water. Everybody relaxes.

A gooselike bird resembling a gannet flies over. It has even-colored brown plumage, except for dark rings around its eyes. Yesterday a jaeger winged by. It was not supposed to be there. Should I inform these birds that they are beyond their prescribed ranges? New fish, new birds, different water color, no sargasso. It all adds up. This voyage *will* end soon. I stare intensely at the horizon until my eyes water.

• • •

[2]His emergency beacon.

April 16, Day 71

The past few days have passed ever so slowly and I have been growing progressively more dim and depressed. We should have reached the islands days
ago. We couldn't have passed between them, could we? No, they are too
close together. I'd have seen at least one. And the birds still come at me from
the west. When do I use the EPIRB for the last time? Even with the short
range it must now have, the massive daytime Caribbean air traffic will hear
the signal. But I must wait until I see land or can last no longer.

I am beginning to doubt everything—my position, my senses, my life itself. Maybe I am Prometheus, cursed to have my liver torn out each day
and have it grow back each night. Maybe I am the Flying Dutchman,
doomed to sail the seas forever and never rest again, to watch my own body
rot and my equipment deteriorate. I am in an infinite vortex of horror,
whirling deeper and deeper. Thinking of what I will do when it is all over
is a bad joke. It will never be over. It is worse than death. If I were to search
the most heinous parts of my mind to create a vision of a real hell, this would
be the scene, exactly.

The last solar still has completely blown, just like the one before. The
bottom cloth has rotted and ripped away. I have a full stock of water, but it
will go quickly. Rainfall is my only well now.

April 18, Day 73

I continue to take note of the positive signs of approaching landfall. The
tiger dorados have gone. A five- or ten-pound mottled brown fish, a triple-
tail, has lumbered around *Rubber Ducky* for two days. I've tried to hit it,
but I've been impatient. I hurried the shots and only managed to poke it
twice, driving it away.[3] There have been more sooty birds in the sky, and
the frigates continue to reel about overhead. I've grabbed two snowy terns,
which landed for a short rest and received a permanent sleep. I've seen another ship, but at night and very far off. Somehow all of these changes do

---

[3]Callahan had improvised an effective speargun out of a butter knife and stray pieces of
plastic and wood.

little for my continued depression. I am the Dutchman. I arise still feeling asleep. There is no time for relaxation, only time for stress. Work harder. Do more. Must it last forever?

I strike my fishing pose yet again. My aching arms grasp the few ounces of plastic and aluminum, the butter knife tied on like a caveman's stone point, but indubitably less effective. Now I can hold the pose only for a minute or so, no longer. The dorados brush against my knees as I push all of my weight down on one knee, then the other. They turn their sides to me as if wanting to show off the target area, and they swing out to the left and right or flip around deep below. Occasionally they wiggle their heads so near the surface that the water welters up. Perhaps one will rise and speak to me like the flounder in the fairy tale. Often I wait a microsecond too long, and the few square inches of bull's eye melt away into the dark water, which is just starting to brighten as the sun rises. This time I strike home, the battle rages, and I win again. The emerald elders court behind the lines like generals who are smart enough not to join in the melee any more.

Clouds race across my world, gray and smeared, too light for a heavy burst of rain, but the light sprinkles and misty air, combined with wave spray stirred up by the wind, prevent my fish from drying properly. Temporarily though, the stock of food allows me to concentrate my energy on designing new water-catchment systems. The first is simple. I stretch plastic from the cut-up still along the shaft of the spear gun. I can hold it out, away from the sheltering canopy, pulling a corner with my mouth. Next I set the blown still on the bow. I punch it into a flat, round plate and curl up the edges like a deep-dish pizza pie. Even in light showers, I can see that the two devices work. A fine mist collects into drops, that streak into dribbles, that run into wrinkled, plastic valleys, where I can slurp them up. I must move quickly to tend to each system and collect water before it's polluted by waves or the canopy. I am far enough west that the clouds are beginning to collect, and occasionally I see a "black cow," as some sailors call squally cumulus, grazing far off, its rain streaking to earth.

I stick with the routine that I've followed for two and a half months. At night I take a look around each time I awaken. Every half hour during the day, I stand and carefully peruse the horizon in all directions. I have done this more than two thousand times now. Instinctively I know how the waves roll, when one will duck and weave to give a clear view for another hundred yards or half a mile. This noon a freighter streams up from astern, a bit to the north of us. The hand flares are nearly invisible in the daylight, so I choose an orange smoke flare and pop it. The dense orange genie spreads its arms out and flies off downwind just above the water. Within a hundred feet it has been blown into a haze thinner than the smoke of a crowded pub. The ship cuts up the Atlantic a couple of miles abeam and smoothly steams off to the west. She *must* be headed to an island port.

April 19, Day 74

I work all the rest of the day and all of the morning of April 19 to create an elaborate water collection device. Using the aluminum tubing from the radar reflector and my last dead solar still, I make *Rubber Ducky* a bonnet that I secure to the summit of the canopy arch tube. The half circle of aluminum tubing keeps the face of the bonnet open and facing aft. A bridle adjusts the angle of the face, which I keep nearly vertical, and the wind blows the bonnet forward like a bag. I fit a drain and tubing that I can run inside to fill up containers while I tend to the other water collectors.

For hours I watch white, fluffy cumulus rise up from the horizon and slowly pass. Sometimes they band together and form dense herds running in long lines. Those that have grazed over the Atlantic long enough grow thick and muscular, rearing up to great billowing heights, churning violently, their underbellies flat and black. When they can hold no more, their rain thunders down in black streaks that lash the sea. I chew upon dried sticks of dorado awaiting the test of my new tools.

But it seems that the paths of the squalls are bound to differ from mine. Sometimes a long line of clouds passes close by. I watch the wispy edges swirl above me and feel a few drops or a momentary sprinkle coming down. It's just enough to show me that my new water collection gear is very effective. I'm convinced that I'll collect several pints, maybe even a gallon, if I can just get directly in the path of a single heavy shower. It's one thing to have a tool and quite another to be in a position to use it. My eyes wander from the horizon to the sky. I'm so tired of always awaiting something.

April 20, Day 75

Seventy-five days—April 20. With the drizzle and the salt spray, my dorado sticks have grown pasty rather than drying. I'm astonished that the dried sticks from one of the first dorados that I caught still seem to be fine. Only a slight whitish haze covers the deep amber, woody interior.

For an hour in late afternoon, I watch a drove of clouds run up from the east. I can tell that they're traveling a little to the south of my course. As they rise up and charge onward, I ready myself, swallowing frequently, though there is no saliva to swallow. I try to wish them into running me down, but they ignore me and begin to sweep by about a mile away, clattering and flashing with lightning. Four separate heavy columns of rain pour down, so dense that they eclipse the blue sky behind. I watch tons of pure water flowing down like aerial waterfalls. If only I could be just a mile from where I am. No sips, no single mouthfuls, but an overflow of water I could guzzle. If only *Ducky* could sail instead of waddle. *I have missed.* My collection devices are bone dry and flutter in the wind.

SEBASTIAN JUNGER

(b. 1962)

From *The Perfect Storm*

Sebastian Junger's challenge, in The Perfect Storm, *was in a sense the antithesis of Steven Callahan's (see previous excerpt). Junger hoped to chronicle the story of a sea disaster in which the protagonists had failed to survive—the six-man crew of the* Andrea Gail, *sunk in 1991 off the coast of New England in a millennial storm that struck without warning. Compounding the challenge was the fact that before writing the book, Junger had never met any of the doomed seamen. That the book was not only a best-seller but a fine piece of writing is largely owing to the author's capacity to empathize and imagine an ultimate horror— even when it means taking the considerable risk of inventing internal monologues.*

In this excerpt, however, which details an attempted helicopter rescue at the height of the storm that turned into a second survival ordeal, Junger benefited from the opportunity to interview the survivors. Yet once again, Junger's empathic skills serve him so well that the reader forgets

the whole scene has been reconstructed. Instead, we find ourselves bob-
bing in the furious sea, rescuers needing to be rescued, clutching des-
perately at our own lifelines.

R uvola has made twenty or thirty attempts on the drogue—a monstrous feat of concentration—when the tanker pilot radios that he
has to shut down his number one engine.[1] The oil pressure gauge
is fluctuating wildly and they are risking a burn-out. The pilot starts in on
the shut-down procedure, and suddenly the left-hand fuel hose retracts;
shutting off the engine has disrupted the air flow around the wing, and the
reel-in mechanism has mistaken that for too much slack. It performs what
is known as an "uncommanded retraction." The pilot finishes shutting
down the engine, brings Ruvola back in, and then reextends the hose. Ruvola lines up on it and immediately sees that something is wrong. The
drogue is shaped like a small parachute, and ordinarily it fills with air and
holds the hose steady; now it is just convulsing behind the tanker plane. It
has been destroyed by forty-five minutes of desperate refueling attempts.

Ruvola tells the tanker pilot that the left-hand drogue is shot and that
they have to switch over to the other side. In these conditions refueling from
the right-hand drogue is a nightmarish, white-knuckle business because the
helicopter probe also extends from the right-hand side of the cockpit, so the
pilot has to come even tighter into the fuselage of the tanker to make contact. Ruvola makes a run at the right-hand drogue, misses, comes in again,
and misses again. The usual technique is to watch the tanker's wing flaps
and anticipate where the drogue's going to go, but the visibility is so low
that Ruvola can't even see that far; he can barely see past the nose of his
own helicopter. Ruvola makes a couple more runs at the drogue, and on
his last attempt he comes in too fast, overshoots the wing, and by the time
he's realigned himself the tanker has disappeared. They've lost an entire

---

[1]At the height of the storm, helicopter pilot Dave Ruvola is attempting to refuel by cou-
pling a hose (called a "drogue") to a tanker plane in midair.

C-130 in the clouds. They are at 4,000 feet in zero visibility with roughly twenty minutes of fuel left; after that they will just fall out of the sky. Ruvola can either keep trying to hit the drogue, or he can try to make it down to sea level while they still have fuel.

We're going to set up for a planned ditching, he tells his crew. *We're going to ditch while we still can.* And then Dave Ruvola drops the nose of the helicopter and starts racing his fuel gauge down to the sea.

John Spillane, watching silently from the spotter's seat, is sure he's just heard his death sentence. "Throughout my career I've always managed—just barely—to keep things in control," says Spillane. "But now, suddenly, the risk is becoming totally uncontrollable. We can't get fuel, we're going to end up in that roaring ocean, and we're not gonna be in control anymore. And I know the chances of being rescued are practically zero. I've been on a lot of rescue missions, and I know they can hardly even *find* someone in these conditions, let alone recover them. We're some of the best in the business—best equipped, best trained. We couldn't do a rescue a little while earlier, and now we're in the same situation. It looks real bleak. It's not going to happen."

While Ruvola is flying blindly downward through the clouds, copilot Buschor[2] issues a mayday on an Air National Guard emergency frequency and then contacts the *Tamaroa,* fifteen miles to the northeast. He tells them they are out of fuel and about to set up for a planned ditching. Captain Brudnicki orders the *Tam's* searchlights turned up into the sky so the helicopter can give them a bearing, but Buschor says he can't see a thing. *Okay, just start heading towards us,* the radio dispatcher on the *Tam* says. *We don't have time, we're going down right now,* Buschor replies. Jim McDougal, handling the radios at the ODC[3] in Suffolk, receives—simultaneously—the ditching alert and a phone call from Spillane's wife, who wants to know where her husband is. She'd had no idea there was a prob-

[2]Graham Buschor.
[3]Operations Dispatch Center.

lem and just happened to call at the wrong moment; McDougal is so pan-icked by the timing that he hangs up on her. At 9:08, a dispatcher at Coast Guard headquarters in Boston takes a call that an Air National Guard he-licopter is going down and scrawls frantically in the incident log: "*Helo [he-licopter] & 130 enroute Suffolk. Can't refuel helo due visibility. May have to ditch. Stay airborne how long? 20–25 min. LAUNCH!*" He then notifies Cape Cod Air Base, where Karen Stimson is chatting with one of her res-cue crews. The five airmen get up without a word, file into the bathroom, and then report for duty out on the tarmac.

Ruvola finally breaks out of the clouds at 9:28, only two hundred feet above the ocean. He goes into a hover and immediately calls for the ditch-ing checklist, which prepares the crew to abandon the aircraft. They have practiced this dozens of times in training, but things are happening so fast that the routines start to fall apart. Jim Mioli has trouble seeing in the dim cabin lighting used with night-vision gear, so he can't locate the handle of the nine-man life raft. By the time he finds it, he doesn't have time to put on his Mustang survival suit. Ruvola calls three times for Mioli to read him the ditching checklist, but Mioli is too busy to answer him, so Ruvola has to go through it by memory. One of the most important things on the list is for the pilot to reach down and eject his door, but Ruvola is working too hard to remove his hands from the controls. In military terminology he has become "task-saturated," and the door stays on.

While Ruvola is trying to hold the aircraft in a hover, the PJs[4] scramble to put together the survival gear. Spillane slings a canteen over his shoul-der and clips a one-man life raft to the strap. Jim Mioli, who finally man-ages to extract the nine-man raft, pushes it to the edge of the jump door and waits for the order to deploy. Rick Smith, draped in survival gear, squats at the edge of the other jump door and looks over the side. Below is an ocean so ravaged by wind that they can't even tell the difference between the waves and the troughs; for all they know they are jumping three hundred feet. As

---

[4]Pararescue jumpers.

horrible as that is, though, the idea of staying where they are is even worse. The helicopter is going to drop into the ocean at any moment, and no one on the crew wants to be anywhere nearby when it does.

Only Dave Ruvola will stay on board; as pilot, it is his job to make sure the aircraft doesn't fall on the rest of his crew. The chances of his escaping with his door still in place are negligible, but that is beside the point. The ditching checklist calls for a certain procedure, a procedure that insures the survival of the greatest number of crew. That Mioli neglects to put on his survival suit is also, in some ways, suicidal, but he has no choice. His duty is to oversee a safe bail-out, and if he stops to put his survival suit on, the nine-man raft won't be ready for deployment. He jumps without his suit.

At 9:30, the number one engine flames out; Spillane can hear the turbine wind down. They've been in a low hover for less than a minute. Ruvola calls out on the intercom: *The number one's out! Bail out! Bail out!* The number two is running on fumes; in theory, they should flame out at the same time. This is it. They are going down.

Mioli shoves the life raft out the right-hand door and watches it fall, in his words, "into the abyss." They are so high up that he doesn't even see it hit the water, and he can't bring himself to jump in after it. Without telling anyone, he decides to take his chances in the helicopter. Ditching protocol calls for copilot Buschor to remain on board as well, but Ruvola orders him out because he decides Buschor's chances of survival will be higher if he jumps. Buschor pulls his door-release lever but the door doesn't pop off the fuselage, so he just holds it open with one hand and steps out onto the footboard. He looks back at the radar altimeter, which is fluctuating between ten feet and eighty, and realized that the timing of his jump will mean the difference between life and death. Ruvola repeats his order to bail out, and Buschor unplugs the intercom wires from his flight helmet and flips his night-vision goggles down. Now he can watch the waves roll underneath him in the dim green light of enhanced vision. He spots a huge crest, takes a breath and jumps.

Spillane, meanwhile, is grabbing some last-minute gear. "I wasn't terrified, I was scared," he says. "Forty minutes before I'd been more scared, thinking about the possibilities, but at the end I was totally committed. The pilot had made the decision to ditch, and it was a great decision. How many pilots might have just used up the last twenty minutes of fuel trying to hit the drogue? Then you'd fall out of the sky and everyone would die."

The helicopter is strangely quiet without the number one engine. The ocean below them, in the words of another pilot, looks like a lunar landscape, cratered and gouged and deformed by wind. Spillane spots Rick Smith at the starboard door, poised to jump, and moves towards him. "I'm convinced he was sizing up the waves," Spillane says. "I wanted desperately to stick together with him. I just had time to sit down, put my arm around his shoulders, and he went. We didn't have time to say anything—you want to say goodbye, you want to do a lot of things, but there's no time for that. Rick went, and a split-second later, I did."

According to people who have survived long falls, the acceleration of gravity is so heart-stoppingly fast that it's more like getting shot downward out of a cannon. A body accelerates roughly twenty miles an hour for every second it's in the air; after one second it's falling twenty miles an hour; after two seconds, forty miles an hour, and so on, up to a hundred and thirty. At that point the wind resistance is equal to the force of gravity, and the body is said to have reached terminal velocity. Spillane falls probably sixty or seventy feet, two and a half seconds of acceleration. He plunges through darkness without any idea where the water is or when he is going to hit. He has a dim memory of letting go of his one-man raft, and of his body losing position, and he thinks: My God, what a long way down. And then everything goes blank.

JOHN SPILLANE HAS the sort of handsome, regular features that one might expect in a Hollywood actor playing a pararescueman—playing John Spillane, in fact. His eyes are stone-blue, without a trace of hardness or indifference, his hair is short and touched with grey. He comes across as friendly, unguarded, and completely sure of himself. He has a quick smile and an offhand way of talking that seems to progress from detail to detail, angle to angle, until there's nothing more to say on a topic. His humor is delivered casually, almost as an afterthought, and seems to surprise even himself. He's of average height, average build, and once ran forty miles for the hell of it. He seems to be a man who has long since lost the need to prove things to anyone.

Spillane grew up in New York City and joined the Air Force at seventeen. He trained as a combat diver—infiltrating positions, securing beaches, rescuing other combat divers—and then left at 21 to join the Air National Guard. He "guard-bummed" around the world for a year, returning to Rockaway Beach to lifeguard in the summer, and then signed up for PJ school. After several years of reserve duty he quit, went through the police academy, and became a scuba diver for the New York City Police Department. For three years he pulled bodies out of submerged cars and mucked guns out of the East River, and finally decided to go back to school before his G.I. Bill ran out. He started out majoring in geology—"I wanted to go stomp mountaintops for a while"—but he fell in love instead and ended up moving out to Suffolk to work full-time for the Guard. That was in 1989. He was 32, one of the most widely-experienced PJs in the country.

When John Spillane hits the Atlantic Ocean he is going about fifty miles an hour. Water is the only element that offers more resistance the harder you hit it, and at fifty miles an hour it might as well be concrete. Spillane fractures three bones in his right arm, one bone in his left leg, four ribs in his chest, ruptures a kidney, and bruises his pancreas. The flippers, the one-man raft, and the canteen all are torn off his body. Only the mask, which he wore backward with the strap in his mouth, stays on as it is supposed to. Spillane doesn't remember the moment of impact, and he doesn't remember the moment he first realized he was in the water. His memory goes from falling to swimming, with nothing in between. When he understands that he is swimming, that is *all* he understands—he doesn't know who he is, why he is there, or how he got there. He has no history and no future; he is just a consciousness at night in the middle of the sea.

When Spillane treats injured seamen offshore, one of the first things he evaluates is their degree of consciousness. The highest level, known as "alert and oriented times four," describes almost everyone in an everyday situation. They know who they are, where they are, what time it is, and what's just happened. If someone suffers a blow to the head, the first thing they lose is recent events—"alert and oriented times three"—and the last thing they lose is their identity. A person who has lost all four levels of consciousness, right down to their identity, is said to be "alert and oriented times zero." When John Spillane wakes up in the water, he is alert and oriented times zero. His understanding of the world is reduced to the fact that he exists, nothing more. Almost simultaneously, he understands that he is in excruciating pain. For a long time, that is all he knows. Until he sees the life raft.

Spillane may be alert and oriented times zero, but he knows to swim for a life raft when he sees one. It has been pushed out by Jim Mioli, the flight engineer, and has inflated automatically when it hits the water. Now it is scudding along on the wave crests, the sea anchors barely holding it down in the seventy-knot wind. "I lined up on it, intercepted it, and hung off the side," says Spillane. "I knew I was in the ocean, in a desperate situation, and I was hurt. I didn't know anything else. It was while I was hanging onto the raft that it all started coming back to me. We were on a mission. We ran out of fuel. I bailed out. I'm not alone."

While Spillane is hanging off the raft, a gust of wind catches it and flips it over. One moment Spillane is in the water trying to figure out who he is, the next moment he is high and dry. Instantly he feels better. He is lying on the wobbly nylon floor, evaluating the stabbing pain in his chest—he thinks he's punctured his lungs—when he hears people shouting in the distance. He kneels and points his diver's light in their direction, and just as he is wondering how to help them—whoever they are—the storm gods flip the raft over again. Spillane is dumped back into the sea. He clings to the safety line, gasping and throwing up sea water, and almost immediately the wind flips the raft over a third time. He has now gone one-and-a-half revolutions. Spillane is back inside, lying spread-eagle on the floor, when the raft is flipped a fourth and final time. Spillane is tossed back into the water, this time clinging to a rubberized nylon bag that later turns out to contain half a dozen wool blankets. It floats, and Spillane hangs off it and watches the raft go cartwheeling off across the wave crests. He is left alone and dying on the sea.

"After I lost contact with the raft I was by myself and I realized my *only* chance of survival was to make it until the storm subsided," he says. "There was no way they could pick us up, I'd just ditched a perfectly good helicopter and I knew our guys would be the ones to come out and get us if they could, but they couldn't. They couldn't refuel. So I'm contemplating this and I know I cannot make it through the storm. They might have somebody on-scene when light breaks, but I'm not going to make it that long. I'm dying inside."

For the first time since the ordeal began, Spillane has the time to contemplate his own death. He isn't panicked so much as saddened by the idea. His wife is five months pregnant with their first child, and he's been home very little recently—he was in paramedic school, and in training for the New York City marathon. He wishes that he'd spent more time at home. He wishes—incredibly—that he'd cut the grass one more time before winter. He wishes there was someone who could tell his wife and family what happened in the end. It bothers him that Dave Ruvola probably died taking the helicopter in. It bothers him they're all going to die for lack of five hundred pounds of jet fuel. The shame of it all, he thinks; we have this eight-million-dollar helicopter, nothing's wrong with it, nobody's shooting at us, we're just out of fuel.

Spillane has regained his full senses by this point, and the circumstances he finds himself in are nightmarish beyond words. It is so dark that he can't see his hand in front of his face, the waves just rumble down on him out of nowhere and bury him for a minute at a time. The wind is so strong it doesn't blow the water so much as fling it; there is no way to keep it out of his stomach. Every few minutes he has to retch it back up. Spillane has lost his one-man life raft, his ribs are broken, and every breath feels like he is being run through with a hot fire poker. He is crying out in pain and dawn isn't for another eight hours.

After an hour of making his farewells and trying to keep the water out of his stomach, Spillane spots two strobes in the distance. The Mustang suits all have strobe lights on them, and it is the first real evidence he has that someone else has survived the ditching. Spillane's immediate reaction is to swim toward them, but he stops himself. There is no way he is going to live out the night, he knows, so he might as well just die on his own. That way he won't inflict his suffering on anyone else. "I didn't want them to see me go," he says. "I didn't want them to see me in pain. It's the same with marathons — don't talk to me, let me just suffer through this by myself. What finally drove me to them was survival training. It emphasizes strength in numbers, and I know that if I'm with them, I'll try harder not to die. But I couldn't let them see me in pain, I told myself. I couldn't let them down."

Believing that their chances will be slightly less negligible in a group, Spillane slowly makes his way toward the lights. He is buoyed up by his life vest and wetsuit and swimming with his broken arm stretched out in front of him, gripping the blanket bag. It takes a long time and the effort exhausts him, but he can see the lights slowly getting closer. They disappear in the wave troughs, appear on the crests, and then disappear again. Finally, after a couple of hours of swimming, he gets close enough to shout and then to make out their faces. It is Dave Ruvola and Jim Mioli, roped together with parachute cord. Ruvola seems fine, but Mioli is nearly incoherent with hypothermia. He only has his Nomex flight suit on, and the chances of him lasting until dawn are even lower than Spillane's.

Ruvola had escaped the helicopter unscathed, but barely. He knew that the rotors would tear him and the helicopter apart if they hit the water at full speed, so he moved the aircraft away from his men, waited for the number two engine to flame out, and then performed what is known as a hovering auto-rotation. As the helicopter fell, its dead rotors started to spin, and Ruvola used that energy to slow the aircraft down. Like downshifting a car on a hill, a hovering auto-rotation is a way of dissipating the force of gravity by feeding it back through the engine. By the time the helicopter hit the water it had slowed to a manageable speed, and all the torque had been bled out of the rotors; they just smacked the face of an oncoming wave and stopped.

Ruvola found himself in a classic training situation, only it was real life: He had to escape from a flooded helicopter upside down in complete darkness. He was a former PJ, though, and a marathon swimmer, so being underwater was something he was used to. The first thing he did was reach for his HEEDS bottle, a three-minute air supply strapped to his left leg, but it had been ripped loose during the ditching; all he had was the air in his lungs. He reached up, pulled the quick-release on his safety belt, and it was then that he realized he'd never kicked the exit door out. He was supposed to do that so it wouldn't get jammed shut on impact, trapping him inside. He found the door handle, turned it, and pushed.

To his amazement, the door fell open; Ruvola kicked his way out from under the fuselage, tripped the CO_2 cartridge on his life vest, and shot ten or fifteen feet to the surface. He popped up into a world of shrieking darkness and landsliding seas. At one point the crest of a wave drove him so far under the surface that the pressure change damaged his inner ear. Ruvola started yelling for the other crew members, and a few minutes later flight engineer Mioli—who'd also managed to escape the sinking helicopter—answered him in the darkness. They started swimming toward each other, and after five or ten minutes Ruvola got close enough to grab Mioli by his survival vest. He took the hood off his survival suit, put it on Mioli's head, and then tied their two bodies together with parachute cord.

They've been in the water for a couple of hours when Spillane finally struggles up, face locked up with pain. The first thing Ruvola sees is a glint of light on a face mask, and he thinks that maybe it's a Navy SEAL who has airlocked out of a U.S. submarine and is coming to save them. It isn't. Spillane swims up, grabs a strap on Ruvola's flotation vest, and clamps his other arm around the blanket bag. What's that? Ruvola screams. I don't know, I'll open it tomorrow! Spillane yells back. Open it now! Ruvola answers. Spillane is in too much pain to argue about it, so he opens the bag and watches several dark shapes—the blankets—go snapping off downwind.

He tosses the bag aside and settles down to face the next few hours as best he can.

• • •

ONE CAN TELL by the very handwriting in the District One incident log that the dispatcher—in this case a Coast Guardsman named Gill—can't quite believe what he's writing down. The words are large and sloppy and salted with exclamation points. At one point he jots down, a propos of nothing: *"They're not alone out there,"* as if to reassure himself that things will turn out all right. That entry comes at 9:30, seconds after Buschor calls in the first engine loss. Five minutes later Gill writes down: *"39-51 North, 72-00 West, Ditching here, 5 POB [people on board]."* Seven minutes after that the tanker plane—which will circle the area until their fuel runs low—reports hearing an EPIRB[5] signal for fifteen seconds, then nothing. From Gill's notes:

> 9:30—*Tamaroa in area, launched H-65*
> 9:48—*Cape Cod 60!*
> 9:53—*CAA [Commander of Atlantic Area]/brfd—ANYTHING YOU WANT—NAVY SHIP WOULD BE GREAT—WILL LOOK.*

Within minutes of the ditching, rescue assets from Florida to Massachusetts are being readied for deployment. The response is massive and nearly instantaneous. At 9:48, thirteen minutes into it, Air Station Cape Cod launches a Falcon jet and an H-3 helicopter. Half an hour later a Navy P-3 jet at Brunswick Naval Air Station is requested and readied. The P-3 is infrared-equipped to detect heat-emitting objects, like people. The *Tamaroa* has diverted before the helicopter has even gone down. At 10:23, Boston requests a second Coast Guard cutter, the *Spencer*. They even consider diverting an aircraft carrier.

The survivors are drifting fast in mountainous seas and the chances of spotting them are terrible. Helicopters will have minimal time on-scene because they can't refuel, it's unlikely conditions would permit a hoist rescue

[5]An emergency crash beacon.

anyway, and there's no way to determine if the guardmen's radios are even working. That leaves the *Tamaroa* to do the job, but she wasn't even able to save the *Satori* crew, during less severe conditions.[6] The storm is barreling westward, straight toward the ditch point, and wave heights are climbing past anything ever recorded in the area.

If things look bad for Ruvola's crew, they don't look much better for the people trying to rescue them. It's not inconceivable that another helicopter will to have to ditch during the rescue effort, or that a Coast Guardsman will get washed off the *Tamaroa*. (For that matter the *Tamaroa* herself, at 205 feet, is not necessarily immune to disaster. One freak wave could roll her over and put eighty men in the water.) Half a dozen aircraft, two ships, and two hundred rescuers are heading for 39 north, 72 west; the more men out there, the higher the chances are of someone else getting into trouble. A succession of disasters could draw the rescue assets of the entire East Coast of the United States out to sea.

A Falcon jet out of Air Station Cape Cod is the first aircraft on-scene. It arrives ninety minutes after the ditching, and the pilot sets up what is known as an expanding-square search. He moves slightly downsea of the last known position—the "splash point"—and starts flying ever-increasing squares until he has covered an area ten miles across. He flies at two hundred feet, just below cloud cover, and estimates the probability of spotting the survivors to be one-in-three. He turns up nothing. Around 11:30 he expands his search to a twenty-mile square and starts all over again, slowly working his way southwest with the direction of drift. The infrared-equipped P-3 is getting ready to launch from Brunswick, and a Coast Guard helicopter is pounding its way southward from Cape Cod.

And then, ten minutes into the second square, he picks up something: a weak signal on 243 megahertz. That's a frequency coded into Air National Guard radios. It means at least one of the airmen is still alive.

The Falcon pilot homes in on the signal and tracks it to a position about twenty miles downsea of the splash point. Whoever it is, they're drifting fast.

---

[6] The *Satori* was another ship needing a rescue in the storm.

The pilot comes in low, scanning the sea with night-vision goggles, and finally spots a lone strobe flashing below them in the darkness. It's appearing and disappearing behind the huge swell. Moments later he spots three more strobes half a mile away. All but one of the crew are accounted for. The pilot circles, flashing his lights, and then radios his position in to District One. An H-3 helicopter, equipped with a hoist and rescue swimmer, is only twenty minutes away. The whole ordeal could be over in less than an hour.

The Falcon circles the strobes until the H-3 arrives, and then heads back to base with a rapidly-falling fuel gauge. The H-3 is a huge machine, similar to the combat helicopters used in Vietnam, and has spare fuel tanks installed inside the cabin. It can't refuel in midflight, but it can stay airborne for four or five hours. The pilot, Ed DeWitt, tries to establish a forty-foot hover, but wind shear keeps spiking him downward. The ocean is a ragged white expanse in his searchlights and there are no visual reference points to work off of. At one point he turns downwind and almost gets driven into the sea.

DeWitt edges his helicopter to within a hundred yards of the three men and tells his flight engineer to drop the rescue basket. There's no way he's putting his swimmer in the water, but these are experienced rescuemen, and they may be able to extract themselves. It's either that or wait for the storm to calm down. The flight engineer pays out the cable and watches in alarm as the basket is blown straight back toward the tail rotors. It finally reaches the water, swept backward at an angle of 45 degrees, and DeWitt tries to hold a steady hover long enough for the swimmers to reach the basket. He tries for almost an hour, but the waves are so huge that the basket doesn't spend more than a few seconds on each crest before dropping to the end of its cable. Even if the men could get themselves into the basket, a shear pin in the hoist mechanism is designed to fail with loads over 600 pounds, and three men in waterlogged clothing would definitely push that limit. The entire assembly—cable, basket, everything—would let go into the sea.

DeWitt finally gives up trying to save the airmen and goes back up to a hover at two hundred feet. In the distance he can see the *Tamaroa*, search-lights pointed straight up, plunging through the storm. He vectors her in toward the position of the lone strobe in the distance—Graham Buschor—and then drops a flare by the others and starts back for Suffolk. He's only minutes away from "bingo," the point at which an aircraft doesn't have enough fuel to make it back to shore.

Two hundred feet below, John Spillane watches his last hope clatter away toward the north. He hadn't expected to get rescued, but still, it's hard to watch. The only benefit he can see is that his family will know for sure that he died. That might spare them weeks of false hope. In the distance, Spillane can see lights rising and falling in the darkness. He assumes it's a Falcon jet looking for the other airmen, but its lights are moving strangely; it's not moving like an aircraft. It's moving like a ship.

THE TAMAROA HAS taken four hours to cover the fifteen miles to the splash point; her screws are turning for twelve knots and making three. Commander Brudnicki doesn't know how strong the wind is because it rips the anemometer off the mast, but pilot Ed DeWitt reports that his airspeed indicator hit 87 knots—a hundred miles an hour—while he was in a stationary hover. The *Tamaroa*'s course to the downed airmen puts them in a beam sea, which starts to roll the ship through an arc of 110 degrees; at that angle, bulkheads are easier to walk on than floors. In the wheelhouse, Commander Brudnicki is surprised to find himself looking *up* at the crest of the waves, and when he orders full rudder and full bell, it takes thirty or forty seconds to see any effect at all. Later, after stepping off the ship, he says, "I certainly hope that was the high point of my career."

The first airman they spot is Graham Buschor, swimming alone and rel-atively unencumbered a half mile from the other three. He's in a Mustang survival suit and has a pen-gun flare and the only functional radio beacon of the entire crew. Brudnicki orders the operations officer, Lieutenant Kristopher Furtney, to maneuver the *Tamaroa* upsea of Buschor and then drift down on him. Large objects drift faster than small ones, and if the ship is upwind of Buschor, the waves won't smash him against the hull. The gunner's mate starts firing flares off from cannons on the flying bridge, and a detail of seamen crouch in the bow with throwing ropes, waiting for their chance. They can hardly keep their feet in the wind.

The engines come to a full stop and the *Tamaroa* wallows beam-to in the huge seas. It's a dangerous position to be in; the *Tamaroa* loses her righting arm at 72 degrees, and she's already heeling to fifty-five. Drifting down on swimmers is standard rescue procedure, but the seas are so violent that Buschor keeps getting flung out of reach. There are times when he's thirty feet higher than the men trying to rescue him. The crew in the bow can't get a throwing rope anywhere near him, and Brudnicki won't order his rescue swimmer overboard because he's afraid he won't get him back. The men on deck finally realize that if the boat's not going to Buschor, Buschor's going to have to go to it. *SWIM!* they scream over the rail. *SWIM!* Buschor rips off his gloves and hood and starts swimming for his life.

He swims as hard as he can; he swims until his arms give out. He claws his way up to the ship, gets swept around the bow, struggles back within reach of it again, and finally catches hold of a cargo net that the crew have dropped over the side. The net looks like a huge rope ladder and is held by six or seven men at the rail. Buschor twists his hands into the mesh and slowly gets hauled up the hull. One good wave at the wrong moment could take them all out. The deck crewmen land Buschor like a big fish and carry him into the deckhouse. He's dry-heaving seawater and can barely stand; his core temperature has dropped to 94 degrees. He's been in the water four hours and twenty-five minutes. Another few hours and he may not have been able to cling to the net.

It's taken half an hour to get one man on board, and they have four more to go, one of whom hasn't even been sighted yet. It's not looking good. Brudnicki is also starting to have misgivings about putting his men on deck. The larger waves are sweeping the bow and completely burying the crew; they keep having to do head counts to make sure no one has been swept overboard. "It was the hardest decision I've ever had to make, to put my people out there and rescue that crew," Brudnicki says. "Because I knew there was a chance I could lose some of my men. If I'd decided not to do the rescue, no one back home would've said a thing—they knew it was almost impossible. But can you really make a conscious decision to say, 'I'm just going to watch those people in the water die?'"

Brudnicki decides to continue the rescue; twenty minutes later he has the *Tamaroa* in a beam sea a hundred yards upwind of the three Guardsmen. Crew members are lighting off flares and aiming searchlights, and the chief quartermaster is on the flying bridge radioing Furtney when to fire the ship's engine. Not only do they have to maneuver the drift, but they have to time the roll of the ship so the gunwale rides down toward the waterline while the men in the water grab for the net. As it is, the gunwales are riding from water-level to twenty feet in the air virtually every wave. Spillane is injured, Mioli is incoherent, and Ruvola is helping to support them both. There's no way they'll be able to swim like Buschor.

Spillane watches the ship heaving through the breaking seas and for the life of him can't imagine how they're going to do this. As far as he's concerned, a perfectly likely outcome is for all three of them to drown within sight of the ship because a pickup is impossible. "My muscles were getting rigid, I was in great pain," he says. "The *Tam* pulled up in front of us and turned broadsides to the waves and I couldn't believe they did that—they were putting themselves in terrible risk. We could hear them all screaming on the deck and we could see the chemical lights coming at us, tied to the ends of the ropes."

The ropes are difficult to catch, so the deck crew throw the cargo net over the side. Lieutenant Furtney again tries to ease his ship over to the swimmers, but the vessel is 1,600 tons and almost impossible to control. Finally, on the third attempt, they snag the net. Their muscles are cramping with cold and Jim Mioli is about to start a final slide into hypothermia. The men on deck give a terrific heave—they're pulling up 600 pounds deadweight—and at the same time a large wave drops out from underneath the swimmers. They're exhausted and desperate and the net is wrenched out of their hands.

The next thing Spillane knows, he's underwater. He fights his way to the surface just as the boat rolls inward toward them and he grabs the net again. This is it; if he can't do it now, he dies. The deck crew heaves again, and Spillane feels himself getting pulled up the steel hull. He climbs up a little higher, feels hands grabbing him, and the next thing he knows he's being pulled over the gunwale onto the deck. He's in such pain he cannot stand. The men pin him against the bulkhead, cut off his survival suit, and then carry him inside, staggering with the roll of the ship. Spillane can't see Ruvola and Mioli. They haven't managed to get back onto the net.

The waves wash the two men down the hull toward the ship's stern, where the twelve-foot screw is digging out a cauldron of boiling water. Furtney shuts the engines down and the two men get carried around the stern and then up the port side of the ship. Ruvola catches the net for the second time and gets one hand into the mesh. He clamps the other one around Mioli and screams into his face, You got to do this, Jim! There aren't too many second chances in life! This is gonna take everything you got!

Mioli nods and wraps his hands into the mesh. Ruvola gets a foothold as well as a handhold and grips with all the strength in his cramping muscles. The two men get dragged upward, penduluming in and out with the roll of the ship, until the deck crew at the rail can reach them. They grab Ruvola and Mioli by the hair, the Mustang suit, the combat vest, anything they can get their hands on, and pull them over the steel rail. Like Spillane they're retching seawater and can barely stand. Jim Mioli has been in sixty-degree water for over five hours and is severely hypothermic. His core temperature is 90.4, eight degrees below normal; another couple of hours and he'd be dead.

The two airmen are carried inside, their clothing is cut off, and they're laid in bunks. Spillane is taken to the executive officer's quarters and given an IV and catheter and examined by the ship's paramedic. His blood pressure is 140/90, his pulse is a hundred, and he's running a slight fever. *Eyes pearled, abdomen and chest tenderness, pain to quadricep,* the paramedic radios SAR OPS [Search-and-Rescue Operations] Boston. *Fractured wrist, possibly ribs, suspect internal injury. Taking Tylenol-3 and seasick patch.* Boston relays the information to an Air National Guard flight surgeon, who says he's worried about internal bleeding and tells them to watch the abdomen carefully. If it gets more and more tender to the touch, he's bleeding inside and has to be evacuated by helicopter. Spillane thinks about dangling in a rescue litter over the ocean and says he'd rather not. At daybreak the executive officer comes in to shave and change his clothes, and Spillane apologizes for bleeding and vomiting all over his bed. Hey, whatever it takes, the officer says. He opens the porthole hatch, and Spillane looks out at the howling grey sky and the ravaged ocean. Ah, could you close that? he says. I can't take it.

The crew, unshaven and exhausted after thirty-six hours on deck, are staggering around the ship like drunks. And the mission's far from over: Rick Smith is still out there. He's one of the most highly trained pararescue jumpers in the country, and there's no question in anyone's mind that he's alive. They just have to find him. *PJ wearing black ¼" wetsuit, went out door with one-man life-raft and spray sheet, two 12-oz. cans of water, mirror, flare kit, granola bar, and whistle,* the Coast Guard dispatcher in Boston records. *Man is in great shape—can last quite a while, five to seven days.*

A total of nine aircraft are slated for the search, including an E2 surveillance plane to coordinate the air traffic on-scene. Jim Dougherty, a PJ who went through training with Smith and Spillane, throws a tin of Skoal chewing tobacco in his gear to give Smith when they find him. This guy's so good, Guardsmen are saying, he's just gonna come through the front door at Suffolk Air Base wondering where the hell we all were.[7]

---

[7]Despite a nine-day search, Rick Smith's body was never found.

THOMAS F. HORNBEIN

(b. 1930)

From *Everest: The West Ridge*

One of the finest deeds in American mountaineering was the ascent of
the west ridge of Mount Everest in 1963 by Willi Unsoeld and Tom
Hornbein, culminating in the first traverse of the world's highest peak.
Himalayan veteran Doug Scott later called the climb the greatest
achievement in Everest history.

After bivouacking just below the summit on the South Col descent
route, Unsoeld suffered such severe frostbite that he ultimately had all
his toes amputated. Hornbein was inexplicably unaffected.

It is exceedingly rare that a great adventurer also turns out to be a
first-class writer, but Hornbein's book about the expedition, so free of
pretension, so vivid in its details, has been universally regarded as a classic since it was published in 1965. In this passage, Hornbein recounts
the daring ascent, as the two good friends pass the point of no return
and deliver themselves over to the mountain's unforgiving mercy.

At four the oxygen ran out, a most effective alarm clock. Two well-incubated butane stoves were fished from inside our sleeping bags and soon bouillon was brewing in the kitchen. Climbing into boots was a breathless challenge to balance in our close quarters. Then overboots, and crampons.

"Crampons, in the tent?"

"Sure," I replied, "It's a hell of a lot colder out there."

"But our air mattresses!"

"Just be careful. We may not be back here again, anyway. I hope."

We were clothed in multilayer warmth. The fishnet underwear next to our skin provided tiny air pockets to hold our body heat. It also kept the outer layers at a distance which, considering our weeks without a bath, was respectful. Next came Duofold underwear, a wool shirt, down underwear tops and bottoms, wool climbing pants, and a lightweight wind parka. In spite of the cold our down parkas would be too bulky for difficult climbing, so we used them to insulate two quarts of hot lemonade, hoping they might remain unfrozen long enough to drink during the climb. Inside the felt inner liners of our reindeer-fur boots were innersoles and two pairs of heavy wool socks. Down shells covered a pair of wool mittens. Over our oxygen helmets we wore wool balaclavas and our parka hoods. The down parka–lemonade muff was stuffed into our packs as padding between the two oxygen bottles. With camera, radio, flashlight, and sundry mementos (including the pages from Emerson's diary),[1] our loads came close to forty pounds. For all the prior evening's planning it was more than two hours before we emerged.

I snugged a bowline about my waist, feeling satisfaction at the ease with which the knot fell together beneath heavily mittened hands. This was part of the ritual, experienced innumerable times before. With it came a feeling of security, not from the protection provided by the rope joining Willi

---

[1]Team member Dick Emerson, a professional sociologist, had asked all the climbers to keep diaries of their reactions to altitude. Rather than carry their whole diaries up the west ridge, Hornbein and Unsoeld tore a few pages out on which to record their thoughts.

and me, but from my being able to relegate these cold gray brooding forbidding walls, so high in such an unknown world, to common reality—to all those times I had ever tied into a rope before: with warm hands while I stood at the base of sun-baked granite walls in the Tetons, with cold hands on a winter night while I prepared to tackle my first steep ice on Longs Peak. This knot tied me to the past, to experiences known, to difficulties faced and overcome. To tie it here in this lonely morning on Everest brought my venture into context with the known, with that which man might do. To weave the knot so smoothly with clumsily mittened hands was to assert my confidence, to assert some competence in the face of the waiting rock, to accept the challenge.

Hooking our masks in place we bade a slightly regretful goodbye to our tent, sleeping bags, and the extra supply of food we hadn't been able to eat. Willi was at the edge of the ledge looking up the narrow gully when I joined him.

"My oxygen's hissing, Tom, even with the regulator turned off."

For the next twenty minutes we screwed and unscrewed regulators, checked valves for ice, to no avail. The hiss continued. We guessed it must be in the valve, and thought of going back to the tent for the spare bottle, but the impatient feeling that time was more important kept us from retracing those forty feet.

"It doesn't sound too bad," I said. "Let's just keep an eye on the pressure. Besides if you run out we can hook up the sleeping T and extra tubing and both climb on one bottle." Willi envisioned the two of us climbing Everest in lockstep, wed by six feet of rubber hose.

We turned to the climb. It was ten minutes to seven. Willi led off. Three years before in a tent high on Masherbrum he had expounded on the importance of knee-to-toe distance for step-kicking up steep snow.[2] Now his anatomical advantage determined the order of things as he put his theory to the test. Right away we found it was going to be difficult. The Couloir,

---

[2]In 1960, Hornbein and Unsoeld had been members of an American expedition that made the first ascent of 25,660-foot Masherbrum in the Karakoram of Pakistan.

as it cut through the Yellow Band, narrowed to ten or fifteen feet and steepened to fifty degrees. The snow was hard, too hard to kick steps in, but not hard enough to hold crampons; they slid disconcertingly down through this wind-sheltered, granular stuff. There was nothing for it but to cut steps, zigzagging back and forth across the gully, occasionally finding a bit of rock along the side up which we could scramble. We were forced to climb one at a time with psychological belays from axes thrust a few inches into the snow. Our regulators were set to deliver two liters of oxygen per minute, half the optimal flow for this altitude. We turned them off when we were belaying to conserve the precious gas, though we knew that the belayer should always be at peak alertness in case of a fall.

We crept along. My God, I thought, we'll never get there at this rate. But that's as far as the thought ever got. Willi's leads were meticulous, painstakingly slow and steady. He plugged tirelessly on, deluging me with showers of ice as his ax carved each step. When he ran out the hundred feet of rope he jammed his ax into the snow to belay me. I turned my oxygen on to "2" and moved up as fast as I could, hoping to save a few moments of critical time. By the time I joined him I was completely winded, gasping for air, and sorely puzzled about why. Only late in the afternoon, when my first oxygen bottle was still going strong, did I realize what a low flow of gas my regulator was actually delivering.

Up the tongue of snow we climbed, squeezing through a passage where the walls of the Yellow Band closed in, narrowing the Couloir to shoulder width.

In four hours we had climbed only four hundred feet. It was 11 A.M. A rotten bit of vertical wall forced us to the right onto the open face. To regain the Couloir it would be necessary to climb this sixty-foot cliff, composed of two pitches split by a broken snow-covered step.

"You like to lead this one?" Willi asked.

With my oxygen off I failed to think before I replied, "Sure, I'll try it."

The rock sloped malevolently outward like shingles on a roof—rotten shingles. The covering of snow was no better than the rock. It would pretend to hold for a moment, then suddenly shatter and peel, cascading down on Willi. He sank a piton into the base of the step to anchor his belay.

I started up around the corner to the left, crampon points grating on rusty limestone. Then it became a snowplowing procedure as I searched for some sort of purchase beneath. The pick of my ax found a crack. Using the shaft for gentle leverage, I moved carefully onto the broken strata of the step. I went left again, loose debris rolling under my crampons, to the base of the final vertical rise, about eight feet high. For all its steepness, this bit was a singularly poor plastering job, nothing but wobbly rubble. I searched about for a crack, unclipped a big angle piton from my sling, and whomped it in with the hammer. It sank smoothly, as if penetrating soft butter. A gentle lift easily extracted it.

"Hmmm. Not too good," I mumbled through my mask. On the fourth try the piton gripped a bit more solidly. Deciding not to loosen it by testing, I turned to the final wall. Its steepness threw my weight out from the rock, and my pack became a downright hindrance. There was an unlimited selection of handholds, mostly portable. I shed my mittens. For a few seconds the rock felt comfortably reassuring, but cold. Then not cold any more. My eyes tried to direct sensationless fingers. Flakes peeled out beneath my crampons. I leaned out from the rock to move upward, panting like a steam engine. Damn it, it'll go; I know it will, T,[3] I thought. But my grip was gone. I hadn't thought to turn my oxygen up.

"No soap," I called down. "Can't make it now. Too pooped."

"Come on down. There may be a way to the right."

I descended, half rappeling from the piton, which held. I had spent the better part of an hour up there. A hundred feet out we looked back. Clearly we had been on the right route, for above that last little step the gully opened out. A hundred feet higher the Yellow Band met the gray of the summit limestone. It had to get easier.

"You'd better take it, Willi. I've wasted enough time already."

"Hell, if you couldn't make it, I'm not going to be able to do any better."

[3] I.e., "Tom"—as Hornbein talks to himself.

"Yes you will. It's really not that hard. I was just worn out from putting that piton in. Turn your regulator clear open, though."

Willi headed up around the corner, moving well. In ten minutes his rope was snapped through the high piton. Discarding a few unsavory holds, he gripped the rotten edge with his unmittened hands. He leaned out for the final move. His pack pulled. Crampons scraped, loosing a shower of rock from beneath his feet. He was over. He leaned against the rock, fighting for breath.

"Man, that's work. But it looks better above."

Belayed, I followed, retrieved the first piton, moved up, and went to work on the second. It wouldn't come. "Guess it's better than I thought," I shouted. "I'm going to leave it." I turned my oxygen to four liters, leaned out from the wall, and scrambled up. The extra oxygen helped, but it was surprising how breathless such a brief effort left me.

"Good lead," I panted. "That wasn't easy."

"Thanks. Let's roll."

Another rope length and we stopped. After six hours of hiss Willi's first bottle was empty. There was still a long way to go, but at least he could travel ten pounds lighter without the extra cylinder. Our altimeter read 27,900. We called Base on the walkie-talkie.

Willi: West Ridge to Base. West Ridge to Base. Over.

Base (Jim Whittaker, excitedly):[4] This is Base here, Willi. How are you? How are things going? What's the word up there? Over.

Willi: Man, this is a real bearcat! We are nearing the top of the Yellow Band and it's mighty tough. It's too damned tough to try to go back. It would be too dangerous.

Base (Jim): I'm sure you're considering all about your exits. Why don't you leave yourself an opening? If it's not going to pan out, you can always start working your way down. I think there is always a way to come back.

Willi: Roger, Jim. We're counting on a further consultation in about two

---

[4]Three weeks earlier Jim Whittaker had climbed the South Col route, becoming the first American to stand atop Everest.

or three hundred feet. It should ease up by then! Goddammit, if we can't start moving together, we'll have to move back down. But it should be easier once the Yellow Band is passed. Over.

Base (Jim): Don't work yourself up into a bottleneck, Willi. How about rappelling? Is that possible, or don't you have any *reepschnur*[5] or anything? Over.

Willi: There are no rappel points, Jim, absolutely no rappel points. There's nothing to secure a rope to. So it's up and over for us today . . .

While the import of his words settled upon those listening 10,000 feet below, Willi went right on:

Willi (continuing): . . . and we'll probably be getting in pretty late, maybe as late as seven or eight o'clock tonight.

As Willi talked, I looked at the mountain above. The slopes looked reasonable, as far as I could see, which wasn't very far. We sat at the base of a big, wide-open amphitheater. It looked like summits all over the place. I looked down. Descent was totally unappetizing. The rotten rock, the softening snow, the absence of even tolerable piton cracks only added to our desire to go on. Too much labor, too many sleepless nights, and too many dreams had been invested to bring us this far. We couldn't come back for another try next weekend. To go down now, even if we could have, would be descending to a future marked by one huge question: what might have been? It would not be a matter of living with our fellow man, but simply living with ourselves, with the knowledge that we had had more to give.

I listened, only mildly absorbed in Willi's conversation with Base, and looked past him at the convexity of rock cutting off our view of the gully we had ascended. Above—a snowfield, gray walls, then blue-black sky. We were committed. An invisible barrier sliced through the mountain beneath our feet, cutting us off from the world below. Though we could see through, all we saw was infinitely remote. The ethereal link provided by our radio only intensified our separation. My wife and children seemed suddenly close. Yet home, life itself, lay only over the top of Everest and down the

[5]Cord, rope.

other side. Suppose we fail? The thought brought no remorse, no fear. Once entertained, it hardly seemed even interesting. What now mattered most was right here: Willi and I, tied together on a rope, and the mountain, its summit not inaccessibly far above. The reason we had come was within our grasp. We belonged to the mountain and it to us. There was anxiety, to be sure, but it was all but lost in a feeling of calm, of pleasure at the joy of climbing. That we couldn't go down only made easier that which we really wanted to do. That we might not get there was scarcely conceivable.

Willi was still talking.

Willi: Any news of Barry and Lute?[6] Over.

Jim: I haven't heard a word from them. Over.

Willi: How about Dingman?[7]

Jim: No word from Dingman. We've heard nothing, nothing at all.

Willi: Well listen, if you do get hold of Dingman, tell him to put a light in the window because we're headed for the summit, Jim. We can't possibly get back to our camp now. Over.

I stuffed the radio back in Willi's pack. It was 1 P.M. From here we could both climb at the same time, moving across the last of the yellow slabs. Another hundred feet and the Yellow Band was below us. A steep tongue of snow flared wide, penetrating the gray strata that capped the mountain. The snow was hard, almost ice-hard in places. We had only to bend our ankles, firmly plant all twelve crampon points, and walk uphill. At last, we were moving, though it would have appeared painfully slow to a distant bystander.

As we climbed out of the Couloir the pieces of the puzzle fell into place. That snow rib ahead on the left skyline should lead us to the Summit Snowfield, a patch of perpetual white clinging to the North Face at the base of Everest's final pyramid. By three we were on the Snowfield. We had been climbing for eight hours and knew we needed to take time to refuel. At a

---

[6]Barry ("Barrel") Bishop and Lute Jerstad were heading up the South Col route at the same time, hoping to meet Unsoeld and Hornbein near the summit and guide them down.

[7]Dave Dingman had turned back on the South Col route.

shaly outcrop of rock we stopped for lunch. There was a decision to be made. We could either cut straight up to the northeast ridge and follow it west to the summit, or we could traverse the face and regain the West Ridge. From where we sat, the Ridge looked easier. Besides, it was the route we'd intended in the first place.

We split a quart of lemonade that was slushy with ice. In spite of its down parka wrapping, the other bottle was already frozen solid, as were the kippered snacks. They were almost tasteless but we downed them more with dutiful thoughts of calories than with pleasure.

To save time we moved together, diagonaling upward across downsloping slabs of rotten shale. There were no possible stances from which to belay each other. Then snow again, and Willi kicked steps, fastidiously picking a route between the outcropping rocks. Though still carting my full load of oxygen bottles, I was beginning to feel quite strong. With this excess energy came impatience, and an unconscious anxiety over the high stakes for which we were playing and the lateness of the day. Why the hell is Willi going so damned slow? I thought. And a little later: He should cut over to the Ridge now; it'll be a lot easier.

I shouted into the wind, "Hold up, Willi!" He pretended not to hear me as he started up the rock. It seemed terribly important to tell him to go to the right. I tugged on the rope, "Damn it, wait up, Willi!" Stopped by a taut rope and an unyielding Hornbein, he turned, and with some irritation anchored his ax while I hastened to join him. He was perched, through no choice of his own, in rather cramped, precarious quarters. I sheepishly apologized.

We were on rock now. One rope length, crampons scraping, brought us to the crest of the West Ridge for the first time since we'd left camp 4W yesterday morning. The South Face fell eight thousand feet to the tiny tents of Advance Base. Lhotse,[8] straight across the face, was below us now. And near at hand, a hundred and fifty feet higher, the South Summit of Everest shone in the afternoon sun. We were within four hundred feet of the

[8]Everest's neighbor, the fourth-highest mountain in the world.

top! The wind whipped across the ridge from the north at nearly sixty miles an hour. Far below, peak shadows reached long across the cloud-filled valleys. Above, the Ridge rose, a twisting, rocky spine.

We shed crampons and overboots to tackle this next rocky bit with the comforting grip of cleated rubber soles. Here I unloaded my first oxygen bottle though it was not quite empty. It had lasted ten hours, which obviously meant I'd been getting a lower flow than indicated by the regulator. Resisting Willi's suggestion to drop the cylinder off the South Face, I left it for some unknown posterity. When I resaddled ten pounds lighter, I felt I could float to the top.

The rock was firm, at least in comparison with our fare thus far. Climbing one at a time, we experienced the joy of delicate moves on tiny holds. The going was a wonderful pleasure, almost like a day in the Rockies. With the sheer drop to the Cwm beneath us,[9] we measured off another four rope lengths. Solid rock gave way to crud, then snow. A thin, firm, knife-edge of white pointed gently toward the sky. Buffeted by the wind, we laced our crampons on, racing each other with rapidly numbing fingers. It took nearly twenty minutes. Then we were off again, squandering oxygen at three liters per minute since time seemed the shorter commodity at the moment. We moved together, Willi in front. It seemed almost as if we were cheating, using oxygen; we could nearly run this final bit.

Ahead the North and South Ridges converged to a point. Surely the summit wasn't that near? It must be off behind. Willi stopped. What's he waiting for, I wondered as I moved to join him. With a feeling of disbelief I looked up. Forty feet ahead tattered and whipped by the wind was the flag Jim had left three weeks before. It was 6:15. The sun's rays sheered horizontally across the summit. We hugged each other as tears welled up, ran down across our oxygen masks, and turned to ice.

• • •

[9] The Western Cwm, a high basin on the Khumbu Glacier, through which the South Col route on Everest proceeds.

JUST ROCK, a dome of snow, the deep blue sky, and a hunk of orange-painted metal from which a shredded American flag cracked in the wind. Nothing more. Except two tiny figures walking together those last few feet to the top of the earth.

For twenty minutes we stayed there. The last brilliance of the day cast the shadow of our summit on the cloud plain a hundred miles to the east. Valleys were filled with the indistinct purple haze of evening, concealing the dwellings of man we knew were there. The chill roar of wind made speaking difficult, heightening our feeling of remoteness. The flag left there seemed a feeble gesture of man that had no purpose but to accentuate the isolation. The two of us who had dreamed months before of sharing this moment were linked by a thin line of rope, joined in the intensity of companionship to those inaccessibly far below, Al and Barry and Dick—and Jake.[10]

From a pitch of intense emotional and physical drive it was only partly possible to become suddenly, completely the philosopher of a balmy afternoon. The head of steam was too great, and the demands on it still remained. We have a long way to go to get down, I thought. But the prospect of descent of an unknown side of the mountain in the dark caused me less anxiety than many other occasions had. I had a blind, fatalistic faith that, having succeeded in coming this far, we could not fail to get down. The moment became an end in itself.

There were many things savored in this brief time. Even with our oxygen turned off we had no problem performing those summit obeisances, photographing the fading day (it's a wonderful place to be for sunset photographs), smiling behind our masks for the inevitable "I was there" picture. Willi wrapped the kata given him by Ang Dorje about the flag pole and planted Andy Bakewell's crucifix alongside it in the snow; Lhotse and Makalu, below us, were a contrast of sun-blazed snow etched against the

[10]One of the youngest team members, Jake Breitenbach had been killed two months earlier when a serac had collapsed on him in the Khumbu icefall. Along with Jake, Al Auten, Barry Corbet, and Dick Emerson had been members of the original summit team.

darkness of evening shadow.[11] We felt the lonely beauty of the evening, the immense roaring silence of the wind, the tenuousness of our tie to all below. There was a hint of fear, not for our lives, but of a vast unknown which pressed in upon us. A fleeting feeling of disappointment—that after all those dreams and questions this was only a mountaintop—gave way to the suspicion that maybe there was something more, something beyond the three-dimensional form of the moment. If only it could be perceived.

But it was late. The memories had to be stored, the meanings taken down. The question of why we had come was not now to be answered, yet something up here must yield an answer, something only dimly felt, comprehended by senses reaching farther yet than the point on which we stood; reaching for understanding, which hovered but a few steps higher. The answers lay not on the summit of Everest, nor in the sky above it, but in the world to which we belonged and must now return.

Footprints in the snow told that Lute and Barrel had been here. We'd have a path to follow as long as light remained.

"Want to go first?" Willi asked. He began to coil the rope.

Looking down the corniced edge, I thought of the added protection of a rope from above. "Doesn't matter, Willi. Either way."

"O.K. Why don't I go first then?" he said, handing me the coil. Paying out the rope as he disappeared below me I wondered, Is Unsoeld tired? It was hard to believe. Still he'd worked hard; he had a right to be weary. Starting sluggishly, I'd felt stronger as we climbed. So now we would reverse roles. Going up had been pretty much Willi's show; going down would be mine. I dropped the last coil and started after him.

Fifty feet from the top we stopped at a patch of exposed rock. Only the summit of Everest, shining pink, remained above the shadow sea. Willi radioed to Maynard Miller[12] at Advance Base that we were headed for the South Col. It was 6:35 P.M.

[11]A kata is a ceremonial scarf supposed by Buddhists to confer good fortune. Ang Dorje was one of the expedition's strongest Sherpas. Andy Bakewell is a Catholic priest and mountaineer, and a good friend of several team members. Nearby Makalu is the fifth-highest mountain in the world.

[12]A glaciologist and team member.

We almost ran along the crest, trusting Lute and Barrel's track to keep us a safe distance from the cornice edge. Have to reach the South Summit before dark, I thought, or we'll never find the way. The sun dropped below the jagged horizon. We didn't need goggles any more. There was a loud hiss as I banged my oxygen bottle against the ice wall. Damn! Something's broken. I reached back and turned off the valve. Without oxygen, I tried to keep pace with the rope disappearing over the edge ahead. Vision dimmed, the ground began to move. I stopped till things cleared, waved my arms and shouted into the wind for Willi to hold up. The taut rope finally stopped him. I tightened the regulator, then turned the oxygen on. No hiss! To my relief it had only been jarred loose. On oxygen again, I could move rapidly. Up twenty feet, and we were on the South Summit. It was 7:15.

Thank God for the footprints. Without them, we'd have had a tough time deciding which way to go. We hurried on, facing outward, driving our heels into the steep snow. By 7:30 it was dark. We took out the flashlight and resumed the descent. The batteries, dregs of the Expedition, had not been helped by our session with Emerson's diary the night before; they quickly faded. There was pitiful humor as Willi probed, holding the light a few inches off the snow to catch some sign of tracks. You could order your eyes to see, but nothing in the blackness complied.

We moved slowly now. Willi was only a voice and an occasional faint flicker of light to point the way. No fear, no worry, no strangeness, just complete absorption. The drive which had carried us to a nebulous goal was replaced by simple desire for survival. There was no time to dwell on the uniqueness of our situation. We climbed carefully, from years of habit. At a rock outcrop we paused. Which way? Willi groped to the right along a corniced edge. In my imagination, I filled in the void.

"No tracks over here," Willi called.

"Maybe we should dig in here for the night."

"I don't know. Dave and Girmi should be at 6."[13]

We shouted into the night, and the wind engulfed our call. A lull. Again we shouted. "Helloooo," the wind answered. Or was it the wind?

[13]Girmi Dorje, another Sherpa.

"Hellooo," we called once more.

"Hellooo," came back faintly. That wasn't the wind!

"To the left, Willi."

"O.K., go ahead."

In the blackness I couldn't see my feet. Each foot groped cautiously, feeling its way down, trusting to the pattern set by its predecessor. Slowly left, right, left, crampons biting into the snow, right, left, . . .

"*Willeee!*" I yelled as I somersaulted into space. The rope came taut, and with a soft thud I landed.

"Seems to be a cornice there," I called from beneath the wall. "I'll belay you from here."

Willi sleepwalked down to the edge. The dim outline of his foot wavered until it met my guiding hand. His arrival lacked the flair of my descent. It was well that the one of lighter weight had gone first.

Gusts buffeted from all directions, threatening to dislodge us from the slope. Above a cliff we paused, untied, cut the rope in half, and tied in again. It didn't help; even five feet behind I couldn't see Willi. Sometimes the snow was good, sometimes it was soft, sometimes it lay shallow over rocks so we could only drive our axes in an inch or two. With these psychological belays, we wandered slowly down, closer to the answering shouts. The wind was dying, and so was the flashlight, now no more than an orange glow illuminating nothing. The stars, brilliant above, cast no light on the snow. Willi's oxygen ran out. He slowed, suddenly feeling much wearier.

The voices were close now. Were they coming from those two black shapes on the snow? Or were those rocks?

"Shine your light down here," a voice called.

"Where? Shine yours up here," I answered.

"Don't have one," came the reply.

Then we were with them—not Dave and Girmi, but Lute and Barrel. They were near exhaustion, shivering lumps curled on the snow. Barrel in particular was far gone. Anxious hungering for air through the previous night, and the near catastrophe when their tent caught fire in the morning, had left him tired before they even started. Determination got him to the top, but now he no longer cared. He only wanted to be left alone. Lute was also tired. Because of Barrel's condition he'd had to bear the brunt of the climbing labor. His eyes were painfully burned, perhaps by the fire, perhaps by the sun and wind. From sheer fatigue they had stopped thinking. Their oxygen was gone, except for a bit Lute had saved for Barrel; but they were too weak to make the change.

At 9:30 we were still a thousand feet above Camp 6. Willi sat down on the snow, and I walked over to get Lute's oxygen for Barrel. As I unscrewed Lute's regulator from the bottle, he explained why they were still there. Because of the stove fire that had sent them diving from the tent, they were an hour late in starting. It was 3:30 P.M. when they reached the summit. Seeing no sign of movement down the west side, they figured no one would be any later than they were. At 4:15 they started down. Fatigue slowed their descent. Just after dark they had stopped to rest and were preparing to move when they heard shouts. Dave and Girmi, they thought. No—the sounds seemed to be coming from above. Willi and Tom! So they waited, shivering.

I removed Barrel's regulator from his empty bottle and screwed it into Lute's. We were together now, sharing the support so vigorously debated a week before. Lute would know the way back to their camp, even in the dark. All we had to do was help them down. Fumbling with unfeeling fingers, I tried to attach Barrel's oxygen hose to the regulator. Damn! Can't make the connection. My fingers scraped uncoördinately against the cold metal. Try again. There it goes. Then, quickly, numb fingers clumsy, back into mittens. Feeling slowly returned, and pain. Then, the pain went and the fingers were warm again.

Willi remembered the Dexedrine I had dropped into my shirt pocket the evening before. I fished out two pills—one for Barrel and one for Lute. Barrel was better with oxygen, but why I had balked at his communal use of Lute's regulator, I cannot say. Lack of oxygen? Fatigue? It was fifteen hours since we'd started our climb. Or was it that my thoughts were too busy with another problem? We had to keep moving or freeze.

I led off. Lute followed in my footsteps to point out the route. Lost in the darkness sixty feet back on our ropes, Willi and Barrel followed. The track was more sensed than seen, but it was easier now, not so steep. My eyes watered from searching for the black holes punched in the snow by Lute's and Barrel's axes during their ascent. We walked to the left of the crest, three feet down, ramming our axes into the narrow edge. Thirty feet, and the rope came taut as Barrel collapsed in the snow, bringing the entire caravan to a halt. Lute sat down behind me. Got to keep moving. We'll never get there.

We had almost no contact with the back of the line. When the rope came taut, we stopped, when it loosened we moved on. Somewhere my oxygen ran out, but we were going too slow for me to notice the difference. Ought to dump the empty bottle, I thought, but it was too much trouble to take off my pack.

Heat lightning flashed along the plains to the east, too distant to light our way. Rocks that showed in the snow below seemed to get no closer as the hours passed. Follow the ax holes. Where'd they go? Not sure. There's another.

"Now where, Lute?"

"Can't see, Tom." Lute said. "Can't see a damn thing. We've got to turn down a gully between some rocks."

"Which gully. There's two or three."

"Don't know, Tom."

"Think, Lute. Try to remember. We've got to get to 6."

"I don't know. I just can't see."

Again and again I questioned, badgering, trying to extract some hint. But half blind and weary, Lute had no answer. We plodded on. The rocks came slowly closer.

Once the rope jerked tight, nearly pulling me off balance. Damn! What's going on? I turned and looked at Lute's dim form lying on the snow a few feet further down the Kangshung Face.[14] His fall had been effectively if uncomfortably arrested when his neck snagged the rope between Willi and me.

We turned off the crest, toward the rocks. Tongues of snow pierced the

---

[14] The savage east face of Everest, in 1963 still unclimbed and unattempted.

cliffs below. But which one? It was too dangerous to plunge on. After midnight we reached the rocks. It had taken nearly three hours to descend four hundred feet, maybe fifteen minutes' worth by daylight.

Tired. No hope of finding camp in the darkness. No choice but to wait for day. Packs off. Willi and I slipped into our down parkas. In the dark, numb fingers couldn't start the zippers. We settled to the ground, curled as small as possible atop our pack frames. Lute and Barry were somewhere behind, apart, each alone. Willi and I tried hugging each other to salvage warmth, but my uncontrollable shivering made it impossible.

The oxygen was gone, but the mask helped a little for warmth. Feet, cooling, began to hurt. I withdrew my hands from the warmth of my crotch and loosened crampon bindings and boot laces, but my feet stayed cold. Willi offered to rub them. We removed boots and socks and planted both my feet against his stomach. No sensation returned.

Tired by the awkward position, and frustrated by the result, we gave it up. I slid my feet back into socks and boots, but couldn't tie them. I offered to warm Willi's feet. Thinking that his freedom from pain was due to a high tolerance of cold, he declined. We were too weary to realize the reason for his comfort.

The night was overpoweringly empty. Stars shed cold unshimmering light. The heat lightning dancing along the plains spoke of a world of warmth and flatness. The black silhouette of Lhotse lurked half sensed, half seen, still below. Only the ridge on which we were rose higher, disappearing into the night, a last lonely outpost of the world.

Mostly there was nothing. We hung suspended in a timeless void. The wind died, and there was silence. Even without wind it was cold. I could reach back and touch Lute or Barrel lying head to toe above me. They seemed miles away.

Unsignaled, unembellished, the hours passed. Intense cold penetrated, carrying with it the realization that each of us was completely alone. Nothing Willi could do for me or I for him. No team now, just each of us, imprisoned with his own discomfort, his own thoughts, his own will to survive.

Yet for me, survival was hardly a conscious thought. Nothing to plan, nothing to push for, nothing to do but shiver and wait for the sun to rise. I floated in a dreamlike eternity, devoid of plans, fears, regrets. The heat lightning, Lhotse, my companions, discomfort, all were there—yet not there. Death had no meaning, nor, for that matter, did life. Survival was no concern, no issue. Only a dulled impatience for the sun to rise tied my formless thoughts to the future.

About 4:00 the sky began to lighten along the eastern rim, baring the bulk of Kangchenjunga.[15] The sun was slow in following, interminably slow. Not till after 5:00 did it finally come, its light streaming through the South Col, blazing yellow across the Nuptse Wall then onto the white wave crest of peaks far below.[16] We watched as if our own life was being born again. Then as the cold yellow light touched us, we rose. There were still miles to go.

---

[15]Third-highest mountain in the world.
[16]Nuptse is a satellite peak of Everest that looms over the Khumbu Glacier.

ART DAVIDSON

(b. 1943)

From *Minus 148°: The Winter Ascent of Mt. McKinley*

The 1967 expedition to attempt the first winter ascent of Alaska's Denali (Mount McKinley) was so audacious an enterprise that few observers gave the team more than a tiny chance of success. The journey
could not have started off more disastrously — for on the team's first day
on the Kahiltna Glacier, Frenchman Jacques Batkin (the party's most
experienced climber) was killed when he fell unroped into a hidden
crevasse. His stunned teammates recovered his body and pondered
abandoning the effort but in the end pushed on.

On the last day of February, Americans Art Davidson and Dave
Johnston and Swiss expatriate Ray Genet (nicknamed "Pirate") reached
the summit. Descending into darkness, they were forced to bivouac in
a hastily dug snow cave at Denali Pass, at 18,200 feet. They had sleeping bags but no foam pads or tents; an old parachute discarded by a
previous expedition served as a bivouac sack. Even so, had the weather
stayed good, the trio would have routinely continued down the next

morning. But a violent windstorm came up in the night, trapping the men for six harrowing days in their bivouac. Their teammates, led by Greg Blomberg, camped only nine hundred feet below, were powerless to help them. At one point the Japanese Shiro Nishimae, the strongest climber in the support party, thrust his head over the crest of the pass but could not fight the wind to clamber above. He saw a single sleeping bag half out of the cave and assumed his friends were already dead.

Using a single tin can both to cook and urinate in, the trio hung on through those six days, while the wind never let up. Davidson and Genet suffered frostbite to both feet and fingers; each man later had several toes amputated. Genet would go on to pioneer the guiding of clients on Denali but would die in a similar emergency bivouac near the summit of Mount Everest.

In this excerpt, covering the fourth and fifth days of the trio's ordeal, Davidson, who had never before written a book, captures the vacillating fears and hopes of the trapped climbers. The apparent deliverance he records on March 5 proved a false alarm: total whiteout prevented heading down, and the three men had to return to their hated cave for a sixth night. Yet in the end, they completed the descent under their own power, for the technology of the day was not yet adequate for a helicopter rescue, and their teammates had given up hope.

The book's title refers to the official windchill minimum recorded on Denali at the height of the storm.

March 4

I woke elated. The wind had stopped. I heard a helicopter.

Just outside the cave I heard the steady whir. Gregg must have gotten a rescue started.[1] It sounded as if the copter had already landed. People must be searching the pass for us. I was afraid they wouldn't find our cave; it was such a small hole in the ice. Maybe they'd give up and leave.

"Dave!" I rolled toward him. "Dave, do you hear the helicopter? We'd better get outside right away."

---

[1] Gregg Blomberg, leader of the expedition.

"Go to sleep . . . it's the wind."

"No! It can't be. It's too steady, too constant. It's a copter . . . Dave . . ."

He didn't answer.

"It's a copter," I repeated to myself. "It's the steady whir of a copter." I listened to be certain; but I wasn't certain. Maybe it was the wind; it couldn't be. I almost asked Dave to listen; but I knew he was right; yet I strained my ears for a voice, any sound that would let me believe there were rescuers outside.

There was only the wind.

After a long silence Dave admitted that he had been susceptible to my delusion; he had convinced himself for several minutes that the sound of the wind really was a rescue helicopter.

"But you know," Dave said, looking toward me, "it makes you feel kind of humble to know a helicopter couldn't possibly get to us."

Dave went on to explain how he felt good to know that no device of technology nor any effort on the part of our companions could conquer the storm, or even reach through it to help us. He said the three of us were alone in this sanctuary of the earth's wilderness, and that our only security lay in ourselves, in our individual abilities to endure, and in our combined capacities of will-power and judgment.

I said, "Dave, it may sound funny, but I feel closer to you than ever before."

Dave beamed and said "Yea, I know what you mean. If we can't fight our way out of this storm, at least we can stick together, and try to live in harmony with it."

I thought to myself how the storm itself was helping to protect us from its own fury. Ever since the McKinley massif had been thrust upward out of a flat land, the wind had been packing the snow and ice of Denali Pass into contours of least resistance. We were sheltered inside ice that conformed to the pattern of the wind. We had suffered and nearly succumbed to the storm that first morning when we had fought it head-on in the open, but now all the force of the wind only pounded more stability into the roof of our cave as it swept across the slope above us.

The altitude riddled our attention span into fragments of thoughts. Discomfort was the only thing on which my mind seemed able to concentrate. My lips were deeply cracked in several places. Moving my tongue along the roof of my mouth I felt clumps of dried-up mucus; other experiences with dehydration had taught me that if I didn't get water soon, the rawest areas in my mouth would begin bleeding. The ligaments in my legs ached as they dried up. It was especially painful to stretch or change positions; unfortunately, the hardness of the ice made my hips and back sore whenever I remained still for more than a few minutes. I complained very little, not because I was naturally stoic, but because there was no one to complain to—each of us experienced the same discomforts; pain had become a natural condition of our life under the ice.

I was probably warmer than either Dave or Pirate because their sleeping bags were icing up faster than mine. Every time Dave had cooked, steam from the warm liquid had been absorbed into his bag, where it soon froze. As the down had matted together, its resilience had disappeared. It was particularly unsettling when Dave pointed out a number of lumps of ice mixed with the down. I didn't see how his bag could retain any warmth. Pirate's bag was a little better, but his down was fast becoming clogged with moisture from his breath because, against Dave's advice and mine, he persisted in burying his head in his bag, where his exhaled moisture had no escape. All of us sorely missed the foam pads. Without them, we were only able to place a spare wind parka or pair of wind pants under our buttocks and shoulders, leaving the rest of our sleeping bags on bare ice.

Pirate's hands were swollen, but he said he was worried most about his feet. He asked about my down booties. Though he didn't say it outright, I could tell he wanted to wear them. I tried to ignore him, acting as if I hadn't heard. My feet were cold with the booties; without them I thought they would surely freeze while I slept, or even while I lay awake. I avoided thinking about it, but that was exactly what was happening to Pirate's feet. He knew I didn't want to give them up, and didn't ask again. As he kicked his feet inside his bag to relieve their numbness, I knew he must be thinking of the warmth of my booties. Pretending to be asleep, I tried to forget about Pirate's feet.

I couldn't remember how many days we had been in the cave. The day we had gone to the summit, then that first day of the wind, the day we ate ham, then a day without water—it must have been the fourth day, but I was uncertain.

Sometime during the middle of the day Dave rationed us each a fig bar and two hard candies. Sucking on the candies brought a few minutes of relief to the rawness in my mouth. I put the fig bar aside. I wanted to save it for later in the afternoon as a break in the monotony of hunger. After about an hour I couldn't wait any longer. I had looked forward to saliva coming back into my mouth as I chewed the fig bar, but the crumbs only stuck to the gums and roof of my mouth. With some effort I swallowed the sticky wad, feeling it tumble into my stomach, where it set off a series of cramps. The pain constructed a morbidly amusing picture of four or five hands in my stomach grabbing for the fig bar, fighting each other for it, tearing and ripping at it. After a few minutes the cramps died down and the usual steady ache returned.

Silently I cursed the punctured cans of food.[2] Some careless climbers must have punched holes in them with their ice axes as they tried to chip away the ice that covered them. We all wished we had never seen the cans. Without them we might have been able to accept our hunger, but knowing that ham and peas, rotten as they were, lay within arm's reach while we were gradually starving was almost unbearable. The cruelest twist to the irony was the uncertainty; the canned food might still be good. Perhaps the food had remained frozen ever since it had been brought to Denali Pass. It was doubtful that there were any bacteria living at 18,200 feet. At least a portion of the ham, peas, and bacon might not be rancid, but to find out would be risking food poisoning.

Early in the afternoon it became obvious that we were going to spend

[2] The trio had found cans of bacon, ham, and peas left by some previous expedition. Some of the cans had been punctured, perhaps by later climbers digging into the cache with their ice axes. By now the three men had eaten all the good food but dared not try the food in the punctured cans for fear of botulism.

another night in the cave. Even if the wind let up toward evening, we wouldn't have the time, nor perhaps the strength, to descend. We knew our dehydration was critical. We hadn't drunk a cup of liquid for more than thirty-six hours. Because our circulation was down we were all chilly inside our bags with all our parkas and wind pants on. Occasionally, I could feel Dave's body tense and shake with shivers. We needed water, which meant we needed gas—which we didn't have.

The only possibility was the gas Dave had cached at Denali Pass three years before.[3] If one of us went for the gallon of gas, he might not make it back through the wind to the cave. The gruesome reality of this possibility had kept us from retrieving the gas, but there was no longer any alternative. One of us had to go for the gas! Who? I couldn't go because of my hands, so I lay quietly in my bag, letting my silence ask someone else to go.

Dave resisted the thought of his going. He had dug the cave. He had cooked for us when there had been gas. He knew his efforts had kept Pirate and me alive. And we knew it.

It wasn't right that Dave go out into certain misery to possibly disappear in the wind. Yet, knowing Dave, I sensed he was struggling with his weariness and fear to find it in himself to go out. Since he was the only one of us who knew for certain where the gas should be, it was logical that he go. Neither Pirate nor I could ask him. Semiconscious from the altitude and the numbing hypnotism of the wind, we retained a sense of justice.

There was another reason we weren't anxious for Dave to go. He was our hands![4] We needed him to cook if we ever got some gas. We would need him to tie the rope around us and hold us on belay when we descended, whenever that might be.

Quietly—I don't remember hearing him say he would go—Pirate got out of his sleeping bag. When he started to pull on his boots, he found it difficult and painful to force his swollen feet into them. I offered him the use of my down booties. He took them and quickly had them tied on. Dave

[3] On Johnston's first ascent of Denali.
[4] By now, Genet and Davidson had frozen their fingers.

described the rocks among which the gas had been cached. Pirate pulled down his face mask.

The wind had become more erratic: there were gusts and then short—ten- to thirty-second—lulls of comparative calm. Pirate lay on his stomach, facing the entrance, listening for the lull that sounded right to him. A resigned determination seemed to be all that was left of his former fierceness. Suddenly, he gave a short and not too loud "Arahhaa!" and began squirming out the entrance, uphill, through loose snow. Dave and I cheered, not loudly, but with all our remaining enthusiasm. For a moment we heard Pirate placing the pack across the entrance again. Then the lull ended abruptly, and all we heard was the wind.

For the longest time Dave and I listened without saying a word. Ten, fifteen minutes passed. We knew Pirate should have returned, but we said nothing. He might call for help only ten feet from the cave and we'd never hear him. I couldn't help imagining what we'd have to do if he failed to return. Maybe Dave would make a try for the gas. Maybe the two of us would attempt to dash down from the pass. If Pirate didn't return within a few minutes there would be no reason to go looking for him. Maybe Dave and I would simply lie in the cave, waiting until Gregg, Shiro, George, and John could reach us,[5] or until we passed into delirium.

We heard a movement at the entrance. Two immediate whoops of sheer joy expressed our relief. A flurry of snow, then a plastic jug shot into the cave, followed by an exhausted Pirate.

"Bad!" He was gasping. "I couldn't stand up, even in the lulls. Something's wrong with my balance." I had never before heard Pirate say anything was rough or dangerous. "I crawled all the way, clawing into the ice with two ice axes. I can't feel my feet now."

We had gas! We could drink water!

With a merriment we'd forgotten ever existed Dave melted chunks of ice and piles of snow. The first can of water, especially, smelled and tasted

---

[5] Team members Gregg Bloomberg, Shiro Nishimae, George Wichman, and John Edwards.

sweet; we did not remember that the sweetness was the scent of urine.[6] Dave heated can after can of water till they became hot. We drank, and drank, and always waited for yet another canful. For the first time in five days we went to sleep with full stomachs. That we were only full of water mattered not at all—or so we thought.

My feet had become colder. I had to constantly wiggle my toes to keep them from becoming numb. Still, I was glad I had not asked Pirate to return my booties after his trip for the gas.

• • •

March 5

The gusts and lulls of the wind sounded hopeful when we woke to another cold, gray morning under the ice. The ragged end of the storm seemed to be blowing itself out, and had we been strong we probably would have tried to dash down from the pass immediately. Unfortunately, we had become so weak that the wind would have to be completely gone before we could descend with any confidence. Yet, regardless of when the wind disappeared, this had to be our last day in the cave, because by the next morning there would be no food at all. For the three of us we had only a handful of gorp, four slices of cheese, and three little hard candies. When this food ran out the cold would take over our bodies unless we could make it down. We lay silent and brooding in our bags; cheerless as our situation was, I felt a curious sense of relief that it was so simple—without food, it was either descend or perish in this wretched cave.

Pirate refused to believe what the wind had done during the night. On going to sleep, he had fixed a rope to the pack which closed the cave's entrance, then tied that rope around his arm to keep the pack from being blown away if a gust dislodged it. He woke to find both the rope and the pack gone. As the wind had begun packing the entrance full of snow, some loose, fine-grained crystals had sifted into Pirate's sleeping bag; the bag had so little warmth that the snow lay in it without melting. Pirate stared at the

---

[6]Because the trio had a single can to use for cooking and urinating.

snow for ten or fifteen seconds, then mumbled hoarsely that he'd leave the snow in his bag because it might help insulate him. His reasoning sounded absurd. I thought of telling him to get the snow out of his bag as fast as he could, but it was easier to lie silent than begin talking. Then I began wondering whether Pirate might be right about the snow helping to insulate him—his bag and Dave's were now little more than matted down and chunks of ice held together by the nylon shell.

Even after Pirate placed his boots and the gas bottle in the entrance to block the blowing snow from sealing us in, snow still blew through every time a gust of wind hit the slope above. Because the entrance wasn't tightly closed off from the storm, a steady draft circulated the $-35°$ air through our cave. With the chill factor increased, I began shivering again. This wasn't particularly painful, but it was unnerving to watch my body shaking uncontrollably. What happens after you lose control of your body? I thought of asking Dave, but said nothing.

My thoughts wandered back to my childhood. I recalled my parents saying that when I was first learning to walk I enjoyed toddling around in the snow naked. I remembered the times when I was eight and nine and we'd run out into the spring windstorms that sweep across the plains of eastern Colorado; with bales of straw we built shelters from the driving wind and dust, and considered ourselves pioneers. In those days it had been great fun to run shouting from tree to tree in a thunderstorm or when the rain turned to hailstones the size of marbles and golf balls. How had those games in storms led to the desperate mess the three of us were trapped in? All I wanted now was to be free of the fear of freezing and being buried under the ice. I started imagining what we'd look like frozen solid. The feel of my mouth on Farine's cold lips came back.[7] I saw his last expression frozen in his cheeks and eyelids. How much of a body could be frozen before the heart stopped? Was I acting cowardly to think this way? It wouldn't happen to us, not to me; yet, there was the cold in our hands and feet.

---

[7]Farine was Jacques Batkin's nickname. Davidson recalls his effort to bring Batkin back to life with mouth-to-mouth resuscitation after Batkin's fatal crevasse fall.

To get these thoughts out of my mind, I asked Dave if it seemed to him that the gusts were becoming less powerful and the periods of calm longer. He said, "Don't think about it." But I couldn't help being attentive to every fluctuation of the wind, even though I knew as well as Dave that it was only depressing to hear every lull end in a blast of wind.

Only food occupied our thoughts as much as the wind, especially the food in the punctured cans. Those cans haunted us. I felt the little holes staring at me whether the cans were in plain sight or hidden under a sleeping bag or out the entrance. After Dave had emptied the cans of their contents, he classified most of the food as definitely rotten, but there remained at least a pound of peas and a half pound of ham that he thought might be edible. He even thawed and heated some of the ham. It didn't smell or look bad; still, it had come from a partly spoiled can.

"Aw, I'm going to eat it," Pirate insisted.

But we wouldn't let him. There was no question in our minds that, weak as we were, food poisoning would do us in. As long as we could just resist the canned food we had a chance; if we gave in and ate the doubtful ham and peas we might eliminate that chance. Of course, the food might be good, and it could easily provide the extra strength we might need to get down.

As our stomachs tightened with cramps and the deafening repetition of gusts and lulls whittled away our patience, each of us changed our minds about eating the canned food. One moment Pirate would declare he was going to eat the ham, and the next he would be restraining Dave or me from trying it. So far we had been able to check ourselves, but every moment of hunger increased the temptation.

We dreamed about feasts, banquets, exotic dishes, all our favorite foods. For what seemed like hours Dave and I listed every type of food we could think of. Sometimes we would be silent for ten or fifteen minutes, as if the conversation had ended; then as soon as I'd mention something like "crab," Dave would say "Wow, oh honcho boncho! I'd forgotten crab!" Another ten minutes might pass before one of us would remember a forgotten delicacy.

Once Dave said, "Stuffed green peppers!"

"Yea . . . with lots of raisins in the stuffing!" I answered.

We tantalized each other with difficult choices between different foods. "Dave," I asked, "would you prefer a mushroom pizza or a pepperoni pizza?"

"Mushroom, and if you could have one fruit, what would it be?"

"Awaarraghaa . . . I want some bloody meat!" Pirate interrupted. There was enough gas to make as much water as we could drink; however, Dave had only enough motivation to make a minimal amount. As our dehydration continued, our frostbite became more severe. The swelling in my fingers had started to go down; I didn't know whether this was a sign of improvement or an indication that my body simply didn't have enough liquid to keep the swelling up. Much as I worried over the blisters, I realized they were my body's way of trying to save the tissue that had been frozen.

Dave couldn't feel the large toe on his right foot, nor parts of several other toes. There was so little he could do for his feet—rub them, wiggle the toes. He said they were becoming steadily colder. The scabby, frostbitten skin on the end of his nose was sickening to look at, but not nearly as frightening as the freezing that was beginning in his feet. The frostbite on his nose was isolated and had come about because he happened to have a long nose which protruded from his face mask, while the frostbite taking hold in his feet was not isolated; it was a sign that the cold was steadily creeping into his body. It was happening to each of us.

At times I was surprised that I wanted Pirate to continue wearing my down booties, which I had previously guarded so selfishly. I knew I hadn't overcome my selfishness; Pirate was sort of included in it. Since his feet had suffered on his trip to get the gas, I had felt almost as protective toward his feet as toward my own. Later in the day Pirate passed one bootie back to me. Perhaps one bootie each would not be a practical way to halt the freezing in our feet, but, even if it was only a gesture, it was still the most touching thing I had ever seen Pirate do.

The one advantage of being dehydrated was that we rarely had to jeopardize ourselves by urinating into the can inside our sleeping bags. Likewise, our lack of food had saved us from the ordeal of a bowel movement

in the wind. Nevertheless, our hour of reckoning came. We had postponed
the moment until it appeared we wouldn't be safe another minute. To go
outside would be risking the possibility of contracting a humiliating case
of frostbite while our pants were down. By comparison, it was almost pleasant to contemplate attempting the feat inside our sleeping bags. Dave's ingenuity developed a technique which produced little packages, nicely
wrapped in toilet paper. With some coaching from him I managed to get
my bundles safely wrapped and out the cave's entrance. However, Pirate,
who hadn't been very attentive, got himself into trouble. Soon after he had
completely disappeared into his sleeping bag we heard him begin to mumble and swear. When the shape of his sleeping bag began shifting frantically, we offered him some advice.

"Oh, you had paper?" he moaned. "I didn't know you guys had used
paper."

During the first days of the wind, sleep had been an effective way of waiting. Now it had become a continual twisting of hips and shoulders away
from the hardness of the ice, a twisting away from the cold that seeped into
our bags from the ice beneath. None of us had even a momentary respite
from hunger cramps and the cramps and aches in our dried-up ligaments
and muscles. Nevertheless, wakefulness continued to be a worse kind of half-
consciousness; pain was felt more acutely by a more alert mind, and we realized that we weren't dreaming, that we were not going to wake up to find
everything friendly and warm.

At times I was unable to tell for certain whether I was awake or asleep.
Dreams of Farine lying on the ice, of John calling from the bottom of that
crevasse,[8] of Shiro coughing, of our hands and feet turning black, filled my
sleep and drifted over into the different levels of wakefulness that stretched
through the day. Hours no longer existed. I once asked Dave how long we
had been trapped under the ice; he said he didn't know.

In the afternoon, during one period of what I thought was clear-
sightedness, it seemed as though the wind was finally dying. The lulls had

---

[8]As the team had recovered Batkin's body.

become much longer, maybe as long as five or six minutes, and the gusts were less frequent and no longer hit with the force which had shaken our cave for so many days. I dozed fitfully, then woke in the dark to a strange sound. I was startled. To ears that had become unaccustomed to quietness, the silence sounded nearly as loud as the wind's roar had that first morning.

"Dave, the wind's gone! We can descend!"

"Yea man, I'm cooking us up a farewell dinner to this awful hole," Dave said. In a moment his headlamp flicked on and several minutes later I heard the cheery purr of the stove. It was all over, we thought; we had made it through. Our farewell dinner was a farewell to the very last of our food, to the cave, and, we hoped, to the wind. Dave passed the hot water and divided up the four slices of cheese.

THEODORA KROEBER

(1897–1979)

From *Ishi in Two Worlds*

On August 29, 1911, a solitary man, nearly naked, driven to the limits of exhaustion and fear, was discovered shortly after dawn crouching outside a slaughter house in Oroville, California. He understood not a word of English, and quietly allowed himself to be handcuffed and taken to the Oroville jail.

Theodora Kroeber's timeless account of what she calls "the last wild Indian in North America" is at once one of the great survival stories in U.S. history and one of its most moving cultural tragedies. Ishi, as white men named him, was the last living Yahi-Yana, a once proud and fiercely independent people who lived in the brush-choked volcanic canyons of Deer and Mill Creeks, southwest of Mount Lassen. After a series of gratuitous attacks and massacres in the 1860s, the Yahi-Yana went into hiding in their homeland, within only a few miles of ranchers' homesteads, successfully avoiding capture and making only rare and fleeting contact with whites. From their secret lairs, the people could

*watch the daily passage of the railroad train up and down the Sacra-
mento valley scarcely fifteen miles to the west.*

*Ishi lived only four and a half years after his "capture," but he had
the good fortune to come under the aegis of two anthropologists from
the University of California at Berkeley—the great A. L. Kroeber and
the assiduous T. T. Waterman. They gave Ishi a "job" as janitor in the
University Museum, where he also took up residence, and they protected
him from the curiosity hounds who would have gladly put him in a traveling circus. During those years, the scholars slowly pieced together the
unbearably sad story of Ishi's decades of concealment and survival, as
one by one he lost every companion in his life.*

*In this excerpt, Theodora Kroeber recounts the fortunes of those forty-
five years, during which the Yahi-Yana so skillfully hid that the Anglo
world concluded they were extinct.*

T he years passed. No Yahi were seen and there were no "Indian troubles." New settlers in the valley assured each other that the Mill
Creeks had long since been exterminated or had died. They
shrugged their shoulders over the mystery of the last massacre as old timers
remembered it. Stories never lost anything in the telling, they said. Even
the old timers, some of them, agreed. Others were not so sure. A sudden
movement in the brush might be a deer or a quail, or it might be a wild
Indian.

The back country was changing, it was filling up. By 1884 ranches, saw
mills, and small permanent settlements with connecting roads instead of
trails mushroomed far upstream into the hills which no longer need be
shunned because of fear of Indians, of whom tales continued nonetheless
to be told, sometimes making the city papers and growing into circumstantial yarns. The rustling in the chaparral increased; owners of cabins
claimed that they were being robbed as in the old days; and once or twice
a man or a boy came in with a story of having seen fleetingly a strange
Indian.

In 1884 the completeness of the concealment began to crack. After twelve years, the Yahi took to raiding again. By this time they had lost most of their few hunters; hunting and gathering had become ever riskier and scantier in returns. The roads, the ranches, and the new hill population of whites impinged ever closer upon Mill Creek. So, once again, calves were missed, or a sheep would be seen in the flock, unscratched but with arrow points caught in its fleece. And, since the arrows were indubitable evidence that wild Indians were at work, so were the cabins emptied of some of their key contents, but with their canned goods left intact. It was only Yahi, as everyone knew, who took all the flour and barley and none of the canned corn and beans. Perhaps canned goods did not appear to them to be food; or perhaps they had once tried some which was spoiled.

It may seem odd at this distance, but it was the raiding of provisions which irritated the cattlemen far more than did the stealing of stock. When a sheep or a calf was successfully "hunted," its owner suffered a loss; when a cabin was stripped of its stored supplies, inconvenience and frustration were added to loss. Pack loads of stock feed, beans, coffee, sugar, bacon, flour, and canned goods were taken to the hill cabins and sheds where they were stored to await the annual roundup. A vaquero might have to search for the scattered cattle and sheep in difficult and remote parts of the hills, and it was understood that at need he was to dip into the supplies in any cabin whether or not it belonged to his boss. But if the Yahi had been there ahead of the vaquero, there would be neither barley for his horse, nor flour for himself. In the more remote areas, and it was those which the Yahi favored, a cabin or two lacking these staples sometimes made a return to the valley for replacements necessary, and that could mean that the roundup would have to be made all over again.

By the 'nineties, Ishi and the two or three companions still able to raid with him must have known precisely the time of arrival of a pack train at a particular cabin: there were some cabins which they seem to have robbed regularly season after season. They also knew that the risk of discovery and death out-of-hand was greater by far than if they were quietly to snare a sheep or a calf. But it was in spring that the pack trains came, and it was in spring that the ground was still covered with snow and that the remnant band was not merely hungry, but starving.

Mr. Norvall, the informant who in 1915 told Waterman about visiting Kingsley Cave after the massacre there,[1] described for him also one of the late Yahi cabin robbings. As he recalled it, it was one day in April, 1885, that he heard someone in his cabin on lower Dry Creek. He went to investigate, and as he came closer he saw four Indians one after another climb out of the cabin's single window. They obviously were not expecting to be confronted by him, and finding themselves caught, lined up quietly against the cabin wall, leaving the next move to him. They had taken only old clothes from the cabin, perhaps because it contained no food except canned goods. One of the four was a young woman wearing three old jumpers of Norvall's and apparently little else. One was an old man, who had taken a shabby overcoat and an ancient rifle barrel from the cabin. There were two young men, one of whom had a crippled foot. Norvall remarked to Waterman that "Rafe Johnson did that," the reference being to the story that "Rafe" was supposed, some years earlier, to have wounded an Indian child in the ankle. The fourth person was Ishi. The woman pointed toward Mill Creek and said something which Norvall thought was *Dos chiquitos papooses* which would be a pidgin Spanish meaning two small children. Norvall was friendly, indicated by signs that the Indians could keep their pathetic loot, and waved them off. They disappeared, and he saw no more of them. Toward fall of the same year, the cabin was again entered. Nothing was missing from it this time, but Norvall found two Yana baskets left there on the table. These he took to be a gift of gratitude for his earlier friendliness, treasuring them as keepsakes until 1915 when he gave them to the University museum as part of an "Ishi" collection.

D. B. Lyon of Red Bluff related to Waterman also in 1915 an experience he had had in 1889 when he was a young boy, and which certainly involved someone of the Yahi band, perhaps Ishi. Lyon did not say how old he was

---

[1]A massacre on a northern tributary of Mill Creek in either 1867 or 1868, in which thirty-three Yahi men, women, and children were killed and scalped.

at the time, probably in his early teens to judge by the anecdote. He was hunting one day on Big Antelope Creek when he heard a rustling in a clump of buckeye. His dog sniffed it and went in but came out uneasily, so Lyon knew that whatever was there was not a deer or rabbit. A noise as of tomcats fighting then came from the buckeye. Lyon threw a rock into the clump, and hit something which responded with a very human "grunt." Encouraged by this, Lyon circled closer, finally edging under the buckeye where he stumbled over a bundle which must have been dropped only seconds ahead of him, the warm sweat of recent handling still clinging to it when he stooped to open it. It consisted of a sheepskin pelt wrapped around half a dozen legs of freshly slaughtered sheep, and a small buckskin bag. As he bent over the bundle, two arrows passed just above his head, one splintering on a boulder, the other falling to the ground in front of him, while a third grazed his cap brim. Whoever was shooting had the distance perfectly and was correcting for height. Hanging onto his treasures, and scooping up the spent arrow from the ground, he ran, nor did he stop until he was well away. When he emptied the contents of the buckskin bag at home, he found it to be a complete Yahi arrow-making outfit. Like Norvall, Lyon still treasured the pelt, the arrow, and the bag with its tools when he told their story to Waterman. Now they, too, form part of the museum's "Ishi" collection. As for the sound as of tomcats fighting which Lyon described, the Yahi experience of domestic house cats was nil, but Ishi and his people could imitate bird songs and wild animal calls and growls, which they used to bring an animal to them or, as in this incident, to scare one off.

It was Lyon who recounted to Waterman one version of the "poisoned wheat" story which turns up in various guises and attributed to different people. According to Lyon, it was Elijah Graham who left a sack of poisoned flour, plainly labeled as poison, in his hill cabin. Many of the white settlers disbelieved that there were Indians in the hills, or were inclined to think that the considerable robbing and pilfering was not done by Indians. The poisoned flour promptly disappeared, which circumstance Graham (or whoever the initiator was in any telling of the tale) took for proof that it was Indians who had made off with it. This is a conundrum without an answer.

The story's popularity may have stemmed from the number of people around Red Bluff and vicinity who failed to share Elijah Graham's faith that it was only Indians who were illiterate.

It was in 1894 as Lyon recalled it that he and his brother tracked someone through the brush toward Mill Creek cañon. The tracks were made by unshod human feet, wide across the toes, with an imprint of deep creases and cracks. These were probably made by a Yahi. To escape the white boys, the pursued one had jumped from the top of the bluff into a bay tree below, and by so doing quickly put a good length of sloping cañon wall between him and the boys. They may of course have imagined this feat, but very likely it happened as Lyon said it did. Ishi's friends of later years were to learn that heights, narrow ledges, and sheer drops bothered him not at all.

The decade of raiding which began in 1884 came to an end ten years later as inexplicably and as suddenly as it had erupted. Silence and emptiness returned to the cañons, and the yarns about wild Indians which had burgeoned once again lost credibility. For the Yahi band itself the ten successive years of raiding were the first and the resistive phase of their last retreat. The Yahi tried to make a life on Mill Creek, to maintain a living space which took in upper Mill and Deer creeks with the ridges, meadows, and smaller streams between; and as the pressure from white encroachment grew unbearably constricting, to fill their emptying baskets from the intrusive and second grade but available food of the white man: his flour and grain and sheep. They failed. And so began the last retreat to Deer Creek.

There were, it is believed, only five Yahi left to make the withdrawal from Mill Creek to Deer Creek, each step of which was a surrender of another piece of heartland, of oak stand, meadow land, fishing place, and upland hunting ground. There remained to them when they at last put down their baskets only two separate but closely adjacent tracts of land on the south side of Deer Creek cañon, which they might with some reason call their own and occupy with relative security. Each tract was not more than half a mile wide and three miles long. The Yahi knew this country intimately, having formerly lived in good village sites close to the creek. Indeed, Ishi was born in one of the old Deer Creek villages. The Yahi could not, in the 'nineties, retreat to any of these old sites, for they were too exposed to view from above and from the north side. Instead, they built two tiny villages above and below the confluence of Sulphur and Deer creeks. The Speegle homestead and ranch were on Sulphur Creek, only a short distance from the new villages, but no one except the Yahi themselves ever entered the thickets of the cañon, which were a surer protection to them than remoteness itself. The sites were chosen for their invisibility and it might be said for their improbability, and because they were where the long and always risky trip to the creek could be made all the way to the water's edge under a screen of laurel. A grizzly bear, or bears, had at one time a den on the site of the larger of the new villages, hence its name, *Wowunupo mu tetna*, Grizzly Bear's Hiding Place.

The site of Wowunupo is a narrow ledge or trough five hundred or more feet above the creek, the only place where even the simplest of shelters could imaginably be built anywhere on the steep cañon wall. Trees grow tall along this ledge, shading it and screening it from below and from the other side. From the ledge to the rim of the cañon, another two hundred feet, is bare cliff, sheer and impassable, which provided the village with a sheltered rear wall and perfect protection from above.

None of the trees and only part of the scrub growth were cleared within the village proper, so that it remained well camouflaged from all prospects. Only the faintest of narrow trails connected the houses, and these were for the most part under an overhead growth. The easternmost building was a tiny house whose framework was of poles lashed together and thatched with boughs of bay. It was shaped like the letter **A**, looking, with its cleverly arranged covering, very like a tree from the outside. Inside, the little house was partitioned to make two rooms, the larger and back one a storage room for baskets of food and other provisions and tools. The door of the house faced downstream.

Because of the shelflike setting, the village was laid out paralleling the creek. Downstream from the first house was a large digger pine in whose shade a rectangular "reservoir" had been dug, three by four feet in diameter and four feet deep. In winter this was kept packed full of snow as an additional source for water.

Beyond the reservoir, one trail led on through the village; another branched off to the creek, five hundred feet below. The trails were the very ones the bears had made and used when Wowunupo was a bear's den. Ishi found that by following the old grizzly trail he came out onto the creek at a good crossing, and that on the north side the fishing was exceptional. It became his regular fishing place, so much so that he ordinarily left his harpoon and other fishing tackle hidden there, instead of carrying them up and down the steep cañon trail.

The trail which meandered through the village led past a very large and sprawling bay tree to a second house, which was built of driftwood from the creek and overlaid with old wagon canvas, heavily smoked. This was where *charqui*[2] was made and salmon was smoked. North of the smoke house, at one of the trail branchings, was the cook house, with a fireplace, stones for grinding acorns, cooking baskets, and cooking stones, paddles, and stirrers. The cook house was sunk in a slight hollow and covered over with a brush roof which served as a sun and rain shelter, and more importantly, to diffuse the smoke, keeping it from rising in a telltale blue spiral. One trail led away from the shelf edge toward the inner side of the site to the third house, another A-shaped structure, strongly lashed together with strips of bark, and thatched with laurel. This might be said to be the principal living house, since it was the tightest built and had the most natural protection. The original bear's den was a part of it. Here, although the space was cramped, there was a living area of sorts, and room for the five to sleep warm and dry when it was cold or stormy out of doors; and here were kept the coon and bearskin capes and the rabbitskin blankets.

Not far from the den house was a shaded and sheltered spot which was Ishi's workroom where he made his arrow and spear points. Enough obsidian and glass refuse from years of chipping accumulated there to fill one of the large carrying baskets of the Yahi. Here the village proper ended. A trail led off from the last house another fifty or more feet to the village toilet, a designated spot downstream.

Neither the swaying of a laurel branch, nor the soft ping of a bowstring

[2]Jerky.

at the instant of release, nor any other sound or movement betrayed that Wowunupo was occupied. The moons of fog and snow, of renewal, of heat and harvest, came and went. With the first of the harvest moon, the five hidden ones made a stealthy trek to Waganupa, a difficult and risky expedition, but it brought them relief from the breathless heat of the cañon as well as hope of filling their baskets on the mountain. No one ever saw them go or come.

The leaves of the calendar on the kitchen wall in the Speegle ranch house were discarded one by one, and the old calendar replaced twelve times. Still living in Bear's Hiding Place were the long-together five: Ishi, his mother, his sister, who was perhaps a cousin in a sister relation to him and whether older or younger is not known, an old man, and a younger one, these last two not related to the others. Then the younger of these men died, and four were left: a man and woman become frail and old; and a second man and woman, able-bodied, strong, and well, but no longer young. Toward the end of the retreat the two old people must have stayed close to the larger and more comfortable of their two villages most of the time while Ishi and his sister-cousin went up and down creeks and hillsides, fishing, gathering, snaring, hunting, foraging.

Sometime late in 1906 a cabin at the Occidental Mine on upper Deer Creek was broken into and a dunnage bag taken. The incident revived rumors about wild Indians; none were seen, but the alarm had been sounded. Some months after this, two white men, a man named Polk and his partner, were camped at the Speegle ranch. Whether or not Polk saw any Indians his account does not make plain, but he heard someone at their "grub," and he and his partner hid under a bluff with their guns cocked. The pilferers took alarm, making a getaway into Deer Creek and out of sight downstream before Polk had a chance to get a shot at them, nor could his dog track them in the water. There can be little real doubt that it was Ishi and a companion, probably his sister: a hat which they dropped was picked up by Polk, who later gave it to the museum; it is patched with bits of hide and sewed with sinew. Characteristically, none of Polk's canned food had been touched; and if further evidence were needed, only Yahi made a highroad of a roaring, boulder-strewn stream.

Some months after Polk's adventure, the Oro Light and Power Company which was contemplating the building of a dam at the junction of Deer and Sulphur creeks, sent engineers there to survey for a flume. In the early evening of November 9, 1908, two engineers were walking back upstream toward their camp at the Speegle homestead. It so happened that they were moving quietly and without talking as they came out onto a sandbank alongside the creek. There before them on a rock in midstream stood a naked Indian fishing with a harpoon. The Indian was Ishi. The engineers remembered somewhat differently Ishi's behavior upon seeing them. One said that he gave a "vicious snarl" and brandished his harpoon threateningly. The other said that he motioned them emphatically back, saying over and over something which surely meant "Go away!" They went away as quickly as they could, excitedly reporting their encounter at camp where it was received with general disbelief: they were tenderfeet, they had been deceived by some trick of evening shadows, they had been listening to too many sheepherders' tales.

One person in camp listened closely to their story. This was Merle Apperson who knew the Yana country well—he was with the surveyors as guide—and who found credible the possibility that there were live Indians on Deer Creek. The next morning he went down the south side of the creek, turning away from the stream after a half mile or more and working up the steep cañon through thick brush. He was making fair progress when an arrow whizzed past, narrowly missing him. He took the pointed hint and turned back, his guess confirmed, and rejoined the crew which was clearing a flume line below Sulphur Creek and along Deer Creek, utilizing the very shelf on which Wowunupo was built. About ten o'clock the same morning, the crew walked directly into the village.

Its four residents had no doubt been observers of the alarming activity around Speegle's place and at the mouth of Sulphur Creek. With an old man who was weak and could not move quickly and an old woman who was bedridden, there was little they could do but watch and keep out of sight. Ishi and his sister must have arranged that in the event of discovery, she would try to escape with the old man who could still walk, while Ishi would remain with his mother.

Ishi was not seen that morning by any of the party of white people, but the old man supported by Ishi's sister were briefly glimpsed as the two of them left the village, half running through the brush toward the edge of the level shelf of land, and then were lost to sight as they dropped downhill. The brush in that part of the cañon was so dense and so impenetrable, that had the surveyors chosen a line even so little as ten or fifteen feet to the right or left, they might have bypassed the village none the wiser that it was there. As a frightened fawn or partridge "freezes" at the approach of an enemy, taking on the look of inanimate nature, the four Indians must have waited the passing of the whites. When they did not pass, the three who could, ran, after covering up the helpless old mother with blankets and hides that she might by chance go unnoticed.

The surveying party searched the village. Under a pile of skins and rags they found Ishi's mother. Her face was deeply wrinkled, her white hair was cropped close to her head in sign of mourning, she seemed to be partly paralyzed, and her swollen legs were wrapped with strips of buckskin. As the strange men uncovered her, she trembled with fear. They tried to talk to her, and, somewhat reassured, she made some response, but she understood no English. The only communication was when Mr. Apperson said sympathetically, "Muy malo?" pointing to her legs, and she repeated, "Malo. Malo." The men looked farther. They found acorns and dried salmon in baskets in the storage room. In the cook house beside the small hearth there was a fire drill as well as the usual complement of Yahi cooking utensils, and in the other houses there were arrow-flaking tools, a deer snare, bow, arrows, quivers, a two-pronged spear, baskets, moccasins, tanned hides, and a fur robe of wildcat pelts. The men gathered together every movable possession, even the food, and for some unfathomably callous reason took it all with them as souvenirs. Merle Apperson was not a party to the looting. He wanted instead to carry the old woman to camp, but the others demurred. He felt that it would be a friendly gesture to leave at least some gift or token behind, but he could find nothing in his own pockets which might serve, and no one else offered anything.

It was too late to return that day, but Apperson came back to Bear's Hiding Place early the next morning; it was much on his mind that a terrible wrong had been done there. The old woman was gone; there was no trace of any Indians, nor were there footprints or any other sign to show where they might have gone. He was sure that they could not be far away, and he and some of the surveyors searched upstream and down without coming on the faintest clue. It should be said that not only was Apperson much troubled by the episode and its outcome, but Robert Hackley, one of the surveyors, wrote to Waterman on September 5, 1911, while the papers were full of the finding of Ishi and of retellings of this earlier discovery of the village. Said Hackley, "The discredit of driving these harmless people from their home does not belong to the survey party altogether as some of the cattlemen [in the party] considered that they had a grievance on account of stolen goods and proceeded to take matters off our hands." Most of the property taken that fateful morning is now with the "Ishi" collection of the museum, easily contained within a single small exhibition case. It was nonetheless four people's total means of livelihood.

The story of the finding of the Indian village was in the papers. Kroeber and Waterman corresponded with the surveyors who had seen it and with anyone else whom they thought might by chance have any leads to the whereabouts of its dispersed inhabitants. The months passed without any sign of them, and in October of the next year, 1909, Waterman tried to find them. With an engineer, G. W. Hunt, and the son of Merle Apperson, he spent a month beating the brush and the faint trails of Deer Creek. He and his party found evidence in plenty of former occupation of the two villages of the retreat, but they turned up no faintest trace of living Indians. The villages looked as they did when Apperson visited them the morning after their discovery a year before, and as they looked in 1914 when Ishi returned for a brief visit. Neither Ishi nor any other person ever occupied them after the forced dispersal.

Waterman returned to the museum after an arduous month of searching, with photographs of the villages and other evidence of a hidden Yahi
life in the wilds of Deer Creek cañon, but with nothing to suggest that there
were any Yahi alive in 1909. Nor were there stories of encounters or suspicions of any unseen Indian presence there until April 13, 1911. On that day
a surveyor, H. H. Hume, happened to notice a bundle hanging high in a
live oak tree. On examination it proved to be several old barley sacks and
pieces of canvas wrapped around a collection of curious objects. The cache,
for so it was, contained tanned deerhides with the hair left on, a pair of much
worn moccasins, little bundles of pine pitch, and pine needles whose
sheathed ends all pointed neatly in one direction. There was also a bar of
unused soap, a cylinder of "sweetened" charcoal about an inch wide and
three inches in length, a few nails and screws tied separately in a rag, and
a sharp piece of steel with an eyehole at the large end. The cache was probably Ishi's. It was found four months before Ishi turned up at the slaughter
house.

After the morning of the invasion of Wowunupo neither Ishi nor anyone
else ever saw his sister and the old man again. Ishi was convinced that they
had not long survived. His sister ran one way, Ishi another, but had she not
met death soon, she and Ishi would have managed to find each other, their
knowledge of familiar places to look being a shared one. Ishi believed that
his sister and the old man had either drowned—the Deer Creek crossing
was treacherous and slippery—or that they had met some other violent
death and been eaten thereafter by a bear or a mountain lion, else he
would have come on some sign of them in all his searching for them. So
he reasoned and so it would seem to be.

Ishi somehow managed to carry his mother out of reach of Apperson's
best efforts to find her. Dr. Pope understood Ishi to have told him that he
took his mother up Waganupa. Perhaps he did carry her in that direction,
but it is most improbable that he could actually have taken her up the
mountain or that the two of them could have lived there had he been able
to go so far. It was then mid-November; Mount Lassen was snow-covered
and food was even scarcer on the mountain than in the foothills. One of

Ishi's early efforts to talk to Waterman involved a pantomime of a woman bending over a fire, throwing heated stones into the water in a cooking basket, and making acorn mush. "Pukka–pukka–pukka" it said as it cooked, Ishi crooking and withdrawing a finger to indicate the bursting bubbles of a cereal boiling and thickening. Waterman could only conjecture the meaning. Was Ishi relating something about his mother? Or was he trying to do no more than identify for Waterman the sex of the person he was talking about?

Ishi and his mother were together until her death which may have been within days of the breaking up of the village. After she was gone, he was without human companionship for the rest of the time, perhaps for almost all of it, from November, 1908, to August, 1911. That Ishi was wearing his hair burned short in sign of mourning in August, 1911, was evidence of a death or deaths in his family, but his mourning may well have been a prolonged one.

ISHI AND HIS people are at the end of their last retreat: the dim trails of the dispersal fade into the chaparral a stone's throw from Wowunupo mu tetna.

The door of the jail cell stands open, Ishi is dressed in the clothes of "civilization," pants and shirt and coat anyway, not shoes as yet. In the near distance a train whistles for the Oroville station stop. The train will carry him into new hazards, new experiences, and new friendships.

• • •

EVE BALL

(1890–1984)

From *Indeh: An Apache Odyssey*

Eve Ball was a schoolteacher who moved to the small town of Ruidoso, New Mexico, in 1942. Gradually she befriended a number of elders on the nearby Mescalero Reservation, including the descendants of some of the Chiricahua Apache who had ridden with Geronimo in 1886, a band of thirty-four men, women, and children who, by successfully eluding eight thousand American and Mexican soldiers for five months, waged the last war fought by free Indians against the U.S. government. Eventually Ball was allowed to collect oral histories from her informants. The fruit of her research—a profound and unique book called Indeh, *first published in 1980—stands as the most coherent account of one of our country's greatest cultural tragedies told from the victims' point of view.*

No episode in that history is more stirring than the escape by Massai, one of Geronimo's warriors, from the train carrying the Chiricahua to a prison camp in Florida, followed by his subsequent wanderings as a hunted man. Although Massai's flight took place in 1886, he survived at large into the twentieth century before succumbing to a posse's attack about 1911. In this excerpt, the remarkable story of Massai's quarter-century evasion of the hated White Eyes (as the Apache called Anglo-Americans) is told by his daughter, Alberta Begay.

Once a week a member of each family went to the agency for supplies.[1] Orders were issued to bring everybody, and this made the Indians suspicious. But they went to the agency, unarmed, and mounted soldiers herded them like cattle into the corral. Then they were put into wagons and hauled north to Holbrook, in Navajo country.[2] There they were driven onto the train and told that they were en route to Florida to join Geronimo, who also had been captured. Chihuahua and many Warm Springs Apaches had also been shipped to Florida. All Chiricahuas were to be sent as prisoners to Florida, whether or not they had been at war with the soldiers. The scouts too were herded aboard the train, headed for exile in Florida.[3] So did the White Eyes[4] reward those Apaches who had betrayed their own people.

From the first moment he was aboard the train Massai was planning to escape. Massai's wife knew that she could not leave the children and escape with her husband, but she urged Massai, and Gray Lizard, to attempt it.

"We will have to loosen the bars on the window when the guards are not close at hand," Massai said. "We will have to choose a time to escape when the train is going up a long slope. Like a horse it will have to slow down. We cannot jump off with it going like the wind, on the level or downhill."

[1]At Fort Apache, on the White Mountain Apache Reservation in Arizona.

[2]In east-central Arizona.

[3]The U.S. government finally defeated the Chihuahua by enlisting as scouts Apaches from other tribes to hunt them down. "It takes an Apache to catch an Apache," was the motto of the day.

[4]Anglo-Americans.

There seemed to be no place suited for the escape attempt, yet they spent three days cautiously loosening the bars when the guards' backs were turned. Then one morning Massai saw low mountains in the east. They were, he guessed, almost a day's journey away. That evening, if ever, he and Gray Lizard must make the attempt to leave the train.

A Chiricahua scout went through the car. A prisoner himself, he taunted the other prisoners. "When you get to Florida, the soldiers will chop your necks off," he gloated. "All who wear red handkerchiefs around their heads will have their necks chopped."

"You wear a red *cord*," retorted Massai. "If the soldiers do not get you first, I will strangle you with it!"

All the scouts wore the red head cord.

When food was brought at noon Massai pretended to eat, but he concealed most of his portion in his breechclout. His wife gave him her share; she would get more that night. Gray Lizard, too, did not eat.

The train began laboring up the slope, moving more and more slowly as it climbed. Massai looked for a place where there was much vegetation in which he could hide. They came to clumps of bushes, with rocks. The train slowed almost to a stop, and Massai and Gray Lizard slipped through the window and dropped to the ground. They rolled down the slope into the thick brush and lay still. Neither was hurt. The train did not stop. They saw it disappear over the hill, then they wriggled through the vegetation to thicker shelter and hid there until dark. Then they walked toward the low mountains to the southwest and by morning had crossed the little valley and were halfway up the slope. There they ate, drank, and slept.

They had hoped to find Indians on those mountains, but they saw no sign of any but white people. When they came near a log cabin they circled around it. They avoided lights until they saw the smoke of a campfire. That might indicate Indians, so they crept close enough to the blaze to smell mutton cooking and coffee boiling. That night, instead of moving on, they lay hidden near the camp.

At daybreak they saw that the campers were white men and suspected that they were miners. If so, they would leave the camp during the day, leaving their supplies unguarded.

Massai and Gray Lizard watched the three men cook breakfast. They could smell the *coche*[5] frying, and the odor made their mouths water. Finally the men finished their breakfast, took their picks and shovels, and went up the mountain.

When they were out of sight, Massai led the way to the camp. There was cold mutton and bread, and even some hot coffee left in the pot. Best of all, there were rifles. Massai and Gray Lizard each took a .30-30 and all the ammunition they could find. They took cartridge belts and two knives. They cut meat from a sheep hanging in a tree and put the food in flour sacks. Each carried one.

They headed ever toward the west, walking until they were tired and hungry, traveling mostly at night until they were out of the wooded country. Still sleeping or resting during the day, they moved on at night through open country. They found a trail where the deer came to water and killed one. They took all the meat they could carry and buried the rest. The stomach of the deer was cleaned for use as a water bag.

I do not know how long it took them to get back to Río Pecos, but it was a long time. Gray Lizard, who was carrying the water, fell against a prickly pear and tore a hole in the bag. Now they had no water, but they kept moving. They hoped to kill an antelope but did not see any although they were in antelope country.

Massai was making medicine, and so was Gray Lizard. And Ussen[6] heard, for soon a heavy rain began to fall. They made a hole in the ground to catch it. After drinking all the water they could, they kept walking to the west. Their guide was the Dipper, for Indians know the stars and use them for directions.

Finally they came to the Pecos. They recognized it by the bad taste of

[5]Pig.
[6]The all-powerful Chiricahua god.

the water. Now they were sure that they were not far from Mescalero country. Next morning they saw a dark cloud looming to the southwest, a cloud that they gradually recognized as distant mountains. The Capitans! They were almost to Apache country. They prayed to Ussen, thanking Him for giving them the strength and courage to reach their homeland. That is the Apache way. There are many who make medicine when they need help, but few who remember to thank Him later, even for saving their lives.

In the Capitans they stopped for a day's badly needed rest, for they knew that the White Eyes could not catch them there. Later they killed a deer and feasted. Some time later they crossed Capitan Gap and saw the beautiful White Mountain.

"It is not far now to Mescal Mountain," said Gray Lizard. "We can make it easily."

"It is there that the soldiers will look for me," Massai said. "I will stay on the White Mountain, at least until the search is ended."

"It will never end," said Gray Lizard. "Our people are there. You want to see your parents, don't you?"

"Yes, but I do not want to be captured and sent away."

"Nor do I. But the scouts said that all but the Chiricahuas are to be turned loose. I am Tonkawa[7] and they will not take me."

"Go to your people, then, if you are so sure that you will not be hunted. I will stay on White Mountain until the search is ended."

But Gray Lizard persisted. "The White Eyes will not know how you look. Your wife said that after our escape she would tell the guards that you are a big tall man like Naiche[8] when they called your name and you did not answer. Maybe that will keep the White Eyes from finding you."

"Perhaps," replied Massai wearily. "But I will stay here awhile. We will go to the north of the White Mountain, and around to the west side. There we will part. I hope that some day we may meet and again be as brothers."

The next day they divided the food and ammunition and filled their new

[7] A separate tribe.

[8] The son of Cochise, nominal chief in the final band led by Geronimo.

deer-stomach water bag for Gray Lizard. They prayed to Ussen for their re-
union and then, in the Apache custom, they embraced and parted.

MASSAI STOOD ON the slope above Three Rivers and watched Gray
Lizard walk away toward the White Sands. He would go, he knew, by the
Malpais Spring and our sacred peak in the San Andreas. Then, since he
was not a Chiricahua, Gray Lizard would be safe with our people at Mescal
Mountain. But Massai would be an exile hunted like an animal as long as
he lived.

Heavy-hearted, Massai climbed the ridge of the White Mountain and
descended the slope into the Rinconada. It was well named,[9] for it is so secluded that to this day few people have seen that beautiful valley, nestled
high on the peak.

In the Rinconada there is a little stream, grass, piñons, mesquite, and
greasewood. Game abounded there. Difficult to reach from any point, it
was a good place for Massai to hide. He found a cave near a little pool where
the deer came to drink and began preparing for winter. He knew that he
was not out of danger even in this wild, lonely spot, for Fort Stanton was
only a few miles away and the cavalrymen liked to hunt. The report of his
rifle might disclose his hiding place to a wandering hunter, so he made a
bow and arrows for killing deer. He dried meat and tanned hides until he
had a good supply. He was free—but terribly lonely. He knew that he would
never see his wife and children again and also that his wife would think him
dead and marry again.

So it was with great happiness that he saw the ripening of the piñons that
fall. Piñons bear perhaps one year out of four or five, but that fall there was
a big crop. Massai knew that the Mescaleros would come to harvest them.
They were Apaches and his brothers. They would not betray his presence
to the soldiers unless they happened to be scouts. He would recognize the
scouts by the red head cords and ammunition belts they wore. Badly as he

[9] "Rinconada" means "corner" or "angle" in Spanish.

needed ammunition, he would not kill a scout unless attacked. Even if a scout were ambushed and killed silently with arrow or knife, his comrades would miss him and track down his slayer.

One morning from his lookout ledge, Massai saw Mescalero women and children riding up on horseback to camp only a short distance from his cave. For three days he watched, but no men joined them. He had food, but the smell of their boiling coffee tantalized him. More than anything else, he craved association with his people. Finally, on an evening when he could stand his loneliness no longer, he slipped quietly toward the camp.

Two women sat by the fire. Little children, wrapped in their blankets, lay with their feet toward the warmth. One of the women was telling them the legends of their people. The scene was so sweet and homelike that Massai felt his eyes mist and a lump come into his throat. He called to the women. They stood in alarm, and the children sat up in their blankets.

"Do not be afraid," he said softly. "I will not harm you."

He arose and walked toward them. When they saw that he was an Apache they were not afraid. The children smiled and the women stood with shyly downcast eyes.

"Will my brother sit and eat?" invited one of the women.

"I have eaten, but I have not tasted coffee for a long time."

She poured the hot liquid into a gourd and handed it to him. He drank slowly, enjoying the delicious flavor.

"Enjuh!"[10] he said. "I cannot say how good it tastes."

Then he sat across the fire from the women and visited with them. They were sisters who had come to gather piñons. There were no White Eyes in that place, so they had nothing to fear.

"You are brave women; don't you fear strange Apaches?"

One of the women, the wife of Big Mouth, smiled and shook her head. "Now that my brother is close, we feel very safe."

Nor was there reason for them to fear Apaches, even strange Apaches;

[10]"Good!"

for they did not molest women. Other bad things they sometimes did, but they did not molest women. Not even white women.

When Massai rose to leave, they gave him all the coffee they had brought. He thanked them and left. As he went back to his cave, he thought of the women and of his lonely life and tried to put the thought out of his mind. He knew, too, that they would not betray him to the White Eyes.

He did not come again to their camp, nor did he visit any of the others who came to harvest the piñon nuts. Nor did he hunt while they were there. But when he thought that all had left the Rinconada, he took his rifle and concealed himself at the pool where the deer came to drink. He concealed himself and waited.

Massai may have slept, for a splash in the pool suddenly alerted him. Three young women were bathing in it. He did not move, for according to age-old tribal law spying upon women was punishable by death. Yet he watched fascinated as the girls bathed; they got out of the water, dressed, and took down their long hair and braided it. An idea possessed Massai. Already he had forfeited his life; he would take one of these young women. He jumped from his place of concealment and reached the startled girls.

"Come!" he ordered the first.

"Do not take me; my baby would die," she pleaded.

He turned to the next. She stood transfixed like a frightened deer, slender and beautiful, poised for flight. Her long braids swept the ground. Massai caught the end of one and motioned her to walk in front of him.

The others followed, pleading with him not to take her. He motioned them to leave. "Do not take her," one begged.

"Shall I take *you* instead?" he asked grimly.

They turned and fled.

With his rifle Massai motioned his captive on. They climbed to the mouth of the cave. He took the knife from her belt and tied her in the cave. Then he took food and water and placed them within reach of her.

"Here you will sleep tonight," he told her. "There are blankets to keep you warm."

He slept lying across the cave entrance that night. Awaking at sunrise, he lay for some time watching the sun brighten the east with its fiery glow and thinking out his future plans. Finally he arose, his mind made up.

Working quickly, Massai packed his supplies on a wild horse he had tamed, then returned to the cave, freed the girl, and motioned for her to make ready for travel.

Both walked beside the laden packhorse, heading up the trail and crossing the ridge between the Rinconada and Three Rivers. All that day they walked. Massai wanted to get beyond reach of pursuit that he knew would come. He took the winding trail between the White Sands and the Malpais, walking on the rock as much as he could. He knew that trail and where to find water. Late that night he tied up the girl and hobbled the horse, and they slept for a few hours.

Before daylight they took the trail again. In the foothills of the San Andreas was water; there they camped and rested. Massai tied the girl to a tree while he hunted, telling her that if she escaped he would follow and kill her.

During the journey she spoke only in answer to questions and then in monosyllables. After a week's traveling, Massai asked, "Have I mistreated you?"

She shook her head.

"Why, then, will you not talk to me?"

She raised her head to look him straight in the eyes. "You brought me by force. An Apache does not do that."

"Would you have come otherwise?"

"No!"

"Listen to me, then! It is true that I took you, but I have respected you. Now, unless you continue the journey to my people willingly, I will give you the horse and food. You will be free to return to your home. If you go to my people, my mother will make the wedding feast for us. It is for you to decide."

She lowered her head.

"Which is it to be?" Massai's voice was stern, but she looked up into his eyes and saw what was in his heart.

"I will go with you," she murmured.

For the rest of the journey she rode the horse. She was happy, for, despite all, she now knew that Massai was a good man.

Massai's mother made the feast he had promised, so that all the people of Mescal Mountain knew that this was a marriage. There were no vows to be broken, as White Eyes do. To Apaches, marriage is a sacred thing—not to be lightly undertaken nor ended. And though Massai had a wife, though he might never see her again, there was no obstacle to his marriage. Such was the custom of my people.

And so they were married.

THE YEARS PASSED and my father and mother were very happy together—happier still when we children came. But still my father had to dodge the White Eyes, for the danger of discovery always threatened him. One dark day we fled Mescal Mountain to seek safety in the back country. Food was scarce on the trail; I remember clearly my father coming back to camp one day empty-handed. He carefully placed his bow and arrows beside the rifle he had left with my mother; then he seated himself with his back against a pine. I ran to him and nestled against his chest. He cuddled me in his strong arms and bent his head over mine.

"My little daughter, I brought no food. The deer have gone to the high mountains."

"You brought yourself; that is better."

"She speaks true, Massai," said Zan-a-go-li-che, my mother. "When you are with us we can endure hunger."

My father smiled tenderly at her. "You are a good wife, and my children are good. I am sorry that you must share my danger."

My mother's face was beautiful to see. "Danger, like happiness, is to be shared, my husband."

As she spoke, she slipped the *tsach* from her back and took the baby from it. My little brother was old enough to walk and he liked to be free of his cradle. Zan-a-go-li-che reached for the buckskin food bag and gave each of us one handful of pulverized dried venison and mesquite bean meal. We dared not build a fire, but this is a good food raw and is very nourishing. Though the portion did not satisfy our hunger, nobody asked for more. Each knew that when food was available there was no need to ask, for our mother fed us when she could.

My older brother, who was later named Albert, had brought a wicker jug of water from the spring. After we had drunk and lain on the ground, my father spoke.

"I should have left Mescal Mountain when the warnings first came. When Ussen speaks, the Apache should obey. He warned me first by the twitching of the eyelid that always means one is in danger. But I knew that old Santos [a Mexican friend of the family] could not live long, and I would not leave him."

He was silent, staring into the darkness.

"Now the White Eyes are on our trail," he went on. "Two mornings past, when I went to the place where I had hidden the horses, a man tried to ambush me. Not till he raised his rifle was I sure that he had seen me. Then I had no choice—I had to kill him. You heard the shots and asked why I wasted bullets on a deer. It was not a deer; it was a man."

My mother spoke, "His horse?"

"It got away."

"It will go home and there will be soldiers on our trail from his place."

"Yes; sheriffs too, perhaps. Cowboys maybe—and those I dread more than any soldiers."

There was silence again for a long moment. "They cannot know who fired the shot," ventured my mother.

My father's laugh was short and bitter. "When has there been a White Eye killed west of the Río Bravo whose death has not been charged to Massai? When have I not been hunted like an animal?"

"But soldiers and Chiricahua scouts, too, came into our *ranchería* and did not find you, even though you were present when they inquired."

"They were looking for a tall man—one like Naiche—not for a short thin one like me."

"Why?"

"My friends, who were left on the train after my escape, must have told them that I was very large to protect me from being caught."

My mother said no more. After a time my father spoke again. "I must tell you that Ussen has again warned me. This time He has spoken clearly so that there can be no mistake.

"I am not to reach Mescalero; I may not reach the Río Bravo with you. But we are only one day's journey from the village of which I have told you."

He turned to Albert.

"My son, you are young to become the protector of your mother and the younger children. But you are well trained. Always I have foreseen the need and have made a brave of you, boy though you are. You are skillful with both bow and rifle. Bullets are swift and far-reaching, but arrows are silent and sure. Remember to use the rifle only when attacked by White Eyes. For game—the bow. It will obtain food for you."

"My father, I hear," replied Albert.

"I may not return in the morning. If I do not, take your mother and children to the Mexican village on the Río. Stay hidden in the brush until dark, for there may be White Eyes at that town. Watch for a house where there is no man, no big boy. Then, after dark, tap on the door and in the language of Santos ask for help.

"I have talked with those who know the place. The railroad crosses the river there on a trail built of logs. You too can cross that trail, no matter if the river is high. Hide by day and travel by night toward the Rising Sun till you reach the spring at the foot of the mountains. Your mother knows that place. Stay by the water until you can kill game. Then head for the White Mountain and skirt it to the south. There you will find a trail into the Rinconada. Your mother knows that place also."

I saw my mother's sad face light in a smile.

"From there she will guide you to her family. Stay on the Mescalero Reservation. It is my order."

"It will be obeyed, my father. But the horses?"

"You may not have the horses. The White Eyes cannot trail us, but they may be able to follow horses. I am telling you what to do if that happens."

My mother pulled the blanket over her face. My father went on, speaking quietly. "In the early morning I will go to the place where we hid the horses. You are to remain here. It is my order."

My brother bowed his head.

"If I do not return, my son, you are not to wait—you are to leave at once. It is safe to travel by day because of the dense undergrowth. Now we must sleep. I have spoken."

When I awoke it was still dark, but my mother was sitting up, listening.

"My brother," I whispered.

She laid her finger on my lips. "He followed your father. Hush."

I huddled close to her in fear and she drew me under her blanket. The others slept. Just as the first gray light stole into the east I heard a shot, then another, crashing loud in the stillness. My mother hugged me to her. She made no noise but her body shook.

It was daylight when I heard the light patter of moccasins. I touched my mother in the darkness. Soon my brother crept through the dense brush and joined us.

"They killed him?"

"I think so. The White Eyes had trailed the horses and were waiting for us. As he reached to untie his bay, there was a shot and he fell. Even as he did so he called to me to run. I did. I crossed the little hill and slid down the high steep bluff. Then I circled widely, walking on the rock ledge so that they might not be able to follow. Let us start now, as he commanded."

My mother shook her head. "He may not be dead. I cannot go until I know."

"They will be hunting for us. We must go!"

"Not even to save you children can I leave now. Take them and I will stay. Go to my people, as he told you. I do not fear death."

"But the baby! My sisters!"

"We will all stay. What does death mean, now that Massai is gone? I hope that he is dead. Death is better than being a captive of the White Eyes."

We lay in the thick brush at the edge of the mesa and watched. There was a camp in the canyon with many men and horses. Scouts left the camp, fanning out in all directions, some on horseback and some walking. Toward evening they came straggling back.

My mother again gave each of us a handful of our emergency rations. We drank from the jug; and with the remaining water mother bathed the baby, warming the water in her mouth and letting it trickle over his little body. Then she wiped him dry with soft, clean grass and packed him again in the *tsach*. He wore no clothing, but she covered him with the soft skin of a lynx before lacing the buckskin straps across him.

The White Eyes were building a big fire—a much bigger fire than was needed for cooking. It burned far into the night and must have been frequently replenished. Not even the White Eyes kept a big fire going all night. I wondered why these were so foolish. Twice I awakened to find my mother still sitting, still watching.

Next morning we could see nothing, for the canyon was filled with fog. When it lifted there were no White Eyes, no horses, and only a little smoke.

My mother spoke. "I will go down and see if I can find his body. It must have burial. No Apache would leave a relative or even a friend to the coyotes and vultures."

"But they may be waiting to ambush us," my brother objected.

"True. We must wait and keep careful watch all day. If we see nothing, we will risk going tomorrow."

"We are almost out of food," said my brother.

"Keep watch. I will try to find something."

"Let me try to kill a rabbit, mother."

"Are we animals, to eat raw meat? You know that we cannot cook it. No Apache would eat raw meat. There is still enough food for each to have a small bit. I will try to find some roots."

"Do not leave us, mother. On the way tomorrow we may find some cactus food."

She sat down beside us and covered her head.

That night we went to bed without eating; the food must be saved for morning so that we would have strength for the walk. We had water—and with that alone an Apache can endure much hunger.

My brother spoke again before we slept. "My father was a good man. Why did the White Eyes hate him, hunt him like a mad wolf, and finally kill him?"

"It is a hard thing to understand, my son. We cannot know why they want to kill all Apaches. Already they have robbed us of everything we had—our game, our land, our freedom. It was not enough. They want our lives also. That is all I can tell you."

"May I go with you to the camp, mother?"

"Yes, my son. Very early in the morning. Try to sleep now."

I think that my oldest sister was about twelve. (We kept no records, of course.) She kept the baby and us three younger girls while my mother and brother were gone. We did not ask to go. We did not cry. Apache children do not disobey, and they do not argue.

We huddled under the blankets until they returned. My mother carried a sack of meal and she gave each of us some of the food before she spoke. We ate it very slowly and when we had finished she gave us more.

"There is some for morning," she said.

We wanted to know about our father, but she did not tell us until later. They had approached the camp cautiously, even after they felt sure that there was no one there. They crept to the still-smoldering fire.

My mother took a long stick and stirred the ashes. There were partially burned sticks among them—and something else. Bones—charred bones. She raked them out of the ashes, laying them aside in a little heap. She tried to get every fragment. With them she found a small, blackened object—the buckle of an ammunition belt. She recognized the buckle by a dent made by a deflected bullet. She held it in her hands and talked to it.

"This is all I have left of you, my husband. All these years you took care of me and the children, and you were kind to us. Now you are nothing but bones and ashes.

"The White Eyes thought you a bad man, and they hunted you like an animal. They shot you down like a wild beast. They burned you so that in Ussen's land you would have no body. But Ussen knows all things and He can make you another body. To Apaches, the man who bravely defends his family, his home, and his people is a good man. He will not walk in darkness. To Ussen you are a good man. To me you are a good man, for I am an Apache. And I call to Ussen to avenge your death.

"I have nothing but this buckle and your memory. That is a good memory—one for your children to cherish. I have nothing to give your children but that memory, but it is enough. It will always give them courage. It will give them respect for the memory of their father.

"Right now your spirit may be here, listening. I cannot go with it on its journey, but always we will be with your memory."

She fastened the buckle to her belt with her knife and firesticks. Then she wrapped the bones carefully in her shawl, and she and Albert scooped out a hole with their hands and a sharp stone and buried what was left of my father there. They heaped stones upon the grave and left him to make The Journey. He had no horse, no weapons, not even a body. But Ussen would know that an Apache and a brave warrior came. Ussen would understand.[†]

We started toward the Río. My mother carried the baby on her back and the rifle in her hands. Albert went ahead with his bow and spear. My oldest sister had one blanket; the rest we had to leave, for we had no way to transport it. Cora had the water jug and the third girl the food bag. I walked till I was exhausted, and then they took turns carrying me for short distances. We kept on the ridge as long as we could, and then we stole from one clump of vegetation to another until we got near the village. We hid in a big

[†]The buckle was given to me for safekeeping by Alberta Begay. In a letter to this author dated April 2, 1957, Mrs. Evelyn Dahl, who carried out years of research on the Apache Kid, stated in part:

The men of the posse who killed Massai were Harry James, Bill Keene, Mike Sullivan, Walter Hearn, and Burt Slinkard. Ed James, Harry's younger brother, caught up with the party but would never admit who actually did the decapitating. Ed James died in '51 or '52. His last letter to me was in March '49. The height and weight he gives were a guess as the man was dead by the time he joined the party but James himself was 36 at the time. Bob Lewis, a sergeant in the first company of the Mounted Police, told me in 1950 before he died that fall, that he rode into the yard at Chloride one day shortly after the killing and found Bill Keene boiling the head in an iron vat. Both of them were sick at the stomach. When I asked Bob if the men had buried the body he said, "Hell no." [Note by author.]

clump of underbrush near San Marcial while my brother crept close and scouted the place.

He was gone about an hour; it was dark when he returned.

"There is one White Eye family at the tepee where the train stops," he reported. "The rest are Mexican. There are men at every house but one—that of an old woman at this edge of the *ranchería*."

"We go to that tepee," said my mother, "and ask for help."

When we tapped on the door a voice asked, "*¿Quién es?*"

In Spanish, mother replied: "A woman and children, cold and hungry."

The door opened.

"*Pasen*," said the old woman.

• • •

LAURENS VAN DER POST
(1906–1996)
From *Venture to the Interior*

Laurens van der Post was one of the last professional swashbucklers. Best known for his book and film, The Lost World of the Kalahari, *van der Post was a Briton born in Africa who served as a soldier for ten years, much of it in guerrilla warfare. (He also spent several years during World War II incarcerated in Japanese prison camps.)*

Van der Post's fame came as a result of his explorations of remote parts of Africa. In 1949, on an official government mission, he set out on foot to penetrate several little-known regions in the center of the continent. Wracked by shortages after the war, Great Britain hoped to use van der Post's discoveries to exploit new sources of food among its colonies. To a swashbuckler, such a mission was a good excuse for an old-fashioned adventure. In May, with companions Dicky Vance and Peter Quillan, both forestry officers for the province, van der Post pushed into the uplands of Nyasaland (today's Malawi) in hopes of climbing Mount Mlanje.

The dangers of mountain climbing are well known. Much under-rated, in contrast—as this account makes starkly clear—are the dangers of crossing rivers to get to the mountains.

Then, on that Friday, May 27, we climbed back on to the highest edge of the Little Ruo valley, about eight thousand five hundred feet high. There Quillan and Vance decided to take a short cut to our camp for the night and to send our bearers round the long, easy, known route with our guide. They did this because there was some unknown country in front that they thought we should see. As we stood on the rim, talking it over, in a cold breeze and under a grey, morning sky, I noticed far away in the plain below the lumber camp, the top of Mount Chiperone covered in cloud. The wind was blowing off it towards us and the weather was rapidly building up round it.

In a flash I remembered Boyd's warning to me in his house at Mlanje: "For God's sake, when that happens on the peak, look out."[1] So I said to Quillan and Vance: "It looks to me as if there is a Chiperone on the way. Don't let's take any chances! I don't like short-cuts anyway. My experience of mountains is that the longest way round is the shortest way there."

They turned round, regarded Chiperone solemnly, for a moment, looked at each other, nodded, and then Quillan said: "It is only a bit of morning mist. It will clear up soon. We'll be in the camp in an hour or two and can spend the afternoon resting. I think we can all do with it."

Because they were experts on the mountain, because it was their mountain and their mountain's weather, and because I have been trained to give priority to what appears to be reasonable, I stifled my instinct and said no more. But if the future had an origin other than in itself, then I believe it was born in that moment. Our decision was a bad decision, it was the

---

[1] Martin Boyd was district commissioner in the town of Mlanje. He had warned van der Post about sudden changes in the weather coming from Mount Chiperone, forty miles away, and bringing storms that lasted about five days; he explained that they called such storms "Chiperones."

wrong decision. Wrong begets wrong, starts a chain of accident and disharmony in circumstances which quickly develop a will of their own. These circumstances exact their own logical toll and must run their time to the bitter end, before the individual is able to break free of them again.

We sent our bearers on their way, kept only Vance's own gun-bearer with us, dropped quickly into the valley below, crossed a wide stream and started up on the other side. We climbed hard and fast. It was eleven o'clock exactly when we came out on the rim close on nine thousand feet. We sat down, ate a piece of chocolate, and prepared to admire the view.

Almost directly underneath us was the greatest of Mlanje's many dark gorges, the Great Ruo Gorge. The water of the Great Ruo river itself plunged down the top end of the gorge; fell with a wild, desperate, foaming leap into an abyss, thousands of feet deep. We could not see the bottom of it. On either side it was flanked by black, glistening, six-thousand-foot cliffs, tapering off into grey peaks nine thousand feet high. The whole of the gorge rustled, whispered, and murmured with the sound of falling water, which at every change of mountain air would suddenly break over us with a noise like the sound of an approaching hail-storm.

"You see that clump of cedars just beyond the fall," Vance said, "our camp is there. We shall be there within the hour."

As he spoke the mist came down. He and Quillan said it would soon lift. We waited. We got colder and colder. The mist rapidly thickened. It began to drizzle. At eleven-thirty we decided to do the best we could. The sun had vanished, the wind had dropped. Neither Vance, Quillan, I, nor, for that matter, any living person, had ever stood before where we then stood. In the sunlight one stone is very like another; but in the mist on Mlanje they were indistinguishable. Because of that terrible gorge we could not go farther down until we were past the head of the waterfall. So we set out along the peaks, keeping as near to their crest as we could.

Worst of all, the mist halo lay like a blanket over the noise of the fall. Not a sound came up to us. We had not even a whisper from it for guidance. The silence was really complete, except for our breathing, our boots squelching on the wet grass and moss or crunching on stone.

From eleven-thirty until four-thirty—and we had been going since seven without rest—we went up one peak and down into a bottom, up the other side and down again.

At half-past four the rifle-bearer said: "It is no good, Bwana; we are lost. Let us make a fire and wait for it to clear."

I said no. I knew it was no mist. It was a Chiperone and it came, so Boyd had said, in multiples of five days. We would be dead of cold before it cleared. I added, "At all costs, we must go down now. The night is not far off. We must get into a valley and then we can consider the next step."

So slowly down we went, down those steep, uneven slopes of Mlanje, listening carefully for the noise of falling water. But the whole mountain had gone as silent as the dead.

We slid and slithered in a way that was neither prudent nor safe. Suddenly at five the mist began to thin. The gun-bearer gave a tremendous shout. A warm golden glow was coming up to meet us and in a few minutes we were in the tawny-grass bottom of the Great Ruo itself, three miles above the gorge and four miles from our camp. We got to our camp at nightfall and the mist changed into a heavy, steady, drumming downpour of rain. The bearers were already in and Leonard had prepared our little mud-and-straw native hut.[2] We lay down by the side of the fire in the middle of the hut, a great glow of gratitude inside us. We were too tired to speak for half an hour or more, and listened to the violence of the rain.

"It is a Chiperone all right now," said Vance: "the point is, how long is it going to last?"

OUR CAMP WAS a disused, discarded lumber camp, the huts which had originally housed the native timber carriers. Once again, as often before in Africa, I thanked Providence for the African hut-builder. These insignificant-looking, brown beehive huts one dashes past by car or train in Africa are amazing. Considering the poor material, the lack of scientific

[2]Leonard was the team's native cook.

equipment and research, the lack of education of their humble builders, they are works of genius. Although the rain now pounded down so violently, not a drop came through the ancient thatch.

When we had recovered sufficiently, we went round to inquire after our bearers and found them, also under dry roofs, cooking their dinners round crackling cedar fires. They were a happy and cheering sight.

We told Leonard to stay with them in the dry. We did not want him splashing round in the wet, trying to wait on us. We went back, dried ourselves out thoroughly, and did our own cooking. I made a kettleful of hot coffee which we drank very sweet, laced liberally with my medicinal cognac. The cognac was a great improvement on the Portuguese brandy and a welcome and complete surprise. It was precisely the anticipation of moments like these that had made shopping in Blantyre such fun, and I drew a glow of reassurance from this slight justification of my planning.

We ate in silence. I myself was too full of an unutterable sense of well-being to attempt to speak. I think the others perhaps felt something else as well, for they both, particularly Vance, looked somewhat reproved by the experience of the day. Then silently we stretched ourselves out beside the fire, with a good heart, to sleep.

But I was too tired to sleep at once. I lay with my ear close to the ground and listened to the rain drumming down on the mountain. Among those vast peaks there was no other sound than this continuous, violent, downpouring of the rain. There was no light of stars or far-off reflection of town or hamlet; only the dying glow of the cedars from a dying world of trees. The night, the mountain, and the rain were woven tightly into a dark prehuman communion of absolute oneness. No leopard, pig, or antelope or elastic mountain gazelle would venture out on a night like this. It is precisely against moments like these that the leopards bury some portion of bird, bush ape, or pig, and leave it near their holes and caves. The summons riding the mountains with such desperate dispatch was not for animal or human hearts. But it was as if the earth underneath my head was slowly beginning to respond to this drumming, this insistent beat of the rain; to take up this rhythm of the rain; to answer this ceaseless knocking at its most secret door, and to open itself to this vast orchestration of its own natural, primeval elements, to begin to quicken its own patient pulse, and deep inside itself, in the core of its mountain, its Jurassic heart, to do a tap-dance of its own. Whenever I rose in the night to make up the fire there was the rain and this manner of the rain; and when I lay down again there was this deep, rhythmical response of the earth.

We woke finally at five and talked over the day while waiting for the kettle to boil. Our plan originally had been to go over the top of the mountain in the direction of Chambe.[3] But we found now that our experience of the day before among the peaks on the far side of the Ruo valley had made us all decide in the night against any more adventures in the clouds while the Chiperone was blowing. In this way the previous day influenced our behaviour. Our guide well knew the way over the top and, had it not been for that short-cut, I do not believe we would have changed our plans.

Vance now said he knew an easy way down off the mountain which led to a large tea estate at the bottom. Quillan said he knew it too, it was the old timber carriers' track. It was steep, but cut out in the side of the Great Ruo gorge and clearly defined. We could not go wrong. Only it meant abandoning the last part of the trip and that, he thought, would be a pity for me. I said firmly "Abandon." Vance then decided to go ahead to the tea-estate and get a truck to take us round by road to Likabula. With luck, he said, we could all be back on the mountain at Chambe that evening.

With our last eggs I made him a quick omelette for breakfast, and sent him off in the rain. Quillan and I followed slowly with the carriers.

We set out at eight but the rain was so thick and violent that there was only a dim, first-light around us. We went slowly. The track was steep and highly dangerous. On the left of us, only a yard or so away, was that deep cleft down to the Great Ruo gorge. The bearers too had great difficulty with their loads. They had to lower themselves down from one level to another by cedar roots and help one another down perilous mud precipices.

As we went down, the noise of falling water all round us became deaf-

---

[3]A fertile valley at the western end of the Mlanje range.

ening. Whenever there was a slight lift of the rain and mist, the half-light, the mepacrine gloom[4] on the mountain would be suddenly illuminated by a broad, vivid flash of foaming white water leaping down the face of smooth black cliffs, thousands of feet high. We had to shout in places to make ourselves heard.

Moreover the mountain itself, the very stones on which we trod, the mud wherein we slid, seemed to begin to vibrate and tremble under this terrible pounding of water. At moments when we rested, the ground shook like a greaser's platform in the engine-room of a great ship. This movement underfoot, combined with the movement of the flashing, leaping, foaming water in our eyes, and driving rain and swirling mists, gave to our world a devastating sense of instability. The farther down we went, the more pronounced it became, until I began to fear that the whole track would suddenly slither like a crocodile from underneath my feet and leave men falling for ever under the rain and Mlanje's cataclysmic water. It needed conscious effort of will to keep me upright, and I found this all the more difficult because of a new complication that was arising. I began to feel as if my very senses were abandoning their moorings inside myself.

Luckily this stage of the journey did not last too long. Two and a quarter hours later our track suddenly became easier and broader.

Quillan said, "We'll soon be off it now."

We came round a bend in the track and there, to our surprise, was Vance. He was sitting at the side of a fast stream of water which was pouring over the track and had evidently held him up. He was joining some lengths of creeper, of monkey rope, together.

"I didn't want to cross this stream without a rope," he said. "I have been up and down this stream as far as possible and this is the best place to try it. It doesn't look difficult. Do you think this will do?"

He handed me his rope of creepers.

"No! Certainly not," I said, and looked at the stream.

Its beginnings, above us, were lost in the mist and rain. Then it suddenly

---

[4]Mepacrine, also known as quinacrine, is an antimalarial drug that can affect mood.

appeared out of the gloom about a hundred yards above, charging down at us at a steep angle, and finally, just before it reached us, smashing itself up behind a tremendous rock, deeply embedded in the side of the gorge. Somewhere behind the rock it reassembled its shattered self and emerged from behind it flowing smoothly. For about twenty yards it looked a quiet, well-behaved stream but, on our left at the track's edge, it resumed its head-long fall into the terrible main Ruo gorge below us. I now went to this edge and looked over, but the falling water vanished quickly in the gloom and told me nothing. Only the ground shook with the movement as my eyes and head ached with the noise.

I came back and found Quillan lighting a fire.

"Our bearers are nearly dead with cold," he explained. "They'll crack up if we don't do something. Two wood-cutter blokes died here of exposure two years ago. But if I can get this fire going for them in the lee of this rock, our chaps will be all right."

The rain poured down even more heavily than before, and it looked darker than ever. The shivering Negroes, the bamboos bent low with rain, the black rocks, were like figures and things moving in the twilight of a dream.

Again I went and looked at the stream above. Vance appeared to have chosen rightly. The stream was swollen but did not look dangerous at that point, particularly with a good rope. Higher up it would have been hopeless.

"I tell you what, Dicky," I said. (It was the first time I had called him that and I don't know why I did, except that we all suddenly seemed to be very close to one another.) "I tell you what, Dicky. We'll take all our ropes, you knot them together and then I'll go across. I am bigger than you."

"I don't think that is necessary," he said. "I know the way. You don't. And with a rope it will be easy."

We joined up the ropes, tested the result in every way, pulling it, leaning on it. It seemed tight and strong. We took Vance's valise straps and added them to the end, just in case; I then tied it round Vance's chest with a knot that couldn't slip. I made sure it could not tighten and hinder his breathing.

As I tied it I said, "Dicky, are you sure you are happy about this and know how to do it, for if you are not I would much rather do it myself?"

"Of course I know," he said with a deep laugh. "I have done it scores of times in Burma. And I must hurry. I want to get those poor black devils under shelter as soon as I can."

"Well, remember," I said, "keep your face to the stream; always lean against it; go into it carefully and feel well round your feet with your stick before you move."

He took up the stout stick that we had cut for him. I called Quillan and two of the bearers. Quillan and I took the rope. I braced my feet against a tree on the edge of the stream, just in case, but I was not at all worried.

Vance waded in. The water came about to his navel. He went steadily on for some distance then, to my bewilderment, turned his back lightly on the stream. It was the first deviation from plan.

He took another step or two, stopped, suddenly abandoned his stick to the stream and yelled to us, "Let out the rope!"

It was the second deviation from plan. I was horrified. What the hell was he up to? Before we had even properly grasped his meaning he had thrown himself on the stream and was swimming a breast-stroke. As was inevitable, the stream at once caught him and quickly swept him to where it foamed and bubbled like a waterfall over the edge of the track. The unexpected speed with which all of this had happened was the most terrifying thing about it. Even so, Vance had got to within a foot of the far bank, was on the verge of reaching it—when the water swept him over the edge and he disappeared from our view.

Quillan and I were braced for the shock. As we saw it coming we both shouted for the bearers, who rushed to our assistance in a body. The rope tightened in a flash. The strain was tremendous. Vance's body, no longer waterborne but suspended out of sight, below the edge of the rocky track, with the weight and stream of water pouring on top of it, strained the rope to the utmost. Yet it held.

I think it would have continued to hold if the angle and violent impact of the water on the body had not now with incredible speed whipped Vance along the sharp edge of the rocks, swung him from the far side over towards our bank and chafed the rope badly in the process. It still held for a second or two. We worked our way along it towards him—were within two yards of him—when the rope snapped.

At that moment we knew that he was dead. Anyone who stood with us in the black rain, amid those black cliffs in that world of storming, falling, rushing, blind water, must have known that he was dead. Quillan turned round, lifted a face to me naked and bare with misery, and said hoarsely, "What to do, now? He is dead, you know!"

I nodded and said, "Please take a search-party as far as you can, Peter, and see what you can see."

He immediately set out. I called Leonard and some bearers and started to undo our baggage. It was obvious we could not cross now. We had lost all our rope; we had lost one body with a rope, we could not risk losing one without a rope. Nor could we stay there.

Quillan was back almost at once. I was not surprised. We were, as I have said before, on the edge of the Great Ruo gorge.

He shook his head. "Not a sign, not a hope. He is dead and there is nothing we can do now except to see that these fellows don't conk out."

He indicated the bearers.

We called them all round us. They were cold and terribly shaken by Vance's death. One old man was crying and they were all shivering as if with malaria. We told them to dump their loads and to start back up the mountain to the huts we had slept in the night before. A moan of despair rose up from them. They said they wanted to sit by the river, wanted to make a fire and wait for the sun. But I knew that that only meant that the spirit had gone out of them, that they had given up hope and were resigned to do no more than sit down and die in comfort.

It was then that Leonard, the puny plainsman, the sophisticated native from the towns, stood up, unsolicited, and lashed them with his tongue. I don't know what he said, but he insulted them into some shape of spirit.

We distributed all our own and Vance's clothes among them. That cheered them. They began to laugh and to tease one another, at the sight of their companions in tennis shirts, grey sweaters too big for them, in green, blue, red, and grey striped pyjamas, and my own green jungle bush-shirts with their red 15 Corps flashes still on them.

I expect it was an incongruous sight in that world of rain, falling water and black, impersonal rock, but I did not find it at all funny. It seemed to me to fill the cup of our misery to overflowing. I expect whatever gods sit on this African Olympus might well find it amusing to kill a young man of twenty-eight in order to dress up some of the despised, ubiquitous outcasts of their African kingdom in silk pyjamas in the pouring rain. To me, just to kill was bad enough; to mock the kill an intolerable perfection of tragedy. I came near to joining in Quillan's tears at that moment, but fortunately I got angry as well, so angry that I believe if my strength had matched my rage I could have picked up the whole of Mlanje and thrown it over the edge of the world into the pit of time itself.

I walked up to the bearers in anger such as I have never known and told them, by looks and gestures, to get the hell up the mountain without delay. In that mood, Quillan and I got them up the steep, slippery sides of the gorge that we had come down only a few moments before.

At half-past twelve we were back in our camp of the night before; we started a great, blazing fire and dried ourselves. The warmth and the sight of fire and smoke effected an amazing revival of spirit among the Africans. I was discussing with Quillan a plan for going out myself through the Fort Lister gap to fetch help, leaving him there with the bearers because he knew the language, when the oldest forester spoke up and said: "You can't do that, Bwana. It is too far. But I know a short way over the top that will bring us to Chambe safely by sundown."

Quillan asked them all if they had heard what the forester said, under-stood, approved, and were prepared to follow him implicitly. They all said emphatically, "Yes!" It was the only thing to do and they would do it.

By one o'clock we were climbing back up the peaks behind our camp, into clouds and into rain which seemed more violent than ever.

Peter Quillan was at his best. He was firm yet patient with the bearers, steadily urged them on, but it could not have been easy. He was heart-broken, and from time to time I could see he was in tears. He was deeply attached to Vance and was blaming himself bitterly for the accident. I did my best to comfort him. I couldn't see how he was to be blamed at all, and if he were, then what about me? He, after all, had not been worried by a sense of the future. It wasn't he who had lain awake at nights half stifled by a sense of death and listening to the dark drummer of Africa beating-up the weather round Mlanje. But as I comforted him and we slowly forced the bearers up the black peaks in front of us, I too was sick at heart and desperately tired.

Without any preliminary training I had been scrambling round these monstrous peaks from dawn until sunset for nine days, and I could now hardly lift my legs. Heaven knows I was fit, my lungs and spirit were all right, and my rage with the mountain and its gorge spurred me on. The problem was purely mechanical. My legs and feet were so abused that the muscles rebelled and would not react instinctively. It seemed to me that all my reflexes had gone. I had to treat each step as a mechanical and separate entity in the movement of my body. I could move only with a deliberate, calculated, conscious, and determined effort of will. At one moment I thought seriously of retiring to the huts lest I should not be able to continue, and so should bring disaster on the others.

Quillan was amazing. His forester's muscles were intact. He cheered and helped me on by word and example. When, afterwards, we told people of this journey over the highest and wildest part of Mlanje they would hardly credit it. But on the day of Vance's death we did nearly twenty miles' climbing. I hope never to do such a journey again.

For two hours after leaving the hut we continued to climb, at the steepest of angles, into deepening cloud and rain. Our guide, the old forester, in his rags and tatters, dripping with water, was unbelievable. He climbed at our head with his stick held in one hand in front of him. Every now and then he parted the grasses with it, peered at them intently, or tapped a stone, listening carefully to its ring, and then changed direction to the left or the right; but he never faltered. Over and over again the rain and mist completely hid him from my view. It was dark, it was black; even at the best of times it was grey all around us.

After two hours, as far as one could judge in the mist, we seemed to pass right over the top of a peak, and our course began to drop slowly down. The relief to my muscles was timely.

Quillan offered me some whisky and water. I do not drink spirits as a rule, but I accepted gratefully and pushed on with renewed energy. At four o'-clock, we suddenly came out of the mist and rain; we walked through it as if it had been a wall. At one minute it was raining; the next we were in the sunlight looking down on the long ledge by Tuchila.

We climbed down there as fast as we could. We had seven miles to go before we reached that razor saddle, and unless we got there before dark we should be unable to cross to Chambe and shelter.

We got down easily enough, but getting up and then down the river gashes and finally up again on to that high steep shoulder by Chambe was for me a bitter and protracted agony. However, we got to the ridge where Val Vance was nearly killed, just as the sun went down.[5]

It was a frightening sunset, a sort of cosmic schism of light and dark-ness. On our left was that immense, dark pile of rain, turning and wheel-ing constantly over the bulk of Mlanje, wheeling in such a manner, with such fantastic contortions of cloud shapes, that to my tired eyes it looked as if the devils of death were charging up and down those peaks on phan-tom, skeleton chargers. Yet to our right lay Chambe with a golden after-glow of sunlight on it, untroubled and serene, as if it had never known death or disaster of any kind. Less than a fortnight before I had seen Mlanje from afar at just such an hour, in such a way with this same pattern of fair and foul, dark and light, on it. Had the same pattern also been in me?

• • •

[5]Dicky and his wife, Valerie ("Val") Vance, along with their two-month-old baby, had been staying at the forestry depot on the mountain when van der Post and Quillan arrived, and Vance decided to join them. He told them of how Val had almost walked off this ridge, not seeing the drop in a thick mist, on her first exploration of the mountain.

MICHAEL RAY TAYLOR

(b. 1959)

"Down to a Sunless Sea"

From *Cave Passages*

If there were any doubt about just how dangerous the relatively new pastime of cave diving is, Michael Ray Taylor's gripping account of the tragedy at Zacatón in east-central Mexico should resolve it. During the last fifty years, cavers and cave divers have performed some phenomenal explorations all over the world. So far, however, at least in English, no literature celebrating those deeds of a quality comparable to the rich narratives of mountaineering and polar exploration has emerged. Taylor, a young journalist and serious caver who writes about his passion for American magazines, seems to be marching in the vanguard of that overdue body of writing.

April 6, 1994

At high noon the *norte* rages. I stand with a handful of reporters and ranchers above an enormous water-filled sinkhole called Zacatón. We stare down

70 feet at the surface of a warm thermal spring. White plumes of sulfur swirl through the water like milk. The sinkhole's diameter is greater than the length of a football field; its contours define a natural arena gouged from stone. We stalk the perimeter of the hole, straining for a glimpse of two men who should soon rise from a world scuba depth record, achieved in absolute darkness over 1,000 feet below the water's surface.

Hot wind snatches hats from our heads and words from our mouths. Bright circles of floating saw grass, 10 to 30 feet in diameter, bounce across the water like slow-motion billiard balls. I try to comprehend the spring's impossible depth. If the Empire State Building sank to the bottom, I could step onto its main observation deck from where I stand. We amble like tourists. Hands in pockets, cameras dangling from straps, we wait for something to happen.

Somewhere down in the water is Sheck Exley, a high school calculus teacher and karate expert from Live Oak, Florida. Exley, forty-five, is also the undisputed master of deep scuba, which is practiced mostly in cave pools and flooded pits. He has logged more than 4,000 successful cave dives, far more than anyone else. It is Exley's own depth record of 867 feet, set in 1989 at another Mexican cave spring called Nacimiento Mante, that he and a colleague, Jim Bowden, have set out to break this morning.

Bowden is a fifty-two-year-old adventurer and dive instructor from Austin. Five years ago, he discovered Zacatón after more than a decade spent searching the springs and caves of Mexico and Central America for deep places where no human had been. Under Exley's tutelage, Bowden has trained for the past year for this moment. He poured thousands of dollars into the equipment needed to make a record descent. He recovered from a case of the bends—suffered on a training dive at Zacatón in November— that would have retired, if not killed, other cave divers.

Closer to the surface, yet hidden from us by the suspended sulfur, three support divers hover, waiting to assist in an anticipated ten-hour decompression. A 1,000-foot descent packs nitrogen into the blood like bubbles in beer; rising too fast would rip joints and muscles from within. The hours of slow ascent, while they breathe precise mixtures of oxygen, helium, and nitrogen at prescribed levels, will let the divers properly outgas, or shed, the excess nitrogen.

Parallel ropes, 25 feet apart, are tied to rocks at the water's edge. They dangle halfway down the pit's plumbed depth — 1,085 feet at this side. (No other soundings along the perimeter have been taken.) The twin ropes hold more than two dozen dive tanks that are to bring Bowden and Exley back to air. Two hours ago the explorers entered the sinkhole by swimming through a 600-foot-long horizontal cave, thus avoiding a difficult rappel down the cliff face. Hidden 30 feet below the floating grass, this natural tunnel carries currents that rise from the depths of Zacatón to spill from a nearby spring.

At last two of the support divers surface. The wind gusts so strongly that none of us above can hear what they are saying. But we can see. We see a woman in a wet suit grabbing the shoulders of another woman, holding her, placating her. We see bubbles, as regular as breath, plopping up near one of the ropes. We see the other rope hanging in water that is chillingly still.

The sun beats down. The hot wind blows. A few others gather at the edge of Zacatón, among them Marcus Gary, who at twenty-three is by far the youngest member of the expedition. "What's going on?" Gary yells to the figures treading water 70 feet below. They don't answer. Perhaps the wind has kept them from hearing.

The third support diver surfaces to join the other two. Beside them, bubbles rise from one line only.

Two photographers use their telephoto lenses to close in on the women in the water. What they see makes them stop snapping frames. "Oh my," one of them says, his voice barely audible in a lapse between gusts.

Gary moves closer to the edge, leaning precariously from a gnarled tree. "What?" he shouts. Again, louder: "Hey! What! Happened!"

The photographer silently lowers his camera and passes it to me. I bring into sharp focus the tear-streaked face of my friend Mary Ellen Eckoff, who once held the women's world scuba depth record and is the longtime companion of Sheck Exley. Just then she looks up and screams, "No!"

The shout echoes from the limestone walls and dies in a sob that the wind carries to us all.

EACH YEAR, AN average of 600 people are certified as cave divers by the National Speleological Society Cave Diving Section, located in Branford, Florida. According to Joe Odom, chairman of the society, there are now[1] more than 14,000 certified cave divers, compared with just 1,000 in 1984. Yet from rank novices to those on the cutting edge of discovery, all cave divers are continually faced with their own mortality.

The sport is to open-water scuba as flying an F-16 is to piloting a Cessna. The difference is that the weekend pilot can't grab the stick of a fighter, while Joe Scuba needs only to find an underwater hole and swim in. It is a sport in which nearly all errors are fatal. Most cave divers with more than five years' experience have participated in at least one body recovery. Sheck Exley made a total of thirty-six recoveries.

The dead are usually open-water divers, sometimes even dive instructors, unaware of the special hazards of submerged caves: loose ceilings; silt that rises from the floor of disturbed passages to darken water that was transparent going in; vertigo induced by huge irregular chambers, confusing some to the point that they literally cannot tell up from down; mind-numbing cold and depth; flashlights that won't operate below shallow depths, or, believe it or not, no light source at all. Bodies have been found within ten feet of a silt-obscured entrance, fingers scraped raw from a last, desperate attempt to claw through solid rock. Sometimes untrained cave divers panic and drown for no discernible reason. At least four died in the past decade with more than thirty minutes of air left in their tanks and an easy way out.

Odom reminds his students: "When you've reached your maximum pen-

[1]In 1996.

etration"—by definition, when a cave diver has used one-third of his air reserves—"you are farther from breathable air than a space shuttle astronaut. NASA could scrub a shuttle mission, de-orbit, and land quicker than you could exit a cave. Your technology needs to be at least as redundant as theirs."

Those who make it through proper cave training and certification enjoy a safety record far better than that of open-water divers. *Basic Cave Diving: A Blueprint for Survival*, published by the NSS-CDS, is one of the first manuals to be read by prospective cave divers. To bring home the danger of the sport, each chapter begins with a terse accident account, illustrating how the flouting of a particular safety procedure needlessly cost a life (or several). Such reading can make even the laziest student suddenly attentive.

The author of this and six other cave-diving texts, and hundreds of published cave-diving articles, is Sheck Exley.

June 29, 1968

Saturday. Wakulla Springs, Florida. Children laugh on the beach. Teenagers jackknife and cannonball from the high dive. Smells of grilled chicken mix with Coppertone and cabbage palms. Somewhere, Jim Morrison sings "Hello, I Love You" on a transistor radio. The 72-degree water hums with the pinging motor of a glass-bottomed boat. Tourists pass over the powerful boil, gawking at the great cave 120 feet below. The water carries another sound too, something distant, metallic, rhythmic: *Hiss. Bubble. Hiss. Bubble.*

Pure water, stuff so clear and clean that it will one day spawn an industry, flows under the whole of North Florida, carving up hard white limestone that rings like a bell, chuckling forth at hundreds of great blue springs, of which Wakulla is the greatest. Today, once again, its deep water has lured the Exley boys, nineteen-year-old Sheck and sixteen-year-old Edward, all the way from Jacksonville.

Irby Sheck Exley, Jr., home from the University of Georgia, dives every weekend, paying for equipment and compressed air with a summer job in the parts department of his father's Volkswagen dealership. In the five years since he took a basic scuba certification course at a YMCA pool, he's gained a reputation among the slow-talking southern boys who hang out at the Panhandle's dive shops. They say Sheck can make a tank of air last longer than it ought to, can keep a calm head at depths that should knock him woozy with nitrogen. Maybe it's the mental discipline of karate—he's only months away from a black belt—that lets him slow his heart and lungs by sheer will, allows him to think straight at 300 feet below. Maybe it's his obsession with gear, the way he rebuilds half the things he buys, finds and corrects potential flaws in regulators designed by naval engineers.

Sheck takes after his father, Irby, in his compact, muscular build and chiseled good looks, in his ability to stare a stranger in the eye and win his trust in an instant. It's as if Sheck inherited along with the face the *confidence* of the man who survived two and half years of infantry service all over the European theater; who walked out of the swamps of Clyo, Georgia, to finish a college education; who worked his way to the top of a Ford tractor dealership before starting his own shop. But put the boys together and Edward's the one who looks the natural athlete. Sixteen and already six feet tall, he's tan as Tab Hunter, good with a basketball. Edward's the one the girls watch from their beach towels as the brothers walk over the sand, carrying their masks and fins into Wakulla.

Sheck might go all afternoon without saying two words.

Edward has the old man's gift of gab, always the center of attention. He flirts at the water's edge. There's an easy and almost infectious wildness about him. Back when ten-year-old Sheck was cataloging—by sex, size, and species—the snakes that lived in the swamp across the street from their suburban home, seven-year-old Edward was slipping them down girls' dresses.

Tanks and regulators sit in the back of Sheck's Beetle, ready for another spring the two plan to visit on the way home. Signs in the Wakulla parking lot prohibit scuba. Old Mr. Ball, of the Du Pont clan, owns the springs and half of Wakulla County. He hasn't let anyone don scuba gear on the property since the 1950s. But Wakulla is a great place for free diving, for the brothers to see how long they can hold their breath and how far they can push the needle on Sheck's new depth gauge. They swim effortlessly out to the deep water, where they take turns strapping the stainless-steel dial on their wrists.

Over and over again they hyperventilate and head for the bottom, waiting until the last possible second to turn and point their bursting lungs toward the Florida sun. Edward pushes the needle to 40 feet. Sheck takes it to 45. Edward makes 52. Sheck focuses his mind, relaxes, and hits 60 feet. Edward laughs and sucks in mighty gusts, hyperventilating to the edge of consciousness. Sheck watches his brother plunge to 60 feet and keep going, swimming deeper than either of them has gone without scuba. He watches Edward start to turn and suddenly go limp. He watches Edward begin to float slowly downward.

Sheck hyperventilates and kicks with everything he's got. It's not enough: The bottom is so very far away. Edward grows smaller in the distance. After three fruitless efforts, Sheck climbs out of the water, shouting for help. He runs to his car for the air tanks, but another swimmer, a certified diver, convinces Sheck that he's too exhausted and panicked to dive. This man straps on the tank, running back down the beach as seconds tick by. He enters the water and pumps his fins. *Bubble. Hiss. Bubble. Hiss.* Risking the bends, the swimmer pulls Edward from the sandy bottom and up to the beach. Before a panicked crowd, Sheck pounds blood-tinged water from his brother's lungs, willing him to live, calmly and correctly breathing life into him. Just life enough to place Edward into an ambulance and onto a machine. Late that night, with his parents standing by the bed, with Sheck and his younger sister Beth nearby, the machine is turned off.

Edward is gone.

June 8, 1972

After Edward's death, Sheck turns his grief into a drive for perfection underwater, for safety and technique, for achievement without mishap. He begins diving with Ned DeLoach, the most experienced cave diver of that time. By 1970, he holds world records for both linear distance traveled and depth achieved in a cave dive. His gear designs and safety procedures are adopted by much older, more experienced divers.

People pay attention to Sheck Exley, pay him compliments. Sheck always turns the compliments around, praising the speaker: *Nonsense, I didn't do anything special. I'm sure you could have done the same. Probably a lot better. The important thing is that we had a safe dive.*

He confides to a friend, "I can't stop diving, but I can make it safer. I've got to. I can't put my parents through that kind of pain again."

Sheck makes his black belt, spends hours a day in exercise. He eliminates every ounce of body fat. He writes, reads poetry, plays the piano, toys with differential equations, listens to Beethoven.

Today he has come home with his business degree. The swamp across the street has been drained, has begun to fill with increasingly prosperous-looking homes. The walls of his father's office have been covered with plaques and certificates, all testifying to a community pillar: head of the Jacksonville Chamber of Commerce, chairman of the annual United Way drive, Sunday school teacher at the Ortega Methodist Church. Sheck sits across from the desk, waiting for his father to come home.

Irby closes the door and sits down. "You wanted to talk?"

"Dad, I'd like a job."

The older man nods. "All right. I've got a question to ask." He looks his son in the eye. "Do you want a job, or do you want a career?"

"What's the difference?"

"Son, a job is coming in at eight, punching the clock, and at five o'clock you punch the clock and leave. If you want to develop a career, you come in at eight o'clock, punch the clock, and at five o'clock, if the business needs you there to do something, you stay and do it for the good of the company. If you want to sit in my chair at my desk, you've got to earn the right. If it's a Friday afternoon, and you see that there's a company need for you to come in the next day, you come in the next day. Even if you have a diving project planned. Now, that is the difference between having a job and developing a career."

"Well, I want that. That's fine."

They shake hands.

April 21, 1980

By the time Sheck has worked his way through parts, sales, and account-ing to assume the position of general manager of Westside Volkswagen, I'm a twenty-year-old senior at Florida State University. With two college room-mates, I have begun to climb and crawl into the air-filled caverns dotting the Florida Panhandle, crystal-lined tunnels scoured by the springs of a pre-vious geologic age. We have joined a university cave club, progressing to the complex passages of Climax Cave, an eight-mile labyrinth in nearby South Georgia.

The muddy rooms of Climax are punctuated with sumps, or cave pools, some of them leading to known tunnels flooded in the 1950s, when con-struction of a dam thirty miles away raised the area water table. Our club suspects that other sumps lead to virgin territory. This weekend, five cave divers and fifty cave sherpas—volunteer labor to hump tanks and gear—have gathered at Climax for a major underwater push. My roommates and I are sherpas. Support teams work ten-hour shifts, hauling gear to and from three distant in-cave sites, unlikely blue holes opening amid muck and limestone.

My job is to lower heavy air tanks down a 30-foot entrance pit and then ferry them, one at a time, through a twisted 300-foot crawlway, a sandy tube punctuated by tight squeezes. Other sherpas move tanks from the end of the crawls to the widely separated pools. We work well in advance of the divers, who are to arrive "fresh" for the penetration effort.

I'm eating a tuna sandwich on the far side of the crawls when the divers begin to trickle in. Several stop to rest, and to check the schedule with the caver in charge of the event. The divers boast varied backgrounds. There's a clean-cut aerospace engineer and a long-haired, tie-dyed Southerner whose main source of income is his own plasma. Yet they all seem pretty much alike. I expected a little macho swaggering—after all, hundreds of volunteer man-hours support this effort. All I see is quiet determination. They joke about the difficulties of the crawl, but each is detail oriented, picky. I watch two of them unpack (each carries three or four large duffels) and gear up for a sump. It is impossible to observe such a highly regi-mented routine without thinking of a preflight check.

One of the quietest in that group is Sheck Exley, introduced to me as "the grand old man of Florida cave diving." He is thirty years old. Of medium height, powerfully built, he looks as if he's stepped from a turn-of-the-century boxing poster: thick mustache balanced on a sharp face; grooved dimples cutting toward an angular jaw; short, wavy brown hair; muscular chest and arms; skin as pale as a shark's belly.

Exley asks my roommate to lead him on to his appointed sump, in the room called Batman's Den. There's no questioning the calm authority in his voice. They push on.

Later I learn that my friend took Exley down a wrong fork. They spent four hours lost, eventually finding their way from the maze of passages to Batman's Den. Exley, fatigued from the difficult caving, decided to call the dive, saying a primary safety rule was to never dive when tired. The other two teams dive without incident, finding only a few hundred feet of new passage.

The haul out proves as long and difficult as the haul in. As I shove an unused tank back through the crawls, a protective valve cover malfunctions. Nudged by the tunnel wall, the valve twists open, spewing air and sand in my face. The sudden wind extinguishes my carbide miner's lamp and shoots sand down my coveralls. I can't reach the valve, so I lie in darkness for the few minutes it takes the tank to empty, eyes shut tight against the grit.

I imagine myself as a diver, the crawlway as a water-filled sump, and this tank as my last. I picture escaping air pooling into bubbles in the ceiling. In water, the sand I lie in would become a brown, enveloping fog. I would float upside down, my face pressed to the roof, and breathe for the five or ten minutes it would take the loose air to retreat into tiny channels in the rock. If I were very near a dry cave, I would hyperventilate, then swim for it. If not, I'd have time to compose a few last words for my dive log.

The tank expires with a hiss. I light my lamp and resume the schlepp out of Climax, resolving never, under any circumstances, to go cave diving.

DIVING FOR DEPTH increases underwater danger geometrically. The tremendous pressure reduces body volume by up to a third, leaving divers swimming inside suddenly huge wet suits. Descent on compressed air can cause nitrogen narcosis (also called rapture of the deep), a dangerous light-headedness that can lead to fatal errors of judgment. Simple tasks become confusing; divers may feel something similar to a drug-induced euphoria. Meanwhile, oxygen becomes increasingly toxic. Dive tanks empty quickly. At extreme depths some of the gases commonly mixed with oxygen—usually helium and nitrogen—themselves become toxic.

As divers push below 600 feet, they are exposed to perhaps the greatest danger of all: high-pressure nervous syndrome (HPNS), a neurological reaction to rapidly increasing pressure. The eyes shrink, causing divers to see flashing auras around people and objects. Accurately depicted in the science-fiction film *The Abyss*, HPNS can cause violent body tremors, convulsions, hallucinations, and death. Naval and oil company divers successfully battle the syndrome by descending slowly, inside submersible habitats—expensive steel capsules that would be impossible to transport into most caves.

Divers with COMEX, a French petroleum firm, have worked successfully below 2,400 feet. But such divers descend in fully equipped habitats over a period of days, acclimating to the depth while watching videos and eating TV dinners. After spending days at the bottom, conducting short dives between long rests, the slow rise to the surface may take weeks. "Open-circuit" divers, with no habitat to retreat to and only minutes of breathing time on their backs, face a near certainty of HPNS from deep descents. The syndrome often hits in combination with a condition called "compression arthralgia," known to navy divers as "no joint juice" because it feels as if their knees, elbows, and wrists have suddenly rusted solid.

December 17, 1989

I sit in my office and dial a Florida number. "I can tell you everything you need to know about Sheck Exley in four letters," says the voice on the line, an easygoing drawl reminiscent of Chuck Yeager. "All you need to know is u-g-l-y."

I've called to ask about joining his surface team on the next Mante effort, and to try to talk the publicity-shy diver into letting a known writer hang around him for a few days. Although I haven't seen Exley since that day in Climax Cave, I've followed his career in the pages of the *National Speleological Society News*. I know that in the mid-1980s, he became intrigued with research on scuba and rapid decompression. He studied a series of rapid submarine dives made two decades earlier by Hans Keller, a pioneer in mixed-gas diving. The deepest point Keller reached in his sub was 305 meters. The diver who accompanied him (a journalist of limited underwater experience) panicked at the bottom and swam away from the habitat until he passed out and died.

Exley had located a number of very deep water-filled caves in Mexico; rapid descent on mixed gas seemed to be the only way to see where they went. He began diving with Jochen Hasenmeyer, a German who had taken away Exley's early depth record in the 1970s. Hasenmeyer had recently set a seemingly unassailable open-circuit (as opposed to a dive aided by submersible habitat) scuba mark of 656 feet.

The deep work involved travel to France, Mexico, the Caribbean, and elsewhere, and travel involved time spent away from the family business. In 1985, Exley resigned as a full partner in his father's dealership and began teaching advanced algebra and calculus at rural Suwanee High School in Live Oak, Florida. He bought Cathedral Canyon, a long and complex underwater cave near Live Oak. A house trailer at the entrance became his home. He established the school's karate club and began leading teenagers in strenuous workouts after school. On weekends, school holidays, and during the summer, he was free to travel to deep sites.

The years Exley spent training advanced divers have helped him develop a passion for teaching. He is popular at the high school, known for drawing smiley faces in his pie charts on the blackboard. When a student misses an answer, "Mr. X" will roll his eyes and say "Noooooo" in a way that puts the class in hysterics. He writes his home number on the board, labels it "Mr. X's Fabulous Hotline." "Call me day or night if this stuff gives you trouble," he says. Many call with troubles that have nothing to do with differential equations. Exley makes personal projects of wild sixteen-year-old boys who've had a brush with the law or are on the verge of dropping out.

One by one, he pulls them into the karate club. He teaches them to avoid danger through physical and mental discipline, to take control of their lives by thinking.

One by one, he calmly breathes life into them.

IN JANUARY 1989, Exley had established the longest distance traveled in a single cave dive, 10,450 feet, going in and out the same route, solo, in his backyard cave. By the time he emerged, he had been submerged for fourteen hours, a third of that in decompression—also a world duration record. That April, in Nacimiento Mante, he surpassed Hasenmeyer's record with a dive to 868 feet.

Unlike other cave divers at the highest levels of achievement—notably, Bill Stone and Wes Skiles—Exley made these record dives without fanfare. He didn't seek support from National Geographic or the BBC. After the Mante dive, *Good Morning America* called to invite him on the show. So did *Today*. Exley turned them down.

One cave diver who stopped by Exley's camp at Mante was Jim Bowden. Like Exley, Bowden had labored for years in a successful family business— an Austin photo studio—and then gave it up for what he called "the old Star Trek syndrome": going where no one has gone before. Traveling through Mexico and Belize on a shoestring, often alone or with only two or three friends, Bowden had discovered and explored more underwater passage than many huge, well-funded expeditions. In 1986, he and a few other divers had formed a small organization called the Proyecto Espeleológico de Buceo Sierra Madre Oriental, through which they solicited official recognition and support from government agencies and corporate sponsors.

Bowden and Exley hit it off. Both loved exploration for its own sake. Both were dive instructors who sought to instill confidence and a dedication to safety in their students. Both had studied literature and loved to quote romantic poetry. And both knew the secret locations of very deep holes that no divers had entered. Sitting in camp at Mante, they arranged to teach a cave-diving class together that summer, and to develop plans for deep dives.

After setting world length and depth records earlier in the year, in October Exley returned to Wakulla Springs, the site of Edward's death, as a member of a National Geographic team. He helped map nearly five miles of underwater cave passage, spending several days camped in a submersible habitat at the cave's entrance. Pulled behind an electric scooter, he glided silently over the bones of drowned Ice Age animals.

WE TALK FOR a while. "You don't really want to write about me, do you? Nobody would read it. I mean, I guess you can come on down here if you want, but I don't think you'll see anything very interesting. Just ugly."

We agree to meet at Mante in March, should he decide to go. Several days later he calls to say that Hasenmeyer, the German who is Exley's only possible competition in the depth record, has been paralyzed during a faulty decompression. Details are sketchy, but Exley will put off any Mante attempt until Hasenmeyer's accident has been carefully analyzed—until 1991, at the earliest. If then.

But he plans some work at a Florida cave, yet another Panhandle spring that might eventually yield a new distance record. If I want to come watch, he guesses it's okay.

February 22, 1990

The Florida sunset spreads out in pastel bands, orange sherbet reaching into pale turquoise. Two metal sheds sit beside Exley's modular home. In front of one shed is a battered Ford cargo van, side and rear doors open. Mexican tourist stickers dot the windshield. I see Exley loading tanks into the back of the van. He walks up to me and says, "Hey there, you must be Mike," as if I am the one person on the planet he most wants to see. "We need to go get some air. Then I thought maybe we could meet M.E. for dinner."

M.E. is Mary Ellen Eckoff, the world's most experienced woman cave diver. A tanned, good-looking woman with a strong southern accent, Eckoff is a grant writer for Florida school boards and has trained over a hundred cave divers, logging more than a thousand dives in the process. In 1987, at Nacimiento Mante, she set a women's depth record of 400 feet.

Eckoff and Exley met in 1977 and were married in 1983. The marriage lasted only three years, but the diving relationship and love have somehow endured.

She and Sheck's usual partner, Paul DeLoach (no relation to Ned), will take part in the coming two-day dive effort. We climb into the van and head down winding blacktop through scrub pine. The console is cluttered with hand tools and cassette tapes: Rachmaninoff, Brahms, and the sound track from *South Pacific*. There are also a couple of swollen, water-warped paperbacks, cheap science fiction with the pages glued together. These Exley uses to pass the time during long decompressions. He can't finish a novel on the surface, after it dries, but next time down, the pages will become pliable once more.

"What's your motivation in going to Mante?" I ask. "Why do such deep dives?"

"I held both the world depth and distance records in 1970," Exley says. "I thought it would be nice to hold them both again before I retire. It just took me nearly twenty years to do it." He pauses before adding, "I'm not sure I'll go back to Mante. I had wanted to reach a thousand feet. It's a nice round number. But that might be pushing it. I'm going to have to hang up my tanks—at least from that sort of thing—pretty soon. I guess the real reason I'm doing it is I just want to know what's down there."

After stopping at a dive shop to fill air tanks and talk with some local cave divers, we drive to a Live Oak barbecue house to meet Mary Ellen. As she and Exley share diving tales over heaping plates of ribs, both display playful sides I've missed from watching divers only in caves. Eckoff describes the small pranks Exley and Paul DeLoach have pulled on each other during decompression. There was, for instance, that time at Cathedral Canyon.

Exley's backyard cave is entered via a flooded pit, 130 feet deep. Twenty feet below the surface, a small ledge cluttered with rotting logs, concrete blocks, and other debris makes a convenient decompression stop after long dives. Once, as DeLoach sat on a log, lightly dozing through the wait, Exley tapped him on the shoulder.

DeLoach looked up to see his partner standing at the edge, a cinder block in his hands. Exley gestured with the block, as if to call it to DeLoach's attention. DeLoach shrugged. Exley shook the block a couple of times. DeLoach shrugged again. Exley grinned around his mouthpiece, then tossed the hunk of cement over the cliff.

Only then did DeLoach notice that the cinder block was tied to a coil of nylon line. Rapidly uncoiling nylon line. While he had napped, Exley had looped the other end around DeLoach's manifold. Water slowed the block's fall to the skewed gravity of a Roadrunner cartoon. DeLoach had just enough time to draw his knife and cut the line before it yanked him over the cliff. Exley blew out great bubbles of laughter.

As Eckoff tells the story, Exley turns a vivid red, grinning behind his mustache.

April 6, 1994

I stand in the hot wind, pointing a telephoto lens into Zacatón. I see Eckoff's face, and I put down the camera. The message is conveyed. The details, I know, will come later.

Bowden's rapid descent went smoothly, but his bottom gas mix—the tank for the deepest portion of his dive—began to run out faster than he anticipated. At the 925-foot-mark on his line, he began his ascent. (His two digital depth gauges later read maximum depths of 915 and 924 feet; a third gauge malfunctioned.) He didn't see Exley, but visibility was poor, and he assumed Exley had continued down to 1,000 feet. As Bowden made his first decompression stops, he realized that he was using gas faster than expected and that he might not be able to put in all the required decompression time.

Hundreds of feet above him waited support divers Karen Hohle and Ann Kristovich. (Kristovich, the team's medical officer, broke Eckoff's depth record with a 554-foot dive in Zacatón in September.) The two women saw Bowden's bubbles and knew he had begun ascent, but there was nothing on Exley's line. Eckoff, who had just entered the sinkhole from the tunnel, saw worried looks on the faces of Hohle and Kristovich.

Where's Sheck? Kristovich asked on her underwater slate.

Eckoff descended to 279 feet, the border of light and darkness. As she stared at Exley's vanishing line, she saw two tiny white squares drifting up toward her. Suddenly, she realized they were the laminated pages of his dive profile, something he would never let go of alive. Somehow, she made it to the surface. More than an hour later, she heads out of the cave.

Bowden is not out of the water yet. He cut seven minutes off one decompression stop because of inadequate gas reserves; at another stop, a free-flowing regulator dumped out several minutes more. At about 250 feet, Bowden realized that he had still not seen Exley. Only then did he understand what that meant. At about 100 feet, Hohle used sign language to confirm the worst. For the next several hours, he will continue his decompression in terrible knowledge.

When he finally emerges in the night, after an extra hour spent on pure oxygen at ten feet, Bowden will suffer his second case of the bends. Using a controversial French technique which proved effective with the first case, Kristovich will treat him with massive intravenous steroids, anticoagulants, and painkillers. By the next morning, Bowden will be on his feet. After a period of reflection and mourning, he will continue deep diving, in Zacatón and elsewhere. Having reached at least 915 feet, Jim Bowden now holds the world open-circuit scuba depth record.

ALL OF THIS will happen later. Long before Bowden leaves the water, I'm driving Mary Ellen the two hours to Tampico. She needs to talk to Sheck's parents. She needs to make arrangements for Paul DeLoach to fly in and help her drive the van home. She needs to buy a spare tire. She needs to be away from Zacatón.

The battered Econoline bounces over the highway, and I don't know what to say or do. Sheck's wallet and glasses lie on the console where he left them, along with tapes of Beethoven, Brahms, and several Broadway musicals.

I don't say it, but I assume—and I suspect Mary Ellen assumes—that Sheck's body will never be recovered, that he continued sinking from the point where the trouble occurred, whatever that trouble was. Zacatón will have to be a fitting tomb for the world's greatest cave diver.

I am wrong. Three days later, when the dive team begins to pull up Exley's unused decompression tanks, they discover him entangled in the guideline. His single depth gauge reads 904 feet. Whether he was conscious when he became entangled or merely drifted into the line later is unknown. In 4,000 cave dives, Exley had certainly became entangled in dive lines before, but had never experienced trouble in extricating himself.

The exact cause of death is unknown. There are several reasonable guesses, high among them drowning as a result of HPNS, but they will remain only guesses. With help from Sergio Zambrano, a celebrated Mexican cave diver, Irby Exley is able to cut through international red tape. He claims his son's body and has it cremated within just twenty-one hours.

April 12, 1994

I join divers from around the world at the Ortega Methodist Church in Jacksonville, Florida. The church bulletin contains an excerpt from Samuel Taylor Coleridge's "Kubla Khan," one of Exley's favorite poems. "Through caverns measureless to man / Down to a sunless sea," read the famous lines. The week before Exley and Eckoff drove to Mexico, Exley's publisher had called to say that his latest book, his memoirs, had gone to the printer. The book's title: *Caverns Measureless to Man*.

After the service, Don Jacobs, a twenty-year-old who studied karate with Exley for seven years, progressing from beginner to black belt under his instruction, sees me taking notes.

"I want you to write this down exactly," he tells me. He thinks for a long minute before saying, "The man taught us to love and respect every individual no matter what race, religion, whatever, the way he loved each of us. He treated us like his own kids. Sheck Exley was the best friend I ever had."

I write it down, exactly like he says.

...

IN 1991, THE National Speleological Society presented Exley with its Stephenson Award for lifetime service—the highest honor in American cave exploration. Exley asked his friend Wayne Marshall to introduce him at the ceremony. Before an audience of 2,000, which included Irby and Victoria Exley, Marshall said, "We honor Sheck as an explorer, as a man who set fifteen world depth and distance records. But we also honor him as a guide and a teacher. This man has done more to promote safe cave diving than any living person. His ideas, books, and personal instruction have saved hundreds if not thousands of lives."

Marshall's is a sentiment I hear echoed dozens of times as I phone cave divers around the country in the days following the memorial service. More than one tells me how Sheck literally saved their lives in past underwater mishaps.

Four days before the fatal dive, as Exley and Eckoff set out on I-10 toward Texas and the Pan-American Highway, she asked him, "Is diving to a thousand feet worth dying over?"

Mr. X rolled his eyes as if she were a slow algebra student. "Nooooo," he said. "Of course not. No dive is worth dying over." The date was April 1, 1994—his forty-fifth birthday.

Two days before the fatal dive, as he, Bowden, and the rest of the team placed the decompression bottles in advance of their attempt, Sheck Exley set his last world record: He descended to 422 feet on compressed air, surfacing with no ill effects. The deepest previous dive on compressed air had been to 410 feet. Underwater, he grinned at Eckoff and pointed to his depth gauge.

She read the numbers and wrote on her slate, "You're crazy."

The morning of his last dive, I watched Exley kit up at his van, which was parked beside the concrete dock at the spring leading into Zacatón. A strong breeze carried the scent of barbecue from across the water. Local villagers, many of whom had befriended team members during earlier expeditions, were preparing a fiesta to celebrate the world record dive. Mante,

Karen Hohle's exuberant husky, splashed in and out of the water, barking playfully at cows on the other side.

I walked over to Sheck. He was stuffing into a net bag plastic tubes full of colorful liquid, the sort of children's treat commonly frozen for after-school snacking. I knew that during the long decompression he needed to drink plenty of fluids in order to ward off dehydration. Sheck had hit upon a well-packaged, inexpensive, and flavorful alternative to the specialty fare available from custom dive shops.

I waited until he had closed the bag and clipped it onto his harness before I asked the question that had just occurred to me. "What do your high school students think of cave diving?"

"I don't let them know about it," he said. "Those kids look up to me, and I wouldn't want one of them to try to make some macho point, prove his manhood or something, trying to copy me."

Ten minutes later, Sheck Exley walked over to the spring and stepped in. He grinned and pushed away from us on the shore, kicking with his back to the current and the *norte*. He swam slowly, back to the breeze, a smile on his face. He grew smaller and vanished underwater.

PETER BOARDMAN

(1950–1982)

From *The Shining Mountain*

One of the great partnerships of modern mountaineering, that of Peter Boardman and Joe Tasker, was forged on their extremely bold two-man expedition to 22,520-foot Changabang, in India, in 1976. Chris Bonington later called their new route on the mountain's west wall "the hardest thing that's been done in the Himalayas." Six years later, in their prime, Boardman and Tasker vanished high on Everest's un-climbed east-northeast ridge.

The most dangerous part of a climb is often the descent. In this excerpt from Boardman's vivid book about Changabang, The Shining Mountain, *the accomplished duo has to pull out all the stops to get down from the summit alive. Then, just as they anticipate relaxing and gorging themselves at base camp, they stumble into the tragedy all mountaineers dread—and find themselves driven to a mission of mercy more macabre than any climb.*

15th–19th October

"We might as well unrope for the first part of the descent," said Joe.

"What—with this storm coming in?" I was incredulous.

"Well, there's not much point in keeping it on if we're not going to belay. If one slips, he'll just pull the other one off."

"I prefer to keep it on and move together, so that it's there and ready in case we come across any tricky bits," I said.

"Well, there aren't any tricky bits and we'll have to abseil[1] as soon as we reach that rock step above the bivouac," said Joe.

"All right then, but you go first and I'll carry the rope," I agreed. "If he can do it, so can I," I thought. Although I could understand Joe's cool rationale, I was repelled by the idea of soloing above the five and a half thousand feet of the West Wall of Changabang. On the summit Joe had become assertive, whilst I had been preoccupied with the view and our arrival. A wave of purpose had rippled between us and I was happy that he led down.

I finished coiling the rope. Joe quickly moved back along the ridge and started down our line of tracks that stretched down the snowslope. As I looked across at him, I could see under the cloud the familiar sight of the Rhamani Glacier, twisting down towards the Rishi Ganga. The walls of the Rhamani before had oppressed me, but now we moved above them, and they were reduced to geographic details. The moraines of the Rhamani, that broke through the ice like the bones of the earth, were now the highway of our return. The beginning of the dark sheltered vegetation of the Rishi Ganga was a promise that sprang from a kindlier planet. There, only tree-tops would be swaying.

The snowslope was easier to climb down than I had feared and, in descent, the altitude had lost its enfeebling effect. Soon the falling snow had imprisoned us in mad, whirling whiteness and we kicked and plunged downwards with increasing urgency. Joe reached the rock step and hastily fixed a sling. I uncoiled the rope and we flung it below us. It snaked out

[1]Rappel.

into the cloud and writhed down among the falling snow and spindrift. The air and snow around us were in constant downward dance, and as we slid down the ropes we joined their momentum.

As we picked up our sacks and sorted our gear at the bivouac site, spindrift was pouring everywhere, into our sack, into our gloves and down our necks. We were retreating under bombardment. The hardware was so cold it stuck to our gloves. "Let's get the hell outa here," echoed a thought in a voice like a John Wayne movie, and with it came the return of the strange realisation that I was actually enjoying myself.

The next two abseils went quickly. By the time I arrived next to Joe, he was fixing the anchor for the next abseil and he threaded it through as I pulled one end of the doubled rope down. The previous time we had used this abseil procedure had been five years before, when we had first met in the Western Alps. Now it was automatic.

We had reached a point half way down the steep pitch I had led the previous day. As I swung down the rope towards him, Joe said, "If I direct the rope right, we should make it in one go to the bottom of the gully from here." He was perched on a couple of footholds and I held on above him. After I had pulled the ropes down I saw his anchor. He had tapped a one and a half inch knife blade into a thin diagonal crack in a rock inlaid in the ice. It had gone in about an inch of its length. And he was about to slide off on it!

"You're not going to just abseil off that are you?" I was aghast.

"Can you suggest anything better?" he replied coldly.

We had left most of the pegs[2] at the top of the fixed ropes and now only had two left with us. The other one was of the wrong size. I could not suggest anything better, and off he went without an upward glance. I clung on to the peg with one of my hands, hoping it would not lever out. Joe did not seem worried:

> I believed that the piton was just adequate to take our weight. I had the impression that we would be all right. We had put everything possi-

---

[2]Pitons.

ble into making sure it was safe, we could do no more; we needed now a little bit of luck.

Joe, out of sight beneath the bulge of the gully, shouted to me that he had reached the snow, and that he was swinging across to the side of the gully to fix an anchor. I was still frightened about the peg, because of my extra weight. However, I knew that once Joe had tied off the end of the rope there was chance of a fall being held after 300 feet.

I went springing over the bulges, and the sun started fighting through the snow clouds. The storm was passing and I knew that with the improving visibility we would find the end of the fixed ropes. But it was a declining sun and brought to the amphitheatre lighting identical to that of the afternoon before; except we had reached the summit in between, and now golden particles of snow were falling through the light.

Reaching the fixed ropes felt like coming into the mouth of the harbour out of a storm-tossed sea. Our faces and clothing were encrusted with ice from the struggle. As we arrived, it stopped snowing but, unfortunately, it also became dark.

"Go and get the brew on, Joe," I said. We had eleven hundred feet of abseiling to do. It would be too dangerous to try and retrieve the rope, and, so, sadly, we would have to leave it behind. Joe went first:

> We did the long, lonely abseils in the dark, without seeing or hearing each other. There was just an awareness, a mental, psychological bond between us. . . . In the thirty-six hours since we had been on the ropes they had been, in parts, affected by the wind. One anchor point on the big flake had lifted off. I had to haul, drag and claw my way back onto course. I replaced the anchor point to make it easier for Pete. . . . Then on down, with my hands stiffening into cramp with the strain of hanging on, finding my way by touch and memory.

We had climbed the West Wall when nobody had thought we could do it, and now I was grimly determined that the mountain would not have the last word. Every knot, peg and ropelength that I unclipped and clipped and heaved my way past was another piece of mountain that could not capture me. Every foot I descended was taking me further away down the mountain that was now an enemy that was trying to cheat us. The circling voices, faces and names returned, accelerating around in my head.

The descending traverses that reversed the tension moves were desperately complicated to negotiate, because the rope was tied off in so many places. I was thankful to reach the three peg crack above the Big Groove. On reaching the top peg I leant down and clipped an etrier[3] into the lower peg and put my foot into it. Then I clipped my waist into the middle peg with a fifi hook[4] and leant out on it and extricated the karabiner brake from the rope above. Suddenly I was being propelled backwards, flopping over head-first, as helpless as a rag doll. "I'm dead. How did that happen? Thwack!" I was winded but I had not fallen. My foot had caught in the etrier. Without a thought, I scrambled and pulled myself upright. The middle peg had come out. It was one that I had put in. "Well, I'm still here—better get moving." This was not the time for prayers of thanksgiving.

Wind and cold were forgotten. The rope in the Big Groove only had to hold my weight once more: and it held. Long engraved disciplined skills took me past obstacles and my detached mind was half-surprised at my progress. Trained homo sapiens, the tool-user, had taken over.

Far below me, Joe had reached Camp Two:

Half-way from the summit, half-way to safety. As usual, I hacked some lumps of ice and put them near the tent doorway, then tumbled into the tent, feeling more exultation than I had ever permitted myself on the summit.

Warm inside my sleeping bags, revelling in the sensual ache of relaxation after exertion, I melted ice, preparing a hot drink for Pete when he

[3]A short nylon ladder used for aid or artificial climbing.

[4]A small metal device that when hooked on a wrinkle of rock can be used to support a climber's weight.

came in. Without a descendeur,[5] it usually took him much longer to descend than it took me to have the water hot. I listened for him, full of things to say for once, wanting to share the satisfaction of knowing we had succeeded. He seemed to be taking longer than usual. The water was hot. For some curious reason, I delayed having a drink myself until he arrived.

I waited. There was no tell-tale jangling of hardware to herald his approach. I looked out into the blackness. Not a sound. I called out. Nothing.

Back inside, I mentally went over the last hour—one and a half hours—to see whether I could recall any sound which might have been Pete falling. With this, I admitted the possibility to myself of what might have happened, but could recall nothing.

Still there was no sound. I asked myself what the hell could I do? I longed to hear the sounds which would banish these morbid thoughts from my mind.

Then the sounds came—a rattling and jangling, a scraping of crampons on rock; not in the sudden rush of catastrophe, but slowly, in control. My fears vanished, but I could not find again quite the same exultation which I had wanted to share two hours earlier.

I saw the fragile, flapping nylon of Camp Two, fifteen feet below me in the darkness. It looked deserted but I knew Joe would be inside, crouched over the stove. Then, far below on the glacier, I saw a green light.

"Hey, Joe," I yelled excitedly. "There's a green flare on the glacier. Can you see it?" But he was too late, for by the time he got his head out the tent door, the light had faded. "Pass me your torch, Joe." I flashed it back down towards the glacier, but there was no reply. I insisted that I had seen it, but Joe was guarded—like a doctor suspecting a patient of concussion.

Inside the tent we talked compulsively, our minds unwinding the ela-

---

[5]A metal device through which the rope is fed on rappels, controlling the speed of descent through friction.

tion of success. We laughed unashamedly at the terrible warnings other climbers had given us. For two hours our egos reigned supreme. We were not off the mountain yet, but the dangers below us were all on known ground.

The morning sun thawed us slowly into action. There was no sense of urgency. The view from the door seemed as friendly as a loved and famil-iar face. It was not the mountains around us that had changed, but our attitude to them. The cold camp we had left with tense resolve two days before was now a warm and comforting haven. We talked on the surface, but there was no need to express the deep contentment that flowed between us. There was no need for blunt confrontation any more, because all the important decisions had been made.

"I suppose we'd better get moving, or we'll get benighted again."

"I don't like the idea of having to hump all this stuff down on our backs."

"We could always roll some of the gear down from here, it'd only bounce a couple of times before landing at the bottom of the Wall, and there aren't many crevasses for it to go in."

"Yes, and it'll be fun to watch too."

"We'd better hang onto our survival gear though, just in case the stuff disappears."

We rolled up the superfluous equipment including the tents, the ham-mocks and the three remaining Gaz cylinders we had left, into red stuff bags and strung them together until they looked like a string of floats for lobster-pots.

"Remember to let go of them when you throw them."

"I wonder what the Mars Bars–eater'll[6] make of these when they plunge out of the sky and land around its ears."

The stuff bags slid off down the icefall with the confidence of an Olympic ski-jumper, launched out above the Barrier, hung momentarily in space, and disappeared from view.

---

[6]An unidentified creature that had attacked Boardman and Tasker's food supply at base camp.

I had to rebandage my three fingers that were most damaged. Once again, Joe offered to go first and rig the abseils on the icefield. He would find it easier than I to find the anchors we had left behind, since he had led this section of the climb.

I am always scared unless I am abseiling off at least two pegs, even if one apparently is a perfect placement. But it did not seem to bother Joe to abseil off just one. Halfway down, he set off on another solitary knifeblade. It was flexing as he went down. This time I was not going to say anything, but I unclipped from it, so that I would not be pulled down after Joe if it came out. At that moment, Joe looked up and saw what I had done.

"Well, if it does come out, you'll be a bit stranded up there without a rope," he shouted cheerfully.

"I'd take my shirt off and wave for help," I shouted back.

Fortunately it was an obedient peg, and stayed where it was to Joe's apparent confidence and to my whispered incantations. I suppressed my worries and drew strength from his attitude. I did not know whether this bluffing of each other was based either on mutual deception or on mutual support. It was like being in a platoon of soldiers, in which nobody really wants to fight, but everybody is doing what he imagines his comrade expects him to do.

Soon we were at the bottom of the icefield and Joe disappeared down the overhanging wall next to the Guillotine. It was half an hour before he shouted for me to come on down. As soon as I moved down over the lip of the icefield I saw the reason for the delay. The abseil rope had not been long enough to reach the end of rope we had fixed through the Toni Kurz pitch,[7] and Joe had found himself dangling and sliding towards the loose ends whilst still a few feet out from the rock. He had tied some slings together and, after knotting them to the end of the abseil ropes, he had swung in and grabbed the peg.

---

[7]Named for the tragic victim of an early attempt on the north face of the Eiger. Kurz had died within a few feet of his would-be rescuers when a knot in the rope he was rappelling jammed.

I found it difficult to retrieve the ropes. Joe pulled me into the rock with the slings on the end of them and held me there whilst I hammered in some pegs. I then hung off these and pulled the ropes through and then abseiled from there down to Joe.

"I'd better go down the Toni Kurz pitch first, in case I get tangled up in karabiners and need to be extricated," I said.

"Don't worry, Uncle Joe'll look after you," came the reply.

It was the first time on Changabang that I had abseiled whilst wearing such a heavy sack. Halfway down I lost my balance and turned completely upside down with a squeak of fright. I hoped that Joe had not heard it, and painfully righted myself. I floundered and thrashed about, trying to unclip and clip the mess of karabiners around my waist so that I could pass the pegs, hoping that I was not unclipping the wrong ones. The torques and tensions the heavy sack had introduced were enormous, it felt as if I were trying to couple up the trucks of a heavy goods train single-handed. But I reached the Balcony before I realised that I could have saved a lot of energy.

"It'd be best to come down on your jumars,[8] Joe. It'd make it much easier getting past the pegs. It's bloody desperate if you try to abseil."

The afternoon had rushed past, and granite was turning red around us as Joe bounced into sight around the overhangs.

"It looks easy angled down there," he said, looking past me at the rock below us. I looked round at it. Yes, compared to the rock and the risk of the Upper Tower, its angle looked gentle. And to think how awe-struck we had been on those early pitches! If only we had known what was to come—how our sense of judgement had changed.

"We'll have to find all the abseil placements in the dark now, though," I said. I was cursing myself for the conceit of our leisurely morning. We had completely underestimated the time the descent would take. "Why does everything always turn into an epic?" I thought. "Why can't anything be simple?" Then Joe announced that while he was overseeing my descent,

[8]Mechanical devices for ascending a rope.

his descendeur had become unclipped from a karabiner and had bounced down into the shadows. A nasty thought sneaked into my mind and had its say before I slammed the door on it. "At least he'll find out how desperate it is abseiling with all these karabiners." It did not matter now who went first, we were both equally slow.

As quickly as we could, we made three abseils in the waning light and were five hundred feet above Camp One when it became dark. The remaining problem was to find convenient abseil points on this mixed ground of snow and rock without straying so far to our right that we went over the North Face, or so far to the left that we missed the ridge altogether. The short sections of rope that we had gleaned from Shipton's Col and hung over some of the rock steps were hidden by the darkness.

One hour after nightfall, the wind started to carry snow with it. Steadily the wind became stronger and the amount of snow in the air increased. Now we had reached the change in angle where the ridge started out of the Wall.

"You'd better go down first," said Joe. "Your eyesight's better than mine in stuff like this. My contact lenses aren't infra red."

"It's finding the point where we go down through that first rock step above the camp that's going to be the tricky bit," I said.

We decided that we would move together, to save time, and I would go first and place as much protection as I could.

I kicked off down the slope. The visibility was so bad that I could not see Joe after the first ten feet. I was scared that I might go through the cornice, and tried to sense that I was just below the crest of the ridge by the angle of the snow. After seventy feet I placed a deadman snow anchor[9] as a runner and, after ninety feet, I stumbled across the blackness of a short rock-step with one of our pegs and marker ribbons in it. I clipped the rope into this and kept going. Soon I felt the rope tug gently, as if there were a fish on the end of the line. Then it slackened off again. Joe was coming.

It was a bitter ordeal—feet frozen, legs shaking with cold, bodies screaming "no more!" Yet we were completely in control, treading the fine line

[9]A metal plate buried in the snow so that when frozen in, it serves as an anchor.

that separates the difficult from the dangerous. It was impossible for us to feel tired whilst we still had one more obstacle to overcome. We knew we were probably only a couple of hundred feet above the camp, and thrilled to the action, for success could not be far away. I was playing to the audience of my mind. The situation was drawing from me the utmost of my skills and strength, and yet more seemed to rush in to compensate, as if I had been created to struggle through to life. "If I've got any sixth sense, it had better start working now," I thought. We were so keyed up by our tantalising position that nothing could have stopped us from finding the tent.

"The rock step must be just below." Joe's voice was muffled by the snow and wind.

I moved down and a few feet below me the slope sheered away. I lowered myself down from my ice hammer and axe, and lunged at the ice below with my feet. It was like kicking concrete. The crampons bounced off hard granite beneath the ice.

"I'm just above it now, I'll traverse around till I find the polypropylene," I shouted. If only it were daylight! Then I recognised something about the way the black outline of rock curved into the slope. I stepped down and brushed away the snow. I could feel two pitons and a length of polypropylene rope. I clipped into them and belayed Joe until he joined me. We quickly rigged an abseil and sped off down it.

"We'll pull the rope down in the morning."

The dark shape of the tent loomed up in front of us through the drifting curtain of snow. We tumbled inside. It was 9.15 P.M. We had been descending for three hours in darkness. We prepared a quick meal with the scraps of food that were there. The air inside the tent quickly warmed up. We started to feel drowsy, and soon flopped into exhausted sleep.

It had been the 17th September, exactly one month before, when we had erected the tent at Camp One. Now it had sunk deep into the snow of the ridge and, in the morning, we hacked it out and packed up all the equipment we had accumulated at the camp.

"To think we carried all this lot up," said Joe, as he thrust the pressure cooker into the top of his bulging sack. I chipped out the sweet papers that were inlaid like a mosaic under the groundsheet.

"We could always do another trundle," I suggested.

Joe seemed slightly shocked. Dropping anything, whether it's part of the mountain or equipment, is frowned upon as bad practice in the crowded Alps, when it is likely that you will hit someone. This accounted for the sense of guilt we had felt when we dropped the gear down from Camp Two. We both peered over the edge of the ridge, like a couple of small, mischievous boys planning to drop something on a train.

"We'll have to throw it well clear of these first rocks," said Joe. We wrapped the tent and our outer sleeping bags and duvets in the foam mats and hurled them into the air. Long seconds later, many objects appeared back into our view on the glacier a thousand feet below. Our carefully tied parcels had disintegrated and now all our jettisoned belongings were running all over the glacier like startled sheep. We tried to watch them all until they stopped, memorised their positions and then shouldered our sacks. We then climbed down the ridge and, taking one last look towards Tibet, started to climb down the ice slope towards the Rhamani Glacier.

It was an effort to summon the concentration to descend the ice slope. Our crampons were worn into blunt and stubby points and hardly bit into the ice. The slope had disintegrated beyond recognition and was still poised on a layer of loose rubble that threatened to behave like ball bearings and roll the sheets of ice off. Joe moved quickly below me, to get out of the way of the stones I was dislodging. He was down it half an hour before I was and, as I descended the last dangerous section, I looked down at him collecting our fallen belongings, envying his safe world of the glacier. At last I was stumbling over the lumpy avalanche debris at the foot of the slope. "Nothing can kill me now," I thought as I walked across the glacier to help him.

"It kept us on our toes till the very end didn't it?" said Joe.

We managed to find nearly all our equipment. The Mars Bar–eater had covered the glacier with more of its tracks whilst we had been on the mountain, and now we added to them in our search. Our full body harnesses and the tent had disappeared.

"We'll come back and look for them in the morning," I said.

"It kept us on our toes till the very end, didn't it?" said Joe.

There was only a tin of corned beef to greet us inside the tent at Advance Camp, and we soon demolished that. Now that we were safe, thoughts of food started to obsess us. It was eleven days since we had eaten our last big meal at Base Camp. However, we knew that we could manage another day without much to eat. There would be plenty of time to celebrate later. It was a marvellous luxury to slide into our sleeping bags before it was completely dark, and to fall asleep without the fear of rolling over.

We woke up hungry, but there was no breakfast. I decided to start on a course of Ampicillin to prevent my fingers from rotting.

"Who's the junkie now?" said Joe, as I took the first pill. "I bet they haven't any calories!"

It was the 18th October, the day the flight we had booked left Delhi. Our parents and our friends would be starting to worry about where we were, since they were expecting us on it. They would not have heard from us since we had sent letters back with Palta[10] for him to post for us, early in September. Obviously, it was a priority to reach Joshimath and send some telegrams. Also, we were bursting to tell someone we had climbed the West Wall. We wondered how the Americans had fared on Dunagiri, and if there would be any of them around at Base Camp. Joe was longing for a change of company as much as I:

> That would be good, to go and relax amongst other people . . . Able to laugh and joke in the knowledge that I had earned the right to laugh completely, that it wasn't a false façade I would be projecting. We had earned the right to relax.

We had wound down from the effort of the route into a lazy passiveness, when it came to turning our talk of descent into action. Food is fuel and we had none, and our stomachs were rumbling as we walked up to the foot

---

[10]Liaison officer for the two-man expedition.

of the West Wall to look for the gear we had lost. Joe saw the harnesses, half buried by snow inside the bergschrund,[11] and lay flat across a snow bridge so that he could lever them out with his ice axe. There was no sign of the tent and, after extensive searching for it, we assumed that it had disappeared down a crevasse.

The amount of equipment at Advance Camp seemed enormous, after we had taken the tent down and accumulated it all in a big pile. We realised that we would not be able to carry it all back down to Base Camp that afternoon, and determined to return for the remainder the following morning. We did not contemplate leaving any behind.

"Ever a little further . . ." muttered Joe, as he hitched his sack up.

"It's 'always a little further,' actually," I said—the title of a book by Alistair Borthwick, from a line in a poem by Flecker.

"Pedant," said Joe. "Typical English student!"

The sun was low in the sky by the time we left the moraine of Advance Camp. Imperceptibly, the days had become shorter with the coming of winter. Our departure offered a scene that would have gladdened the heart of any film producer, had he been there. Our sacks were piled high on our backs and the sun was glittering on the ice of the glacier, casting our long shadows into the shadows of the mountains around us. We crunched downwards with slow, wandering steps, whilst white-walled Changabang loomed high behind us, cold and aloof, looking as awe-inspiring as it had on first sight.

It was dark when we reached the top of the valley. I always regarded Base Camp with a strange mixture of feelings, for it was both a welcome home and a misty Bleak House at the same time. It had been a refuge of recovery, but also a hiding place after defeat. Now I was in a silent mood of trepidation, although we had both just been complaining to each other about being ravenously hungry. As the angle of the descent changed, and our feet started thumping the soft earth of the moraine instead of harsh grey ice and stones of the glacier, Joe suddenly stopped.

[11]A crevasse that separates the mountain proper from the glacier beneath it.

"Can you hear voices?" he said. We both listened, but there were no living noises in the eddying air. "I'm sure I heard something. Oh well, perhaps not."

We were walking closely together, as if for security. A few hundred feet lower down, I was convinced I could smell woodsmoke. Then we both definitely heard voices. Our pace quickened involuntarily. We rounded the boulders abruptly and saw a hillside aglow with lights and fires. Our forty days of self-imposed isolation had ended and we were back in the world of people. We shouted hallos. No reply. We became dubious. "Perhaps someone's raiding our tent," I said.

We approached with caution. Nothing seemed out of place. The tent was still fastened up. The note was still underneath the stone.[12] We dropped our sacks and hurried, tripping and falling, and a little uncertain, across to the fire. A large tent loomed up; there were lights inside and voices chattering away. "They sound Japanese," said Joe. I pulled back the flap.

The inside was bright with candlelight, and I saw a blur of red sweaters and dark, bearded faces. It was a big tent and they were all sitting around the sides. In the middle of them was a table made of boxes, with an enormous primus stove belching away with a large pot on top of it. Everyone shuffled around and room was made for Joe and me. Rabbi Corradino introduced himself as the leader of the Italian Garhwal expedition, from Turin, and then introduced his seven fellow-members. Joe and I found ourselves sitting next to a woman, who told us she was from the American Dunagiri expedition. Cups of hot tea, biscuits and Italian cheese were thrust into our hands and we chatted in a mixture of broken French and English.

The Italians had come to climb Kalanka, but their porters, disliking the idea of the long trek around into the Sanctuary and up the Changabang Glacier, had brought them here to the foot of the Rhamani. The Italians

[12]On September 14, as Boardman and Tasker set out from their base camp to go up on Changabang, they left a "To whom it may concern" note in a plastic bag, under a stone, explaining their intentions to any possible passersby.

had tried to cross the ridge but had not realised the circuitous manœuvres that the Indo-British expedition had made to cross Shipton's Col. Two of them had reached the ridge by a snowslope between Shipton's Col and Rishi Kot, but the other side had been too difficult for them to contemplate descending. Then the expedition had seen signs of fixed rope on the Japanese route on the South-West Ridge and, hoping that it was all in place, had been across to attempt a second ascent. However, the ropes had stopped after a few hundred feet and so they had not got very far. And now they were going back and their porters were due in two days' time. It had not been a very successful expedition for them, but they did not seem too bothered.

Yes, they knew we had climbed the West Wall, they had seen us coming down. Had they any news of the South Face expedition? Apparently they had reached the summit about ten days before we had, by a new route on the south side, although they did not think it was the actual South Face. We were hungry for more news, and our achievement and experiences were changing in value to us, for the outside was bringing new perspectives. I had organised a climbing trip to Britain, the previous year, for eight Italian mountaineers from all over Italy, and now I repeated their names to them. Yes, they knew them all, and it was good to talk about mutual friends. Joe they knew of by his reputation, mainly because of his second ascent of the Gervasutti route on the East Face of the Grandes Jorasses. It was an ascent that had been widely acclaimed in Italy, and an article by Joe about it had been published in an Italian mountaineering magazine.

And what of the Dunagiri expedition? Had they climbed their mountain? Why was the woman next to us the only American here? Where were the others? We thought that they would have left days before. Had they been delayed? The American woman, Ruth Erb, had a quiet voice and it was difficult to hear her against the background hubbub of the Italians.

"We had an accident," she said.

"I'm sorry to hear that," said Joe. "Was anybody hurt?"

"Yes, four of us were killed three days ago. I'm the only one left."

Slowly her words penetrated our bemused confusion of fatigue and elation. I winced as if I had been slapped in the face. Had we heard correctly?

Her voice seemed so calm, so measured, it seemed to belie the content of her words.

"Was anyone related to you?" asked Joe.

"Yes, my husband."

"How did it happen?" I asked, suddenly unsure of myself, not knowing if she would want to talk about it. Our happiness, our intoxication at our success, started to feel inane.

Ruth talked objectively, as if with an enormous effort she was holding the full implication of the tragedy off from her consciousness. On 12th October they had established a camp at 19,850 feet, at the foot of the rockstep on the South-West Ridge. By the 15th, the day Joe and I had reached the summit of Changabang, six of the team had to leave because their available time was growing short or for various other reasons. Ruth had stayed at the 19,850 foot camp while the remaining four climbers, Graham Stephenson, the leader, Arkel Erb, John Baruch and the Mexican climber, Benjamin Casasola, had set out to establish a camp on the ridge above, from which they hoped to reach the summit the next day. On the afternoon of the 16th, Ruth had been watching Arkel and John descending the snow ridge between 21,000 and 22,000 feet, when she saw them slip and fall. They had appeared to be trying to brake their fall with their ice axes on the slopes but had failed, and had disappeared from view. They fell about two thousand feet. Ruth had moved to a point on the edge of the ridge where she could look down onto the glacier below, and saw not only the bodies of her husband and John, but also those of Graham and Ben.

Ruth had spent the next two nights alone at the camp, hoping that the expedition porters at Base Camp would come up to see what was wrong and to help her down. The previous day, the 17th, she had noticed someone about a thousand feet below her. She had shouted and whistled and thought he had heard her, but was shattered when he went back down. However, the man (Yasu)[13] had gone down to Base Camp to get help. He had found the Italian climbers and that day three of them had gone up with

_____

[13]A porter.

Yasu and helped her down. She had arrived at Base Camp one hour before we had.

Joe stumbled out of the tent, in search of Yasu, who was a good friend of his. For me, the Italians had drifted into the background. They were tactfully talking amongst themselves. I asked Ruth if she had any children. She had a twenty-two year old son. Had she thought what she was going to do now? She hoped there might still be some members of the expedition in Delhi, and would leave the mountains with the Italians. However, she was worried about the bodies. Someone ought to go up and find them. I felt overcome with the pain of listening to her and hardly dared look at her face. I told her I was going to get something to eat and left the tent.

Outside, I stretched upwards into a clear, starry night. I shivered from the cold and went to our tent, which was still in darkness. Joe appeared.

"Hey, Pete, come over here to Yasu's tent," he said. "He's got masses of food. His mate Balu's here from Joshimath."

We wanted to talk the whole thing over together, and as we walked over to Yasu's tent Joe told me what he had been able to find out. Yasu had been able to see the bodies in the distance on the glacier, below the South-West Ridge, and they wanted Joe and me to go back up to them the next day. Joe's knowledge of the geography of Dunagiri would be a great help.

"Yasu was incredibly pleased to see me," said Joe. "I think that since they'd acted as agents and negotiated porters for the expedition, they feel responsible about the whole thing. I don't know how experienced they are, and they seem a bit subdued. Yasu's only about twenty and Balu must be around the same age. Somebody has to take decisions for Ruth at the moment, and its easier for us to discuss with her since she speaks English."

Yasu gave me some packets of freeze-dried food that the Americans had left behind. "They have no need of it now," he said.

The stream that flowed through the meadow had dried up and Joe set off up the hill to fetch some water. I flopped inside the tent with a confusion of thoughts racing through my head. I put on my down suit and lay down, looking at the pattern of the candlelight on the tarpaulin of the shelter. It was half an hour before Joe arrived.

"Haven't you got the primus lit? What have you been doing all this time? I had to go bloody miles to get the water." He was furious.

I shook myself into action and rushed about, lighting the stove and preparing the meal whilst Joe crouched outside self-righteously. Yasu had come over to talk to Joe and I saw the teeth of his smile gleam in the darkness.

"You know the Monkey God, Hanuman? He has servants who are also monkeys and who rush about and do everything for him. Just like Pete is for you!"

Joe had quickly focused on a plan of action. I was amazed at the speed with which he had absorbed all that had happened, and had decided exactly what we had to do. We would leave at seven the next morning with Yasu and Balu, climb up to Dunagiri and reach the bodies. If it seemed the best thing to do, we could bury them in a crevasse after collecting as much of their personal belongings as possible, and after photographing them in case there were any legal problems about proving their deaths. We considered walking up the Changabang branch of the Rhamani Glacier, and collecting the rest of our equipment afterwards, but realised we probably would not have enough time. Joe went and consulted Ruth about the plan. She was desperately anxious that the bodies should not be just left on the glacier. She could only speak for her husband, but felt that the other relatives would, if they knew, entrust us with the task and the decisions that would be involved.

I was in awe of Joe's honest compassion and the direct simplicity with which he had immediately offered to help. How crass my bumbling professions of sympathy seemed in comparison!

"It could be a bit gruesome," I ventured.

Joe just shrugged a sigh. "It's just something we've got to do," he said.

• • •

EDWARD ABBEY

(1927–1989)

From *Desert Solitaire: A Season in the Wilderness*

More than any other book, Edward Abbey's seminal classic Desert
Solitaire, *published in 1968, helped turn the American Southwest from
a little-known, sparsely populated region into a de rigueur "destination"
for wilderness enthusiasts. Late in life, Abbey expressed regret that his
own writings had helped unleash a flood of backpackers, climbers, river
runners, and mountain bikers.*

Desert Solitaire *remains Abbey's finest book, alternatingly lyrical
and satiric as it weaves a paean to the author's favorite landscape in
the world. This short passage recording a jaunt in Havasu Canyon in
Arizona mordantly captures the kind of predicament familiar to every
desert wanderer who has flirted too seriously with seductive slickrock.*

Most of my wandering in the desert I've done alone. Not so much from choice as from necessity—I generally prefer to go into places where no one else wants to go. I find that in contemplating the natural world my pleasure is greater if there are not too many others contemplating it with me, at the same time. However, there are special hazards in traveling alone. Your chances of dying, in case of sickness or accident, are much improved, simply because there is no one around to go to for help.

Exploring a side canyon off Havasu Canyon one day, I was unable to resist the temptation to climb up out of it onto what corresponds in that region to the Tonto Bench. Late in the afternoon I realized that I would not have enough time to get back to my camp before dark, unless I could find a much shorter route than the one by which I had come. I looked for a shortcut.

Nearby was another little side canyon which appeared to lead down into Havasu Canyon. It was a steep, shadowy, extremely narrow defile with the usual meandering course and overhanging walls; from where I stood, near its head, I could not tell if the route was feasible all the way down to the floor of the main canyon. I had no rope with me—only my walking stick. But I was hungry and thirsty, as always. I started down.

For a while everything went well. The floor of the little canyon began as a bed of dry sand, scattered with rocks. Farther down a few boulders were wedged between the walls; I climbed over and under them. Then the canyon took on the slickrock character—smooth, sheer, slippery sandstone carved by erosion into a series of scoops and potholes which got bigger as I descended. In some of these basins there was a little water left over from the last flood, warm and fetid water under an oily-looking scum, condensed by prolonged evaporation to a sort of broth, rich in dead and dying organisms. My canteen was empty and I was very thirsty but I felt that I could wait.

I came to a lip on the canyon floor which overhung by twelve feet the largest so far of these stagnant pools. On each side rose the canyon walls, roughly perpendicular. There was no way to continue except by dropping into the pool. I hesitated. Beyond this point there could hardly be any returning, yet the main canyon was still not visible below. Obviously the only sensible thing to do was to turn back. I edged over the lip of stone and dropped feet first into the water.

Deeper than I expected. The warm, thick fluid came up and closed over my head as my feet touched the muck at the bottom. I had to swim to the farther side. And here I found myself on the verge of another drop-off, with one more huge bowl of green soup below.

This drop-off was about the same height as the one before, but not overhanging. It resembled a children's playground slide, concave and S-curved, only steeper, wider, with a vertical pitch in the middle. It did not lead directly into the water but ended in a series of steplike ledges above the pool. Beyond the pool lay another edge, another drop-off into an unknown depth. Again I paused, and for a much longer time. But I no longer had the option of turning around and going back. I eased myself into the chute and let go of everything—except my faithful stick.

I hit rock bottom hard, but without any physical injury. I swam the stinking pond dog-paddle style, pushing the heavy scum away from my face, and crawled out on the far side to see what my fate was going to be.

Fatal. Death by starvation, slow and tedious. For I was looking straight down an overhanging cliff to a rubble pile of broken rocks eighty feet below.

AFTER THE FIRST wave of utter panic had passed I began to try to think. First of all I was not going to die immediately, unless another flash flood came down the gorge; there was the pond of stagnant water on hand to save me from thirst and a man can live, they say, for thirty days or more without food. My sun-bleached bones, dramatically sprawled at the bottom of the chasm, would provide the diversion of the picturesque for future wanderers—if any man ever came this way again.

My second thought was to scream for help, although I knew very well there could be no other human being within miles. I even tried it but the sound of that anxious shout, cut short in the dead air within the canyon

walls, was so inhuman, so detached as it seemed from myself, that it terrified me and I didn't attempt it again.

I thought of tearing my clothes into strips and plaiting a rope. But what
was I wearing?—boots, socks, a pair of old and ragged blue jeans, a flimsy
T-shirt, an ancient and rotten sombrero of straw. Not a chance of weaving
such a wardrobe into a rope eighty feet long, or even twenty feet long.

How about a signal fire? There was nothing to burn but my clothes; not
a tree, not a shrub, not even a weed grew in this stony cul-de-sac. Even if I
burned my clothing the chances of the smoke being seen by some Huala-
pai Indian high on the south rim were very small; and if he did see the
smoke, what then? He'd shrug his shoulders, sigh, and take another pull
from his Tokay bottle. Furthermore, without clothes, the sun would soon
bake me to death.

There was only one thing I could do. I had a tiny notebook in my hip
pocket and a stub of pencil. When these dried out I could at least record
my final thoughts. I would have plenty of time to write not only my epitaph
but my own elegy.

But not yet.

There were a few loose stones scattered about the edge of the pool. Taking the biggest first, I swam with it back to the foot of the slickrock chute
and placed it there. One by one I brought the others and made a shaky little pile about two feet high leaning against the chute. Hopeless, of course,
but there was nothing else to do. I stood on the top of the pile and stretched
upward, straining my arms to their utmost limit and groped with fingers and
fingernails for a hold on something firm. There was nothing. I crept back
down. I began to cry. It was easy. All alone, I didn't have to be brave.

Through the tears I noticed my old walking stick lying nearby. I took it
and stood it on the most solid stone in the pile, behind the two topmost
stones. I took off my boots, tied them together and hung them around my
neck, on my back. I got up on the little pile again and lifted one leg and
set my big toe on the top of the stick. This could never work. Slowly and
painfully, leaning as much of my weight as I could against the sandstone
slide, I applied more and more pressure to the stick, pushing my body up-

ward until I was again stretched out full length above it. Again I felt about for a fingerhold. There was none. The chute was smooth as polished marble.

No, not quite that smooth. This was sandstone, soft and porous, not marble, and between it and my wet body and wet clothing a certain friction was created. In addition, the stick had enabled me to reach a higher section of the S-curved chute, where the angle was more favorable. I discovered that I could move upward, inch by inch, through adhesion and with the help of the leveling tendency of the curve. I gave an extra little push with my big toe — the stones collapsed below, the stick clattered down — and crawled rather like a snail or slug, oozing slime, up over the rounded summit of the slide.

The next obstacle, the overhanging spout twelve feet above a deep plunge pool, looked impossible. It *was* impossible, but with the blind faith of despair I slogged into the water and swam underneath the drop-off and floundered around for a while, scrabbling at the slippery rock until my nerves and tiring muscles convinced my numbed brain that *this was not the way.* I swam back to solid ground and lay down to rest and die in comfort.

Far above I could see the sky, an irregular strip of blue between the dark, hard-edged canyon walls that seemed to lean toward each other as they towered above me. Across that narrow opening a small white cloud was passing, so lovely and precious and delicate and forever inaccessible that it broke the heart and made me weep like a woman, like a child. In all my life I had never seen anything so beautiful.

The walls that rose on either side of the drop-off were literally perpendicular. Eroded by weathering, however, and not by the corrasion of rushing floodwater, they had a rough surface, chipped, broken, cracked. Where the walls joined the face of the overhang they formed almost a square corner, with a number of minute crevices and inch-wide shelves on either side. It might, after all, be possible. What did I have to lose?

When I had regained some measure of nerve and steadiness I got up off my back and tried the wall beside the pond, clinging to the rock with bare toes and fingertips and inching my way crabwise toward the corner. The watersoaked, heavy boots dangling from my neck, swinging back and forth with my every movement, threw me off balance and I fell into the pool. I swam out to the bank, unslung the boots and threw them up over the drop-off, out of sight. They'd be there if I ever needed them again. Once more I attached myself to the wall, tenderly, sensitively, like a limpet, and very slowly, very cautiously, worked my way into the corner. Here I was able to climb upward, a few centimeters at a time, by bracing myself against the opposite sides and finding sufficient niches for fingers and toes. As I neared the top and the overhang became noticeable I prepared for a slip, planning to push myself away from the rock so as to fall into the center of the pool where the water was deepest. But it wasn't necessary. Somehow, with a skill and tenacity I could never have found in myself under ordinary circumstances, I managed to creep straight up that gloomy cliff and over the brink of the drop-off and into the flower of safety. My boots were floating under the surface of the little puddle above. As I poured the stinking water out of them and pulled them on and laced them up I discovered myself bawling again for the third time in three hours, the hot delicious tears of victory. And up above the clouds replied—thunder.

I emerged from that treacherous little canyon at sundown, with an enormous fire in the western sky and lightning overhead. Through sweet twilight and the sudden dazzling flare of lightning I hiked back along the Tonto Bench, bellowing the *Ode to Joy*. Long before I reached the place where I could descend safely to the main canyon and my camp, however, darkness set in, the clouds opened their bays and the rain poured down. I took shelter under a ledge in a shallow cave about three feet high—hardly room to sit up in. Others had been here before: the dusty floor of the little hole was littered with the droppings of birds, rats, jackrabbits and coyotes. There were also a few long gray pieces of scat with a curious twist at one tip—cougar? I didn't care. I had some matches with me, sealed in paraffin (the prudent explorer); I scraped together the handiest twigs and animal droppings and built a little fire and waited for the rain to stop.

It didn't stop. The rain came down for hours in alternate waves of storm and drizzle and I very soon had burnt up all the fuel within reach. No matter. I stretched out in the coyote den, pillowed my head on my arm and suffered through the long long night, wet, cold, aching, hungry, wretched, dreaming claustrophobic nightmares. It was one of the happiest nights of my life.